Introduction

Comprehensive and engaging, this textbook introduces students not only to foundational sociological work, but also to insights from contemporary sociological theory and research. This combined approach ensures that students become familiar with the **core of sociology**: key concepts, theories, perspectives, methods and findings. Students will acquire the ability to **think like a sociologist**, to **investigate** and **understand** complex social phenomena.

This text presents a **complete sociological toolkit**, guiding students in the art of asking good sociological **questions**, devising a sophisticated **theory** and developing methodologies to **observe** social phenomena. The chapters of this book build cumulatively to equip students with the tools to quickly understand **any** new sociological topic or contemporary social problem.

The textbook also **applies** the sociological toolkit to **selected key sociological issues**, showing how specific sociological topics can be easily investigated and understood using this approach. Taking a **global and comparative perspective**, the book covers a rich diversity of sociological topics and social problems, such as crime, immigration, race and ethnicity, media, education, family, organizations, gender, poverty, modernization and religion.

The book presents a range of helpful pedagogical features throughout, such as:

- **Chapter overview** and **learning goals** summaries at the start of every chapter;
- **Thinking like a sociologist** boxes, encouraging students to reflect critically on learning points;
- **Principle** boxes, summarizing key sociological principles;
- **Theory schema** boxes, presenting sociological theories in a clear, understandable manner;
- **Stylized facts** highlighting key empirical findings and patterns;
- **Key concepts** and **summary** sections at the end of every chapter; and
- **A companion website** providing additional material for every chapter for both instructors and students, including PowerPoint lecture notes, discussion questions and answers, multiple-choice questions, further reading and a full glossary of terms.

This clear and accessible text is essential reading for students taking introductory courses in sociology. It will also be useful for undergraduate and graduate courses in other social science disciplines, such as psychology, economics, human geography, demography, communication studies, education sciences, political science and criminology.

Frank van Tubergen is Professor of Sociology at Utrecht University, where he teaches introduction to sociology. His current work is focused on social networks, immigration and religion.

"Frank van Tubergen's excellent introduction delivers a fresh and unique approach to the key challenge of teaching Sociology: how can we combine the fascination for all the many social phenomena with the virtue of clear and systematic thinking, step by step? It was more than time to have such a textbook available."

Frank Kalter, University of Mannheim, Germany

"I've been waiting for an introduction like this for years. It introduces students to sociology's overarching themes and shows how the principles of asking sociological questions, formulating and testing sociological ideas, and thus building knowledge applies across the seemingly different topics in our broad discipline. If you're looking for an introduction that helps your students understand and engage with state-of-the-art (academic) sociology, look no further. This is an excellent introduction for students wishing to understand the key principles of building sound sociological knowledge and applying the sociological perspective across a wide range of topics. I will be recommending this to all our graduate students – whether they already took an intro to sociology or not."

Christiaan Monden, University of Oxford, UK

"Finally a free-of-dust introduction to state-of-the-art sociology. Van Tubergen presents an excellent and most engaging overview of the discipline and shows beginners how to think as sociologists. An indispensable book to teach and learn the sociology that really matters."

Javier G. Polavieja, University Carlos III of Madrid, Spain

"Frank van Tubergen's *Introduction to Sociology* is an invitation to think like a sociologist, written with a passion for the discipline and a mastery of the sociological toolkit. The book is a beacon for the aspiring sociology student and an inspiring and positive call for sociology as a science."

Christofer Edling, Lund University, Sweden

"Prof. van Tubergen's *Introduction to Sociology* is very original in the understanding of social phenomena with the scheme of common themes such as norms, groups, networks, stratification, etc., which cuts across various institutional lives. The organization of the textbook is also very innovative and coherent in its approach to introducing students sociological imagination."

Ping-Yin Kuan, National Chengchi University, Taiwan

Introduction to Sociology

Frank van Tubergen

Routledge
Taylor & Francis Group

LONDON AND NEW YORK

First published 2020
by Routledge
2 Park Square, Milton Park, Abingdon, Oxon OX14 4RN

and by Routledge
52 Vanderbilt Avenue, New York, NY 10017

Routledge is an imprint of the Taylor & Francis Group, an informa business

British Library Cataloguing-in-Publication Data
A catalogue record for this book is available from the British Library

Library of Congress Cataloging-in-Publication Data
Names: Van Tubergen, Frank, 1976- author.
Title: Introduction to sociology / Frank van Tubergen.
Description: Milton Park, Abingdon, Oxon ; New York, NY : Routledge, 2020.
   I Includes bibliographical references and index.
Identifiers: LCCN 2019043292 (print) I LCCN 2019043293 (ebook) I ISBN
   9780815353843 (hardback) I ISBN 9780815353850 (paperback) I ISBN
   9781351134958 (ebook)
Subjects: LCSH: Sociology.
Classification: LCC HM586 .V36 2020 (print) I LCC HM586 (ebook) I DDC
   301—dc23
LC record available at https://lccn.loc.gov/2019043292
LC ebook record available at https://lccn.loc.gov/2019043293

ISBN: 978-0-8153-5384-3 (hbk)
ISBN: 978-0-8153-5385-0 (pbk)
ISBN: 978-1-351-13495-8 (ebk)

Typeset in Sabon
by Swales & Willis, Exeter, Devon, UK
www.routledge.com/cw/tubergen

Printed and bound in Great Britain by
TJ Books Limited, Padstow, Cornwall

Contents

Preface   ix
Acknowledgments   xiii
About the author   xv
Abbreviations   xvi

Part 1   Thinking like a sociologist   1

1   **Questions**   3
   1.1   The sociological perspective   4
   1.2   Social problems   13
   1.3   Three aims of sociology   16
   1.4   Three types of sociological questions   20
   1.5   The art of asking good sociological questions   21
   1.6   Sociology and common sense   26
   1.7   Sociology as cumulative science   32
   1.8   Chapter resources   34

2   **Theories**   37
   2.1   Birth month and success in sports   38
   2.2   Theories and explanations   41
   2.3   What are useful sociological theories?   46
   2.4   Durkheim's theory of suicide   53
   2.5   Concepts   58
   2.6   Causality   62
   2.7   Conceptual models   64
   2.8   Formal models   68
   2.9   Chapter resources   70

3   **Methods**   73
   3.1   Is your smartphone making you stupid?   74
   3.2   Measurement quality   76
   3.3   External validity   82
   3.4   Internal validity   87

Contents

	3.5	Exploratory research	88
	3.6	Qualitative and quantitative methods	91
	3.7	Case study research	91
	3.8	Administrative research	94
	3.9	Survey research	96
	3.10	Big data research	98
	3.11	Experimental research	100
	3.12	Replication	103
	3.13	Chapter resources	106

4	**Perspectives**		**109**
	4.1	The origins of sociological perspectives	110
	4.2	Sociological themes and topics	114
	4.3	Causal explaining or subjective understanding?	123
	4.4	Multilevel framework	127
	4.5	Chapter resources	132

| **Part 2** | **Culture** | | **137** |

5	**Opinions**		**139**
	5.1	Why is Harry Potter so popular?	140
	5.2	Self-fulfilling prophecy	142
	5.3	Conformity	146
	5.4	Informational and normative social influence	153
	5.5	Social learning theory	156
	5.6	Popularity of cultural products	162
	5.7	Diffusion of innovations	165
	5.8	Chapter resources	170

6	**Norms**		**179**
	6.1	College binge drinking: a social problem?	180
	6.2	What are social norms?	182
	6.3	Social control theory	183
	6.4	Internalized norms	189
	6.5	Legal norms	191
	6.6	Why do norms emerge?	192
	6.7	Cultural maladaptation and norm change	199
	6.8	The dynamics of group distinction	206
	6.9	Chapter resources	210

| **Part 3** | **Social relations** | | **217** |

7	**Networks**		**219**
	7.1	The friendship paradox	220
	7.2	Personal networks	222

7.3	Network size and hubs	226
7.4	Network density and transitivity	230
7.5	The small-world phenomenon	235
7.6	Network change: loss-of-community?	240
7.7	Networks and social cohesion	242
7.8	Networks and social capital	246
7.9	Chapter resources	252

8 Groups — 259

8.1	Groups unite and divide	260
8.2	Group segregation	264
8.3	The causes of group segregation	268
8.4	In-group favoritism	274
8.5	Social context and in-group favoritism	277
8.6	Group threat theory	281
8.7	Chapter resources	288

Part 4   Inequality — 297

9 Stratification and mobility — 299

9.1	What makes you happy?	300
9.2	Social class and status	303
9.3	Income and wealth	307
9.4	Long-term changes in stratification	312
9.5	Social mobility	314
9.6	Ascription and achievement	318
9.7	Modernization and mobility theory	319
9.8	Cultural reproduction theory	322
9.9	The *Great Gatsby* Curve	324
9.10	Chapter resources	328

10 Resources — 333

10.1	Human capital	334
10.2	Social capital	336
10.3	Group affiliation and discrimination	343
10.4	Inequality of outcomes, opportunities and returns	345
10.5	Gender inequality	347
10.6	Chapter resources	359

Part 5   Topics — 365

11 Immigration and integration — 367

11.1	Immigration and integration: a social problem?	368
11.2	International migration	369
11.3	Integration: what does it mean?	376

11.4	Integration: changes over time?	379
11.5	Integration: social context effects?	382
11.6	Case study: culture of honor	385
11.7	Integration: selective or spillover effects?	388
11.8	The dynamics of residential segregation	393
11.9	Chapter resources	397
12	**Modernization**	**407**
12.1	Is the world getting worse?	408
12.2	Wealth and health	410
12.3	Peace and safety	413
12.4	Rationalization	415
12.5	Technological progress	417
12.6	Scientization	423
12.7	McDonaldization	429
12.8	Value change	431
12.9	Population change	440
12.10	The dynamics of modernization	444
12.11	Chapter resources	450
13	**Religion**	**457**
13.1	What is religion?	458
13.2	Did religions solve the problem of human cooperation?	462
13.3	The stickiness factor of religion	464
13.4	Secularization in Western Europe	468
13.5	Modernization and secularization	471
13.6	Existential insecurity theory	475
13.7	Chapter resources	483
Glossary		**489**
Index		**501**

Preface

Why are today's youth soccer players of the national teams often born in January and rarely in December? Why are many people satisfied with their own life, but think the world is getting worse? Why is binge drinking so common in college, whereas the majority of students are against it? Why are your friends so similar to you? Why are citizens of the United States more religious than those in Western Europe?

Sociology is a science that studies a wide range of fascinating topics such as these. I have had the pleasure of giving introductory courses for many years, sharing sociological insights with first-year students. However, I have always felt uncomfortable with the completely out-of-date sociological ideas and findings presented in textbooks. As has been frequently noted by others as well, there are "two sociologies." On the one hand, there is sociological knowledge presented in textbooks, which presents a picture of the discipline of sociology as it was decades ago and which has long been abandoned by sociologists. On the other hand, there are sociological insights published in contemporary sociological journals and books, presenting cutting-edge theories and research findings, but this state of the art is not incorporated in sociology textbooks.

I have written this book in the spirit of uniting the "two sociologies," to write a textbook which not only addresses foundational sociological work but also integrates insights from contemporary sociological research. I think this book presents a more accurate picture of what current sociology is actually about and also proves more useful to students for understanding and mitigating social problems. It is written primarily as an introduction to sociology, which means that the materials are presented in a highly accessible and engaging way. It covers a rich diversity of sociological topics and social problems, such as crime, immigration, race and ethnicity, media, education, family, organizations, gender, poverty, modernization and religion.

My hope is that, after reading this book, students have become familiar with *key knowledge* in sociology. This means that students get to know several core sociological concepts, theories, perspectives, methods and findings. Furthermore, I hope that this textbook will help students learn *to think like a sociologist*. My hope is that this book offers students a "sociological toolkit," a set of useful insights, tools and principles that will enable them to do research like a sociologist themselves. Thinking like a sociologist means that students have not only familiarized themselves with key sociological knowledge, but that, for example, they are able to develop a new theory themselves, or that they can formulate interesting sociological questions about a certain topic. Being able to think like a sociologist helps to analyze *any* sociological topic and *any* contemporary social problem—even those with which one is as yet unfamiliar.

Only you—students and colleagues—can tell whether this textbook has succeeded. I invite you to let me know your thoughts about the book, whether, for example, important developments, theories or findings that are currently omitted should be part of this introductory textbook. Do tell me if I have not explained something clearly, or if I have made mistakes somewhere. Please send me your comments and suggestions for improvement. I will consider your feedback carefully and use it constructively for the next edition. Receiving your feedback will make this book a collaborative effort, and this "wisdom of the crowd" will greatly contribute to presenting an accurate picture of the state of the art of sociology in textbooks.

Frank van Tubergen
textbook.sociology@uu.nl

The structure of the book

Part 1 introduces you to the building blocks of *Thinking Like a Sociologist*. It covers the key tools and principles for becoming a sociologist. Thinking like a sociologist means, first, that you understand the unique sociological perspective on human behavior and that you are able to ask sociological *questions* (Chapter 1). Sociological thinking also implies understanding what sociological *theories* are and that you acquire tools to develop theories yourself (Chapter 2). In addition, this part reviews key sociological *methods* and helps you to understand their pros and cons (Chapter 3). Lastly, thinking sociologically implies that you can apply different sociological *perspectives* (Chapter 4). It provides an introduction to the multilevel perspective, which studies the interplay between individuals (micro) and their social context (meso and macro). It also introduces three sociological themes that can be used as unique perspectives on human behavior, namely: Culture, Social relations and Inequality (CSI). Parts 2, 3 and 4 elaborate on Part 1 as it introduces key sociological knowledge with respect to each of these three themes.

Part 2 deals with the first of these three themes, namely *Culture*. This part introduces you to key sociological knowledge on culture: core concepts, theories and findings. It addresses, first, sociological knowledge of *opinions*, which encompasses people's beliefs, cognition, values and attitudes (Chapter 5). Subsequently, this part covers the "rules of the game" in society, i.e., the informal, moral and formal *norms* that shape human behavior (Chapter 6).

Part 3 covers the second theme: *Social relations*. This theme relates to concepts like social cohesion, cooperation, trust and conflict. Part 3 provides an introduction to key sociological concepts, theories and findings on *social networks* (Chapter 7) and *groups* (Chapter 8).

Part 4 addresses the third general theme in sociology, which is *Inequality*. It gives an overview of core sociological concepts, theories and findings with respect to research on *stratification and mobility* (Chapter 9) and to the role *resources* play in generating inequality (Chapter 10).

Part 5 deals with *Topics*. This part brings together all previous parts. It provides an illustration of how *thinking like a sociologist* (Part 1) and *key sociological knowledge* that has accumulated within the three major themes in sociology (Parts 2–4) is used to understand sociological topics. The three sociological themes of Culture, Social relations and Inequality (CSI) can be combined and used like a "crime scene investigation," so that taking different perspectives helps in solving puzzles of what happened. This part applies sociological thinking and the CSI approach to three sociological topics. These are: *immigration and integration* (Chapter 11), *modernization* (Chapter 12) and *religion* (Chapter 13).

Pedagogical features

Throughout the book I introduce a rich variety of sociological puzzles, social problems and sociological topics to make the materials more engaging to students like you. When you read this book you'll come across several pedagogical features:

- **Principles**
  These are boxes that contain useful guidelines, tools, insights or practices for thinking like a sociologist. You can add these to your sociological toolkit.
- **Stylized facts**
  Sociologists study many social phenomena. When there is sufficient ground to think they observe a robust empirical pattern, when the evidence is strong, they call this a "stylized fact." I have included a number of stylized facts in this book, also in boxes, and I have given them names, which makes it easier to refer to them.
- **Thinking like a sociologist**
  To engage you more while reading the chapters, I have inserted, in boxes, "thinking like a sociologist" questions.
- **Learning goals**
  At the beginning of each chapter I mention key learning goals. You can check if, after reading the chapter, you're able to respond to these goals.
- **Chapter overviews**
  Also, at the beginning of each chapter, I have included a short outline so that you can quickly grasp the content of the chapter.
- **Summaries**
  At the end of the chapter you can find a summary that highlights the main insights.
- **Key concepts**
  In each chapter I identify key concepts in bold and give definitions. These are concepts that are often used in sociology and it is important for you to understand their meaning.

Companion website

There is a companion website for the book that contains much information and resources for both students and instructors.

For students

- **Multiple-choice questions**
  These provide a quick test of your knowledge of the key materials of each chapter.
- **Glossary**
  A list of all key concepts and their definitions for each chapter.
- **Further reading**
  A list of essential readings for each chapter.

- **Appendix**
  Some chapters have an online appendix. These appendices provide coverage of some topics that are not essential to the core argument of the chapter, but which you may find interesting to read as more in-depth material and for further strengthening your skills to think like a sociologist.

For instructors

- **Test bank**
  A collection of multiple-choice questions that can be used to test sociology students' knowledge of the materials.
- **Discussion questions with answers**
  Discussion questions (with answers) that more deeply reflect on the materials presented in the textbook.
- **PowerPoint**
  For each chapter, customizable PowerPoint slides have been made.

Acknowledgments

Many people contributed to the process of producing this textbook and the companion website. I would like to thank the Routledge editorial team, and especially Emily Briggs, for taking great care of this project. I am incredibly grateful to the reviewers recruited by Routledge and to other scholars as well for taking the time to thoroughly read the chapters and give their detailed feedback. I have learned so much from each of you! Special thanks go to the following people for reviewing the book:

Professor Vincent Buskens, Utrecht University
Dr Rense Corten, Utrecht University
Professor Andreas Flache, University of Groningen
Dr Fenella Fleischmann, Utrecht University
Dr Sara Geven, University of Amsterdam
Professor Nan Dirk de Graaf, Oxford University
Professor Frank Kalter, University of Mannheim
Dr Antonie Knigge, Utrecht University
Professor Ping-Yin Kuan, National Chengchi University
Professor Richard Layte, Trinity College Dublin
Professor Marco van Leeuwen, Utrecht University
Professor Tanja van der Lippe, Utrecht University
Dr Zoltán Lippényi, University of Groningen
Professor Marcel Lubbers, Radboud University Nijmegen
Professor Ineke Maas, Utrecht University
Dr Jornt Mandemakers, Utrecht University
Dr Roza Meuleman, Radboud University Nijmegen
Professor Christiaan Monden, Oxford University
Dr Wojtek Przepiorka, Utrecht University
Professor Werner Raub, Utrecht University
Dr Anne Roeters, The Netherlands Institute for Social Research
Professor Arnout van de Rijt, European University Institute
Professor Stijn Ruiter, Utrecht University
Dr Tobias Stark, Utrecht University
Dr Jordi Tena, Universitat Autònoma de Barcelona
Dr Wilfred Uunk, University of Bamberg
Professor Ellen Verbakel, Radboud University Nijmegen

Acknowledgments

Professor Beate Völker, University of Amsterdam
Professor Herman van de Werfhorst, University of Amsterdam
Dr Pascale van Zantvliet, Fontys University of Applied Sciences

I wish to thank Renae Loh Sze Ming for providing support for creating the graphics of this book and Judith Harvey for editing the entire book. Several people assisted me in producing the materials for the companion website. Special credits go to Kevin Wittenberg, Marissa Bultman, Nick Wuestenenk, Jos Slabbekoorn and Sara Marcora.

About the author

Frank van Tubergen is Professor of Sociology at Utrecht University (Netherlands), where he has taught introduction to sociology for many years. His current work is focused on social networks, immigration and religion. His work has appeared in top journals including *American Sociological Review*, *American Journal of Sociology*, *European Sociological Review* and *Demography*. He has received numerous awards for his scientific work and he is a Fellow of the European Academy of Sociology.

Abbreviations

B(sp)	Background: social problem
B(k)	Background: scientific knowledge
Q	Question
Q(d)	Descriptive question
Q(t)	Theoretical question
Q(a)	Application question
O	Observation
T	Theory
P	Proposition
H	Hypothesis
C	Condition

Part 1

Thinking like a sociologist

Chapter 1

Questions

Chapter overview

Science starts with curiosity, with raising questions about what's happening and why. Questions are at the very beginning of any research, and the kind of questions scientists ask more or less defines their discipline. There are many different scientific disciplines, however, such as physics, biology, psychology, anthropology and sociology. So what sort of questions, then, do sociologists ask? This chapter is about sociological questions: what they are, what makes good questions and how they differ from questions in other disciplines. As we will see, underlying sociological questions is a certain perspective, which is called the "sociological perspective" and the "sociological imagination". I explain how the sociological view differs from an individual perspective on human behavior (1.1). Then I discuss how sociological questions are related to social problems, which are often the main starting point for sociological research (1.2). After this, I introduce the three aims of sociology, namely to accurately describe social phenomena, to understand underlying processes and to apply sociological insights (1.3), and we will see that these three aims concur with three types of sociological questions—descriptive, theoretical and application questions (1.4). I then review the art of asking good sociological questions (1.5). Subsequently, I bring in the idea that all human beings are "private sociologists" themselves, as they participate in social life continuously and wonder every day about what's happening and why. At the same time, however, this does not mean that sociological questions and insights are common sense. I discuss why people sometimes mistakenly think so and what this means for "academic sociology," i.e., the scientific study of social life (1.6). I end with a discussion of sociology as a cumulative science, i.e., theories and observations of earlier studies are incorporated in the work of successive sociological studies (1.7).

> ## Learning goals
>
> After reading this chapter, check if you are able to:
>
> - Describe the difference between sociological and individual perspectives on human behavior.
> - Explain what is meant by proximate and ultimate causes of human behavior.
> - Describe the difference between micro, meso and macro level.
> - Describe the similarities and differences between a social problem and a social phenomenon.
> - Describe the three aims of sociology.
> - Differentiate between normative and scientific questions.
> - Formulate descriptive, theoretical and application questions.
> - Reformulate ill-defined questions into more precise questions.
> - Describe the meaning of societal and scientific relevance.
> - Describe how private sociologists differ from academic sociology.
> - Describe how cumulative sociological science works.

1.1 The sociological perspective

When you look around, at your friends, family and other people you know, it might sometimes strike you how much people differ from each other in what they possess, how they think and the things they do. You might know some people, I guess, who are wealthy and have a high social status and you might also know others who are less affluent. You might also know people who uphold norms and values that you don't share, and people who do not go to university like you, or who spend more (or less) time with friends and family than you normally do. You might also have noticed how similar people are sometimes. People who share the same religion and lifestyle, for example, or who have the same political preferences.

How could we understand the fact that sometimes people differ in their behavior? And why do some people resemble each other? In short: how can we explain human behavior? In answering these questions, sociologists take a specific perspective. To illustrate what this perspective entails, let's take an example of a phenomenon they study: obesity. Why are some persons obese and others not? Before answering this question, we need to be clear what we mean by "obesity." The World Health Organization (WHO) defines obesity as "abnormal or excessive fat accumulation that may impair health" (WHO, 2015) and it uses the Body Mass Index (BMI), which is a person's weight in kilograms divided by the square of that person's height in meters, to classify overweight (BMI ≥ 25) and obesity (BMI ≥ 30). According to statistics of the WHO 39% of adults aged 18 years and over across the world were overweight in 2014 and 13% were obese.

THINKING LIKE A SOCIOLOGIST 1.1

How would you explain that some people are obese and others are not? What would be the reason do you think?

Let's make things simple and say we know one obese person. Let's call him John. Then assume we know another person who is not obese: Kaito. We can ask ourselves: why is John obese and not Kaito?

One explanation could be that John eats too much and that he is having too little physical exercise. Maybe Kaito takes more care about his food intake than John and he goes to work by bike instead of by car as John does. One could argue that a lack of "self-control" is the cause of John's obesity, which means that John is eating impulsively too often and cannot control his short-term desires for food intake—unlike Kaito. Or, maybe, it is that John has a negative self-concept and feels some relief from his "mental pain" by eating, whereas Kaito does not suffer from this. Another explanation for why John is obese could be that brain or body dysfunctions play a role; genetically inherited dispositions that make John more vulnerable to being overweight than Kaito.

Suppose that one day, John becomes dissatisfied with his extreme overweight and wants to lose weight. What could he do? We identify several possible explanations for his obesity and the first step to be taken is to discover the exact cause in the case of John. Is it indeed a lack of self-control from which John suffers? Does he have a negative self-concept or is something else the cause of his obesity? Maybe it appears that not just one but a combination of factors causes his excessive overweight. Having identified the causes, John could then take action and try to reduce his body weight. One solution to do something about the excessive overweight could be that John uses a self-help book and follows its suggested treatment program. In fact, such self-help books ("lose weight in eight weeks!") are popular nowadays and used by many as an attempt to control their eating behavior. Another way for John to combat his obesity is to ask for the help of a dietitian regarding the right food intake. Or he could start psychological therapy to increase his self-control and gain a more positive self-concept.

This example gives you an idea of how one could explain human behavior. And it gives clues about possible remedies and treatments as well. All the explanations for obesity seem plausible and its corresponding solutions and treatment programs might indeed work. It is, however, important to realize that the explanations for obesity and its corresponding "solutions" take a specific perspective. What they have in common is that they frame John's overweight as an *individual problem*. This means that the causes of John's extreme overweight are to be found in his individual characteristics, like his personal eating pattern, his own lack of self-control, his negative self-concept and/or his biological disposition. And, given these individual causes, the solutions and treatments should be targeted towards the individual and therefore can differ from person to person. This, in short, is called an **individual perspective** on the causes and treatments of obesity, and indeed one could use such an individual perspective to explain any kind of human behavior.

Sociologists, by contrast, adopt a different perspective on human behavior. They do not deny that there are individual causes of obesity and they are aware of the merits of individual treatments. That said, they would come up with different explanations and solutions. The unique perspective taken by sociologists is to understand the behavior of persons by considering their **social context**. Classic sociologists such as Durkheim, Weber, Simmel, Marx and Engels emphasized this particular way of looking at human behavior. The American sociologist C. W. Mills famously coined the term **sociological imagination** to signal that the task for sociologists is to identify *social causes* of human behavior (Mills, 2000 [1959]). Thus, the **sociological perspective** seeks to explain human behavior by the social contexts individuals share. In short, it identifies social causes as opposed to individual causes.

What might this "social context" be? One particular context which sociologists frequently study is the country in which people live. If the country, as a social context, plays a role in understanding obesity, then we should expect to see that countries differ in how many people are obese. Is this indeed the case? To answer this question we can again consult data provided by the WHO, but now differentiated by country (WHO, 2016b). Table 1.1 presents the percentage of the population 18 years and older that are overweight and obese for a selected number of countries in the world. Note that the numbers for overweight include those who are obese.

There are striking differences across countries. At the top of the ranking we find the United States, where 66.9% of the population over 18 are overweight and 34.9% obese. The figures are much lower in China, Japan, India and Indonesia. For example, in China 5.5% of the population are obese and in Japan it is 3.9%. Apparently where you are born matters in determining your "risk" of overweight and obesity. Sociologists would therefore argue that, when studying the causes of overweight and obesity, one should not consider these as pure individual problems.

individual perspective type of explanation of human behavior which focuses on individual causes.

social context social environment in which people are embedded.

sociological imagination (also **sociological perspective**) type of explanation of human behavior which focuses on social causes.

Table 1.1 Percentage of population aged 18+ overweight and obese (2014).

	Overweight	Obese
North America		
United States	66.9	34.9
Canada	63.2	28.3
Mexico	63.9	27.8
South America		
Argentina	61.8	27.3
Brazil	55.3	21.1

Asia		
China	30.8	5.5
India	18.6	3.5
Indonesia	26.5	6.1
Japan	26.4	3.9
Pakistan	27.0	7.8
Africa		
Nigeria	27.6	8.1
Egypt	62.2	30.6
South Africa	52.5	27.2
Europe		
France	58.6	20.8
Germany	56.0	21.5
United Kingdom	62.7	26.6
Italy	57.6	19.3
Russia	56.3	22.5
Oceania		
Australia	63.6	27.9

Source: WHO, 2016b.

Countries are not static entities, however: the country where you live today may differ from your country a few decades ago. Sociologists say that social contexts change and they study the human consequences of such changes. Consider, for example, Figure 1.1, which presents the overweight rate among adults in various countries between 1975 and 2016. As you can see, in each of these countries the share of the population with overweight significantly increased. For example, in China fewer than 10% of the population were overweight in 1975, but this has increased to more than 30% in 2016. The overweight and obesity rates have increased not only for these five selected countries; they have increased worldwide. The WHO has called this trend "globesity," i.e., the global epidemic of obesity (WHO, 2016a), and warns that "if immediate action is not taken, millions will suffer from an array of serious health disorders."

You might wonder, in the meantime, where John and Kaito fit into this sociological perspective – if they do so at all. This is an important question. The sociological perspective is different from the individual perspective not only because it focuses on *social causes* of behavior (instead of individual characteristics), but also because it considers *collective outcomes* (instead of the behavior of a few individuals). What sociologists actually study is not why John is obese and Kaito is not. That is to say, sociologists do not aim to understand the behavior of each unique individual, John and Kaito. That is the purpose of the individual perspective. The sociological perspective instead examines **social phenomena**.

social phenomenon
collective human behavior.

Thus, what sociologists aim to understand is how, first, human behavior *typically* results from shared contextual conditions and how, subsequently, this gives rise to collective outcomes. Sociologists may point out that John is living in the US and that obesity is a common pattern for people living in his country. They may argue that Kaito is different from John, because Kaito is born and raised in Japan—a country in which obesity is rather uncommon. Thus, the cases of "John" and "Kaito" can be interpreted as collective human

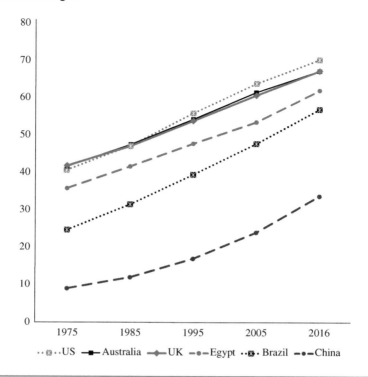

Figure 1.1 Percentage of population aged 18+ overweight, 1975–2016.
Source: WHO, 2016b.

behavior typically occurring when living in the US and Japan, respectively. Thus, sociologists argue that behavior has social causes and that such shared social contexts result in collective outcomes (Coleman, 1990; Hedström & Swedberg, 1998; Raub, Buskens, & Van Assen, 2011). Sociologists are therefore interested in describing and understanding, for example, how the crime *rate* changed in a country, why *group* violence occurs, how entire *societies* and *cultures* change. Let's summarize the differences between the individual and the sociological perspective on human behavior (Table 1.2):

Table 1.2 Differences between the individual perspective and the sociological perspective.

	Individual perspective	*Sociological perspective*
Phenomena of interest	Individual phenomena, individual behavior (Why is John obese?)	Social phenomena, collective behavior (Why is obesity increasing in society?)
Explanations for behavior	Individual characteristics (e.g., genes, personality)	Social context, social causes (e.g., country, neighborhood, school, family)

What does this mean for you when you want to use a sociological perspective to study human behavior? It means that you consider the role social contexts play in shaping behavior rather than focusing on individual characteristics like personality. Whatever kind of behavior you study—crime, corruption, peer relations and so forth—you can always apply this unique sociological perspective. Let's summarize this as a useful principle:

PRINCIPLE 1.1

The Sociological Perspective
Sociology is the scientific study of social phenomena. This means that, if you want to give a sociological explanation of human behavior, you need to consider the influence of social contexts and study the resulting collective human behavior.

How is this sociological perspective on human behavior related to the individual perspective? Do they supplement each other or are they in conflict? Let's use our obesity example to answer these questions. There are, generally speaking, three possible relations between the two perspectives.

Supplemental perspectives

Often, sociologists argue that the sociological perspective *supplements* the individual perspective. They are not in conflict, but the two perspectives together provide a more comprehensive explanation of human behavior. Thus, one may argue that obesity is a phenomenon that we cannot understand if we only adopt an individual perspective. The differences across countries in the rates of overweight and obesity suggest that social contexts do indeed matter and so do the observed changes in the obesity rate within countries over time.

There is another source of evidence which suggests that a pure individual perspective on behavior falls short and needs to be supplemented with a sociological perspective. If only individual causes underlie behavior then individual treatments should be highly effective. In reality, however, such treatments fail all too often. Many people buy self-help books and follow treatment programs to lose weight, give up this program after a certain time and gain weight again. Or they make plans to change their food intake but never realize them. Some people start doing more physical exercise, only to discover after a while that they haven't done so for a long time. Even with the help of a psychologist or dietitian, many people who are obese do not succeed in losing weight structurally. Why do individual treatments often fail for people like John? To answer this question one needs to consider a sociological perspective, too.

Alternative perspectives

The individual and sociological perspectives can also be framed as *alternative perspectives*. For example, one may claim that social contexts do not matter at all in explaining human behavior and that, in fact, only individual causes matter. Or that there are only social causes and no individual causes to behavior.

For example, one may argue that we can very well explain obesity with individual characteristics and that social conditions do not matter. In other words, what drives obesity are individual factors such as biological-genetic inheritance, personality and so forth. Consequently, the observed variation across social contexts in the rates of obesity are in fact due to these and other individual factors. The argument would be, for example, that a higher percentage of citizens in the US are obese than in Japan because the populations differ in their genetic disposition for obesity.

Sociologists would be inclined to recognize the importance of individual biological factors. However, they would also argue that context differences are hard to *completely* explain with individual factors. In the case of obesity, for example, it is difficult to completely explain with individual factors the differences in obesity across countries. Moreover, sociologists would argue that social phenomena change over time – as we have seen with respect to the obesity "epidemic" in the US. Our brains and biological makeup do not evolve that quickly and personal characteristics are likewise rather constant over time. If obesity is *only* caused by individual factors then we would expect no change in obesity over short periods in time. The evidence, however, shows that prevalence of obesity in many countries is strongly changing in a very short time span. Because human nature did not change in such a short period, the individual perspective can't explain this increase. Instead, *changing societal conditions* must have contributed to that *change in the rate of obesity*, and thus contexts affect our risk of obesity as well.

Proximate and ultimate causes

Next to the idea that individual and sociological perspectives can supplement each other and are seen as alternatives at other times, there can be a third relationship between the two. Sociologists sometimes argue that individual causes of human behavior are "proximate" causes of behavior, not ultimate causes. **Proximate causes** are the factors that are "close to" the phenomena the researcher wants to explain, whereas ultimate causes are factors that are "deeper," "hidden" in the background (Lieberson & Silverman, 1965; Mayr, 1961). Proximate causes are explained by **ultimate causes** (also called "distal causes").

proximate causes
factors that are close to the phenomenon to be explained.

ultimate causes
factors that underlie proximate causes.

For example, one could explain individual differences in obesity with individual differences in negative self-view: those individuals who have more negative self-image are more likely to gain excessive body fat (Figure 1.2). It could well be that research indeed shows that this explanation makes sense, and that therefore having a "negative self-concept" is a factor that affects obesity. However, one could legitimately ask the question why someone develops a negative self-concept in the first place. From a sociological perspective, one could argue that social contexts affect the development of a negative self-concept and that this negative self-concept subsequently results in distorted eating behavior. For example, it could be that problematic situations in the family or being bullied in school result in the development of negative self-views. In this latter case, the school context, and the bullying that takes place in this context, is the ultimate cause: social contexts affect individual predispositions (i.e., "negative self-concept") and these predispositions in turn affect obesity.

This example also shows that when sociologists refer to "social contexts" they can have different things in mind. Sociologists often consider the country in which people live as an

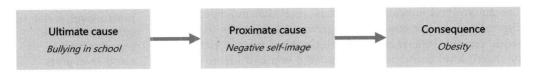

Figure 1.2 An example of ultimate and proximate causes.

important social context that shapes human behavior. Much sociological work compares countries and the changes within countries (Coleman, 1990; Nolan & Lenski, 2011), as we have done above. It is important to realize, however, that sociologists also study other social contexts besides countries. Sociologists consider families and schools as social contexts, but also neighborhoods and organizations. People who are raised in the same family, who attend the same school, who live in the same neighborhood, or belong to the same organization share certain social contexts. This means, for example, that people's "risk" of becoming obese may not only be affected by the country in which they are living, but also by the family they grow up in, by their peers in school and so forth.

There is a difference, however, between countries on the one hand and families, schools, neighborhoods and organizations on the other hand. The difference has to do with the *scale*, or *level*, of the social context (Alexander, Giesen, Munch, & Smelser, 1987). Let's see why this is the case, taking schools in the US and Japan as an example (Figure 1.3). Pupils *P1* and *P2* are exposed to the same conditions at school—they share the same school context *S1*, which may be different from conditions in schools *S2*, *S3* and so forth. This school context is of small scale: typically, there are somewhere between 100 and 1,000 pupils per school. But pupils are also citizens of a country (in this case: the US or Japan) and, as such, they share another social context—albeit on a much larger scale. There are multiple schools, neighborhoods and families within a country, but not the other way around. Countries are, so to say, of a "larger" scale and "higher" level than neighborhoods and families.

micro level the level at which individuals operate.

To designate these differences in scale (level), sociologists have coined the concepts *micro*, *meso* and *macro level*. The **micro level** refers to the lowest level, namely individuals and their behavior, attitudes, resources and so forth. The **meso level** designates social conditions that individuals share in their immediate environment. Examples are: family, neighborhood, school, work organization, religious community, political organization and social networks.

meso level social contexts at the intermediate level. Examples: families, neighborhoods, schools, organizations.

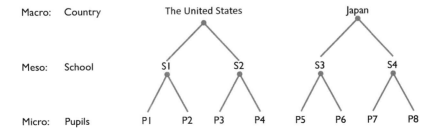

Figure 1.3 An example of the micro, meso and macro level.

The **macro level** indicates the highest level that individuals share. Typically these are countries or groups of countries (continents, world regions). Social contexts can therefore refer to either meso- or macro-level contexts. Consequently, you can identify at both levels ultimate causes for behavior. For example, when trying to explain obesity, you can study meso-level factors like the socializing role of parents (family context), the impact of living near to fast-food restaurants (neighborhood context), the social norms of peers (school context) and so forth. And one can study how the macro environment shapes low-exercise (e.g., elevators, motorways) or high-exercise infrastructure (e.g., stairs, cycle paths).

> **macro level** social contexts that are broader than meso level units. Examples: nations, groups of nations, continents.

In reality, the exact scale cannot be captured with three levels. For example, some neighborhoods may be small, others may be larger. And larger neighborhoods may group together multiple families, so that it seems more appropriate to speak of four or more levels. That said, it is important to remember that you can identify social contexts at different levels—from microscopically small (like the family) to bigger contexts that millions of people share (like the country). As a rough indication of this important difference, it is helpful to distinguish between meso and macro. Sometimes, however, you'll see that sociologists make reality even more simple than this threefold distinction and use only the concepts "micro" and "macro" to differentiate between individuals and their social context. If so, you should keep in mind that, in such cases, "macro" can refer to various levels: either the meso or macro level.

BOX 1.1

Durkheim's study: *Suicide* (1897)

One of the most famous studies in sociology is Durkheim's *Suicide*, which was published in 1897. Many sociologists today regard this classic work as an exemplary study of how to apply the sociological perspective to understand human behavior. In this renowned study, the topic of investigation—suicide—was considered an immoral act at the time of writing, similar to alcoholism, prostitution and crime. However, before the 19th century, suicide was considered just that: an immoral act, but no one thought of studying the possible causes of suicide (Giddens, 1965).

This changed in the 19th century and gradually suicide became the subject of scientific investigations. Most scholars at that time, however, adopted an individual perspective on suicide. For example, Esquirol, writing in 1838, argued that "Suicide shows all the characteristics of mental disorders of which it is in fact only a symptom" (Esquirol, 1838). The predominant view at the end of the 19th century was that suicide is purely driven by individual causes, such as mental alienation, alcoholism and heredity.

At the same time, however, more and more population-level administrative data on suicide rates were collected and analyzed by so-called moral statisticians (Morselli, 1881; Quetelet, 2013 [1835]). These data were used by Durkheim for his study as well, and with more vigor than anyone else of his time. In Part I of *Suicide*, Durkheim systematically criticizes these "extra-social factors." He presents statistics on suicide rates that challenge the individual perspective. For example, he shows that European countries differ enormously in their suicide rates—how could that be explained by individual causes? And if alcoholism is a major individual cause of suicide, why are the suicide rates then lower in areas within France where alcohol consumption is high? Durkheim shows that these observations are not in line with expectations derived from the individual perspective.

After having eliminated the supposed individual causes of suicide one by one, Durkheim shows in Part II that contextual conditions greatly affect suicide. He systematically builds up a theory in which he outlines the influence of the family, the religious group and other social contexts. At the end of his book, Durkheim also addresses the possibility that individual characteristics such as depression and alcoholism affect suicide, but he argues that these proximate causes are in turn explained by socio-structural conditions (i.e., ultimate causes). Durkheim tests his theory with empirical data and shows that his theory succeeds very well. In Chapter 2, we will take a more in-depth look at his theory of suicide.

Durkheim's study *Suicide* has stimulated many follow-up studies on suicide, including the work of his nephew Halbwachs (2002 [1930]), Henry and Short (1954), Gibbs and Martin (1964) and continues to do so today (Pescosolido & Georgianna, 1989; Stack, 2000). According to the counts on Google Scholar in 2019 (June), *Suicide* has been cited in more than 20,000 studies. Most of these studies are not on suicide, however. Rather, many of these follow-up studies cite *Suicide* as a classic work which outlined the sociological perspective on human behavior and continue in that tradition.

1.2 Social problems

What motivates sociologists to investigate social phenomena? Why do they study obesity as a social phenomenon, for example? An important reason for sociologists to study certain topics is when these are considered social problems. But what are social problems? A **social problem**, also named **public issue**, is commonly understood as a problem that (Mills, 2000):

1   goes beyond the individual (it affects many people),
2   is an issue about which many people are concerned (it is in conflict with certain values).

Social problems are more severe the more people are affected (criterion 1) and the more strongly they conflict with prevalent values (criterion 2). In the case of John, his obesity might be called **personal trouble**, when he personally feels dissatisfied with his extreme overweight and when only individual causes underlie his overweight. In that case it would be, in other words, a problem of John himself.

> a **social problem** (also **public issue**) is one that:
>
> 1 goes beyond the personal troubles of the individual (it affects many people);
>
> 2 is an issue about which many people are concerned.
>
> **personal trouble** problem related to the personal life of an individual.

But the "problem" of John's obesity might also go beyond the individual and indicate a social problem. If many people are obese in the country in which John lives, sociologists would argue that the obesity of a person like John is "typical" for people who live over there. If obesity is generally regarded as a problem—because people find it undesirable and it conflicts with certain values—it is called a social problem, a public issue (Mills, 2000).

What is identified as a social problem varies from time to time, from context to context. One reason social problems fluctuate over time and differ across societies is that the problems with which people are confronted equally change over time and space. Obesity wasn't a major social issue in the world in the 1960s because at that time few people were obese. Another reason is that what most people consider as "desirable" changes over time and across contexts, i.e., mainstream values are not a universal constant but rather differ across time and space. What might be a social problem in one country might not be so in another, and even within the same social context people may disagree about whether something is a social problem or not. What people consider as a social problem depends on their values.

Let's review another contemporary social problem, namely poverty. While obesity is increasing worldwide, it is typically a social problem seen in affluent countries. In poorer nations, overweight is often not the main issue of concern—but underweight certainly is. There are, even today, many countries in the world where people suffer and even die because of poverty. Undernutrition and insufficient health care are a major cause of death for many children in the world. According to UNICEF, an organization that is concerned with the rights and wellbeing of children across the world, more than 16,000 children die every day from "preventable or treatable causes" (UNICEF, 2015). Worldwide, UNICEF statistics show that around three million children under the age of five die each year due to undernutrition. In some countries such child deaths are much more common than in other nations. To see how large these differences are, consider Table 1.3, which presents the under-five mortality rate per 1,000 live births in 2015.

Table 1.3 Under-five mortality rate per 1,000 live births (2015).

	Mortality rate
North America	
United States	6.8
Canada	5.3
Mexico	14.8
South America	
Argentina	11.4
Brazil	15.7
Asia	
China	10.8
India	44.1
Indonesia	27.2
Japan	3.0
Pakistan	79.5
Africa	
Nigeria	107.5
Egypt	23.7
South Africa	40.3

Europe

France	4.2
Germany	3.9
United Kingdom	4.5
Italy	3.5
Russia	8.6
Oceania	
Australia	3.8

Source: UNICEF, 2016.

In Japan—a highly developed country—three out of 1,000 children died in 2015 before they were five years old. In other affluent nations the mortality rate is in the same direction. Compare these figures with those of poorer nations, where many children suffer from under-nutrition and insufficient health care. In Nigeria, 107 out of 1,000 children die before they are five years old. The most disadvantaged country in the UNICEF 2015 ranking is Angola, where 162 out of 1,000 children die before they are five years old. The under-five mortality rate is indicative of poverty more generally and in many countries poverty is one of the main social problems, particularly for the poorer nations like Angola but not exclusively so: also in highly developed nations poverty is an issue of concern to a large group of people.

Image 1.1 Poverty, as a social problem, is the starting point of sociological studies.

The two examples of social problems introduced so far—the obesity epidemic and poverty—are issues that involve large segments of societies. Other social problems could be more locally concentrated, such as in certain neighborhoods, families and organizations, or only relate to specific segments or "social categories" within societies, such as women or ethnic minorities. For example, it could be that certain neighborhoods in the country are confronted with violence and poverty, whereas other neighborhoods do rather well. In that case, one could be tempted to not call this a "social problem" as not many people in the country at large are affected (criterion 1), or concerned about it (criterion 2). However, within the neighborhoods that are plagued by violence and poverty it is considered a social problem. A more inclusive approach to social problems, which I adopt in this textbook, does consider these more locally concentrated problems, as well as problems pertaining to only certain categories in society, as true social problems. Thus, a longer list of social problems could include:

- Corruption in organizations
- Crime and unsafety in neighborhoods
- Bullying at school
- Violence and abuse in families
- Excessive income inequality
- Inter-ethnic tensions
- War and collective violence
- Refugee crisis
- Societal polarization
- Discrimination
- Mental health problems
- Erosion of social connections
- Terrorism
- High unemployment rate
- Global warming and pollution.

THINKING LIKE A SOCIOLOGIST 1.2

Can you think of other social problems? What are currently, according to you, the three most important ones in your country? Can you also come up with something that used to be a social problem but is not so any longer?

1.3 Three aims of sociology

What is the role of sociologists when we talk about social problems? How are social problems related to the work of sociologists? Governments often try to solve social problems and political parties typically offer different strategies and solutions to do so. But also specialized organizations can target certain social problems in society. We might wonder, then, what sociologists have to offer.

Generally speaking, one can say that the aim of sociologists is to come up with accurate scientific descriptions and theoretical explanations for social phenomena, and to apply their

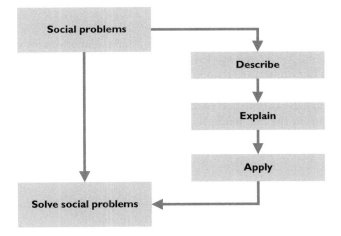

Figure 1.4 Social problems and the core aims of sociology.

knowledge. In other words, there are three core aims of sociology, i.e., to *describe*, to *explain* and to *apply*. Figure 1.4 helps to clarify the relationship between social problems and the aims of sociology.

Social problems typically become the target of governments and organizations, which attempt to mitigate these problems. Once obesity is considered as a public issue, as something that is seen as an undesirable collective outcome, government agencies develop policy measures and interventions. However, in order to come up with interventions that are effective, one needs to get an insight into the nature and causes of the social problem. To assess how large the social problem is, what causes the problem and which interventions are effective, the work of sociologists is needed.

What sociologists do is often motivated by contemporary social problems, and they approach social problems, from a scientific perspective, as social phenomena. Why are "social problems" and "social phenomena" different? Social problems have a *normative* dimension: desirable goals or values are threatened, people want to solve this problem and politicians, policy makers and organizations offer various measures and interventions to do so. In sociology, social problems are studied as social phenomena, which means that they are not studied as a normative problem but as a scientific phenomenon of interest. Understanding social phenomena thereby contributes to understanding and solving social problems.

Describe

The first aim for sociologists is, then, to come up with accurate descriptions of social phenomena. This is an important contribution to the understanding of social problems because people could uphold erroneous beliefs about it. For example, there could be a major concern in society about the "rising crime rates among youth," which is regarded as a social problem. Sociological studies might come up with accurate descriptions of changing crime rates: how strong is the change? What sorts of crime are committed by youth? Is there, indeed, an increase in crime? To get a good understanding of the nature of social problems we need to have accurate descriptions to begin with. Sociologists play an important role in this. The first important task for sociologists is therefore to provide accurate descriptions of social phenomena.

Explain

The second aim of sociologists is to come up with scientific explanations for social phenomena. What causes "globesity," i.e., the epidemic increase in obesity worldwide? How can we explain phenomena like crime, poverty and violence? Sociologists come up with explanations and subsequently use empirical data to examine whether these explanations are true. If politicians and policy makers want to solve social problems effectively, they need to know what causes these problems in the first place. If crime is rising among youth, how can we explain that? What social conditions set these forces in motion?

Apply

The third aim of sociology is to apply and share its insights. By doing so, it returns to the normative domain, to the public concern about social problems.

First, sociological work can be valuable for coming up with *predictions*, i.e., sociological findings can be used to describe what is likely to happen. It could be that sociological studies provide evidence to suggest that some social problems will disappear, whereas others will become more pressing. For example, sociological studies can predict how the crime rate will develop in the near future—with certain probabilities and within certain boundaries. To illustrate, it is a well-established empirical finding that youth are more likely to commit crime than elderly people. Younger people, particularly around the ages of 15–25, show a peak in crime levels—what is known as the "age-crime curve." Sociological studies may look deeper into this phenomenon and relate the age-crime curve to societal changes in age composition. This will allow sociologists to predict what will happen to the crime rates in the future. If fertility rates steadily decrease and populations become older, there are simply fewer youth who can commit crime—thereby lowering the overall crime rate.

The second way in which sociologists apply their knowledge is to develop and evaluate **social interventions**. Interventions are subject to scientific insights and empirical work and are targeted towards reducing social problems. Let's take an example of a social problem to illustrate this. Imagine that the *disadvantaged employment position of women* is seen as a social problem in society: women have lower-paid jobs and earn less than men, and many people find this undesirable. Suppose that in public debates there is a discussion about what to do about this and policy makers are struggling about arriving at appropriate measures. Sociologists could then be of value, by evaluating various proposed social interventions as well as developing alternative ones.

social intervention
social policy
measure.

Imagine, for example, that one proposed intervention is to implement *positive discrimination*, i.e., to hire disproportionally more women. Sociological studies could then clarify the following issues:

a   Do positive-discrimination policies lead to a boost in the career of women or not?
b   How large are the costs and benefits of such positive-discrimination policies?
c   Are there unintended consequences of positive-discrimination policies?
d   Which alternative interventions can be developed to boost the career of women?

Based on sociological explanations and theoretical insights, sociologists can evaluate what the outcome will be of the various interventions and if these outcomes concur with what is seen as desirable by politicians and the public at large. They can inform social policy makers on whether the outcomes would be as desired, how much the costs and benefits of the measures will be, and whether such policies will have other, possibly unintended consequences. Possibly, sociological studies would show that the career of women can be more improved by providing extensive child care facilities, or that such measures are cheaper and do not have unwanted side-effects.

When sociological work is carried out in view of current social problems that exist in society, their work has so-called **societal relevance**. The relevance of sociology to society is the scientific knowledge they produce in light of social problems. Their contribution is, first of all, to come up with accurate *descriptions* of social phenomena. This is critically important, as public misperceptions about social problems happen all too often. Second, sociologists dig

societal relevance relevance of sociological work for the understanding of social problems.

deeper into the processes that underlie social phenomena. They systematically construct and test *explanations*, leading to a better understanding of what causes the social phenomena. And then, third, they can *apply* their knowledge such that they give scientifically grounded predictions of what will happen, as well as developing and evaluating social interventions.

Ultimately, it is up to society, to politicians, policy makers, organizations and the general population to decide which intervention, if any, should be used. From describing and understanding social life (*what is*) one cannot infer how social life *should be*. It is a *normative* issue (1) whether one finds it desirable or not to boost the employment position of women (i.e., what one identifies as a social problem) and (2) which interventions should be favored, if any, to enhance the employment position of women (i.e., how one solves the problem).

Societal relevance, therefore, does not imply that sociologists should pursue normative statements or engage in social activism (Weber, 1919). Sociology is a science, not a political ideology, although some sociologists in the past, most prominently Marx, have had such a moral-political agenda (i.e., the ideology of communism, "Marxism"). Sociologists, and scientists more generally, may have their personal opinions about "what are the major social issues" and "what should be" done, but such views, when expressed publicly, are actually normative positions and can be seen as statements of scientists *as citizens* (Borjas, 2005). That does not mean that sociologists cannot engage *as scientists* at all in public normative discussions. Sociologists fulfill the important role of informing the public debate and policy makers with scientific knowledge. It is "public sociology" without a political-normative ideology. And when sociologists do not work in academia, but as *professionals* in governmental and non-governmental organizations, they can give valuable scientific advice on how to mitigate the social problems their organization is concerned about.

It is important to realize that social problems are often complex and have multiple causes, including not only social conditions but also non-social factors. This means that sociological insights contribute to our knowledge of social problems, but that a full understanding of social problems also includes the work of other scientists. Take, for example, global warming, which is seen by many as one of the most urgent contemporary social problems on our planet. Scientific studies show that global warming results in extreme weather, massive flooding, the extinction of species, long-term droughts in certain areas of the world, the melting of the land-based ice in the Arctic and rising sea-levels, amongst other problems. Global warming is caused by greenhouse gases, which result from a variety of human activities such as fossil-fuel burning. To combat climate change, scholars emphasize that a mixture of actions is needed: laws to protect the environment, the improvement of technologies for solar and wind energy, but also social changes as people need to adopt the new technologies and change their lifestyle. The societal relevance of sociological work on these complex social problems shows itself in conjunction with the work of other scientists.

1.4 Three types of sociological questions

We have seen that the core aims of sociology are to describe and explain social phenomena and to apply this knowledge. Each sociological study starts with asking a question, which is related to one of these aims or to several of them. *Scientific* questions, therefore, need to be differentiated from *normative* questions. Typically, questions

normative question question that entails value judgments.

on social problems are framed in a normative way. Social problems are accompanied with **normative questions** about what "should be done." When sociologists study social problems as social phenomena, these normative elements are set aside and instead the scientific aspects of it are underlined. Consider the following examples of normative questions that could be related to social problems:

1 "Should we reduce income inequality?"
2 "Should we do more to combat the rise in crime?"
3 "Should we adopt positive-discrimination policies to boost the career of women?"

Each of these three questions are about what one *should* do; answers to normative questions entail value judgments, i.e., about what people consider as good or bad for themselves or for society at large. Some people think it is the role of the government to actively reduce income inequalities, whereas other people approve of larger inequalities in society and are more in favor of free markets and minimal government interference. Answers to normative questions such as those mentioned above typically differ between people, depending on people's own beliefs, goals, norms and values. Those questions naturally belong to the realm of politics, they are at the core of the public debate and they can be the subject of personal contemplation.

scientific question question that does not entail value judgments. There are three types of scientific questions, namely: descriptive, theoretical and application.

Sociology is not a normative ideology, hence you need to verify that your questions are targeted towards social phenomena. It is therefore helpful to differentiate the normative element of social problems from the scientific aspects of it. This allows you to ask **scientific questions**.

PRINCIPLE 1.2

Scientific questions
Sociologists study the scientific aspects to social problems. This means that, rather than asking normative questions, they address scientific questions about social phenomena.

After you have verified that your question is a scientific one about social phenomena, you need to be clear about the underlying *aim* of your question. To which of the three aims in sociology is your question related? Is the aim to describe social phenomena? To explain? Or is it to apply the knowledge you have acquired about the social phenomena? Let's call the questions sociologists raise Q. I will discuss three *types* of questions Q that sociologists address: *descriptive*, *theoretical* and *application* (Table 1.4).

descriptive question type of scientific question targeted towards describing phenomena.

The first type of questions sociologists ask are so-called **descriptive questions**, *Q(d)*. These are questions that are concerned with

Table 1.4 Three types of sociological questions.

Type of question	Symbol	Nature of the question	Examples
Descriptive	Q(d)	How much, many? What is happening?	How high is the crime rate in Brazil and Canada?
Theoretical	Q(t)	Why is this happening?	Why is the crime rate higher in Brazil than in Canada?
Application	Q(a)	What will happen in the future? What are the consequences of a certain social intervention?	How will the crime rate develop in Brazil? Which interventions reduce crime?

describing social phenomena. They are "how much, how many" questions, or "what is happening" questions. Examples are: "How much crime is there in Brazil?" or "How much did the divorce rate change in Germany?" In order to answer such descriptive questions, sociologists carefully observe what is actually happening. They use all sorts of scientific data to look at what is going on. They scientifically *observe* and describe social phenomena. Let's call these scientific observations O, as they are a crucial element in sociological work.

The second type of questions are called **theoretical questions,** *Q(t)*, also called "explanatory questions," "why questions," and "theory questions." Examples are: "why is the crime rate lower in Canada than in Brazil?" or "Why is there an increase in divorce?" Theoretical questions are therefore "why" questions. The answers to such questions are theories, which we designate with the symbol *T* and which provide explanations for social phenomena and from which one can derive hypotheses to test those explanations. In Chapter 2 we will discuss in great detail what theories are. In Chapter 3 we will then go into the next step of the sequence, which is that sociologists make observations to test their explanations. These scientific observations, O, tell us whether our explanations are confirmed by evidence or that, instead, the data suggest that our explanations were wrong.

theoretical question type of scientific question targeted towards understanding phenomena.

The kind of questions sociologists address when they apply their knowledge are called **application questions,** *Q(a)*. These questions can be targeted towards predictions (what will happen in society) or towards social interventions. Examples are: "how will the crime rate develop in Brazil in the coming five years?" and "What would be effective social interventions to mitigate crime?" The answers to these questions are sociological applications, such as predictions and interventions.

application question type of scientific question targeted towards applying scientific knowledge.

1.5 The art of asking good sociological questions

Now that you know what a scientific question is and how it differs from a normative one, and you know that there are three types of sociological questions (descriptive, explanatory, application), it is helpful to pay attention to asking good sociological questions. How do you formulate a good sociological question? This seems easy but practice proves otherwise. Asking good sociological questions is difficult. It is, however, important to acquire the art of asking good questions because questions are at the very beginning of any sociological study you will do. There is no cookbook with recipes for asking good questions, but there are, nevertheless, some guidelines that may help you in formulating and identifying good sociological questions.

Two elements for developing a good sociological question are *precision* and *relevance*. Let's start with precision. What can go wrong is that the question you formulate is vague and subject to multiple interpretations. The art of asking good questions is to reformulate such **ill-defined questions** into **precise questions**. The more precisely you have formulated a question, the better it becomes. This means that the question you raise is clear; that you make explicit what you are interested in rather than leaving things implicit and vague. How does this work? Consider the following ill-defined question:

> **ill-defined question**
> question which is vague and ambiguous.

> **precise question**
> question which has clear interpretation.

"How high is the crime rate?"

Do you think this is a good scientific question? Well, one could say yes because (1) it is a sociological question and not a normative question and (2) the aim is clear: it is a descriptive question. That said, however, would you know how to answer this question? The question leaves many things open: it is an ill-defined question, too vague, and you would have no idea how to answer it.

Although reformulating ill-defined questions into precise questions is not like reading a cookbook with clear recipes, as mentioned, there are some important ingredients that you could consider. The more explicitly and specifically these ingredients are addressed in the question, the more precise it becomes. There are four **question ingredients** that can be considered when you formulate your question:

> **question ingredients**
> elements of a question which can be specified. These are: (1) behavior of interest, (2) social contexts, (3) period and (4) populations.

1 The human behavior you are interested in
2 The social context
3 The period
4 The population.

Let's use these four ingredients to re-formulate the ill-defined question "how high is the crime rate?" into a more precise one. The first ingredient asks you to be clear about the *human behavior* you are interested in. In this case it is the "crime rate," but it could also be other phenomena like poverty, the divorce rate and so on. Here, we use a broad definition of human behavior, so that it also includes people's attitudes, beliefs, values, resources and so forth. Regarding our example, we could ask ourselves "what do we mean by 'crime'"? Do we mean *all* types of crime? Or do we have a particular kind of crime in mind, say homicide? Suppose we come up with a definition of crime, argue that there are different sorts of crime and that we are actually interested in homicides only. So, a more precise descriptive question is the following:

"How high is the homicide rate?"

This question is still too imprecise. For one thing, it remains unclear what the *social context* would be that we are talking about. Is it the homicide rate in, say, Italy that we are interested in? Do we mean instead that we want to describe the homicide rates across a number of countries and, if so, which ones? Or is the idea to observe the homicide rates within countries, such as across neighborhoods or other meso-level contexts? Let's say we are interested in England only, so we can make our question more precise:

"How high is the homicide rate in England?"

Answering this question would still pose difficulties because we have not specified the *period* we are interested in. Do we want to know the homicide rate in England in a particular year and, if so, which one? Or do we want to know how the homicide rate developed over a longer time period? For now, let's assume we are interested in the homicides that occurred very recently, say in the year 2015:

"How high was the homicide rate in England in the year 2015?"

As you can see, we have arrived at a question we can answer. Sometimes, however, sociologists go one step further and specify the *population* of individuals they have in mind. In this case, one might wonder if what we aim to know is the homicide rate of the entire population in England (in 2015), or instead if we are more interested in subpopulations, i.e., specific groups of individuals. Do we want to know the homicide rate of men and women together, or separately, or of only one of the two groups? The homicide rate of all age groups or only those between 15 and 65 years old? An example of a further specification would be the following, when the aim is to describe the homicide rate among men only:

"How high was the male homicide rate in England in the year 2015?"

This question, which is formulated in a scientific and precise way, is an example of a descriptive question $Q(d)$ sociologists may ask. And it will guide subsequent research and descriptive observations O in a straightforward manner.

THINKING LIKE A SOCIOLOGIST 1.3

Imagine someone comes up with the following question: "How much poverty is there?" Do you think this is a good question? Can you make it more precise?

When it comes to formulating theoretical questions, the same four question-ingredients can be considered, as in the case of descriptive questions. For example, the question "Why is there social order?" is too general and impossible to answer. The question "Why was the homicide rate among men higher than among women in England in 2015?" is much more precise, as we have specified each of the four question ingredients.

In summary, the first element in the art of asking good questions is to formulate questions as precisely as you can. What helps is to answer the following four questions: (1) What is the human behavior you want to describe? (2) What is the social context you are interested in? (3) What period do you want to cover? (4) Which population do you want to include? Although reality is more complex than that, these four questions will often prove fruitful.

PRINCIPLE 1.3

Precise questions

Formulate sociological questions as precisely as you can. In developing more-precise questions, specify the following question ingredients: (1) the human behavior you want to describe, (2) social context, (3) period and (4) population.

The second element of a good sociological question is *relevance*. Not all questions are equally relevant or interesting. Your sociological question becomes more relevant when you can relate it to social problems that exist in society—and the more pressing these problems are, and/or the more you can relate your question to societal problems, the more societally relevant will be your sociological question. We have seen that sociological studies are typically motivated by the existence of social problems.

Societal relevance, however, is not always the primary motivation for sociological studies. Sociological studies can also be conducted in view of their **scientific relevance**. By this, scholars indicate that a sociological study is conducted in order to accumulate sociological knowledge. The contribution can be diverse—such as coming up with new findings, new theories and explanations, or improving sociological methods. Such knowledge, in turn, can eventually be used to understand social problems—but social problems are not the

scientific relevance
relevance of sociological work for the accumulation of sociological knowledge.

primary motivation of the study. In other words, although sociological studies can be engaged in a certain scientific discussion that seems unrelated to social problems, the scientific knowledge that is produced may be used in other sociological studies to understand social problems.

It is helpful to differentiate between two types of backgrounds, *B*, to which sociological studies can be relevant, namely: scientific knowledge, *B(k)*, and social problems, *B(sp)* (Figure 1.5).

Let's consider three challenges to the relevance of a sociological question—and what we can learn from this.

We already know it! Suppose you are interested in crime and you'd like to study how the crime rate has developed over time in a certain country. The thing you'd like to avoid is that you will address a question that has been asked before—and to which we know the answer already. That would lead to an irrelevant question. It is therefore essential that before you conduct your sociological study you get an overview of what has been done before, i.e., the background knowledge. If you don't do this, then you take the risk that you will be doing exactly the same thing as has been done before. Therefore, it is highly recommended that you do a **literature review** before you start working on your own study. In a literature

literature review
systematic overview of the theories and observations that are known (background knowledge), typically in a certain specialized field of research.

review, you summarize the existing knowledge about a certain well-defined topic, i.e., the state-of-the-art knowledge from studies that have been conducted at that time in that area, and you identify possibilities to contribute to what is already known.

That's a false question! In some cases you can use as a starting point some descriptive observation that you'd like to explain. Say that you raise the following theoretical question:

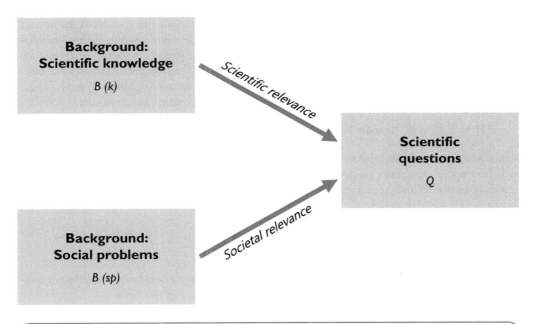

Figure 1.5 Scientific and societal relevance of sociological work.

"Why did church attendance in West-European societies increase in the period between 1950 and 2010?" This question, however, presupposes that there was such an increase in church attendance in Western Europe. And this assumption is false—in reality, church attendance rates have gone down. This means that you raise a **false theoretical question**, which aims to explain something that does not exist. The lesson we can take from this example is that we need to be sure that, when presupposing certain social phenomena, our descriptions of these social phenomena are correct. Only then can we move on to explain these social facts.

false theoretical question
theoretical question which aims to explain something that does not exist.

That's just one case! Suppose a sociologist raises the following question: "How high was the male homicide rate in England in the year 2015?" The question is precisely formulated, but not very relevant. The reason is that the question is about a *single* social context (England), a *single* year (2015) and a *single* population (men). Although sociologists do formulate and answer such questions on single cases, more typically they are interested in questions that entail some kind of social comparison, i.e., **comparative-case questions**. The reason why sociologists find these comparative-case questions more attractive than questions about a single case is that they are

comparative-case question
question which includes some comparison of cases, such as multiple social contexts, multiple moments in time and/or multiple populations.

more aligned to the sociological perspective. If social conditions shape human behavior, we should see that under different social conditions people act differently. By studying comparative cases we can discover such social causes.

Let's see how you can make questions more attractive by introducing some comparison. First of all, you can vary the *social context*, such as countries (macro level) or organizations, families and neighborhoods (meso level). You can compare the same behavior across a number of countries and such cross-country comparative questions stimulate one to look at the impact of countries as social contexts. As we have seen above, the obesity rate strongly differs between contemporary societies and such observations can tell us more about how social conditions are related to human behavior. Equally we can, at the meso level, study differences across organizations or neighborhoods. Are there any differences in crime across neighborhoods? To come back to our example, we could compare England to another country, say Australia:

"How high was the male homicide rate in England and Australia in the year 2015?"

Even within the same social context, you could make interesting comparisons. Sociologists study how social contexts change *over time*, to discover *societal trends*. They study long time periods to establish long-term trends, but also periodical events or other kinds of fluctuations over time. This is an example:

"How did the male homicide rate in England develop in the period between 1950 and 2000?"

Finally, within the same social context you could make a comparison between different *subpopulations*, such as between men and women or age groups. For example:

"How high was the male and female homicide rate in England in the year 2015?"

In summary, the most relevant questions are those that are directly important to society (as they address contemporary social problems) and also those that significantly contribute to scientific knowledge.

PRINCIPLE 1.4

Relevant questions
Formulate sociological questions to be as relevant as you can. In developing more-relevant questions, pay attention to their (1) societal relevance and (2) scientific relevance.

1.6 Sociology and common sense

Isn't sociology just common sense? It could be a friend who raises this question with you, a family member or someone else to whom you talked about sociology. Sociology is a relatively young discipline compared with other sciences such as physics and biology, starting off in real spirit roughly around the year 1900. In slightly more than 100 years it has witnessed an enormous growth of scientific observations and explanations, and has become a respected social science with clear societal relevance.

However, sometimes people are not aware of the progress that has been made in sociology and think that sociological work is no different from common sense and conventional wisdom. Why are people sometimes thinking this way?

Let's return to our example on obesity and let's invite your skeptical friend, who does not believe in the relevance of sociology, to join in. What, so your friend might say, has sociology to offer if the observations and explanations it provides are obvious and common sense? When thinking about the sociological imagination, and trying to identify the social causes of obesity, sociologists might come up with a list of sociological explanations. They could argue that the ultimate sociological causes of obesity are not to be found in personal characteristics like self-control, but rather in changes in the messages in mass media and in increasing opportunities for food intake. Assume that sociologists have extensively studied these possible explanations and that their observations indeed show that these are important social conditions that affect obesity.

Perhaps, however, when you tell your friend about these explanations, your friend replies that all this is **common sense** and "obvious." Your friend might respond: "of course obesity is affected by mass media and increasing opportunities for food intake, everyone knows that. We don't need to have sociologists to tell us that! Sociology is explaining in complex ways things that are obvious to me." In public discussions we now and then encounter this kind of critique. Is this critique justified? In order to convince your friend you could do a short experiment through which your friend will learn that sociology is not just common sense.

common sense everyday thinking, intuitions, beliefs and perceptions.

In the first step of the experiment, you present your friend with a sociological finding. You can tell the story like this:

> Sociologists have studied global trends in extreme poverty. Before they started their work they had in mind three possibilities. Namely: in the last 20 years, the proportion of the world population living in extreme poverty has …
>
> A   Almost doubled
> B   Remained more or less the same
> C   Almost halved.
>
> The sociologists conducted research over several years, they worked together in large groups, published scientific reports about their methodologies and findings, and in the end they concluded that the share of the world population living in extreme poverty has doubled in the last 20 years—hence sociological work shows that A appears true. They were good social scientists so they took the time to share their insights with the public. A newspaper recently reported their main conclusion: "A sociological study has shown that poverty levels in the world has increased in the past decades."

Now that your friend has listened carefully to what you have told them, you have to ask your friend the following two questions:

1   Were you surprised that sociology has found this increase in the proportion of people living in extreme poverty?
2   How would you explain this increase?

Probably your friend, being skeptical of sociology, comes to the following *sociology-is-obvious* conclusion:

> Well of course! Everyone who reads the newspapers and who is able to think understands that the share of world population living in extreme poverty is increasing. That is pretty obvious and we need no sociologists to find that out. We can see this on TV every day. And, yes, of course I can understand why this is happening. Think about the conflicts in Iraq and Syria, for example, how devastating they are to millions of people and then there are so many conflicts elsewhere.

At the end of this experiment you have to confront your friend with slightly uncomfortable news (which your friend can handle, hopefully!):

> Okay, I have to tell you that I played a little trick. Sociologists did not find that extreme poverty has been increasing. That's not true. It has also not remained more or less the same. What research shows is that, in the last 20 years, the proportion of the world population living in extreme poverty has almost halved. So C is true, not A.

Now it is possible that your friend can explain this fact too. "OK, wait a minute" your friend might reply, "This makes sense. And I can explain it." But here is the problem with which you have to confront your friend: if it is equally obvious (to your friend) that extreme poverty has decreased *and* increased (and your friend can explain *both* as well), then something is wrong with the labels "obvious" and "common sense."

This kind of experiment, which helps people to realize that sociology is not so obvious, was introduced by the American sociologist Paul Lazarsfeld in 1949. In his review of the sociological study *The American Soldier* (Stouffer et al., 1949)—which was based on a survey of no less than 600,000 American soldiers during and shortly after WWII—he presented to the imaginative reader several findings that came out of this massive study. One of these was that "Men from rural backgrounds were usually in better spirits during their army life than soldiers from city backgrounds." Of course, people would respond, that makes sense! Those guys are used to tough circumstances. Why waste so much money on sociology to tell me these obvious facts? In reality, however, the facts were exactly the opposite. It was not soldiers from rural backgrounds who were in better spirits, but those from the city (Lazarsfeld, 1949).

In his book *Why Everything is Obvious—Once You Know the Facts*, the sociologist Duncan Watts argues that common sense helps us with practical issues that we encounter on a daily basis (Watts, 2011). For example: how should we behave when talking to people, how do we navigate through the traffic to our work and how to keep relationships going on well. We use common sense often implicitly, intuitively and it helps to solve all kinds of small things. However, he also makes clear that such common-sense thinking is often utterly wrong when it comes to understanding social phenomena. What is worse, people often think that *only other people* are subject to the failure of common sense, whereas everyone happens to be prone to failures of common-sense thinking.

Watts, who trained as a mathematician and physicist before he turned to sociology, makes the interesting observation that few people nowadays would dare to apply common-sense thinking regarding physics—which often shows counterintuitive findings—whereas many people still do so when it comes to social phenomena. It is easy to come up with explanations for human behavior, as we are human beings, rather than to imagine oneself being an electron, for example, and explain the way electrons behave. Watts argues that people have too much confidence in their common sense when it comes to understanding such social behavior:

> The consistency with which our common sense physics fails us has one great advantage for human civilization: It forces us to do science. In science, we accept that if we want to learn how the world works, we need to test our theories with careful observations and experiments, and then trust the data no matter what our intuition says ... But when it comes to the human world, where unaided intuition is so much better than it is in physics, we rarely feel the need to use the scientific method. ... Unlike problems in physics, biology, and so on, when the topic is human or social behaviour, the idea of

running expensive, time-consuming, 'scientific' studies to figure out what we're pretty sure we already know seems largely unnecessary.

(Watts, 2011)

Sociological knowledge often challenges common sense, i.e., people's *descriptions* of reality and their *explanations*. Indeed, an important role for sociologists is to debunk myths and uncover social patterns that are sometimes surprising and counterintuitive. To illustrate, let's return to our experiment, which we started with a question about trends in extreme poverty. This question has actually been asked, in a project coordinated by Hans Rosling and associates (Rosling, Rosling, & Rosling Ronnlund, 2018), to thousands of people in a number of countries. Figure 1.6 presents the percentage of people, per country, who came up with the right answer (C, "almost halved"). It appears that very few people came up with the correct answer, on average only 9%. In Hungary, only 2% gave the correct answer, in Spain 3%. In Norway and Sweden, 25% had it right, which is much better—but you should keep in mind that if people randomly select an answer, they should score 33% (as there are only three answer categories). This is why Rosling and his team added a benchmark which they called "chimpanzees." And, as you can see, the chimpanzees, choosing randomly either "A," "B" or "C," clearly outperformed *Homo sapiens* on this question.

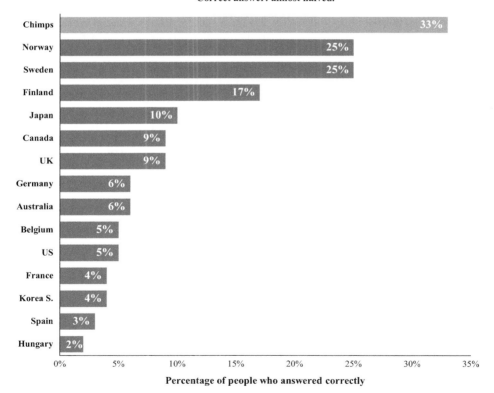

Question: "In the last 20 years, the proportion of the world population living in extreme poverty has ...."
Correct answer: almost halved.

Percentage of people who answered correctly

Figure 1.6 Question 3 from the Gapminder Test 2017
Source: Gapminder, 2019; Rosling et al., 2018.

What we can learn from our little experiment is that there is a difference between what we may call **private sociologists** and **academic sociology**. All of us, as human beings, are private sociologists, because we engage in social life and develop our own, private, beliefs about social phenomena, about what's happening and why. For many daily situations, our common-sense thinking is sufficiently accurate, however there is a major gap between this common-sense thinking of private sociologists on the one hand and academic sociology on the other hand. One difference is that, in academic sociology, knowledge becomes available to others, it becomes public, "objective," and hence the subject of critique and systematic inquiries by many people.

The importance of such public discussions has been noted by the philosopher of science Karl Popper:

> It is very important to appreciate the huge difference between a thought that is only subjectively or privately thought or held to be true, which is a dispositional psychological structure, and the same thought when formulated in speech (perhaps also in writing) and thus presented for public discussion. My thesis is that the step from my unspoken thought: 'It will rain today' to the spoken proposition 'It will rain today' is a hugely important step, a step over an abyss, so to speak. At first this step, the expression of a thought, does not seem great at all. But to formulate something in speech means that what used to be part of my personality, my expectations and perhaps fears, is now objectively to hand and therefore available for general critical discussion … It can be experimentally endorsed by others as well as by myself, but it can also be experimentally disputed.
>
> (Popper, 1999 [1994])

private sociologists the way human beings, in daily life, make sense of the social world. As such they are prone to, among other things, intuitive thinking, implicit reasoning, development of incoherent and vague ideas, keeping knowledge private and searching for confirmations.

academic sociology the way academic institutions describe and explain the social world. Characteristics are the systematic way of gathering knowledge, making explanations public and subject to criticism, the development of coherent theories and rigorous testing.

In academic sociology, the ideas that scholars have about social phenomena become public knowledge, open to discussion, revisions and improvements. Academic sociology is the collective knowledge generated by many scholars in an attempt to filter out inaccurate descriptions of reality and theories that are wrong. Such collective filtering mechanisms are lacking when we keep our knowledge private.

As private sociologists, we rely on intuition and story thinking. People can easily come up with descriptions and explanations for certain social phenomena. It does not take much effort to come up with picturing a reality in which extreme poverty levels have increased in the past 20 years, nor to come up with an explanation for this. Even within a few minutes most people can create a story that makes sense to them. And if we are confronted with facts that oppose our prior assumptions, such as hearing that poverty rates have decreased instead of increased (as we thought), we are capable of understanding that too. Psychologists call this *hindsight bias* as, after being presented with the facts or explanations, people think it makes sense and is obvious. The human imagination is extremely powerful, particularly when it comes to the social life of which all of us are a part. Every day we observe the behavior of other people, make sense of what is happening, create our private explanations and act accordingly. This means that the subject of sociology—social phenomena—is the very same subject that we contemplate in our daily activities. The fact that human beings can easily come up with descriptions and explanations of social phenomena is clearly an incredible source upon which many sociological studies build.

However, it is important to realize that coming up with descriptions and explanations of social phenomena does not imply that they are true. These are different things. Our private knowledge could be wrong—indeed, people can explain phenomena that do not exist (such as why poverty is increasing, which it isn't). This is at the core of sociological work: to systematically, critically study whether our descriptions and understandings of social phenomena are true or false. However, when we privately describe or explain some sort of social phenomenon, we often feel that our personal impressions are true and we rarely do the sorts of systematic research to validate our beliefs. Our private thoughts are therefore not just a possibility—just an idea, an imagination of the human mind. No, the act of describing and understanding a social phenomenon is often at the same time believing that this is reality.

Often people feel little need to test their beliefs and to see if they are right or not. Instead, when they do confront their thoughts with reality, they often search for observations that confirm their ideas and disregard facts that might undermine their ideas—what has been called *confirmation bias*. In sociology, by contrast, explanations are seen as possible explanations, which can be true or wrong, and sociologists pay much attention to the systematic testing of these explanations. Explanations for social phenomena are not kept private—to a single person—but rather shared in the academic setting. This means that explanations are made explicit, precise, coherent and subject to critique. And rather than focusing only on evidence that might confirm their ideas, as we may do as private sociologists, in academic sociology theories are open to criticism and counterevidence.

In academic sociology, intuitive ideas become subject to systematic and rational discussion, incoherent ideas are made coherent and precise, descriptions and explanations for social phenomena are not taken as self-evident and true, but rather seen as possibilities that can be true or false, and empirical testing—which is open to provide counterevidence—is seen as key. Table 1.5 summarizes the important differences we have reviewed.

Table 1.5 Differences between human beings as "private sociologists" and sociology as a science.

Private sociologists	Academic sociology
Subject: social phenomena	Subject: social phenomena
Private knowledge	Public knowledge
Intuitive and story thinking	Systematic and rational discussion
Incoherent and vague ideas	Coherent and precise
Descriptions and explanations are true	Descriptions and explanations can be true or false
Little need for empirical testing	Importance of empirical testing
Search for confirmations	Open to counterevidence

1.7 Sociology as cumulative science

What sociologists know today about social phenomena is based on more than 100 years of scientific progress, of authors elaborating on the work of their predecessors, of developing new theories, of confronting ideas with empirical observations and of improving methods of research. Sociology is a **cumulative science**, i.e., theories and observations of earlier studies are incorporated in the work of successive studies (Weinberg, 2015).

cumulative science the practice that theories and observations of earlier studies are incorporated in the work of successive studies.

It would therefore not be very insightful for you to become an expert in the work of just a few classic sociological scholars such as, say, Locke, Marx and Pareto. It would mean that you would remain ignorant of the progress that has been made in sociology. Rather than focusing on "great classical sociologists" and making a few *scholars* the center of attention, it is much more important to study *scientific ideas and observations*. And, in doing so, it is important to realize that ideas have been developed in response to earlier ideas. Thus, rather than thinking that studies are conducted in isolation from one another, it is essential to see sociology, in fact any science, as cumulative science. The growth of knowledge takes an evolutionary path as new studies bring to light that previous theories were wrong and need to be replaced by better ones (Popper, 1972). Insofar as the ideas of classical sociologists like Durkheim, Marx and Weber have "survived" 100 years of critique, you will see them presented in this book. If some of their ideas have been improved or rejected, you'll see the contemporary state of the art instead—but then realize that their ideas were of importance at a certain moment in time.

So how does cumulative science work? We can visualize scientific progress by using our abstract scheme of research questions Q, theoretical explanations T and observations O. Let's say that Scholar 1 raised a certain descriptive sociological question, for example: "are there any differences between Indonesia and Norway in the frequency of interethnic violence in the period 1950–2000?" To answer this question, Scholar 1 studied both societies and it appeared that in Indonesia there was more interethnic violence than in Norway. Let's call the scientific question $Q(d)_1$ and the descriptive observations O_1. Scholar 1 published a book on this work, let's call it Study 1 (see Figure 1.7).

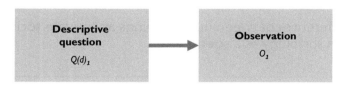

Figure 1.7 Study 1: descriptive question and observations.

Suppose now that Scholar 2 read this book, became interested in the topic and then decided to pursue research on the very same issue. However, Scholar 2's starting conditions differed from that of his predecessor. At the time Scholar 2 became interested in the topic, O had already been observed, whereas this was not the case before Study 1 was conducted. This means that what we can label as the **background knowledge** (Popper, 2005) of Scholar 2 encompasses the work done before, i.e., observation O_1. By background knowledge,

background knowledge the theories and observations that are known before the study commences.

we indicate all knowledge (i.e., observations and theories) at the time of study. Scholar 2 might attempt to *contribute* to the background knowledge. There are different ways in which this could happen, but one way is to come up with an explanation for the observed facts. Scholar 2 might ask: "Why is there more interethnic violence in Indonesia than in Norway in the period 1950–2000?" and develop a possible theory, T_1, which argues that "societies—such as Indonesia—which are nearer to the equator than others—such as Norway—are more violent because of higher temperatures, which stimulates aggression." Scholar 2 published a book on this topic and his explanation; let's call it Study 2.

In Figure 1.8 we get the following update of the scheme:

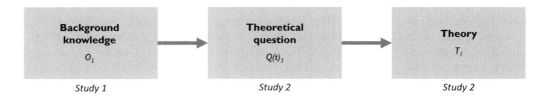

Figure 1.8 Cumulative science: Study 2 contributes to Study 1.

Maybe, after some time, there is another scholar, Scholar 3, who reads the by-then classic observations documented in Study 1 and the subsequent theory proposed in Study 2. Scholar 3 becomes intrigued about the topic, but also rationally criticizes current knowledge and does not believe that theory T_1 is true. Scholar 3 starts collecting data on interethnic violence in many countries, O_2, thereby directly testing the theory and, after doing some carefully conducted research, the study indeed appears not to be in line with T_1. In the same work, Scholar 3 also offers an alternative theory, T_2, which might possibly prove to fit reality better than T_1 (see Figure 1.9):

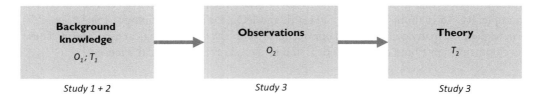

Figure 1.9 Cumulative science: Study 3 contributes to Study 1 and 2.

And so scientific progress continues. Study 4 will elaborate on Studies 1, 2 and 3. Study 4 is conducted in view of the background knowledge at that time and it will again aim to increase our scientific knowledge. It can raise new research questions (Q), elaborate on prior theories (T) and/or on observations (O). It can question old explanations and propose new ones (e.g., T_3), but it can also come up with new descriptions or tests of theories—for example, because better methods and data have become available in the meantime. When new explanations are proposed, they compete with older explanations and, gradually over time, the better explanations will survive. It is therefore important to realize that new studies are always conducted in an attempt to contribute to what is already known.

Critically important for science to be cumulative is that scholars make their knowledge public and do not keep it private. Only when knowledge is made public and shared with others is it possible to elaborate on that knowledge. The discipline of sociology progresses by publishing theories and observations in academic books and peer-reviewed journals. The oldest journal is the *American Journal of Sociology*, which was established in 1895 and which publishes state-of-the-art, highly innovative sociological research. It is still considered as one of the most important sociological journals nowadays. Meanwhile, more and more journals have appeared. Some examples of general sociological journals are *Social Forces* (founded in 1922), *American Sociological Review* (1936), *European Sociological Review* (1985) and *Sociological Science* (2014).

Next to these more general journals, more specialized journals have appeared, such as *Journal of Marriage and Family* (1939), *Journal for the Scientific Study of Religion* (1961), *Sociology of Education* (1963), *Criminology* (1963), *International Migration Review* (1964), *Journal of Mathematical Sociology* (1971), *Social Networks* (1978), *Gender and Society* (1987), *Journal of Artificial Societies and Social Simulation* (1998), *New Media and Society* (1999) and *Research in Social Stratification and Mobility* (2001).

Equally important for science to progress is that sociologists work together in academic communities, where they can share ideas and collaborate. In the early beginnings of "sociology," when Comte had not yet proposed the label "sociology," important ideas were already developed that stimulated scholars thereafter. At that time, however, scholars such as Ibn Khaldun and, much later, Hobbes, worked rather independently. With the establishment of sociology as a scientific discipline, roughly around 1900, sociologists could work together in universities and academic communities and elaborate on prior work in a more organized way. Nowadays, the discipline of sociology is well established in most countries and many universities have their own Department of Sociology and offer Bachelor's and Master's courses in Sociology.

Today, the sociological community is professionally organized in various sociological associations. The International Sociological Association (ISA) was founded in 1949 and it organizes conferences and seminars, it publishes various journals, it provides opportunities for fellowships and grants, it has its codes of ethics and it has its 55 research committees (RC), which bring together groups of sociologists who share their interest in a specialized area. For example, RC-15 is about Sociology of Health and RC-27 is about Sociology of Sport. In addition to the ISA, many countries and continents have their own sociological association. These developments contribute to sharing ideas and to cumulative sociological science.

1.8 Chapter resources

Key concepts

Individual perspective	Personal trouble	Question ingredients
Social context	Social intervention	Scientific relevance
Sociological imagination	Societal relevance	Literature review
Sociological perspective	Normative question	False theoretical question
Social phenomenon	Scientific question	Comparative-case question
Proximate causes	Descriptive question	Common sense
Ultimate causes	Theoretical question	Private sociologists
Micro, meso, macro level	Application question	Academic sociology
Social problem	Precise question	Cumulative science
Public issue	Ill-defined question	Background knowledge

Summary

- The sociological perspective explains human behavior with social contexts that individuals share and thereby differs from the individual perspective.
- The sociological perspective can be supplemental to the individual perspective, it can offer an alternative and it can provide ultimate causes that are to be distinguished from proximate causes.
- Individuals (micro level) share social contexts, which can be identified at the meso level (e.g., neighborhoods, families) and macro level (e.g., countries).
- Social problems are problems that go beyond the individual and about which many people are concerned.
- Sociologists study the scientific element to social problems, i.e., they study social phenomena.
- Rather than asking normative questions, sociologists raise scientific questions.
- The aims of sociology are to come up with accurate scientific descriptions and theoretical explanations for social phenomena, and to apply this knowledge.
- There are three types of sociological questions, namely: descriptive questions (what is happening?), theoretical questions (why is this happening?) and application questions (how can we apply our knowledge?).
- Ill-defined questions can be reformulated into more precise questions by considering question ingredients.
- Questions can increase in relevance by relating them to societal relevance and scientific relevance.
- There is a difference between private sociologists and academic sociology.
- Sociology is a cumulative science, as theories and observations of earlier studies are incorporated into the work of successive studies.

References

Alexander, J. C., Giesen, B., Munch, R., & Smelser, N. J. (Eds.). (1987). *The micro-macro link*. Berkeley and Los Angeles, CA: University of California Press.

Borjas, G. J. (2005). *Labor economics* (3rd ed.). New York, NY: McGraw-Hill.

Coleman, J. S. (1990). *Foundations of social theory*. Cambridge, MA: Harvard University Press.

Esquirol, É. (1838). *Des maladies mentales considérées sous les rapports médical, hygiénique et médico-légal*. Paris: JB Baillière.

Gapminder (2019). www.gapminder.org/data.

Gibbs, J. P., & Martin, W. T. (1964). *Status integration and suicide: A sociological study*. Eugene, OR: University of Oregon.

Giddens, A. (1965). The suicide problem in French sociology. *The British Journal of Sociology*, *16*(1), 3–18.

Halbwachs, M. (2002 [1930]). *Les causes du suicide*. Paris: Presses universitaires de France.

Hedström, P., & Swedberg, R. (Eds.). (1998). *Social mechanisms*. Cambridge: Cambridge University Press.

Henry, A. F., & Short, J. F. (1954). *Suicide and homicide: Some economic, sociological and psychological aspects of aggression*. New York, NY: Free Press.

Lazarsfeld, P. F. (1949). The American soldier: An expository review. *Public Opinion Quarterly*, *13*(3), 377–404.

Lieberson, S., & Silverman, A. R. (1965). The precipitants and underlying conditions of race riots. *American Sociological Review*, 30(6), 887–898.

Mayr, E. (1961). Cause and effect in biology. *Science*, 134(3489), 1501–1506.

Mills, C. W. (2000 [1959]). *The Sociological imagination*. New York, NY: Oxford University Press.

Morselli, E. A. (1881). *Suicide: An essay on comparative moral statistics*. London: C.K. Paul & Company.

Nolan, P., & Lenski, G. (2011). *Human societies: An introduction to macrosociology* (11th ed.). Boulder, CO: Paradigm Publishers.

Pescosolido, B. A., & Georgianna, S. (1989). Durkheim, suicide, and religion: Toward a network theory of suicide. *American Sociological Review*, 54(1), 33–48.

Popper, K. (1972). *Objective knowledge: An evolutionary approach*. Oxford: Clarendon Press.

Popper, K. (1999 [1994]). *All life is problem solving*. Abingdon: Routledge.

Popper, K. (2005 [1935]).*The logic of scientific discovery*. New York, NY: Routledge.

Quetelet, A. (2013 [1835]). *A treatise on man and the development of his faculties*. Cambridge: Cambridge University Press.

Raub, W., Buskens, V., & Van Assen, M. A. (2011). Micro-macro links and microfoundations in sociology. *The Journal of Mathematical Sociology*, 35(1–3), 1–25.

Rosling, H., Rosling, O., & Rosling Ronnlund, A. (2018). *Factfulness*. London: Sceptre.

Stack, S. (2000). Suicide: A 15-year review of the sociological literature part II: Modernization and social integration perspectives. *Suicide and Life-Threatening Behavior*, 30(2), 163–176.

Stouffer, S. A., Lumsdaine, A. A., Lumsdaine, M. H., Williams, J. R., Smith, M., Janis, M. B., Star, S. A., & Cottrell, L. S., Jr. (1949). *The American soldier: Combat and its aftermath. Volume II*. Princeton, NJ: Princeton University Press.

UNICEF (2015). Introduction to UNICEF's work on statistics and monitoring. Retrieved from www.unicef.org/statistics.

UNICEF (2016). UNICEF data: Monitoring the situation of women and children. Retrieved from www.data.unicef.org/resources.

Watts, D. J. (2011). *Everything is obvious: Once you know the answer*. New York, NY: Crown Business.

Weber, M. (1919). *Wissenschaft als beruf*. Munich: Duncker & Humblodt.

Weinberg, S. (2015). *To explain the world: The discovery of modern science*. London, UK: Penguin Books.

WHO (2015). Obesity and overweight. Retrieved from www.who.int/mediacentre/factsheets/fs311/en.

WHO (2016a). Controlling the global obesity epidemic. Retrieved from www.who.int/nutrition/topics/obesity/en.

WHO (2016b). Global health observatory data. Retrieved from www.who.int/gho/ncd/risk_factors/overweight/en.

Chapter 2

Theories

Chapter overview

In Chapter 1 we learned about different types of sociological questions. One of these is the theoretical question, which is concerned with understanding social phenomena: why is something happening? How can we explain social phenomena? The answers to such theoretical questions are theories and this chapter is about what theories are, what makes a theory a useful one and what tools sociologists use to represent theories. The overarching aim is that you learn how you can translate the intuitions we all have about social phenomena into sociological theories. This means that we need to make our stories, which are often implicit and incoherent, both explicit and coherent, and analytically decompose its various elements. All this means that you start thinking like a sociologist about theories. The chapter is organized as follows. I begin with an example of a social phenomenon, namely the puzzling relationship between birth month and success in sports (2.1). Then I provide an explanation for this observation and, in doing so, discuss what theories are (2.2). Coming up with a theory is one thing, however it is something else that the theory is also useful. I introduce several principles which we can use to evaluate how useful a theory is (2.3). Subsequently, I describe Durkheim's classic theory of suicide in more detail, as it nicely illustrates a useful theory (2.4). After this, I review in more depth the key elements of sociological theories. These are concepts and typologies (2.5) and hypotheses and causality (2.6). At the end of this chapter I introduce various tools that sociologists use to systematically represent their theories. In particular I discuss the use of "conceptual models" (2.7) and "formal models" (2.8).

Learning goals

After reading this chapter, check if you are able to:

- Describe what a sociological theory is.
- Use a theory schema to represent sociological theory, hypotheses and observations.
- Describe criteria by which one could evaluate the usefulness of a sociological theory.
- Describe how concepts are related to sociological theory.
- Describe the notion of causality and explain how it is related to sociological theory.
- Use a conceptual model to represent various types of causal relations.
- Describe the pros and cons of various theory tools.

2.1 Birth month and success in sports

Every country has its own sports at which it excels. In some countries it is tennis, in others it is swimming and in yet others it is football. In Canada it is ice hockey and they are extremely good at it. On May 22, 2016, Canada defeated Finland in the gold medal game of the World Championship for men, thereby winning their 26th gold medal. Russia ended in third place and the United States ended fourth. Ice hockey is an extremely popular sport in Canada and many kids start playing at a young age—as early as age 10. These children compete with one another to become the stars of their team and many of them hope that they will make it to the highest divisions in ice hockey and even one day play for their national team. Being such a popular sport, however, means that selection is highly competitive and only a few are selected for the best teams. These selections, one might presume, are based on the quality and skills of the players. Most prominently, one might think that those who are faster, physically stronger, technically more gifted and those who have better coordination and overview of the game, but also a better mindset, are the ones who are more highly skilled and therefore selected for the top leagues and the national team. Part of these skills are genetically inherited whereas, for the rest, the amount of effort and training accounts for the quality of the player.

The idea that good genes and individual effort together determine success in ice hockey perfectly fits with the individual perspective on human behavior. After all, only individual characteristics account for who is eventually to become successful and who fails. And it seems pretty obvious to argue that selection is based on individual qualities only. So it seems indeed. But is it true?

At the beginning of the 1980s, Canadian social scientists discovered something unusual in the selection for the highest ice hockey leagues in their country. They analyzed the birth records of the 1982/1983 players from three major hockey leagues (Barnsley, Thompson, & Barnsley, 1985). One of these was the Ontario Hockey League (OHL), which is the major

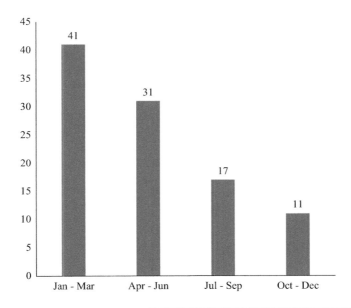

Figure 2.1 Players in the 1982/1983 "Junior A" Ontario Hockey League in Canada by birth-month (%).
Source: Barnsley et al., 1985.

Junior A developmental league for the adult professional National Hockey League. After coding the 15 teams of these top young players in the OHL, it appeared to the social scientists that some birth months were highly overrepresented. Figure 2.1 presents their findings, grouped in birth-month quarters.

The results show that 41% of the OHL players were born in just three months: January, February and March. By contrast, those born in October, November or December made up only 11% of the talented players. In other words, there are approximately four times as many young Canadians born in the first three months of the year in the OHL compared with their peers born in the last three months. The researchers analyzed two data sources on birth months of the Canadian top ice hockey players and they discovered the same pattern. The researchers were puzzled that birth month was related to success in Canadian ice hockey and, furthermore, that it did so in such a strong way. For his book *Outliers: The Story of Success*, the journalist and writer Malcolm Gladwell interviewed Roger Barnsley, one of the researchers who discovered this link (Gladwell, 2008). Barnsley admitted that: "I have never run into an effect this large … You don't even need to do any statistical analysis. You just look at it" (Gladwell, 2008, p. 23). Hence, the researchers found strong evidence that birth month was related to success in ice hockey in Canada. Let's summarize their observation, O, and give this particular finding a name (*hockey and birth month in Canada*) to identify it later on:

> O. Individuals born in January–March were overrepresented among the youth top ice-hockey players in Canada in 1982. (*hockey and birth month in Canada*)

In a follow-up study, Barnsley and his team wanted to know whether in countries other than Canada success in sports also depends on birth month (Barnsley, Thompson, & Legault, 1992).

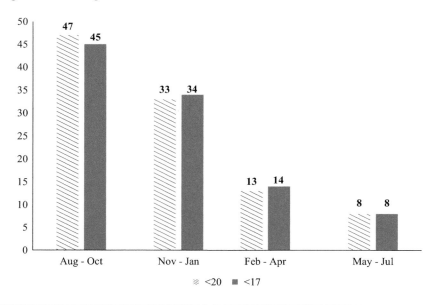

Figure 2.2 Soccer players of the 1989 World Tournament Under-20s and Under-17s, by birth month (%).
Source: Barnsley et al., 1992.

Ice hockey, however, is not a popular sport in many countries and data were not easily available. For their purposes, then, soccer appeared to be the ideal subject of study, as soccer is very popular in many countries and they discovered nice data sets which included birth month of youth top players—highly similar to their ice hockey study. Specifically, they looked at the rosters of the national football teams who participated in the Under-17s and Under-20s World Tournaments, which took place in 1989 in Saudi Arabia and Scotland respectively. Again, they grouped together birth months of the players in quarters. Figure 2.2 presents their findings.

Again, the researchers found that birth month is strongly related to success in sports. Almost 50% of the youth top soccer players were born in just three months: August, September and October. This pattern holds true for both the Under-17s and Under-20s. Individuals born in May, June or July were, with a few exceptions, absent from the tournament. The study therefore reveals that also outside Canada and in sports other than ice hockey birth month and sports success are related. Surprisingly, however, the top players in soccer are not born at the beginning of the year—as they are in Canadian ice hockey. Let's also summarize this finding:

O. Individuals born in August–October were overrepresented among the youth top soccer players in the World Tournament in 1989. (*soccer and birth month 1980s*)

The descriptive research of the Canadian scientists resulted in the observation of these two surprising social phenomena. Although interesting on its own, most people are inclined to ask the logical follow-up question: why is this happening? The findings suggest that an individual perspective on success in sports is insufficient and that—somehow—social conditions related to birth month play a role too. Such questions, as we have seen in Chapter 1, are theoretical questions, $Q(t)$. They are "why questions." Why is something happening? Why

Image 2.1 Surprisingly, birth month is related to success in soccer and other sports.

do we observe these social phenomena? How can we explain them? Let's formulate theoretical questions about the two social phenomena we have observed:

$Q(t)_1$. Why were individuals born in January–March overrepresented among the youth top ice-hockey players in Canada in 1982?

$Q(t)_2$. Why were individuals born in August–October overrepresented among the youth top soccer players in the World Tournament in 1989?

THINKING LIKE A SOCIOLOGIST 2.1

How would you explain these social phenomena? Write down your thoughts.

2.2 Theories and explanations

In trying to answer "why questions," scientists across all disciplines—ranging from physics, astronomy and biology to economics, psychology and sociology—develop theories. The famous physicist Isaac Newton formulated a theory of gravity to explain why objects fall down on earth. The well-known biologist Charles Darwin constructed the theory of evolution to explain the origins and variety of species. Likewise, sociologists develop theories to explain social phenomena. Thus, although the phenomena that sociologists want to explain differ from those studied by physicists and biologists, they resemble each other in their aim to come up with theories that explain certain phenomena. Theories and explanations are the core of science and a key contribution to public understandings of what is happening in the world:

> In times past questions as to the what and the why of the empirical world were often answered by myths; and to some extent, this is so even in our time. But gradually, the myths are displaced by the concepts, hypotheses, and theories developed in the various branches of empirical science, including the natural sciences, psychology, and sociological as well as historical inquiry.
>
> (Hempel, 1962)

What does a scientific explanation look like? In his influential work *The Logic of Scientific Discovery*, the philosopher of science Karl Popper came up with an answer to that question (Popper, 2005 [1935]). Popper argued that "It is from the universal statements in conjunction with initial conditions that we deduce the singular statements" (Popper, 2005 [1935]). This sentence may seem quite abstract, so some further explanation is needed. To begin with, what does Popper mean by "universal statements?" Popper states that these are "hypotheses of the character of natural laws" (Popper, 2005 [1935]) and today it is common to call these universal statements **propositions**. But what does "proposition" mean? And what is an "initial condition" and a "singular statement?" It is helpful to organize what Popper said in a so-called **theory schema** (see Figure 2.3).

We start at the bottom of the schema, where you place the observation, O, that you'd like to explain. This is the "fact," "phenomenon," "pattern" in which you're interested and, in the case of sociology, this is a social phenomenon. Popper called this the "singular statement" and it is also called the *explanandum* (Hempel, 1965), i.e., the thing you would like to explain. Beyond the horizontal line we then put the explanation—hence, you work from the bottom to the top. An observation is explained by a combination of propositions, P, and initial conditions, C. Instead of "initial conditions" I will more often use the term **conditions** or mention "assumptions" about conditions. Together, the propositions and the (assumptions about the) conditions are the explanation—also called *explanans*. The propositions and conditions together offer a

proposition
universal statement, i.e., statement about the causal relations between two or more concepts.

theory schema
type of theory tool in which propositions, conditions, hypotheses and observations are written out as a coherent set of verbal statements.

condition
assumption about the specific setting which relates propositions to observations and hypotheses.

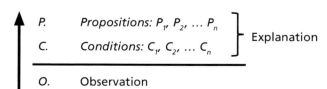

Figure 2.3 Theory schema and scientific explanation.

potential explanation for the observation, as the observation can be logically deduced from propositions and conditions. This is why this type of explanation is called the **deductive-nomological explanation** (Hempel, 1965; Hempel & Oppenheim, 1948).

Now that we have introduced this terminology, it helps to use an example to see how such an explanation, consisting of a proposition and condition, works. Theory schema 2.1 gives a simple example:

deductive-nomological explanation form of explanation of phenomena using proposition(s) and conditions.

P. Every time and everywhere it rains ("R"), people who are outside get wet ("W").

C. It rained on June 13, 2016, between 10–12 am in Oxford ("R" is the case).

O. On June 13, 2016, people who were outside in Oxford between 10–12 am got wet ("W").

Theory schema 2.1 Example of an explanation.

In this example, the *observation*, O, is the fact that on June 13, 2016, those people who were outside in Oxford between 10–12 am got wet. How can we explain this? The theory schema postulates a proposition, P, which argues that *every* time and *everywhere* it rains, people who are outside get wet. The proposition has a general character, in the form of *if* R ("every time and everywhere it rains"), *then* always W ("people who are outside get wet"). And now the condition, C, comes into play, as it specifies the circumstances, the conditions that occurred on that specific day in Oxford ("It rained on June 13, 2016"). On that day, between 10–12 am, R was true. And that means that, because *if* R always leads to W and *if* R is the case here, *then* we should expect W as well. The deduction is called a *syllogism*, in which the observation can be logically deduced from the proposition and the condition.

To see how this type of deductive explanation works in sociology, let's return to the relationship between birth month and sports success. We observed two social phenomena which we called *hockey and birth month in Canada* and *soccer and birth month 1980s*:

O. Individuals born in January–March were overrepresented among the youth top ice-hockey players in Canada in 1982. (*hockey and birth month in Canada*)

O. Individuals born in August–October were overrepresented among the youth top soccer players in the World Tournament in 1989. (*soccer and birth month 1980s*)

Let's start with ice hockey first. A possible explanation for the relationship with birth month is that, in 1982, the cut-off date for selecting individuals for a certain ice-hockey team in Canada was January 1st. This means that youth born on or shortly after that date were relatively older compared with the peers within their team, particularly those who were born just before January 1st. At the age of, say, 10 or 12, a one-year difference in age, or even 6 months, is substantial. The relatively older youth players are physically stronger, faster, mentally more mature and so forth. It is possible that coaches are not so well aware of these age differences between the pupils in the team, and consequently mistake relative age differences for "talent." The more "talented" players are then selected for the best teams, whereas the relatively younger players are not.

We might therefore come up with the proposition which states that *relatively older individuals in general are more often selected for the best sports teams*. Let's call this proposition P, the **relative age effect**. The condition C then links this proposition on the relative age effect to the *observation*, as it describes the specific circumstances in Canada in the 1980s, at which time the cut-off date for ice hockey selection was January 1st. Theory schema 2.2 presents this explanation in a scientific way. Again, the arrow goes from the bottom to the top, to illustrate that we start with the *observation*, and then move upwards towards the explanation.

P. The relatively older individuals are, compared with their peers, more often selected for the best sport team. (*relative age effect*)

C. In Canada, in the 1980s, those individuals born in January–March were relatively older compared with their peers in the ice-hockey teams.

O. Individuals born in January–March were overrepresented among the youth top ice-hockey players in Canada in 1982. (*hockey and birth month in Canada*)

Theory schema 2.2 An explanation of the relationship between birth month and success in ice-hockey.

As becomes clear from this schema, the phenomenon we wanted to explain is seen as a *specific* case of a more *general* "law-like" process. The phenomenon (singular statement) can be deduced from, and is thereby explained by, the proposition (universal statement) in conjunction with the condition. Because such propositions are universal statements, they subsume multiple phenomena. In this case, the relative age effect, which explained the relationship between birth month and success in hockey, can *also* explain the second observation (*soccer and birth month 1980s*). It can do so with the help of the assumption that in the 1980s conditions were such that soccer team selections were based on the cut-off date of August 1st. This means that youth born in August, September or October were the relatively oldest in their soccer team, leading to the same advantage as the relatively oldest ice-hockey players in Canada that we discussed before. The relative age proposition therefore explains both observations in the same way. We get the following theory schema:

P. The relatively older individuals are, compared with their peers, more often selected for the best sport team. (*relative age effect*)

C. In the 1980s, those individuals born in August–October were relatively older compared with their peers in the soccer teams.

O. Individuals born in August–October were overrepresented among the youth top soccer players in the World Tournament in 1989. (*soccer and birth month 1980s*)

Theory schema 2.3 An explanation of the relationship between birth month and success in soccer.

It should be emphasized that the proposition, in conjunction with the two conditions, provides a *potential* explanation for both social phenomena. One could come up with other explanations as well. How could one know whether the relative age explanation is true or not? This is a complicated question and we will come back to this question in Chapter 3, when we discuss sociological methods and observations.

At this moment it is important to mention that, following the work of Popper, scientists aim to deduce a new **hypothesis** or "prognosis" (Popper, 2002 [1944]) from the same proposition, and then study whether that hypothesis is in line with observations or not. The new prediction is called a hypothesis because, at the moment the researcher derives this prediction, the phenomenon is a purely *hypothetical* case and it is unclear if it really happens or not.

hypothesis
testable prediction, derived from theory.

Importantly, deriving a hypothesis, *H*, works in the opposite direction of explaining a phenomenon. Thus, instead of starting at the bottom of the theory schema and going up to the propositions and assumptions, when it comes to deducing new hypotheses one follows the route from top to the bottom. Thus, one starts with the proposition and then derives a new hypothesis (prediction) of what will happen under specific conditions.

Let's see how this works. We use the same proposition on the *relative age effect*, which, if it is true, describes a universal pattern. Then we study the consequences of this universal pattern under conditions not explored before. An interesting change of societal conditions happened, namely that in many countries the cut-off date for selection in soccer changed in the 1990s from August 1st to January 1st. This means that, if the proposition on the relative age effect is indeed true, these slightly different conditions should result in a change in team selection: nowadays the soccer players in the best youth teams should be born at the beginning of the year. Theory schema 2.4 schematically presents how the new prediction is deduced from the same proposition. The arrow emphasizes that in this case one works from the top to the bottom.

P . The relatively older individuals are, compared with their peers, more often selected for the best sport team. (*relative age effect*)

C . In the 2000s, those individuals born in January–March were relatively older compared with their peers in the soccer teams.

H . Individuals born in January–March were overrepresented among the youth top soccer players in 2000s. (*soccer and birth month 2000s*)

Theory schema 2.4 **Hypothesis deduced from the same proposition.**

The hypothesis plays a role in assessing the truth of the theory. The reason is that, if researchers find that observations are *not* in line with the hypothesis, in other words that individuals born in January–March are *not* overrepresented among the youth top soccer players in the 2000s, this would be a direct challenge to the theory of the relative age effect. The reason is that *if* one assumes that the general proposition *P* and the condition *C* are both true, *then* the hypothesis (*soccer and birth month 2000s*) should be true. That is a logical syllogism. This means that if the research shows that the hypothesis is *not* true, then either the proposition

P or the condition *C*, or both, should be false. This is the so-called **modus tollens** of classical logic (Popper, 2005 [1935]) and virtually all scientific studies rely on this logic. Scholars derive hypotheses from proposition(s) and then test if these predictions are confirmed or not.

Propositions and hypotheses are part of sociological **theory**. There are two aspects which deserve attention when we speak of a theory. First, there should be *coherence* between the entire set of propositions and assumptions about conditions. This means that the propositions and conditions form an interrelated, consistent set, rather than a fragmented collection of propositions and conditions which may be partly conflicting as well. Sometimes people say that theories are just stories. In a certain way they are: both stories and theories are mental constructions; they are the product of human imagination. A crucial difference between the two, however, is that theories are by definition coherent, whereas stories are often not so. The propositions and conditions that make up a theory should be logically connected to each other, hence internal contradictions and inconsistencies are impossible. When telling stories in ordinary language, however, we often say things at one moment (A is the cause!) and later on effectively say the exact opposite (A is not the cause!).

Second, a theory *explains* phenomena as well as *predicts* new phenomena. We have seen both elements (explaining and predicting) in the example on relative age effects in sports. A theory is therefore more than an explanation for certain facts. Theoretical propositions also allow the deduction of hypotheses, which can be either confirmed or not.

> **modus tollens** logic rule which states that if it is hypothesized that *A* leads to *B*, and it is observed that *B* is not true, then *A* cannot be true either.

> **theory** coherent set of propositions and assumptions about conditions which can explain certain phenomena and which generate hypotheses (predictions) on other (yet unobserved and hypothetical) phenomena.

2.3 What are useful sociological theories?

Now that you know what a sociological theory is, we should ask ourselves what makes a *useful* sociological theory. Sociologists have proposed many theories, but they are not all equally useful. In order to start thinking about how useful theories are, it is helpful to compare theories with maps you can find on your phone. Imagine that you are in a city you have not been to before and you want to find your way to a certain building. You know the building is somewhere on the other side of the city, but you don't know how to find your way. A useful map guides you to that building. It presents the roads, the names of the streets, shows you where the rivers and lakes are, the railway stations, major buildings and a few more essential things. And it gives you a legend so that you understand the symbols, the scale and so forth. With just a very simple map on your phone you are able to navigate through a dazzling large and complex city.

How is that possible? What is happening here? There are two key elements which determine together how useful the map on your phone is. First, the map should be *true* not false. Second, and less obvious at first sight, is that it should also be *informative*. Both elements need to be explained in more detail, which we will do now.

Truth

To begin with truth. When you think about maps on your phone, what you definitely do not want to have is a map which contains a lot of errors. No, you want the map to be a true representation of reality. The names of the streets should be correct, a lake on the map should

Image 2.2 You can compare theories with maps on your phone.

be there in reality and if there is a new major building it should be on the map as well. Thus, truth reflects the correspondence between what the map shows and what is there in reality (do the streets really exist?). In a similar way, theories can correspond to reality—and the more they do so, the more useful they are. This means that the better, more useful, theories are those that explain observations and in which hypotheses that are derived from the propositions are confirmed. To be precise, this criterion is not a matter of yes or no, true or false. A map can have one street wrong, but if the rest of the map is true, it is still a good one. If the map has four streets wrong, it is further removed from truth; and in the extreme case that none of the map corresponds to reality, we say it is completely false.

In this context, scholars often talk about the **empirical success** of a theory. If we go back to the theory of the relative age effect, we can assess its empirical success by looking at what is subsumed under the proposition (see Figure 2.4).

empirical success
the degree
of empirical
confirmation of a
theory.

There are two *observations* explained by the proposition on the relative age effect. Then there is one hypothesis derived from the proposition. This hypothesis (*soccer and birth month 2000s*) can be true or false, and it is up to empirical investigations to come up with the verdict. It appears that sociological studies consistently find support for this hypothesis. Findings reveal that nowadays youth top soccer teams in countries all over the world, be it England, Italy, Germany, but also outside Europe, consist of a disproportionately large group of players born at the beginning of the year—exactly in line with the hypothesis (Cobley, Schorer, & Baker, 2008; Helsen, Van Winckel, & Williams, 2005; Simmons & Paull, 2001). This means that not only are the two observations in line with the relative age proposition, but also the hypothesis derived from this proposition

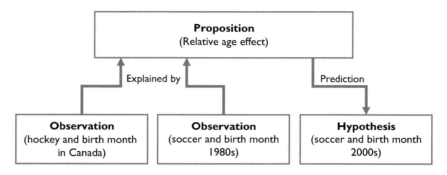

Figure 2.4 Schematic presentation of the theory on relative age effects in sports.

is confirmed empirically. Drawing on this evidence, one could say an empirical success of three out of three, or 100%. If instead, say, the hypothesis would have been refuted empirically, one would say that the theory is less successful empirically.

Truth, therefore, is a major criterion for judging the usefulness of a theory. We say that truth is a *regulative idea*, i.e., a principle by which we can evaluate the value of theories (Popper, 1999 [1994]). It can well be that the theory is strongly supported by empirical findings, but it can also be the case that only sometimes is the theory supported, or that the theory is consistently refuted. The regulative idea on truth states: the higher the empirical success of theories, the more useful they are.

Information

Truth, however, is not the only regulative idea which is used to evaluate theories. In fact, if theories were only judged by their empirical success, one would get theories that are useless. To see why, let's return to the metaphor of theories as maps. Imagine that you would like to have a map which is a completely true representation of reality, and the only thing you care about is that. If so, you'll have to zoom into the map on your phone so much that it will show you each tree in the city, all the houses, traffic lights, etc., in short, all the details of the city. The map would be incredibly detailed and it would not be very helpful for you when trying to find your building on the other side of the city. What does this tell us? Useful maps are simple and not complex. They present the relevant essentials, ignoring the complexity of the city that is irrelevant for finding your way. And, here again, the issue is a matter of degree, not yes or no: if your map zooms too much into the details, it becomes less useful.

Scientists talk about the degree of **information content** of a theory (Popper, 1999 [1994]). The higher the information content of a theory, the more useful it is. Information content is the second regulative idea in the evaluation of theories (Popper, 1972, 2014 [1963]). But what does "information content" mean exactly? To build up an intuition of this concept, imagine that we had to evaluate a theory which predicts that "tomorrow it will rain, or it will not rain." Clearly, this theory will always be confirmed: whatever happens, it will be true. But it is also a completely uninformative theory. It is a so-called *tautology*, i.e., a statement which is logically true. In other words, this theory does *not exclude* any

information content
the degree of theoretical precision and theoretical scope of a theory.

possible phenomenon in reality and is therefore impossible to *falsify*, i.e., to be false. Therefore, it is good to have a theory which can be falsified, and the more it can be falsified—the higher the information content—the better it is.

> **theoretical precision** the degree to which the theory excludes possibilities of what could happen with respect to a particular case.

But how do we get such a theory with a higher degree of information content? One way to increase the information content of a theory is to make the theory more *precise*. To illustrate the meaning of **theoretical precision** let's compare two propositions, P_1 and P_2:

P_1. "Couples will or will not divorce within 10 years after marriage."
P_2. "Couples do not divorce within 10 years after marriage."

Proposition 2 makes precise predictions about what will happen to married couples. This means that the proposition *excludes possibilities of what could happen in that particular case*. It is falsifiable and has a higher information content than Proposition 1, which is imprecise. Effectively, Proposition 1, being a tautology, does not exclude any possibility at all and it is impossible to falsify.

To see the consequences for predictions derived from both propositions, imagine that we study seven couples. One group of scholars is in favor of Proposition 1 and they say, "well, yes, some couples will divorce, but others will not." The other group of scientists use Proposition 2 instead and predict that "no couple will divorce within 10 years after marriage." Table 2.1 summarizes the predictions derived from both propositions.

Proposition 1 ("Some couples divorce, others do not") will do very well empirically. For each couple, predictions based on this proposition will be confirmed, as it always correctly predicts the outcome. This means that the proposition is confirmed 7 out of 7 observations. The reason it is so is because the hypothesis is very imprecise: it does not exclude any possibility at all. The proposition will *always* be true as there is, logically speaking, no way for it to be untrue. How useful is such a theory? It won't help scientists to understand which couples will end up in a divorce and which not. The theory is said to be uninformative, unfalsifiable.

By contrast, Proposition 2 is precise and falsifiable. The proposition states that no couple will divorce within 10 years of marriage and thereby excludes the possibility for each couple

Table 2.1 Predictions derived from three propositions.

Couple	Condition: years of marriage	Prediction: Divorce yes or no?		
		P_1 (tautology)	P_2 (Precise)	P_3 (Precise + broader scope)
1	2	Yes or No	No	No
2	5	Yes or No	No	No
3	1	Yes or No	No	No
4	16	Yes or No	?	Yes
5	12	Yes or No	?	?
6	8	Yes or No	No	No
7	22	Yes or No	?	Yes

within that period to do otherwise. There are four couples which fall in this range of being married for less than 10 years and, for these cases, the predictions based on the proposition can go wrong. For the other couples, the proposition did not predict anything.

> **theoretical scope**
> the degree to
> which the theory
> is applicable to
> a wider range of
> cases: phenomena,
> populations and
> settings.

And this brings us to the second way of increasing information content. This second element is called **theoretical scope**, i.e., the degree to which the theory is applicable to a wider range of cases: phenomena, populations and settings. Consider the following proposition, for illustrative purposes:

> P_3. "Couples do not divorce within 10 years of marriage, but all of them eventually will be divorced when they are married for 15 years."

Proposition 3 has a *broader scope* than Proposition 2, because it contains all the predictions we can derive from that proposition *and adds two more* (see Table 2.1). Specifically, it will predict that couples 4 and 7 will also be divorced, whereas such predictions could not be derived from Proposition 2. We say that Proposition 3 has a higher information content than Proposition 2, which is restricted in scope.

Theories which have a broader scope are very useful, because you can apply them to a wide range of phenomena. You can use the same idea to understand different things. You don't need to think again and again about how to explain something. This means that if your theory explains, say, certain crime patterns in France, it would be great if the same theory also explains crime patterns in Italy, Australia and Kenya. That is more useful than having to think about three new theories: one for Italy, one for Australia and one for Kenya. Similarly, if your theory not only explains a certain *crime* pattern, but also other social phenomena such as *religion* and *health*, it is more useful than if the theory is only applicable to crime.

We can illustrate this idea with the theory of relative age effects. So far, we have discussed how this theory could be applied to understand why birth month is related to youth top-teams: (1) ice hockey in Canada, (2) soccer in the 1980s and (3) soccer in the 2000s. However, researchers have discovered that the relative age theory may actually be broader in scope and can be applied to a wider range of phenomena. Scholars have found that the *relative age effect* occurs in sports other than ice hockey and soccer too (Cobley, Baker, Wattie, & McKenna, 2009). And, perhaps surprisingly, researchers have argued that the theory can also be used outside the domain of sports, suggesting relative age patterns in education (Bedard & Dhuey, 2006; Bernardi & Grätz, 2015; Dhuey & Lipscomb, 2008; Verachtert, De Fraine, Onghena, & Ghesquière, 2010), self-esteem (Thompson, Barnsley, & Battle, 2004) and even suicide risks (Thompson, Barnsley, & Dyck, 1999). We will come back to this more general theory of relative age effects in Chapter 5.

Developing theories that have a broader scope is thus desirable. But how does that work in practice? Let's try finding out. Consider the following two propositions:

> P_4. "The higher people are educated, the more liberal their worldviews are."
> P_5. "The higher people are educated, the more liberal their worldviews are and the more active they are politically."

Here, Proposition 5 has a broader scope and is therefore more informative, because it makes the same predictions as Proposition 4 and *adds another one*. Another way of saying

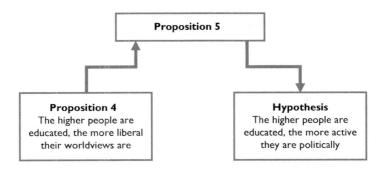

Figure 2.5 Proposition 5 is broader in scope than Proposition 4.

this is that Proposition 5 *excludes more possibilities* than Proposition 4. This may sound a bit counterintuitive, so let's rewrite Proposition 4:

P_4. "The higher people are educated, the more liberal their worldviews are and the less/ more/equally active they are politically."

As you can see, Proposition 4 doesn't say anything about political activism, whereas Proposition 5 does. We can visualize the difference between the two propositions graphically, to see that Proposition 5 is more general and has a broader scope than Proposition 4 (see Figure 2.5). Proposition 5 can explain the same phenomena as Proposition 4, but also adds to this a prediction that cannot be derived from Proposition 4.

The scope of a theory can therefore be expanded if you increase the range of predictions which can be derived from it. You can realize this by making the theory applicable to a wider range of outcomes. But you can also broaden the scope of the theory by expanding the populations and settings to which it is applicable. Compare the following two propositions:

P_6. "Income inequality increased in the United States between 1950–2010."
P_7. "Income inequality increased in all Western countries between 1950–2010."

Clearly, Proposition 7 is more informative as it not only states that income inequalities have increased in the United States but also in *all* Western countries. Proposition 6 is only applicable to one setting or population (the United States), whereas Proposition 7 has a much larger scope. In summary, sociological theories that have a higher information content are the ones scientists prefer; they are more useful because they are more precise and they can be applied to a wider range of social phenomena.

Where does all this lead us to? Scientists want theories that are both true and informative. They are the useful maps that guide you through the city. And we need to distinguish them from maps that are not true (the street has a new name, not on the map yet!), or not informative (the map is full of detailed stuff, I do not find my way!). In practice, theories are rarely completely true or false, nor are theories perfectly informative or pure tautologies. Both truth and information are a matter of degree and that's why scientists consider the empirical success and information content of theories. Taking this into consideration, we can formulate a principle about what determines how useful a sociological theory is (Opp, 2005; Popper, 2014 [1963]):

PRINCIPLE 2.1

Useful sociological theories

Sociological theories are not equally useful. The principles by which we judge the usefulness of a sociological theory are truth and information. Sociological theories are considered more useful when: (1) they have a higher empirical success—the theory is more in line with empirical findings—and (2) when they have a higher information content—the theory is more precise and covers a wider range of phenomena.

Although scientists aim to develop theories that are highly informative and whose predictions are supported by observations, in reality developing such theories is often incredibly difficult. The reason is the tension between truth and information content. A highly informative theory excludes many possibilities that could happen in reality and hence its predictions are likely to be disconfirmed many times. Likewise, when we develop a theory with the aim of having a perfectly true one, we might end up with just describing reality in its full complexity, or even provide a tautology, and hence have an unfalsifiable, uninformative theory.

In the cumulative growth of scientific knowledge, theories compete with each other in an evolutionary process (Popper, 1999 [1994]). Theories that are less successful empirically are replaced by others which are more empirically successful. Theories which are rather imprecise and restricted are replaced by theories that are more precise and which have a broader scope. The most useful theories, ultimately, are the ones which are highly empirically successful and highly informative at the same time. One might call the discovery and construction of such theories the big adventure of science, from physics and biology to sociology. Powerful theories are those that simplify reality such that they cover a huge range of phenomena and, at the same time, their predictions are supported by research findings.

The scientific community contains numerous theories that compete for success and so one could say that the best theories survive (Lakatos, 1978). When Newton proposed his theory of gravity in the 17th century there were other theories out there that explained why objects fall. However, the theory of gravity was much more informative than competing theories: it could not only explain why objects fall to earth, but also to any two objects in the universe. And his theory proved empirically very successful: empirical tests across a wide range of conditions confirmed the hypotheses derived from his theory. That's why the theory of gravity won the battle over other theories. Only in certain conditions, as Einstein showed 300 years later, does Newton's theory not hold. Einstein's theory of relativity further generalized the theory of gravity, arriving at an even more informative theory than that of Newton. Thus, in the evolution of theories, where theories compete for being more informative and being nearer to the truth, we see that sometimes a theory beats an alternative theory and that sometimes a theory is "eaten up" by another one that is more general. Newton's theory of gravity and Darwin's theory of evolution are such exceptionally powerful theories. They are very simple and elegant (informative!) and successful empirically (true!).

2.4 Durkheim's theory of suicide

Now let's review a classic example of a useful sociological theory, which is Durkheim's theory of suicide. One of the founding fathers of sociology, Emile Durkheim proposed his famous theory of suicide at the end of the 19th century (Durkheim, 1961 [1897]). Let's see how we can use a theory schema to represent part of his sociological theory and explicitly address his sequence of asking questions, making observations, offering explanations for those observations and testing these explanations.

In the beginning of his book, Durkheim raised a descriptive question:

> *Q(d)*: "How large are the suicide rates in various European countries, between 1866–1878?"

Using administrative data, he compared suicide rates across a number of countries (Table 2.2). As it appears, there were strong country differences in the *suicide rate*, i.e., the number of suicides per one million people. In some countries, such as Italy and Belgium, the suicide rate was rather low, whereas in countries like Denmark and Saxony it is much higher. These country differences seem rather stable over a longer period.

Table 2.2 Suicide rates per one million inhabitants and their rankings in European countries, 1866–1878.

	Suicide rates			Country ranking		
	1866–1870	1871–1875	1874–1878	1866–1870	1871–1875	1874–1878
Italy	30	35	38	1	1	1
Belgium	66	69	78	2	3	4
England	67	66	69	3	2	2
Norway	76	73	71	4	4	3
Austria	78	94	130	5	7	7
Sweden	85	81	91	6	5	5
Bavaria	90	91	100	7	6	6
France	135	150	160	8	9	9
Prussia	142	134	152	9	8	8
Denmark	277	258	255	10	10	10
Saxony	293	267	334	11	11	11

Source: Durkheim, 1961 [1897].

Having observed these country differences, Durkheim then wondered why they exist. Why are there more suicides in Denmark than in Belgium, for instance? How can we explain this? In sum, he addressed a theoretical question:

> *Q(t)*: "What explains the country differences in suicide rates between 1866–1878 in Europe?"

Durkheim argued that the differences in the suicide rate had to do with the dominant religion in these countries. More specifically, Durkheim speculated that the suicide rate is generally higher

THINKING LIKE A SOCIOLOGIST 2.2

How would you explain country differences in suicide? Write down your thoughts.

in Protestant regions than in Catholic regions, and that regions with a mixed Protestant–Catholic population should fall in between these two extremes. This would explain, for example, why the suicide rate at this time was higher in Saxony—a Protestant region—than in Italy—a Catholic country. We can reconstruct his explanation in a theory schema (see Theory schema 2.5):

P. Suicide rates are higher in Protestant regions than in Catholic regions. (*religion and suicide*)

C. In the 19th century, Saxony was largely a Protestant region, whereas Italy was predominantly Catholic.

O. In the 19th century, the suicide rate was higher in Saxony than in Italy. (*suicides in Saxony and Italy*)

Theory schema 2.5 Explanation of suicide differences across regions.

Durkheim classified the countries according to their dominant religion and found that, indeed, the average suicide rates in Protestant countries (190 per 1 million) exceeded the suicide rates in Catholic countries (58), and that mixed Protestant–Catholic countries were in between (96). To come up with a new test of his proposition on *religion and suicide*, Durkheim argued that, *if* this proposition is true, one would predict that also *within* countries Protestants have a higher suicide rate than Catholics. He hypothesized that provinces in Bavaria and Prussia in which there are more Protestants should have higher suicide rates than in provinces in which there are more Catholics. Furthermore, he made similar predictions regarding regional differences in Switzerland. Let's formulate one such prediction that Durkheim made in a theory schema (see Theory schema 2.6):

P. Suicide rates are higher in Protestant regions than in Catholic regions. (*religion and suicide*)

C. In the 19th century, the Bavarian Province Rhenish Palatinate counted less than 50% Catholics, whereas at the same time the Bavarian Province Upper Palatinate had more than 90% Catholics.

H. In the 19th century, the suicide rate in the Bavarian Province Rhenish Palatinate was higher than the suicide rate in the Bavarian Province Upper Palatinate. (*Bavarian suicides*)

Theory schema 2.6 New hypothesis derived from the religion and suicide proposition.

In line with this prediction, Durkheim found that in the Rhenish Palatinate the suicide rate (167) was indeed higher than in the Upper Palatinate (64). All the other hypotheses derived from his *religion and suicide* proposition were confirmed as well. Given the abundance of empirical success for this proposition, Durkheim subsequently raised the question of how we can understand that the suicide rates are higher in Protestant regions. Durkheim wondered:

Q(t): "Why are the suicide rates in Protestant regions higher than in Catholic regions?"

THINKING LIKE A SOCIOLOGIST 2.3

Is this a single-case question or a comparative-case question? See Chapter 1 for more on this topic.

Durkheim noted that Protestant and Catholic religious groups equally prohibit suicide and condemn it as an immoral act, which means that this norm cannot explain the difference in suicide rate. Instead, he argued that the suicide rate in Protestant regions is higher because Protestants have "fewer common beliefs and practices," i.e., the Protestant group is weaker and less integrated than the more cohesive Catholic group. In the words of Durkheim:

> We thus reach the conclusion that the superiority of Protestantism with respect to suicide results from its being a less strongly integrated church than the Catholic church.
>
> (Durkheim, 1961 [1897])

The stronger bonds in the group of Catholics mean that Catholics more strongly conform to the norm that one should not commit suicide than Protestants do. Thus, although both groups have the same norm, the stronger integration in the Catholic religious group results in stronger norm-conformity. We can represent this explanation in a theory schema (see Theory schema 2.7):

P . The more cohesive the group, the more strongly people in that group conform to the norm which prohibits suicide, and the lower the suicide rate in that group. (*group integration and suicide*)

C . The group of Protestants are less cohesive than that of Catholics.

P . The suicide rates are higher in Protestant regions than in Catholic regions. (*religion and suicide*)

Theory schema 2.7 Proposition on group integration and suicide explains religion and suicide proposition.

This might seem confusing as there are now two propositions within a single theory schema. What is the difference between the proposition on the effect of group integration on suicide (on the top) and the impact of religion on suicide (at the bottom)? The difference between the two is the "level of universality" (Popper, 2005 [1935]). Both are propositions, but the proposition at the bottom (*religion and suicide*) is of *lower* universality than the *more general* proposition from which it is deduced (*group integration and suicide*).

This is an example of what is called a **deeper explanation**. In a deeper explanation, a proposition is explained with an *even more general* proposition and regarded as a specific case of a more general process. Propositions differ in their degree of universality and, in this case, Durkheim explains his *religion and suicide* proposition with his even more general *group integration and suicide* proposition. In doing so, he was increasing the *scope* and thereby the *information content* of his theory on suicide. According to the philosopher of science Hempel, such more general theories increase the breadth and depth of explanations:

> **deeper explanation**
> type of explanation in which one proposition is explained by another, more general, proposition.

> Subsumption under broader laws or theories usually increases both the breadth and the depth of our scientific understanding. There is an increase in breadth, or scope, because the new explanatory principles cover a broader range of phenomena; for example, Newton's principles govern free fall on the earth and on other celestial bodies, as well as the motions of planets, comets, and artificial satellites, the movements of pendulums, tidal changes, and various other phenomena. And the increase thus effected in the depth of our understanding is strikingly reflected in the fact that, in the light of more advanced explanatory principles, the original empirical laws are usually seen to hold only approximately, or within certain limits.
>
> (Hempel, 1965)

A more comprehensive proposition specifies the **scope condition** of the less general proposition. Suicide rates are higher in Protestant regions than in Catholic regions, *only under the condition* that Protestants are a less-integrated group than Catholics (Van Tubergen, Te Grotenhuis, & Ultee, 2005). In 19th-century Europe, Durkheim provided evidence to suggest that this was indeed the case. However, in another place or context in which a Protestant group is more cohesive than a Catholic group, one would expect to find that Protestants commit suicide less often than Catholics.

> **scope condition**
> set of conditions to which a certain theory is applicable.

Durkheim used his *group integration and suicide* proposition to derive other propositions. In order to do so, he posited that, next to *religious* groups, there are other types of groups. Durkheim argued that there are *families* and *political groups*, and that these groups can also be less or more cohesive. He assumed that married couples make a more cohesive family than singles. With respect to political groups, he assumed that during wartime people would be more strongly integrated politically than in more peaceful times. From his general *group integration and suicide* proposition, Durkheim derived two hypotheses that are more specific: one on marriage and another on war (see Theory schema 2.8):

P. The more cohesive the group, the more strongly people in that group conform to the norm which prohibits suicide, and the lower the suicide rate in that group. (*group integration and suicide*)

C. Married couples are a more cohesive group than singles are.

C. Countries at war are a more cohesive group than countries not engaged in war.

H. Married couples have a lower suicide rate than singles. (*marriage and suicide*)

H. Countries at war have a lower suicide rate than countries not engaged in war. (*war and suicide*)

Theory schema 2.8 Hypotheses derived on family and war.

The findings he presented are in line with these predictions. Married couples do indeed have lower suicide rates than singles and so too does the suicide rate go down when countries go to war. For example, Durkheim observes that:

> in 1866 war breaks out between Austria and Italy, and suicides drop 14 per cent in both countries.
>
> (Durkheim, 1961 [1897])

Based on his theory and observations, Durkheim concludes:

> So we reach the general conclusion: suicide varies inversely with the degree of integration of the social groups of which the individual forms a part. But society cannot disintegrate without the individual simultaneously detaching himself from social life, without his own goals becoming preponderant over those of the community … The more weakened the groups to which he belongs, the less he depends on them, the more he consequently depends only on himself and recognizes no other rules of conduct than what are founded on his private interests. If we agree to call this state egoism … we may call egoistic the special type of suicide springing from excessive individualism.
>
> (Durkheim, 1961 [1897])

Durkheim's theory discussed here is only one of his theories on suicide. It relates to what Durkheim calls *egoistic* suicides and, in *Suicide*, Durkheim constructs theories on yet three other types of suicides: altruistic, anomic and fatalistic.

What can we conclude about his theory of egoistic suicides, which I will refer to as **Durkheim's integration and suicide theory**? His theory is quite complicated because it consists of different propositions, hypotheses and observations. To clarify his theory, Figure 2.6 presents an overview of the different parts that we have reviewed. It reveals how his propositions, hypotheses and observations are related to each other. His *integration and suicide* theory consists of a *coherent* set of interrelated propositions and hypotheses. His theory is very useful because it is both informative and empirically successful. It is

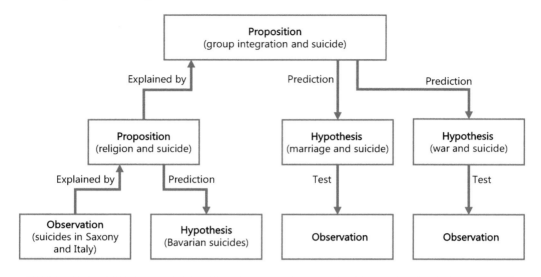

Figure 2.6 Structure of (part of) Durkheim's integration and suicide theory.

informative because the theory excludes possibilities that can happen in reality. It consists of propositions of different levels of universality and his most general *group integration and suicide* proposition is broad in scope. The theory is *empirically successful* because the hypotheses subsumed under the theory are in line with observations. It is therefore with good reason that many scholars regard *Suicide* as a brilliant sociological work. Elsewhere in this textbook we will discuss how contemporary sociological studies have elaborated on this work, and it provides a nice illustration of the idea that sociological knowledge has cumulated over the years.

2.5 Concepts

What status do concepts have in sociological theories? Are concepts the same as theories? It is time to take a closer look at concepts, which are the building blocks of theories. Consider once more Durkheim's theory of suicide. His general *group integration and suicide* proposition states that:

> P. The more cohesive the group, the more strongly people in that group conform to the norm which prohibits suicide, and the lower the suicide rate is in that group (*group integration and suicide*).

This proposition is made up of key concepts such as "group," "conformity," "norm" and "suicide." It is for this reason that scientists say that concepts are the elements, the building blocks, of theories. Examples of commonly used sociological concepts are "social control," "values," "inequality," "culture," "role" and "religion." In everyday life we also make use of concepts all the time, such as "food," "table" and "clothes." Although everyone has an intuition about what concepts are, it is helpful to clarify some of the features of concepts (Jaccard & Jacoby, 2010).

First, concepts are abstractions. This means that concepts refer to a number of specific instances. For example, the concept *food* applies to all sorts of things that we can eat, like fish, fruit and so on. Despite the fact that food differs in color, size, shape and in various other ways, we are able to have a general idea about what food is and what, in reality, all these different things have in common. Some concepts are more abstract and multidimensional than others (Goertz, 2006). For example, the concept "culture" is more abstract than the concept of "age." In Chapter 3 we will discuss the level of generality of concepts, the notion of conceptualization and the way one could differentiate between the dimensions that make up more general, complex concepts.

Second, concepts are hypothetical. This means that concepts are mental constructs, the ideas that we have in our mind and that we share with others. Concepts are not reality but ideas about reality. If concepts were reality, it would mean that we would have food and tables in our head, whereas we only (fortunately) have the concepts of food and tables in our head. Concepts are representations of reality, not reality itself.

Third, concepts contain categories, attributes. For example, the concept of *food* distinguishes between things in reality that classify as *food* and the rest, which is *non-food*. Scientists often talk about concepts as *variables*, which have different *values* (*categories*, *attributes*). In the example above, there are two values: food and non-food. In sociology, **concepts** are called **theoretical variables** and they are different from *measurement variables*. Although the measurement variable may approximate the theory variable to a high degree,

> **concept**
> (also **theoretical variable**)
> hypothetical abstraction that contains certain categories.

this is not necessarily the case. Theoretical variables are part of the theory, they are the theory concepts, whereas measurement variables are the variables used in empirical research and sociological observations that are supposed to represent those theoretical concepts. In Chapter 3 we will give a more detailed discussion of measurement variables.

Concepts are hypothetical abstractions that contain certain categories. In order to use concepts in constructing theories, it is important to be clear about the meaning of the concepts involved. If two persons are discussing a theory which contains the concept "religion" for example, but both attach completely different meanings to that concept, it will result in misunderstanding. It is therefore helpful to give a *definition* of the concept to avoid that kind of confusion. A definition is a description of the concept using other words. In the beginning of *Suicide*, Durkheim gives a definition of suicide:

> The term suicide is applied to all cases of death resulting directly or indirectly from a positive or negative act of the victim himself, which he knows will produce this result.
> (Durkheim, 1961 [1897])

Definitions are in a sense normative. Two people can give a different definition of the concept "suicide," and it is a matter of convention, which definition people agree on. In sociology there is agreement about the definitions of many concepts, but, at the same time, there are also a number of concepts that are defined in different ways. This means that it is helpful to make sure which definition you use for a certain concept, to avoid that someone else may have a different definition in mind, which would result in conceptual misunderstanding.

In this textbook I give explicit definitions for key concepts, keeping in mind that, in some cases, different definition conventions exist. As a general rule I tend to use definitions that are *most commonly* used (follow the majority!), definitions which use *clear* language (keep it simple!) and definitions which are *sufficiently distinctive* from definitions of other concepts (avoid overlap!). It should be realized, however, that in some cases alternative definitions might equally have been given. Importantly, this means that when you read sociological studies, you will come across definitions that might be different from the ones presented in this textbook and you will also see that definitions vary between studies.

Why, so you might legitimately ask, do we not pay more attention to definitions of concepts, to dig deeper and thereby get to the "essence" and truth of theories? After all, concepts are the building blocks of theories, so why not find the truth in the definitions? Can't we think harder about the concept of, say, "religion" and come up with the essential characteristics of this concept? It is certainly wise to be clear and explicit about the meaning of a concept. However, thinking harder about concepts, as if this brings us nearer to the essence and thereby to the truth, is a mistake. A definition is a description of a concept and so it introduces new words, which we then need to further define as well, and so on, as an infinite regress—and it will not lead us to the truth.

There is therefore little to be gained in answering questions of the type "What is the *essence* of X?" A definition cannot be "true" or "false" in the sense that one definition comes closer to the truth. There is no way in which we can falsify a definition and discussions about which definition of a concept is the right one are often fruitless. Definitions are longer descriptions of concepts, which are therefore just a *shorthand* for such descriptions (Popper, 2014 [1963]). That said, however, it is important to be explicit about the definition you use for a concept, and that you use simple language to avoid conceptual miscommunication (Hedström, 2005) and to avoid developing theories that are obscure (Boudon, 2002).

PRINCIPLE 2.2

Concepts and definitions
Concepts are building blocks of theories. To avoid confusion, it is important to be clear about what the key theoretical concepts mean. Give a definition of concepts, preferably one that is clear, sufficiently distinctive from other concepts and in line with common standards.

Sometimes a concept is mistakenly seen as being a theory. This happens quite often when people talk about so-called **typologies**. A typology is a way of classifying people, countries, phenomena or other things in several "clusters." For example, one could make a typology of countries in terms of their welfare state regime. This typology results in several clusters of countries. The sociologist Esping-Andersen (2013 [1990]) distinguished these three types of welfare state:

typology a way of classifying reality, often done by combining concepts.

1 Liberal:
   o The state offers limited social welfare provisions.
   o Examples: US, Canada and Australia.
2 Social-democratic:
   o Strong state involvement and support.
   o Examples: Scandinavian countries.
3 Conservative-corporatist:
   o Family is key in giving support and the state only interferes when the family cannot.
   o Examples: Austria, Germany, France and Italy.

This typology might be a useful part of a theory. A typology in itself, however, is not a theory yet, as it does not explain anything and nothing can be predicted from a typology (Hedström, 2005). Typologies are similar to concepts and they are of great use in helping to order and classify things. In the case above, "welfare state provisions" is the concept and it has three different values (liberal, social-democratic and conservative-corporatist). The countries are then classified according to this typology, in one of the three clusters. Such a typology, or concept, does not explain *why* countries end up in a certain cluster or what kind of social consequences there are to being part of one type of welfare state and not another. The question of why Austria became a conservative-corporatist welfare state and Sweden a social-democratic state is not answered by this typology. Typologies and other concepts do not answer such theoretical questions. The conceptual stage in theory development is a necessary first step because concepts are the building blocks of theories. But concepts are not theories yet.

BOX 2.1

Merton on anomie and deviance: typology or theory?

In 1938, the American sociologist Robert Merton published a paper on "Social structure and anomie" (Merton, 1938). In the article, Merton proposed a typology to study deviance. The typology differentiated between five different groups, each group classified on the acceptance or rejection of culture goals and institutionalized means (see Table 2.3).

Table 2.3 Merton's typology.

	Culture goals	Institutionalized means
Conformity	+	+
Innovation	+	−
Ritualism	−	+
Retreatism	−	−
Rebellion	±	±

By "culture goals" Merton had in mind the American Dream of becoming successful and wealthy. By "institutionalized means" he indicated the legitimate ways to obtain such goals. In the *conformity group* we find people who accept the American Dream of making good money and who also manage to reach that goal via legitimate, institutionalized means. This group works hard, in other words, and they conform to mainstream norms. Then there is the group of *innovative* people who also want to realize the American Dream, but they want to do so in illegal ways and hence to deviate from what is seen as acceptable in society. The *ritualists* form a third category. They are people who conform to the norms, but they don't make big money and they have given up on the American Dream. Then there is a group of people, according to Merton, who *retreat* from society and who have given up both the culture goals and the institutionalized means. One could think of junkies or homeless people here. Finally, there are people who *rebel* against society and who develop new cultural goals and new means as alternatives to what is seen as acceptable by the majority. These are radicals or terrorists. Although Merton himself mentioned in the 1938 paper that his typology was not a theory yet, as it does not contain any propositions, confusingly in follow-up studies it is sometimes called Merton's "strain theory" or "anomie theory."

2.6 Causality

A hypothesis, as we have seen, is a testable statement about the association between concepts that has been logically derived from theory. When researchers stipulate these kinds of relationships, they typically have in mind that these relationships are *causal*. What does this mean?

Let's take an example. Suppose you formulate a hypothesis about the expected relationship between "attending college education" and "criminal activities," such that "people who attend college education are less often involved in criminal activities than those who did not attend college education." This hypothesized relationship might be true, but it could also be false—that makes good science. More importantly, what you have in mind is the idea that attending college education has a *causal* effect on criminal activities. It is a statement on the *effect* of the **independent variable** "attending college education" (called X) on the **dependent variable** "criminal activities" (Y).

> **independent variable** variable which has an effect on another variable (dependent variable).

> **dependent variable** variable which is affected by another variable (independent variable).

There are different definitions in the literature of "causality" (Morgan & Winship, 2015). One common interpretation goes like this. Say you take a group of 1,000 persons and then randomly divide them in two groups of 500. One group you send to college (let's call this the *treatment* group, say $X=1$) and the others you don't (let's call this the *control* group, say $X=0$). Because you randomly divided the individuals over the two conditions, you could think of each individual having two *potential outcomes*, namely: criminal activities when attending college and criminal activities when not attending college.

Of course, each individual could have been observed in only one condition: either the treatment (attending college, $X=1$) or the control group (not attending college, $X=0$). But for each individual you could ask the *what-if* question about a *counterfactual* situation: what would have happened to someone, if that person had been exposed to the other condition? If there is a causal impact, then you would expect, for example, that those attending college education (treatment) are less criminal than those not attending (control). A causal impact of attending college implies that those who attend college ($X=1$) should turn out to be less criminal on average than those who don't attend college ($X=0$). In other words, the people you send to college would have been more criminal if you had not sent them to college. And vice versa: those whom you didn't send to college would have been less criminal if they had been in college.

This notion of **causality** between X and Y contains several ingredients, of which three we discuss here (Mill, 1884; Shadish, Cook, & Campbell, 2002).

> **causality** idea that an independent variable (X) has an effect on a dependent variable (Y).

1 *Association*

The first criterion states that the independent (X) and dependent (Y) variables must be associated with each other. If we think about the example above, this means that those people who are exposed to the treatment condition (college, X=1) should be less criminal than those who are in the control condition (no college, X=0). If both groups (X=0 and X=1) have the same level of criminal activities on average (i.e., they score the same on the dependent variable Y), then there is no causal impact of X on Y.

2 *Time order*

Stipulating a causal impact of X on Y means more than stating that X and Y should be associated. The second ingredient of causality is that the cause should *precede* the effect. Thus, the independent variable X should precede the dependent variable Y in time. If we say that X causes Y, it means that we claim that differential conditions in X sets something in motion, which then changes the outcome, Y. People are sent to college (X=1) or not (X=0) and then this affects their criminal activities Y.

3 *Non-spuriousness*

Saying that X causes Y also means that different conditions of X result in differential outcomes in Y—and nothing else. To illustrate what this means, consider our example. Suppose that after we have divided the population into a group that goes to college (X=1) and the other group that doesn't (X=0), we treat both groups differently. Say that we decide that we give those who attend college ten "pro-sociality" training sessions (something they normally won't get in college), whereas for those who do not attend college we will not give such training sessions. If in the end we see that those who attend college are less criminal than those who didn't attend college, we cannot conclude that X affected Y, because there is a third variable Z (pro-sociality training) which could entirely explain the difference between X=1 and X=0. In that case, the relationship between X and Y could be spurious. Thus, if we have a hypothesis that posits a causal impact of college education on crime, we have in mind that various conditions in college education (X=1 versus X=0) result in differential outcomes in Y, and not that these differential outcomes are the result of another variable Z.

Causal statements about X and Y are thus different from spurious relationships between X and Y. There could be cases in which there is (1) an association between X and Y, or even that (2) X precedes Y, but still X does not cause Y—because the relationship is spurious. For example, consider the relationship between shoe size X and math skills Y (Babbie, 2015). Typically, those with bigger shoes (call them X=1) outperform those with smaller shoes (X=0) and, possibly, shoe size precedes math skills too. But, clearly, your math skills do not become better *because* your shoes become bigger. If you go from X=0 to X=1, what impacts your math skills is age (and what that brings about: maturity, cognitive capacity, learning). So, age is the third variable Z, which completely explains that shoe size is associated with math skills, and that shoe size has no causal impact at all on math skills (Figure 2.7).

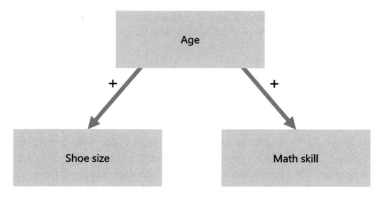

Figure 2.7 Example of a spurious relationship.

2.7 Conceptual models

How can you represent sociological theories in a scientific way? So far, I have introduced one way of doing so, namely using a *theory schema*. With the use of such a schema you can easily identify what are the *propositions*, *conditions* (which you can place above the line) and what are the *observations* and *hypotheses* (which you can place below the line). Using such a schema helps you to make sure your theory is *coherent*, an issue which is especially important when theories become complex.

A theory schema is an example of a **theory tool**. Having theory tools in your toolbox will help you to clarify your theories and avoid obscurities and inconsistencies. If you read a complex book or article in which the theoretical propositions, conditions and hypotheses remain rather implicit or are not spelled out well, you may want to use a theory schema to organize everything. To be sure, a theory tool is not a theory in itself, but rather something that helps you to organize and represent theories in a more *systematic* and *explicit* way.

theory tool tool which helps to systematically present a theory. Three often-used theory tools are: theory schema, conceptual model and formal model.

A theory schema is not the only way in which you can represent theories. A second tool that you might want to have in your toolbox is a **conceptual model**. A conceptual model, which is also called *path model* and *causal figure*, can provide a clear overview of the relationships between various concepts (Jaccard & Jacoby, 2010; Opp, 2005). These relationships can refer to theoretical propositions as well as to the hypotheses derived from the theory. Conceptual models are particularly helpful when there are many concepts involved and also

conceptual model type of theory tool in which the causal relationships between concepts are visualized.

when there are many relationships between the concepts specified. In these cases using a theory schema appears less useful because it cannot handle many relationships at the same time.

So, how do you use a conceptual model for representing theories and the hypotheses derived from theory? With a conceptual model you visualize causal relations between the key concepts. Take, for example, the following hypothesis which could have been derived from theory:

H. The more frequently people have interethnic contacts, the more positive their interethnic attitudes are.

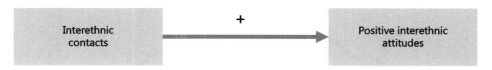

Figure 2.8 Example of a direct causal relationship.

We can visualize this hypothesis by focusing on the independent variable X—in this case "interethnic contacts"—and the dependent variable Y—"interethnic attitudes" and the specified relationship between these theoretical variables—which, in this case, is positive. We then represent this causal relationship in a conceptual model, as is done in Figure 2.8. The "+" symbol designates a positive relationship, meaning that interethnic contacts have a positive effect on positive interethnic attitudes. If the symbol "-" had been used, it would mean that more frequent interethnic contacts decrease positive interethnic attitudes. The arrow shows the direction of the causal relationship, i.e., from X to Y.

This type of relationship between two variables is called a **direct causal relationship**, also known as a *direct effect*. And these kind of relations can also be handled easily with a theory schema.

The usefulness of conceptual models becomes clear when we increase the complexity of the relationship between X and Y a little bit. Imagine that we had the following hypothesis in mind:

> *H.* The more frequently people have interethnic contacts, the more positive experiences people get with out-group members and, in this way, people will have more positive interethnic attitudes as a result.

The relationship between X and Y is now a little more complex, because we add another concept Z that is mediating the two. This theoretical variable is called a **mediator**. The idea is that X has a causal impact on Z, and that subsequently Z sets Y in motion. It is thus a "chain" of multiple causal relations instead of a single direct causal relation between X and Y. With the help of a conceptual model one can easily visualize this causal chain. In fact, a conceptual model helps you to clarify one issue here that can remain ambiguous in a theory schema. The issue is that one could interpret the mediating effect in two different ways.

First, if you say that Z mediates the impact of X on Y, it could mean that Z *fully* mediates the relationship between X and Y. In that scenario, X has no effect on Y *other than via* Z. This is called **complete mediation**. In our example, it means that interethnic contacts (X) have a positive effect on positive experiences with out-group members (Z), and this in turn affects positive attitudes (Y), and there is no other way in which X affects Y than via Z. The influence of interethnic contacts on positive interethnic attitudes is said to be *indirect*, via Z, i.e., there is no direct effect of X on Y but only an indirect effect, via Z (Figure 2.9).

direct causal relationship a relationship between two variables X and Y, such that changes in X have a direct effect on changes in Y.

mediator a variable Z that mediates the relationship between variables X and Y, such that changes in X impact changes in Z, which then results in changes in Y.

complete mediation the impact of X on Y is completely accounted for by a third variable, Z, such that there is no other way that X affects Y than via Z.

partial mediation the impact of X on Y is partially accounted for by a third variable, Z, such that X affects Y via Z, but also via other variables.

Figure 2.9 Example of full mediation: indirect causal relationship.

The second interpretation is slightly different. In that scenario, the third variable Z *partly* mediates the relationship between X and Y. In that case, scientists talk about **partial mediation** of X and Y via Z. In our example, this means that interethnic contacts (X) affect positive interethnic attitudes (Y) via positive experiences with out-group members (Z), but also that there is a direct effect of interethnic contacts (X) on positive interethnic attitudes (Y). There is, in other words, both a direct and indirect effect of X on Y (Figure 2.10).

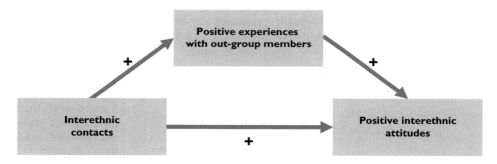

Figure 2.10 Example of partial mediation: direct and indirect causal relationship.

Sometimes researchers argue that the relationship between concepts X and Y is not in one direction, but rather state that both theory variables influence each other. Consider the relationship between frequency of interethnic contacts (X) and positive interethnic attitudes (Y) again. So far, we have argued that people who more often have contacts with members of another ethnic group than their own tend to develop more positive attitudes towards that group—which is a well-known theory in sociology and social psychology (Allport, 1954). At the same time, however, one could hypothesize that Y also affects X: people who have more positive attitudes towards other ethnic groups more often develop interethnic contacts, which implies that there might also be an effect in the opposite direction. These kind of two-way causal relationships are called **bidirectional** or **feedback relations** (see Figure 2.11) and in this case it is argued that there is a *positive* direct causal relation both ways.

bidirectional relation (also **feedback relation**) relation between two variables X and Y, such that changes in X result in changes in Y, and changes in Y result in changes in X.

Figure 2.11 Example of bidirectional causal relationship.

Scientists sometimes hypothesize that a relationship between two variables is dependent on a third variable Z. This means that the effect of X on Y differs, depending on values of Z. Scientists call these **moderation** or **interaction effects**. In an extreme case, such a moderator variable can specify conditions which turn the relationship between X and Y on or off. For example, one could think of the effect of electricity (X) on the light of a lamp (Y): the electricity gives the lamp light, but this only happens when the switch (Z) is turned on. Let's consider another example:

moderation effect (also known as **interaction effect**) the relationship between X and Y is dependent on variable Z.

H. The more frequently people have interethnic contacts, the more positive their interethnic attitudes are, and this effect is stronger among ethnic majority members than it is among ethnic minority members.

In this example, "ethnic majority status" is called the moderator or interaction variable Z. It does not say that there is no effect at all among ethnic minority members of interethnic contacts on positive attitudes. Instead, it states that the effect is *less* strongly present among this group, compared with majority members. Figure 2.12 depicts this moderation effect.

In summary, using conceptual models is a helpful tool to represent theories and the hypotheses that are derived from them. It does so especially in cases where there are statements about more complicated relationships between concepts, such as indirect effects, bidirectional effects and moderating effects. These more complicated relationships are difficult to handle with a theory schema and you might therefore want to use a conceptual model

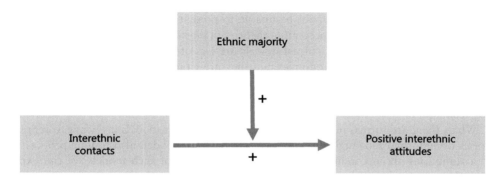

Figure 2.12 Example of moderated causal relationship.

instead. Using conceptual models also has some pitfalls, however. A conceptual model does not differentiate between propositions and hypotheses, thus between theoretical statements and the predictions you can derive from the theory. A theory schema clearly identifies the propositions and conditions on the one hand and the hypotheses on the other hand, but this is not the case in a conceptual model.

2.8 Formal models

A theory schema and a conceptual model are two well-known theory tools. The third theory tool you can use to represent theories is a **formal model** (Bonacich & Lu, 2012). That might sound a little scary, but often formal models help us to represent theories in a simple and explicit way. Moreover, formal models can express more than we normally can do with a theory schema or conceptual model. The reason is that a theory schema and conceptual model still rely heavily on natural language, i.e., on verbal reasoning, and when hypothesized relations become more complicated, our natural language fails on us. In their textbook *Matrices and Society: Matrix Algebra and Its Applications in the Social Sciences*, Ian Bradley and Ronald Meek nicely illustrate this issue:

formal model type of theory tool in which theories are expressed with formalized language.

> Translating the following simple mathematical argument into English would not produce anything intelligible:
>
> $$x^2 - 5xy + 6y^2 = 0$$
> $$(x - 2y)(x - 3y) = 0$$
> $$x = 2y \ or \ 3y$$
>
> The translation might start something like this. 'Suppose there are two quantities. They are such that if the first one is multiplied by itself and from this is subtracted five times the product of the two quantities, and then to this result is added six times the second quantity multiplied by itself then we will end up with nothing.' This is bad enough but just try making the logic of the next step in English!
>
> (Bradley & Meek, 2014 [1986])

Indeed, a theory schema and a conceptual model, both relying on natural language and lacking a set of abstract symbols, would be unable to present this formal model. Such formal models are the standard way of presenting theories in physics and other natural sciences like chemistry. In the social sciences, formal models are less often used for theory construction, however they are common in economics and they are gaining in popularity in other social sciences, including sociology (Bonacich & Lu, 2012; Coleman, 1964, 1990; Edling, 2002; Fararo, 1973). Furthermore, in empirical research, social scientists heavily use statistical modelling techniques.

What, then, are formal models? Well, in a nutshell, such models are ways to represent theories using formalized language. This means that formal models also contain propositions and assumptions about conditions, and that with the help of such models we can explain social phenomena and deduce new hypotheses. In that sense they are similar to a theory schema and conceptual model. The main difference from a theory schema and conceptual model is that such models are more formalized, i.e., they typically make use of abstract symbols and equations. And it is exactly for that reason that sociologists sometimes switch to such models, because the theory schema and conceptual model have reached their upper limits. Thus, formal models can be useful for constructing and representing sociological theories when the other two theory tools—theory schema and conceptual model—which rely more heavily on natural language, cannot do so any more. Such formal models can more easily handle exponential, logarithmic or power functions (Swedberg, 2001), and more complex (dynamic) relations between different concepts.

So, which theory tools can you expect in this textbook? The general strategy I use is the following. The default theory tool used in this textbook is the theory schema, because this one is not only the most intuitive but it also helps us to clearly differentiate between propositions, conditions and hypotheses, all very well organized in simple natural language. I then switch to a conceptual model, in case there are too many concepts or when more complex relations between concepts are specified—something the theory schema cannot handle well. When both the theory schema and the conceptual model appear not to be useful any more, when attempting to represent the theory in natural language fails and makes things excessively complicated, I will present a formal model.

PRINCIPLE 2.3

Theory tools
Sociologists use different tools to present theories in a more systematic (coherent, precise) way, namely: (1) theory schemes, (2) conceptual models and (3) formal models. It is helpful to be able to use all three tools and to be aware of their pros and cons.

BOX 2.2

Sociological puzzles

At the end of this chapter on theories, you might want to try to construct sociological explanations for several interesting theoretical questions. You can try to play with the different theory tools discussed in this chapter. Below, you'll find part of a longer list of intriguing questions that the sociologist Diego Gambetta compiled in the context of his course on sociological analysis at Oxford University. Gambetta called these "sociological puzzles" and students had to verify first whether the puzzle was true or spurious. Although for some questions this could not be decided for sure, most of them do rely on reliable sources of evidence.

Gambetta's puzzles:
    Why do women wear high heels?
    Why do teenagers in Britain drink more than most other European teenagers?

Why is the suicide rate higher in Scotland than in England?
Why do more people file for divorce after the holidays?
Why do science students live longer than art students?
Why are couples who marry after cohabitation more likely to divorce?
Why is the number of women suicides higher than that of men only in China?
Why are theology books more frequently stolen from libraries than books on other subjects?
Why is the frequency of having sex inversely related to education?

2.9 Chapter resources

Key concepts

Proposition	Deeper explanation	Partial mediation
Theory schema	Scope condition	Bidirectional relation
Condition	Theoretical variable	Moderation effect
Deductive-nomological	Typology	Formal model
explanation	Theory tool	Feedback relation
Hypothesis	Conceptual model	Interaction effect
Modus tollens	Direct causal relationship	Concept
Empirical success	Mediator	Independent variable
Information content	Causality	Dependent variable
Theoretical precision	Theoretical scope	
Theory	Complete mediation	

Key theories

- Relative age effect
- Durkheim's integration and suicide theory.

Summary

- In order to explain social phenomena, to answer "why questions," sociologists come up with theories. A sociological theory is a coherent set of propositions and assumptions about conditions which can explain certain social phenomena and which generate hypotheses (predictions) on other (yet unobserved and hypothetical) social phenomena.
- The two criteria to evaluate the usefulness of sociological theories are truth and information and both are a matter of degree. Hence, sociologists talk about the degree of empirical success and level of information content. The higher the empirical success and the information content of a theory, the more useful that theory is.
- Theories have a higher information content when they have more theoretical precision and when they have a broader theoretical scope.
- A deeper explanation, provided by an even more comprehensive proposition, specifies the scope conditions for the less general proposition.

- Concepts are the building blocks of theories. They are hypothetical abstractions that contain certain categories. Theoretical variables (concepts) are to be distinguished from measurement variables.
- The notion of causality implies that at least three criteria must be met for there to be a causal impact of an independent variable X on a dependent variable Y: there must be an association between X and Y, the time order is such that X precedes Y and differential conditions in X result in Y and nothing else (non-spuriousness).
- With the help of conceptual models one could specify different kinds of relationships: direct, mediation, moderation/interaction and bidirectional/feedback.
- There are three theory tools which you can use when you want to present a theory in a coherent way, namely: theory scheme, a conceptual model and a formal model.

References

Allport, G. W. (1954). *The nature of prejudice*. Cambridge, MA: Addison-Wesley Publishing Company.

Babbie, E. (2015). *The practice of social research* (14th ed.). Boston, MA: Cengage Learning.

Barnsley, R. H., Thompson, A. H., & Barnsley, P. E. (1985). Hockey success and birthdate: The relative age effect. *Canadian Association of Health, Physical Education and Recreation Journal*, 51, 23–28.

Barnsley, R. H., Thompson, A. H., & Legault, P. (1992). Family planning football style: The relative age effect in football. *International Review for the Sociology of Sport*, 27(1), 77–87.

Bedard, K., & Dhuey, E. (2006). The persistence of early childhood maturity: International evidence of long-run age effects. *The Quarterly Journal of Economics*, 121(4), 1437–1472.

Bernardi, F., & Grätz, M. (2015). Making up for an unlucky month of birth in school: Causal evidence on the compensatory advantage of family background in England. *Sociological Science*, 2, 235–251.

Bonacich, P., & Lu, P. (2012). *Introduction to mathematical sociology*. Princeton, NJ: Princeton University Press.

Boudon, R. (2002). Sociology that really matters: European academy of sociology, first annual lecture, 26 October 2001, Swedish cultural center. *European Sociological Review*, 18(3), 371–378.

Bradley, I., & Meek, R. L. (2014 [1986]). *Matrices and society: Matrix algebra and its applications in the social sciences*. Princeton, NJ: Princeton University Press.

Cobley, S. P., Baker, J., Wattie, N., & McKenna, J. (2009). Annual age-grouping and athlete development. *Sports Medicine*, 39(3), 235–256.

Cobley, S. P., Schorer, J., & Baker, J. (2008). Relative age effects in professional German soccer: A historical analysis. *Journal of Sports Sciences*, 26(14), 1531–1538.

Coleman, J. S. (1964). *Introduction to mathematical sociology*. London: Free Press of Glencoe.

Coleman, J. S. (1990). *Foundations of social theory*. Cambridge, MA: Harvard University Press.

Dhuey, E., & Lipscomb, S. (2008). What makes a leader? Relative age and high school leadership. *Economics of Education Review*, 27(2), 173–183.

Durkheim, E. (1961 [1897]). *Suicide*. New York, NY: Free Press.

Edling, C. R. (2002). Mathematics in sociology. *Annual Review of Sociology*, 28, 197–220.

Esping-Andersen, G. (2013 [1990]). *The three worlds of welfare capitalism*. New York, NY: John Wiley & Sons.

Fararo, T. J. (1973). *Mathematical sociology: An introduction to fundamentals*. New York, NY: John Wiley & Sons.

Gladwell, M. (2008). *Outliers: The story of success*. New York, NY: Little, Brown and Company.

Goertz, G. (2006). *Social science concepts: A user's guide*. Princeton, NJ: Princeton University Press.

Hedström, P. (2005). *Dissecting the social: On the principles of analytical sociology*. Cambridge, UK: Cambridge University Press.

Helsen, W. F., Van Winckel, J., & Williams, A. M. (2005). The relative age effect in youth soccer across Europe. *Journal of Sports Sciences, 23*(6), 629–636.

Hempel, C. G. (1962). Frontiers of science and philosophy. In Colodny (Ed.), *Explanation in science and in history* (pp. 9–19). Pittsburgh, PA: University of Pittsburgh Press.

Hempel, C. G. (1965). *Aspects of scientific explanation and other essays in the philosophy of science*. New York, NY: The Free Press.

Hempel, C. G., & Oppenheim, P. (1948). Studies in the logic of explanation. *Philosophy of Science, 15*(2), 135–175.

Jaccard, J., & Jacoby, J. (2010). *Theory construction and model-building skills: A practical guide for social scientists*. New York, NY: Guilford Press.

Lakatos, I. (1978). *The methodology of scientific research programmes*. Cambridge: Cambridge University Press.

Merton, R. K. (1938). Social structure and anomie. *American Sociological Review, 3*(5), 672–682.

Mill, J. S. (1884). *A system of logic: Ratiocinative and inductive*. New York, NY: Harper.

Morgan, S. L., & Winship, C. (2015). *Counterfactuals and causal inference: Methods and principles for social research* (2nd ed.). New York, NY: Cambridge University Press.

Opp, K. (2005). *Methodologie Der Sozialwissenschaften: Einführung in Probleme Ihrer Theorienbildung Und Praktischen Anwendung* (6th ed.). Wiesbaden: Springer-Verlag.

Popper, K. (1972). *Objective knowledge: An evolutionary approach*. Oxford: Clarendon Press.

Popper, K. (1999 [1994]). *All life is problem solving*. London: Routledge.

Popper, K. (2002 [1944]). *The poverty of historicism*. New York, NY: Psychology Press.

Popper, K. (2005 [1935]). *The logic of scientific discovery*. New York, NY: Routledge.

Popper, K. (2014 [1963]). *Conjectures and refutations: The growth of scientific knowledge*. New York, NY: Routledge.

Shadish, W. R., Cook, T. D., & Campbell, D. T. (2002). *Experimental and quasi-experimental designs for generalized causal inference*. Belmont, CA: Wadsworth Cengage Learning.

Simmons, C., & Paull, G. C. (2001). Season-of-birth bias in association football. *Journal of Sports Sciences, 19*(9), 677–686.

Swedberg, R. (2001). Sociology and game theory: Contemporary and historical perspectives. *Theory and Society, 30*(3), 301–335.

Thompson, A. H., Barnsley, R. H., & Battle, J. (2004). The relative age effect and the development of self-esteem. *Educational Research, 46*(3), 313–320.

Thompson, A. H., Barnsley, R. H., & Dyck, R. J. (1999). A new factor in youth suicide: The relative age effect. *Canadian Journal of Psychiatry, 44*, 82–85.

Van Tubergen, F., Te Grotenhuis, M., & Ultee, W. (2005). Denomination, religious context, and suicide: Neo-Durkheimian multilevel explanations tested with individual and contextual data. *American Journal of Sociology, 111*, 1412–1457.

Verachtert, P., De Fraine, B., Onghena, P., & Ghesquière, P. (2010). Season of birth and school success in the early years of primary education. *Oxford Review of Education, 36*(3), 285–306.

Chapter 3

Methods

The core aims of sociology, as we have seen in Chapter 1, are to accurately describe social phenomena, to understand underlying social processes and to apply sociological knowledge. In order to fulfill these aims, sociologists conduct empirical research: they observe social reality. This chapter introduces you to sociological methods of observation. Three important things to ask are therefore: (1) which sociological research methods can you use? (2) how should you decide which method to use? and (3), which principles can help you in evaluating empirical evidence? In this chapter the aim is to answer these questions. I begin with an outline of the three aims of sociological research, namely to describe social phenomena, to test hypotheses and to explore (3.1). Then, before reviewing the various research methods that sociologists use, I introduce three principles which help you to evaluate the quality of empirical studies that aim to describe social phenomena and test hypotheses. These three principles are: measurement quality (3.2), external validity (3.3) and internal validity (3.4). After this, I discuss in more detail the idea of exploration as a research aim (3.5) and qualitative and quantitative methods (3.6). Subsequently, I will introduce a variety of sociological methods one by one, namely: case study research (3.7), administrative data (3.8), surveys (3.9), big data (3.10) and experiments (3.11). I end this chapter with a discussion of the role of replication in sociology (3.12).

Learning goals

After reading this chapter, check if you are able to:

- Describe and use key concepts on sociological methods.
- Describe three goals of sociological research.
- Describe and use criteria to evaluate evidence from sociological research.
- Describe various sociological methods.

3.1 Is your smartphone making you stupid?

"Please put your smartphone away!" It may well be that you have heard that phrase before, or even more than once—maybe it was directed to you or to someone you know. Increasingly, there is concern among teachers that students are distracted during class because they are checking their online messages instead of making notes. Parents worry that their kids use their smartphone so often at home that they do not spend enough time on their homework anymore. The increasing smartphone use and its potential harmful effects on education can be regarded as a social problem. And this public issue raises a number of urgent societal and policy questions: should we indeed be concerned about excessive smartphone usage? Should we regard smartphones in classrooms as a bad thing? Is this problem getting worse?

Against the background of this social problem, sociologists conduct their research. Research on smartphone usage and the consequences thereof for education have clear societal relevance. But, rather than engaging in normative discussions on whether we should see smartphones as good or bad, sociologists pose scientific questions that are related to this public issue and which underlie and inform the normative discussion. Suppose this debate about smartphones is about a specific group, say, youth aged 15–20 in your country. Let's formulate descriptive and theoretical questions which are relevant in this context:

Q(d). How frequent is smartphone usage among youth aged 15–20 in your country nowadays?

Q(t). What is the effect of smartphone usage on educational performance among youth aged 15–20 in your country nowadays?

After answering these questions, sociologists have acquired knowledge which can be *applied* to get a better understanding of the social problem. If you want to implement interventions for solving a problem, you first want to know if there is indeed a problem and, if so, how much of a problem and what are the underlying mechanisms. Say that, maybe, the study shows that smartphone usage indeed lowers educational performance but is only having a marginally small effect that is hardly noticeable— so, who cares? But if the study shows that smartphone usage is having a big impact then we may want to do something about it. If you want to solve social problems you need to have solid evidence and good understanding before you act.

So, where do sociologists get their evidence from? The answer is: sociological observations, O. Sociology is an empirical science. This means that sociologists use data and observe reality. Sociologists look at what people actually do, they interview people and observe social processes. There are three purposes of sociological research (Babbie, 2015):

1 to accurately describe social phenomena,
2 to strongly test hypotheses,
3 to explore.

The first purpose of sociological research is the follow up to the first aim of sociology, which is answering descriptive questions, $Q(d)$, about social phenomena. This is called **descriptive research** and the goal is to come up with accurate descriptions of social phenomena. This is a critical task for sociology because people's perceptions of social reality may be biased. Thus, teachers and parents may overestimate (or underestimate) the actual smartphone usage of students as their perceptions are subject to cognitive biases. Let's focus on the descriptive question which sociologist aim to answer in their research. The task they have to perform is to come up with:

descriptive research research whose purpose is to come up with accurate descriptions of social phenomena.

> Highly accurate *descriptions* of the frequency of smartphone usage among youth aged 15–20 in your country.

The second purpose of doing research, namely strongly testing hypotheses, is related to theoretical questions, $Q(t)$. When sociologists construct theories, they want to find out how much truth there is in the predicted hypothesis—and, by confronting the hypothesis with empirical research, they will find this out. This is called **explanatory research**. Suppose that from sociological theory a hypothesis is derived which posits that frequency of smartphone usage has a *negative* effect on educational performance among youth. Then sociological research is needed to find out whether this hypothesis is confirmed by empirical observations. Thus, the task to be completed in empirical research is to come up with:

explanatory research research whose purpose is to rigorously test hypotheses.

> Strong empirical tests of the *hypothesis* that smartphone use has a negative effect on educational performance among youth aged 15–20 in your country.

The third purpose of empirical research, *to explore*, is not to directly answer descriptive and theoretical questions. Rather, the idea of **exploratory research** is to discover new phenomena and to construct new theories. This, in the end, helps to answer descriptive and theoretical questions, albeit indirectly. We'll come back to the purpose of exploratory research (See 3.5).

exploratory research research whose purpose is to discover new phenomena and to construct new theories.

Suppose you were presented with several sociological studies right now, from different research teams, each team claiming that they have succeeded in coming up with highly accurate descriptions and strong empirical tests of hypotheses. In other words, they claim: "Yes, now we know it! Our study answers your descriptive and theoretical questions regarding smartphone usage and its impact on educational performance."

Thinking like a sociologist means that you don't take the conclusions drawn in their studies as given. Rather, in the spirit of academic sociology, you critically review the *empirical evidence* that is presented for the *claims* and *arguments* that are made in the studies. In other words, to substantiate the *argument* that each study makes with respect to (1) the descriptions of smartphone usage and (2) to the test of the hypothesis, it has to come up with *convincing empirical evidence*. This raises a question: what are *criteria* you can use to evaluate whether the argument made in the study is convincing in light of the empirical research presented? It is helpful to think about the arguments relating to three components, namely: concepts, population and causal effects (Figure 3.1).

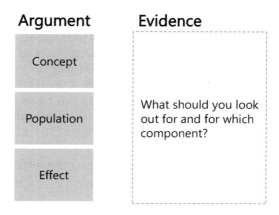

Figure 3.1 Between arguments and empirical evidence.

When do the claims regarding concepts, population and causal effects make sense? In the following sections we will review three criteria which are commonly regarded as being important for evaluating scientific evidence, each of these corresponding to one component. With respect to claims made about *concepts*, you can consider *measurement quality*. Regarding *population*, you can think of *external validity*. And when claims are made about *causal effects*, you have to consider *internal validity*. These criteria are not equally important for each research goal, however. As we will see, for accurately describing social phenomena two components play a role, namely: concepts and population. Consequently, measurement quality and external validity are relevant to consider for descriptive research purposes. When it comes to explanatory research, however, you need to consider these two criteria, but also the third one as well, namely internal validity. And when the aim is to do exploratory research, each of these criteria is less important than it is for descriptive and explanatory research.

3.2 Measurement quality

Let's start with the first criterion that you can use to judge empirical evidence coming from sociological research, and which is particularly relevant when it comes to accurate descriptions of social phenomena and explanatory research. It is concerned with the measures that are used in the research and sociologists call it **measurement quality**. In fact, this quality is an outcome of two different aspects of measurement, which are called the *validity* and *reliability* of the measures (Figure 3.2)

measurement quality quality of the measures. This depends on the validity and reliability of the measures.

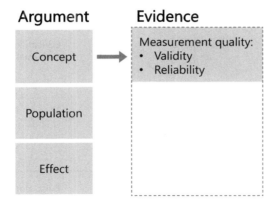

Figure 3.2 Between argument and empirical evidence: the role of measurement quality.

Let's start with **measurement validity**. It refers to the degree to which the empirical study comes up with measures that accurately capture the concepts of the study. Suppose we look in more detail at an imaginary sociological study of smartphone usage in society and the impact of smartphones on education. In the study, the sociologists needed to come up with measures of the concepts in which they were interested. With respect to the descriptive question, the key concept is *smartphone usage*, which they defined straightforwardly

measurement validity the degree to which measures reflect the theoretical concept that they are intended to measure.

as "the duration with which the smartphone is used." With respect to the hypothesis they have another concept as well, namely *educational performance*. They defined this concept as "the combined cognitive skills and educational credentials acquired by students in the school environment."

Suppose that the sociologists were in a hurry and that they did not pay so much attention to the development of the measures as they should. To measure the concept *smartphone usage*, they asked students whether they were satisfied with how often they use their smartphone; and to capture *educational performance*, they asked them what their educational aspirations were (Figure 3.3). They then proceeded with these measures, carried out their research and came up with the *argument* that they had accurately described frequency of smartphone usage and that they had provided a strong test of the hypothesis that smartphone usage has a negative effect on education.

The key question we have to ask ourselves here is: are we convinced by their arguments given their empirical evidence? The evidence is clearly flawed because the measures are invalid. The measures used in the study do not represent the concepts that they are intended to measure. When you ask students how satisfied they are with how often they use their smartphone, it will give information about their satisfaction with their phone and not about how often they use their phone. And educational aspiration is not the same as educational performance—someone may aspire to go to university but not actually attend university.

What we can learn from this example is the important difference between concepts and measures. We use *concepts* (*constructs*, *theoretical variables*) in theoretical and descriptive

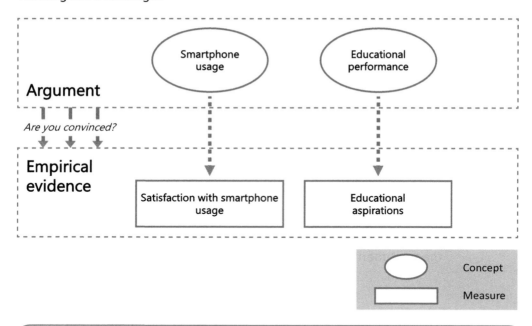

Figure 3.3 Example of measurement invalidity.

statements, and we use **measures** (also called **indicators, empirical variables, proxies**) of those concepts in empirical research. Measures are supposed to represent concepts, and the better the measures represent concepts, the higher the measurement validity. Thus, sociologists develop measures that are (approximately) representing concepts. This process is called **operationalization**, i.e., the translation of concepts into measures (Neuman, 2014).

It is helpful to make a distinction between two different types of concepts, namely *simple* and *complex* ones. For **simple concepts**, it is easy to develop valid measures. Think about the following simple concepts:

- Age
- Body weight
- Marital status
- Income.

measure (also **indicator, empirical variable, proxy**) variable used in empirical research.

operationalization translation of theoretical variables (concepts) into empirical variables (indicators).

simple concept theoretical concept that can be easily measured with empirical variables.

These and many other sociological concepts can often be measured accurately. We can ask straightforwardly about someone's age, for example. Likewise, we can quite easily come up with unproblematic measures of body weight, marital status and income. These are examples of simple concepts. Complex concepts are more difficult to translate into valid measures. Take a look at these sociological concepts:

- Social cohesion
- Social norms
- Crime

- Inequality
- Educational performance.

When sociologists develop measures for **complex concepts**, they face two threats to validity. First, they could come up with measures that capture *something else* than the concept they are supposed to measure. It is thus important to check if, on face value, the measures are indeed measuring what we want them to measure. Second, threats to validity arise when measures only *partly* capture the concept.

complex concept
theoretical concept
that consists
of different
dimensions.

Suppose, for example, that we measure the concept "educational performance" with a variable that indicates whether or not a student has "completed secondary education." Although having completed secondary education is indeed indicative of "educational performance," it does so only partly. The complex concept "educational performance" is much *broader* than what is measured with "completing secondary education."

Therefore, an important step to be taken before operationalizing complex concepts like "educational performance" is to disentangle the various **dimensions** that make up the concept (Goertz, 2006). Complex concepts consist of *multiple* dimensions and these need to be differentiated first in a process called **conceptualization** (Neuman, 2014). Thus, in this process, you use the definition of the complex concept to differentiate between the various dimensions which make up this concept.

dimension
an aspect of theory
variables.

conceptualization
the differentiation
of various
dimensions
of theoretical
variables. Relevant
for complex
concepts.

For example, we can differentiate between two dimensions of educational performance. First, the concept refers to the totality of the *cognitive skills* students acquire during their school career. This refers to everything they learned about mathematics, language, geography, physics and so forth. Then, second, educational performance includes the *education credentials* that are obtained during the school career.

After we have differentiated between these dimensions, we can come up with an operationalization of both dimensions. Suppose that we measure cognitive skills with pupils' test scores (say, on math and literacy tests), whereas we operationalize educational credentials by not only the completion of secondary education but also the completion of tertiary education (see Figure 3.4).

Thus, if we only measure whether pupils have completed secondary education or not, we would be capturing only part of the dimension "educational credentials," and entirely miss the other dimension: cognitive skills. When we use *multiple measures* instead of only one measure, we increase the validity of our measurement of this complex concept. To be sure, the four measures (indicators) in conjunction are still not perfectly representing the abstract concept of "educational performance," but together they are much more valid measures than the single measure "completing secondary education."

PRINCIPLE 3.1

Measurement validity

The better the measures that are used in the empirical research represent the concepts they intend to capture, the better the empirical evidence. Measurement validity is under threat when measures capture something different than they are intended to do and when they only partly reflect concepts.

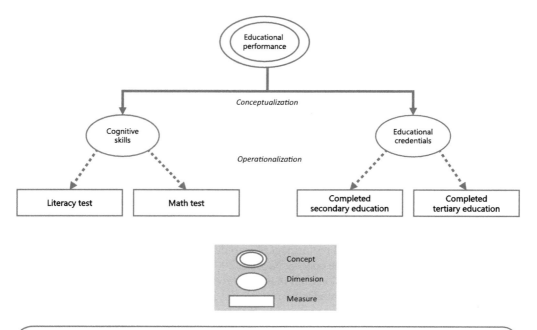

Figure 3.4 Different dimensions of educational performance and possible measures.

The second criterion with which sociologists evaluate the quality of measures has to do with reliability. The concept of **measurement reliability** indicates the tendency to get the *same* data when repeating the observation of the same phenomenon (Shadish, Cook, & Campbell, 2002). The reliability of the measure depends on the instrument that we use to collect the data. When we say that we have a measurement instrument that generates a very reliable measure, it means that we can trust that the measurement instrument will give us the same data every time we use it.

measurement reliability the degree to which the measurement instrument gives the same result when repeating the observation of the same phenomenon.

Let's see how this works. Suppose researchers wanted to measure smartphone usage among youth. They divided the teams with the plan to measure students in three locations. By combining the data from the three locations, the researchers argued that they would be able to say more about smartphone usage among youth in the entire country. In each location there is one researcher who collects the data. The researchers have not received instructions on how to proceed, so the researcher at location A may observe how often the students use their smartphone during school hours and during breaks, the researcher at location B may talk to students about their smartphone usage and the third researcher at location C may install an app on the students' phones to monitor their smartphone behavior (Figure 3.5).

Would you be convinced by the empirical evidence the researchers provide based on this research? The issue you and I should be concerned about in this case is that the measure of their study is unreliable. The researcher in location A may only speak to a select group of students and the students may misreport on their frequency of smartphone usage. Furthermore, the researcher may not be able to observe what happens to all students, or may simply misperceive what's happening because of cognitive biases. Students could also adjust their behavior in

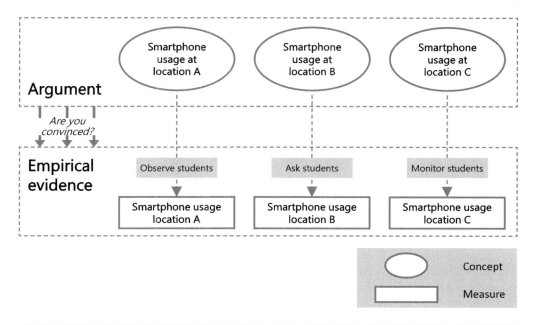

Figure 3.5 Example of measurement unreliability.

response to the presence of the researcher in class. If the researcher had not been seen by the students, different conclusions would have been drawn. And, very likely, if the researcher in location A had used the methods used in locations B or C, results would have been different. The researchers in the three locations each used their own method, giving rising to artificial differences between the three locations. The empirical findings for each location may then depend on which researcher visited that location, and combining the data from the three locations would not give us an accurate picture for the population at large. These are problems of reliability.

Having reliable measures makes the empirical evidence from your study stronger. How can you come up with more reliable measures? One way to do this is very straightforward: **standardization**. This means that you make sure that the procedures, questions, answer categories and other aspects of the measurement instrument are identical between observations (Babbie, 2015). You could standardize the way data on smartphone usage are collected among students. For example, you could use the method of the researcher in location C: develop an app that students install on their phone and that records for how long students use their phone each day. This would rule out the biased, subjective observations of a single researcher and the misperceptions of the students about their own smartphone usage. But you could also standardize the process of observation (in location A) and that of interviewing (in location B). For example, if researchers get strict instructions on the interviewing process, measures become more reliable. Measurement reliability is under threat when interviewing happens in an unstructured way. The *way* questions are asked to the respondent, the specific *words* that are used, the *answer categories* that are specified, but also the *order* in which questions are addressed significantly affects the answers given by respondents (Neuman, 2014). In order to avoid unreliable measures, you should ask identical questions, use identical answer categories and ask questions in the same order each time.

standardization process of making identical procedures, questions, answer categories and other aspects of the measurement instrument.

PRINCIPLE 3.2

Measurement reliability
The more reliable the measures that are used in the empirical research, the better the empirical evidence. There are different ways to increase reliability, but the gold standard is standardization of the measurement instrument.

In summary, the quality of measures depends on both their validity and their reliability. You can evaluate the quality of an empirical study, and the claims that are made based on that study, with the help of these two criteria. The higher the validity *and* reliability of the measurement in a sociological study, the stronger the evidence for the claims of that study.

The first thing you can do when you read a study in which it claims to provide highly accurate descriptions and a strong empirical test of hypotheses, is to consider the quality of the measures. Do you think the measures are valid? Reliable? Let's summarize the importance of measurement validity and reliability when the aims are to accurately describe social phenomena and to strongly test hypotheses.

PRINCIPLE 3.3

Measurement quality
When you evaluate the empirical evidence for (1) descriptions of social phenomena and (2) tests of hypotheses, it is important to consider the quality of the measures used in the empirical study. The better the measurement quality, the more convincing the evidence. Measurement quality depends on measurement validity and measurement reliability.

3.3 External validity

The quality of the evidence from an empirical study also depends on the *generalizability* of the observations of the study to the population about which it makes claims: to what extent can the findings of the study be generalized to the population of interest? (Figure 3.6). Scientists call this **external validity** (Shadish et al., 2002).

> **external validity** the validity of inferences about whether the results of the study are generalizable beyond a specific study.

In doing research, sociologists are often not (only) interested in the cases that they study, but rather the aim of their research is to use the specific cases they study to make more general claims. If their research is on a certain neighborhood, for example, what they want to do is to say something about neighborhoods more generally, about those that didn't participate in their research. The evidence from their study (a single neighborhood) is then used to make claims about many other neighborhoods. In the words of sociologist Goldthorpe:

The methods of enquiry that are used across the natural and social sciences alike are informed by what might loosely be called a common "logic of inference" – a logic relating evidence and argument ... We aim to obtain information about this world that we can take as a basis for inferences that extend beyond the data at hand, whether in descriptive or explanatory mode.

(Goldthorpe, 2000)

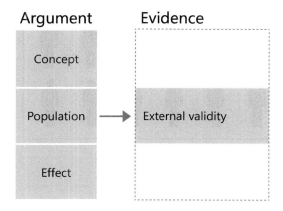

Figure 3.6 Between argument and empirical evidence: the role of external validity.

When sociologists generalize, they move from the specific observations in their study and use these to make inferences about some larger population. By **population**, sociologists mean the entire set of individuals or groups *about which the researcher wants to draw conclusions*. Sometimes, scholars talk about the *target population*. This can be all inhabitants in a country but also a more specific group of people.

population the entire set of cases about which the researcher wants to draw conclusions.

In our example of smartphone use, the target population is *youth, aged 15–20, in your country*. This means that we want to conduct empirical research in such a way that it allows us to come up with accurate descriptions and a strong test of the hypothesis *among this target population*. Suppose that a research team takes up this task and interviews 50 female students aged 18 on their university campus. If the team did so, we would not be convinced by the evidence it provides because external validity is threatened here. The group that was the focus of the study (female students aged 18 on a university campus) is not representative of the population aged 15–20 in your country. It is very likely that this group of female students aged 18 use their smartphone differently than others aged 15–20.

biased sample sample for which observations in the study cannot be generalized to the population.

This is what we call a **biased sample** and it undermines the evidence coming from the study. So how could you make sure that your sample is representative and not biased? You first need to make sure that you know what a **sample** is. These are the people, the observations, that are in your study (Figure 3.7). The sample of individuals

sample a small set of cases a researcher selects from the population.

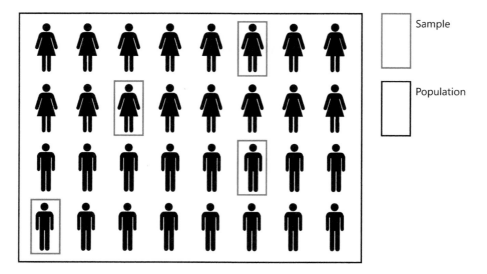

Sample

Population

Figure 3.7 Population and sample.

who participate in the study should be a **representative sample** of all individuals in the target population. If that is the case, if the sample is indeed representative, you can make inferences from a relatively small group of individuals (say 500 people) to the larger population (say 1 million people). However, not all samples are representative, and when observing or interviewing a group of people that is not representative of the larger population the researcher cannot say much about the target population.

representative sample sample for which observations in the study can be generalized to the population.

How do you get a representative sample? One necessary requirement is that you use a **probability sample** (Babbie, 2015). This might sound a little technical and scary, but the idea is simple. Imagine we have a population of 20,000 persons: 10,000 men and 10,000 women. We take a sample of that population, say 200 people. Clearly, what we do not want is to get a selective (non-representative, biased) sample, say 200 men and no women. Therefore, in order to get a representative sample, men and women need to be equally represented.

probability sample sample drawn by giving individuals in the population equal chance to participate in the study.

A common strategy to get such a representative sample is to give all individuals in the population *an equal chance* of being selected in the sample (Babbie, 2015). If we have 20,000 people and we want to select 200 subjects for our study, then each of the 200 individuals in the population should have a probability of participating in the study of 200/20,000 = 0.01. This means that in our example we will get around (0.01 × 10,000 =) 100 women and (0.01 × 10,000 =) 100 men in our sample. In practice, there might be a little more than or fewer than 100 women in the sample. By chance it will happen that sometimes we get a sample of 90 women and 110 men, or 105 women and 95 men. When the size of the sample goes up, for example if we did not have 200 persons in the sample but 2,000, we would get a sample that will be closer to the 50:50 distribution. By using random probability sampling a crucial step is taken to make more conclusive inferences from the sample to the larger population.

How to draw a random sample from a population? How could you make sure that, in this example, every individual in the population has a probability of 0.01 to be involved in the sample? To do so, you need to have a list of people who make up this population. This could be a roster with all their names on it, numbered from 0 to 20,000. You give each individual on that list a probability of 0.01 and then draw your sample.

In practice, sociologists often order their target population in several *strata* before they take a probability sample. A stratum can be a neighborhood, for example, but also gender, ethnic groups, social class or characteristics of schools can serve as strata. Figure 3.8 gives an example in which gender and education are used as strata to categorize the population. Within each of these strata, a probability sample is then taken. By ordering the population in such a **stratified sample**, you can more easily make sure that each subgroup in the population is well-represented in the survey. Moreover, sometimes researchers are interested in particular smaller subgroups, say ethnic minorities, and they can then oversample this group to make sure they have a sufficient number of respondents from this group. In the analysis after the data collection, this oversampling is then taken into account.

> **stratified sample** sample based on dividing the population into subpopulations (strata).

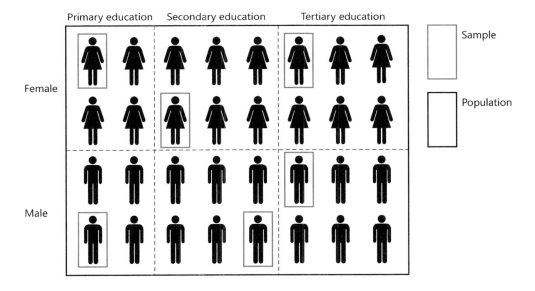

Figure 3.8 Example of stratified sample by gender and education.

When you use a representative sample, you have powerful empirical evidence that allows you to generalize the findings from the study to the target population. By contrast, if you have a biased sample then the evidence is suspicious. Consider Figure 3.9, which presents an imaginary sample of female university students among whom data are collected on smartphone use. You can see that, from the population, the researcher selected a very specific sub-sample that is presumably not representative of the target population—in this case all 15–20 year olds in your country. In other words, the study ends up with a *biased sample* that is not representative and conclusions based on this sample cannot be generalized to the target population.

Thinking like a sociologist

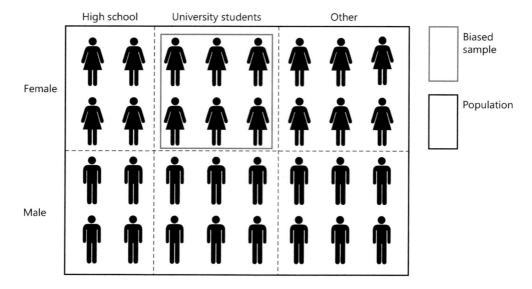

Figure 3.9 Example of a non-representative (biased) sample.

A biased sample is not only problematic for descriptive research purposes. Such biases also hinder strong tests of hypotheses. The reason is that, if you have a biased sample, the study can only observe whether a relationship exists among the respondents in the study, such as female university students aged 18 years old. Suppose the study reveals that among this particular group there is no effect of smartphone use on educational outcomes. The problem is that we cannot conclude from these findings that the same is true for the rest of the population. Possibly, smartphone use is having a negative effect on educational performance among boys or only among youth aged 15–17. As long as your sample is biased, so will be the claims that you make about the larger population.

In summary, another issue you may consider when evaluating empirical evidence is external validity. When sociological studies aim to accurately describe social phenomena and to strongly test hypotheses in a certain population, the empirical evidence of the study should be generalizable to that target population.

 PRINCIPLE 3.4

External validity
When you evaluate the empirical evidence for (1) descriptions of social phenomena and (2) tests of hypotheses, it is important to consider external validity. The better the external validity, the more convincing the empirical evidence. External validity depends on the degree to which the observations of the study can be generalized to the target population.

3.4 Internal validity

When the aim of sociological research is to *test hypotheses*, there is a third criterion you can use to evaluate the empirical evidence, namely **internal validity** (Figure 3.10). By this, researchers mean how strongly you can infer from the empirical findings in the study that there is a causal impact of X on Y (Shadish et al., 2002). Internal validity is therefore not a relevant issue to consider when it comes to describing social phenomena. But when the aim of your study is to find out whether X affects Y, then not only measurement quality and external validity, but also internal validity is something you have to take into account.

> **internal validity** the validity of inferences about whether an observed association between X (independent variable) and Y (dependent variable) reflects a causal relationship from X to Y.

The criterion of internal validity applies to the context in which the study was conducted. This means that when internal validity is strong, the researcher has good reasons to make claims about whether or not X has a causal impact on Y *within the context of investigation*. Such a context can be the laboratory of the researcher, for example, but also an organization or a specific neighborhood. Strong internal validity does not imply that there is strong external validity too, or that the measurements are of high quality. These three criteria operate independently from each other. For example, it is possible that a study has high internal validity but low external validity, and vice versa.

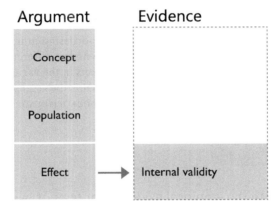

Figure 3.10 Between argument and empirical evidence: the role of internal validity.

Suppose a research team aims to test the hypothesis that smartphone usage has a negative effect on educational performance. Let's give them some credit and assume they develop good measures and use a representative sample. The researchers interviewed all students on a particular day, asking them about how frequently they use their smartphone on that day, as well as measuring how well they perform in education. They then analyzed their data and found that those students who indicated that they use their phone very frequently are doing less well in education. The researchers then make the following claim, which they report in a scientific journal: "our study clearly demonstrates that smartphone usage among students has a negative effect on educational performance."

The question we can ask is: do we find the evidence this study provides convincing for the claim that is made? Would you say that the research team has come up with a strong test of the hypothesis that smartphone use X has a negative effect on educational performance Y?

One problem from which their study suffers is that the researchers have only demonstrated that there is an *association* between X and Y. The notion of causality contains two other ingredients which need to be addressed (see Chapter 2), namely that X should *precede* Y in time and that different conditions in X result in differential outcomes in Y—and nothing else (*non-spuriousness*). With respect to these two aspects, the study fails to provide convincing evidence and, as a consequence, we are uncertain about whether or not there is or there is not a causal impact of smartphone usage on educational performance.

For example, it could be that it is not the case that X affects Y, as the study claims, but rather the opposite: those students who perform worse in education (Y) start using their smartphone more often (X). If so, this would indeed lead to a negative relationship between X and Y, but then the causal impact goes from Y to X and not from X to Y. Furthermore, it could also be the case that there is actually no causal impact at all of X on Y, or from Y to X, even though X and Y are associated—as the study finds. This scenario could happen if there is a third variable Z that sets in motion the association between X and Y. Possibly, parents who exert more social control have children who use their smartphone less and do better in education as well. In that case, the relationship between X and Y would be entirely spurious.

What can we learn from this? The example tells us that when a study wants to come up with a strong test of an hypothesis, it needs to address all three elements of causality. That is, it needs to establish whether there is an association between X and Y, that X comes before Y and that it is indeed X that leads to changes in Y. In practice, it appears that coming up with a study that finds whether there is an association or not is not so difficult. To examine whether X precedes Y, the study should at least have some time-ordering in it, such that X and Y are repeatedly measured instead of only once. To find out whether different conditions in X set Y in motion, the gold standard is to randomly assign subjects in the various conditions of X and then observe whether this results in differences in Y. That is the essence of doing experiments and we will come back to this when we discuss different experimental methods (See 3.11).

 PRINCIPLE 3.5

Internal validity

When you evaluate the empirical evidence for tests of hypotheses, it is important to consider internal validity. A study has a higher internal validity when it is able to convincingly determine whether X and Y are associated or not, whether or not X precedes Y in time, and whether or not it is differential conditions of X which result in differential outcomes in Y—and nothing else.

3.5 Exploratory research

Sociological research helps us to accurately describe social phenomena, as well as to test hypotheses about these phenomena. It can inform social policy making, such as when sociologists have come up with solid empirical evidence on how smartphone use is changing in society and how it can have disruptive effects on education, health and wellbeing.

In addition to these two purposes of sociological research, there is a third reason to do research which we have not discussed in detail so far. The third reason is called exploration. A major aim of exploratory sociological research is to discover *new* social phenomena and to construct *new* typologies and theories (Abbott, 2004; Swedberg, 2014b). Exploratory research *supplements* the aim to come up with accurate descriptions and strong tests of hypotheses.

To see how, we can have a little conversation with our imaginary research team. We may ask them:

> where does your hypothesis come from, which you want to test? You expect that smartphone use is doing no good to the education of students. But why would you think so?

The research team might then very well respond by saying that:

> well, we have deduced this hypothesis from the theory. That theory contains certain propositions and assumptions. Specifically, the theory posits that people need to have time and energy for learning, and that checking online messages disrupts that learning process. Furthermore, we make the assumption that students are using their smartphone during school hours. We follow the rule to deduce testable hypotheses and then apply modus tollens—if the hypothesis is refuted by empirical research, so is the theory.

All that makes sense and is good sociological research. But it begs an important question, namely: *where did this research team get its ideas and theory from?* After all, the research team must have discovered at some point that students are using their smartphones during college hours. And the propositions that make up the theory cannot have come out of nowhere. Of course, the researchers could say that the theory they used was developed by another scholar and that they were only applying and testing it. But this only shifts the problem—where did this other scholar get the theory from? The point is that sociologists also discover and learn about *new* social phenomena and they develop *new* theories.

The sociologist Swedberg calls this stage the *art of theorizing* (Swedberg, 2014a). Theorizing typically starts with making observations and inductive reasoning. By **induction**, scientists mean the inferences that are made from observations of only a limited number of cases to a more general, universal pattern (Neuman, 2014). This is something we do all the time, although most of the time it happens implicitly. Say, for example, if a friend of yours has repeatedly come too late for appointments in the past then you might generalize his behavior and state that "He *always* comes too late." This is a case of inductive reasoning, as now you also claim that, for future meetings, your friend will come too late. Furthermore, you might compare his behavior with that of three other friends of yours who always come on time. They happen to be three girls and this leads you to hypothesize that "Boys tend to come too late, girls tend to be there on time." Effectively what you have been doing is precisely what is happening in inductive theory construction: you use a few observations to make more general claims (Wallace, 1971). The data lead you to construct theories. As Sherlock Holmes once proclaimed:

induction
inferences that are made from observations of only a limited number of cases to a more general, universal pattern.

> I have no data yet. It is a capital mistake to theorize before one has data. Insensibly one begins to twist the facts to suit theories, instead of theories to suit facts.
>
> (Doyle, 1892)

Exploration means that you use your observations for the purpose of theory development, that you work from single cases to more universal patterns and that you construct new theories based on the patterns that you see. Where your data comes from does not matter—as long as it helps you in your creative process of generating new insights. For exploratory research, one can therefore use various research methods and data sources. In the words of Swedberg:

> At the beginning of the research the information should come from a very broad range of sources. It can come from interviews, archives, newspapers, bar codes, autobiographies, data sets, dreams, movies, poems, music ... Anything goes!
>
> (Swedberg, 2014a)

Why are criteria of measurement quality, external validity and internal validity less useful for evaluating exploratory research? The answer is that the aims of exploratory research on the one hand and, on the other hand, the aim of coming up with accurate descriptions and strong tests of hypotheses, are of different natures. Philosophers of science have labeled this the distinction between the *context of discovery* and the *context of justification* (Popper, 2005; Reichenbach, 1938). A key purpose of exploratory research is to discover possibly new and important social phenomena and to construct new theories. This means that in exploratory research no claim is made by the researchers that they have come up with an accurate description of social phenomena, nor that they have provided rigorous tests of hypotheses. This is unlike descriptive and explanatory research which, as we have seen, makes claims about accurately describing social phenomena and strongly testing hypotheses.

Exploratory research is supplemental to descriptive and explanatory research—they work together in a *cycle*. Exploratory research discovers new and interesting phenomena and gives impetus to theory development. But because exploratory research rests on inductive reasoning, one cannot infer the truth of the theory (Popper, 1972, 2005). It could very well be the case that, someday, we observe something that is not in line with the theory. From the observation that three girls arrive on time we cannot infer that girls arrive on time more so than boys do. Logically speaking, inductive reasoning does not prove that the theory is true. That is the problem of induction.

But, then, that is not a problem when combined with descriptive and explanatory research. One can use the newly developed theory and *deduce* hypotheses from it. Using rigorous empirical research, we can then test whether observations confirm or refute the hypothesis—and thereby the theory. If empirical findings consistently refute the hypotheses we may want to develop another theory, and for this we can use exploratory research again. And so forth, working in tandem, in a cycle of developing and testing.

 PRINCIPLE 3.6

Exploratory research
The purpose of exploratory research is to discover new social phenomena and construct new theories. For this purpose, you can use various data sources and inductive reasoning.

3.6 Qualitative and quantitative methods

Sociologists uses a myriad of methods and it is helpful for you to become familiar with the various methods you can use. Sometimes the methods sociologists use are divided into two categories, namely *qualitative* and *quantitative* methods. Although the distinction is often made, there is no consensus among scholars about the meaning of these two terms and in practice they are used in various ways. Some scholars use these words to make a contrast between (quantitative) methods that are used for counting and comparing things and (qualitative) methods in which counting and comparing are not important. Others use the distinction to differentiate large-scale research, using administrative data, surveys and big data (i.e., quantitative) from small-scale case study research (i.e., qualitative). Yet another use of these words relates to the difference between deductive research (quantitative) versus inductive research (qualitative), or to the distinction between explaining behavior (quantitative) and understanding behavior (qualitative).

Differences between qualitative and quantitative approaches—however defined—can be interpreted as a matter of degree rather than a simple dichotomy. For example, contemporary qualitative studies not only rely on case-study methods but also administrative data and big data. Similarly, so-called "quantitative studies" not only use surveys and big data, but also carry out case studies. Furthermore, some qualitative research uses only a handful of unstructured interviews, but other qualitative research uses larger samples and structured interviewing.

The approaches can also be regarded as supplementary to each other. For example, qualitative approaches may show a greater interest in *exploratory research* than quantitative approaches. This generates new ideas about social phenomena and contributes to the development of new theories. Quantitative approaches may focus more on accurately *describing social phenomena* and *rigorously testing hypotheses*. It is therefore useful to combine insights from both approaches rather than focusing on one beforehand.

If you go beyond the dichotomy between qualitative and quantitative methods, you'll see that there are many methods available for you to use—not just two. The most common ones are: case study research, administrative data, surveys, big data and experiments. Importantly, each of these methods has its strengths and weaknesses. Therefore, it would be unwise to exclusively rely on a single method for whatever social phenomenon you study. Rather, it would be much more valuable to have multiple methods at your disposal and, each time you plan to conduct empirical research, to decide which method you think is the best one *given the specific aims of your research*.

Thus, rather than *first* selecting a method and *then* applying this method to answer questions, it is more useful for you to first consider the aims of the research (descriptive, explanatory, exploratory) and use these to select the appropriate method. For example, some methods are better suited for answering descriptive questions than testing hypotheses. Other methods are more useful for testing hypotheses. In the words of sociologist Firebaugh: "Let method be the servant, not the master" (Firebaugh, 2008).

3.7 Case study research

case study research research that is an in-depth examination of an extensive amount of information about very few units or cases.

One method sociologists use is **case study research** (Marshall & Rossman, 2014). This method typically focuses on one or just a few well-defined cases, such as an organization, a criminal gang, a school, or a neighborhood (Yin, 2013). These cases are then studied in depth, such that the researcher extensively interviews the actors and/or observes what is happening (Hammersley & Atkinson, 2007). This can generate rich data on how the actors are related to each other, how these relations develop over time and how the context in which they participate plays a role therein. For example, one could conduct a case study of an organization by interviewing the employees and employers and observing how they interact within the workplace.

An example of a classic case study is Willem Foote Whyte's *Street Corner Society* (Whyte, 2012[1943]). Whyte carried out his research in the late 1930s in the North End district of Boston, which was predominantly inhabited by people with Italian roots. His research took three and a half years and, during these years, Whyte himself closely participated within one of the criminal gangs (the Nortons) in this district. His study describes in rich detail this community, how gangs operate, as well as the broader social structure and politics within this community. For example, using his data he was able to construct in detail the social network relations of the Nortons' street gang (Figure 3.11).

For this study, Whyte actively engaged within the community. This element is called *participant observation* and it means that the researcher observes the behavior of the subjects in their natural setting and uses this source of personal information for the investigation. At the beginning of his research, Whyte had no clear idea how he would approach his subject nor who, in the end, the subject of his investigations would be. After several failures to connect with local people, eventually a member of a criminal gang accepted him, introduced him to his gang and let him make notes. This allowed him to get inside knowledge about how this criminal gang operated. Whyte then interviewed the gang members and other actors in the

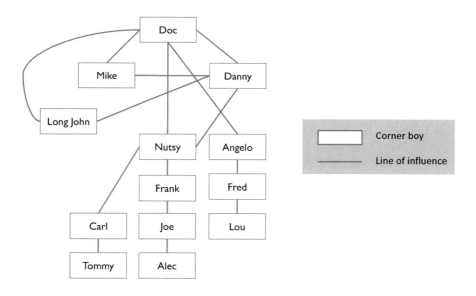

Figure 3.11 Social network of the Nortons' gang. Note: the higher the position of the box in the network, the higher the status. "Doc" is the leader of the gang.

Source: Whyte, 2012[1943].

Image 3.1 In case study research, the researcher not only interviews the respondents but sometimes also actively participates in the setting.

community. To this end, he did not use a set of questions that were constructed and standardized beforehand, but rather used unstructured, open questions.

The case study method is typically used for two research purposes. First, to generate what is called **thick description** (Geertz, 1973). These are detailed descriptions of persons, their behaviors, motivations, meanings, social processes and personal relationships *within a well-defined case*. Second, when the aim is to discover new phenomena and develop new theories. Case study research can be used for exploratory purposes, such that the researcher uses the observations made within the case study to generate more general ideas.

thick description
detailed description of persons, their behaviors, motivations, social processes and personal relationships within a well-defined case.

Case study research is less-suited for generalizing the findings *beyond* what is studied (Goldthorpe, 2000). Whyte's study gives a rich and detailed account of the North End district of Boston in the late 1930s, but the empirical evidence provided in *Street Corner Society* is not such that one could convincingly claim that the study gives insights of what happens in other districts and neighborhoods in the US—let alone in other countries. It may well be that the patterns of social interaction, the organization of criminal gangs and so forth is very different in the cases that were not studied by Whyte. One could argue that the *external validity* of the study is low, because Whyte studied only one case (the North End district of Boston) and this particular case is unlikely to be representative of other cases in the population.

This critique of case study research needs to be seen in perspective. Importantly, as we discussed before, the issue of external validity is about the possible mismatch between the *sample* from which you take your observations and the *target population* about which you draw your conclusions. This means that if Whyte used his observations from within a *single* district in the US (sample) to draw inferences about what is happening in *all cases* in the US (target population), then one would not be convinced by the evidence. However, this is not what Whyte claimed or intended to do: he was interested in describing the people living in a slum neighborhood—and in the end his claims are about the social processes and structures in the North End district of Boston. His sample and target population coincided.

Furthermore, case study research is done in a variety of ways. Whyte's study is a classic, but case study research can use different designs. It may be carried out by a single researcher—as in *Street Corner Society*—but it may involve teamwork as well, such that a group of researchers together study the same case. It can be conducted in a more open, unstructured way, as Whyte did, or be more standardized, using well-defined guidelines on whom to interview and how to approach the subjects, as well as structured questionnaires. It can be targeted towards a single case—such as the North End district of Boston—but it can also cover more cases such as, say, several neighborhoods. And it can use participant observation, as Whyte did, but can also be done without this.

Some case study designs are more appropriate for generalizing the observations beyond what is studied. When the researcher studies a single case it is hard to make claims beyond that case. But when a group of researchers work together and study more than one case, the evidence to generalize becomes stronger. This is particularly so if more and more cases are studied, and if the cases are well-chosen such that they provide a representative group of cases of the target population. This would then involve more rigorous, standardized procedures for data collection, such as using standardized questionnaires to compare the findings from the various cases with each other. Whether or not to opt for such an approach depends on the purposes of the research. If the aim is to generalize beyond the observations of the study, this is an attractive strategy. But if the research purpose is to provide thick descriptions of the processes within the case that is studied, and/or to discover new phenomena and develop new theories, then it makes perfect sense to focus on a single case.

3.8 Administrative research

Another source for sociologists is administrative data. **Administrative research** relies on data on human populations that come from official institutions such as governments, schools, hospitals, police departments and other organizations. Schools keep records of the grades and school progress of their pupils, police departments record suspects of a crime and so forth. In Durkheim's famous study on suicide (Chapter 1 and 2), he used data on suicide rates in various states and regions. These figures were obtained from the government. In contemporary research on suicide such official records remain an important data source for sociologists.

> **administrative research** research in which the researcher uses data on human populations that are provided by official institutions such as governments, schools or hospitals.

Administrative data provide a rich source for historical sociological research, such as to describe long-term trends in societies, but also for contemporary analyses and more in-depth studies of particular events and cases. To illustrate, the sociologists Padgett and

Image 3.2 Archival records are an important source of data for sociologists.

Ansell used data on marriage records and financial transactions in 14th- and 15th-century Florence to study the social connections of the De Medici family (Padgett & Ansell, 1993). With the use of such archival records, they were able to show how the status and power of the De Medici changed over time and that this was related to the social connections of this family.

There are different sorts of administrative data and one sort that is frequently used is the *population census*. Census data are collected among (almost) the entire adult population in a country via standardized questionnaires that respondents fill in. To interview all citizens in a country is, as you can imagine, a gigantic operation. It costs a lot of money and requires a strong organization to do the fieldwork. Nevertheless, many countries do have a population census because governments consider it important to gather information about the population.

Sociologists use population census data mainly for descriptive research purposes and hypotheses testing. A key strength of census data is that they are collected among all citizens in the country, which means that the data have strong external validity. A limitation of census data is that researchers are constrained by the information that is collected by the government. Typically, governments use the census to collect information on core socio-demographic characteristics such as age, gender, marital status, place of living, ethnicity, country of birth, employment status, occupation and income. For these characteristics, census data provide a rich data source for research purposes.

BOX 3.1

IPUMS-International

Census data have been collected all over the world, in many countries and for a long time period. Because census data cover entire populations and often contain data on core sociological topics like education and occupation, migration and race, they are a rich source for sociologists. At the Minnesota Population Center (USA) a team of researchers has been collecting as much census data from all over the world as they can. They have been integrating these census data from various countries into a cross-national comparative data set, which allows researchers to compare sociological processes across these nations. In 2019, the Integrated Public Use Microdata Series (IPUMS) International, as it is officially called, covered data from 94 countries, based on 365 censuses and more than one billion person records. Every year, new censuses are added to the project. The data are free to use for scientists. More information on this project can be found on the website of the IPUMS project, see: https://international.ipums.org/international.

3.9 Survey research

Another method of data collection is surveys (Fowler, 2013). In **survey research**, sociologists interview people with the help of questionnaires. How people are interviewed varies from survey to survey, as there are different ways of doing so. In some surveys, interviews are conducted by phone, in others this is done face to face or via self-completion questionnaires in hardcopy or online. Traditionally, surveys were mainly done face to face, using the home of the respondent as the interview setting. Nowadays, more and more surveys are conducted online, with questionnaires that can be filled out on the internet or phone.

> **survey research** research in which the researcher uses questionnaires to collect data from respondents.

Survey might sound the same as a population census but there are two important differences. Censuses are largely designed by the government and are mainly done to get information on core socio-demographic characteristics of the population. Surveys, by contrast, are designed by researchers. This flexibility allows the researcher to study social phenomena that are often missing in census data, such as attitudes, norms, values and so forth.

Another important difference between a census and a survey is that in a census the entire population of a country is interviewed, as we saw above, while in a survey only a sample of individuals participate. A potential issue is therefore *external validity* if the aim of the study is to generalize beyond the observations to some larger target population. To mitigate this problem, one can draw a random probability sample and survey the individuals within that representative sample. Sociological surveys are able to ensure a high degree of external validity when they are based on such probability samples and when biases due to systematic non-response are minimized.

Image 3.3 Sociologists use surveys as a method of observation.

Survey data collection can be done in a more unstructured way, using open questioning. And it can be collected in a highly standardized way, which ensures strong *measurement reliability*. To make sure that the measures that are used in the survey are valid, one can first do a pilot study among a smaller group of respondents. This helps to assess whether the variables indeed measure what they are supposed to measure. Only the validated measures are then used in the survey. In summary, survey data have the potential to come up with strong *measurement validity*.

Surveys are often used for providing descriptions of social phenomena and for testing hypotheses. Over the years, different sorts of surveys have been developed. To study trends in society, so-called *repeated cross-sectional surveys* have been developed. These surveys are conducted with a certain interval (e.g., once every five years) and, when identical questions are asked to a representative sample of the same population each time, one can use such survey data to discern societal changes over longer time periods. To study the role of social contexts within society, *multilevel surveys* have been invented that allow you to compare the importance of meso-level conditions. For example, you can study how crime differs across neighborhoods, how work satisfaction differs across organizations and thus how such meso-level social contexts impact the behavior of individuals. *Cross-national surveys* have been developed to compare macro-level cases, which means that you can compare people living in different countries. Finally, *panel surveys* have been developed in which the same individuals are repeatedly surveyed. This allows sociologists to study life-course changes and also to come up with tests of causality that are stronger than when individuals are observed only once.

European Value Survey (EVS) and World Values Survey (WVS)

The European Value Survey (EVS) is a large-scale, cross-nationally comparative survey. In the year 1981 this survey was conducted for the first time. It then included nine European nations. Since then it has been repeated several times. The focus of the research was the values, attitudes, opinions and beliefs of Europeans. The fourth wave, which was conducted in 2008, was carried out in no less than 47 European societies and 70,000 people were interviewed. Meanwhile, the World Values Survey (WVS) expanded the scope of EVS and also included societies outside Europe, i.e., in North and South America, Asia, Oceania and Africa. Together, WVS and EVS carried out representative national surveys in 97 societies containing almost 90% of the world's population. It is a rich source for sociologists who want to describe how cultures differ across societies, but also cultural changes over time. The data from the EVS and WVS are accessible for researchers. For more information, visit the official websites:www.europeanvaluesstudy.eu and www.worldvaluessurvey.org.

3.10 Big data research

A growing source of data for sociologists are so-called *big data* (Golder & Macy, 2014; Lazer et al., 2009), also referred to as *digital data*, *online data* and, when using these kind of sources for research, as **big data research** or *computational social science* (Lazer et al., 2009). There is no consensus about the definition of big data (Salganik, 2017), but one common interpretation is that it refers to the unstructured data coming from the Internet (e.g., social media, websites), digital communication (e.g., emails, text messages) and digital traces (e.g., GPS location, web-tracking). Most prominently,

big data research research in which the researcher uses (unstructured) data from the Internet, digital communication and digital traces.

the Internet provides a massive amount of big data for sociologists, such as Facebook, Twitter, Instagram, YouTube, LinkedIn, blogs and other websites. Digital data, however, entails much more than what can be found on the Internet. It also includes email records, SMS text messages, mobile phone communications, MSN, GPS location tracking and more. The sociologist Duncan Watts argued that these new sources are promising for sociological research:

> [J]ust as the invention of the telescope revolutionized the study of the heavens, so too by rendering the unmeasurable measurable, the technological revolution in mobile, Web, and Internet communications has the potential to revolutionize our understanding of ourselves and how we interact ... [T]hree hundred years after Alexander Pope argued that the proper study of mankind should lie not in the heavens but in ourselves, we have finally found our telescope. Let the revolution begin.
>
> (Watts, 2011)

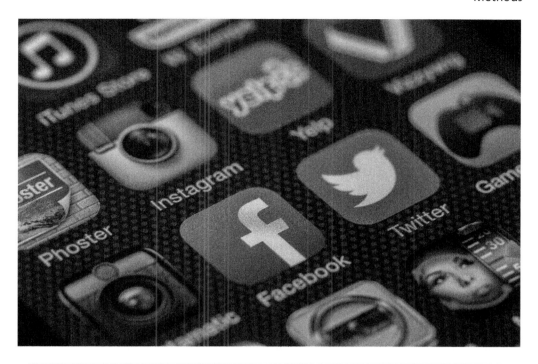

Image 3.4 More and more, sociologists use online data to study social processes.

How useful big data are for sociological research purposes is difficult to evaluate in a simple statement as the data sources are so diverse—from Twitter to emails to GPS location tracking—and because the field is rather new and progresses strongly. What can be said is that, in various ways, big data offer some unique opportunities and challenges.

Big data can create opportunities to study social phenomena on a unprecedentedly large scale, in continuous time and using behavior data. *Large scale*, because some big data, such as from Twitter or Facebook, or phone records, cover millions of people. *Continuous time*, because some big data provide data without intervals. Data from Facebook and Twitter are available all the time; every minute, so to speak, the researcher can study their subjects on such social media. By contrast, traditional methods are often conducted at certain points in time with (large) intervals in between measurements. For example, the researcher conducts a survey in a certain year and then re-interviews the same respondents again one year later. What has happened between these two measurement moments often remains unknown to the researcher. *Behavioral data*, because some big data contain information about what people do and this may provide interesting supplemental data to—or even more precise data than—what people self-report in surveys. For example, one can ask students how often they interact with peers using a survey, but you can also install an app on their phone measuring very precisely where they are (using GPS, wi-fi and Bluetooth) and from these big data infer precisely how often they meet their peers (Eagle, Pentland, & Lazer, 2009; Mastrandrea, Fournet, & Barrat, 2015).

There are several challenges to using big data (Golder & Macy, 2014). One has to do with sampling and external validity. If one studies a social media platform like Facebook or Twitter, for example, the users are not representative of the population at large as this also includes those not using Facebook or Twitter. It then makes sense to generalize to the population of Facebook or Twitter users only. Even then, however, there are challenges because, for example, Facebook users may use privacy settings for their account. This means that their information is not available in the public domain, hence the researcher can only observe those who have public profiles. Consequently, this creates another challenge to external validity. In principle, these barriers could be overcome if the researcher has access to all social media user data, but the reality is that social media companies often restrict researchers' access to their user data.

BOX 3.3

Big Data: Twitter

Big data come in a variety of forms—from social networking sites like Facebook to GPS location tracking from smartphones. Among this huge diversity in data sources is Twitter. In one study published in the journal *Science*, sociologists Golder and Macy (2011) analyzed Twitter data to study people's mood, i.e., their positive affect (e.g., enthusiasm, delight) and negative affect (e.g., fear, anger). Using data from millions of public Twitter messages and counting the number of times people use positive and negative affect words, they found that people's mood is best in the morning and deteriorates as the day progresses. Furthermore, they found that people are happier on weekends than during the week. With their analyses of these behavioral data, continuous in time and large in scope, Golder and Macy provided new insights to earlier research on mood, which had heavily relied on traditional data sources.

3.11 Experimental research

Another sociological method is the experiment (Cox & Reid, 2000), which is regarded as the gold standard in testing hypotheses. **Experimental research** is often contrasted with **observational research**, which relies on case studies, surveys, administrative records and big data.

In a typical experiment, participants are randomly assigned, at t_0, to either the *experimental condition* (E) or the *control condition* (C). In practice, there can be more than two conditions to which subjects are assigned. In the experimental condition, participants are exposed to a certain "treatment," such as handing in their phone during class. The participants in the control group can keep their phone during class. To do the experiment properly, the two groups have the same instructor but they attend classes in different sessions. The instructor has been trained very well so that the lectures are the same for both groups.

Suppose we are interested in whether there is a difference between the experimental group and the control group in the grade for the course. Did those who had to hand in their phone during class outperform those who did not? After the experiment has been conducted, we can measure the outcome "course grades" among

experimental research research in which the researcher manipulates conditions for some research participants but not others and then compares group responses to see whether doing so made a difference.

observational research research in which the researcher relies on non-experimental observations.

participants in the experimental and the control group. Suppose that at t_0, the groups (E) and (C) are similar with respect to their course grades. Then, by comparing the course grade of the two groups, i.e., (E) and (C), *after* the experiment has been completed at t_2, researchers can infer to what extent the treatment has resulted in a change of outcomes (Babbie, 2015). Figure 3.12 illustrates how this works.

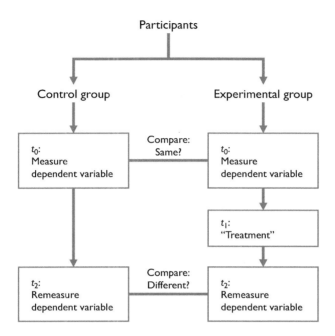

Figure 3.12 **Key elements of an experiment.**

Sociologists use experiments mainly for testing hypotheses, because experiments can have strong *internal validity*. This is because, first, researchers can use an experiment to manipulate the *time order* between X and Y—as opposed to observational data in which the data are given and it is more difficult to convincingly show that X precedes Y. In the above example, we manipulate X (hand in your phone yes/no) at $t = 1$ and then study whether that makes a difference in Y (course grade) at $t = 2$.

Second, experiments can rule out spuriousness effectively. This is because in an experiment subjects are *randomly assigned* to the control and treatment condition. This is important because the difference between the control and treatment group in the outcome at $t = 2$ is then the result of the treatment and not due to the two groups being already different before the study began. Because it is only chance that decides where individuals end up, the initial condition (at t_0) will be such that the group of individuals in the experimental condition will be similar to those who fall into the control condition. Often, however, researchers check whether this is indeed the case (see Figure 3.12 above) and, if it is not, they can correct for this initial imbalance. Having a control group and an experimental group that are similar before the treatment occurred (at t_1) is important, since it assures the researcher that differences observed between the groups after the treatment (at t_2) are caused by the treatment and nothing else.

The potential threat to experiments in sociological research is *external validity*. The classic setting in which experiments take place is the laboratory (Falk & Heckman, 2009; Webster & Sell, 2014; Willer & Walker, 2007). Such *laboratory experiments* are common in psychology but they have also found their way into other social sciences such as sociology. One threat to external validity is that the *participants* in the experiment are a specific group. Scholars have labelled them **WEIRD people**, i.e., the typical participants in laboratory experiments in the social sciences are: Western, Educated, Industrialized, Rich and Democratic (Henrich, Heine, & Norenzayan, 2010). Such intelligent, highly educated, western participants are not representative of the larger population. Second, it could be that the nature of the *setting* affects the results. The laboratory setting differs in many ways from the real world and in various ways

WEIRD people typical participants in laboratory experiments in the social sciences are: Western, Educated, Industrialized, Rich and Democratic. Due to their specific characteristics, they are not representative of the larger population.

Image 3.5 Can you really study an army in the laboratory (Zelditch, 1969)?

this could mean that patterns found in the laboratory do not travel to those outside the lab. For these reasons, laboratory experiments in the social sciences often face problems of external validity.

As a response to the issue of external invalidity of laboratory experiments, social scientists use *field experiments* (Harrison & List, 2004) or, relatedly, *natural experiments* (Dunning, 2012). These are experiments conducted in natural settings instead of the laboratory and that also often use more representative samples of participants. An example is the field experiments on ethnic discrimination in the labor market that were first developed in the 1960s by British sociologists (Daniel, 1968). The experimental design is such that the researcher selects real job vacancies and then submits multiple applications from fictitious job seekers. These applications consist of a fake resume and accompanying letter and these resumes and letters are made similar to one another. This means that the candidates do not differ in their quality or skills: they are all equally qualified. Importantly, the fictitious job seekers are randomly assigned a certain "ethnicity" or "race," which can be signaled via their name, nationality or country of birth. The dependent variable in many of these experiments is whether the applicant is invited for an interview or not. If it appears that ethnic minority applicants systematically receive such an invitation less often than ethnic majority members this is seen as experimental evidence for the existence of discrimination (Pager, 2007). Such field experiments have been conducted on other types of discrimination, such as age and gender, as well as in other social domains such as housing (Pager & Shepherd, 2008). The attractive feature of such field experiments for hypothesis testing is that they do well on both internal validity and external validity.

3.12 Replication

The use of a plurality of methods in sociology, each having their typical strengths and weaknesses, means that in practice descriptive and theoretical questions are often not answered at once with a single method. Rather than a single sociological study, which relies on one method, providing definite answers to a certain question, more often several studies using different methods are conducted sequentially. This is true for both descriptive and theoretical questions. Let's come back to the two sociological questions we addressed at the beginning of this chapter:

Q(d). How frequent is smartphone usage among youth aged 15–20 in your country nowadays?

Q(t). What is the effect of smartphone usage on educational performance among youth aged 15–20 in your country nowadays?

THINKING LIKE A SOCIOLOGIST 3.1

Suppose you were asked to answer the descriptive question *Q(d)* and theoretical question *Q(t)*. Which method(s) would you prefer to use? How would you carry out the research (e.g., which sample and data source would you use)?

By now you know that to answer sociological questions like these you can use various methods: case study research, administrative data, surveys, big data and experiments. And you know that the criteria of measurement quality and external and internal validity can help you in choosing particular methods and in designing your research plans.

Let's take another example to illustrate why sociologists typically use multiple studies, using various methods, to get a better view of what's going on. Consider the following descriptive question:

> Q(d). To what extent was there a change in physical aggression in Spain from 1950 to 2019?

Study 1 could use *administrative data*, obtained from police records or hospitals, to answer this question. Suppose the observations from these sources suggest a steady decline over time in physical aggression. In that case researchers might still doubt the conclusion. For example, they may question the quality of these official data, arguing that the change is artificial because policing practices may have changed. Hence they want to check whether these conclusions are supported by other methods. For this reason, Study 2 relies on *repeated cross-sectional survey* data about victimization from the same period. In these surveys, respondents can confidentially report about incidents of physical aggression and therefore this method is not subject to the same (potential) bias from which administrative data suffer. But then, another team of researchers argues that the measures from these surveys were not valid. Study 3 therefore conducted *small-scale research*, interviewing a group of respondents and improving measures. Study 4 incorporated these more fine-grained measures, again using *repeated cross-sectional survey* data. When researchers find that different methods, and different or improved measures, come to the same conclusions, they have more confidence in their conclusions. Thus, although administrative and survey data are subject to sources of bias, together they provide a more accurate description of social phenomena.

Sociologists call this **replication**, i.e., redoing studies on the same topic by using different data, methods or measures (Firebaugh, 2008). Such replication research is also highly relevant with respect to hypotheses testing for various reasons. One reason is that sociological hypotheses are often difficult to test with experiments and sociologists therefore use observational data. As we have seen, experimental studies give more conclusive evidence for the corroboration or rejection of hypotheses than observational studies. This means that in sociology one needs to consider even more explicitly how convincing the evidence is which comes from observations.

replication
redoing studies on the same topic, theory or hypothesis using different data, methods or measures.

Another reason for doing replication research is that findings published in academic journals tend to be biased (Ioannidis, 2005). Not all studies which have been conducted by scientists appear in journals. Sometimes the scientists themselves decide not to submit their paper to a journal and, even when they do, their paper can be rejected by reviewers and the editorial team. What appears to happen in this publication process is that those papers that tend to confirm hypotheses are more likely to be published eventually than papers disconfirming hypotheses (Ioannidis, 2005). By doing replication research, scientists can find out whether the results drawn in previous studies are corroborated or not.

In this context, two concepts are relevant to understand, namely: *false positives* and *false negatives*. What do we mean by these concepts and why are they important for you? Let's illustrate their meaning and importance with a concrete example. Imagine that you have developed a specific hypothesis, based on the information you got from the media, on poverty levels in the world and their possible connection to political institutions. Imagine you come up with the following hypothesis:

H. The development of democratic institutions in a country results in declining poverty levels.

Let's call this the "democracy and poverty" hypothesis and you now want to know whether this prediction is true or not. As we have seen in this chapter, there are several kinds of data sources you can use. Suppose you use government statistics and you find time-varying information on the development of democratic institutions and poverty levels in 50 nations in the period 1960–2000. In your analysis, you relate the development of democratic institutions (X) and poverty levels (Y) to each other. There are then two empirical outcomes possible.

Outcome A: confirmation

What should you conclude if your "democracy and poverty" hypothesis is supported by your observations? You might reason that in that case the hypothesis is confirmed, that you can trust your empirical research and that no further research is needed. Most researchers, however, would think otherwise. They would agree that after having seen these findings you can have somewhat more confidence in the truth of the hypothesis. But they would also remain cautious, as they realize that something could be wrong with the observations or analysis. You could have a case of a **false positive**: in reality the hypothesis is false, but the observations from the research nevertheless suggest the hypothesis is true. You might have wrongly concluded that your hypothesis is true for various reasons. For example, it is possible that what you find is merely an association between levels of democracy (X) and poverty (Y), but that this relationship is caused by a third variable (Z) that you did not take into account in your study. In that case, the association between democracy and poverty is a "spurious" relationship and you need to reject your hypothesis. With observational data, the threat of internal invalidity is always something to take into account. But also errors in measurement and external invalidity could result in "supporting evidence" for a hypothesis which is actually wrong.

> **false positive**
> a research finding which suggests the hypothesis is true, whereas in reality the hypothesis is false.

Outcome B: rejection

What if your findings are *not* in line with the prediction? When that happens, you could conclude that your hypothesis was wrong. Often, however, when researchers are confronted with evidence that does not corroborate the hypothesis, they don't immediately infer from that observation that their hypothesis is false. The reason for that is that although they acknowledge that their hypothesis could be wrong, they argue that something could be wrong with the observations as well. If that is indeed true, we call this a **false negative**: the hypothesis is correct, but nevertheless it is rejected by the observations.

> **false negative**
> a research finding which suggests the hypothesis is false, whereas in reality the hypothesis is true.

How could that happen? Again, this could occur when you have made a mistake in your observations or analysis. Imagine that poor measurement quality has disturbed your observations, for example if the data you got from some governments on their poverty levels was highly biased; non-democratic governments provided statistics that strongly underreport their true poverty levels. If this is the case, your observations are biased and your conclusions may be wrong. You have compared the true poverty levels of democratic nations to the artificially low poverty levels of non-democratic nations, possibly finding no difference between the two whereas there is one in reality. This is an example of a false negative: we reject a prediction because the observations say so, but in reality the prediction is true and the observations were wrong.

The possibility of false positives and false negatives is a major issue with which scientists are confronted, and it appears that papers in scientific journals tend to over-report false positives (Ioannidis, 2005). Replication is thus important. Follow-up studies on the same hypothesis can use different measures, different data sources and different techniques, thereby questioning the conclusions drawn in previous studies. Not a single test, nor a single study, can either refute or confirm a theory (Lakatos, 1978). Science progresses slowly, step by step, by the accumulation of a vast body of observations centering around the same theory. Only after many observations have been made can we come up with an empirical assessment of the theory. When hypotheses derived from a theory are *repeatedly* rejected by observations, using different methods and analyses, can we come to the conclusion that the theory might be wrong. When it is *repeatedly* found that a theory is confirmed by observations, using different measures, data sources and techniques, and which really tested the predictions using rigorous tests, can we believe with good reasons that the theory is true.

3.13 Chapter resources

Key concepts

Measurement quality	Standardization	Thick description
Measurement validity	External validity	Administrative research
Measure	Population	Survey research
Indicator	Biased sample	Big data research
Empirical variable	Sample	Experimental research
Proxy	Representative sample	Observational research
Operationalization	Probability sample	WEIRD people
Simple concept	Stratified sample	Replication
Complex concept	Descriptive research	False positive
Dimension	Explanatory research	False negative
Conceptualization	Exploratory research	Internal validity
Measurement reliability	Case study research	Induction

Summary

- There are three purposes of sociological research: to accurately describe social phenomena (descriptive research), to strongly test hypotheses (explanatory research) and to explore (exploratory research).
- In order to come up with accurate descriptions of social phenomena and strong tests of hypotheses, measurement quality and external validity are important principles that guide the quality of the empirical evidence.

- Measurement quality depends on measurement reliability and measurement validity.
- The issue of external validity relates to the population to which you want to generalize and the sample you actually use in your research.
- When testing hypotheses, the researcher additionally needs to consider the principle of internal validity.
- Sociologists use a myriad of data sources, of which the major ones are: case study research, administrative data, surveys, big data and experiments.
- Replication research is an essential element of science and is important for both description and hypothesis testing. Because of the issue of false positives and false negatives, sociologists often do repeated research on the same topic, theory and hypothesis.

References

Abbott, A. (2004). *Methods of discovery: Heuristics for the social sciences.* New York, NY: WW Norton & Company.

Babbie, E. (2015). *The practice of social research* (14th ed.). Boston, MA: Cengage Learning.

Cox, D. R., & Reid, N. (2000). *The theory of the design of experiments.* Boca Raton, FL: CRC Press.

Daniel, W. (1968). *Racial discrimination in England.* Middlesex, UK: Penguin Books.

Doyle, A. C. (1892). *Adventures of Sherlock Holmes.* Harper: New York and London.

Dunning, T. (2012). *Natural experiments in the social sciences: A design-based approach.* Cambridge: Cambridge University Press.

Eagle, N., Pentland, A. S., & Lazer, D. (2009). Inferring friendship network structure by using mobile phone data. *Proceedings of the National Academy of Sciences of the United States of America, 106*(36), 15274–15278.

Falk, A., & Heckman, J. J. (2009). Lab experiments are a major source of knowledge in the social sciences. *Science, 326*(5952), 535–538.

Firebaugh, G. (2008). *Seven rules for social research.* Princeton, NJ: Princeton University Press.

Fowler, J. F. J. (2013). *Survey research methods.* London: Sage publications.

Geertz, C. (1973). Thick description: Toward an interpretive theory of Culture. In C. Geertz (Ed.), *The interpretation of cultures: Selected essays* (pp. 3–30). New York: Basic Books.

Goertz, G. (2006). *Social science concepts: A user's guide.* Princeton, NJ: Princeton University Press.

Golder, S. A., & Macy, M. W. (2011). Diurnal and seasonal mood vary with work, sleep, and daylength across diverse cultures. *Science,* 1878–1881.

Golder, S. A., & Macy, M. W. (2014). Digital footprints: Opportunities and challenges for online social research. *Annual Review of Sociology, 40,* 129–152.

Goldthorpe, J. H. (2000). *On sociology: Numbers, narratives and the integration of research and theory.* Oxford: Oxford University Press.

Hammersley, M., & Atkinson, P. (2007). *Ethnography: Principles in practice.* Abingdon: Routledge.

Harrison, G. W., & List, J. A. (2004). Field Experiments. *Journal of Economic Literature, 42*(4), 1009–1055.

Henrich, J., Heine, S. J., & Norenzayan, A. (2010). The weirdest people in the world? *Behavioral and Brain Sciences, 33*(2–3), 61–83.

Ioannidis, J. P. (2005). Why most published research findings are false. *PLoS Med, 2*(8), e124.

Lakatos, I. (1978). *The methodology of scientific research programmes.* Cambridge: Cambridge University Press.

Lazer, D., Pentland, A., Adamic, L., Aral, S., Barabási, A. L., Brewer, D., Christakis, N., Contractor, N., Fowler, J., Gutmann, M., Jebara, T., King, G., Macy, M., Roy, D, Van Alstyne, M. (2009). Life in the network: The coming age of computational social science. *Science, 323*(5915), 721–723.

Marshall, C., & Rossman, G. B. (2014). *Designing qualitative research.* London: Sage publications.

Mastrandrea, R., Fournet, J., & Barrat, A. (2015). Contact patterns in a high school: A comparison between data collected using wearable sensors, contact diaries and friendship surveys. *PloS One, 10*(9), e0136497.

Neuman, L. W. (2014). *Social research methods: Qualitative and quantitative approaches (seventh edition).* Essex: Pearson.

Padgett, J. F., & Ansell, C. K. (1993). Robust action and the rise of the medici, 1400-1434. *American Journal of Sociology, 98*(6), 1259–1319.

Pager, D. (2007). The use of field experiments for studies of employment discrimination: Contributions, critiques, and directions for the future. *The Annals of the American Academy of Political and Social Science, 609*(1), 104–133.

Pager, D., & Shepherd, H. (2008). The sociology of discrimination: Racial discrimination in employment, housing, credit, and consumer markets. *Annual Review of Sociology, 34,* 181–209.

Popper, K. (1972). *Objective knowledge: An evolutionary approach.* Oxford: Clarendon Press.

Popper, K. (2005 [1935]). *The logic of scientific discovery.* New York, NY: Routledge.

Reichenbach, H. (1938). *Experience and prediction: An analysis of the foundations and the structure of knowledge.* Chicago, IL: University of Chicago Press.

Salganik, M. J. (2017). *Bit by bit: Social research in the digital age.* Princeton, NJ: Princeton University Press.

Shadish, W. R., Cook, T. D., & Campbell, D. T. (2002). *Experimental and quasi-experimental designs for generalized causal inference.* Belmont, CA: Wadsworth Cengage Learning.

Swedberg, R. (2014a). *The Art of social theory.* Princeton, NJ: Princeton University Press.

Swedberg, R. (Ed.). (2014b). *Theorizing in social science: The context of discovery.* Stanford, CA: Stanford University Press.

Wallace, W. L. (1971). *The logic of science in sociology.* New Brunswick, NJ: Transaction Publishers.

Watts, D. J. (2011). *Everything is obvious: Once you know the answer.* New York, NY: Crown Business.

Webster, M., & Sell, J. (2014). *Laboratory experiments in the social sciences.* Oxford: Elsevier.

Whyte, W. F. (2012 [1943]). *Street corner society: The social structure of an Italian slum.* Chicago, IL: University of Chicago Press.

Willer, D., & Walker, H. A. (2007). *Building experiments: Testing social theory.* Stanford, CA: Stanford University Press.

Yin, R. K. (2013). *Case study research: Design and methods.* London: Sage publications.

Zelditch, J. M. (1969). Can you really study an army in the laboratory? In A. Entzioni (Ed.), *A sociological reader on complex organizations* (pp. 528–539). New York, NY: Holt, Rinehart and Winston.

Chapter 4

Perspectives

Chapter overview

Sociologists study many different topics such as education, crime, organizations, health, family, work, immigration, to name only a few. One way to introduce you to this variety of topics is to simply discuss each topic one by one. However, it is also fruitful for you to see some common patterns between this variety of topics. First, you can study any topic by relating it to overarching sociological themes. A theme emphasizes certain characteristics of a topic and it can be used as a perspective that helps you to see common patterns between topics. Second, you can study any topic by adopting a multilevel perspective, which is useful for understanding the interplay between social contexts and individuals. To introduce you to the themes and multilevel perspective, this chapter starts with a brief history of sociology (4.1). In the course of history, sociologists have developed different perspectives on what they consider key sociological themes. I briefly introduce you to three: culture, social relations and inequality (4.2). Subsequently, we will see that divergent perspectives have been developed with respect to the model of sociological explanation (4.3) and that nowadays sociologists often combine these divergent perspectives in a multilevel framework (4.4).

Learning goals

After reading this chapter, check if you are able to:

- Describe three sociological themes: culture, social relations and inequality.
- Relate sociological topics to sociological themes.
- Reflect on understanding and explaining in sociology.
- Describe and apply the multilevel framework.

4.1 The origins of sociological perspectives

In Chapter 1 we discussed the unique sociological perspective on human behavior and how it differs from individual perspectives on human behavior. When did the sociological perspective develop? What are the origins of sociology? When did sociology become an academic discipline? In answering these questions, we will see that in the history of sociology not one but various perspectives have been developed. These perspectives differ in what they consider key *themes* in sociology and also in what they see as the *model of sociological explanation*. We will first briefly sketch the origins of sociology and then reflect more systematically on the different perspectives that have been developed.

When did sociology emerge as a science? To define the exact beginning of sociology is difficult. We might fix it to the year 1838, when the word "sociology" was first coined by the French scholar Auguste Comte (1789–1857), or somewhat later, in 1873, when the English scholar Herbert Spencer (1820–1903) started publishing books that included "sociology" in the title for the first time. The word sociology is derived from the Latin word *socius*, which means "together" and the Greek word *lógos*, "knowledge."

However, claiming that sociological thoughts started to develop after the beginning of the 19th century would ignore social theorists long before that time (Collins, 1994). The Greek philosopher Aristotle (384–322 BC) is a very early thinker who, in some of his works, wrote about the historical development of societies. The sociological perspective was not central to his work, however. Much later in time, but still long before Comte, the Tunisian social theorist Ibn Khaldun (1332–1406) was much more oriented towards the sociological perspective. Some scholars regard him as one of the founding fathers of sociology, as he developed explicit ideas on how social conditions influence behavior. In one of his works, Ibn Khaldun coined the concept of *asabiyyah*, which means something like "social cohesion" and "solidarity," and he developed theories on the group dynamics of conflict and solidarity.

Against the background of the English Civil War (1641–1651), questions on social order became central to the English philosopher Hobbes (1588–1679). In his classic work *Leviathan* (1651), Hobbes sketches life in the "state of nature," which has no state authority and which, according to him, is characterized by "continual fear and danger of violent death, and the life of man, solitary, poor, nasty, brutish, and short" (Hobbes, 1994 [1651]). Subject to the power of a central authority, the Leviathan, people will be punished for their aggressive behavior and therefore refrain from such acts.

Another English philosopher, John Locke (1632–1704), elaborated on this theory of Hobbes in his *Two Treatises of Government* (Locke, 1988 [1689]), which appeared one year after the Glorious Revolution (1688). One of the main insights of Locke was that a Leviathan does not necessarily lead to a reduction of violence and disorder. Centralized authorities in the form of dictators could also abuse their power and oppress their citizens. Locke argued that only democracy, and rulers who have the legitimacy of the population, result in social order and the protection of human rights. Much later in time, the French social thinker Alexis de Tocqueville (1805–1859) argued that even democratic systems are vulnerable to injustice and suppression. The French Revolution in 1798 initially shifted power from aristocracy to democracy, but soon despotism reappeared in France. While travelling to the US, where in 1776 democracy became the new political system, Tocqueville observed that there democracy did succeed. To explain these differences between France and the US, he argued that whereas in his home country civil society—families, churches, organizations—more or less became marginal with the Revolution, such social groups remained strong at the other side of the Atlantic Ocean. Tocqueville claimed that such civil communities and organizations are therefore critical for retaining social order and preventing democratic systems turning into despotism.

The Scottish philosopher Ferguson (1723–1816) was one of the first who wrote about social inequality in *An Essay on the History of Civil Society* (Ferguson, 1980 [1767]). In that book he addressed the inequalities between various social groups, such as between men and women and fathers and their children. Another Scottish philosopher, Millar (1735–1801), pursued this line of social thought about inequality and, even more prominently, so did the German scholars Karl Marx (1818–1883) and Friedrich Engels (1820–1895), who often published together. As so many social thinkers before them, the social problems that Marx and Engels observed around them greatly motivated their scientific work. The context in which Marx and Engels wrote their work was that of rapid social changes in Europe, which was characterized by industrialization and growing levels of poverty.

In work by Marx and Engels, such as *The Communist Manifesto* (1848) and *Capital* (1867–1894), a number of theories and observations on social inequality were proposed that have inspired numerous scholars and still do so nowadays. One of their core ideas was that inequalities between the capitalists (owners) and laborers (proletariat) were becoming larger over time, because the capitalists had more power and could accumulate their wealth. But also competition among the capitalists, so they predicted, would result in the centralization of capital and wealth in the hands of the super-rich. Eventually, they argued, the poor will not accept suppression and poverty any longer, the proletariat will join forces to revolt against the ruling capitalists and, after the revolution, communism will bring social equality. In their work, Marx and Engels were explicitly arguing against insights from mainstream economics and (Hegelian) philosophy, thereby paving a way for the development of sociology as a new social science (Collins, 1994).

Another famous sociologist, Emile Durkheim (1858–1917), did something similar in his own works—but then delineated his approach from a more psychological perspective. Although the word "sociology" was coined by Comte in 1838, the *discipline* of "sociology" did not exist at that time. Durkheim wrote the now classic study *Suicide* (Durkheim, 1961 [1897]) in an attempt to prove the need for this new social science discipline, as he argued that a purely individualistic perspective on suicide falls short of understanding that social conditions are strongly correlated to suicide rates (see Chapter 1). Apparently Durkheim was successful in realizing this goal of establishing the new academic discipline of sociology, as he established the first chair in sociology in Europe at the beginning of the 20th century.

Around the time Durkheim wrote his masterpiece on *Suicide,* another scholar greatly contributed to the development of the sociological perspective and to sociology as an independent social science, namely the German Max Weber (1864–1920). Weber's most famous study is *The Protestant Ethic and the Spirit of Capitalism* (1905), in which he studied the relationship between religious "worldviews" in society and the consequences thereof for economic growth (Weber, 2002 [1905]). Weber argued that people's religious beliefs and values affect their work behavior, their efficiency and rationality, and that this could explain why West-European (Protestant) nations did so well economically from 1500 onwards. Weber outlined the long-term process of rationalization and what this means for politics, organizations, science and other societal domains. Table 4.1 provides a summary of early social thinkers and classical sociologists, as well as some classical works.

There is something to say for the claim that the sociological perspective commenced around 1900 in Western-Europe, and that the key founding fathers of sociology are Durkheim, Weber and Marx. The work of these three sociologists has inspired many students subsequently, more so than the work of other earlier thinkers. And indeed, since around 1900, sociology as a discipline became established in academia. After around 1900, the discipline of sociology was growing rapidly in Europe, the US and eventually in many other parts of the world, and now we would not be able to present the many authors and works in a simple table.

That said, to identify Durkheim, Weber and Marx as founding fathers of sociology and to state that the sociological perspective started around 1900 is also an oversimplification for various reasons. First of all, as we have seen, there were social theorists long before Durkheim, Weber and Marx developed their ideas, and the three "founding fathers" were elaborating on their work rather than starting from scratch. Second, many other social theorists

Table 4.1 Selective overview of early social thinkers, sociologists and key works, 1377–1905.

Name	Country of birth	Key works
Ibn Khaldun	Tunisia	*Muqaddimah* (1377)
Hobbes	England	*Leviathan* (1651)
Locke	England	*Two Treatises of Government* (1689)
Ferguson	Scotland	*An Essay on the History of Civil Society* (1767)
Millar	Scotland	*Observations concerning the Distinction of Ranks in Society* (1771)
Comte	France	*A General View of Positivism* (1844)
Tocqueville	France	*Democracy in America* (1835–1840)
Marx and Engels	Germany (Prussia)	*The Communist Manifesto* (1848) *Capital* (1867–1894)
Spencer	England	*The Study of Sociology* (1873)
Durkheim	France	*The Division of Labor in Society* (1893) *Suicide* (1897)
Weber	Germany (Prussia)	*The Protestant Ethic and the Spirit of Capitalism* (1905)

around or shortly after 1900 could also be named as being founding fathers of sociology, or at least to have contributed greatly to the discipline. Table 4.1 lists some key scholars, but one could think of many and many more, including Vilfredo Pareto (1848–1923), Georg Simmel (1858–1918) and Norbert Elias (1897–1990) in Europe, for example, and Lester Ward (1841–1913) in the United States. Third, there is some evidence to suggest, according to the sociologist Collins, that although Marx is often considered more famous today than Engels, and often regarded as the most important scientist of these two scholars, it is actually Engels who was the true original sociologist of the two (Collins, 1994). Some of the works which are today credited to the intellect of Marx and published under his name, for example, were actually written by Engels and not Marx.

Besides the question of *when* sociology exactly started, or the debate on *who* we should identify as the true founding fathers of sociology, one could also consider the *ideas and insights* that sociology has produced over time. The current body of sociological knowledge is the result of a long process of accumulation of scientific observations, theory development and testing. The insights of classical sociological studies have been incorporated, as background knowledge (Chapter 1), in successive sociological studies. These insights include theories, research findings and research methods, but also a distinct sociological perspective on human behavior, as opposed to an individual perspective.

A closer look, however, reveals that although sociologists share a common sociological perspective that is different from an individual perspective on human behavior, they have also developed different sociological perspectives. It is useful for you to become familiar with these different perspectives.

To address this issue, we should clarify the concept of perspective in more detail first. What actually is a perspective? Simply stated, a **perspective** is a certain way of looking at things. For example, if you think of a house, then you could focus on its market price, which is one way of looking at a house. But you could also take a different perspective, say, focusing on its architecture, floor area, neighborhood, decoration and so forth. The same object can be viewed,

perspective (also **framework** or **paradigm**) certain way of looking at things.

studied and analyzed in different ways, taking different perspectives. To be sure: perspectives are *not* theories, i.e., perspectives don't offer a coherent set of propositions that can explain social phenomena. Perspectives are also *not* the same as research findings. Focusing on the price of a house doesn't determine its value. Instead, perspectives can be regarded as heuristic tools; they help you *to focus* on certain things, to orientate your thinking (Johnson, 2008). Taking a certain perspective will push you in a certain direction, i.e., you ask certain questions, develop certain concepts, theories and research methods in the spirit of your perspective (Lakatos, 1978). Perspectives provide the boundaries for the things you consider important to examine. In a research context, other words having (more or less) the same meaning as perspective are **framework** and **paradigm**.

In the history of sociology one can identify distinct perspectives (frameworks and paradigms) which have been developed over time.

First, various perspectives emerged, each addressing a key sociological *theme*. Three themes have attracted the attention of sociologists, namely: *culture*, *social relations* and *inequality*. If you consider the writings of Weber, Durkheim and Marx/Engels, then, with some simplification one could say that the theme of *culture* was key in the writings of Weber, the theme of *social relations* appeared prominent in the works of Durkheim and the theme of *inequality* was at the core of the writings of Marx and Engels (Craib, 1997; Morrison, 2006).

Second, different perspectives emerged with respect to the model of *sociological explanation*. Again, with some simplification, one could argue that Weber advanced the perspective focusing on *individual behavior* (i.e., micro level) and *subjective understanding* (in German: "*Verstehen*"), while Durkheim was more oriented towards *collective behavior* (i.e., meso and macro level) and *causal explanations*. Sociologists before and after Weber and Durkheim have been attracted to either of these two perspectives, some focusing on subjective understanding of human behavior at the micro level, whereas others are more oriented to causal explanations of collective phenomena.

In getting to start thinking like a sociologist, it is useful for you to become familiar with these perspectives as they have evolved around (1) sociological themes and (2) models of sociological explanation. Perspectives should not be seen as alternatives, although they are sometimes presented in that way. In contemporary sociological research it appears useful to see perspectives as complementary, to combine different perspectives rather than focusing time and again on the same perspective. To have multiple perspectives in your toolbox is useful because it allows you to play with different perspectives, to approach the same phenomenon from different angles. When buying a new house, it is advisable not to focus on its price only, but also to consider whether you like the house, to consider the quality of the environment and so forth. The same is true for understanding complex social phenomena.

4.2 Sociological themes and topics

Let's start with the various perspectives that have developed with respect to sociological themes. What are themes actually? And why are they useful for you to know? To answer these questions, we need to go back to what we mentioned in Chapter 1, namely that many sociological studies are conducted in light of social problems. Social problems are often the starting point for sociological research. We also discussed that social problems change over time, differ from country to country and from locality to locality. Social problems come and go. Today, obesity is seen as a social problem in many western countries, but this was not so 50 years ago. And what is considered as a social problem in, say, India, might not be a problem at all in, say, France. One could make a list of old and current social problems in the world, but it would become excessively long.

This multitude of social problems that sociologists study is reflected in a huge diversity of **sociological topics** (Boudon, 1981). Topics are specific areas of research and they have a close link to specific social problems. For example, if there is great concern in society about the increasing prevalence of depression, this social problem will receive attention from sociologists of health. In this specific area of research, sociologists have built up expertise in understanding how social conditions influence people's health and well-being. And, to give another example, if many people are concerned about interethnic tensions in society, this public issue may motivate sociologists of immigration and integration, who have expertise in this area, to conduct new research and to advise policy makers about effective social interventions.

sociological topic
a specific subject matter in sociology. Examples: crime, ethnicity, globalization, gender.

There are many different social problems and so, too, are there many sociological topics. A complete list of all topics that sociologists study would be too long to include here. To give you an impression of some of them:

- Family
- Organizations
- Immigration and integration

- Youth
- Ethnicity and race
- Health
- Neighborhoods
- Crime
- Gender
- Social change and modernization
- Religion
- Education
- Social movements.

This huge variety of topics might give you the impression that there is no coherence in sociology; that the topics—and their associated social problems—are too different and studied in isolation. To a certain extent this is true; there exists, for example, a sociology *of the family*, a sociology *of youth*, a sociology *of organizations*, a sociology *of immigration and integration* and so forth. Within each of these specialty areas sociologists have built up a body of knowledge. It may seem, therefore, that each topic should be studied in isolation from others; that family sociology is entirely different from organizational sociology and so forth.

On closer inspection, however, the variety in sociology is only superficially there. If you look more closely, you can discover three **sociological themes** that—in the footsteps of Weber, Durkheim, Marx, Engels and many others—are recurrently addressed in each of these various areas of research: *Culture*, *Social relations* and *Inequality* (in short: CSI). A sociological theme acts like an umbrella and helps you to relate diverse, specific topics to each other in a more abstract way (Ultee, 2001). A theme works like a perspective and helps you to see common patterns among seemingly unrelated topics and social problems.

sociological theme complex concept which helps to relate diverse, specific topics to each other in a more abstract way. Three main sociological themes are: culture, social relations and inequality.

Let's address these three themes one by one and consider, first, the theme of culture. We can relate this theme to any topic and to any social problem. To illustrate, let's take the first three topics from the list above: family, organizations and immigration and integration (Figure 4.1). Although these are clearly different topics, related to different social problems, if you take the underlying theme of culture you can see that sociologists study these topics from the same angle. Namely, they consider within families how norms and values are transmitted from parents to children and how norms and values shape family relations. They study how norms and values play a role in organizations and how ethnic majority and minority populations may have different norms and values. A recurrent theme in each of these specific fields of research is therefore the role of norms and values, which are ingredients of culture.

So what actually is culture? Some have claimed that "culture is one of the two or three most complicated words in the English language" (Williams, 2014 [1976]). In daily language, culture is often interpreted as "high culture," like art or classical music. Although these are certainly elements of culture and are also subject to investigation by sociologists, this definition is too narrow. Culture comprises far more. Culture is everywhere, but often we are not aware of it. We grow up in a certain culture and regard everything that comes with it as so normal that it is difficult to define.

Maybe the meaning of culture is the most clear when you are on holiday in another country. You might, for instance, realize that you do not speak the language of the country, traffic is driving on the other side of the road, the etiquette is different and people listen to

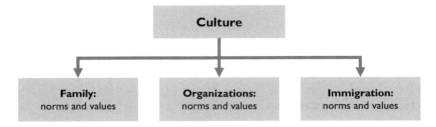

Figure 4.1 Unity in diversity: three different topics, overarching theme of culture.

other music. You might also realize that the roads are of poorer quality (or actually better), certain technological products are unfamiliar or houses are constructed in a different way.

If you look a little closer at the culture of the country where you are taking your holiday, it may also be that you find out that the inhabitants have completely different views on fundamental questions like men–women roles, social inequality, religion and spirituality. It is for good reason that people often call it a *culture shock* when they have been to a country where the culture strongly differs from what they are used to. It is especially in the confrontation with other cultures that we realize what culture actually means. We can hardly identify the things that we have come to experience as usual in our own culture. Whatever you have been considering as self-explanatory suddenly turns out not to be so common.

Image 4.1 Greeting conventions are part of our culture.

There are many different definitions given in the literature of culture and there is no consensus on a single definition. Some definitions are very broad, others are more narrow. A very broad definition of culture is to say that it includes everything that is more than nature. This is a firm point of departure and also reveals how comprehensive an understanding of culture might be. Earth and its natural laws bring us plants, trees, animals, rivers, etc. That is quite something, but also very little if you consider all the things you now see in this world which man has thought up and created: boats, roads, aircraft, computers, schools, hospitals, political parties, beliefs, guns, rockets, judges, maps, satellites, chairs and tables, rituals, writing systems and so on.

Some scholars restrict the definition of culture to that which is acquired via social learning (Mesoudi, 2011). Thus, in *so far as* the beliefs and values of a group are socially acquired, it is called culture. Cultures indeed develop and change as a result of social learning and social transmission, but not only so, as we will see. In this book, social learning is not used as a way to define culture, but instead is used to explain patterns of culture.

In this textbook, I regard culture, and the two other themes (social relations and inequality), as complex concepts (Chapter 3). This means that they consist of several sub-dimensions, called **sociological subthemes**. In conceptualizing the complex concept of **culture**, one can distinguish two subthemes, namely *opinions* and *norms*.

sociological subtheme subdimension of a sociological theme.

Culture is, first, about **opinions** of human populations. The concept of opinion is used in a generic way, such that it refers to both cognitive beliefs (what people think) as well as to preferences, attitudes and values (what people want, like and dislike). Cognitive beliefs can be true or false, more rational or highly irrational (Nolan & Lenski, 2011). People have ideas about reality; they have a certain understanding of nature and society; they have cognitive belief systems; cognition; perceptions; knowledge. When I speak about "beliefs," I refer to "descriptive" or "cognitive" beliefs—not to "normative" beliefs (Boudon, 2001). Thus, sociologists are interested in how social conditions shape beliefs, perceptions, knowledge; for example, why people believe in supernatural beings or why in premodern Europe many believed in the existence of witches. Sociologists study the transmission of knowledge, the way information, perceptions and beliefs are diffused between people.

culture sociological theme on opinions, norms and corresponding behavior.

opinion cognitive beliefs, preferences, attitudes and values.

Opinions also include the attitudes, preferences, ideology and values of people, i.e., what is seen as "appropriate," desirable, good and bad, right and wrong (Hofstede, 2001 [1980]; Rokeach, 1973). Such attitudes and values are subjective evaluations, which indicate how people feel about certain states of affairs. Values, attitudes and preferences are therefore not the same as knowledge, information, beliefs and cognitions. They are also in the human mind, but if I say that Madrid is the capital city of Spain then this is not a value or preference but rather a statement of fact. It is knowledge. Preferences, attitudes and values are emotionalized, subjective judgments which prioritize (assign a value) to something. It includes people's attitudes towards divorce, for example, but also attitudes towards gender roles and political attitudes. Consequently, opinions are also about what people consider good or bad, attractive or unattractive, liked and disliked.

The second subtheme of culture relates to **norms**, which regulate and constrain human behavior (Bicchieri, 2005; Brennan, Eriksson, Goodin, & Southwood, 2013; Elster, 2009; Gibbs, 1965; Hechter & Opp, 2001; Opp, 2001). Norms can be highly formal—written in legal documents and enforced by official authorities—but they can also exist as informal rules, such as the dos and

norm rules of the game in society.

don'ts within groups. Other types of norms include conventions, which are not enforced but nevertheless guide social life by shaping people's expectations about what to do in a certain setting. Sociologists study how norms come to exist and how such cultural rules shape human behavior.

In summary, when you want to understand a certain social problem, or a certain sociological topic, you can take the theme of culture as a perspective, which helps you to focus on the role that opinions and norms play. Whether you study corruption, crime, or any other social problem or sociological topic, you can use the sociological theories and research findings that have been developed with respect to the two subthemes of culture: opinions and norms (see Figure 4.2). We will review key concepts, theories and findings on opinions (Chapter 5) and norms (Chapter 6) and illustrate how you can apply these to social problems and topics.

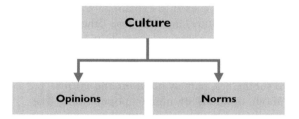

Figure 4.2 Two subthemes of culture: opinions and norms.

The second sociological theme is about *social relations* in society, about social cohesion and patterns of social order, cooperation, trust and conflict at the level of individuals, groups and entire societies. Let's apply this theme to the same first three topics from our list (Figure 4.3). Within family sociology, much research is done on marriage and divorce, for example, but also on relationships between parents and their children. Marriage indicates a positive social relation between two persons, whereas divorce indicates a negative relationship. In organizational literature, sociologists study how well workers cooperate with each other, but also look at gossiping and negative work relations. In research on immigration and integration, scholars examine friendships and contacts between ethnic majority and ethnic minority members. In short, in each area of research scholars study very similar phenomena which have to do with the theme of social relations.

Figure 4.3 Unity in diversity: three different topics, overarching theme of social relations.

The theme of **social relations** encompasses different dimensions. One can distinguish two subthemes: social networks and groups. The subtheme of **social networks** is about the connectivity of people, i.e., with whom people interact, how often and how personal ties tend to cluster (Scott, 2017 [1991]; Wasserman & Faust, 1994). This includes such daily interactions between people at work, in the family, at school, in the neighborhood and online. Sociologists study the formation and consequences of social networks. Why is it that some people are rather isolated, whereas other people have more social connections? How can we explain that some individuals have many negative ties and are bullied by their peers? How important are social networks for the diffusion of opinions and norms? What role do networks play in getting a job and well-being?

social relations
sociological theme on social networks and groups.

social network
a set of actors and the ties between them.

The second subtheme of social relations concerns **groups**. People are affiliated to groups, such as religious groups, political entities, ethnic groups and status groups. Individuals have more than one social identity—they belong to a web of group affiliations (Simmel, 1955). We belong to a certain ethnicity, but also gender, socioeconomic status group and so forth. Groups may unite people and serve common interests, but they may also divide societies and create conflicts. How can we understand the formation of groups? When do group boundaries and conflicts emerge?

group social category with which people can affiliate.

When sociologists study topics and social problems, the theme of social relations is one to which they pay attention. Whether you look at sociology of family, sociology of youth, sociology of organizations and so forth, common subthemes are networks and groups (Figure 4.4).

Image 4.2 A common theme in sociology is the study of social relations.

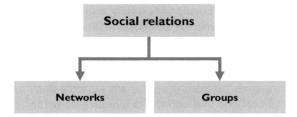

Figure 4.4 Two subthemes of social relations: networks and groups.

We will address the key concepts, theories and findings of the two subthemes of social relations in more detail in Chapter 7 (Networks) and Chapter 8 (Groups).

The third theme in sociology that can be applied to a wide variety of topics is called social inequality, or simply **inequality**. In the literature you will find concepts that are very closely related, such as "stratification," "poverty," "social mobility" and "power" (Grusky, 2001). Irrespective of the specific label that one uses, I guess that everyone has an intuition about what inequality is. We all know that some people are incredibly rich, whereas others are less affluent and yet others live in poverty. Inequality is about the distribution of these and other valued goods in society. Typically, sociologists want to describe the degree of inequality in society and they want to understand the processes that generate inequality.

inequality
sociological
theme on social
stratification,
social mobility and
resources.

Inequality is a recurrent theme in various sociological topics. To illustrate, let's consider once more sociology of the family, organizations and immigration (Figure 4.5). When you take an inequality perspective and use this in the study of families, you would focus on, for example, the inequality in the household—such as between husband and wife in the amount of paid and unpaid work, or the inequality between parents and children in authority, for example. In studying organizations, one could focus on the unequal careers of men and women, or on the income gap between the employer and employees. And when studying immigration and integration, one could examine ethnic inequalities in education and the labor market.

The theme of inequality is complex and it is useful to differentiate three subthemes. The first subtheme of inequality is **social stratification**

social stratification
unequal
distribution of
valued goods.

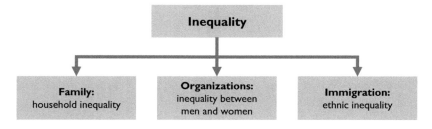

Figure 4.5 Unity in diversity: three different topics, overarching theme of inequality.

(in short: stratification), which refers to the unequal distribution of "valued goods." These are goods that are seen as desirable by people. Sociologists tend to say that there are many goods, that, in other words, social stratification is multidimensional (Grusky, 2001). There can be *economic* inequalities, which refer to the unequal distribution of economic goods, such as income or wealth. Some people earn more than others or have enormous wealth, whereas others deal with debts and live in poverty. *Health* is another example. People differ in their life expectancy, quality of life, mental problems and so forth. Some people live longer in good health, whereas others have numerous health problems and die at a younger age. These are only examples—there are many other kinds of valued goods (Grusky, 2001).

The second subtheme of inequality is **social mobility** (in short: mobility), which is about the inequality in changing one's social position (Blau & Duncan, 1967). For example, some people are born poor and climb up the social ladder and become rich. But others are born poor and remain so for the rest of their life. That's a difference in social mobility and sociologists study such patterns of mobility over time, across countries and by social backgrounds.

social mobility movement of people from one position to another in the stratification system.

The subtheme of mobility is related to, but is different from, another subtheme of inequality, which is about **resources**. This subtheme captures concepts like "capital," "opportunities" and "power" and it focuses on the resources that people have to realize their goals (Hout, 2015). If you want to get a good job in the labor market, for example, having a university education may help you in realizing that goal. In this context, a "university degree" is a resource. Such resources are unequally distributed in societies: some people have access to university whereas others do not. Obtaining a resource like a university degree may, subsequently, generate inequalities in realizing valued goals.

resources capital, opportunities and power one can use to realize one's goals.

We will discuss the subtheme of inequality (Figure 4.6) in more depth in Chapter 9 (Stratification and mobility) and Chapter 10 (Resources).

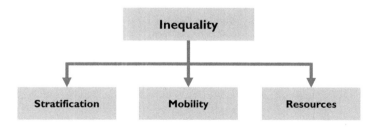

Figure 4.6 Three subthemes of inequality: stratification, mobility and resources.

Subsuming the many different sociological topics and social problems under three overarching sociological themes helps you to see how these seemingly unrelated topics and social problems are related. You can see the bigger picture. The themes serve as umbrellas for the various topics and problems. You can relate any topic, and any social problem, to these overarching themes.

PRINCIPLE 4.1

Sociological themes

The long list of topics that sociologists study may seem fragmented and may bewilder you. On a more general level, however, sociological studies show a continuous interest in three themes, which we can loosely label as Culture, Social relations and Inequality (CSI). It is often helpful to relate the topic of your interest to these overarching themes.

Once you have mastered the CSI themes in sociology, and their key concepts, theories and findings, you can apply these themes, and the knowledge that is accumulated within each, to any topic and social problem. You can study patterns of *social relations* in the sociology of health, crime, ethnicity, gender and so forth. But it is important not to focus too narrowly; that in the end you can only think of a *single* theme and apply that theme to each and every topic you come across. Then you would become a child who got a hammer and everything looked like a nail. It is more fruitful to consider each CSI theme when you study a certain topic or social problem.

Take, for example, the topic of family sociology (Figure 4.7). Adopting a *cultural* perspective, you could study which norms and values parents transmit to their children. Using a *social relations* perspective, you could focus instead on patterns of social interaction, such as the social bonds between the family members. And when you use an *inequality* perspective, then you can pay attention to yet other aspects, such as levels of income and poverty in families. When you want to study a certain topic—such as families—changing perspectives can be helpful. You can ask yourself: "OK, what if I use a cultural perspective instead of focusing on inequality, what would I look for then? And what if I consider the role of social relations, i.e., social networks and groups?"

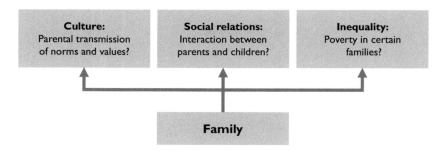

Figure 4.7 Examples of relating the topic of "family" to overarching sociological themes on culture, social relations and inequality.

You can use the CSI themes in two ways. First, you can study them as *outcomes*, i.e., how can we understand certain patterns of culture, social relations and inequality? Second, you can study them as *social conditions*, which have consequences, i.e., what is the impact of culture, social relations and inequality on human behavior? In the course of this book we will outline the CSI themes in more detail and discover the accumulated body of theoretical and empirical sociological knowledge about culture, social relations and inequality: how they emerge and change and what the consequences thereof are for individuals. We will review key sociological insights on *Culture* (Part 2), *Social relations* (Part 3) and *Inequality* (Part 4). We will see, by way of illustrations, how you can apply these broader themes to topics like family, organizations, crime and so forth. And then in Part 5 we will apply the CSI themes to three sociological topics in more detail. These topics are: immigration and integration, modernization and religion.

In summary, when you study a new social problem or a topic that is new to you, you don't need to start from scratch if you have familiarized yourself with the common themes in sociology. You can use the CSI perspectives and rely on the theoretical and empirical knowledge sociologists have acquired about culture, social relations and inequality. And, therefore, if you study a new topic like family or organizations, you can use the theories developed about CSI themes and apply these to your research topic. And, similarly, if you study a new social problem, you can rely on the CSI themes as well. With the sociological CSI approaches in mind, you can come up with three different perspectives on social phenomena, and use the theories and empirical findings that are known about culture, social relations and inequality. Social problems come and go and there is an overwhelmingly large variety of sociological topics, but the three sociological perspectives, and the theories that have been developed within these perspectives, have a much longer and more stable history.

PRINCIPLE 4.2

Themes as perspectives

Sociological themes can also help you to explain social phenomena. A theme can act as a unique perspective on social reality, which means that you get a better orientation on where to look for causes and also to rely on theories that have been developed before.

4.3 Causal explaining or subjective understanding?

In the history of sociology, so we have seen, sociologists have articulated different perspectives on key sociological themes. But different perspectives have been developed with respect to the *model of sociological explanation* too. We may characterize these perspectives as follows. The first one focuses on *causal explanations*, relating *variables* to each other and typically focusing on *collective* outcomes (meso and macro level). The second one is more concerned with *subjective* understanding, at *individual outcomes* (micro level) and paying attention to *human actions*. Let's take a closer look at these perspectives and assess whether they should be seen as opposites or if they can somehow be combined.

To introduce you to the two perspectives, consider the following example. Suppose we're interested in explaining the emergence of capitalism in societies. How can we explain the rise of capitalism in Western Europe? Why did capitalism develop so early there and not elsewhere? Say that a scholar comes up with the idea that capitalism arises in countries which shifted to Protestantism, and that this is the explanation for the fact that in the 16th century Western-European countries became capitalistic societies. We can depict this explanation in a conceptual model (Figure 4.8).

Figure 4.8 Ecological explanation: Protestantism affects capitalism.

Such an explanation is an example of a so-called **ecological explanation**, because both the independent variable (Protestantism) and the dependent variable (capitalism) are at the collective, ecological level. Ecological explanations provide an explanation for a certain meso- or macro-level outcome with attributes at the meso or macro level. Because this type of explanation relates two or more *variables* to each other, it is also sometimes called **variable sociology** (Esser, 1996). Variable sociology is characterized by stipulating causal relationships between independent and dependent variables. It is an attempt to explain a certain variable Y with certain variables $X1$, $X2$ and so forth.

ecological explanation type of explanation in which both the dependent and independent variable(s) are at the collective level (meso or macro).

variable sociology type of sociology which focuses on causal relationships between variables.

At first sight, these "ecological," "variable sociology" kind of explanations seem to make sense. It is conceivable, for example, that a shift towards Protestantism resulted in the emergence of capitalism. In other words, the rise of Protestantism (X) has caused the rise of capitalism (Y) and this may explain why capitalism emerged in 16th-century European nations. We may summarize the explanation in a theory schema, using the well-known deductive-nomological type of explanation:

P.   In countries that shift towards Protestantism, capitalism will emerge.

C.   Western European countries shifted towards Protestantism in the 16th century.

O.   Capitalism emerged in Western European countries in the 16th century.

Theory schema 4.1 Explanation of the rise of capitalism in Western Europe.

In the history of sociology, a certain type of sociological perspective has been developed—sometimes associated with the writings of Durkheim—which focuses on these kinds of ecological explanations and which pays attention to the causal impact of one variable on the other. According to this model of explanation, the researcher succeeds in explaining behavior Y if he or she is able to find variable X, which has a causal impact on Y.

This type of ecological explanation and variable sociology is criticized, however (Coleman, 1990). The main critique is that the ecological and variable type of explanations suffer from a lack of understanding. It is not clear why, for example, countries that shift to Protestantism would become capitalistic societies. What is missing in the explanation is a theory on why the variables are related to each other, in other words, why and under which conditions does X set Y in motion? When such a theory is available, we would be able to understand why X and Y are related and to specify conditions under which X does *not* result in Y. Ecological and variable type of explanations are sometimes called **Black Box explanations** because the *theoretical mechanism* which links X to Y is missing. What, for example, is the mechanism, the theoretical reasoning, underlying the causal effect of X (Protestantism) on Y (capitalism)?

black box explanations type of explanation in which Y is explained by X, but the theoretical mechanism linking X to Y is missing.

Precisely these questions are core to another perspective which has been developed in sociology. This perspective focuses more at micro-level processes and at the subjective understanding of human behavior. This perspective—often associated with the work of Weber, amongst others—argued that sociology should aim to understand the actions of humans. Thus, rather than focusing on "variables" or "ecological" relations at the collective level, this perspective considers "actors," "humans" at the micro level.

Weber's idea of understanding (in German: "**Verstehen**") is typically contrasted with the model of explanation that focuses on causal relations (in German: Erklären). Weber's notion of *Verstehen* is that the researcher should make sense of why individuals behave in a certain way, given their subjective interpretations of the specific situation in which they are embedded. The model of sociological explanation, according to this perspective, entails that you are able to interpret people's behavior from people's subjective understanding of the world.

verstehen type of explanation in which subjective understanding plays a key role.

This view emerged from what is called the tradition of "interpretative sociology," of which Weber was the founding father and to which scholars like George Herbert Mead (1863–1931) and Erving Goffman (1922–1982) belong. It is a research tradition which is also called, or at least is very similar to, "symbolic interactionism." Within the tradition of interpretative sociology and symbolic interactionism, scholars emphasize the importance of developing a theory of human action. Weber's work has inspired many sociologists who have carefully paid attention to the way people interpret their environment, i.e., how they attach meaning to their environment, to their subjective perceptions and their values.

PRINCIPLE 4.3

Weber's Verstehen Principle

In trying to come up with explanations which are also understandable, it is useful to develop theories that consider the beliefs, values and behavior of humans.

The two perspectives on sociological models of explanation are typically contrasted with each other. The idea is that causal explanations for human actions (*Erklären*) and understanding behavior (*Verstehen*) cannot be combined. The idea of *Verstehen* is sometimes contrasted with a *positivistic* perspective on science, which is supposed to ignore the subjective meaning people attach to their behavior and which adopts a pure "physics type" of theory with no room for people. According to this point of view, it would be impossible to capture with theoretical tools the unique way in which people define and interpret their own situation; that the general propositions of theories do not reflect the perceptions of individuals, but rather those of the outsider, the researcher. Therefore, so the argument goes, in sociology one should not come up with theories, but rather *describe* the subjective understanding of behavior from inside, from the perspective of the actors, and this is impossible to capture in a theoretical model (Schütz, 2013 [1932]). A potential pitfall of the focus on subjective understanding, however, is that one may no longer construct theories that stipulate causal relations. The consequence would be that sociology ends up merely describing how people are themselves interpreting their situation and their behavior.

In contemporary sociology, however, the divide between causal explaining (*Erklären*) and subjective understanding (*Verstehen*) is no longer seen as a choice between two alternatives. Although the history of sociology can be characterized by the development of the (Durkheimian) perspective that focuses on causal explanations and the (Weberian) perspective that is more concerned with subjective understanding, most sociologists nowadays integrate both perspectives.

Scholars agree, first, that as a science, sociology should develop theories that contain causal statements. But it is also acknowledged that variable sociology is undesirable and that one should pay attention to micro-level processes. At the micro level, however, one may not need to go so far as to rely on people's subjective understanding of their own situation as a requirement for sociological explanations. What is relevant is that sociological theories contain explicit *assumptions* of the researcher about how study subjects perceive their situation, what their preferences are and so forth. Something like this is what researchers aim for when they develop theories that also provide an understanding of the phenomena they aim to explain:

> *if* an individual named Michael is in social context A, and *if* we assume that this context A can be characterized by this and that (e.g., certain social norms prevail), and *if* we assume that people in general perceive their social environment in a certain way (e.g., they respond to social norms), well yes, *then* I understand why in that situation Michael (and people like him in the same situation) did that!

In the words of Raymond Boudon, this type of explanation is saying that: "I could have easily done the same thing he did if I had been in the same situation" (Boudon, 1987). In this way, sociologists respond to Weber's call for *Verstehen*. Rather than ending up in infinite descriptions of people's own interpretations of the situation, the researcher makes some simplifying assumptions—which, nevertheless, make sense in understanding people's behavior.

When scholars solve the Black Box problem in this way, they make behavior understandable and have a systematic theory at the same time. Typically, we respond to such theories by saying "ah, yes, now I get it!" or "that makes sense to me!" And, again, this is not to say that you and I, or the subject we study, would behave exactly in the way it is assumed by theory. Rather it is understanding in a *hypothetical* way, i.e., *given* certain assumptions about the situation people are in, as well as about their beliefs, values, opportunities and so forth, the observed human decisions make sense to us.

It has been claimed, therefore, that the kind of explanations that include propositions about subjective meaning, beliefs, interpretations and opportunities are no different from causal explanations in physics and chemistry (Hempel & Oppenheim, 1948). The combination of explaining and understanding behavior at the same time, of overcoming the supposed contrast between *Erklären* and *Verstehen*, can be found in the work of many sociologists and social theorists. For example, in his work *The Poverty of Historicism*, published in 1957, Karl Popper argued that social scientific explanations should seek to understand the behavior of people by explicitly taking into account the social context in which people participate (Popper, 2002 [1944]). Such a "situational analysis," as Popper named it, should make the decisions and actions of people meaningful in light of the opportunities and restrictions they face.

Similarly, other "positivist" sociologists have called for explanations that include statements about people and to develop theories in which people are perceived as "purposive agents" (Coleman, 1990). The research tradition called *analytical sociology*, largely initiated by sociologist Peter Hedström, explicitly calls attention to the notion of "social mechanisms," which are causal stories that provide explanations for social phenomena by including the beliefs, preferences and constraints of human actors (Demeulenaere, 2011; Hedström, 2005; Hedström & Bearman, 2009; Hedström & Swedberg, 1998). In addition, a related line of research in sociology, *sociological rational choice models*, likewise pays explicit attention to people's beliefs, preferences and restrictions (Coleman, 1990; Goldthorpe, 1998; Heath, 1976; Kroneberg & Kalter, 2012; Wippler & Lindenberg, 1987; Wittek, Snijders, & Nee, 2013).

In summary, Weber's call for *Verstehen* is nowadays widely shared in sociology and it has been fruitfully combined with the Durkheimian perspective that emphasizes causal explanations. Although some sociological traditions carry Weber's or Durkheim's legacy more explicitly than others, the boundaries between these traditions are not so strong as they are sometimes presented. Moreover, the boundaries have blurred over time and nowadays most sociologists do not identify themselves so strongly with certain traditions. Rather, they develop interesting theories and most agree that paying attention to human agency (Weber) while developing theories that contain causal statements (Durkheim) are both indispensable parts of a good sociological explanation of social phenomena.

4.4 Multilevel framework

Many scholars nowadays integrate causal explaining and subjective understanding, as we have seen. But how does that work in practice? How can you combine both perspectives? The key way they do so is by integrating the study of *collectives* (meso and macro level) with the study of processes at the *individual level* (micro level). Whereas the collective level is typically the focus of variable sociology, the individual level is core to the interpretative tradition. By integrating these levels, you can pay attention to the interplay between the individual and the collective, between micro and macro.

An early formulation of such a combined micro–macro framework was developed by McClelland in his study on *The Achieving Society* (McClelland, 1961). In this study he presented a conceptual model in which he argued that Max Weber's *The Protestant Ethic and the Spirit of Capitalism* (Weber, 2002 [1905]) can be interpreted in such a way that his study contains propositions that stipulate causal relations at the macro and micro level, as well as between these two levels. In other words, Weber, although typically focusing on micro-level processes and subjective understanding, actually also paid attention to macro-level conditions and to causal propositions. In various writings, James Coleman used the same example as McClelland to show how Weber's study actually connected micro and macro levels (Coleman, 1990).

So, how can we interpret Weber's work on *The Protestant Ethic* in this way? Let's take the version of Weber's study presented by James Coleman, because this is the well-known version (Coleman, 1990). Weber, so Coleman argued, attempted to answer the question of why capitalism developed in Western-European nations rather than somewhere else. The starting point of Weber's research was a macro-level relationship: the rise of Protestantism was associated with the emergence of capitalism (arrow 4, Figure 4.9). This, so we have seen, is an ecological relationship between two variables at the macro level.

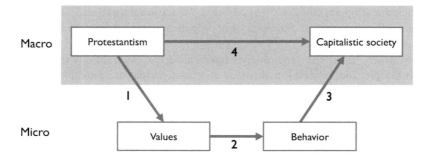

Figure 4.9 Protestantism and the rise of capitalism.

But Weber did not stop here, McClelland and Coleman point out. Weber wondered: why would the rise in Protestant religion contribute to the rise of a capitalistic system? This relationship is far from obvious and as an explanation it is not an informative theory. Weber then considered the values, perceptions and actions of individuals. Weber argued that the rise of Protestantism (macro level) changed the values of people (micro level), such that, in Protestant countries, people are socialized into the Protestant doctrine of having a strong work ethic, an attitude towards hard working, to perform one's duty in a calling (arrow 1). He then argued that when people value hard working, they will indeed work harder, save more and so forth (arrow 2). Finally, as a result of people working long hours, saving money and other economic behavior, the society changed into a capitalistic system (arrow 3).

Seen in this way, Weber explained the ecological relationship (arrow 4) with macro-micro, micro-micro and micro-macro propositions. By going to the level of individuals, and considering the way people in European societies at that time were affected by their social context, he was able to make the ecological relationship understandable. Rather than merely linking variables to each other at the collective level, and determining whether they are causally related as in variable sociology, Weber invoked theoretical mechanisms about how individuals' values are shaped by their social context and how, in turn, this affected their behavior.

Connecting the macro level to the micro level therefore helps to make behavior understandable. An additional advantage of connecting the macro level with the micro level is that you get a deeper explanation. One criterion for evaluating theories is their information content (Chapter 2). When theories are more general and apply to a wider range of phenomena, they are to be preferred above theories that have a smaller scope. Precisely for this reason, explanations that include human actions are to be preferred above ecological explanations.

If we look at Figure 4.9 we can understand how this works. Weber started with the macro-level relationship between Protestantism (X) and the rise of capitalism (Y). When we include the actions of individuals (Z), however, something important happens: the proposition that relates Protestantism to capitalism (i.e., $X \rightarrow Y$, arrow 4) becomes the *thing Weber wanted to explain*. When taken together, the propositions on the impact of macro conditions on micro conditions (arrow 1), micro conditions to micro outcomes (arrow 2) and micro outcomes to macro outcomes (arrow 3), explain the macro-level relationship (arrow 4). They provide what we have called in Chapter 2 a *deeper explanation*, i.e., a more general explanation, which is applicable to a wider range of cases. With a theory schema we can represent Weber's deeper explanation as follows:

P.   In Protestant countries, people are more inclined to develop a strong work ethic, an attitude towards hard working (Arrow 1).

P.   The more people have a strong work ethic, the harder they work and the more money they save (Arrow 2).

P.   The harder people work, and the more they save, the more likely that a capitalistic economy emerges (Arrow 3).

P.   In countries that shift towards Protestantism, capitalism will emerge (Arrow 4).

> **Theory schema 4.2** Explanation of the link between Protestantism and capitalism.

In contemporary sociology, this kind of conceptual model, which contains propositions at the collective and individual level, and which combines causal explanation with subjective understanding, is used very often. Whatever social phenomena you study, in contemporary sociology it is argued that it is preferred to bring in the actions of *individuals*, as then we arrive at a deeper explanation and a better understanding at the same time (Coleman, 1990; Raub, Buskens, & Van Assen, 2011; Wippler & Lindenberg, 1987).

The conceptual model, which integrates the macro and micro levels, is sometimes known as "Coleman-boat" or "Coleman's bathtub" after Coleman published his *Foundations of Social Theory* in 1990 (Coleman, 1990). But since the origins of this micro-macro diagram can be found already in the work of McClelland in the 1960s (McClelland, 1961) and in the writings of other sociologists in the 1970s and 1980s such as Lindenberg and Boudon (Raub & Voss, 2017), I will use the more generic term **multilevel framework**.

multilevel framework a framework which considers the interplay between individuals and their social environment.

You can use the multilevel framework to study any sociological topic or any social problem: families, neighborhoods, organizations, crime, population change and so forth (Billari, 2015; Coleman, 1990; Hedström & Swedberg, 1998; Raub et al., 2011). With this perspective, you can study the interplay between individuals and their social environment, between the micro level and the macro (or meso) level. If you take a look at the topics of family, organizations, crime and so forth, you'll see that sociologists often use this multilevel framework either explicitly or implicitly. Thus, in addition to using overarching *themes* like culture, social relations and inequality, you could also use the *multilevel* perspective to study any topic you like.

Let's review the various elements of the multilevel framework in more detail (Figure 4.10).

First, with the help of a multilevel framework, you can study **social contexts effects** (arrow 1). These type of propositions relate social conditions (macro or meso level) to the individual level. Social context effects relate to individual outcomes *in so far as* they are shaped by social conditions, whatever these social conditions may be: the peer group to which individuals belong, parental resources, the neighborhood in which individuals live, the wider set of institutions in society. Thus, individual differences (i.e., micro level) are explained by social conditions, which can be as small

social context effect influence of social conditions on individual outcomes.

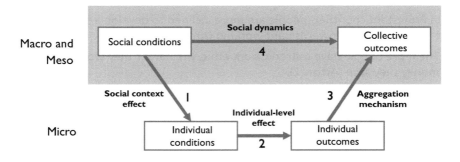

Figure 4.10 Multilevel framework.

as a family, neighborhood or organization (meso level), and as big as an entire country or beyond (macro level). The task for the sociologist is nicely captured by the concept of "sociological imagination," i.e., to discover social causes of human behavior. That is not to say that such sociological studies want to fully explain all individual differences in human behavior. It is recognized that there are also individual characteristics that play a role, such as people's genetic predispositions, their personality, emotions, cognitions, but also human agency, free will and independent choices and decisions.

Using a multilevel framework, you can study how social conditions *directly* shape individual outcomes, such as their values, beliefs, resources and so forth. In the example of the *Protestant Ethic*, this relationship stated that Protestantism affects the development of certain values. But these values were not the "outcomes" of interest in the study. Rather the study was concerned with human behavior, and for that reason one can add at the individual level a relationship between individual conditions and individual outcomes (arrow 2). In the multilevel framework (Figure 4.10), this additional step is included to represent such so-called **individual-level effects**. These type of propositions refer to processes at the individual level, such as whether someone's frustration affects aggression, or how certain perceptions affect behavior, how one's opportunities affect social relations, or how financial resources influence educational choices. Sometimes scholars refer to the theories that are related to the individual level as "micro models," "theories of action" or simply "micro-level propositions."

individual-level effect type of propositions which refer to processes at the micro level.

Importantly, it depends on your theory as to whether or not you need to posit an individual-level effect (arrow 2), as in some cases there might only be a direct social context effect, whereas in other cases you may want to specify how social conditions affect certain individual conditions (arrow 1) and how subsequently these individual conditions affect individual outcomes (arrow 2). Furthermore, it could also be the case that your theory is more complex at the individual level, which means that you will have more than one individual-level relationship. For instance, one could argue that an economic recession in the country leads to more workers becoming unemployed (social context effect); that becoming unemployed leads to a reduction of financial resources (individual-level effect), that having fewer resources leads to more frustration and anger (individual-level effect), and that more frustration and anger leads to a higher risk of crime (individual-level effect). Thus, depending on your theory, you may specify one or more individual-level propositions. More generally, you can use the multilevel framework in multiple ways, specifying on each level one or more propositions (Page, 2015).

What about arrow 3? How should we interpret this type of relationship? In the literature these are called transformation or **aggregation mechanisms**. It specifies propositions which relate the individual level to collective outcomes; they stipulate how social phenomena at the meso or macro level emerge from micro-level processes. Thus, sociologists study the segregation of ethnic groups in society, the polarization of cultural attitudes and differences in the rates of overweight and obesity across countries. Segregation, polarization and rates of overweight and obesity are attributes of populations, aggregations of individuals, and therefore social phenomena instead of individual phenomena. But they are the result of micro-level processes; from people's social interactions, how people create larger groups, communities, collectives and so on.

> **aggregation mechanism** proposition which relates the individual level to collective outcomes.

Broadly speaking, sociologists distinguish between two classes of aggregation. The first one is called **simple aggregation** and it is the most intuitive. If you use simple aggregation, then you say that the collective is simply the sum of its parts. This happens in those situations in which the behavior of people is independent, i.e., the decisions you make do not depend on what others do. For example, you can go shopping at 2 pm or 5 pm, but whatever you decide to do, it will not significantly affect the behavior of other people—at least not the collective. It will not change the behavior of other people today, or tomorrow, or at least not significantly at the collective level (you may affect the behavior of a friend, for example, if you decide to go together).

> **simple aggregation** idea that collective outcomes are no more than the sum of their parts.

When large numbers of individuals in a population behave independently with respect to a certain outcome, it results in very predictable and stable collective outcomes. Often, you'll see a normal distribution emerging in these cases, such that many people cluster together around a certain average, and that the further apart from that average, the fewer people there are. An incidental strong deviation from the average collective behavior, as when an unexpectedly high number of people go shopping at 2 pm on a certain day, will not impact subsequent courses of action. The next day at 2 pm one would expect to see again the average number of people shopping as used to be the case in the weeks and months before. The same pattern will happen again and again at the collective level—as long as people are by and large making their decisions independently. It typically leads to a normal distribution, which fits well with the stable and predictable social phenomena we often encounter in daily life.

However, simple aggregation cannot be used for all collective phenomena. It rests on one crucial assumption, namely that actors make decisions *independently* from each other. In other words: there are no social context effects. In social life, however, this condition of independency (no social context effects) is often violated. In fact, in quite a few cases, social contexts effects exist and people respond to the beliefs, values, norms and behavior of others. There are many such cases of **social interdependency**, i.e., cases in which (observed or expected) actions of individuals affect those of yet other individuals. Social interdependency thus happens when actions of individuals change social conditions at t_1 and, as a result of these new social conditions, it affects yet other individuals at t_2.

> **social interdependency** situations in which actions of individuals affect those of yet other individuals.

What does this interdependency mean when we want to understand the transition from the individual to the collective? It means that collective outcomes are subject to a complex interplay between the individual and the social and that, as a result of that, collective outcomes can be harder to predict and even are collectively unforeseen and unwanted. It also means that history matters: conditions at a certain point in time affect subsequent outcomes. We cannot simply aggregate from the individual to the collective level. Simple aggregation, which often leads to the normal curve, does not work here. Instead, this is a dynamic process which results in **complex aggregation**, i.e., social phenomena that are not simply the aggregation of individuals because their macro- (and meso-) level properties interact. We will address various examples of complex aggregation in this textbook.

complex aggregation idea that collective outcomes result from complex interplay between individuals and their social context.

Finally, let's review arrow 4. This arrow is about **social dynamics** and this concept can refer to two types of relations. First, it can indicate relationships between two social phenomena, such as between Protestantism and capitalistic societies. This we have called ecological relationships and we have seen examples in Weber's study on the *Protestant Ethic*. But social dynamics can also refer to social trends, i.e., collective change, developments at the level of groups or societies. For example, one can study changes in social relations in a certain society, changes in opinions and norms, and changes in social stratification and mobility. Either way, social dynamics can be understood by considering various pathways of the multilevel perspective. Thus, you may consider that ecological relationships and collective changes are caused by a combination of social contexts effects (arrow 1), individual level effects (arrow 2) and aggregation mechanisms (arrow 3).

social dynamics ecological relationships and collective changes.

In the following chapters we will frequently use the multilevel framework. And we will combine this framework with the study of the sociological CSI themes.

PRINCIPLE 4.4

Multilevel framework

When you integrate the CSI themes in a multilevel framework, you can study the interplay between individuals and social phenomena, between micro and macro (meso).

4.5 Chapter resources

Key concepts

Perspective	Social network	Verstehen
Framework	Group	Multilevel framework
Paradigm	Inequality	Social context effect
Sociological topic	Social stratification	Individual-level effect
Sociological theme	Social mobility	Aggregation mechanism
Culture	Resources	Simple aggregation
Opinion	Ecological explanation	Complex aggregation
Norm	Variable sociology	Social interdependency
Social relations	Black Box explanations	Social dynamics

Summary

- In the history of sociology, various perspectives (frameworks, paradigms) have been developed with respect to the key sociological themes and models of explanation.
- Sociological themes are general perspectives on social phenomena.
- Three such themes are: culture, social relations and inequality. Themes consist of subthemes.
- Sociological themes can be applied to sociological topics to emphasize certain aspects of them. Sociologists study a wide variety of topics, such as family, organizations, crime and immigration.
- With respect to models of explanation, some scholars focus more on ecological explanations and causal relations at the collective level. Others instead are more concerned with subjective understanding and micro-level processes.
- Using a multilevel framework, you can integrate these perspectives and study the interplay between individuals and their social context, between micro and macro (meso).
- The multilevel perspective responds to Weber's call for *Verstehen*, which is that one should bring in human agency (people's beliefs, values, actions) in understanding social phenomena.
- Using a multilevel framework, you can identify social context effects, individual level effects and aggregation mechanisms.

References

Bicchieri, C. (2005). *The grammar of society: The nature and dynamics of social norms*. New York, NY: Cambridge University Press.

Billari, F. C. (2015). Integrating macro- and micro-level approaches in the explanation of population change. *Population Studies*, 69(1), 11–20.

Blau, P., & Duncan, O. D. (1967). *The American occupational structure*. New York, NY: Free Press.

Boudon, R. (1981). *The logic of social action: An introduction to sociological analysis*. London: Taylor & Francis.

Boudon, R. (1987). The individualistic tradition in sociology. In J. C. Alexander, B. Giesen, R. Munch, & N. J. Smelser (Eds.), *The micro-macro link* (pp. 45–71). Berkeley and Los Angeles, CA: University of California Press.

Boudon, R. (2001). *The origin of values: Essays in the sociology and philosophy of beliefs*. New Brunswick, NJ: Transaction Publishers.

Brennan, G., Eriksson, L., Goodin, R. E., & Southwood, N. (2013). *Explaining norms*. Oxford, UK: Oxford University Press.

Coleman, J. S. (1990). *Foundations of social theory*. Cambridge, MA: Harvard University Press.

Collins, R. (1994). *Four sociological traditions: Selected readings*. Oxford, UK: Oxford University Press.

Craib, I. (1997). *Classical social theory*. Oxford, UK: Oxford University Press.

Demeulenaere, P. (Ed.) (2011). *Analytical sociology and social mechanisms*. New York, NY: Cambridge University Press.

Durkheim, E. (1961 [1897]). *Suicide*. New York, NY: Free Press.

Elster, J. (2009). Social norms and the explanation of behavior. In P. Hedström & P. Bearman (Eds.), *The Oxford handbook of analytical sociology* (pp. 195–217). Oxford, UK: Oxford University Press.

Esser, H. (1996). What is wrong with 'variable sociology'? *European Sociological Review*, *12*(2), 159–166.

Ferguson, A. (1980 [1767]). *An essay on the history of civil society*. New Brunswick, NJ: Transaction Publishers.

Gibbs, J. P. (1965). Norms: The problem of definition and classification. *American Journal of Sociology*, *70*(5), 586–594.

Goldthorpe, J. H. (1998). Rational action theory for sociology. *British Journal of Sociology*, *49*(2), 167–192.

Grusky, D. B. (2001). The past, present, and future of social inequality. In D. B. Grusky (Ed.), *Social stratification in sociological perspective: Class, race & gender* (2nd ed., pp. 1–51). Boulder, CO: Westview Press.

Heath, A. (1976). *Rational choice and social exchange: A critique of exchange theory*. Cambridge, UK: Cambridge University Press.

Hechter, M., & Opp, K. (Eds.). (2001). *Social norms*. New York, NY: Russell Sage Foundation.

Hedström, P. (2005). *Dissecting the social: On the principles of analytical sociology*. Cambridge, UK: Cambridge University Press.

Hedström, P., & Bearman, P. (Eds.). (2009). *The Oxford handbook of analytical sociology*. Oxford, UK: Oxford University Press.

Hedström, P., & Swedberg, R. (Eds.). (1998). *Social mechanisms*. Cambridge, UK: Cambridge University Press.

Hempel, C. G., & Oppenheim, P. (1948). Studies in the logic of explanation. *Philosophy of Science*, *15*(2), 135–175.

Hobbes, T. (1994 [1651]). *Leviathan*. Indianapolis, IN: Hackett Publishing.

Hofstede, G. (2001 [1980]). *Culture's consequences: Comparing values, behaviors, institutions and organizations across nations* (2nd ed.). Thousand Oaks, CA: Sage Publications.

Hout, M. (2015). A summary of what we know about social mobility. *The Annals of the American Academy of Political and Social Science*, *657*(1), 27–36.

Johnson, D. P. (2008). *Contemporary sociological theory: An integrated multi-level approach*. New York, NY: Springer.

Kroneberg, C., & Kalter, F. (2012). Rational choice theory and empirical research: Methodological and theoretical contributions in Europe. *Annual Review of Sociology*, *38*, 73–92.

Lakatos, I. (1978). *The methodology of scientific research programmes*. Cambridge, UK: Cambridge University Press.

Locke, J. (1988 [1689]). *Locke: Two treatises of government*. Cambridge, UK: Cambridge University Press.

McClelland, D. C. (1961). *Achieving society*. New York, NY: Free Press.

Mesoudi, A. (2011). *Cultural evolution: How Darwinian theory can explain human culture and synthesize the social sciences*. Chicago, IL: University of Chicago Press.

Morrison, K. (2006). *Marx, Durkheim, Weber: Formations of modern social thought* (2nd ed.). Ontario: Sage Publications Ltd.

Nolan, P., & Lenski, G. (2011). *Human societies: An introduction to macrosociology* (11th ed.). Boulder, CO: Paradigm Publishers.

Opp, K. (2001). How do norms emerge? An outline of a theory. *Mind & Society*, *2*(1), 101–128.

Page, S. E. (2015). What sociologists should know about complexity. *Annual Review of Sociology*, *41*, 21–41.

Popper, K. (2002 [1944]). *The poverty of historicism*. New York, NY: Psychology Press.

Raub, W., Buskens, V., & Van Assen, M. A. (2011). Micro-macro links and microfoundations in sociology. *The Journal of Mathematical Sociology*, *35*(1–3), 1–25.

Raub, W., & Voss, T. (2017). Micro-macro models in sociology: Antecedents of Coleman's diagram. In B. Jann & W. Przepiorka (Eds.), *Social dilemmas, institutions, and the evolution of cooperation* (pp. 11–36). Berlin, Germany: De Gruyter.

Rokeach, M. (1973). *The nature of human values*. New York, NY: Free Press.

Schütz, A. (2013 [1932]). *Der Sinnhafte Aufbau Der Sozialen Welt: Eine Einleitung in Die Verstehende Soziologie*. Vienna: Springer-Verlag.

Scott, J. (2017 [1991]). *Social network analysis* (4th ed.). London, UK: Sage.

Simmel, G. (1955). *Conflict and the web of group affiliations*. New York, NY: Free Press.

Ultee, W. (2001). Problem selection in the social sciences: Methodology. In N. Smelser & P. Baltes (Eds.), *International encyclopedia of the social and behavioural sciences* (pp. 12110–12117). Amsterdam: Elsevier.

Wasserman, S., & Faust, K. (1994). *Social network analysis: Methods and applications*. Cambridge, UK: Cambridge University Press.

Weber, M. (2002 [1905]). *The protestant ethic and the spirit of capitalism and other writings*. New York, NY: Penguin Books.

Williams, R. (2014 [1976]). *Keywords: A vocabulary of culture and society*. Oxford, UK: Oxford University Press.

Wippler, R., & Lindenberg, S. (1987). Collective phenomena and rational choice. In J. C. Alexander, B. Giessen, R. Munch, & N. J. Smelser (Eds.), *The micro-macro link* (pp. 135–152). Oakland, CA: University of California Press.

Wittek, R., Snijders, T., & Nee, V. (Eds.). (2013). *The handbook of rational choice social research*. Stanford, CA: Stanford University Press.

Part 2

Culture

Chapter 5

Opinions

What shapes your preferences? Why do you believe in certain things? This chapter is about opinions, i.e., our beliefs, values and attitudes, and about behavior that corresponds to opinions. As an introduction to this subtheme of culture, I begin with a puzzling observation, namely that the popularity of "cultural products" (books, music, songs and movies) is incredibly unequal. Most of the cultural products produced no one has heard of, while just a few are known by almost everybody. How can we explain the dazzling success of the Harry Potter books? (5.1). I introduce the idea that people's opinions are affected by their social context and discuss self-fulfilling prophecies, which result from a dynamic interplay between the individual and the social context (5.2). Then I discuss classic laboratory experiments which show that, in small-scale settings, people conform to the opinions of others in their direct social environment. Subsequently, I will show that the same pattern occurs in the family, among peers in school and when people are exposed to media. I will identify conformity as a stylized fact, i.e., the human tendency to conform to the opinions of other people in their social environment (5.3). Then, I will outline two mechanisms which can explain conformity, namely: learning from other people (informational social influence) and complying with norms (normative social influence) (5.4). It is the idea of informational social influence that sociologists have generalized into a more comprehensive theory on social learning. I will discuss this theory and identify several social learning biases, i.e., conditions that modify the tendency to conform (5.5). With this knowledge on social learning theory and social learning biases, we are then able to understand the success of Harry Potter and other popular cultural products (5.6). I end with a discussion of how this theory is used to understand the diffusion of innovations, which are opinions on new ideas and products (5.7).

> ## Learning goals
>
> After reading this chapter, check if you are able to:
>
> - Describe and use key sociological concepts on opinions.
> - Describe self-fulfilling prophecies.
> - Describe stylized facts on opinions.
> - Describe and apply social learning theory.
> - Describe the dual-process model of social learning.
> - Describe and apply social learning biases.
> - Describe Tarde's diffusion theory.

5.1 Why is Harry Potter so popular?

Have you read the *Harry Potter* books? Or seen the Potter movies? In sociology, a striking observation has been made regarding what are labelled "cultural products" such as books, movies, art, music and songs (Salganik, Dodds, & Watts, 2006; Salganik & Watts, 2008). A feature of these products is that some are extremely popular, whereas the rest almost nobody knows about. Take books, for example. There are a few books that have millions of readers, and many more books that hardly sell more than a few hundred copies. The first book by J. K. Rowling, *Harry Potter and the Philosopher's Stone* (1997), has sold more than 100 million copies worldwide. Sales of the *Harry Potter* book series together exceeds 400 million copies. Another success was Dan Brown's book *The Da Vinci Code* (2003), which sold more than 80 million copies.

Similarly, some movies have become incredibly popular, like *Avatar* (2009) for example, with box office sales of more than USD $700 million in 2014, whereas many movies flop and don't get any fame at all. The situation is no different in art. There is an enormous number of paintings that do not receive any popularity at all. Some are exposed in a museum, but many attract only a few visitors. How different is the success of the few stars. The *Mona Lisa*, painted around 1500 AD by Leonardo da Vinci and today exhibited at the Louvre Museum in Paris, is known by almost everybody in the world. It is clearly the top painting

STYLIZED FACT 5.1

Popularity of cultural products
The popularity of cultural products in contemporary industrialized societies is highly skewed, i.e., a very small minority of books, songs, movies and art products gain incredible success, whereas the overwhelming majority gain very little.

of the collection, attracting around 20,000 visitors *each day*, and many believe it to be the most valuable painting in the world. We can summarize the ***popularity of cultural products*** as a stylized empirical fact (see previous page).

Why is it that some books are read by many people and others are not? Why are some books so popular? Why *Harry Potter*? What explains the dazzling success of *Harry Potter*, *Avatar* and the *Mona Lisa*? Why have these cultural products become so much more popular than all other books, movies and paintings? Let's formulate this as a theoretical question:

> $Q(t)$: Why is the distribution of popularity of cultural products in contemporary industrialized societies highly skewed?

THINKING LIKE A SOCIOLOGIST 5.1

Can you come up with an explanation? Is this a sociological explanation?

An obvious answer is that popular products have certain unique qualities that distinguish them from the rest. Who cannot see the *Mona Lisa* without wondering about her mysterious smile, without admiring the beautiful contrast of dark and light, and witnessing the work of a true master? And isn't it simply the unique talent of Rowling that made her *Harry Potter* books so good and popular? A common-sense explanation of the popularity of certain cultural products is that these products, such as the *Mona Lisa*, are of much higher quality than other products that are less popular. Quality and talents breed success.

Here is a fact that might lead you to doubt this common-sense explanation that takes an individual perspective: for a long time in history, the *Mona Lisa* was not a famous painting at all (Watts, 2011). In fact, many other paintings were more popular and some of these paintings hardly attract any visitors today. Seen from an individual perspective, in which "individual quality is all that matters," this fluctuation in popularity is hard to explain because the quality of the product remains constant. Here is another fact that might question the common-sense, individualistic, thinking: editors who had received the book proposal of Rowling repeatedly rejected it, as they thought it was not good enough and that it would not be profitable. It was not just one editor who had the opinion that the first *Harry Potter* book was of insufficient quality, or even two. No less than 12 editors thought so (imagine how much they must regret their decision now!) before finally an editor saw some merit in the book and it was published.

Clearly, the quality of the cultural product is not a satisfactory explanation for whether it will become highly popular or not. How is that possible? Why did 12 editors reject a book that eventually sold more than 400 million copies? Book editors are skilled and experienced people who should be able to distinguish good from bad writing, profitable from unprofitable books, and certainly they should have an eye for the superstars in their field. Why could they not predict its success? And if the quality of books, songs and movies does not explain their popularity, what does?

Image 5.1 The book *Harry Potter and the Philosopher's Stone* was rejected by 12 editors before it was finally published. Then it suddenly sold millions of copies worldwide. What explains this puzzling success?

5.2 Self-fulfilling prophecy

To understand the unequal popularity of cultural products, we need to take a sociological perspective. This means, first, that we need to understand the process called "self-fulfilling prophecy." A **self-fulfilling prophecy** occurs when behavior based on false beliefs about a situation cause that situation in the end. In the words of sociologist Robert Merton, who coined this idea:

self-fulfilling prophecy when behavior based on false beliefs about a situation cause that situation in the end.

> The self-fulfilling prophecy is, in the beginning, a false definition of the situation evoking a new behavior which makes the original false conception come true.
>
> (Merton, 1948)

The self-fulfilling prophecy phenomenon can be found in various areas, such as in health, education, organizations and sports. In health, for example, the *placebo effect* is a well-known case of a self-fulfilling prophecy (Biggs, 2009). The way placebos work is that the patient receives a certain treatment and the patient is informed that this treatment has proven health benefits (whereas in reality it has no medical effect). Because the patient *believes* that this treatment will work, that the treatment is based on evidence for medical effects, the patient will behave accordingly, resulting in positive health outcomes. In education, a similar pattern has been observed with respect to fear of exams. In this case, if students believe they will not perform well, even though they have enough knowledge to perform well, their false belief will result in the behavior of which they are afraid. In these two cases (placebo and fear of exams), self-fulfilling prophecies emerge because of self-expectations. This is called the **Galatea effect**, i.e., people who have higher self-expectations will have more positive outcomes (Hancock, Adler, & Côté, 2013).

Self-fulfilling prophecies also emerge when *other* people place higher (or lower) expectations on someone or some group. In sociology of education, this has been observed with respect to the educational performance of pupils. In class, teachers have expectations about the abilities and talents of the children: for some they have high expectancies, for others less so. In 1968, Rosenthal and Jacobson used an experimental design to examine what may be the consequences of such differential expectations. They observed that when teachers have higher expectations of a child in class at t_0, that child performed better at the end of the one-year period, at t_1, in terms of IQ growth, compared with equally talented children of whom they had lower expectations (Rosenthal & Jacobson, 1968).

Similar self-fulfilling prophecies have been observed in the sociology of organizations, ethnicity, crime and health. When people uphold certain positive (or negative) beliefs about other groups, they will act accordingly—whether these initial beliefs were true or false. This will affect members of the other group in such a way that these expectations become true or almost so. Such dynamics have been found with respect to the positive (and negative) expectations an employer may have about some of his employees (Eden, 1984, 1990), the general trust people have in members of other groups and social stigma (Goffman, 1986; Link & Phelan, 2001), interethnic prejudice and stereotyping (Blumer, 1958), and labelling of certain groups in society, such as racial and ethnic minority groups, as potential criminals (Scheff, 1966).

In these cases, self-fulfilling prophecies emerge because of expectations created by *other people*. Scholars call this the **Pygmalion effect**, i.e., the idea that when other people place greater expectations on an individual or a group, it will result in greater outcomes attained by the individual or group. The *Pygmalion effect* often interacts with the *Galatea effect*. For example, when teachers have high expectations of boys' math skills (and lower expectations of girls), they may put extra effort into facilitating the development of math skills of boys. They may also give compliments to boys about their mathematical talents, more so than to the equally math-gifted girls. These differential expectations from teachers (*Pygmalion effect*), subsequently impact the self-expectations of boys and girls (*Galatea effect*). The higher (lower) self-confidence of boys (girls) regarding their math skills may then confirm and even amplify the expectations of their teachers.

The *Pygmalion* and *Galatea effects* provide a deeper explanation for the relative age effect, as they can explain the puzzling observation that birth month is related to success in sports (Chapter 2). The key actors in sports are coaches, who might not be well aware of the exact age differences within a team. A one-year difference in the age of pupils who are young, say around the ages of 7 to 15, can make a big difference is terms of physical and cognitive maturity. The coach might then mistakenly believe that a pupil is very talented at sports, much more so than his team-mates, whereas in reality this pupil is just older. The coach might give more praise to the performance of the relatively oldest in the team, and thereby stimulate the development of the oldest more so than that of the others, eventually resulting in higher chances for the older players to be selected for the better teams (Hancock et al., 2013;

Musch & Grondin, 2001). Let's summarize this explanation with the help of a theory schema, focusing, for simplicity, only on the *Pygmalion effect* to explain the *relative age effect* in sports.

P.   Greater expectations placed on an individual or group by others will result in greater outcomes attained by the individual or group. (*Pygmalion effect*)

P.   The relatively older individuals are, compared with their peers in the sport teams, the more positive are the expectations of others (coaches, etc.) that are placed on them (about their talents, etc.).

P.   The better individuals perform, the more often they are selected for the best sport teams.

P.   The relatively older individuals are, compared with their peers, the more often they are selected for the best sport teams. (*Relative age effect*)

> **Theory Scheme 5.1** Explanation of the relative age effect.

The *Pygmalion* and *Galatea effects* can likewise explain differences in education performance by birth month. Pupils who are the relatively oldest at the moment of entering primary school are the ones who attain the best outcomes in education: they get better grades and go to university more often. The explanation for this phenomenon is that teachers have more positive expectations of the relatively oldest pupils. Teachers are not always aware of the age differences within a class and hence they might erroneously believe that a pupil is more talented, whereas in reality the pupil is only a bit older than his peers and hence more cognitively mature. The false beliefs of the teacher might have important consequences. Teachers treat the relatively oldest pupils *as if* they are more talented, which results in a positive feedback process, whereby teachers' positive interactions with the relatively older pupils result in more self-confidence of the pupils, which in turn leads to even higher expectations and more rewards from the teacher, and so forth (Verachtert, De Fraine, Onghena, & Ghesquière, 2010).

What can we learn from Merton's idea of self-fulfilling prophecies and how this works out via self-expectations (*Galatea effect*) and expectations set by others (*Pygmalion effect*)? First, we can learn from these examples about an *individual-level effect*, namely that beliefs, and opinions more generally, impact behavior. The opinions people have affect their behavior and can have consequences for how they behave towards others—even if their opinions are false. How people "define their situation" is a key element in understanding the course of subsequent actions (Goffman, 1959, 1974). If we want to explain behavior, we need to consider the perceptions, beliefs, attitudes and values of people; how they "frame" or perceive the situation they are in. A famous saying of the sociologists William Thomas and Dorothy Swaine Thomas nicely captures this link between opinions and behavior: "if men define situations as real, they are real in their consequences" (Thomas & Thomas, 1928). In other words: the perceptions people have about reality influence subsequent choice of actions. And whether these perceptions match reality or not is not what matters: people act *as if* their beliefs are reality. This is what the **Thomas and Thomas Theorem** teaches us.

thomas and thomas theorem
if men define situations as real, they are real in their consequences.

Second, these examples of self-fulfilling prophecies suggest *social context effects* and *complex aggregation* mechanisms. We should consider the interplay between the individual and the social context, between micro and macro (meso) level. For example, when a teacher in school (i.e., meso-level social context) does not expect much of a certain student (i.e., micro level), whereas the student has much potential, it can negatively affect the performance of the student. The negative opinion of the teacher may be directly shared with other teachers or observed by other teachers. Either way, the teachers may collectively lower their expectations, thereby affecting the student's performance. This, in turn, could shape (even) lower expectations of this student among peers and teachers. In such cases, what other people do—their behavior—is often taken to reveal their opinions—what they believe, value, prefer.

Robert Merton, in his treatment of self-fulfilling prophecies, gave the example of a bank run to reveal the interplay between social conditions and individuals (Merton, 1948). Figure 5.1 presents this scenario in a multilevel framework. A bank run happens when at a certain point in time a person (A_1) starts to believe that the bank is insolvent (I). Suppose that this is not true, at least not *at that moment*, but that nevertheless this person acts *as if* he is right and hence withdraws his money from the bank (W). This is an *individual-level effect*. But, as a result of his new beliefs and behavior, the collective has also changed: at t_1 a higher percentage of the population believe that the bank is insolvent and acts accordingly (they have withdrawn their money from the bank). Because of social interdependency, we see *complex aggregation*. The beliefs and behavior of one person affect the beliefs and behavior of other persons. Person (A_1) affects other persons in the population, such as A_2: a *social context effect*. Possibly this person has talked to A_1 and shared ideas, or A_2 has observed the behavior of A_1 and from this infers that A_1 believes that the bank is insolvent.

Now assume that this person also becomes convinced of the financial instability of the bank and hence goes to the bank to take out his money. But that means that, collectively, a new situation has occurred, namely that (at t_2) an even higher proportion of the population believes that the bank is insolvent and has withdrawn their money. This meso-level change is depicted as an arrow relating collective outcomes at t_1 with collective outcomes at t_2. The process will not stop here, of course. The increasing share of the population that has taken their

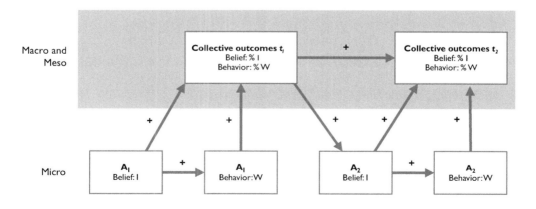

Figure 5.1 Bank run as a self-fulfilling prophecy process.

money from the bank affect the beliefs and behavior of yet other people and so forth, until, in the end, the collective outcome is that the initially false belief becomes reality: the bank collapses.

5.3 Conformity

Self-fulfilling prophecies show us how opinions shape behavior (individual-level effects) and that the emergence and change of collective cultural opinions can be understood as resulting from the interplay between individuals and their social context (social context effects and complex aggregation). In Merton's example of the bank run, it is assumed that people *conform* to the opinions—and corresponding behavior—of other people in the environment; that, in other words, people tend to copy the opinions and behaviors of other people in their environment. This conformity assumption is key to understanding the bank run, but this is only an example—which, moreover, has not occurred so frequently in reality. We may therefore ask: what is the empirical evidence for the proposition that people conform their opinions (and corresponding behavior) to the opinions (and behavior) of others?

Research on conformity started in the 1940s and 1950s, when social psychologist Solomon Asch conducted a series of experiments in the laboratory with male college students (Asch, 1956, 1961). Asch investigated what happens to people's opinions when others in their direct environment publicly express an opinion that is false. Will people copy that wrong belief or do they ignore that and rely on their own belief? The experiments Asch conducted are nowadays known as the classic *line-judgment experiments*. The set-up of these experiments was fairly simple. To begin, it consisted of a group of seven to nine individuals who gathered in a classroom and who were instructed to match the length of the standard line with one of three other lines (see Figure 5.2). Only one of the three lines matched the standard, the other two were wrong. The experiment consisted of 18 comparisons (i.e., each individual had to do the same thing 18 times), all similar to the one presented in Figure 5.2.

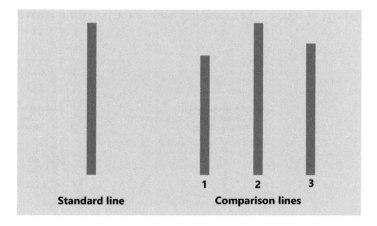

Standard line   **1   2   3**
                      Comparison lines

Figure 5.2 Example of an Asch line judgment trial: which of the three lines matches the standard line?

The participants were asked to announce their judgment publicly, one-by-one, and in the order in which they were seated.

All participants *except one* were informed beforehand by the experimenter about the true purpose of the experiment. They were instructed to respond on certain trails with wrong and unanimous judgments. They were the actors, so to speak, and they formed the majority. The participant who was not instructed beforehand, and who was the subject of Asch's investigation, was therefore not aware of the nature of the experiment.

A consistent observation of the line judgment experiments was that the subjects of the investigation tended to conform to the opinions of the majority—even though this majority view was clearly wrong (Asch, 1956, 1961). Specifically, in 37% of the trials, subjects conformed to the wrong estimates given by the majority group. Clearly, this means that people did not always follow the majority, for still in around 63% of the estimates the subjects were correct and hence relied on their own independent judgment. Nevertheless, these findings reveal the power of conformity in this line judgment setting, because if a majority states that a certain line is correct, say line (1), there is a much higher chance that the subject will take that line (1) as the correct line instead of line (2) or (3)—compared with the counterfactual situation in which the majority stated that line (2) or (3) was correct. In a control group, in which subjects did *not* know the judgments of others, subjects made errors in less than 1% of the comparisons. Taken together, these findings suggest that the judgments of subjects can be influenced by the majority opinion—even when the majority express false beliefs.

Image 5.2 Are people influenced by the opinions of other people when they have to estimate the length of a line?

In the decades after Asch conducted his line judgment experiments these have been replicated by other researchers many times—in different societies, cultures, groups and time-periods, using different populations and procedures. The overall finding of these studies confirms what Asch had reported in the 1950s, namely that there is a tendency for subjects to conform to the misjudgments of the majority group (Bond & Smith, 1996). Thus, even when it comes down to such a simple task, namely to judge the length of a line, which subjects do without errors if they are on their own, when being exposed to the judgments of others subjects tend to conform to this majority belief. Based on this extensive empirical evidence, coming from a myriad of sources, we can speak of a stylized fact of *conformity in judgment* to the majority group in small-scale settings:

STYLIZED FACT 5.2

Conformity in judgments
There is a tendency of people to conform to the publicly revealed judgment of the majority group in small-scale settings, even when this majority judgment is false.

The Asch studies revealed how people conform to cultures that prevail in microscopically small settings such as the laboratory. Do these patterns of opinion conformity also exist outside the laboratory setting, such as in the family, in organizations and neighborhoods? Do they also emerge with respect to opinions other than line judgments? To what extent are cultural opinions transmitted? These questions on culture are key for sociologists. Let's review empirical findings on cultural transmission in three areas of research: (1) *family sociology*, (2) *sociology of youth* and (3) *sociology of media and communication*.

In family sociology, scholars study how opinions—and corresponding behavior—are transmitted from parents to their children. The guiding proposition is called *parental socialization* or *parental transmission*, and it posits that children tend to conform to the opinions and behaviors of their parents. There is strong evidence supporting this proposition. Specifically, extensive research has shown that children tend to conform to parents' beliefs (Vollebergh, Iedema, & Raaijmakers, 2001), family values (Yi, Chang, & Chang, 2004), political preferences (Jennings, 1984; Jennings & Niemi, 1968; Jennings, Stoker, & Bowers, 2009; Nieuwbeerta & Wittebrood, 1995), gender roles (Moen, Erickson, & Dempster-McClain, 1997; O'Bryan, Fishbein, & Ritchey, 2004), ethnic identity (Casey & Dustmann, 2010; Hughes et al., 2006), ethnocentrism (Duriez & Soenens, 2009; Epstein & Komorita, 1966) and substance use (Bantle & Haisken-DeNew, 2002; Chassin et al., 2008; Kandel & Wu, 1995; Webb & Baer, 1995).

Let's consider one study in more depth. In 2012, Dohmen and co-authors published the results of a study on parental transmission in Germany (Dohmen, Falk, Huffman, & Sunde, 2012). They used the 2003 data from the German Socio-Economic Panel Study, a nationally representative survey which contained interviews with over 3,000 parents and their children. Parents and children were interviewed separately, to avoid the risk that they would affect each other's answers. Also, the survey did not only include young children or teenagers; the average age of the child was 25 years and many were not living at home anymore.

The researchers were interested in whether social trust may be transmitted from parents to their children. Therefore, they asked the following:

> Subjects were asked to indicate on a four-point scale to what extent they agree or disagree with the following statements: (1) In general, one can trust people. (2) These days you cannot rely on anybody else. (3) When dealing with strangers, it is better to be careful before you trust them. The four answer categories were labelled: strongly agree, agree somewhat, disagree somewhat, strongly disagree.
>
> (Dohmen et al., 2012)

The researchers collected the answers of the parents and their children on the trust question. Then they examined how strongly these attitudes are associated. The findings for the mothers and their children are presented in Figure 5.3. As you can see, there is a strong positive correlation between the two: when mothers have more trustful attitudes, their children have more trustful attitudes as well. Mothers who show low levels of trust, who think you should be careful when dealing with strangers for example, have children with lower levels of trust. The results for the fathers and their children are very similar. The study by Dohmen et al. (2012) nicely illustrates how strong intergenerational transmission is. And, similar to the Asch experiment, this study—as well as other research on parental transmission—shows that there is conformity, but also that there are individual deviations from this overall tendency. Importantly, however, these deviations from the general pattern do not refute the idea of parental transmission. The *parental transmission* proposition does not state that each child exactly copies their parents. Rather the proposition states that there is a general *tendency* towards transmission from parent to child—and this is exactly what is found in family sociology.

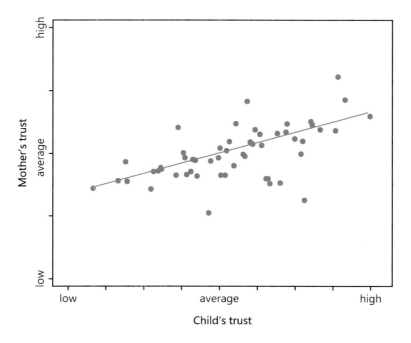

Figure 5.3 Mother–child transmission of trust attitudes in Germany.
Source: Dohmen et al., 2012.

In sociology of youth, the *peer transmission* proposition states that students conform to the opinions and behavior of their peers. This proposition has often been tested with experimental data, as well as with panel data in which youth were followed over time. The evidence generally supports the peer transmission proposition (Veenstra, Dijkstra, & Kreager, 2018). For example, it has been found that students conform to their peers' smoking behavior (Kobus, 2003; Mercken, Snijders, Steglich, Vartiainen, & De Vries, 2010; Steglich, Sinclair, Holliday, & Moore, 2012), alcohol consumption (Borsari & Carey, 2001), delinquent activities (Knecht, Snijders, Baerveldt, Steglich, & Raub, 2010; Weerman, 2011) and drug use (Kirke, 2004). There is also evidence to suggest that eating problems and body image concerns are transmitted by peers (Hutchinson & Rapee, 2007), as well as depression and negative thinking (Brechwald & Prinstein, 2011; Giletta et al., 2012; Van Zalk, Kerr, Branje, Stattin, & Meeus, 2010). Other studies show that students conform to their peers' academic motivations and achievements (Wentzel, Barry, & Caldwell, 2004) and to problematic school behavior (Geven, Weesie, & Van Tubergen, 2013). It has also been found that students conform to the interethnic attitudes of their peers (Poteat, Espelage, & Green, 2007).

The sociology of media and communication examines to what extent media messages impact people's opinions and behavior. The origins of speculations about media effects—broadly conceived—can be traced to the German writer Johann Wolfgang von Goethe in the 18th century. At age 24, he wrote his first novel, *Die Leiden des Jungen Werther* (The sorrows of young Werther). The book, published in 1774, is about a young man, Werther, who falls in love with Lotte. Much to his regret, however, Lotte marries another man. Not being able to accept that his love was unattainable, at the end of the book Werther commits suicide with a pistol. The book became very popular in Europe and at once Goethe manifested himself as a famous writer. The shock was immense when stories appeared suggesting that people imitated Werther's suicide. Confronted with this news, Goethe remarked that:

> My friends … thought that they must transform poetry into reality, imitate a novel like this in real life and, in any case, shoot themselves; and what occurred at first among a few took place later among the general public.
>
> (Phillips, 1974)

In literature on media, the guiding idea on conformity is called the *media transmission* proposition, which posits that people conform to the opinions and behavior expressed in media. Research findings generally support this proposition—indeed, advertisements are based on it. But does it go so far as to even affect suicide? At the time of Goethe, the evidence for such a media effect was purely anecdotal. A century later, the French sociologist Tarde published *The Laws of Imitation* (Tarde, 1903 [1890]) in which he advocated this idea and argued that media have the potential to have such detrimental consequences. A few years later, Durkheim argued against this idea of media imitation effects in *Suicide* (Durkheim, 1961 [1897]). Both authors, however, did not provide strong empirical evidence in favor of their own claims and against alternative interpretations.

It was the publication of an article in 1974, in the scientific journal *American Sociological Review* by sociologist David Phillips, that resulted in a breakthrough (Phillips, 1974). Phillips collected information on the publication of suicides in the major newspapers in Britain and the United States in the period 1947–1968. He found that, directly after a suicide story had been publicized in the newspaper, the suicide rate in the nation increased. Phillips named this the Werther effect after Goethe's novel.

Since the famous publication of Phillips in 1974, more than 100 studies have been done on the Werther effect. These follow-up studies have been conducted in other countries besides

Image 5.3 Did the publication of Goethe's novel *The Sorrow of the Young Werther* in 1774 result in a rise in suicide in Europe?

Britain and the US, they have used more advanced methodologies and techniques, they have used not only newspapers and books, but also television, film and music, and they have considered both completed and attempted suicides (Gould, 2001; Phillips, 1979; Pirkis, 2009; Pirkis, Burgess, Francis, Blood, & Jolley, 2006; Stack, 2005). The verdict of this massive amount of replication research is that there is ample evidence in favor of the Werther effect. Goethe was probably right in his concern that the publication of his novel had resulted in more suicides. And Durkheim was wrong in that he thought that such mass media influence of publicized suicide does not exist. Let's summarize this **Werther effect** as a stylized fact.

STYLIZED FACT 5.3

Werther effect
Suicides reported in mass media increase the likelihood of actual suicides.

The study on the Werther effect is exemplary of research on the transmission of messages, images and stories portrayed in the media to its audience. In very different areas of research, communication scientists, psychologists and sociologists find that people copy the opinions and corresponding behavior of people portrayed in the media. The media transmission proposition is generally supported by empirical evidence. The Werther effect is a specific case of this more general media transmission proposition.

Taken together, there is an impressive amount of empirical sociological research that provides evidence to suggest that, as a general tendency, people tend to conform to the opinions and behavior of others in their environment. This pattern of conformity is observed in sociology of the family (*parental transmission* proposition), sociology of youth (*peer transmission* proposition) and sociology of media and communication (*media transmission* proposition). The findings of these three different research areas can therefore be taken together and subsumed under the pattern of conformity. Figure 5.4 summarizes these findings.

There exists persuasive evidence for this pattern of conformity in other areas of research as well. Generally speaking, people tend to conform to the opinions and behavior of other actors in their direct environment, like their spouse, co-workers and so forth (Katz & Lazarsfeld,

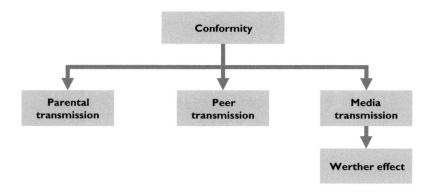

Figure 5.4 Overview of findings on conformity in three areas of research.

1955; Lazarsfeld, Berelson, & Gaudet, 1948). This empirical pattern has been given different names, such as *cultural transmission* (Henrich, 2001), *imitation* (Machiavelli, 2010 [1514]; Tarde, 1903 [1890]), *social contagion* (Christakis & Fowler, 2013) and *conformity* (Cialdini & Goldstein, 2004). Because the empirical evidence suggesting this particular regularity is so strong, we can summarize it as a stylized fact called *conformity* (Cialdini & Goldstein, 2004):

STYLIZED FACT 5.4

Conformity
There is a general human tendency to conform to the opinions and behavior of actors in their social environment.

These patterns help us to understand why cultural opinions and behaviors typically "cluster" within social contexts. Why people often have the same beliefs and values as their friends have. Why parents and children share similar cultural beliefs and practices. Why citizens living in the same country tend to share core cultural views. Why cultures differ across families, peer groups and countries. And, therefore, why, for example, people in Sweden and Uganda tend to have such different cultures.

Conformity is a specific *case* of what is called **social influence** more generally. Social influence refers to the process by which people's opinions and behavior are affected by others. This is in contrast to situations in which people are developing their opinions and behavior independently, i.e., situations in which people's opinions and behavior are not dependent on those of others. In the case of conformity, people adjust their opinions and behavior in such a way that their opinions and behavior become more similar to those of others. Conformity is therefore also called **positive social influence** (Flache et al., 2017). There can also be cases of **negative social influence**, which means that people's opinions and behavior develop in the opposite direction to the opinions and behavior of other actors in their environment. In Chapter 6 (Norms), we will review cases in which this happens. The most common pattern, however, is that of conformity—deviations from this empirical pattern occur less frequently.

social influence process by which people's opinions and behavior are affected by others.

positive social influence process by which people's opinions and behavior develop in the same direction as the opinions and behavior of other actors in their environment.

negative social influence process by which people's opinions and behavior develop in the opposite direction to the opinions and behavior of other actors in their environment.

5.4 Informational and normative social influence

Now that we have seen that conformity is a social pattern that we come across in various social settings—such as the family, school and media—we may wonder *why* this pattern is so robust and widespread? How can we explain these stylized empirical findings? Why do subjects in the Asch experiment conform to the opinions of the other actors, even when false? Why do sociologists observe more generally that people imitate the opinions and behavior of others in their social environment? It is time to take a closer look at this social context effect and to try to understand *why* positive social influence happens (see Figure 5.5).

Culture

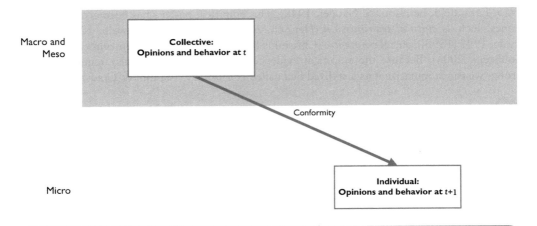

Macro and
Meso

Micro

Figure 5.5 Social context effect: what explains conformity?

To answer this question, we can go back to Asch's line judgment experiments. After the experiments Asch interviewed his subjects, asking them *why* they conformed to the majority group and gave wrong estimates (Asch, 1956, 1961). Roughly speaking, the participants gave two kinds of answers. One group of subjects answered that they thought they must have misperceived the length of the line in some way, and hence followed the group opinion. Therefore they believed the group was right and their own judgment was wrong. The other group of subjects, however, believed they had it right personally, hence they did not agree with the group. Nevertheless, they conformed to the group judgment—so they adjusted their behavior—because they feared social disapproval when they stated their own opinions publicly.

In a follow-up study to the work of Asch, Deutsch and Gerard argued that these two kinds of responses by the subjects of the Asch experiment reflect two mechanisms which can explain positive social influence (Deutsch & Gerard, 1955). First, there is what they call **informational social influence**, which they defined as "influence to accept information obtained from another as evidence about reality". Second, there is **normative social influence**, which is "influence to conform to the positive expectations of another". This kind of influence is based on the desire to receive *social approval* from peers, and to avoid social sanctions and punishment from the group when not conforming to the social norms. Thus, in the Asch experiment, subjects who believed they were right and others were wrong might have decided to conform to the beliefs of others and thereby avoid possible negative sanctions of the others in the classroom. In this

informational social influence influence to accept information obtained from another as evidence about reality.

normative social influence influence to conform to the positive expectations of another.

case, beliefs about reality—factual statements—are normative, i.e., statements in the form of "X is true" are not neutral but normative and not agreeing with them can have social consequences. Sociologists have developed the *social control theory* around this idea and applied it to numerous social phenomena. In Chapter 6 (Norms) I will explore this social control theory in more detail.

In this chapter I will elaborate on the first mechanism, i.e., *informational social influence*. According to this mechanism, people conform to others' opinions and behavior because they want to be *accurate* in their opinions. The opinions and behavior of others is used as a source of information about what is true and false, possible and impossible, and this piece of information can supplement, or even correct, the private beliefs people have. Getting accurate information about nature and social life is often of key importance and the human motivation for accuracy is assumed to underlie informational social influence (Cialdini, 2007; Cialdini & Goldstein, 2004; Deutsch & Gerard, 1955). People try to acquire more information and more accurate opinions because it is rewarding.

Hence, some subjects in the Asch experiment adjusted their own opinion to that of the majority because they thought the majority must have had it right. And, indeed, in follow-up studies, when subjects did *not* have to publicly announce their beliefs but instead were instructed to write down their judgments anonymously (so no sanctions would occur as they did not have to reveal their deviant opinion), there was *still* evidence that people conformed to the opinions of the majority, although less so compared with the original condition (Campbell & Fairey, 1989; Deutsch & Gerard, 1955). Apparently, both informational and normative social influence explain the conformity in the line judgment experiments.

In this textbook I will outline that this *informational social influence* mechanism belongs to the more comprehensive *social learning theory*. However, it should be noted that there exists both a broad and a narrow conception of social learning theory in the literature. In the *broad* version, social learning theory is about how people learn from and imitate others in their environment, via rewards and punishments. People acquire their beliefs, values, norms and copy the behavior of socializing agents in a process of learning via observations and imitation, rewards and punishments, things that work out well and others that do not. If children do not copy the behavior of their parents this might result in a sanction, so the next time the child does conform to the wishes of their parent. That is social learning, broadly conceived.

The problem with this version is that it does not disentangle the two different mechanisms of conformity, namely informational and normative social influence. For that reason, in this textbook, I will use a *narrow* version of social learning theory, in order to better differentiate between the two different mechanisms that are at work. When I talk about social learning theory, I have in mind only the informational social influence. Figure 5.6 summarizes the two different mechanisms which can explain positive social influence.

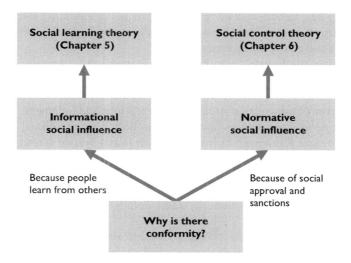

Figure 5.6 Two mechanisms that explain conformity.

5.5 Social learning theory

In *social learning theory*, it is stated that learning from others is motivated by the idea of getting a more accurate picture of reality (Bandura & McClelland, 1977). Social learning is contrasted with **individual learning**, which refers to the things people try out themselves and figure out on their own, without being influenced by others. Social learning can be a particularly attractive strategy when people are confronted with uncertain situations, i.e., when they have little idea of what to do or how things work, and then rely on the

individual learning things people try out themselves, without being influenced by others.

opinions and behavior of others instead of individual learning. Social learning theory states that people tend to conform to opinions of others in their environment because people learn from others—which makes people more similar.

Social learning theory makes a distinction between *direct* and *observational* social learning. Direct social learning happens when people learn via communication with others. People share their opinions, they exchange facts and arguments. Children can learn from their parents about the risks of smoking and drinking, for example, when their parents inform them about these risks. But social learning not only occurs via such direct transmission of opinions. People also learn when they *observe* the behavior of others. The behavior of other people—parents, peers and so forth—reveals information about what is a wise thing to do and about the presumed underlying opinions of others as well (Bikhchandani, Hirshleifer, & Welch, 1992, 1998). In Merton's classic bank-run case, for example, people copy the behavior of other people (namely to withdraw their money) even if they do not talk to other people—just seeing other people withdrawing their money can be a sufficient signal to believe that the bank will go bankrupt.

Contemporary research shows that direct and observational social learning can operate in different ways, corresponding to different parts of the human brain. The *dual-process model* considers two modes of social learning (Evans, 2008; Kahneman, 2003, 2011; Kroneberg, Yaish, & Stocké, 2010; Miles, Charron-Chénier, & Schleifer, 2019; Vaisey, 2009). First, people can process information they acquire from their social environment in a highly rational way. This happens largely deliberately, consciously and slowly. It is the part of human cognition that can be characterized as *rational*, i.e., it is, for example, able to process large chunks of information, to consider all evidence that is available, to think abstractly, to make logical deductions and to reason statistically.

The second way the human brain processes information is very different: it happens quickly, automatically and largely unconsciously. This is the more *irrational, intuitive* part of the human brain, which is associative, relies on rules of thumb, simple heuristics and framing, and is prone to errors of information processing, perceptions and judgment. The dual-process model posits that people can process information in both a more rational and a more irrational way. Psychologist Kahneman calls these *System II* and *System I*, respectively. Evidence suggests that, most of the time, System I is at work—the more irrational, intuitive part of the human brain. System I takes less energy than System II and using this intuitive, unconscious part of the brain works out pretty well. However, it also means that people typically tend to process information not very systematically and carefully and are therefore prone to cognitive errors (Kahneman, 2011).

In research elaborating on the classic social learning theory, scholars have developed propositions on so-called **social learning biases** (Mesoudi, 2011). Such biases emerge when the typical process of social learning is somehow distorted or biased. This can happen, for example, if people copy the opinions of some *actors* in the social

social learning biases conditions that modify the degree of conformity.

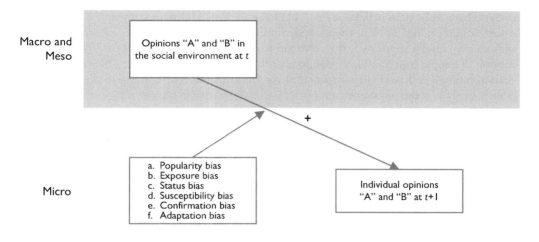

Opinions "A" and "B" in the social environment at t

Figure 5.7 Social learning biases: conditions that affect tendency to copy opinions.

context more strongly than those of other actors in their environment. Or when certain *opinions* in the environment are more likely to be copied than other opinions. These biases can be the result of System II errors, but, in some cases, they also emerge when System I is at work.

Such social learning biases moderate the default social learning process. Figure 5.7 illustrates how this works, using a simplified situation in which the social context consists of just two opinions, namely "A" and "B". These can be opinions like "more refugees should be accepted in our country," or "climate change is not caused by humans" and so forth. Clearly, the standard expectation of social learning theory is that people conform. Thus, people who are exposed to opinions "A" and "B" are more likely to adopt those opinions, as compared with the counterfactual situation in which the social context consists of other opinions, say "C" and "D." But, on top of this general conformity tendency, social learning biases may operate. They can be seen as *moderating* conditions that affect this general tendency to copy certain opinions from the social environment; for example, why opinion "A" is copied more often than opinion "B" although both opinions "A" and "B" are present in the environment.

Let's review each social learning bias one by one.

Popularity bias

One condition that affects the degree of conformity to a certain opinion that exists in the social environment is how popular that opinion is in that social environment. The popularity of an opinion is indicated by the number of supporters of that opinion. The ***popularity bias*** proposition, also known as the ***bandwagon effect***, states that people's tendency to copy opinions from their social environment is positively affected by the number of supporters for a certain opinion (Cialdini, 2007). When a certain opinion receives much support in the population, other people will take this popularity as a signal of "quality," of being the "right" or "accurate" opinion. The more popular a certain opinion, the more likely it will be adopted by yet others.

In the most simple version of this proposition (which we may call the *popularity effect*), this means that when people live in a social context in which 20% of the population believe in "A," they will be more likely to also believe in "A" than if they had been in another context where only 10% believe in "A." Let's say the probability of copying "A" is 20% in the first condition and 10% in the second. Similarly, if "A" and "B" are opposite opinions, and both are equally supported, then one can expect that each opinion has a 50% chance of adoption. If people copy randomly opinions of their environment, then the chance of copying a certain opinion is directly proportional to the frequency of that opinion in the population (Table 5.1). This is the *popularity effect*.

Table 5.1 Popularity biases: popularity effect and majority effect.

Social context	Belief population	Frequency belief "A"	Social learning	
			Popularity effect	Majority effect
1	AAAA	100%	P(A) = 1	P(A) = 1
2	AABB	50%	P(A) = 0.5	P(A) = 0.5
3	AAAB	75%	P(A) = 0.75	P(A) > 0.75

Other versions of the popularity bias proposition also exist. One of these is what we can call the *majority effect*. According to this version, opinions that receive majority support are copied *disproportionately* more often (Mesoudi, 2011). Thus, when a certain opinion is shared by more than 50% of the population—say 75%—the chance that others adopt this opinion as well is not 75%—as in the simple *popularity effect*—but more than 75% (Table 5.1). In this view, majority opinions are not only attractive because they are supported by many—these opinions get an attractiveness bonus on top of that.

The popularity bias proposition has also been applied to observational social learning. When a group of people in the environment does something in the same way, it becomes what is called **social proof** (Cialdini, 2007). What the crowd does contains a certain clue, it reveals an opinion about what is a wise thing to do in a certain setting. Even when people do not speak to others, or exchange information in other direct ways, they nevertheless take the behavior of a group of people as information about what it is wise to do. And when *many* people act in the same way, this makes us believe that what they do is the right thing to do, even though we don't know why. In particular, when there is little time for people to make a decision on their own, but it is important to do something, people often follow the behavior of others, for example if fire breaks out and people have to find their way to the exit doors.

social proof the "evidence" individuals perceive which arises when a group of people in the environment does something in the same way.

Exposure bias

The second social learning bias considers people's degree of *exposure* to certain opinions in the social environment. The ***exposure bias*** proposition states that the more strongly people are exposed to a certain opinion in the population, the more likely they are to conform to that opinion. This proposition is important because people are not equally exposed to all opinions in the population. If 20% of the population supports opinion "A," but individuals are never exposed to that opinion, they will be unlikely to learn this opinion from others. Learning from others is thus conditional upon the degree of exposure to opinions, their *visibility* (Friedkin, 1998) and *observability* (Rogers, 2010).

The *exposure bias* can be observed in many social contexts. Adolescents learn from what their peers in school are doing, but they interact with some peers in school more than with others. They learn most from their friends, with whom they interact most, and less so from other peers in school that they hardly meet. This is one of the reasons why adolescents are strongly affected by the opinions of their friends, but not so much, or not at all, by other peers in their environment (Veenstra et al., 2018). Similarly, children learn from their parents, but they do so more strongly when parents and children frequently interact. The degree to which children adopt the opinions of their parents is therefore a direct function of how strongly children are exposed to the opinions of their parents. For example, if children of divorced parents are raised by their mother and hardly see their father, they will be more strongly exposed to the opinions of the mother than to those of the father and, as a result, will adopt mother's opinions more strongly than father's. Likewise, people are affected by what they see on TV and on the Internet, but this conformity depends on how many hours they spend watching TV or browsing the Internet, and the content thereof as well.

Status bias

Opinions expressed in the social environment of the individual come from different actors. They may be parents, peers, neighbors and colleagues, but also police officers, celebrities, politicians and so forth. The status of these persons may not be seen as equal and social learning may depend on the status position of each actor. The *status bias* proposition states that people conform more strongly to a certain opinion when higher status figures support that opinion (as compared with status figures not supporting it). The higher people perceive the status of someone else to be, the more likely it is that they will adopt the opinions of that person.

Status is not an objective characteristic, however, but rather something people perceive subjectively. Moreover, two people may disagree on the criteria to judge someone's status. What, exactly, determines status may therefore differ from person to person.

For some, *authority* and *expertise* count as criteria for status. If that is the case, then those people may rely on the opinions of authority figures and experts. If an expert in a certain field supports opinion "A" and not "B," whereas a layperson supports "B" and not "A," then the *status bias* proposition states that people will tend to conform to opinion "A" rather than "B." People can place great confidence in experts and authority persons having more accurate knowledge (Cialdini, 2007). For this reason, children often trust the opinions of their parents more than the opinions of other people (up to a certain age) and people pay for consulting professionals and experts, such as brokers and financial experts for example, to gain valuable information and knowledge.

Status may also be associated with *positive affect*. Thus, when people more strongly like another person, they will be more likely to copy their opinions. This process is typically seen among good friends: they are not only strongly exposed to the opinions of each other (exposure bias), but they also like each other (status bias), which means that they are very likely to conform to each other's opinions (Veenstra et al., 2018). But the same process happens also in wider circles, such that people conform their opinions to those of celebrities and public figures they personally like. When, for example, a president, CEO, famous soccer player, YouTube or Instagram influencer, singer or other well-known person publicly expresses their opinion, their supporters will be likely to conform to that opinion, indeed much more so than to opinions expressed by others in their social environment. Positive affect can also be related to the group to which someone belongs. In general, people have more favorable attitudes towards in-group members than to out-group members, which means that when confronted with opinions from in-group members or in-group sources, they will more strongly conform to these opinions than when the opinions are coming from out-group members or out-group sources (Druckman, Levendusky, & McLain, 2018; Greene, 2014; Kahan, Jenkins-Smith, & Braman, 2011; Kahan et al., 2012).

Susceptibility bias

Whether people copy a certain opinion is also related to how susceptible they are. According to the *susceptibility bias* proposition, the more strongly individuals in a certain social condition are susceptible ("open") to adopting opinions, the more likely it is that they will conform to the opinions in that social context. Susceptibility and openness can have different sources. It can be a highly *personal characteristic*; some people are highly unsure about themselves and about their own judgments. Their personal uncertainty and vulnerability results in more strongly relying on the opinions of others (on social learning) than other people do who are more self-confident and who use individual learning more strongly instead (Brechwald & Prinstein, 2011).

Susceptibility can also depend on the *uncertainty of the situation*. People are not always to the *same* degree uncertain about their opinions, about what to believe is true or false, for example. In some settings, people have fairly good knowledge about their environment and they have no need to learn from others—they trust their own opinions. In more uncertain conditions, however, about which people have little knowledge, people are more susceptible. For example, when people are on vacation in another country, they may not know how things work or what is the right thing to do. Or, when they have to make a judgment about a complex issue, about which they have little knowledge, they may feel uncertain about their own opinion. In such social conditions people are more susceptible to learning from others.

Some scholars argue that susceptibility may also be related to the *nature of the opinion*, making a difference between simple and complex contagion (Centola, 2010; Centola & Macy, 2007). Some opinions are about simple facts, such as "Madrid is the capital of Spain" and "this store opens at 9 am." If you don't know the capital of Spain, you may consult Wikipedia. In this case it makes a lot of sense to accept the information you retrieve from Wikipedia. Possibly, you also check with a friend who knows. But why ask more and more people about such simple facts? Getting the information from only one (or two) source(s) should be sufficient to adopt that opinion—in the same way you can get the flu by being infected by contact with a single "infected" person. We're highly susceptible to adopting opinions from our social environment that are about simple facts and factual statements. Only one or two contacts with an information source is sufficient to transmit the opinion. This is called **simple contagion**.

simple contagion diffusion of opinions that need few sources.

There are other types of opinions, however, to which we are not so easily susceptible to adopting. Consider, for example, the situation where Elise has a certain illness and current medication is not working very effectively. Then, a friend of Elise argues that she should try a new drug that has become available. The friend is very excited about this—but will Elise follow her opinion? Taking a new drug can be very risky and cause much harm. Elise probably wants to collect more opinions on this new drug—what are the experiences of other people who tried this new drug? What are doctors saying? Clearly, changing your opinion on a topic like this (i.e., from using current drugs to believing the new drug is better) is different from changing your opinion on what is the capital city of Spain. It is argued that for opinions that are more consequential and risky, people are less susceptible. One needs to receive social affirmation from not one (or two) source(s) but (many) more, before one adopts that opinion. This is called **complex contagion**.

complex contagion diffusion of opinions that need more sources.

Confirmation bias

The tendency of people to copy certain opinions can also be affected by the attractiveness of the *content* of these opinions. According to the **confirmation bias** proposition, people "seek and find confirmatory evidence in support of already existing beliefs and ignore or reinterpret disconfirming evidence" (Shermer, 2011). This type of cognitive bias has been studied for decades and overwhelming experimental evidence suggests that the confirmation bias is strong and occurs in all areas of social life (Nickerson, 1998). Once you have taken a position on an issue, your aim becomes to defend that position. This means that human beings tend to restrict their attention to a favored position or hypothesis, rather than exposing themselves to opposite ideas. Thus, confirmation bias results in *exposure bias* on purpose: people selectively expose themselves to those opinions—information, beliefs, attitudes, arguments—in their environment that are in line with their own opinions.

This pattern of selective exposure to similar opinions can be seen in media attention. For example, an experimental study (Iyengar & Hahn, 2009) showed that conservatives and Republicans in the US preferred to read news reports attributed to conservative/Republican news sources (Fox News) and to avoid liberal/Democratic news sources (CNN and NPR). Democrats and liberals exhibited exactly the opposite syndrome—dividing their attention equally between CNN and NPR, but avoiding Fox News. The contemporary social media landscape suggests the same pattern. Ideologically different political bloggers in the US hardly communicate with each other online (Adamic & Glance, 2005); similarly, Twitter users in the US predominantly follow and retweet within their own political affiliation (Garimella & Weber, 2017); and climate skeptics and non-skeptics blog separately (Elgesem, Steskal, & Diakopoulos, 2015; Häussler, 2017). News consumption of Facebook users around Brexit in the UK revealed the formation of echo chambers (Del Vicario, Zollo, Caldarelli, Scala, & Quattrociocchi, 2017) and Facebook users are segregated into consuming either scientific or conspiracy news (Del Vicario et al., 2016). These patterns of online segregation are partly due to social media algorithms (suggesting like-minded pages) and, more strongly, they are caused by selective self-exposure, whereby users and organizations seek to confirm their initial views and prefer to connect to like-minded pages (Bakshy, Messing, & Adamic, 2015).

Confirmation bias also means that people tend to preferentially treat evidence supporting existing opinions. Cases that support their views are overweighted, whereas negative evidence is underweighted. People also see what they are looking for: they can see patterns for which they are looking, even when such patterns are not there in reality. A new opinion is generally regarded as more attractive when it is more in line with people's existing opinions (Rogers, 2010). New ideas that are seen as incompatible and implausible are dismissed more often than opinions that fit well with what people know already. The confirmation bias has been labeled the mother of all cognitive biases.

Adaptation bias

Scholars have also argued that some opinions are more attractive to adopt when these opinions are better adapted to the social context in which people are embedded (Boudon, 2001; Harris, 1989; Mesoudi, 2011). One can have the opinion that "cars are always slower than horses," but that opinion is not particularly useful because it is plainly false. One can believe that "Madrid is the capital of Italy," but if that opinion creates confusion each time you share it, then it appears more useful to drop it. Human beings prefer to adopt opinions that work better, that are more useful in a certain social context (Rogers, 2010). The *adaptation bias* proposition states that the more certain opinions are adapted to the social environment, more useful so to speak, the more likely it is that people will conform to those opinions.

This proposition thereby assumes that there are *good reasons* for people to adopt a certain opinion in a certain setting. Thus, given a set of available opinions "A" and "B," people more often adopt those opinions that appear the best, or most useful, to them given the material, social, political context they are in. This can be seen as an "evolutionary process" in which alternative opinions (values, beliefs, etc.) "compete" and those opinions that are most effective in a certain social condition are chosen (Inglehart & Welzel, 2005). This could mean that as social conditions change so people may change their opinions too.

*

In summary, social learning theory explains the human tendency to copy the opinions of actors in their social environment. Individuals learn from others. However, this copying tendency varies with certain conditions. Opinions are copied more often when they are popular, when people are strongly exposed to opinions, when opinions are expressed by high-status persons and in-group sources, when people are more susceptible, when opinions confirm existing opinions and when opinions are well-adapted to their context.

The social learning biases operate in System I and II. The adaptation bias proposition assumes rationality that is characteristic of System II. People rationally weigh the pros and cons of adopting certain opinions in a certain social context. But this kind of information processing is in itself costly and human beings often tend to shift to the more intuitive thinking System I. This gives rise to all sorts of irrationality, such as selectively searching for evidence that confirms our pre-existing opinions (confirmation bias) or relying on certain opinions just because they are expressed by a famous singer (status bias).

What happens when we consider all these social learning biases at the same time? In some cases they reinforce each other as they can work in the same direction. For example, if opinion "A" is very popular in the population, and high-status people like the president and celebrities equally express the same opinion "A," then it is very likely that those who have not yet adopted opinion "A" will do so. But social learning biases can also work in opposite directions. If opinion "A" is very popular in a population, but certain individuals in that population admire a celebrity who argues against "A," then two social learning biases (popularity bias and status bias) have opposite effects. In that case, the tendency to copy a certain opinion can be subject to conflicting forces.

5.6 Popularity of cultural products

Now that we have reviewed social learning theory and social learning biases, let's see how we can use these insights to understand the phenomenon with which we started this chapter, namely the puzzling success of *Harry Potter*. According to sociologists Salganik and Watts, it is conformity based on the mechanism of social learning that explains the success of the *Harry Potter* books—and which more generally drives the success and failure of books, movies, art products, music and songs (Salganik et al., 2006; Salganik & Watts, 2008).

Specifically, following the *popularity bias* proposition, they argued that people buy books that are popular. The reason people do so is that they are faced with uncertainty about the quality of the books. There are way too many books on the market for people to judge on their own before they make a decision and buy a book that is well-written, interesting, informative, exciting and so forth. Therefore, people look at the behavior of others, at what other people have bought, and from their behavior infer the quality of the product: the most popular books must be the best books. That is *social proof* at work.

Likewise, when people visit the Louvre in Paris, they have to make a decision as to which paintings to visit and which ones they don't want to see. As many people have no perfect information about the quality of each of the many paintings in the museum, they rely on the information and behavior of other people. They therefore tend to go to the most popular painting, the *Mona Lisa*, and when back at home they tell their friends they saw the *Mona Lisa*. This leads friends to also view the *Mona Lisa* and so on.

Thus, the cultural market, with its overwhelming number of books, songs, music and movies creates uncertainty among its consumers: which are the interesting books and which ones are not? Which songs are great and which ones are not worth listening to? When there are more than one million books on the market, individual learning is very costly and time-consuming. It is not an option to read all the reviews of books before you buy one. Hence, people tend to learn from what others have done or said and, in particular, people tend to go for the most popular ones. Therefore, Salganik and Watts argue that social learning theory could explain the inequality in the popularity of cultural products.

The question, however, is whether their explanation is supported by empirical evidence. To test their claims, they designed websites where people could download, for free, new (unknown) songs from unknown artists. One group was exposed to a website where they did not see what other visitors had done. This is the *independent condition*, i.e., the control group. The other visitors were in the *social influence condition*, i.e., the experimental group. In this social influence condition, visitors could see how many people before them had downloaded a certain song. The researchers created not one but eight websites for this social influence condition. Participants were randomly assigned to the website in the control group or to one of the eight websites in the experimental group. The visitors to the website could not see each other's names and could not communicate with each other. People who participated in the study remained anonymous, which means that the mechanism of normative social influence (social control) does not play a role.

The only type of social influence that could occur is informational and, more specifically, information based on observing the *behavior* of other people (i.e., the songs that were downloaded by visitors to the website). Figure 5.8 presents their design.

Salganik and Watts first examined what happened in the independent condition. They observed a ranking of songs in terms of popularity: some songs were often downloaded,

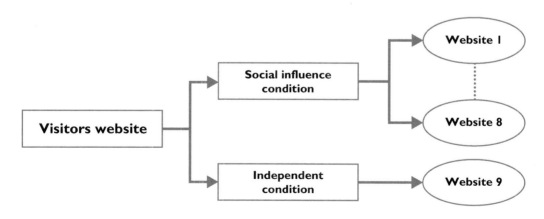

Figure 5.8 The Salganik-Watts study on success in cultural markets.
Source: Salganik et al., 2006.

others less so. Because visitors to this website downloaded the songs independently from what others had done, the scholars took this popularity ranking as an assessment of the quality of each song. When visitors liked a song, they would download it.

Subsequently, the researchers then examined whether this ranking (observed at the website with the independent condition) was also found on the eight websites on which visitors could see how often songs had been downloaded before them by other visitors. If it is only the quality of the song that determines success, its popularity, then that is what you would expect. However, it appeared that the ranking of the songs on the websites in the social influence condition was very different from the ranking in the independent condition. Indeed, the same song could be highly popular on one website, but end up in the middle on another website. Quality mattered only in so far that the worst evaluated songs never became the winners and that the best evaluated songs never ended lowest. But, other than that, quality seemed not to predict the success of a song.

What, then, can explain a song's popularity? In line with social learning theory and the *popularity bias* proposition, Salganik and Watts found that people were affected by what other people had chosen: when a song had been downloaded often, new visitors downloaded that song more often than other songs. As a result of that, the popular song became even more popular, attracting yet more people and so forth, a dynamic interplay between the individual and the social context, involving social context effects and complex aggregation. This social learning process, therefore, resulted in a positive feedback loop, in which popular songs received more and more attention.

Figure 5.9 illustrates this dynamic interplay between the individual and the social context. At t_0, the first visitor to the website (X_1) has no information about the songs from others as nobody has downloaded a song before her. She then downloads a song, S_1. As a result of this, the collective outcomes of the popularity of songs changes, as S_1 now becomes the most commonly downloaded song. The next visitor to the website (X_2) observes what the previous visitor has done and, from the behavior of the previous visitor, he infers that S_1 must be worth listening to, more so than the other songs. He will therefore decide to also listen to S_1 and this makes the song even more popular, and this positive feedback process will continue with the other visitors. So, what explained the success of a song? It appeared to be prior success. Success breeds success.

In many situations in which positive social influence processes occur, feedback effects exist. When the phenomena that are studied are related to some kind of *success*, like popularity,

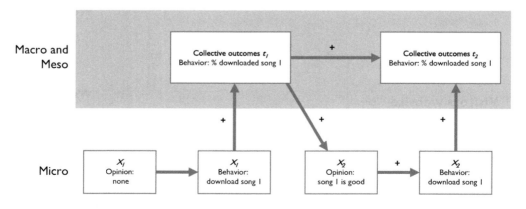

Figure 5.9 Social learning in cultural markets.

prestige, reputation or wealth, these positive feedback effects are called **cumulative advantages** or simply the **Matthew effect**, a term coined by Merton in 1968 (Merton, 1968, 1988) after Matthew 25:29: "For unto every one that hath shall be given, and he shall have abundance: but from him that hath not shall be taken even that which he hath."

> **cumulative advantage** (also **Matthew effect**) positive feedback process in which prior success increases likelihood of successive success.

The consequence of cumulative advantages can be dramatic at the collective level (DiPrete & Eirich, 2006). First, there is high *inequality in success*: some songs became very popular in the study and many, many songs had no or only a few downloads. Songs that have more supporters become yet more popular. It is a *winner-takes-all* social phenomenon, in which the distribution of supporters is far from normal. The outcome of the Salganik-Watts experimental study exactly matches the observations in real-life cultural markets, namely the huge inequality in success. On the website on which visitors could not see how often songs had been downloaded by others, the inequality in popularity was much smaller. In other words, social influence amplifies inequality and creates superstars such as Rowling and Da Vinci.

Second, exactly *which* song would become famous was largely *unpredictable* at the beginning of the experiment, precisely because of the positive feedback process. If on website "1" a song happened to have been downloaded a few times in the beginning, say eight times, it would attract the attention of others and become famous. If, however, the same song was not noticed in the early stages on website "2" and downloaded only two times on website "2", it would not become popular on that website (whereas it was on website "1"). Thus, Salganik and Watts suggest that some books, and cultural products more generally, can become highly popular because of social influence, even if they are of mediocre quality, and that highly popular ones can remain so for a longer time.

In their study on social learning, Sushil Bikhchandani, David Hirshleifer and Ivo Welch describe the following case which illustrates this process:

> In 1995, management gurus Michael Treacy and Fred Wiersema secretly purchased 50,000 copies of their business strategy book *The Discipline of Market Leaders* from stores across the nation. The stores they purchased from just happened to be the ones whose sales are monitored to select books for *The New York Times* bestseller list. Despite mediocre reviews, their book made the bestseller list. Subsequently, the book sold well enough to continue as a bestseller without further demand intervention by the authors. Presumably, being on a bestseller list helps a book sell more because consumers and reviewers learn from the actions of previous buyers.
>
> (Bikhchandani et al., 1998)

5.7 Diffusion of innovations

Social learning theory can also be useful to understand diffusions of innovations. An **innovation** is a new opinion, or some new practice or object, that is based on new opinions (knowledge), which is aimed to solve a certain problem (Rogers, 2010). Because innovations are *new* by definition, it also comes with uncertainty about its potential benefits and pitfalls, i.e., whether the innovation is an advantage or not over existing ideas, practices and objects. When adopting an innovation, people take a certain risk—they have to trust that the

> **innovation** a completely new belief, or some new practice or object, that is based on new beliefs (knowledge), which is aimed to solve a certain problem.

new opinion (and/or the object, tool, practice, technology) that is based on this knowledge is better than what they are used to. It is an example of complex contagion.

The literature on innovations is extensive and covers disciplines such as sociology, management and business science, economics, organizational theory and communication science (Rogers, 2010). In many areas, the diffusions and adoptions of innovations are studied. In particular, technological innovations are researched, such as the adoption of new medicines or mobile devices, but also many other ideas, practices and objects, such as new teaching methods and new scientific insights.

Each day, many new innovations are made, some of them are welcomed by citizens, consumers or organizations and they become popular, whereas other innovations do not. An important question in the literature is how innovations are diffused, i.e., how new ideas (and tools, practices and objects based on this novel knowledge) are transmitted from person to person in the population at large. Typical questions that are addressed in the literature on the **diffusion** of innovations are (Rogers, 2010):

diffusion the transmission and spread of something.

- How fast is the rate of adoption of the innovation in the population?
- Who are the first adopters, who are the followers?
- Why do some innovations become popular and others do not?

One of the first to write about the diffusion of innovations was the French sociologist Gabriel Tarde. The point of departure for Tarde was social learning theory and the idea that people tend to imitate other people because they learn from what others do (Tarde, 1903 [1890]). Importantly, however, Tarde speculated about the possible consequences of this learning tendency for collective outcomes. Tarde reasoned that the human tendency to imitate others should lead to a diffusion of ideas and innovations in society at large. Specifically, he maintained that the cumulative adoption of an innovation follows an *S-shaped curve*, as presented in Figure 5.10.

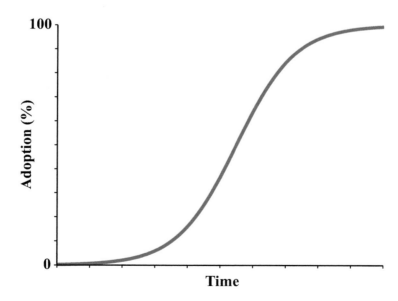

Figure 5.10 Tarde's speculation: the S-shaped curve of adoption of innovations.

In the words of Tarde, the S-shaped curve represents three stages of the diffusion process. *Tarde's diffusion theory* expects "Slow progress at the outset, fast progress of regular acceleration in the middle, before final gradual deceleration down to the end" (Tarde, 1903 [1890]). In other words, the diffusion process starts with a rather long period in which only a few people adopt the innovation. Then, after a certain period, a large group of people follows and many people in the population rapidly adopt the same innovation. At the end of the diffusion process the speed of adoption slows as it reaches the remaining group of people in the population. That is to say, the S-shaped curve of cumulative adopters comes down to a normal distribution of the number of new adopters through time: in the beginning a few new adopters, then in the middle the most newcomers and, at the end, again a few new adopters. Nowadays, the earliest group of adopters is called the *innovators* and they represent the first 2.5% of the individuals who adopt an innovation (Rogers, 2010). They are followed by the *early adopters* (13.5% of the population), the *early majority* (34%) and the *late majority* (34%). At the end come the *laggards* (16%), who are the last to adopt the innovation.

Tarde's intuition that diffusion follows an S-shaped curve could be formally modelled with a simple diffusion model (See the online Appendix for this chapter). The question is, however, if in reality diffusion does indeed follow this process. Is there empirical evidence for *Tarde's diffusion theory*? What do sociological observations say about this?

For decades Tarde's proposition did not receive much attention until two American sociologists, Ryan and Gross, came up with the first empirical test of it in 1943 (Ryan & Gross, 1943, 1950). What they studied was a particular technological innovation at that time, namely the adoption of hybrid corn in two agricultural communities in Iowa during the period 1926–1941. In 1926 it was a new seed, developed by agricultural scientists of Iowa State University, which could be used by farmers instead of the then widely used pollinated varieties. Hybrid seeds had some clear advantages over the seeds used traditionally. But at the same time it also required farmers to buy seeds each year instead of using their own crop to provide the seeds for each year's planting.

The adoption of this new corn was actively encouraged by both commercial and educational agencies, thus farmers were not only *exposed* to the new product (Ryan & Gross, 1943, 1950) but also certain *status figures* supported these products. Scientific reports provided yet another *status-based* source, as they showed that the new seed was superior to existing ones and these reports were used by salesmen to commercialize the product. Overall, the new seeds were thus also better. According to the *adaptation bias* proposition, it would therefore be more attractive for farmers to change their opinion and to use the new seeds. What may have gone against adopting the new seeds was *confirmation bias*: farmers selectively focusing on the drawbacks of the new seed and ignoring its advantages, tending to favor what they had been doing from generation to generation. And, possibly, some farmers may not have regarded scientists as high-status figures, but rather regarded them as outgroup members that they distrusted. Perhaps these farmers may have been more trusting of farmers they knew personally. In summary, the diffusion of innovations may be subject to a number of social learning biases.

What Ryan and Gross wanted to know was: did farmers adopt this innovation and, if so, how many did so over the passage of time? Did the adoption rate indeed follow the S-shaped curve, as predicted by Tarde?

In 1941, the researchers interviewed all the farmers in the two communities using structured questionnaires. They asked the farmers if they had decided to adopt hybrid corn and, if so, in what year that had been. They also asked about a number of other things, including the date on which they first heard about the new corn. In the end, they were able to analyze the year of adoption of 259 farmers. They found that only 2 out of the 259 farmers had not

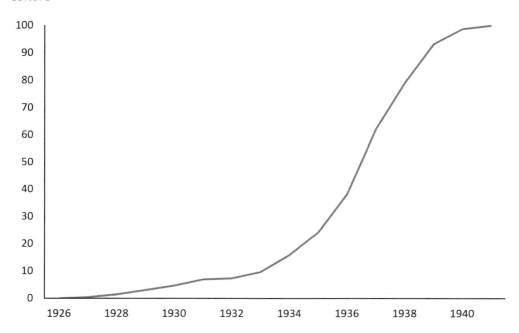

Figure 5.11 Percentage of adopters of hybrid corn in two Iowa
communities, 1926–1941.
Source: Ryan & Gross, 1943.

adopted the new hybrid corn in the period between 1928 and 1941. Moreover, they found strong evidence for Tarde's S-shaped diffusion hypothesis. Figure 5.11 shows the cumulative percentage of the farmers that adopted hybrid corn. It appears that in the earliest period (1926–1929) the new seeds were adopted by only a small fraction of the farmers, not more than 3%. They were the *innovators*. Then, the hybrid corn was adopted by a larger group of *followers* (around 13%), so that in the year 1934 15.8% used the new corn. From that moment, the adoption rate accelerated and within just four years (1934–1938) a large group of farmers (65%, i.e., the *early* and *late majority*) decided to adopt hybrid corn as well, and the cumulative adoption rate rose to 80%. In the final stage, the adoption rate lowered and almost all of the last 20% of the farmers (the *laggards*) finally switched to this new technique.

Ryan and Gross discovered that there was a certain delay between the time that farmers first got to hear about the hybrid corn and the time that they actually used this new seed. Hearing about the innovation diffuses like a *simple contagion*. But acquiring information is one thing, adopting the opinion is yet another. Effectively, this seems to concur well with the idea that adopting the new seed follows the pattern of *complex contagions*: farmers needed to have more "proof" before they decided to actually adopt the innovation. And when farmers were interested in the new corn and started to believe in it, they experimented with it on a smaller scale to find out for themselves if it worked. When interviewing the farmers about why they did not immediately adopt the innovation after they heard about it, they received the following typical explanations (Ryan & Gross, 1943):

- "I just figured I'd let the neighbors try it first."
- "A man doesn't try anything new right away."
- "Well, I had a good open-pollinated seed, so why change?"

Thus, the process of information diffusion in the Iowa communities happened first, and it was largely initiated by the commercial and educational agencies. Soon, the entire farm communities were aware of this new seed. But then, at first, most farmers did not adopt it—on average, the gap between the percentage of the population hearing about the innovation and the percentage accepting it was five years. The diffusion of the adoption was strongly affected by farmers actually seeing other farmers using it—waiting for *social proof*. Indeed, when asking the farmers who was the most influential source for them in deciding to adopt the new corn, 46% of them mentioned their neighbors and 32% salesmen. From neighbors who had adopted the corn, or at least who had experimented with it on a small scale, they could see that it worked and that the innovation was indeed very attractive and profitable.

These findings confirm Tarde's diffusion theory and social learning theory. Because the hybrid corn was superior to its existing alternative, it was attractive for farmers to adopt it and, after they learned about the new corn from others, it eventually replaced the old corn—despite counterforces such as confirmation bias. Thus, rather than being the result of individual trial-and-error learning, the hybrid corn diffused as a social process (Henrich, 2001). The classic work of Ryan and Gross stimulated work on the diffusion of innovations. In 1962, sociologist Rogers summarized the more than 500 studies that had appeared on the sociology of diffusion in his by now classic book *Diffusion of Innovations*, which was updated several times (Rogers, 2010). He concluded that many studies had found support for the S-shaped diffusion theory of Tarde.

In the past few decades, however, significant advances have been made in understanding diffusion processes (Valente, 2010; Young, 2009). In particular, scholars have begun to realize the importance of *social relations*. This theme will be covered in Part 3 of this book, but let us review some notions on the role of relations in studying diffusion—and processes of social influence more generally.

In the simple diffusion theory, such as the one proposed by Tarde, individuals learn from each other via direct contact. This is so-called *one-to-one* social transmission. But nowadays, and also at the time Ryan and Gross performed their study, mass media plays a role in at least disseminating the information about the innovation. Hence, this kind of *one-to-many* social influence is ignored in the simple diffusion theory. A large literature has emerged in the past decades in which both types of influences, one-to-many from mass media and one-to-one in personal interactions, are both taken into account (Bass, 1969, 2004; Katz & Lazarsfeld, 1955; Lazarsfeld et al., 1948; Mahajan, Muller, & Bass, 1990; Mesoudi, 2011; Watts & Dodds, 2007).

In more recent literature, scholars have also studied the *many-to-many* type of social influence on the Internet and on social media platforms in particular (Bail et al., 2018; Bond et al., 2012; Centola, 2010; Sunstein, 2017; Törnberg, 2018). One area of research is the diffusion of conspiracy theories, pseudoscience, anti-science, misinformation and fake stories (Del Vicario et al., 2016, 2017) and the emergence of echo chambers. Given people's inclination to seek confirmation for their opinions (*confirmation bias*), they selectively expose themselves to the information that supports their ideas (Bakshy et al., 2015; Iyengar & Hahn, 2009). It has been argued that, as a consequence, they become online-segregated into echo chambers, i.e., social media communities in which members only confirm each other's ideas (Bessi et al., 2015; Del Vicario et al., 2016; Halberstam & Knight, 2016; Jasny, Waggle, & Fisher, 2015). Echo chambers may increase polarization in opinions, such as with respect to climate change (Jasny et al., 2015), because people receive more arguments in line with their opinion (Sunstein, 2017) and people mainly see like-minded people expressing their approval for their opinion (*social proof*). The World Economic Forum stated in 2013 that digital misinformation is one of the major global risks. The many-to-many transmission on social media and the selective exposure to the information people seek to confirm their opinions could result in the emergence of collective misperceptions and opinion polarization (Sunstein, 2017). This could pose a challenge to having a well-informed population of citizens who demand that their governments solve problems that matter, and also to trusting science and evidence-based policy measures.

Another questionable assumption of the simple diffusion theory is that social interactions between any two persons in the population are random. Isn't it more plausible to think of social relations being clustered in certain groups and social networks? That people meet their friends more often than strangers? Furthermore, some people have many social ties and might be central in the community, while others might have fewer connections. In 1957, the sociologists Coleman, Katz and Menzel published a now classic work on diffusion, which shows the role of social networks in shaping the adoption of a new medicine (Coleman, Katz, & Menzel, 1957). Soon, many other studies followed on the impact of networks on diffusion (Granovetter, 1973; Valente, 1995). In Part 3, we will look more closely at social networks and groups.

5.8 Chapter resources

Key concepts

Self-fulfilling prophecy	Informational social	Simple contagion
Thomas and Thomas	influence	Complex contagion
Theorem	Normative social influence	Cumulative advantage
Social influence	Individual learning	Matthew effect
Positive social influence	Social learning biases	Innovation
Negative social influence	Social proof	Diffusion

Key theories and propositions

- Galatea effect
- Pygmalion effect
- Social learning theory
- Dual-process model

- Popularity bias
- Bandwagon effect
- Exposure bias
- Status bias

- Susceptibility bias
- Confirmation bias
- Adaptation bias
- Tarde's diffusion theory.

Key stylized facts

- Popularity of cultural products
- Conformity in judgments
- Werther effect
- Conformity.

Summary

- The success of cultural products is highly unequal; a few are very popular, most are hardly known.
- A self-fulfilling prophecy occurs when behavior based on false opinions (beliefs) about a situation cause that situation in the end. This can happen via self-expectations (Galatea effect) and expectations set by others (Pygmalion effect).

- The Thomas and Thomas Theorem says that people's opinions and perceptions of reality have behavioral consequences; "if men define situations as real, they are real in their consequences."
- Asch's classic laboratory experiments showed that there is conformity in line judgments in small-scale settings. The stylized pattern of conformity has likewise been found in sociology of the family (parental transmission), youth (peer transmission) and media (media transmission).
- There are two mechanisms which can explain conformity: people can learn from others (informational social influence) and people can conform to the expectations of others (normative social influence).
- Social learning is different from individual learning. Social learning can happen directly, but also via observing behavior.
- The dual-process model states that direct and observational social learning occurs in two ways: (a) rationally, consciously (System II) and (b) intuitively, unconsciously (System I).
- Social learning biases emerge in the process of social learning. Social learning theory includes the following biases: popularity bias, exposure bias, status bias, susceptibility bias, confirmation bias and adaptation bias.
- Popularity bias can give rise to cumulative advantage and the Matthew effect, which creates increasing inequalities in popularity of certain opinions, behaviors and products over time.
- Innovations are new opinions (practice, products) which aim to solve certain problems. Adopting such innovations may entail some risk. Research has confirmed Tarde's diffusion theory, i.e., such innovations attract few adopters in the beginning, then there is a sudden growth of adopters, while at the end the number of new adopters declines.

References

Adamic, L. A., & Glance, N. (2005). The political blogosphere and the 2004 US election: Divided they blog. Paper presented at the *Proceedings of the 3rd International Workshop on Link Discovery*, Chicago, IL.

Asch, S. E. (1956). Studies of independence and conformity: I. A minority of one against a unanimous majority. *Psychological Monographs: General and Applied*, 70(9), 1–70.

Asch, S. E. (1961). Effects of group pressure upon the modification and distortion of judgments. In M. Henle (Ed.), *Documents of gestalt psychology* (pp. 222–236). Berkeley: University of California Press.

Bail, C. A., Argyle, L. P., Brown, T. W., Bumpus, J. P., Chen, H., Hunzaker, M. B. F., Lee, J., Mann, M., Merhout, F., & Volfovsky, A. (2018). Exposure to opposing views on social media can increase political polarization. *PNAS*, 115(37), 9216–9221.

Bakshy, E., Messing, S., & Adamic, L. A. (2015). Exposure to ideologically diverse news and opinion on Facebook. *Science*, 348(6239), 1130–1132.

Bandura, A., & McClelland, D. C. (1977). *Social learning theory*. Englewood Cliffs, NJ: Prentice-Hall.

Bantle, C., & Haisken-DeNew, J. P. (2002). Smoke signals: The intergenerational transmission of smoking behavior. *DIW Berlin, German Institute for Economic Research, Discussion Paper No. 277*. Retrieved from www.diw.de/sixcms/detail.php?id=diw_02.c.226678.de

Bass, F. M. (1969). A new product growth for model consumer durables. *Management Science*, 15(5), 215–227.

Bass, F. M. (2004). Comments on "A new product growth for model consumer durables the bass model". *Management Science*, 50(12 supplement), 1833–1840.

Bessi, A., Coletto, M., Davidescu, G. A., Scala, A., Caldarelli, G., & Quattrociocchi, W. (2015). Science vs conspiracy: Collective narratives in the age of misinformation. *PloS ONE*, *10*(2), e0118093.

Biggs, M. (2009). Self-Fulfilling Prophecies. In P. Hedström & P. Bearman (Eds.), *The Oxford handbook of analytical sociology* (pp. 294–314). Oxford, UK: Oxford University Press.

Bikhchandani, S., Hirshleifer, D., & Welch, I. (1992). A theory of fads, fashion, custom, and cultural change as informational cascades. *Journal of Political Economy*, *100*(5), 992–1026.

Bikhchandani, S., Hirshleifer, D., & Welch, I. (1998). Learning from the behavior of others: Conformity, fads, and informational cascades. *The Journal of Economic Perspectives*, *12*(3), 151–170.

Blumer, H. (1958). Race prejudice as a sense of group position. *The Pacific Sociological Review*, *1*(1), 3–7.

Bond, R., & Smith, P. B. (1996). Culture and conformity: A meta-analysis of studies using Asch's (1952b, 1956) line judgment task. *Psychological Bulletin*, *119*(1), 111–137.

Bond, R. M., Fariss, C. J., Jones, J. J., Kramer, A. D., Marlow, C., Settle, J. E., & Fowler, J. H. (2012). A 61-million-person experiment in social influence and political mobilization. *Nature*, *489*(7415), 295–298.

Borsari, B., & Carey, K. B. (2001). Peer influences on college drinking: A review of the research. *Journal of Substance Abuse*, *13*(4), 391–424.

Boudon, R. (2001). *The origin of values: Essays in the sociology and philosophy of beliefs.* New Brunswick, NJ: Transaction Publishers.

Brechwald, W. A., & Prinstein, M. J. (2011). Beyond homophily: A decade of advances in understanding peer influence processes. *Journal of Research on Adolescence*, *21*(1), 166–179.

Campbell, J. D., & Fairey, P. J. (1989). Informational and normative routes to conformity: The effect of faction size as a function of norm extremity and attention to the stimulus. *Journal of Personality and Social Psychology*, *57*(3), 457–468.

Casey, T., & Dustmann, C. (2010). Immigrants' identity, economic outcomes and the transmission of identity across generations. *The Economic Journal*, *120*(542), F31–F51.

Centola, D. (2010). The spread of behavior in an online social network experiment. *Science*, *329*(5996), 1194–1197.

Centola, D., & Macy, M. (2007). Complex contagions and the weakness of long ties. *American Journal of Sociology*, *113*(3), 702–734.

Chassin, L., Presson, C., Seo, D., Sherman, S. J., Macy, J., Wirth, R., & Curran, P. (2008). Multiple trajectories of cigarette smoking and the intergenerational transmission of smoking: A multigenerational, longitudinal study of a midwestern community sample. *Health Psychology*, *27*(6), 819.

Christakis, N. A., & Fowler, J. H. (2013). Social contagion theory: Examining dynamic social networks and human behavior. *Statistics in Medicine*, *32*(4), 556–577.

Cialdini, R. B. (2007). *Influence: The psychology of persuasion.* New York, NY: Harper Collins Publishers.

Cialdini, R. B., & Goldstein, N. J. (2004). Social influence: Compliance and conformity. *Annual Review Psychology*, *55*, 591–621.

Coleman, J., Katz, E., & Menzel, H. (1957). The diffusion of an innovation among physicians. *Sociometry*, *20*(4), 253–270.

Del Vicario, M., Bessi, A., Zollo, F., Petroni, F., Scala, A., Caldarelli, G., Stanley, H.E., Quattrociocchi, W. (2016). The spreading of misinformation online. *PNAS*, *113*(3), 554–559.

Del Vicario, M., Zollo, F., Caldarelli, G., Scala, A., & Quattrociocchi, W. (2017). Mapping social dynamics on Facebook: The Brexit debate. *Social Networks*, *50*, 6–16.

Deutsch, M., & Gerard, H. B. (1955). A study of normative and informational social influences upon individual judgment. *The Journal of Abnormal and Social Psychology*, *51*(3), 629–636.

DiPrete, T. A., & Eirich, G. M. (2006). Cumulative advantage as a mechanism for inequality: A review of theoretical and empirical developments. *Annual Review of Sociology*, *32*, 271–297.

Dohmen, T., Falk, A., Huffman, D., & Sunde, U. (2012). The intergenerational transmission of risk and trust attitudes. *The Review of Economic Studies*, *79*(2), 645–677.

Druckman, J. N., Levendusky, M. S., & McLain, A. (2018). No need to watch: How the effects of partisan media can spread via interpersonal discussions. *American Journal of Political Science*, *62*(1), 99–112.

Duriez, B., & Soenens, B. (2009). The intergenerational transmission of racism: The role of right-wing authoritarianism and social dominance orientation. *Journal of Research in Personality*, *43*(5), 906–909.

Durkheim, E. (1961 [1897]). *Suicide*. New York, NY: Free Press.

Eden, D. (1984). Self-fulfilling prophecy as a management tool: Harnessing Pygmalion. *Academy of Management Review*, *9*(1), 64–73.

Eden, D. (1990). *Pygmalion in management: Productivity as a self-fulfilling prophecy*. Lexington, UK: Lexington Books.

Elgesem, D., Steskal, L., & Diakopoulos, N. (2015). Structure and content of the discourse on climate change in the blogosphere: The big picture. *Environmental Communication*, *9*(2), 169–188.

Epstein, R., & Komorita, S. (1966). Childhood prejudice as a function of parental ethnocentrism, punitiveness, and outgroup characteristics. *Journal of Personality and Social Psychology*, *3*(3), 259–264.

Evans, J. (2008). Dual-processing accounts of reasoning, judgment, and social cognition. *Annual Review of Psychology*, *59*(1), 255–278.

Flache, A., Mäs, M., Feliciani, T., Chattoe-Brown, E., Deffuant, G., Huet, S., & Lorenz, J. (2017). Models of social influence: Towards the next frontiers. *Journal of Artificial Societies & Social Simulation*, *20*(4). doi:10.18564/jasss.3521

Friedkin, N. E. (1998). *A structural theory of social influence*. Cambridge, UK: Cambridge University Press.

Garimella, V. R. K., & Weber, I. (2017). A long-term analysis of polarization on Twitter. Paper presented at the *Proceedings of the Eleventh International AAAI Conference on Web and Social Media*.

Geven, S., Weesie, J., & Van Tubergen, F. (2013). The influence of friends on adolescents' behavior problems at school: The role of ego, alter and dyadic characteristics. *Social Networks*, *35*(4), 583–592.

Giletta, M., Scholte, R. H., Prinstein, M. J., Engels, R. C., Rabaglietti, E., & Burk, W. J. (2012). Friendship context matters: Examining the domain specificity of alcohol and depression socialization among adolescents. *Journal of Abnormal Child Psychology*, *40*(7), 1027–1043.

Goffman, E. (1959). *The presentation of self in everyday life*. New York, NY: Doubleday.

Goffman, E. (1974). *Frame analysis: An essay on the organization of experience*. Harvard: Harvard University Press.

Goffman, E. (1986). *Stigma: Notes on the management of spoiled identity*. New York, NY: Simon and Schuster.

Gould, M. S. (2001). Suicide and the media. *Annals of the New York Academy of Sciences*, *932*(1), 200–224.

Granovetter, M. (1973). The strength of weak ties. *American Journal of Sociology*, *78*(6), 1360–1380.

Greene, J. (2014). *Moral tribes: Emotion, reason, and the gap between us and them*. London: Atlantic Books.

Halberstam, Y., & Knight, B. (2016). Homophily, group size, and the diffusion of political information in social networks: Evidence from Twitter. *Journal of Public Economics*, *143*, 73–88.

Hancock, D. J., Adler, A. L., & Côté, J. (2013). A proposed theoretical model to explain relative age effects in sport. *European Journal of Sport Science*, *13*(6), 630–637.

Harris, M. (1989). *Cows, pigs, wars, & witches: The riddles of culture*. New York, NY: Random House.

Häussler, T. (2017). Heating up the debate? Measuring fragmentation and polarisation in a German climate change hyperlink network. *Social Networks*, *54*, 303–313.

Henrich, J. (2001). Cultural transmission and the diffusion of innovations: Adoption dynamics indicate that biased cultural transmission is the predominate force in behavioral change. *American Anthropologist*, *103*(4), 992–1013.

Hughes, D., Rodriguez, J., Smith, E. P., Johnson, D. J., Stevenson, H. C., & Spicer, P. (2006). Parents' ethnic-racial socialization practices: A review of research and directions for future study. *Developmental Psychology*, *42*(5), 747–770.

Hutchinson, D. M., & Rapee, R. M. (2007). Do friends share similar body image and eating problems? The role of social networks and peer influences in early adolescence. *Behaviour Research and Therapy*, *45*(7), 1557–1577.

Inglehart, R., & Welzel, C. (2005). *Modernization, cultural change, and democracy: The human development sequence*. Cambridge, UK: Cambridge University Press.

Iyengar, S., & Hahn, K. (2009). Red media, blue media: Evidence of ideological selectivity in media use. *Journal of Communication*, *59*, 19–39.

Jasny, L., Waggle, J., & Fisher, D. R. (2015). An empirical examination of echo chambers in US climate policy networks. *Nature Climate Change*, *5*(8), 782–786.

Jennings, M. K. (1984). The intergenerational transfer of political ideologies in eight Western nations. *European Journal of Political Research*, *12*(3), 261–276.

Jennings, M. K., & Niemi, R. G. (1968). The transmission of political values from parent to child. *American Political Science Review*, *62*(1), 169–184.

Jennings, M. K., Stoker, L., & Bowers, J. (2009). Politics across generations: Family transmission reexamined. *The Journal of Politics*, *71*(3), 782–799.

Kahan, D. M., Jenkins-Smith, H., & Braman, D. (2011). Cultural cognition of scientific consensus. *Journal of Risk Research*, *14*(2), 147–174.

Kahan, D. M., Peters, E., Wittlin, M., Slovic, P., Ouellette, L. L., Braman, D., & Mandel, G. (2012). The polarizing impact of science literacy and numeracy on perceived climate change risks. *Nature Climate Change*, *2*(10), 732.

Kahneman, D. (2003). Maps of bounded rationality: Psychology for behavioral economics. *American Economic Review*, *93*(5), 1449–1475.

Kahneman, D. (2011). *Thinking, fast and slow*. New York, NY: Farrar, Straus and Groux.

Kandel, D. B., & Wu, P. (1995). The contributions of mothers and fathers to the intergenerational transmission of cigarette smoking in adolescence. *Journal of Research on Adolescence*, *5*(2), 225–252.

Katz, E., & Lazarsfeld, P. F. (1955). *Personal influence: The part played by people in the flow of mass communications*. New York, NY: Free Press.

Kirke, D. M. (2004). Chain reactions in adolescents' cigarette, alcohol and drug use: Similarity through peer influence or the patterning of ties in peer networks? *Social Networks*, *26*(1), 3–28.

Knecht, A., Snijders, T. A. B., Baerveldt, C., Steglich, C. E. G., & Raub, W. (2010). Friendship and delinquency: Selection and influence processes in early adolescence. *Social Development*, *19*(3), 494–514.

Kobus, K. (2003). Peers and adolescent smoking. *Addiction*, 98(s1), 37–55.

Kroneberg, C., Yaish, M., & Stocké, V. (2010). Norms and rationality in electoral participation and in the rescue of Jews in WWII: An application of the model of frame selection. *Rationality and Society*, 22(1), 3–36.

Lazarsfeld, P. F., Berelson, B., & Gaudet, H. (1948). *The people's choice: How the voter makes up his mind in a presidential campaign*. New York, NY: Columbia University Press.

Link, B. G., & Phelan, J. C. (2001). Conceptualizing stigma. *Annual Review of Sociology*, 27, 363–385.

Machiavelli, N. (2010 [1514]). *The prince*. Chicago, IL: University of Chicago Press.

Mahajan, V., Muller, E., & Bass, F. M. (1990). New product diffusion models in marketing: A review and directions for research. *The Journal of Marketing*, 54(1), 1–26.

Mercken, L., Snijders, T. A., Steglich, C., Vartiainen, E., & De Vries, H. (2010). Dynamics of adolescent friendship networks and smoking behavior. *Social Networks*, 32(1), 72–81.

Merton, R. K. (1948). The self-fulfilling prophecy. *The Antioch Review*, 8(2), 193–210.

Merton, R. K. (1968). The Matthew effect in science. *Science*, 159(3810), 56–63.

Merton, R. K. (1988). The Matthew effect in science, II: Cumulative advantage and the symbolism of intellectual property. *Isis*, 79(2), 606–623.

Mesoudi, A. (2011). *Cultural evolution: How darwinian theory can explain human culture and synthesize the social sciences*. Chicago, IL: University of Chicago Press.

Miles, A., Charron-Chénier, R., & Schleifer, C. (2019). Measuring automatic cognition: Advancing dual-process research in sociology. *American Sociological Review*, 84(2), 308–333.

Moen, P., Erickson, M. A., & Dempster-McClain, D. (1997). Their mother's daughters? The intergenerational transmission of gender attitudes in a world of changing roles. *Journal of Marriage and the Family*, 59(2), 281–293.

Musch, J., & Grondin, S. (2001). Unequal competition as an impediment to personal development: A review of the relative age effect in sport. *Developmental Review*, 21(2), 147–167.

Nickerson, R. S. (1998). Confirmation bias: A ubiquitous phenomenon in many guises. *Review of General Psychology*, 2(2), 175.

Nieuwbeerta, P., & Wittebrood, K. (1995). Intergenerational transmission of political party preference in the Netherlands. *Social Science Research*, 24(3), 243–261.

O'Bryan, M., Fishbein, H. D., & Ritchey, P. N. (2004). Intergenerational transmission of prejudice, sex role stereotyping, and intolerance. *Adolescence*, 39(155), 407–426.

Phillips, D. P. (1974). The influence of suggestion on suicide: Substantive and theoretical implications of the Werther effect. *American Sociological Review*, 39(3), 340–354.

Phillips, D. P. (1979). Suicide, motor vehicle fatalities, and the mass media: Evidence toward a theory of suggestion. *American Journal of Sociology*, 84(5), 1150–1174.

Pirkis, J. (2009). Suicide and the media. *Psychiatry*, 8(7), 269–271.

Pirkis, J., Burgess, P., Francis, C., Blood, W., & Jolley, D. (2006). The relationship between media reporting of suicide and actual suicide in Australia. *Social Science & Medicine*, 62(11), 2874–2886.

Poteat, V. P., Espelage, D. L., & Green, H. D., Jr. (2007). The socialization of dominance: Peer group contextual effects on homophobic and dominance attitudes. *Journal of Personality and Social Psychology*, 92(6), 1040–1050.

Rogers, E. M. (2010). *Diffusion of innovations*. New York, NY: Simon & Schuster Inc.

Rosenthal, R., & Jacobson, L. (1968). Pygmalion in the classroom. *The Urban Review*, 3(1), 16–20.

Ryan, B., & Gross, N. C. (1943). The diffusion of hybrid seed corn in two Iowa communities. *Rural Sociology*, 8(1), 15–24.

Ryan, B., & Gross, N. C. (1950). *Acceptance and diffusion of hybrid corn seed in two Iowa communities*. (No. Research Bulletin 372). Ames, IA: Iowa State College of Agriculture and Mechanic Arts.

Salganik, M. J., Dodds, P. S., & Watts, D. J. (2006). Experimental study of inequality and unpredictability in an artificial cultural market. *Science, 311*(5762), 854–856.

Salganik, M. J., & Watts, D. J. (2008). Leading the herd astray: An experimental study of self-fulfilling prophecies in an artificial cultural market. *Social Psychology Quarterly, 74*(4), 338–355.

Scheff, T. J. (1966). *Being mentally ill: A sociological theory*. Chicago, IL: Aldine.

Shermer, M. (2011). *The believing brain: From ghosts and gods to politics and conspiracies*. London: Robinson.

Stack, S. (2005). Suicide in the media: A quantitative review of studies based on nonfictional stories. *Suicide and Life-Threatening Behavior, 35*(2), 121–133.

Steglich, C., Sinclair, P., Holliday, J., & Moore, L. (2012). Actor-based analysis of peer influence in a stop smoking in schools trial. *Social Networks, 34*(3), 359–369.

Sunstein, C. R. (2017). *#Republic: Divided democracy in the age of social media*. Princeton, NJ: Princeton University Press.

Tarde, G. (1903 [1890]). *The laws of imitation*. New York, NY: Henry Holt and Company.

Thomas, W. I., & Thomas, D. S. (1928). *The child in America: Behavior problems and programs*. New York, NY: Knopff.

Törnberg, P. (2018). Echo chambers and viral misinformation: Modeling fake news as complex contagion. *PloS ONE, 13*(9), e0203958.

Vaisey, S. (2009). Motivation and justification: A dual-process model of culture in action. *American Journal of Sociology, 114*(6), 1675–1715.

Valente, T. W. (1995). *Network models of the diffusion of innovations*. Cresskil, NJ: Hampton Press.

Valente, T. W. (2010). *Social networks and health: Models, methods, and applications*. New York, NY: Oxford University Press.

Van Zalk, M. H., Kerr, M., Branje, S. J., Stattin, H., & Meeus, W. H. (2010). It takes three: Selection, influence, and de-selection processes of depression in adolescent friendship networks. *Developmental Psychology, 46*(4), 927–938.

Veenstra, R., Dijkstra, J. K., & Kreager, D. (2018). Pathways, networks, and norms: A sociological perspective on peer research. In W. M. Bukowski, B. R. Laursen, & K. H. Rubin (Eds.), *Handbook of peer interactions, relationships, and groups* (pp. 45–63). New York, NY: Guilford.

Verachtert, P., De Fraine, B., Onghena, P., & Ghesquière, P. (2010). Season of birth and school success in the early years of primary education. *Oxford Review of Education, 36*(3), 285–306.

Vollebergh, W. A., Iedema, J., & Raaijmakers, Q. A. (2001). Intergenerational transmission and the formation of cultural orientations in adolescence and young adulthood. *Journal of Marriage and Family, 63*(4), 1185–1198.

Watts, D. J. (2011). *Everything is obvious: Once you know the answer*. New York, NY: Crown Business.

Watts, D. J., & Dodds, P. S. (2007). Influentials, networks, and public opinion formation. *Journal of Consumer Research, 34*(4), 441–458.

Webb, J. A., & Baer, P. E. (1995). Influence of family disharmony and parental alcohol use on adolescent social skills, self-efficacy, and alcohol use. *Addictive Behaviors, 20*(1), 127–135.

Weerman, F. M. (2011). Delinquent peers in context: A longitudinal network analysis of selection and influence effects. *Criminology, 49*(1), 253–286.

Wentzel, K. R., Barry, C. M., & Caldwell, K. A. (2004). Friendships in middle school: Influences on motivation and school adjustment. *Journal of Educational Psychology*, 96(2), 195–203.

Yi, C., Chang, C., & Chang, Y. (2004). The intergenerational transmission of family values: A comparison between teenagers and parents in Taiwan. *Journal of Comparative Family Studies*, 35(4), 523–545.

Young, H. P. (2009). Innovation diffusion in heterogeneous populations: Contagion, social influence, and social learning. *The American Economic Review*, 99(5), 1899–1924.

Chapter 6

Norms

Chapter overview

Why is binge drinking so common among university students? In this chapter, we will study binge drinking as a cultural phenomenon, as something that is driven by norms. The main aim of the chapter is to introduce you to key concepts, theories and findings on norms. This chapter starts with what some people regard as a social problem, namely excessive alcohol intake by college students (6.1). Often, students indicate that they do so because drinking is seen as "something you should do." This is an example of a social norm (6.2). I introduce social control theory, which explains when and why people adhere to social norms (6.3). Then, I describe two other types of norms, namely: "internalized norms" (6.4) and "legal norms" (6.5). I then ask how norms emerge. It is argued that certain types of norms often emerge for good reasons, that these norms solve problems of collective behavior and hence benefit the group. Sociologists argue that injunctive norms solve cooperation problems, whereas descriptive norms provide solutions to coordination problems (6.6). I will then review cases of existing norms that do not benefit the collective, or may even cause harm. In discussing these cases, I will identify two mechanisms that scholars have proposed to explain such "unpopular norms," namely cultural inertia and pluralistic ignorance (6.7). At the end of the chapter, I will apply the insights of this chapter to understand changes in fashion, habits and traditions (6.8).

Learning goals

After reading this chapter, check if you are able to:

- Describe and use key sociological concepts on norms.
- Describe similarities and differences between social norms, internalized norms, legal norms and descriptive norms.
- Describe and apply social control theory.
- Explain the emergence of norms.
- Describe the difference between cooperation and coordination problems.
- Explain the existence of unpopular norms.
- Describe and apply trickle-down theory.

6.1 College binge drinking: a social problem?

A well-known fact in western countries is that, when young people enter college, their alcohol intake levels increase (Kypri, Cronin, & Wright, 2005). Excessive drinking—i.e., short periods of extremely high alcohol consumption—is rather common in this group. To illustrate, one study reported "very high rates of alcohol use disorders and hazardous drinking" (together around 60%) among a convenience sample of 770 undergraduate students from seven universities in England in 2008–2009 (Heather et al., 2011). Another study among undergraduate students from a university in Australia in 2007 found that 34% met criteria for hazardous drinking (Hallett et al., 2012). Among US adults aged 18 to 22 enrolled full time in college, 39% were past-month "binge" alcohol users in 2011 (White & Hingson, 2013), where binge drinking was defined as consuming five or more drinks in an evening. Such high levels of hazardous drinking by university students has been reported in many other western countries (Wicki, Kuntsche, & Gmel, 2010).

These alcohol consumption patterns among students have major consequences (White & Hingson, 2013). For example, in the US each year:

- More than 1,800 college students die from alcohol-related causes (Hingson, Zha, & Weitzman, 2009).
- Around 600,000 students are injured under the influence of alcohol (Hingson et al., 2009).
- An estimated 97,000 students are victims of alcohol-related sexual assault or date rape (Hingson et al., 2009).
- Around 400,000 students had unprotected sex and nearly 110,000 students report having been too intoxicated to know if they consented to having sex (Hingson, Heeren, Zakocs, Kopstein, & Wechsler, 2002).

In addition to these consequences, numerous other alcohol-related harms have been documented (White & Hingson, 2013), such as increased health problems, suicide attempts,

Image 6.1 Binge drinking is common among students. Why is this the case?

drunk driving, memory loss, property damage and involvement with police. About one in four college students report academic consequences of their drinking, such as missing class and doing poorly in exams (Wechsler et al., 2002).

THINKING LIKE A SOCIOLOGIST 6.1

How would you explain the fact that binge drinking is common among university students?

Although many students enjoy (excessive) drinking, it is seen as a public health risk by others, as a *social problem* that needs to be addressed. The World Health Organization closely monitors alcohol consumption levels of this age group and that of adults in general, and governments in western countries implement policies to remedy this social issue. This appears rather difficult. In the aim to reduce alcohol intake among college students, it has been frequently noted that students perceive (excessive) drinking as something they "should do when entering college," that "getting drunk is cool" and that they feel the expectation that they "should join their peers and drink together." These are an example of what sociologists call "social norms" and they are social forces that strongly impact behavior.

6.2 What are social norms?

Social norms are ubiquitous in social life. We could spend hours making a list of all the social norms that we have to deal with every day. Think about the following social norms which might sound familiar to you:

1 "If someone helps you, help that person in return when he or she needs it."
2 "Do not arrive late for an appointment."
3 "You must not swear."
4 "Do not jump the line at the register."
5 "Do the dishes every day."
6 "Don't interrupt people when they are speaking."
7 "Don't steal."
8 "Go to church every week."
9 "Do your homework."
10 "Don't drink alcohol."

Social norms are an element of culture (Patterson, 2014) and affect people's behavior. They are widely studied in sociology, across a variety of sociological topics, such as in the sociology of religion (Sherkat, 1997; Sherkat & Ellison, 1999), the sociology of the family (Billari & Liefbroer, 2007; Liefbroer & Billari, 2010), the sociology of youth and adolescents (Veenstra, Dijkstra, & Kreager, 2018), the sociology of crime (Sutherland, 1947), the sociology of organizations (Blau, 1955) and sociological studies on collective violence (Bauman, 2005 [1989]). Some would even go so far as to claim that sociology *is* the scientific study of social norms. And indeed, in the "classic" interpretation of *homo sociologicus*, "man" was seen as completely determined by social norms (Dahrendorf, 2010 [1959]). Nowadays, sociologists no longer maintain such an extreme view, nor do they argue that sociology is *only* about social norms. That said, social norms are still a central element in many sociological investigations.

What, then, are social norms? Unfortunately, there is no consensus in the literature about the definition of social norms—the concept of "social norms" is used in different ways (Bicchieri, 2005; Brennan, Eriksson, Goodin, & Southwood, 2013; Elster, 2009; Gibbs, 1965; Hechter & Opp, 2001; Opp, 2001). It is, however, common to regard *social* norms as one specific type of *norms*, which we defined as the rules of the game in society (Chapter 4). This means that there are different types of norms, of which social norms are a specific sub-category. We can distinguish the sub-category *social* norms from other types of norms (Figure 6.1).

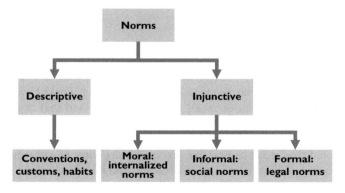

Figure 6.1 Classification of norms.

Social norms are a sub-category of **injunctive norms**, also called **prescriptive norms** and **oughtness norms** (Hechter & Opp, 2001). Injunctive norms are rules of the game that contain statements about how people *should and should not* behave; all that is taboo or allowed; right and wrong. The Ten Commandments from the Bible, for instance, are injunctive norms: "thou shalt not steal" (norm number 7 in our list above). What they have in common is that they are *normative statements*, that is to say that the directives express what people should or should not do. When we speak of an injunctive norm, then, there is always an "ought," something people "should" do in a certain situation.

> **injunctive norm** (also **prescriptive norm** or **oughtness norm**) normative statement specifying what a person should do or not do.

Although the "should" commonly refers to behavior, to how people should *behave*, it can also be expanded to what people should *think and say*, i.e., what kind of opinions (beliefs, values) they should have (Opp, 2001). For example, an injunctive norm could be "you should believe in God" or "you should value men and women equally." Thus, normative statements are often directed towards how people should behave, but social norms can also pertain to opinions. Violating injunctive norms results in some sort of sanction. Injunctive norms are in that sense different from descriptive norms (conventions, customs, habits).

There are various types of injunctive norms. Social norms are different from moral norms (also called internalized norms) because moral norms operate within individuals, whereas a characteristic of social norms is that they are informal statements made in groups. Social norms are also different from formal norms (also called legal norms), which refer to laws imposed by the state rather than norms within social groups. Thus social norms are similar to moral and legal norms in so far as all these three sub-categories are injunctive norms—but social norms operate in groups whereas moral norms work internally and legal norms are imposed by the state.

Social norms are thus not formal rules but rather informal directives. Such rules to live by are usually not written down, although sometimes they are, as in the Bible. Social norms are made in groups, such as in religious groups, peer groups, organizations, criminal gangs, in families and so forth. As a consequence, such informal statements can differ between groups and contexts, and they can change over time. Whatever applies as a social norm in one group may be entirely different in another.

Let us look at an example from our list, number 3: "you must not swear." This social norm applies in some groups. It is a norm that many religious groups uphold, certainly when it is swearing that is related to (their) religion and faith. It is, nevertheless, not a general rule. There are groups in which swearing is allowed and, in others, for instance certain youth cultures, swearing and cursing might even be the social norm everyone ought to follow. Similarly, statement number 10 ("don't drink alcohol") may be a social norm in some groups (parents, teachers) but not in others (e.g., among college students). Social norms may, in other words, apply in a specific group, such as a family, ethnic and religious community, school, organization, neighborhood, among friends and, even more generally, in society as a whole. In conclusion, when we speak of **social norms**, we have in mind informal, normative statements specifying what a person should do or not do.

> **social norm** informal, normative statement specifying what a person should do or not do.

6.3 Social control theory

Why do people actually follow social norms? What determines whether people conform to the social norms of the group in some cases and not in other cases? When and under what circumstances do people deviate from social norms? To answers these questions, sociologists working on different topics, such as crime, family, religion and suicide, have come up with rather similar ideas and what I will call the *social control theory*. The origins of this theory are diverse and not that of a single author. It can be traced back to Durkheim's "social integration theory" of suicide, published in 1897 (Durkheim, 1961), which we discussed in Chapter 2. But similar ideas can also be found in Sutherland's "differential association theory" of crime, which was developed in the 1930s and 1940s (Sutherland, 1947) and which was then elaborated on by other scholars (Akers, 1996; Bruinsma, 1992; Opp, 1989). Other sources are the classic studies of Homans on human groups, published in 1950 (Homans, 2017 [1950]), and that of Blau on organizations in 1955 (Blau, 1955).

According to social control theory, people adhere to social norms because deviations from social norms can be answered by **social sanctions**. Social sanctions are **external sanctions** imposed by other people of the group in which the social norm applies. These are so-called **third parties** and they can be parents, peers, teachers or any other member of the social group. Take another look at the examples in the list above and imagine what could happen if you were to break these social norms.

social sanction punishment for behavior diverging from social norms.

external sanction sanctions imposed by third parties, i.e., other people of the group in which the social norm applies.

Let us consider number 4: "do not jump the line at the register." Suppose you are aware of this social norm and know that it is impolite to cut in line, but you are in a hurry and deviating from the norm has direct benefits (jumping the queue saves you time or gets you a better seat). There are thus incentives, good reasons, for you to deviate from the norm and suppose, for once, you decide to do so. This behavior, however, can result in social sanctions: chances are that the clerk, as well as the people who are patiently waiting their turn, will call you to account for your deviant behavior. Perhaps you will receive a verbal reprimand or see people shake their heads in disapproval. The clerk might punish you by insisting that you go to the back

third party other members of the same group to which certain norms apply.

of the line. In the worst-case scenario, you will be moved by force. These are all examples of social sanctions. In reality, there are far more types of social sanctions, which differ in their *severity*. Some of these are relatively mild, such as a verbal reprimand, a disapproving gesture, and suchlike. However, social sanctions can also be extremely intrusive, like exclusion from the group, reputation damage, verbal abuse, the loss of resources and means and physical punishment even as far as death. Because people *fear* such punishment, they will tend to conform to social norms.

Deviating from social norms can therefore be "costly." But there are also "benefits" from following social norms. When people adhere to social norms, they can count on the approval and appreciation of others in their group—they can count on **social approval** or "behavioral confirmation." A mother might compliment her daughter ("good girl!") when she follows the social norm set by her parents to "work hard and do your homework;" an adolescent can express his approval ("cool man!") when his friend has *not* prepared for the exam—and thereby follows the norm of the peer group "don't work too hard."

social approval rewards and appreciation by other group members for following social norms.

However, social sanctions and social approval are not always effective. They are not effective if behaviors are not observed by the group members, i.e., by third parties who can impose sanctions. Therefore, the theory states that social control becomes effective if the behavior of the individuals belonging to a certain group is also visible to third parties. Therefore, researchers often use the words "safeguarding" or, somewhat milder, **monitoring** of someone's behavior and the beliefs and values they express. If "swearing is not allowed" is the social norm in the group, people may still swear without suffering any social sanctions if, for instance, they do so outside anyone's earshot. And, likewise, if an adolescent did not prepare for the exam—thereby following the social norm of his peer group—he will only receive social approval when his peers learn about his behavior. Monitoring is not simply a matter of present or absent—more often it is a matter of degree. In some groups, people strongly monitor what others are doing, whereas in other groups this is less so. Thus, the *degree* of monitoring behavior is critical in understanding why people follow social norms in the group: the more strongly people are monitored in their group, the more strongly they follow the social norms of that group.

> **monitoring** the behavior of an individual within a group is visible to third parties.

It has also been realized, however, that actual monitoring may not always be commensurate with people's perceptions of it. It could be the case that, for example, *objectively* speaking, there is little monitoring of behavior in a group, but nevertheless people in that group *believe* they are consistently monitored. What matters in the end are not the "objective" sanctions and monitoring within the group, but rather people's *subjective expectations*, because that's what is determining their behavior. Say, for example, that it might be objectively true that, if person A violates a social norm in his group, the probability that his peers will notice his deviant behavior is very low, say 0.01. However, the more realistic version of social control theory postulates that it is not objective but rather subjective expectations that are critical for understanding social norm adherence. If person A *believes* that the probability of detection is 0.5, then he is much more likely to adhere to the social norm than if he thinks it is 0.01. Similarly, the theory claims that *perceived* social sanctions and *expected* social approval play a role, rather than the objective sanctions and approval. When taking into account people's subjective perceptions rather than the objective conditions alone, we might call this, with good reasons, the *subjective* social control theory.

We have now identified two core parameters in the social control theory, namely: (1) expected sanctions/approval and (2) expected monitoring. The theory argues that these two elements together determine whether members of a group will comply with the social norms. The interplay between these two forces is illustrated in Table 6.1. In this example, expected social sanctions range from "severe" (-100) to "nothing happens" (0). All positive feedbacks from adhering to social norms score beyond 0 and the more positive the feedback the higher the score. The expected probabilities of being monitored by peers ranges from 0 to 1. When combining expected sanctions/approval and monitoring, one can see the expected "costs" and "benefits" of norm-deviation and norm-conformity. If a person expects that norm-deviance results in high sanctions (-100), but also that the probability a third party will notice is very low (P=0.01), then the expected costs (-100 x 0.01 = -1) are the same as in the case of low expected sanctions (-2) and high monitoring (P = 0.5). For this reason, the theory claims that it is critical to always consider both the severity of sanctions/approval *and* monitoring.

According to this sociological social control theory, it can therefore be "rational" to conform to group norms. For example, if someone expects high social costs of norm-deviance—which exceed personal benefits in the case of deviating from the norm—then obeying the social norm makes sense. This insight sheds light on a longstanding discussion in the social sciences, in which it was claimed that sociological theories of norms (the *classic* interpretation

Table 6.1 Illustration of the interplay between sanctions/approval and monitoring.

	Expected sanctions/approval		Expected probability (P) of being monitored	
			Low (P = 0.01)	High (P = 0.5)
Deviate				
	High	−100	−1	−50
	Low	−2	−0.02	−1
Conform				
	High	50	0.5	25
	Low	2	0.02	1

of "*homo sociologicus*") are opposite to a "rational" perspective on human behavior (typically identified with "*homo economicus*"):

> One of the most persistent cleavages in the social sciences is the opposition between two lines of thought conveniently associated with Adam Smith and Emile Durkheim, between *homo economicus* and *homo sociologicus*. Of these, the former is supposed to be guided by instrumental rationality, while the behavior of the latter is dictated by social norms.
>
> (Elster, 1989)

The social control theory takes away the sharp boundaries between these positions. It considers the role of social norms but does not presuppose a sort of "irrational" purely norm-following and passive perspective of human beings. Instead, the social control theory assumes human agency and it explains why people obey social norms and why it makes sense to do that at all. Norm conformity is a choice, sometimes a good one, which makes sense from the perspective of the actor, but not something that automatically follows from group membership. Moreover, social control theory makes norm compliance *contingent*, i.e., the likelihood that people adhere to the social norms of their group *depends* on the severity of expected sanctions and monitoring. Thus, the theory can explain when people conform to group norms and when they don't. In reality, of course, there are numerous other reasons for people to either adhere to the social norms of their group or not. For example, strong monetary incentives may lead someone to not follow a certain social norm ("do not steal"), even under conditions of high social control. Thus, criminal activities may be subject to social control, but also to other forces such as monetary incentives.

It is helpful to systematically formulate the social control theory and for this I use a theory schema. The most general idea of this theory (the *social control* proposition) can be formulated as follows:

> P. The higher people's expected social sanctions in a group in case of norm-deviance, and the higher their expected social approval in case of norm-compliance, the more likely they are to conform to the social norms of that group. (*social control*)

Why would you need to know social control theory? My view on this is that it is a simple though incredibly powerful theory that you can use to understand different social phenomena. You will come across this theory in various areas of research in sociology. Whatever sociological topic you study (family, religion, crime and so forth), the chances are high that the ideas conveyed in this simple general proposition about social norms can be applied to your area of research.

For example, let's return to *Durkheim's integration and suicide* theory (Chapter 2). The most general proposition we have identified in his theory (*group integration and suicide*) can be seen as a particular *application* of the social control theory, as becomes evident when using a theory schema:

P . The higher people's expected social sanctions in a group in case of norm-deviance, and the higher their expected social approval in case of norm-compliance, the more likely they are to conform to the social norms of that group. (*social control*)

P. The more cohesive the group, the higher people's expected social sanctions in case of norm-deviance, and the higher their expected social approval in case of norm-compliance.

C . Generally speaking, groups specify the social norm which says that suicide is prohibited.

P. The more cohesive the group, the more strongly people in that group conform to the norm which prohibits suicide, and the lower the suicide rate in that group. (*group integration and suicide*)

> **Theory schema 6.1** Explanation of the link between group integration and suicide.

In other words: Durkheim's integration and suicide theory is the same as social control theory but then applied to the topic of suicide. The social control theory is more general, it has a broader scope (Chapter 2), as it can be applied to a larger variety of sociological topics, such as crime, religion, family, organizations and so forth. In these specific sociological areas of research, the social control theory operates under different names. In short, the social control theory is a general, highly informative, theory that is applicable to a wide variety of social phenomena.

The social control theory can also explain the stylized fact of *conformity* which we identified in Chapter 5 (Opinions). This empirical pattern, this stylized fact, was summarized as follows:

> There is a general human tendency to conform to the opinions and behavior of actors in their social environment. (*conformity*)

In Chapter 5 I showed that this human tendency to copy other's opinions (and behavior) can be partly explained by social learning processes—so called *informational* social influence. But the conformity pattern can also be explained, at least sometimes, in terms of social control, i.e., *normative* social influence. That is to say, people sometimes copy what others do in their environment because this behavior is the social norm in the group; deviating from this norm can be sanctioned whereas following the social norm results in social approval. And as we have seen, opinions can also become the subject of social norms, which means that people can also copy the opinions of others because they are supposed to do so. For example, if people in the social environment believe that "the earth is flat," and if they regard that belief as the one and only appropriate belief, then it becomes a social norm ("it is forbidden to think that the earth is not flat;" "it is wrong to think that the earth is not the center of the universe," etc.) and people are expected to conform. We can summarize how social control theory can explain the stylized pattern of conformity using a theory schema:

P. The higher people's expected social sanctions in a group in case of norm-deviance, and the higher their expected social approval in case of norm-compliance, the more likely they are to conform to the social norms of that group. (*social control*)

C. Generally speaking, groups impose the social norm that their members should adjust their opinions and behavior to those of their own group.

C. Generally speaking, people expect that in case of norm deviance, there will be at least some social sanctions in the groups of which they are a member, whereas norm-compliance is expected to result in social approval.

O. There is a general human tendency to conform to the opinions and behavior of actors in their social environment. (*conformity*)

Theory schema 6.2 Explanation of conformity with social control theory.

In this way, social control theory makes sense of *why* people have a tendency to adjust their own behavior and opinions to the behavior and opinions of people in their environment. Take, for example, the empirical observation that children tend to copy the opinions and behavior of their own parents (more so than those of other parents). Why are the opinions and (corresponding) behavior typically transmitted from parents to their children? Why is this happening? Why do children copy their parents? The answer to that, says social control theory, is social norms. Thus, children who are raised by conservative parents may be faced with social norms like these two:

- *Opinion*: "you <u>should</u> believe in the existence of God."
- *Behavior*: "you <u>should</u> vote for a conservative political party."

These are dos and don'ts, with which the children may or may not comply, depending on their subjective expectations of parental control. Generally speaking, parents reward their children when their children adopt their opinions and behavior, and punish their children when they deviate from that. What the parents think and do is regarded as the social norm and violations of this norm result in social sanctions. Parents are, so to speak, the third-party "agents" that control their children "externally." They monitor what their children say and what they do, reward norm-conformity and sanction norm-deviance. Hence, social control theory can explain *why* parental transmission happens.

Similarly, social control theory can explain the social influence exerted by other third parties and groups. Just like parents, teachers have their control opportunities as well. Social norms, such as to behave well in class and to perform well academically, are enforced by monitoring and sanctioning mechanisms, such as expelling pupils from class and grading their performance. Peers have such control mechanisms as well. The label "youth culture" is often used in this context to express the fact that peers can develop a kind of social norm that differs from their parents' and teachers' norms. For example, it can be the norm among peers that "smoking is OK" or that "skipping classes is cool" and deviators from this norm can expect punishment by peers. They monitor each other's behavior and impose sanctions if needed, such as excluding peers from friendship networks, bullying and gossiping. Because of these expected sanctions, children would be likely to comply with the social norms of their peers.

In summary, social control theory can explain why and when people follow social norms, the theory is applied to a wide variety of topics, such as crime and religion, and the theory can explain the stylized fact of conformity.

6.4 Internalized norms

The social control theory, however, is confronted with an empirical puzzle it cannot explain: sociologists have observed that people sometimes—though not always—comply with the social norms of their group even in the absence of any social control. Children often obey the rules of their parents even when their parents are not around, so when there is no monitoring at all. For example, most parents teach their children that they should not steal money from other people (norm number 7); that, more generally, they should act pro-socially and in an altruistic way. Studies have shown that, later in life, many adults comply with this pro-social, altruistic social norm when there is nobody in their environment who observes their behavior and there is no one who could possibly sanction deviations from this norm. So, the puzzle is:

> Why do people stick to social norms when they could deviate from that norm without risk and thus do whatever they prefer to do?

THINKING LIKE A SOCIOLOGIST 6.2

Why would you think this happens?

According to one influential line of thought, the reason is that, uniquely, human beings have a kind of *internal control* mechanism, i.e., when people belong to a certain group and are repeatedly exposed to its social norms, they gradually *internalize* these social norms. For this reason, these are so-called **internalized norms** or **moral norms** (Brennan et al., 2013). Such internalized norms emerge when the social norm in the group has become part of people's intrinsic set of prescribed things one "should" do. Internalized norms can also become part of one's personal preferences and **values**, i.e., the things that people "want" and "appreciate." Either way, social norms can become something people *intrinsically see* as the good things to do—irrespective of the social sanctions and approval they might receive from the group.

internalized norm (also **moral norm**) norm that has become part of people's intrinsic set of things one should do or prefer to do.

value things that people want and appreciate.

For example, if parents have socialized their children such that they repeatedly told their children they should "go to church every week" (norm number 8), this social norm could eventually become part of the set of internalized norms ("I should go to church every week") or values ("I want to go to church every week"). An external social norm has become internalized; it is something children think is the right thing to do and that they will do even in the absence of parental social control. When no longer living with their parents, the child will nevertheless go to church every week, because doing so has become *intrinsically rewarding*; the social norm has become part of the child's moral and value system. This is similar to the social approval gained from norm-compliance, but different in the sense that it is not approval from others but rather from oneself. Moral norms are similar to social norms in the sense that both are injunctive norms, but they are different because the "should" in moral norms comes from the person themselves, whereas in social norms the "should" is coming from third parties. The positive reason for following internalized norms is that it gives good conscience, which is similar to receiving approval from peers in the case of social norms.

The flipside of the coin is that when people deviate from an internalized norm, they "sanction" themselves by feeling guilt or shame (Benedict, 1934; Durkheim, 1961; Gintis, 2009; Nisbett & Cohen, 1996; Parsons, 1967). Whereas deviance from social norms can result in *external* sanctions when others notice, not obeying norms that are internalized leads to **internal sanctions**. People feel bad (shame, guilt, bad conscience) when violating these moral norms, i.e., people suffer from "psychological costs." In cases where moral norms become one's values, then not acting according to these values may not raise issues of guilt and shame but feelings of frustration, anger and unfulfillment. Thus, even in the absence of social control (monitoring and external sanctions), it makes sense for people to conform to the norms of their group as they want to avoid either the psychological costs of violating the corresponding moral norms or the feelings of not acting according to one's values (Welzel, 2013).

> **internal sanction**
> feeling of shame, guilt and bad conscience resulting from deviation from internalized norms.

Moral norms and values motivate human behavior. Research findings suggest that internalized norms and values predict individual actions across a wide range of domains (Datler, Jagodzinski, & Schmidt, 2013; Miles, 2015; Schwartz, 2010), although the relationship is not always perfect (Ajzen, 1991; Ajzen & Fishbein, 1977). There are many reasons for moral norms/value–action (or attitude–behavior) inconsistencies. For example, situational conditions may interfere, such that people will not act according to their values or people are confronted with conflicting values and they prevail one over the other.

At the macro and meso level, dominant moral norms and values also have consequences for collective behavior. For example, Inglehart and Welzel show that countries in which gender equality values are endorsed by an increasing share of the population subsequently develop more rights for women and measures to combat gender inequality, and that these rights and measures, in turn, result in reduced gender inequalities in education and the labor market (Inglehart & Norris, 2003; Inglehart & Welzel, 2005; Welzel, 2013). Thus, moral norms and values have consequences; they affect behavior, deeds and actions at the individual and collective level (Hitlin & Piliavin, 2004; Miles, 2015; Patterson, 2014; Rokeach, 1973).

People need not always be aware of their internalized norms and value system. The dual-process model of human cognition (Chapter 5) posits that, for the most part, human behavior is based on relatively automatic, fast and unconscious processes, based on prior learned and deeply ingrained cognitions, moral norms and values (Evans, 2008; Haidt, 2001; Kahneman, 2011; Miles, 2015). People are therefore *not always aware of their own software, of their own moral norms and values*; this could be the case, but often it is not so. Moral norms and values are often so deeply ingrained that people take their own perspectives for granted and thereby this affects their behavior automatically and unconsciously (Patterson, 2014). This means that people rarely deliberatively reflect on their own moral norms and values, and act according to them without thinking.

In this context, it is relevant to mention the concept of **habitus**, which was coined by the French sociologist Pierre Bourdieu (2010 [1979]). Although the concept is controversial and not clearly defined, as pointed out by several scholars (Hedström, 2005), it can be integrated in the dual-process model (Vaisey, 2009). Specifically, one could understand habitus as behavioral dispositions that are based on cognitions, moral norms, values and cultural scripts that remain largely unconscious and which impact behavior in an automatic way. What you are inclined to do automatically, based on your internal preference system in conjunction with learned cognitions, is therefore your habitus. Consequently, the insight that moral norms and values often shape behavior automatically and unconsciously implies that they shape actions more strongly than people think they do, even when reporting in interviews and survey questionnaires (Vaisey, 2009).

> **habitus** behavioral dispositions based on cognitions, moral norms, values and cultural scripts.

6.5 Legal norms

Social norms and moral norms provide society with an important set of "rules," but there is more. Typical of social norms, as we have established, is that they are informal and that any violations will be penalized through social sanctions. Moral norms are similar, but subject to internal sanctions. Apart from social and moral norms, there are also formal norms, called **legal norms** or **laws** (Brennan et al., 2013), whose observance is watched by a formal authority such as the state, and which, if violated, may be punishable by **formal sanctions** (Bicchieri, 2005). Take, for instance, the two following norms:

> **legal norm** (also **law**) formal, normative statement specifying what a person should do or not do.

> **formal sanction** punishment for behavior diverging from legal norms.

1 "you may not hit others."
2 "you may not run a red light."

In the first case (1), the violation will often be answered by social disapproval and informal sanctions. It may well be that if someone is aggressive toward others then this person may count on social sanctions. This may also happen when someone runs a red light. It is, however, not only purely social norms that apply here, but also formal norms that have been set by the state. The punishments following the violation of these norms are, therefore, not solely informal. Whoever hits, physically abuses or kills another (and thus violates norm number 1) probably breaks the law that is applicable in society and will, therefore, be punished by a prison sentence, fine, corporal punishment or even death.

You may wonder why people actually obey legal norms and why people sometimes do not comply with them. There are several forces at work here. First, law-enforcement authorities may or may not effectively *monitor* whether people obey legal rules and they may or may not impose severe *sanctions* in case of legal disobedience. Thus, when legal authorities strongly monitor citizens and sanctions are high, then people are more likely to follow the rules. These ideas should sound familiar to you as they very much resemble social control theory. The difference is that, whereas social norms are enforced informally by parents, peers and other third-party actors in *social* groups, legal norms are commanded by the *state* and legitimately enforceable by the state. Let's formulate this idea in what we may call the *formal control* proposition:

> P. The higher people's expected legal sanctions in case of legal disobedience, the more likely they are to conform to legal norms. (*formal control*)

Second, legal norms may or may not be supported by social norms (and their corresponding moral norms). If certain laws are not seen as OK among certain groups, then members of these groups may not obey these formal norms. For example, criminal gangs may not believe in the legitimacy of state authority and may not respect the law. They may endorse a general anti-police, anti-government attitude and share social norms that oppose legal norms. Legal obedience is more likely if social norms are in line with general or particular legal obedience. If parents, for example, instruct their children that they "should always obey the law," that they "should never hurt someone" and that they "should never steal someone else's property" legal norms are supported by social and moral norms.

Another concept used in the literature for legal norms and laws is formal institution. Formal institutions are distinguished from informal institutions, which correspond to what we have called social norms. When used in this way (formal and informal) institutions are therefore more or less similar to norms (Esser, 2000). You can see *norms* and *institutions* as "rules of the game" or the "grammar of society" (Bicchieri, 2005). A well-known definition in line with this broad conception is given by economist Douglass North:

> Institutions are the rules of the game in a society, or more formally, are the humanly devised constraints that shape human interaction. In consequence they structure incentives in human exchange, whether political, social, or economic. Institutional change shapes the way societies evolve through time and hence is key to understanding historical change.
>
> (North, 1990)

Sociologist Orlando Patterson comes up with a similar definition of norms and institutions:

> Institutions are thoroughly cultural. They are norms or an ensemble of norms, understood in the broader sense of both the prescriptive weight (i.e., the nature and degree of approval or penalty) and the social objects to which they are directed.
>
> (Patterson, 2014)

However, you should keep in mind that there is no consensus in the literature about the meaning of norms and institutions and that they are used in different ways. Some scholars use norms and institutions interchangeably, others do not. In this book, I follow scholars who talk about (informal and formal) institutions in such a way that they correspond to what are called (social and legal) norms.

6.6 Why do norms emerge?

Given the influence of social, moral and legal norms on human behavior, it is relevant to understand how they came about in the first place. Why do norms emerge? What are their origins? These are difficult questions and sociologists, as well as other social scientists, study them up to today.

One influential approach to answer this question is to argue that norms emerge as a solution to collective problems. Certain norms are more adaptive, more useful than other norms in certain social conditions, in the sense that they benefit the collective (Boudon, 2001; Ullmann-Margalit, 2015 [1977]). This approach resonates well with the idea of adaptation bias in social learning (Chapter 5), which argues that people tend to copy particularly those opinions that seem to be better adapted to their current social context. But whereas this type of bias in social learning plays a role at the individual level, and responds to problems of the individual, norms can be seen as solutions to problems at the collective level. Norms may emerge to solve two kinds of collective problems, namely: (1) cooperation problems and (2) coordination problems.

Let's start with cooperation problems. This issue can be illustrated with the example of a student dorm. Suppose that you live in a dorm with 25 students and each year, as the academic year begins, new students come in and others leave. Imagine that, in addition to your private room in the dorm, you share a common room there with the other students, in which you can relax, cook and do the dishes. Now assume that you, like other students, don't like cleaning and doing the dishes. But suppose that you also prefer, as others do, to have a common room that is clean and in which you can cook with clean plates. We can depict this situation with the help of a simple matrix (Table 6.2).

Table 6.2 Cooperation problem in student dorm.

		Another student	
		Cleaning	Always relax
You	Cleaning	8,8	4,10
	Always relax	10,4	5,5

Note: Entries in each cell of the matrix represent the student's payoffs, in this case happiness on a scale from 0 to 10. The first number is your payoff, the second is the payoff of another student.

In this matrix I specify how happy you and a randomly taken student living in the same dorm are with certain outcomes, using a happiness scale that runs from 0 (lowest) to 10 (highest). You and the other student have two options: either do the cleaning now and then or always relax, which means never cleaning anything! Each cell gives the happiness score for you (left side) and the other student (right side). The best outcome for you is that you relax, whereas the other student does the dishes and cleans the common room. This will give you a clean common room, while you need do nothing for it. This gives you a 10 on the happiness scale while the other student gets 4. A bad outcome for you would be that both of you do nothing. Although that situation may seem nice for a moment, or even a day or two, you'll get a dirty common room and you'll not be able to cook anymore. It gives the outcome (5,5), which means that you (5) and the other student (5) are both unhappy with the situation.

Exactly that situation is likely to happen in your student dorm. To see why, let's consider your options and those of the other student. Suppose that the other student decided to clean the common room: what would you prefer to do? In that case, it is more attractive to relax (which gives you a perfect 10) rather than also cleaning the common room (which ends up in an 8). But what would you do in case the other student always relaxes? Then you would also be inclined to relax, because relaxing makes you still happier (5) than the alternative, which is cleaning the common room while the other student relaxes (4). Thus, regardless of what the other student does, you will decide to relax instead of cleaning. This is called a **dominant strategy** in the terminology of "game theory" (see the online Appendix for Chapter 6): a strategy that is favorable to choose irrespective of what the other will do. The other student will reason in exactly the same way; you have the same dominant strategy.

dominant strategy strategy that is favorable to choose irrespective of what other people do.

Therefore, what will happen in this particular situation is that both of you will not clean the common room. Paradoxically, this collective outcome (5,5) is not the most desirable collective outcome, which would be that both you and the other student now and then clean the common room (8,8). This simple example suggests that there can be social conditions in which, if persons act rationally and

free-ride type of behavior in which one prefers personal gains above the interest of the group.

pursue their material self-interest, the collective outcome can be suboptimal. In this case, students tend to relax and let other people do the dishes rather than that they contribute themselves to the common good. They do not act cooperatively, but rather choose what gives the greatest personal benefits – they **free-ride**. Because everyone is doing the same, as a collective they are worse off.

These are called **cooperation problems**, or **social dilemma** situations, i.e., certain conditions in which rational self-interest behavior results in collective problems because individuals are tempted to free-ride. Social dilemma situations are ubiquitous in social life (Merton, 1936). A classic example was given by Hardin, which he called the *Tragedy of the Commons* (Hardin, 1968). Suppose, he said, there is a pasture somewhere, open to herdsmen. Each herdsman has the choice to add more animals to their herd or not. Being rational beings pursu-

cooperation problem (also **social dilemma**) certain condition in which rational self-interest behavior results in collective problems.

ing their self-interest, it is more attractive to add more and more animals of their own. Each herdsman realizes that there is a risk of overgrazing but, individually, they cannot make a difference to the collective outcome if they would, say, have one animal less. Hence, for every herdsman individually, it is rational to free-ride and get more and more animals rather than to act cooperatively and take care of the common good. As everyone is following this free-rider strategy, the result is collective overgrazing and everyone is worse off.

Consider the following empirical examples in which such cooperation problems play a role:

- *Environment*: suppose you have the choice between airplane transportation or alternative, more environmentally friendly modes of transportation. These alternative forms of transport are less attractive from a purely selfish, materialistic viewpoint: they are more expensive and take more time. Moreover, so one could reason, what difference would it make to the environment if you decide not to fly but everyone else still does? Seen from that perspective, it would be attractive to keep using airplane transport. However, if every individual reasons in this way, the long-term consequences are global warming and environmental damage—a collectively undesirable outcome.
- *Traffic*: people may prefer to take the car instead of public transport because they reason that it is cheaper and more comfortable, and that if they are the only ones taking public transport it will make no difference to the environment. The collective problems are traffic jams, pollution and environmental damage.
- *Not-in-my-backyard*: people object to windfarms in their neighborhood, but as people in other neighborhoods are equally opposed to such windfarms near their houses, then collectively everyone is worse off.

- *Littering*: on a sunny day people are enjoying the weather and relaxing in the park. However, after a while, all the garbage cans in the park are full. If people want to dump their waste, they need to search for garbage cans outside the park or they leave it in the park. Following short-term self-interest, they are inclined to litter in the park—which makes the park a dirty place.

In many social settings cooperation problems occur. Injunctive norms can emerge as *solutions* to these cooperation problems (Boyd & Richerson, 1988; Ullmann-Margalit, 2015 [1977]). If people obey social, moral and legal norms they may be better off as a collective than they would be without such norms (Bicchieri, 2005; Hechter & Opp, 2001; Voss, 2001). For example, in a student dorm, norms may emerge such as "everyone should do the dishes each day" and "once a week, you help cleaning the common room." If such social norms, such house rules, are sufficiently enforced by social control mechanisms, they create a solution to the cooperation problem in the student dorm. The reason is that free-rider behavior (always relaxing) will be sanctioned, whereas cooperative behavior (cleaning) will receive social approval. This will lead to a change in strategy, such that students will be more inclined to clean the house and, in doing so, the student dorm is better off.

The problems of human cooperation may operate at different levels, i.e., at the level of groups and entire societies. Social norms emerge as solutions to cooperation problems within groups, such as in a student dorm, whereas legal norms arise as solutions to social dilemma problems of large-scale populations. The difference between social and legal norms is therefore one of scope: social norms operate in groups, whereas legal norms transcend groups. Thus, social norms—and the eventual internalization thereof—emerge as solutions to cooperation problems in groups (e.g., family, ethnic, religious). They appear particularly effective in smaller groups, because in smaller groups people can better monitor and control each other's behavior. Social norms, therefore, work well in overcoming human cooperation in smaller groups, but they are less suited to overcome cooperation in large-scale societies.

Many legal norms emerged as solutions to large-scale cooperation problems. They are, therefore, similar to social norms in overcoming social dilemma situations and the temptations of individuals to free ride and defect. Many legal norms emerged to serve the **public good**, such as safety and security, and to solve collective undesirable outcomes. Governments can set rules to mitigate the temptation of citizens to steal property, for example. If there are no laws that prohibit this then stealing from others could be more attractive than being nice and cooperative. And if everyone is reasoning in this way, the collective result would be the outbreak of collective chaos, plundering and suffering. Therefore, the legal norms we often see like "it is forbidden to steal someone's property," "you may do no harm to other people" and "you may not exceed speed limits" are more adaptive, more useful to the collective, than legal norms like "you may do whatever you like," "you may randomly kill people" and so on. To establish the administration needed to build a strong government—an army, police force and so forth—legal norms emerged such as "you should pay taxes."

public good good that serves collective benefits, such as national safety and environmental protection.

A clean and sustainable natural environment is also a public good. Therefore, national and global environmental issues may become the subject of governmental laws. Legal norms like "you are not allowed to dump your garbage on the street" may be regarded as a solution to the collective problem that arises if such norms do not exist. The way they do so is by sanctioning the free-rider option, making this a less-attractive strategy

Table 6.3 Fishing cooperation problem, without formal sanctions.

| | | Fisher B | |
		Limited	Unlimited
Fisher A	Limited	9,9	3,10
	Unlimited	10,3	4,4

than cooperative behavior. Let's see how this works by taking another example, namely that of fishers who are tempted to catch as many fish as they can. The situation is similar to that of the herdsmen in the *Tragedy of the Commons* (Hardin, 1968; Ostrom, 2015 [1990]). Table 6.3 presents this cooperation problem of fishers in a stylized way, such that each fisher has the choice of either limited or unlimited fishing. Again, I use a simple well-being scale, ranging from 0 to 10, indicating how content each individual is with a certain outcome.

If the fishers pursue their own self-interest, this social dilemma situation will result in unlimited fishing by everyone. The reason for this is that unlimited fishing is more attractive than the alternative, which is that fishers restrict their fishing. Thus, Fisher A reasons:

> if Fisher B opts for limited fishing, I go for unlimited fishing (which makes me perfectly happy: 10!) instead of limited fishing (9). And if Fisher B goes for unlimited fishing, then unlimited fishing is also more beneficial for me (4) than limited fishing (3).

Thus, the dominant strategy is to fish without limits. Because Fisher B reasons in exactly the same way, for both of them unlimited fishing is the most attractive option. But the collective result is that they end up in a situation that does not serve the collective interest (4,4).

In this social dilemma situation, legal norms like "fishers may not exceed the fish quota" may emerge and these particular norms may be regarded as attractive to enforce—more so than other norms that do not solve this social dilemma. What would happen if there is such a law that prohibits (and sanctions) unlimited fishing? It would mean that the free-rider strategy becomes less attractive, because doing so violates the law and results in sanctions. Table 6.4 presents one possible scenario.

In this new social condition, unlimited fishing is no longer the dominant strategy. Instead, it is more attractive for fishers to stick to the fish quota—whatever other fishers are doing.

Table 6.4 Fishing cooperation problem, with formal sanctions.

| | | Fisher B | |
		Limited	Unlimited
Fisher A	Limited	9,9	3,8
	Unlimited	8,3	2,2

The collective outcome is that everyone will limit their number of fish (9,9), which is better than the situation before legal norms emerged (4,4).

In summary, injunctive norms can therefore be regarded as solutions to problems of human cooperation—small scale and large scale. They have the potential to solve the conflict between (often short-term) self-interest and (often longer-term) collective interest, and thereby promote collective health, the environment, national safety and well-being (De Swaan, 1988; Pinker, 2011; Welzel, 2013). This does not imply that *each* social and legal norm that emerged and which was enforced, is a solution to a social dilemma situation, that it was adaptive to its social context, but in many cases it is fruitful to consider this evolutionary approach in order to understand why a certain injunctive norm emerged and is sustained.

PRINCIPLE 6.1

Injunctive norms and cooperation

If you want to understand the emergence of particular injunctive norms, it is often fruitful to see them as solutions to cooperation problems.

There is a second explanation for norms to emerge, which is that they can also solve **coordination problems**. To illustrate, consider how you greet someone. Suppose you're meeting someone for the first time. What do you do? There are many ways to greet, such as handshaking, hugging, bowing, kissing, to name only a few. And you can give one kiss, two, or even more and also combine various styles (e.g., hugging and kissing). Let's see what we get if we focus, for the moment, on two of these greeting options, namely handshaking and bowing (Table 6.5).

coordination problem certain condition in which people want to do the same thing, but are uncertain about the behavior of each other.

In a coordination problem like this one, everyone benefits from doing the same thing as the others do, but what others will do is uncertain. Thus, if you and the other person choose handshaking, then you're both content (10,10). But it could be that the other person bows instead, while you were trying to give a handshake, which would be a collectively undesirable outcome (5,5). And if you opt for bowing, it could still be that the other person opts for handshaking, again leading to a suboptimal outcome (5,5). What is the best thing to do will depend on what the other person does. There is, therefore, no dominant strategy. Both you and the other person want to do the same, but the problem is that you and the other person may not know what the other person will do.

Table 6.5 Coordination problem: handshaking or bowing?

		Other person	
		Handshaking	Bowing
You	Handshaking	10,10	5,5
	Bowing	5,5	10,10

Situations like these generate a demand for norms. But these are not the injunctive norms we have reviewed so far but rather are **descriptive norms** (Hechter & Opp, 2001). These are norms too, as they specify what people are expected to do in certain circumstances. Unlike injunctive norms, however, violating such norms does not lead to sanctions. Deviance from injunctive norms results in some kind of sanction, as we have seen: either externally (social norms), internally (moral norms) or formally (legal norms). Such sanctioning is applied because individuals are tempted to free-ride in cooperation situations. But in the case of coordination problems, such sanctioning is not needed as everyone benefits from doing the same as others do. Descriptive norms are therefore different from injunctive norms in that the expectations have no normative connotation.

> **descriptive norm** statement specifying what a person is expected to do.

Descriptive norms about greeting styles can be regarded as solutions to coordination problems (Lewis, 2008 [1969]; Schelling, 1980; Ullmann-Margalit, 2015 [1977]). The descriptive norm "always shake hands instead of bowing" solves the problem of how to coordinate actions when you meet someone. If this norm is common, everyone benefits from sticking to this convention instead of deviating from it. The descriptive norm solves the coordination problem. Unlike cooperation problems, individuals have an incentive to stick to the convention as their self-interest is exactly the same as the interest of the group. There is no temptation to free-ride and so sanctions are not needed.

Many conventions, habits and traditions can be seen as descriptive norms that emerged as solutions to coordination problems. Consider the following empirical examples of descriptive norms:

a "if you drive on the street, you keep to the right"
b "if you meet someone, you shake hands"
c "eat with a knife and fork"
d "always speak English"
e "measure distance in miles"
f "quantify temperature in Celsius"
g "office hours start at 9 am."

When the descriptive norm prevails that says "if you drive on the street, you keep to the right" the coordination problem has been solved, because everyone knows what they are expected to do and they know that others know what to do as well. Interestingly, "driving on the right side" is not the only descriptive norm which could solve the coordination problem that is typical in traffic. Different descriptive norms can emerge to solve the same coordination problem. Thus, the descriptive norm "if you drive on the street, you keep to the left" equally solves the problem of coordinating traffic. For each of the examples above (a–g), you can think of alternative descriptive norms which have evolved and which provide alternative solutions to the underlying coordination problems.

We may wonder why different descriptive norms emerged for the same coordination problem. Why did the norm "drive on the left" become dominant in Great Britain, for example, and "drive on the right" in France? Why speak English in Ireland, Chinese in China and Arabic in Morocco? These norms depend on historical contingencies that come about through "exogenous" and "endogenous" processes (Voss, 2001). Sometimes, descriptive norms emerge "exogenously", top-down, and when this happens they are called **decrees** (Ullmann-Margalit, 2015 [1977]). Exogenous parties, such as the state, could take action and establish decrees that solve coordination problems. But descriptive norms often emerge by human action as well, by "endogenous" forces and not by human design

> **decree** top-down change in descriptive norm.

(Bicchieri, 2005). These refer to bottom-up processes from repeated interactions of individuals who themselves can come up with a generally accepted rule, which then becomes self-enforcing.

For example, imagine we go back a few centuries to when people used a horse and carriage. Imagine that two persons (A and B) crossed their paths on a certain day and, by coincidence, both opted for the left side—and everything went well. When, on their way back, they meet each other again, they opt again for the left side—remembering how that worked well last time. Then, on a certain day, person A encounters another person (C). Person A is by now used to going left, but what does person C do? If C also chooses the left side, then three persons are already coordinating their actions according to the same rule. If, instead, person C makes a different choice, it will hurt C and A. The next time person C will act differently, knowing that person A will drive left, and, when new persons enter this situation, they will do so as well, as they have observed that the norm is to keep to the left. Some conventions emerge in this way, endogenously, bottom up. And, as you can see, the process could easily have unfolded differently, namely when the first person opted for driving right rather than left. Once established, the descriptive norm is self-enforcing: everyone benefits from doing the same as the majority.

PRINCIPLE 6.2

Descriptive norms and coordination
If you want to understand the emergence of particular descriptive norms, it is often fruitful to see them as solutions to coordination problems.

6.7 Cultural maladaptation and norm change

It has been argued so far that norms emergence can be seen as solutions to collective problems and that cultures are rational adaptations to challenges of human coordination and cooperation. In this social evolutionary approach, the emergence of norms can be understood as solutions to various problems of collective behavior which serve the (often long-term) collective benefits. The emergence of certain norms can make sense in a way, as they can benefit the group and the society at large.

However, certain norms exist which do not serve the interest of the collective. There can be norms which cause harm and undermine well-being. And, less severely, norms can exist which are suboptimal solutions, i.e., people would profit more from alternative norms. They are called **unpopular norms** (Centola, Willer, & Macy, 2005; Willer, Kuwabara, & Macy, 2009) and they belong to the broader category of **cultural maladaptation** (Mesoudi, 2011), i.e., the existence of norms, and also opinions, which do not fit their social environment well. You may wonder why this is happening. What explains unpopular, maladaptive norms? And when, and under which conditions, do they change into norms that serve the interest of the collective? There are several explanations for cultural maladaptation. Two important reasons are: (1) *cultural inertia* and (2) *pluralistic ignorance*.

unpopular norm
norm which is not serving collective benefits.

cultural maladaptation
norms and opinions which do not fit their social environment well.

Cultural inertia

Maladaptation can be due to **cultural inertia**, the time-lag that can exist between changing social conditions and adapting new norms and opinions which are better suited to the new conditions. Cultural traits (norms, opinions), which emerged as adaptive, rational responses to certain conditions, may only slowly change or even persist after the initial conditions in which they emerged disappear (Lieberson, 1987, 2000). This need not be problematic but, in some cases, norms persist

cultural inertia time-lag between changing social conditions and adapting new norms and opinions.

that are harmful to people or that do not give the best collective outcomes. Let's review several empirical cases in which unpopular norms persisted and identify when they changed.

Driving on the wrong side

We have seen that driving on the right or left side can be seen as a coordination problem and that descriptive norms ("always drive left!") solve these kinds of collective problem. The issue, however, is that the descriptive norm ("always drive left!") may serve the collective interest at one point in time but, when conditions change, it may no longer be the best response. This is exactly what happened in Sweden in the 1960s. Traditionally, the descriptive norm in Sweden was that "people should drive on the left of the road," which is, as we have seen, no problem, because everyone benefits from following a descriptive norm.

However, this descriptive norm was increasingly conflicting with another descriptive norm, namely the one that prevailed in neighboring countries. At that time, citizens of neighboring countries Finland and Norway were expected to drive on the right side instead of the left side. Because of increasing traffic and mobility across neighboring countries, the casualties caused by these two conflicting descriptive norms were becoming more and more of a collective problem. We can present this "multiple" coordination problem for Sweden using a matrix (Table 6.6). Clearly, the descriptive norm "drive left" is not the collectively worst outcome, but also not the optimal outcome, which is "drive right," because this norm solves the problem of coordination within Sweden and the coordination problem between countries.

The conflicting norms "drive on the left side" (Sweden) and "drive on the right side" (Finland, Norway) persisted for many years, despite the fact that these norms were suboptimal responses. Many traffic accidents and casualties could be prevented if the countries could agree on the same descriptive norm. Changing from one (suboptimal) descriptive norm to another (optimal) norm can be difficult, as such norms tend to *lock-in*, i.e., an equilibrium has emerged that is hard to change. Individuals have no incentive to deviate on their own from the descriptive norm because that would be risky. Governments may not want to change either because it

Table 6.6 Coordination problem of driving on the left or right side of the road: Sweden in the 1960s.

		Person B	
		Right	Left
Person A	Right	10,10	0,0
	Left	0,0	7,7

may incur significant costs in making the change. Imagine a country changing its entire traffic system, from an infrastructure designed to drive on the left side to the right side (or vice versa).

Eventually, on September 3, 1967, the Swedish government decided to accept the transition costs and make this gigantic change. They enforced the rule of "driving on the right," despite the fact that over 82% of the Swedish population voted against this norm. Once this norm was established, the opposition quickly disappeared and within no time the Swedes were happy to drive safely on the right side of the road. Once a new descriptive norm is established, it is self-enforcing: everyone benefits from following the norm.

Holy cows and pig taboos

Scholars have described in detail various cases in which norms persist, despite that the initial cause for the norm has disappeared. The anthropologist Marvin Harris mentions several of such examples regarding eating practices: "holy cows" in India, "pig haters" among Jews and Muslims and "pig lovers" in New Guinea and the South Pacific Melanesian islands (Harris, 1989). Why do Hindus worship cows? Why do the Bible and the Koran, and their adherents to the present day, condemn pigs? Harris argues that these and other food norms emerged for good ecological reasons a long time ago, as local solutions to problems of the conflict between (short-term) individual benefits and (long-term) collective outcomes. For example, Harris mentions that pigs were:

> ill-adapted to the hot, dry climate of the Negev, the Jordan Valley, and the other lands of the Bible and the Koran. Compared to the cattle, goats, and sheep, the pig has an inefficient system for regulating its body temperature. Despite the expression "To sweat like a pig", it has recently been proved that pigs can't sweat at all … To compensate for its lack of protective hair and its inability to sweat, the pig must dampen its skin with external moisture. It prefers to do this by wallowing in fresh clean mud, but it will cover its skin with its own urine and feces if nothing else is available.
>
> (Harris, 1989)

Keeping and eating pigs was not a collective beneficial strategy in the hot habitat of the Middle East. It was the wrong place to raise pigs, but people may have been tempted to raise pigs for their meat—a luxury good that serves immediate short-term benefits. The taboo on eating pigs among Jews and Muslims may have evolved a long time ago as a social norm in these local conditions. And although the ecological objections to eating pigs may no longer apply, Jews and Muslims, even when not living in the Middle East, observe these food taboos. One reason for this, Harris suggests, is that the social norm in itself may have become a way for members to think of themselves as a distinctive group (Harris, 1989).

Footbinding

Another example of a norm that persisted for a long time while not serving the interest of the collective is footbinding. The footbinding practice persisted for around 1,000 years in China, until it eventually disappeared in a few decades. Sociologist Gerry Mackie describes this practice in detail:

> Beginning at about age six to eight, the female child's four smaller toes were bent under the foot, the sole was forced to the heel, and then the foot was wrapped in a tight bandage day and night in order to mold a bowed and pointed four-inch-long appendage. Footbinding was extremely painful in the first 6 to 10 years of formative treatment.

Complications included ulceration, paralysis, gangrene, and mortification of the lower limbs; perhaps 10 percent of girls did not survive the treatment.

(Mackie, 1996)

According to Mackie, footbinding became a convention which solved coordination problems in the marriage market, namely how to signal to potential marriage partners that you are faithful. Mackie describes that, from around 960 to 1900, bound feet were regarded as a sign of "gentility" and that footbinding became a persistent inferior convention in which the population became trapped:

Both men and women would be better off marrying without the mutilating practice, but they are trapped by the inferior convention. However the custom originated, as soon as women believed that men would not marry an unmutilated woman, and men believed that an unmutilated woman would not be a faithful partner in marriage, and so forth, expectations were mutually concordant and a self-enforcing convention was locked in.

(Mackie, 1996)

Footbinding persisted for hundreds of years, even though it was an unpopular maladaptive norm that did much harm. The reason it persisted for such a long time is similar to the reason people in Sweden kept driving on the left side of the road. Descriptive norms tend to be self-enforcing, even when, after a certain time, they appear no longer needed or even harm people. In 1912, the Nationalist Revolution eventually banned footbinding by decree and through various campaigns advancing natural feet. In no time at all, people adopted the new convention which better served the collective interest (Mackie, 1996).

Immigrant cultures

Unpopular norms can persist for a considerable time. This phenomenon of cultural inertia has been observed in studies of immigrant groups as well. Immigrants are a particularly interesting group to study in this context because immigrants have been socialized in the culture of their country of origin, whereas their children grow up in the destination country— which may have very different social conditions in which the norms of the previous generation may no longer be useful. What scholars have found is that the prevalent norms of immigrant groups persist for many immigrant generations and only slowly change.

This process unfolds as follows. It begins with immigrants who have internalized the norms from their country of origin. When arriving in a new country they pass on the old norms (which were adaptive in the origin country) to their children, even if such norms are maladaptive in the new context. Children internalize the norms acquired from their parents and pass on these norms to the next generation and so forth, following the process of parental transmission (Chapter 5). But norms that were adaptive in the previous (parental) generation need not necessarily be useful in the next (child's) generation. People, however, also learn from their own experience that parental norms may not be that effective in the current context. Within each generation, individuals thus acquire new information and they may learn that the old norms are not the best strategies anymore. This means that the old norms are learned in childhood and are then updated with some new information that people acquire from individual learning (Inglehart, 1990). A combination of "old" and "new" knowledge is then passed on to the next generation. This means that each new generation is socialized into norms that are better and better adapted to current conditions. Consequently, norms of immigrant groups only slowly change in the direction of the dominant norms of the majority population (Greeley & McCready, 1975).

This pattern of long-term ethnic-cultural heritages—and slow adaptations to changing environmental conditions—has been found with respect to a wide range of norms, opinions and corresponding behavior (Giavazzi, Petkov, & Schiantarelli, 2019; Rice & Feldman, 1997). For example, immigrant groups whose ancestors migrated from societies that had very conservative cultures—such as highly unequal gender roles—tend to only slowly change to adopt the mainstream progressive norms of their highly progressive host societies (Alesina, Giuliano, & Nunn, 2013; Finseraas & Kotsadam, 2017; Polavieja, 2015). Children of immigrants whose parents were born and raised in low-trust societies tend to have lower trust than children of immigrants who come from high-trust societies (Dinesen, 2011; Helliwell, Wang, & Xu, 2016; Ljunge, 2014; Nannestad, Svendsen, Dinesen, & Sønderskov, 2014).

Putnam observed such long-term cultural legacies in his study of civic traditions in the south and north of Italy (Putnam, Leonardi, & Nanetti, 1993). Inglehart and other researchers have pointed out the slow changes of values over long periods of time and the persistent value differences in supranational, cultural zones (Inglehart & Baker, 2000; Inglehart & Welzel, 2005). Cultural norms can change in society due to changing societal conditions, but typically the process of cultural change is slow. Norms—even when maladaptive—can persist for long periods of time.

Pluralistic ignorance

The existence of norms that do not serve collective interests can also be the result of collective misperceptions. This happens when many people *believe* that the majority supports a certain norm, whereas in reality this is not the case. But because of collective misperceptions, people collectively believe that the costs of norm-deviance are high and they therefore comply with the norm.

How can this happen? Why can a norm persist that is rejected by the majority of people? Let's return to the case of binge drinking, which happens so frequently among university students. It has often been noted that students *think* that (excessive) drinking is "cool," that it is something they "should do when entering college." Why these social norms? Well, you could argue that there is a collective demand for such a "drinking norm." If that is the case—if the majority supports this norm—then the norm may have emerged for good reasons. Yet scholars have shown that, when asked privately, most students were more uncomfortable with alcohol practices than they believed others to be (Borsari & Carey, 2001; Prentice & Miller, 1993). In other words, most students don't like the social norm of excessive drinking, yet they believe that others do. Despite the fact that most students do not like to drink a lot, the norm "you should drink excessively" exists and the students collectively adhere to this norm.

What is happening here is what is called a situation of **pluralistic ignorance** (Katz & Allport, 1931). These situations have the following characteristics:

A   the majority of people privately reject a certain norm;
B   but they incorrectly believe that others privately support the norm.

The key issue in understanding why such maladaptive norms can persist is the distinction between *private preferences* and *public behavior* (Kuran, 1997, 1991). Private preferences are things people personally prefer (value, desire, support). Public behavior is what people express in public, i.e., what they say or do in the presence of other people. It is not necessarily the case that public behavior corresponds to

> **pluralistic ignorance** situation in which the majority of people privately reject a certain norm, but incorrectly believe that others privately support the norm.

private preferences. It could well be that a person prefers "A" but for whatever reason does "not-A" in public. Because people commonly rely on observational learning and social proof (Chapter 5), they take the public behavior of other people as revealing information about their private preferences. Thus, if someone *does* "A" in public, people infer from this behavior that that person *prefers* "A."

However, in the case where someone's public behavior is not congruent with his or her private preferences, other people may *misperceive* his/her *private* preferences. When, in a certain social context, people do not express their private preferences in public, people have to rely on what others are doing in *public*. This public behavior is then used to infer what peers prefer in private. But public behavior might not always concur with what people support privately.

Scholars have argued that this incongruency might well play a role in students' excessive drinking patterns (Borsari & Carey, 2001; Prentice & Miller, 1993). Students think that their peers prefer excessive drinking, but this is wrong. They (incorrectly) come to believe this because they see their college peers drinking a lot in public, hence they assume that their peers prefer such behavior. Many students dare not express their personal preferences in public—thus violating the norm—so private reasons remain something to be inferred from public behavior. And as students do not speak up, so they will conform to what others are doing: they will also drink excessively, thereby signalling to yet other peers that they approve of the norm.

Such scenarios of pluralistic ignorance can contribute to the phenomenon called the **bystander effect**. This refers to the phenomenon that people are less likely to help other people in a critical situation when passive bystanders are present (Darley & Latane, 1968). In real life this phenomenon often happens in various ways: a person falls in the water, he cannot swim, many bystanders witness the person struggling, but nobody interferes. Or, a person is lying on the ground in a busy street shouting for help as she needs medical assistance, but those passing by ignore her. Why is this happening? Why are people not helping when such helping could be done without any danger to the individual and could save someone's life?

bystander effect phenomenon in which people are less likely to help other people in a critical situation when passive bystanders are present.

Scholars have argued that different processes contribute to the bystander effect (Fischer et al., 2011), one of them being pluralistic ignorance (Latané & Nida, 1981). When bystanders are passive and do not interfere, people may believe that the bystanders *prefer* such passive behavior; that others believe the best response to the "crisis" situation is to do nothing. In fact, research findings suggest that the bigger the group of passive bystanders, the more strongly people come to believe this and the less likely they are to intervene (Latané & Nida, 1981). Apparently, when bystanders are passive, people may believe that there is no crisis or that, somehow, the problem will be solved without the help of the bystanders. In turn, people will remain passive as well, thereby further confirming the norm that "one is not expected to interfere." Privately, they may have their doubts or, in fact, they may want to interfere but, given that the majority of people are not doing anything, they remain passive as well.

Maladaptive, unpopular, norms that may even do more harm than good to the collective can emerge and persist because of pluralistic ignorance. They occur in social contexts in which there is a discrepancy between people's private preferences and their public behavior, by the lack of expression of private preferences and interpersonal communication, creating an "illusion of support" for the norm. People are wrongly believing that other people support the norm. This can happen in peer groups in which students incorrectly believe that the majority supports the norm of excessive drinking, or in bystander situations, such as on a busy street, when strangers think that passive behavior is what others prefer.

Maladaptive norms that are due to pluralistic ignorance can erode quickly when the sole force is the collective misperception of each other's beliefs. In these cases, once people discover that there is no majority support for the norm, that, in fact, everything was a lie or public misunderstanding, the norm collapses. If a student speaks up, tells his peers that he does not want to drink and his behavior is not ridiculed, this could break down the "excessive drinking norm."

Sometimes, however, maladaptive norms can become stable. This can happen when *false enforcement* emerges: people enforce the norm in public, and hence sanction deviance, even when they privately reject the norm (Centola et al., 2005; Willer et al., 2009). Thus, people may not only *conform* to a norm they reject in private, but they may also actively *punish* others who do not comply and reward conformity. People may do this—enforce norms they do not support in private—to show that they have complied out of conviction; that they are "genuine supporters" (Centola et al., 2005; Willer et al., 2009) or "true believers" (Henrich, 2009). In fact, people who reject a social norm but believe the majority supports that norm may display behaviors that signal their credibility. They may become fanatic in sanctioning those who do not comply to the norm and they may themselves over-act just to signal to others that they truly believe in and support the norm.

Consider again the binge-drinking norm among students and suppose there is a group of four students (A, B, C, D), all of them publicly supporting this norm. Suppose that none of them actually wants to binge drink—this is their private preference—and that student A dares to speak up and reveal to her peers her private preference, that she does not want to drink that much. What can happen, in a situation of pluralistic ignorance, is that one of her peers, say student B (although agreeing with A in private), might *sanction* A nevertheless. By so doing, B is showing to peers A, C and D that not only does she conform to the drinking norm because of peer pressure but that, in addition, she *sincerely believes* it is a good norm. More than this, B may signal her true belief in this norm by drinking a lot, on many occasions, and speaking very often and positively about her own binge drinking behavior. In such cases, the norm to drink excessively can become stable—even though the majority rejects it privately.

Even entire societies can become locked in to such maladaptive norms for long periods of time, until they break down eventually. A case in point is the Communist political system that prevailed in Eastern Germany for several decades, under the rule of the (former) Soviet Union. To the surprise of the majority of East Germans, this political ideology collapsed in the October 1989 revolution (Kuran, 1991). Many citizens had not seen this revolution coming. The reason why is that, up to that date, the majority of people believed that the population supported the regime.

These collective misperceptions were deliberately promoted by public rituals organized by the government. Broadcasting large-scale ceremonies created the illusion of majority support for the regime because everyone in the population knew about these public events. They were "ritual signs of dominance," creating the illusion of massive support for the regime (Chwe, 2013). In this context, citizens in Eastern Germany actively signalled that they were genuine supporters. For example, they would not just attend communist party meetings, but would also actively engage in the party by publishing materials that supported the communist ideology and by chasing down and reporting people to the authorities when they criticized communism—even if those persons were friends and family members. Hence, everyone was showing to everyone else how fantastic the communist system was—whereas, in private, most people rejected the system. In this **spiral of silence**, people dared not speak up and

spiral of silence people's tendency to remain silent and not express their private preference when they believe that their private preferences deviate from the majority's preferences.

express their private preferences as they (wrongly) believed that they deviated from the majority opinion (Noelle-Neumann, 1993; Scheufele & Moy, 2000). The revolution, then, came as a surprise to the East Germans. When a small group dared to challenge the ideology this group was soon followed by a larger group, and soon almost everyone was protesting against the ruling system (Kuran, 1997).

6.8 The dynamics of group distinction

Thus far, we have seen evidence suggesting that descriptive norms tend to persist for long periods of time because everyone benefits from the status quo. Conventions, customs, traditions and habits solve coordination problems and they tend to be self-enforcing. Several sociologists, however, such as Elias, Veblen, Bourdieu, Durkheim and Simmel, have noted that descriptive norms can become subject to dynamics of *group distinction*, i.e., the intended process of differentiating oneself from other groups. Let's see how we can understand such processes of distinction by using the insights from this chapter.

One particular often-discussed idea in this field of research is the so-called **trickle-down theory** (Durkheim, 1887; Elias, 2000 [1939]; Simmel, 1957). This theory can be summarized as a coherent set of propositions and assumptions:

1 There are *multiple* groups in society and these groups differ in their descriptive norms (habits, conventions, customs).
2 Groups are *hierarchically* ordered: they differ in their subjective "social standing" and "prestige."
3 Descriptive norms are *symbolic expressions* of group identity.
4 Higher status groups *invent* new descriptive norms to symbolically differentiate their group from lower-status groups.
5 Lower-status groups *imitate* these new descriptive norms to symbolically associate themselves with high-status groups.
6 The more strongly lower-status groups have adopted the high-status descriptive norms, the less attractive these descriptive norms are to high-status groups, resulting in new inventions (return to step 4).

According to the trickle-down theory, therefore, some descriptive norms are *dynamic* and in constant flux. They diffuse from high- to low-status groups. Once they are widely adopted by low-status groups, they lose their attraction to the high-status groups, which then invent new ones and so forth. This is a dynamic process in which high-status groups aim to agree on the *same* descriptive norm—all members benefit from doing the same as the other members of their own group—and at the same time this norm should be *distinctive* from those of low-status groups, i.e., high-status groups deliberately aim *not* to coordinate their behavior with lower-status groups. It is thus a matter of (within-group) *coordination* and (between-group) *distinction* at the same time.

Sociologists, in earlier works of those such as Durkheim (1887) and Simmel (1957), have argued that this process is typical of the dynamics in *fashion*. The kind of clothes people wear, hair style and so forth is in constant change. It is, strictly speaking, a matter of "taste" whether, for example, one wears a hat or not. However, wearing a hat could also be a symbolic expression of group identity; it is a *signal*. Imagine that in a certain society, at t_0, no one wears a hat and there are only two groups: one of low status and another of high status. We can represent this situation in a matrix as "dynamics of distinction and imitation"

Table 6.7 Dynamics of group distinction and imitation.

		High-status	
		Wear hat	No hat
Low-status	Wear hat	8,4	4,8
	No hat	4,8	8,4

(Table 6.7). Under these conditions, it may become a strategy for the high-status group to start wearing a hat at t_1, as this then becomes a signal that they are different from low-status groups. The descriptive norm within the high-status group is then "wear a hat!" and all members benefit from doing this. But then low-status members will copy this behavior, say at t_2, and hence wearing a hat loses its attraction. High-status members will then invent a new fashion, at t_3, such as wearing not simply a hat but a hat of a certain "exclusive" type and so forth. Sociologists have found evidence that at least in some societies trickle-down processes in fashion have taken place (Barber & Lobel, 1952; Fallers, 1954).

Such "dynamics of distinction and imitation" have also been observed in *first naming*. Although giving a name to the newborn child might seem a purely personal choice, sociologists have long recognized hidden social forces in name-giving. Indeed, the trickle-down process has been observed in name-giving. In this case, new names invented by high-status groups are subsequently adopted by low-status groups. High-status groups invent yet other names and so forth. This pattern has been observed in France (Besnard, 1979), Germany (Gerhards & Hackenbroch, 2000) and the United States (Lieberson, 2000; Lieberson & Bell, 1992). Similar processes of distinction and imitation have been observed in *consumption* (Veblen, 2017), *language usage* and admiring certain *art* (Bourdieu, 2010 [1979]).

One of the most impressive sociological studies on the trickle-down theory was *The Civilizing Process* written by the German sociologist Norbert Elias (2000 [1939]). The book was originally published in German in 1939 and, when the war began in Germany, Elias fled to England and years went by before his book was noted by other scientists. It was in 1969 that the book was finally translated into English and it soon became a classic. Coincidentally, Elias was already 70 by then.

Elias' study became famous because he asked the virtually impossible question of how *behavioral manners* had changed over a period of 500 years. Elias studied so-called "etiquette books" (in their widest sense, books on "manners") from Western Europe, as well as poems, paintings and literature from the periods roughly between 1200 and 1850. Such etiquette books comprised a system of norms; of all the behaviors that you were, and were not, expected to do. Such etiquette books were written for high-status groups, i.e., for nobles and aristocrats.

By comparing these books on proper manners over time, Elias was able to trace back changes in norms. What was regarded as good or bad behavior in the 13th century? How did this change over time? Elias reasoned that if something was *not* allowed according to an etiquette book, this meant that the specific behavior *often occurred* in practice. Behavior from the Middle Ages now comes across as weird; because such behavior is now truly unimaginable we no longer have to tell one another that such behavior is not okay.

In order to arrive at a systematic comparison over time, Elias focused on topics that appeared in all the books. In this regard, he referred to "universal human challenges," i.e., the basic human needs to eat, drink, sleep and relieve ourselves. How do people deal with these universal human functions? In all societies, across all times, people have to somehow deal with them and Elias said that by studying the changes in how they did, we can trace back cultural differences.

Let us examine some examples more closely. Let us begin with: what did people across the ages think about "table manners?" It is striking that on this topic there were few rules to be found in the manner books of the Middle Ages (500 to 1500). Almost anything was allowed, we may conclude. Whatever they said about "correct" behavior would be found self-explanatory nowadays. Take, for instance, these two:

> Anyone who hawks up during dinner and blows their nose in the tablecloth: I consider them not very well mannered.
>
> (13th century)

> I consider anyone blowing their nose and spraying the table or wiping their nose with their hand to be a boor who knows no better manners.
>
> (13th century)

Image 6.2 Table manners are part of the etiquette. According to Elias, such table manners have changed over time.

Using your hands was usual; the fork and one's own spoon did not come in until the 16th century. It was not until the 17th century that handkerchiefs were widespread. In the 18th century, the elite gradually started to eat with new spoons, knives and forks for each dish. The manner in which people relieved themselves changed. You only have to read what was written on this subject in the 16th century:

> It is rude to greet someone who is urinating or relieving themselves.
>
> (1530)

Apparently, in 1530, some people greeted one another while they pooped and peed. And how about the following clues on proper behavior:

> Likewise it applies that no one whomsoever may pollute the spiral staircases, other staircases, corridors, or rooms with urine or any other filth during, after or before the meal, whether early or late, but that one is supposed to go to the appropriate, appointed places to perform these necessary functions.
>
> (1598)

> Do not show your most intimate body parts openly; that is shameful and wicked, despicable and rude.
>
> (1619)

By systematically comparing the rules regarding etiquette across the ages on the basis of relevant books, literature and paintings, Elias discovered that the standards for good behavior were set gradually higher. He referred to this development as the *civilization process*, a long-term development in which the norms "thou shalt not ..." became increasingly strict. Therefore, "civilized" also meant "well mannered," "refined," "decent," "well bred," "adult" and "modest," and was often set off against "unrefined," "barbaric," "primitive," "childish," "impulsive" and "bestial."

This change, however, did not occur in all segments of society at the same time. Elias describes that higher-status groups invented "refined" manners of behavior (such as eating with a spoon), which were subsequently adopted by lower-status groups. The civilization campaign first emerged among the court aristocracy (i.e., the elite) and subsequently found its way to the bourgeoisie (middle classes) and eventually to the farmers and the lowest classes— as a trickle-down, spiraling process:

> For it is precisely the chief function of the court aristocracy to distinguish themselves, to maintain themselves as a distinct formation, a social counterweight to the bourgeoisie. They are completely free to spend their time elaborating the distinguishing social conduct of good manners and good taste ... They [the bourgeoisie] ape the nobility and its manners. But precisely this makes modes of conduct developed in court circles continually become useless as means of distinction, and the noble groups are forced to elaborate their conduct still further. Over and over again customs that were once 'refined' become 'vulgar'.
>
> (Elias, 2000[1939]: 424–425)

In short, descriptive norms on behavioral manners were vertically diffused, from the top to the bottom, in line with the trickle-down theory.

6.9 Chapter resources

Key concepts

Social norm	Moral norm	Coordination problem
Injunctive norm	Value	Descriptive norm
Prescriptive norm	Habitus	Decree
Oughtness norm	Legal norm	Unpopular norm
Social sanction	Formal sanction	Cultural maladaptation
External sanction	Internal sanction	Cultural inertia
Third party	Dominant strategy	Pluralistic ignorance
Social approval	Free-ride	Bystander effect
Monitoring	Cooperation problem	Spiral of silence
Internalized norm	Public good	

Key theories and propositions

- Social control theory
- Trickle-down theory

Summary

- There are different types of norms in society. A common distinction is that between descriptive norms and injunctive norms.
- Injunctive norms include moral norms, social norms and legal norms.
- The social control theory explains why and under which conditions people follow social norms.
- Injunctive norms can emerge as solutions to cooperation problems and social dilemma situations.
- Descriptive norms can emerge as solutions to coordination problems.
- Sometimes, norms persist even though they do not fit their social environment well. These are unpopular norms and they are part of the phenomenon called cultural maladaptation.
- Cultural maladaptation can be due to cultural inertia and pluralistic ignorance.
- The trickle-down theory argues that descriptive norms can change due to dynamics between group distinction and imitation.

References

Ajzen, I. (1991). The theory of planned behavior. *Organizational Behavior and Human Decision Processes*, 50, 179–211.

Ajzen, I., & Fishbein, M. (1977). Attitude-behavior relations: A theoretical analysis and review of empirical research. *Psychological Bulletin*, 84(5), 888–918.

Akers, R. L. (1996). Is differential association/social learning cultural deviance theory? *Criminology*, 34(2), 229–247.

Alesina, A., Giuliano, P., & Nunn, N. (2013). On the origins of gender roles: Women and the plough. *The Quarterly Journal of Economics*, 128(2), 469–530.

Barber, B., & Lobel, L. S. (1952). Fashion in women's clothes and the american social system. *Social Forces*, 31(2), 124–131.

Bauman, Z. (2005 [1989]). *Modernity and the holocaust.* Cambridge, UK: Polity Press.

Benedict, R. (1934). *Patterns of culture.* New York, NY: Houghton Mifflin Harcourt.

Besnard, P. (1979). Pour une étude empirique du phénomène de mode dans la consommation des biens symboliques: le cas des prénoms. *European Journal of Sociology/Archives Européennes De Sociologie, 20*(2), 343–351.

Bicchieri, C. (2005). *The grammar of society: The nature and dynamics of social norms.* New York, NY: Cambridge University Press.

Billari, F. C., & Liefbroer, A. C. (2007). Should I stay or should I go? The impact of age norms on leaving home. *Demography, 44*(1), 181–198.

Blau, P. (1955). *The dynamics of bureaucracy.* Chicago, IL: University of Chicago Press.

Borsari, B., & Carey, K. B. (2001). Peer influences on college drinking: A review of the research. *Journal of Substance Abuse, 13*(4), 391–424.

Boudon, R. (2001). *The origin of values: Essays in the sociology and philosophy of beliefs.* New Brunswick, NJ: Transaction Publishers.

Bourdieu, P. (2010 [1979]). *Distinction: A social critique of the judgement of taste.* Abingdon, UK: Routledge.

Boyd, R., & Richerson, P. J. (1988). *Culture and the evolutionary process.* Chicago, IL: University of Chicago Press.

Brennan, G., Eriksson, L., Goodin, R. E., & Southwood, N. (2013). *Explaining norms.* Oxford, UK: Oxford University Press.

Bruinsma, G. J. (1992). Differential association theory reconsidered: An extension and its empirical test. *Journal of Quantitative Criminology, 8*(1), 29–49.

Centola, D., Willer, R., & Macy, M. (2005). The emperor's dilemma: A computational model of self-enforcing norms. *American Journal of Sociology, 110*(4), 1009–1040.

Chwe, M. S. (2013). *Rational ritual: Culture, coordination, and common knowledge.* Princeton, NJ: Princeton University Press.

Dahrendorf, R. (17th ed.). (2010 [1959]). *Homo sociologicus: Ein versuch zur geschichte, bedeutung und kritik der kategorie der sozialen rolle.* Wiesbaden, Germany: Springer Fachmedien.

Darley, J. M., & Latane, B. (1968). Bystander intervention in emergencies: Diffusion of responsibility. *Journal of Personality and Social Psychology, 8*(4), 377–383.

Datler, G., Jagodzinski, W., & Schmidt, P. (2013). Two theories on the test bench: Internal and external validity of the theories of Ronald Inglehart and Shalom Schwartz. *Social Science Research, 42*(3), 906–925.

De Swaan, A. (1988). *In care of the state: Health care, education, and welfare in Europe and the USA in the modern era.* Cambridge, UK: Polity Press.

Dinesen, P. T. (2011). Where you come from or where you live? Examining the cultural and institutional explanation of generalized trust using migration as a natural experiment. *European Sociological Review, 29*(1), 114–128.

Durkheim, E. (1887). La science positive de la morale en allemagne. *Revue Philosophique De La France Et De L'Étranger, 24,* 113–142.

Durkheim, E. (1961[1897]). *Suicide.* New York, NY: Free Press.

Elias, N. (2000 [1939]). *The civilizing process: Sociogenetic and psychogenetic investigations* (2nd ed.). Oxford, UK: Blackwell Publishers.

Elster, J. (1989). Social norms and economic theory. *Journal of Economic Perspectives, 3*(4), 99–117.

Elster, J. (2009). Social norms and the explanation of behavior. In P. Hedström & P. Bearman (Eds.), *The Oxford handbook of analytical sociology* (pp. 195–217). Oxford, UK: Oxford University Press.

Esser, H. (2000). *Soziologie. spezielle grundlagen. band 5: Institutionen* (5th ed.). A. M. Frankfurt, Germany: Campus Verlag.

Evans, J. (2008). Dual-processing accounts of reasoning, judgment, and social cognition. *Annual Review of Psychology, 59*(1), 255–278.

Fallers, L. A. (1954). A note on the 'trickle effect'. *The Public Opinion Quarterly, 18*(3), 314–321.

Finseraas, H., & Kotsadam, A. (2017). Ancestry culture and female employment: An analysis using second-generation siblings. *European Sociological Review, 33*(3), 382–392.

Fischer, P., Krueger, J. I., Greitemeyer, T., Vogrincic, C., Kastenmüller, A., Frey, D., Moritz, H., Wicher, M., Kainbacher, M. (2011). The bystander-effect: A meta-analytic review on bystander intervention in dangerous and non-dangerous emergencies. *Psychological Bulletin, 137*(4), 517–537.

Gerhards, J., & Hackenbroch, R. (2000). Trends and causes of cultural modernization: An empirical study of first names. *International Sociology, 15*(3), 501–531.

Giavazzi, F., Petkov, I., & Schiantarelli, F. (2019). Culture: Persistence and evolution. *Journal of Economic Growth, 24*(2), 117–154.

Gibbs, J. P. (1965). Norms: The problem of definition and classification. *American Journal of Sociology, 70*(5), 586–594.

Gintis, H. (2009). *The bounds of reason: Game theory and the unification of the behavioral sciences*. Princeton, NJ: Princeton University Press.

Greeley, A. M., & McCready, W. C. (1975). The transmission of cultural heritages: The case of the Irish and the Italians. In N. Glazer & D. P. Moynihan (Eds.), *Ethnicity: Theory and practice* (pp. 209–235). Cambridge, MA: Harvard University Press.

Haidt, J. (2001). The emotional dog and its rational tail: A social intuitionist approach to moral judgment. *Psychological Review, 108*(4), 814–834.

Hallett, J., Howat, P. M., Maycock, B. R., McManus, A., Kypri, K., & Dhaliwal, S. S. (2012). Undergraduate student drinking and related harms at an australian university: Web-based survey of a large random sample. *BMC Public Health, 12*(37), 1–8.

Hardin, G. (1968). The tragedy of the commons. *Science, 162*(3859), 1243–1248.

Harris, M. (1989). *Cows, pigs, wars, & witches: The riddles of culture*. New York, NY: Random House.

Heather, N., Partington, S., Partington, E., Longstaff, F., Allsop, S., Jankowski, M., ... St Clair, G. A. (2011). Alcohol use disorders and hazardous drinking among undergraduates at English universities. *Alcohol and Alcoholism, 46*(3), 270–277.

Hechter, M., & Opp, K. (Eds.). (2001). *Social norms*. New York, NY: Russell Sage Foundation.

Hedström, P. (2005). *Dissecting the social: On the principles of analytical sociology*. Cambridge, UK: Cambridge University Press.

Helliwell, J. F., Wang, S., & Xu, J. (2016). How durable are social norms? Immigrant trust and generosity in 132 countries. *Social Indicators Research, 128*(1), 201–219.

Henrich, J. (2009). The evolution of costly displays, cooperation and religion. *Evolution and Human Behavior, 30*(4), 244–260.

Hingson, R. W., Heeren, T., Zakocs, R. C., Kopstein, A., & Wechsler, H. (2002). Magnitude of alcohol-related mortality and morbidity among US college students ages 18–24. *Journal of Studies on Alcohol, 63*(2), 136–144.

Hingson, R. W., Zha, W., & Weitzman, E. R. (2009). Magnitude of and trends in alcohol-related mortality and morbidity among US college students ages 18–24, 1998–2005. *Journal of Studies on Alcohol and Drugs*, July(16), 12–20.

Hitlin, S., & Piliavin, J. A. (2004). Values: Reviving a dormant concept. *Annual Review of Sociology, 30*, 359–393.

Homans, G. C. (2017 [1950]). *The human group*. Abingdon, UK: Routledge.

Inglehart, R. (1990). *Culture shift in advanced industrial society*. Princeton, NJ: Princeton University Press.

Inglehart, R., & Baker, W. E. (2000). Modernization, cultural change, and the persistence of traditional values. *American Sociological Review*, 65(1), 19–51.

Inglehart, R., & Norris, P. (2003). *Rising tide: Gender equality and cultural change around the world*. Cambridge, UK: Cambridge University Press.

Inglehart, R., & Welzel, C. (2005). *Modernization, cultural change, and democracy: The human development sequence*. Cambridge, UK: Cambridge University Press.

Kahneman, D. (2011). *Thinking, fast and slow*. New York, NY: Farrar, Straus and Groux.

Katz, D., & Allport, F. H. (1931). *Student attitudes*. Syracuse, NY: Craftsman.

Kuran, T. (1991). Now out of never: The element of surprise in the East European Revolution of 1989. *World Politics*, 44(1), 7–48.

Kuran, T. (1997). *Private truths, public lies: The social consequences of preference falsification*. Cambridge, MA: Harvard University Press.

Kypri, K., Cronin, M., & Wright, C. S. (2005). Do university students drink more hazardously than their non-student peers? *Addiction*, 100(5), 713–714.

Latané, B., & Nida, S. (1981). Ten years of research on group size and helping. *Psychological Bulletin*, 89(2), 308–324.

Lewis, D. (2008 [1969]). *Convention: A philosophical study*. Oxford, UK: Blackwell Publishers.

Lieberson, S. (1987). *Making it count: The improvement of social research and theory*. Berkeley and Los Angeles, CA: University of California Press.

Lieberson, S. (2000). *A matter of taste: How names, fashions, and culture change*. New Haven, CT: Yale University Press.

Lieberson, S., & Bell, E. O. (1992). Children's first names: An empirical study of social taste. *American Journal of Sociology*, 98(3), 511–554.

Liefbroer, A. C., & Billari, F. C. (2010). Bringing norms back in: A theoretical and empirical discussion of their importance for understanding demographic behaviour. *Population, Space and Place*, 16(4), 287–305.

Ljunge, M. (2014). Trust issues: Evidence on the intergenerational trust transmission among children of immigrants. *Journal of Economic Behavior & Organization*, 106, 175–196.

Mackie, G. (1996). Ending footbinding and infibulation: A convention account. *American Sociological Review*, 61(6), 999–1017.

Merton, R. K. (1936). The unanticipated consequences of purposive social action. *American Sociological Review*, 1(6), 894–904.

Mesoudi, A. (2011). *Cultural evolution: How darwinian theory can explain human culture and synthesize the social sciences*. Chicago, IL: University of Chicago Press.

Miles, A. (2015). The (re)genesis of values: Examining the importance of values for action. *American Sociological Review*, 80(4), 680–704.

Nannestad, P., Svendsen, G. T., Dinesen, P. T., & Sønderskov, K. M. (2014). Do institutions or culture determine the level of social trust? The natural experiment of migration from non-western to western countries. *Journal of Ethnic and Migration Studies*, 40(4), 544–565.

Nisbett, R. E., & Cohen, D. (1996). *Culture of honor: The psychology of violence in the south*. Boulder, CO: Westview Press.

Noelle-Neumann, E. (1993). *The spiral of silence: Public opinion, our social skin* (2nd ed.). Chicago, IL: University of Chicago Press.

North, D. C. (1990). *Institutions, institutional change and economic performance*. Cambridge, UK: Cambridge University Press.

Opp, K. (1989). Economics of crime and the sociology of deviant behaviour: A theoretical confrontation of basic propositions. *Kyklos, 42*(3), 405–430.

Opp, K. (2001). How do norms emerge? An outline of a theory. *Mind & Society, 2*(1), 101–128.

Ostrom, E. (2015 [1990]). *Governing the commons: The evolution of institutions for collective action.* Cambridge, UK: Cambridge University Press.

Parsons, T. (1967). *Sociological theory and modern society.* New York, NY: Free Press.

Patterson, O. (2014). Making sense of culture. *Annual Review of Sociology, 40,* 1–30.

Pinker, S. (2011). *The better angels of our nature: A history of violence and humanity.* London: Penguin.

Polavieja, J. G. (2015). Capturing culture: A new method to estimate exogenous cultural effects using migrant populations. *American Sociological Review, 80*(1), 166–191.

Prentice, D. A., & Miller, D. T. (1993). Pluralistic ignorance and alcohol use on campus: Some consequences of misperceiving the social norm. *Journal of Personality and Social Psychology, 64*(2), 243–256.

Putnam, R. D., Leonardi, R., & Nanetti, R. Y. (1993). *Making democracy work: Civic traditions in modern Italy.* Princeton, NJ: Princeton University Press.

Rice, T. W., & Feldman, J. L. (1997). Civic culture and democracy from Europe to America. *The Journal of Politics, 59*(4), 1143–1172.

Rokeach, M. (1973). *The nature of human values.* New York, NY: Free Press.

Schelling, T. C. (1980 [1960]). *The strategy of conflict.* Cambridge, MA: Harvard University Press.

Scheufele, D. A., & Moy, P. (2000). Twenty-five years of the spiral of silence: A conceptual review and empirical outlook. *International Journal of Public Opinion Research, 12*(1), 3–28.

Schwartz, S. H. (2010). Basic values: How they motivate and inhibit prosocial behavior. In M. Mikulincer & P. Shaver (Eds.), *Prosocial motives, emotions, and behavior:The better angels of our nature* (pp. 221–241). Washington, DC: American Psychological Association Press.

Sherkat, D. E. (1997). Embedding religious choice: Preferences and social constraints into rational choice theories of religious behavior. In L. A. Young (Ed.), *Rational choice theory and religion: Summary and assessment* (pp. 65–82). New York, NY: Routledge.

Sherkat, D. E., & Ellison, C. G. (1999). Recent developments and current controversies in the sociology of religion. *Annual Review of Sociology, 25,* 363–394.

Simmel, G. (1957). Fashion. *American Journal of Sociology, 62*(6), 541–558.

Sutherland, E. H. (1947). *Principles of criminology.* Chicago, IL: Lippincott.

Ullmann-Margalit, E. (2015 [1977]). *The emergence of norms.* Oxford, UK: Oxford University Press.

Vaisey, S. (2009). Motivation and justification: A dual-process model of culture in action. *American Journal of Sociology, 114*(6), 1675–1715.

Veblen, T. (2017 [1899]). *The theory of the leisure class.* New York, NY: Routledge.

Veenstra, R., Dijkstra, J. K., & Kreager, D. (2018). Pathways, networks, and norms: A sociological perspective on peer research. In W. M. Bukowski, B. R. Laursen & K.H. Rubin (Eds.), *Handbook of peer interactions, relationships, and groups* (pp. 45–63). New York, NY: Guilford.

Voss, T. (2001). Game-theoretical perspectives on the emergence of social norms. In M. Hechter & K. Opp (Eds.), *Social norms* (pp. 105–136). New York, NY: The Russell Sage Foundation.

Wechsler, H., Lee, J. E., Kuo, M., Seibring, M., Nelson, T. F., & Lee, H. (2002). Trends in college binge drinking during a period of increased prevention efforts: Findings from 4

Harvard school of public health college alcohol study surveys: 1993–2001. *Journal of American College Health*, *50*(5), 203–217.

Welzel, C. (2013). *Freedom rising: Human empowerment and the quest of emancipation.* Cambridge, UK: Cambridge University Press.

White, A., & Hingson, R. (2013). The burden of alcohol use: Excessive alcohol consumption and related consequences among college students. *Alcohol Research: Current Reviews*, *35*(2), 201–218.

Wicki, M., Kuntsche, E., & Gmel, G. (2010). Drinking at European universities? A review of students' alcohol use. *Addictive Behaviors*, *35*(11), 913–924.

Willer, R., Kuwabara, K., & Macy, M. W. (2009). The false enforcement of unpopular norms. *American Journal of Sociology*, *115*(2), 451–490.

Part 3

Social relations

Chapter 7

Networks

Chapter overview

Who do you regard as your best friends? How important are your friends and other social connections for your well-being, trust and for enforcing norms? These are questions about social networks. In the past decades, sociology has witnessed a tremendous increase in research on social networks. To introduce you to this literature, I start with a puzzle that is known as the Friendship Paradox (7.1). I then describe key social network terminology, focusing on personal networks. We come across the distinction between strong and weak ties (7.2). Then I examine a property of personal networks, namely their size. How many friends do people have? How much variation is there between individuals in the size of their personal networks? (7.3). Subsequently, we will discover that personal networks tend to be highly clustered, i.e., that your connections also know each other (7.4). After that, we go beyond the discussion of personal networks. I introduce you to the "small-world phenomenon," i.e., any two persons in contemporary large-scale societies are connected to each other via just a few intermediates. We will see that the combination of high clustering of personal networks and weak ties that provide shortcuts to other communities helps us to understand the small-world phenomenon (7.5). I then address societal changes in network structures. Do people have fewer friends nowadays? Are people visiting their neighbors less often? We will discuss the loss-of-community proposition (7.6). Then I will relate the insights from the literature on social networks to the concepts of "social cohesion" (7.7) and "social capital" (7.8).

Learning goals

After reading this chapter, check if you are able to:

- Describe and use key sociological concepts on social networks.
- Represent a social network as a graph and matrix.
- Explain the tendency towards transitivity.
- Describe and explain the small-world phenomenon.
- Describe the strength-of-weak-ties proposition.
- Describe the loss-of-community proposition.
- Relate social networks to the concept of social cohesion.
- Relate social networks to the social capital paradigm.

7.1 The friendship paradox

Let's start this chapter with a question. Think about the following and try to come up with the right answer:

On Facebook, you can see how many friends your friends have. Do you think that people on Facebook on average have as many friends as their friends have on average?

a   Yes, on average people have as many friends as their friends have on average.
b   No, on average people have more friends than their friends have on average.
c   No, on average people have fewer friends than their friends have on average.

THINKING LIKE A SOCIOLOGIST 7.1

What do you think is the right answer? Write down your answer and give a reason why you think this is the correct answer.

When people are asked this question, most tend to choose answer (a). It seems intuitive that people have the same number of friends as their friends have on average. But is it true? You can find it out empirically by checking the number of friends you have on Facebook (or another social media platform you use) and then compare the answer with, say, 20 friends of yours to whom you are connected on Facebook (or another social media platform). Chances are high that your friends will have more friends on average than you have. The correct answer is (c), which clearly puzzles many people.

In 1991, the sociologist Scott Feld published a paper on this topic in the *American Journal of Sociology* (Feld, 1991). He showed that the average number of friends people have is *lower* than the average number of friends of friends. Feld, writing long before the era of the Internet and Facebook, explained the puzzle in the following way. Imagine that there are two persons: person A, who has a large personal network of say 50 friends, and person B who has only 2 friends. Now you can ask yourself: if you were person C, to whom would it be more likely you'd be connected? Person A or B? The answer, of course, is person A, because A has a much larger network than B. And that means that you're more likely to be connected to persons who have larger networks. Because this pattern is true in general (Grund, 2014), on average people's friends have more friends than they have. This "friendship paradox" illustrates once more that sociological insights can prove counterintuitive and sometimes debunk common sense. Let's summarize this *friendship paradox*:

STYLIZED FACT 7.1

Friendship paradox
People have fewer friends on average than their friends do on average.

The friendship paradox is not just a funny story—it can be used for mitigating social problems and policy interventions too. Sociologists Christakis and Fowler argued that the insights from this paradox can be cleverly integrated into current tools to monitor and predict contagious outbreaks, such as the flu, which is critical for implementing effective interventions (Christakis & Fowler, 2010). Because, on average, the friends of randomly selected people have more friends than the person who named them, the researcher could monitor the friends of randomly selected individuals to better detect early signals of contagions. One's friends have larger networks, hence they are more likely exposed to diseases. To study this empirically, the researchers studied the flu outbreak at Harvard College in 2009. They followed 744 students who were divided into two groups: (a) a group of randomly chosen students and (b) the friends of those students. In line with the friendship paradox, they found that the progression of the epidemic in the friends group (b) occurred 13.9 days in advance of the randomly chosen group (a).

What we can learn from the friendship paradox more generally is that social networks —a subtheme of social relations—is a key element in understanding many social phenomena. The past decades have seen a tremendous growth of studies on the science of social networks (Bonacich & Lu, 2012; Bruggeman, 2013; Degenne & Forsé, 1999; Kadushin, 2012; Scott, 2017 [1991]) and on network science across disciplines: physics, economics, computer science and biology, amongst others (Barabasi, 2016; Easley & Kleinberg, 2010; Jackson, 2008; Newman, 2010).

Sociologists study *social* networks, of course, but you should realize that such networks need not only be *online* social networks, such as your friendship network on Facebook, Instagram or in your WhatsApp group. Although such online networks are becoming more and more the subject of study in social network research, the study of social networks also includes *offline* networks, such as the face-to-face ties people have with family members, friends and neighbors.

Today, in various areas of research, sociologists study the role of networks: in the study of organizations, family relations, crime, neighborhoods, education and so forth. It is found that social networks are important ways for understanding each of these various domains of research. Given the consequences social networks have for human behavior, it is valuable for you to learn more about the study of social networks.

7.2 Personal networks

A useful starting point in the study of social networks is the concept of personal networks. You can think of your personal network as the ties you have with your friends, family, neighbors and so forth. In social network studies, such connections between people are often presented in a **graph**, also called a **sociogram** (Scott, 2017 [1991]; Wasserman & Faust, 1994). In social network studies individuals in the network are called **nodes** or actors and they are connected to each other via **edges** or ties (Scott, 2017 [1991]; Wasserman & Faust, 1994). A social network is simply a set of actors (nodes) and the ties between them (edges).

Figure 7.1 presents a particular type of social network, namely the **personal network**. This is an ego network which presents all the ties of a certain person (*ego*) with other persons (*alters*). Each (possible) relationship between ego and alter is called a **dyad** (Scott, 2017 [1991]). In this personal network *ego* (A) can reach all *alters* (B, C and D) in one step; there is one degree of separation between them. This is identical to saying that ego A and alter B are at distance, radius or chain(path) length of one. Personal networks are therefore also called 1.0 degree networks, because ego is only one degree away from the alters in his network. Figure 7.1 gives an example of a graph, in which person A is connected to persons B, C and D. This could be an example of a network which represents all close friendships of person A.

We can extend the ego network to a 1.5 degree network. Such a network adds all the connections between the alters to whom ego A is directly connected. Figure 7.2 gives an example of such a 1.5 degree network. As you can see, there is a tie between alters C and D. There are no ties between B and C or between B and D.

When studying personal networks, another commonly made distinction is that between *directed ties* and *undirected ties* (Scott, 2017 [1991]). Directed ties are ties in which the direction of the relationship between actors is specified. Say we study friendship relations among

graph (also **sociogram**) a visual representation of relations between actors in a network.

nodes actors within the network. In social networks, these are often individuals.

edges the ties in the network.

personal network a network presenting all the ties that a certain person (ego) has to others (alters).

dyads each (possible) relationship between ego and alter.

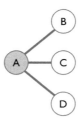

Figure 7.1 Example of a 1.0 degree network.

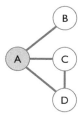

Figure 7.2 Example of a 1.5 degree network.

adolescents and we ask them to nominate the five peers in class they like most. These are directed ties, or *arcs*, as the relationship between two actors is directed and can be asymmetrical. This means that if actor A nominates B as a friend, it could be that B does not nominate A as a friend. In a case where you have only a network of undirected ties (such as on Facebook), all ties are two-sided by definition. But with network data on directed ties, you can study whether A and B nominate each other as friends—or if the friendship is perceived on one side only.

An example of a directed graph, in short a *digraph*, is given in Figure 7.3, in which the arrows represent friendship nominations. Suppose these nominations come from a study on six children who are in the same school class, which consists of only those six children, and each child is asked to report on his or her friends in their class. There is an arrow from Person 1 to Person 2, which means that Person 1 regards Person 2 as a friend. There is also an arrow in the opposite direction, which means that Person 2 also sees Person 1 as a friend. In social network terminology, these are *reciprocal* relations (i.e., two-sided, symmetrical). The relation between Person 2 and Person 3 is an example of an *asymmetrical* relationship, because Person 2 nominated Person 3 as a friend, but not vice versa. When we study undirected ties, as in Figure 7.2, we cannot study such asymmetrical relationships.

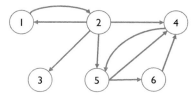

Figure 7.3 Example of a directed graph.

Graphs represent the relations between nodes (actors) in a given network. These are nice tools to visualize the network structure. Another way to present social networks is with the use of matrices. Table 7.1 presents the same social network of directed ties (digraph) as depicted in Figure 7.3, but now using a matrix of rows and columns. Using this matrix, you can find the persons who nominate another person in the rows. They are called the *sender* and, in this case, the nominations indicate friendships. The persons whom they nominate as friends are the *receivers*. They can be found in the columns. Such a matrix is called an **adjacency matrix**, because it represents who is "next to" (adjacent to) whom in the social network (Wasserman & Faust, 1994).

adjacency matrix
a matrix representing who has a relation to whom in a network.

Table 7.1 Example of an adjacency matrix.

			Receiver			
Sender	1	2	3	4	5	6
1	–	1	0	0	0	0
2	1	–	1	1	1	0
3	0	0	–	0	0	0
4	0	0	0	–	1	0
5	0	0	0	1	–	1
6	0	0	0	1	0	–

With the use of an adjacency matrix, we can quickly assess properties of the actors and the overall network. Researchers often consider indegree and outdegree as two relevant properties of the social networks of actors (Scott, 2017 [1991]). **Indegree** is simply how often a person is nominated by others in the network. For example, in Table 7.1, we can see that Person 2 is nominated only by Person 1 as a friend. This means that his indegree is 1. **Outdegree** indicates how often a person nominates other persons. For Person 2, the outdegree is 4.

indegree the number of nominations a person receives from others.

outdegree the number of nominations a person makes.

THINKING LIKE A SOCIOLOGIST 7.2

If you take indegree as an indication of popularity, who is the most popular actor in this network (Table 7.1)?

In network studies, a distinction is often made between strong ties and weak ties (Granovetter, 1973). This distinction is based on the degree of *emotional closeness*, *frequency of interaction* and *reciprocity* between two persons (Granovetter, 1973; Marsden & Campbell, 1984). People who are emotionally close share intimate and personal information, they are a source of social support and they trust each other. Frequency of interaction typically, but not exclusively, refers to face-to-face encounters. Reciprocity indicates equivalence between individuals, i.e., that the relationship is balanced and that favors are returned. Importantly, both strong and weak ties refer to *positive relations* between people, which are to be distinguished from *negative relations*. In negative relations, people undermine the well-being, personal development and resources of the other person.

strong ties positive relationships in which people feel emotionally close to one another, trust each other and help each other out when needed.

Strong ties are, then, conceived as those positive relationships in which people feel emotionally close to one another, trust each other and help each other out when needed; relationships in which people often interact with each other face to face and in which the investments and commitments are reciprocated and not one-sided. They are warm, mutually beneficial, socially supportive relationships. The relationship between spouses, friends and close family members are usually conceived of as strong ties, although these relationships are not always strong ties. For example, sometimes spouses, family members and friends hardly support each other at all or even develop negative relationships.

Weak ties are more superficial or instrumental relationships. We speak of a weak tie between two persons when they see each other not so often, when investments are not necessarily reciprocated and when people are emotionally less close to each other. They do, however, fulfil the minimum requirement of being a positive tie. Typically, these weaker ties are called *acquaintances* and they can include (non-befriended) peers at school, colleagues at work, contacts in the neighborhood, co-members from voluntary organizations and so forth. It is the group of people we personally know on a first-name basis and with whom we have some kind of positive relationship, but we would not call them strong ties.

weak ties
a more superficial or instrumental relationship between two people who see each other not that often and are emotionally less close to one another.

This dichotomy, although often used in network studies, is a gross simplification of reality of course. After all, not all strong ties are alike and not all weak ties are the same. It is important that you realize that the strength of a social tie between two persons can be ranked in a much more refined way, based on the degree of *emotional closeness*, *frequency of interaction* and *reciprocity* between the two persons (Degenne & Forsé, 1999; Granovetter, 1973). On the other hand, it is often difficult to exactly determine the strength of ties in this more nuanced way because researchers often cannot measure precisely the degree of emotional closeness, number of interactions and reciprocity between people.

Some scholars have proposed a "middle way" between these two extremes—still a simplification of reality, but also more realistic than the dichotomy between strong and weak ties (Mac Carron, Kaski, & Dunbar, 2016). They distinguish between five categories of tie strength instead of only two. And they then consider these categories as being ordered in *hierarchical network layers* of tie-strength between ego and alter (Arnaboldi, Conti, Passarella, & Dunbar, 2017). Figure 7.4 visualizes this idea.

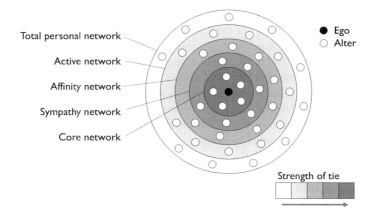

Figure 7.4 Five layers in personal networks.

The larger the layer, therefore, the lower the tie-strength and hence the lower the emotional closeness, contact frequency, reciprocity, trust and social support. Each larger layer includes the previous (smaller) layer(s). The following categories are distinguished:

1 *Core network*. The first layer consists of the core network. These are the "strongest" social ties, i.e., the most valued and intimate ties, such as with the spouse and a few best friends.
2 *Sympathy network*. This is the second layer. These are all strong ties and include the core network, but also add to this some ties that are not perceived to be as intimate as in the core network. It adds the wider circle of close family members and other friends.
3 *Affinity network*. This layer adds peers, more-distant family members and others with whom people have relatively frequent contact.
4 *Active network*. This layer includes the total number of persons with whom a person maintains an active relation.
5 *Total personal network*. This is the entire personal network. It includes all strong ties, but also people merely known on a first-name basis and with whom people have hardly any contact.

7.3 Network size and hubs

Having friends, knowing many people and occupying a central position in the social network can be an important resource in social life. Being isolated and not having close friends who can give social support when needed can be disadvantageous and restrict people in realizing their goals. In social network studies, therefore, attention is paid to network degree, i.e., the size of personal networks. How many friends do people actually have? How many people are socially isolated? How many acquaintances do people know? How much variation is there among people in their personal network size? Let us write down the descriptive questions we want to answer:

> *Q(d)*. How large are personal networks in contemporary industrialized societies? And how much do the sizes of personal networks vary among individuals within these societies?

To answer these questions, we can use the idea of hierarchical layers, i.e., people have smaller circles of strong ties, which are then nested in larger layers of increasingly weaker ties. With this more refined classification system in mind, scholars try to estimate how large each layer is. How large is the first layer, i.e., the core network? And how big is the second layer and so forth? The answer to these questions is difficult for two reasons. First, much depends on the specific measures that are used in research—as we will see. Second, to date, most studies have been conducted in the US and hence little is known about other countries. Therefore, the following empirical presentation of studies should be seen as building up some evidence-based intuition of the size and variation of personal networks in contemporary societies.

Let's begin with the first layer, the *core network*. How many core network members do Americans have? One way scholars have attempted to answer this question is to ask respondents about the people with whom they "discuss important matters." This is typically done as part of a representative survey of the population, in which respondents are introduced to a short preamble and then asked to name the people with whom they discuss matters important to them. In the 1985 General Social Survey, a large-scale survey conducted among a sample of Americans, respondents were introduced to the following question (Burt, 1984):

Image 7.1 With how many people do you discuss matters important to you?

From time to time, most people discuss important matters with other people. Looking back over the last six months—who are the people with whom you discussed matters important to you? Just tell me their first names or initials.

This is an example of a **name generator**, i.e., a survey question that asks respondents to mention the names or initials of alters in their personal network. Using this name generator, scholars then simply count the number of alters that are mentioned by respondents. The various studies which use this measure estimate that Americans have on average a core network of around 2–5 people, typically consisting of the spouse/partner and a best friend (Marsden, 1987; McPherson, Smith-Lovin, & Brashears, 2006; Paik & Sanchagrin, 2013).

name generator
a survey question which asks the respondent to mention the names or initials of alters in their personal network.

THINKING LIKE A SOCIOLOGIST 7.3

Who would you count as your core network? Write down their names.

The measure of the "core discussion network" does not count all strong ties, of course. People have strong ties with persons they did not discuss important matters with in the past six months. So, how large is the *sympathy network*, which consists of the core network and another layer of slightly less intimate ties? One survey on personal networks of Americans, which was conducted in 2004, measured the number of "very close relationships," which they defined as:

> the people to whom Americans turn to discuss important matters, with whom they are in frequent contact, or from whom they seek help.
>
> (Boase, Horrigan, Wellman, & Rainie, 2006)

This definition comes close to what we call the core network, but it is slightly more inclusive, because it not only asks Americans to name people they discuss important matters with, but also to name (yet others) with whom they are in frequent contact or from whom they seek help. Using this measure, it appeared that Americans have a mean of 23 core ties (Boase et al., 2006). However, the researchers found that this average was influenced by a small number of people reporting a very large number of strong ties. Therefore, it is better to look at the median and the median number of strong ties is 15. In other words, one-half of Americans have 15 or more ties that fall in the sympathy network.

A similar conclusion was drawn in a follow-up survey conducted in 2006. In this study, a slightly different prompt was used to elicit information about the sympathy network:

> Now I'm going to ask you some questions about people that you trust, for example good friends, people you discuss important matters with, or trust for advice, or trust with money.
>
> (DiPrete, Gelman, McCormick, Teitler, & Zheng, 2011)

Again, this measure is broader and more inclusive than the "core discussion network." And although this "trust network" might differ from people's "sympathy network," empirically they appear to largely overlap—the people you trust are the people you feel sympathy for in your strong tie network. The scholars found that Americans have a median of 17 trust ties, i.e., half of the Americans have 17 or more strong, "high trust," social ties (DiPrete et al., 2011).

Beyond this circle of around 15 ties, scholars have estimated that the *affinity network* consists of around 50 people (Arnaboldi et al., 2017). The next layer—*the active network*—contains all individuals with whom people actively maintain social contacts. Analyses of the number of Christmas cards people sent—in the old days—(Hill & Dunbar, 2003) and—more relevant today—of the number of active contacts on social media, such as on Facebook, with whom people actively communicate, reveal a quite robust number of 150 (Dunbar, Arnaboldi, Conti, & Passarella, 2015; Gonçalves, Perra, & Vespignani, 2011). Nowadays, scholars refer to this number (150) as "Dunbar's number," after Robin Dunbar, who argued that because of the cognitive constraints of the human brain, people are not able to actively maintain more than 150 relations at a non-negligible level of intimacy.

Finally, how many people are in the *total personal network*? Studies relying on the total number of "friends" people have in online social websites such as Facebook—i.e., their strong and weak ties—suggest that most people have around 300 ties (Dunbar et al., 2015; Gonçalves et al., 2011). People do not have all their offline ties online of course, which means that the total number of personal ties is underestimated. Using innovative methods (Bernard et al., 1990), recent work in this area has estimated that the median American person is acquainted with 472 (McCormick, Salganik, & Zheng, 2010), 550 (DiPrete et al., 2011) or 610 people (Zheng, Salganik, & Gelman, 2006).

Let's summarize the empirical findings as a stylized fact:

STYLIZED FACT 7.2

Personal network size in the US

For the majority of citizens of the United States, the sizes of each subsequent ego network layer—decreasing in tie strength—consist of roughly 5 alters (core network)—15 alters (sympathy network)—50 alters (affinity network)—150 (active network)—500 alters (total personal network).

This stylized fact should be taken with caution as the estimated numbers of each layer may be subject to the specific way in which questions are probed and asked. Possibly, you may want to generalize this finding as a stylized fact of western industrialized societies *in general*, or even to other (non-western non-industrialized) societies. However, more research is needed to conclude that these observations are robust. At present, few studies have been done on personal network sizes in industrialized societies other than the US and measuring each layer precisely is also very difficult and needs more testing.

That said, if you were asked to make a *guestimate* about the personal network size of citizens of another country, say Japan, France, China, Brazil or Australia, probably the best thing to do is to use the figures of the United States as *baseline* and guess that it will look more or less the same somewhere else. Until you have strong reasons to think otherwise, it seems like a defensible strategy. Indeed, a recent study measured the total personal network of the general population of Spain, finding 536 acquaintances on average—very much in line with the total personal network size of American citizens (Lubbers, Molina, & Valenzuela-Garcia, 2019).

There is another stylized fact which emerges from research in this area, namely the strong inter-individual variation in network degree. There are a few people who have much larger networks than the rest of society. For example, it has been found that most Americans have fewer than 20 trusting ties, but a very small group has many more trusting ties—beyond 40 (DiPrete et al., 2011). Similarly, studies on the total network size, as we have seen, estimate that most people have around 500 ties, but a very small group of people have many more personal ties (DiPrete et al., 2011; McCormick et al., 2010).

Figure 7.5 depicts the typical pattern that has been found for the total personal network size (DiPrete et al., 2011). As you can see, most people know around 500 people; the proportion (p) of the population with network size (k) peaks at around 500. Some know slightly fewer (say 400), others a few more (600), but within that range (400–600) you can find the large majority of the population. Then, however, there are a few individuals who know many more people: 1,000, 1,500, 2,500, even more than 3,000.

They are an example of what are called **hubs**, i.e., highly connected central nodes (actors) in the network. The distribution of personal network size is, as you can see, far from being a normal distribution. A normal distribution has a peak at the mean and deviations from that average are symmetrical. Here, however, the distribution is highly *skewed* and there

hub highly connected central nodes in a network.

is a long *tail* to the right of the mean—where we can find the hubs. This typical pattern (highly skewed distribution, long tail) is known as a power-law distribution (Barabasi & Albert, 1999; Price, 1965, 1976). Personal networks reveal this typical skewed distribution. A few people have many more connections than the rest. Let's formulate these observations as a stylized fact.

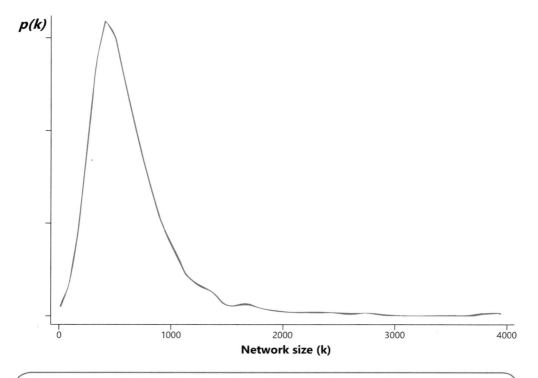

Figure 7.5 Typical distribution of total personal network size.
Source: DiPrete et al., 2011.

STYLIZED FACT 7.3

Hubs in personal networks
The distribution of personal network size follows a power law (highly skewed, long tail). A small number of individuals (hubs) have very many social ties.

7.4 Network density and transitivity

We have established, to the best of current knowledge, estimates for the size of personal networks in the US, which we can use as our best guestimate for the network size of citizens in contemporary large-scale industrialized societies. We have also seen that some individuals have much larger networks than others. However, these insights do not tell us anything about whether our friends or acquaintances also know each other. That is to say, thus far we have not addressed the issue of how strongly one's friends are befriended; how many alters know each other. Let's write this down as a descriptive question:

Q(d). To what extent are alters in personal networks connected to each other in contemporary industrialized societies?

In network studies, scholars capture such links among alters with the concept of **network density**, d (Kadushin, 2012). Generally speaking, network density captures the ratio of all realized ties in a network to the number of possible ties in that network (Scott, 2017 [1991]). In a network with *directed* ties, there are $k(k-1)$ unique directed ties between actors possible, where k is the number of actors. In an *undirected* network, there are $k(k-1)/2$ unique ties between actors possible. The network density measure, d, ranges from 0 (there

> **network density**
> the ratio of all realized ties in a network to the number of all possible ties in the same network.

are no ties between actors) to 1 (all actors are connected to each other). One can apply the concept of network density to any type of network, such as, for example, to core networks, the total personal network, networks among employees in an organization and so forth.

To illustrate the concept of network density, consider Figure 7.6. It presents the 1.5 degree network of ego A, who has three friends: B, C and D. How large is the network density among these friends? Because in this case we have an undirected network with three actors, there are [3(3 – 1)/2 =] 3 unique ties possible between the friends. If there are no ties between friends B, C and D, the density coefficient d is (0 realized tie/3 possible ties =) 0. If one pair of friends have a tie, the network density is (1 realized tie/3 possible ties =) 0.33. If there are two ties then the density is 0.67, and if all three friends of ego have ties with each other, then the network density among the three friends of ego is 1.

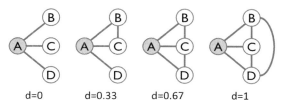

d=0   d=0.33   d=0.67   d=1

Figure 7.6 Network density among three friends of ego A: four examples.

What does empirics tell us about the density of personal networks? Let's try to answer this question by focusing on the inner circle of the hierarchical layer: *the core network*. What is the *core network density*? To answer this question, we need to study the 1.5 degree network and measure how strongly the alters are connected to each other.

A classic study that tried to examine this for the first time was Edward Laumann's *Bonds of Pluralism*, which was published in 1973 (Laumann, 1973). In this book, Laumann presents his findings on a survey conducted among 988 white men in Detroit (USA), in the year 1966. To capture core network density, the following question was posed to the respondents:

Of your three best friends, how many of them are good friends with one another?

The study found that the average core network density was around 0.42. This means that 42% of ego's friends were good friends with one another or, similarly, when you randomly pick two of ego's friends from the study, then there is a 42% chance that they are good friends too.

THINKING LIKE A SOCIOLOGIST 7.4

Look at the persons you considered as your core network: how many of them are befriended with each other? What is the density in your core network?

Following in the footsteps of Laumann, other scholars have also examined the network density in core networks. To illustrate, consider the following four studies:

- A study among 845 adults in Toronto, Canada, from the year 1968 found a mean density among six closest intimates ("the persons outside your home that you feel closest to") of 0.33 (Wellman, 1979).
- In 1977–1978, another research study was carried out among 1,050 adults in northern California, US (Fischer, 1982). In this survey, respondents were asked whether the persons to whom they felt close "know each other well." This group of close friends and/or family members consisted of up to five persons. The study found an average core network density of 0.44.
- Another study found an average density of 0.61 for the core discussion network, using data from the 1985 US General Social Survey (Marsden, 1987).
- The same density (0.61) was observed with the core network module in a 1999–2000 survey in the Netherlands—indicating whether alters "know each other well" (Mollenhorst, Völker, & Flap, 2011).

Taken together, and simplifying a bit, these studies tell us that densities in the *core network* are around 0.5 and typically fall in the range between 0.33 and 0.61. This means that of your best friends—who make up your core network—around 50% are befriended with each other as well. The figures, however, underestimate core network density because they only count the *strong ties* between your friends, such as being friends or "knowing each other *well*." If you were to ask instead if your friends merely "know each other," then you would find ties among your friends to be more common because some of your friends may just know each other but not be friends. Indeed, studies suggest that, when taking this minimum definition of "knowing each other," the clustering among alters in the core network goes up significantly and studies find a quite consistent density of around 0.75 (Davis, 1970; Louch, 2000; Mollenhorst et al., 2011; Robinson & Balkwell, 1995).

These research findings gives us insight into the structure of core networks, namely that they tend to have high density. Chances are high that most of your friends know each other. You can look at this finding from the perspective of a network consisting of three actors: yourself and two of your friends. Such a network of three actors and the (possible) ties between them is called a **triad**. If all three actors are connected to each other, then we speak of **triadic closure** and **transitivity**. This means that ego A has a tie to B and C, and B and C have a tie to each other as well. Researchers often find that transitivity occurs in core networks.

triad a network of three actors and the (possible) ties between them.

triadic closure (also **transitivity**) the situation in which the two alters of one ego are also connected to each other.

This is a puzzling phenomenon once you consider that nowadays most people live in large-scale 10+ million societies. What are the chances *any two random people know each other*? Taking two random individuals would be very unlikely to capture a friendship relation. In fact, the chances are *negligible* (e.g., < 0.00001) that the two would even know each other by name. But if we look at people's friends, the chance that any two of their friends know each other is 0.75 and the probability that they are friends is 0.50. This clearly shows extremely high levels of clustering within core networks: many of your most intimate ties, your friends, know each other as well or are even friends—far more than you would expect if networks are made at random. This high degree of network clustering is a well-known empirical regularity found in social networks studies and can be called the *transitivity tendency* (Davis, Holland, & Leinhardt, 1971).

STYLIZED FACT 7.4

Transitivity tendency

If ego A has ties to alters B and C, then B and C are more likely to be (positively) connected compared with the situation in which ego A has a tie to either B or C (or to neither). In simple language: your connections likely know each other as well.

How can we understand that transitivity occurs so often in core networks? How can we explain the fact that your friends also know each other and are often befriended too—even though two random individuals have a minimum chance of knowing each other? There are three mechanisms of social tie-formation that explain the driving forces behind the transitivity tendency in core networks (Granovetter, 1973). Note that we will discuss these mechanisms in more detail in Chapter 8 (Groups).

1   *Meeting opportunities*: social ties are created in contexts of interaction, i.e., there must be an opportunity for persons B and C to meet each other in order to know each other (Blau, 1977; Feld, 1981). Because ego A has strong ties to both B and C, it means she often interacts with B and C. This could mean that B and C share the same context as A, such as attending the same school or living in the same neighborhood, and therefore they also know each other. But it could also mean that B and C meet each other because they often interact with ego A (e.g., they are invited by ego A to her parties). Either way, meeting opportunities for B and C are high and one would expect transitivity in core networks.

2   *Homophily*: typically people prefer to develop strong ties to others who are like themselves (Byrne, 1971). This means, for example, that friends are chosen because they share the same political or religious views and opinions, or belong to the same ethnic group. For this reason, ego A will probably be quite similar to both B and C. But that also means that B and C are quite similar to one another and therefore they find each other more attractive than a random stranger.

3   *Structural balance*: another mechanism underlying transitivity in core networks is that ego A will be uncomfortable having friends B and C who are not having such positive ties with each other and, in particular, when her friends have a negative relationship. Scholars have argued that this unbalanced situation creates psychological strain for ego A and she will strive towards a balanced network, in which her friends B and C maintain a mutually positive relation (Cartwright & Harary, 1956; Heider, 1946; Homans, 2017 [1951]).

With these three arguments in mind, sociologist Mark Granovetter explained why the transitivity tendency is so common in core networks (Granovetter, 1973). He illustrated this robust empirical pattern with a simplified sociogram, consisting of only ego A and her two friends B and C (Figure 7.7). He called triads in which ego A has strong ties to both B and C, but in which no tie exists between B and C, a **forbidden triad**.

forbidden triad
a triad in which ego A has strong ties to alters B and C, but in which no tie exists between B and C.

Empirically, we have seen that forbidden triads now and then occur in core networks. Roughly 25% of the friends do not know each other. However, the very point Granovetter wanted to make by introducing the concept of *forbidden triad* is to clarify that transitivity is not a universal characteristic, something you find equally across

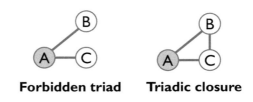

Forbidden triad   Triadic closure

Figure 7.7 Core discussion networks: forbidden triad and triadic closure.

strong ties and weak ties. Specifically, he stated that the transitivity tendency is particularly high in core networks and increases with tie-strength. Granovetter argued that the transitivity tendency is "a function of the strength of ties, rather than a general feature of social structure" (Granovetter, 1973).

Why did Granovetter come to this conclusion? To understand why, you need to consider again the three mechanisms which were used to explain the transitivity tendency in the first place: opportunities, homophily and structural balance. If you go through these arguments again you'll see why one would expect lower levels of transitivity with decreasing tie strength. It is helpful to use the simple dichotomy between strong ties (e.g., your friends) and weak ties (e.g., an acquaintance) here:

1 *Meeting opportunities.* If ego A has weak ties to alters B and C, it means she less often interacts with them than if these had been strong ties. Hence, there are fewer opportunities for B and C to meet each other than if they had belonged to the core network of ego A.
2 *Homophily.* In the case of weak ties, people do not have a strong preference to interact with others who are similar to them. Such weak relations are more "superficial" and "instrumental," as with neighbors or acquaintances. Being different in terms of political, religious and normative opinions is then less troublesome than in the case of more intimate ties. Consequently, if ego A has weak ties with B and C, then she is more likely to be different from them. Therefore, B and C also differ from one another and there is little common ground for them on which to develop a social tie.
3 *Structural balance.* In the case of weak ties, people are not so concerned that their connections are not mutually befriended or don't know each other, as they are in the case of their most intimate social ties. You can know your neighbor (B) superficially and another person from the tennis club (C), but there is no psychological strain for you if B and C don't know each other. Hence, there are no or few pressures for you to introduce B and C to each other.

For these three reasons, Granovetter argues that tie-strength between ego A and alters B and C *moderates* the transitivity tendency (Granovetter, 1973). In other words, the stronger the tie of ego A to alter B and C, the more likely it is that B and C are connected too. If one goes from the strongest ties typical of the core discussion network into the larger layers of weaker ties, it becomes less likely that alters in those layers are connected. Your friends know each other, in other words, but your acquaintances not so often. Triadic closure occurs in your core network, but not so often in the affinity network.

Empirically, studies have found that, indeed, the transitivity tendency increases with tie-strength: triadic closure is more common among strong ties (such as in the core network) than among weaker ties (Granovetter, 1973). This does not mean that the weakest ties of ego A, such as mere acquaintances, never know each other: in fact, they are still more likely connected to each other than two random persons in the population at large (Girvan & Newman,

2002; Granovetter, 1973; Newman, 2010). But, compared with your core network, triadic closure is less common among weaker ties. Let's call this the *forbidden triad tendency*.

STYLIZED FACT 7.5

Forbidden triad tendency
Transitivity increases with tie strength. It is highly common in core networks. The more you go up to the larger layers in personal networks (from strong ties to weaker ties), the less often transitivity occurs.

7.5 The small-world phenomenon

We have reviewed personal networks, their degree and density. Sociologists also study the connections *between* different personal networks and examine the structure of larger social networks. Research in this field has discovered the so-called small-world phenomenon (de Sola Pool & Kochen, 1978; Schnettler, 2009b). What is this phenomenon about?

As you probably know, for the most part in the history of *Homo sapiens*, humans have lived in hunter-gatherer communities, which were very small in size. Not surprisingly, when people spent their entire life in the same tight-knit group, everyone was connected to everyone else and hence everyone knew each other on a first-name basis. It was a small world with extremely high levels of clustering in such communities ($d = 1$). Today, however, most people live in large-scale anonymous societies typically consisting of populations with over 10 million people. This raises the question about how personal networks in contemporary highly industrialized societies are connected to each other. There are some who think quite pessimistically about this and believe that more and more people are anonymous strangers to each other. Others are more optimistic and think that, even in such large-scale societies, people are still socially connected to each other. Which ones are right?

This is, of course, a broad question and there are no easy answers to it. Let's try one way to formulate a question on this important societal matter:

> what are the chances that, when we randomly pick two people (A and Z) in a society, they will know each other personally?

In the hunter-gatherer societies, the chances are high that people know each other. But in contemporary large-scale 10 million+ populations, as we have seen, these chances are negligible. It may thus seem as if the pessimists are right. But, we may also formulate the question somewhat more broadly and ask what the chances are that any two persons are *indirectly* connected, via their acquaintances and friends. Persons A and Z might not know each other *directly*, but A might have a friend B, who happens to know person C and so forth, until someone is personally linked to Z. If, somehow, two random strangers are connected with each other in this way in just a few steps, then we can say that there is still some social glue that holds people in large-scale societies together. Thus, you may ask:

> when we randomly pick two persons in the population, how many intermediate friendship or acquaintance links are needed before A and B are connected?

In the 1960s, this intriguing question was taken up empirically, for the first time, by social psychologists Stanley Milgram and Jeffrey Travers (Milgram, 1967; Travers & Milgram, 1969). They designed an innovative study to assess how many intermediary people (B, C, …) are needed to connect a random person "A" ("starting person") to another random person "Z" ("target person"). They conducted their study in the United States, which, at that time, had approximately 200 million inhabitants. This is how they set up their 1969 study:

> An arbitrary "target person" and a group of "starting persons" were selected, and an attempt was made to generate an acquaintance chain from each starter to the target. Each starter was provided with a document and asked to begin moving it by mail toward the target. The document described the study, named the target, and asked the recipient to become a participant by sending the document on. It was stipulated that the document could be sent only to a first-name acquaintance of the sender. The sender was urged to choose the recipient in such a way as to advance the progress of the document toward the target; several items of information about the target were provided to guide each new sender in his choice of recipient. Thus, each document made its way along an acquaintance chain of indefinite length, a chain which would end only when it reached the target or when someone along the way declined to participate. Certain basic information, such as age, sex and occupation, was collected for each participant.
> (Travers & Milgram, 1969)

The puzzling outcome of their study was that the starting persons needed on average only 5.2 intermediaries to reach the target person, which means 6.2 steps (degrees of separation) in total. Their findings thereby suggest that even large-scale societies with 200 million citizens are still a "small world": two random people are connected with each other in just 6 steps. As has become a famous saying later on, any two people in contemporary large-scale anonymous societies are "six degrees of separation" away from each other on average (Watts, 2003).

However, before one can draw such a firm conclusion, more research is needed. One issue that could raise concern is that the Travers–Milgram study was concerned with only *one* target person—a male stockbroker in Boston. What would their results have looked like if they had used a different target person? To answer this question, follow-up studies used other target persons, and they also used different starters, varied contextual conditions and also used different ways to forward the message: phone and email instead of regular mail. The findings of these replication studies confirm the Travers–Milgram study: in large-scale societies, any two persons are connected via only a few intermediaries—typically 4 or 5 (Dodds, Muhamad, & Watts, 2003; Guiot, 1976; Korte & Milgram, 1970; Lundberg, 1975; Schnettler, 2009a).

It seems that by now we can claim that we still live in a "small world." However, scholars have identified a potential weakness common to studies leading to this conclusion: it appears that many starters *do not reach their target persons* (Kleinfeld, 2002; Schnettler, 2009a). In the original Travers–Milgram study, for example, of the 296 people who participated and who were asked to send on the document to friends or acquaintances so that eventually the document would reach the target person, only 64 (22%) were in the end successful. This means that the overwhelming majority of chains (78%) were not completed. This could occur, for example, if starting person A sends the document to friend B, but then B does not send the document to another person—ending the chain unsuccessfully. Possibly, the reason for such interrupted chains is a lack of motivation to participate in the study, but it could also be that person B—and so many other persons in the study like B—was unable to send the document to someone else that would bring the document closer to the target person. If that is the case, then the world might not be as small as these studies seem to suggest.

So, what should we conclude? Is the world still "small" or should we reject the conclusions from the Milgram–Travers study?

In 2011, a new breakthrough in this debate came from an unexpected source: Facebook. Scholars used data on Facebook to overcome the pitfalls with the design of earlier work, which studied letters or emails (Backstrom, Boldi, Rosa, Ugander, & Vigna, 2012). They used a massive data set on a staggering number of 721 million active users across the world and a total of 69 billion "friendship" links. Such friendship connections on Facebook contain "true" friendships, but they can also be acquaintances and family members; in any case, persons that people know by their first name. Using this enormous dataset, the researchers came to the following astonishing conclusion:

> Any two randomly chosen people in the world are connected via only 3.74 intermediaries (4.74 steps), on average.

Thus, although the researchers used a totally different method than before (i.e., in the Milgram–Travers study), the authors arrived at the same conclusion: it is indeed a small world. Anonymous strangers are connected in less than 5–6 steps. It means that you are connected, via only a few intermediaries, to a farmer in Chili, to a police officer in Moscow, to a 15-year-old child somewhere in Kenya. Specifically, the study showed that 92% of the pairs of individuals can be reached in five or fewer steps. Bearing in mind that not everyone in the world is an active member on Facebook and that those who are members might not include all the people they personally know in their list of Facebook connections, this is a remarkable finding. Apparently we still live in a small world as, on average, people are connected in even fewer than six steps. Given the empirical evidence we have reviewed, it seems legitimate to formulate the *small-world phenomenon* (also known as *six degrees of separation*) as a stylized fact.

 STYLIZED FACT 7.6

Small-world phenomenon
In large-scale contemporary societies, two randomly chosen individuals are personally connected in only a few steps (around 5–6 steps on average), via their friends, acquaintances and family.

At first, the small-world phenomenon seems easy to explain. The upper layer of personal networks, as we have seen, typically consists of 500 people. This means that, if social connections are made *at random*, then the average person—having 500 connections in the upper layer—could be connected to 500 x 500 = 250,000 persons in two steps. Or even slightly more than this number, because our friends have more friends than we have. Disregarding this for a moment, one could reach (500 x 500 x 500 =) 125 million people in just three steps. For most large-scale industrialized nations, this would mean that any two individuals are connected to each other in no more than three steps. Hence, it seems that we can easily explain the small-world phenomenon and that it was not puzzling after all.

However, such an explanation for the small-world phenomenon overlooks the *transitivity tendency*, i.e., many of your social connections know each other. In the inner circle, the core network, 75% of your connections know each other. But also in the other layers a considerable number of people know each other. This means that among the 500 people you know, quite a number of them will know each other. And although your connections know more people than you do, they will not come up with 500 connections that are unknown to you. What's more, your friends' friends' friends may be also known to you and so forth.

To capture this clustering of social relations in "webs of inter-related personal networks," scholars have coined the concept of **community** (Girvan & Newman, 2002). A community is a cluster of nodes that are more connected internally than externally, either *directly* (distance 1) and/or *indirectly* (say, at distance 2 or 3). This may sound a bit abstract so let's illustrate this concept with an example. Figure 7.8 displays a social network consisting of individuals A–O and the social ties between them. Suppose, you are actor A and your friends are B, C and H. Look at the network of your friend B. B is befriended with C, so there is some overlap (transitivity!). But your friend B also has some ties with people you don't know, such as with F. However, this person F is somehow connected to you, not only via your friend B but also via friend C. So, even if you may not know person F, you are connected to F via several friends. If you zoom out a bit from your own 1.5 degree network, you see that there is a cluster of social ties among persons A to H. This is what we may call *community 1*. Together A to H form a community because they have many ties with each other directly and/or indirectly, rather than with people outside their community, such as with actors I to O, who together make up another community.

> **community**
> a cluster of nodes that are more connected internally than externally, either directly and/or indirectly.

How can we understand the small-world phenomenon—that two random strangers are connected to each other in just a few steps—while people find themselves embedded in a community of clustered social connections? We can see how this can happen by considering Figure 7.8 again. Suppose that you (ego A) and a random stranger (O) live in a 10+ million society. Both of you (A and O) navigate in different communities, i.e., your connections tend to know each other and ties outside the community are less common. The ties between people *within* the same community are called **community-bonding ties**. People have many of them but, now and then, people also have ties outside their community. Such ties with members of *another* community are called

> **community-bonding ties** ties between people within the same community.

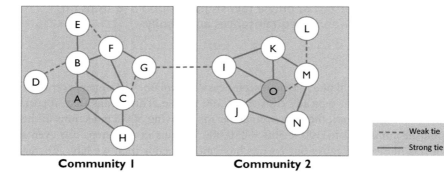

Community 1   **Community 2**

- - - - Weak tie
——— Strong tie

Figure 7.8 Example of a social network consisting of two communities.

community-bridging ties. As a consequence of these bridging ties, you (ego A) and the random stranger (ego O) can reach each other in just a few steps. You are connected, indirectly, in just four steps via intermediaries C–G–I. The crucial tie in this chain that connects A and O is the relation between alters G and I, as they establish a tie that connects communities (1) and (2). If you take any other pair of persons in the networks in Figure 7.8, you'll see that they can reach each other in only a few steps. We say that the average path length is low: everyone is connected in 5–6 steps.

> **community-bridging ties** ties between people of different communities.

> **small-world network** a network that is characterized by a high level of local clustering and low average path length.

Thus, the small-world phenomenon in contemporary societies is a combination of strong clustering of social relations in so-called communities and the existence of a few community-bridging ties creating low average path length (Watts, 1999; Watts & Strogatz, 1998). This social structure is called the **small-world network** (Watts, 1999). The small-world network is located somewhere between *order* and *randomness*. If order ruled the social world, then personal networks would be completely transitive and there would be completely fragmented communities (only community-bonding ties) with no links between them (no community-bridging ties). It would be a "caveman world" (Watts, 2003) in which people could not "escape" their own community.

The opposite of such a completely *ordered* social world would be a world in which networks are formed entirely *randomly*. This would result in a small world too, but also in a world that is totally unrealistic: the chances that your friends know each other would be similar to any two random persons knowing each other. We have seen that, empirically, this is not the case. On the contrary, the chances that your friends know each other are very high (>75%), whereas such chances for two random strangers knowing each other are negligible. In reality, social networks do not emerge at random and they exhibit strong patterns of transitivity and clustering.

Thus, the small-world network is neither a perfectly ordered world nor a perfectly random world: our social networks are in-between these extremes. Locally, we live in dense webs of social ties (clustering, communities) but, because some ties provide shortcuts to completely different communities, we can also reach out very far and connect to people totally different from ourselves—which makes it a small world too.

You may wonder what *type* of ties connect different communities. Are these bridging ties different from community-bonding ties? According to Granovetter, there is indeed an important difference. He argued that because the transitivity tendency pertains in particular to strong ties, such strong ties tend to be more often community-bonding ties. Weak ties, however, tend to be less transitive, as we have seen, and hence tend to act as a bridge between different communities more often than do strong ties. In his own words: "No strong tie is a bridge. All bridges are weak ties" (Granovetter, 1973).

This statement is perhaps a bit too strong, as we have seen that sometimes strong ties are not transitive; the "forbidden triad" happens in reality now and then. But Granovetter was right in that typically, though not always, the community-bridging tie is a weak tie. In Figure 7.8 the bridging tie between actors G and I is a weak tie. This potential of weak ties to provide shortcuts to different communities makes them very important, so "strong" in the words of Granovetter. He therefore coined the expression "strength-of-weak-ties," arguing that weak ties, because of their typical bridging function, connect people to other communities rather than to people within their own community network. Weaker ties in particular create linkages to other communities and thereby connect random strangers via a few intermediate persons. The "strength" of weak ties is therefore that they reach far; they connect us to people who are embedded in different communities than our own. Let's summarize this *strength-of-weak-ties* proposition:

P. Weak ties more often create bridges to other communities than do strong ties. (*strength-of-weak-ties*)

In Chapter 10 we will see how Granovetter used this proposition to understand how job information diffuses in social networks. In particular, he argued that weaker ties may have an advantage compared with strong ties, because weaker ties may access novel information gathered from other communities.

7.6 Network change: loss-of-community?

Thus far we have assumed that personal networks in large-scale industrialized societies have not changed over time. But is there really no reason to believe that, for example, the networks in the year 1920 were very different from what they are today? This question is a topic of discussion amongst sociologists. Specifically, this area of research focuses on potential changes in the strength of personal ties. Do people nowadays have mainly weaker ties? Or are the social ties in personal networks as strong as they used to be in 1920?

One theory that addresses these questions has a long history and originates from the 1887 study by the German sociologist Ferdinand Tönnies. He argued in this study that, over time, there is a shift from *Gemeinschaft* to *Gesellschaft* (Tönnies, 1957 [1887]). A Gemeinschaft is characterized by order: strong interpersonal bonds, solidarity and trust. In such a society, people are strongly embedded in communities, i.e., there are many community-bonding ties and such ties tend to be strong, enduring and supportive. In a Gesellschaft, however, social ties erode and become weaker, more loose and instrumental.

According to Tönnies this change from Gemeinschaft to Gesellschaft, from social "order" to more "randomness" in social relations, has to do with population growth. In small-scale societies, people often meet each other face-to-face; they interact with the same people repeatedly, which strengthens social ties, creates trust and promotes reciprocity. As societies become larger, the opportunities for interacting with the same people shrink. People become more geographically mobile, which means that their friends and family members could relocate and settle in areas far away. Larger societies are also more urban, which

P. The larger the size of the population, the fewer opportunities people have for repeatedly meeting the same people face-to-face.

P. The more opportunities people have for repeatedly meeting the same people face-to-face, the stronger people are embedded in communities.

C. Over time, population size has increased.

P. Over time, people have become less-strongly embedded in communities. (*loss-of-community*)

Theory schema 7.1 Tönnies' theory of the loss-of-community

likewise reduces opportunities for repeated interactions with the same individuals. We can summarize Tönnies' ideas in a theory schema (see previous page).

The *loss-of-community* proposition argues that the tie-strength in personal networks has reduced and that people tend to have more weaker rather than stronger ties. It also argues that personal networks are becoming less transitive because, as we have seen, transitivity is a positive function of tie strength. More broadly, it is argued that people are less strongly embedded nowadays in dense clusters of social ties, that the community is lost. Hence, the proposition states that people have more and more weaker ties rather than stronger ties and that one's (direct and indirect) connections are less often related to each other—at least less so than they used to be.

Tönnies' loss-of-community proposition received new impetus more than 100 years later when Robert Putnam published his study *Bowling Alone* (Putnam, 2000). In it he also claimed a decline in community, but then suggested other forces that might cause this decline. One of them was the rise of modern communication technology. Putnam mentioned the rise of the TV as breaking down social ties, as more and more people tend to watch TV instead of visiting their friends and family. In line with this argument, and extending it to modern technology, one could argue that the recent rise of the Internet, mobile devices and social media has created more and more alternatives to the enduring face-to-face interactions that are typical of strong ties. Hence, one would predict that the rise of modern communication technology results in a shift from strong ties to weak ties. I summarize these ideas with the following theory schema.

P.	The more often people make use of modern communication technology (TV, Internet, mobile devices), the fewer opportunities they have for repeatedly meeting the same people face-to-face.
P.	The more opportunities people have for repeatedly meeting the same people face-to-face, the stronger people are embedded in communities.
C.	Over time, people use modern communication technology more often.

P.	Over time, people have become less-strongly embedded in communities. (*loss-of-community*)

Theory schema 7.2 Putnam's theory of the loss-of-community.

Notice that, if you compare the theories of Tönnies and Putnam, the proposition they derive is the same (*loss-of-community*). But the causal mechanisms that set this process in motion are different according to the two scholars. While Tönnies emphasises the anonymity of living in large-scale populations in which people become strangers to each other, Putnam argues that it is modern technology that drives people away from establishing and maintaining strong ties.

The question, of course, is: are these scholars right? Is there indeed evidence for the *loss-of-community* proposition? In *Bowling Alone*, Putnam comes up with several empirical tests of this proposition. To illustrate, consider the following findings with respect to friendships, family ties and contacts with neighbors.

1 *Friends*. If the loss-of-community proposition is right, people should have fewer contacts nowadays with their friends. This is indeed what Putnam observes. Using survey data between 1975 and 1998 in the United States, he finds that during this period, people less often have friends over for the evening and also less frequently went to the home of friends.

2 *Family*. Also in line with the proposition, Putnam finds that between 1977 and 1999 Americans' family dinners have become less frequent. This suggests a declining strength of family ties, i.e., from strong family ties to weaker ties, as family members see each other less often.

3 *Neighbors*. If the loss-of-community proposition is true, then it could be hypothesized that over time the ties to neighbors should have become weaker or merely non-existent. To examine this, Putnam studied how often people spent a social evening with someone who lives in their neighborhood. He finds that between 1974 and 1998 this fell by about one-third.

The findings of *Bowling Alone* suggest that, in line with the loss-of-community proposition, the tie-strength of personal networks has been reduced in the past decades: strong ties become weak ties and weak ties become even weaker or disappear. Together this means the erosion of communities as one's connections know each other less often. The work of Tönnies and Putnam has sparked great interest in sociology.

However, scholars have not yet come to a consensus about whether the loss-of-community proposition is true: this is still a topic of ongoing investigation. Some studies confirm the proposition and others provide contradictory evidence (Fischer, 1982; Laumann, 1973; McPherson et al., 2006; Paik & Sanchagrin, 2013). There is, furthermore, an ongoing discussion about the presumed role of population size and urbanization in possibly reducing tie-strength (Fischer, 1982) and about the potential impact of modern communication technology (Wang & Wellman, 2010). In short: it is hard to distill stylized facts as this area of research is bound to too many uncertainties and any firm conclusions cannot be drawn.

7.7 Networks and social cohesion

The studies on the small-world networks and loss-of-community are part of a more general research interest in sociology, namely in describing and explaining the degree of *cohesiveness* of social relations—which I will also refer to as **social cohesion**. Ever since the work of sociologists like Tönnies, scholars have examined social structures in light of this particular property. Intuitively speaking, they want to examine whether societies make up cohesive entities, which exhibit positive ties between its inhabitants and where there is *order*, *trust*, *solidarity*, *social support* and *cooperation* between people. Such a cohesive society is then seen as the opposite of a *fragmented*, *disintegrated* society, in which there are many *conflicts*, *negative ties*, *distrust* and *uncooperative behavior*. These are, of course, two extreme opposites. The cohesiveness of social structures is not a matter of either/or but one of *degree*.

The study of personal networks is part of the more overarching question about the degree of social cohesion in society. If people have strongly positive relationships, then their network consists of people they can rely on, who provide social and emotional support when needed, who they trust and with whom they cooperate. If scholars then observe that over time the number of strong ties in personal networks declines at the expense of weak ties, it indicates that social cohesion in society is under threat. And when weak ties, in turn,

social cohesion the degree to which individuals and groups have (strongly) positive relationships with each other, as opposed to no/neutral relationships or (strongly) negative relationships.

disappear, then people become more socially isolated—which means they do not have people they can rely on, people with whom they can discuss matters important to them and who are willing to help them in case they need it.

That said, however, social cohesion is a broader concept that not only captures *positive* relationships. The small-world literature and the Tönnies–Putnam line of research on loss-of-community typically focus on positive ties. The Tönnies–Putnam studies document whether positive ties change in strength—from strong to weak—or become absent, but they do not consider *negative ties*. These are ties that undermine the well-being, personal development and resources of individuals. The more common these kind of negative ties are in personal networks, the lower the social cohesion in society.

It is helpful to differentiate between three possible relationships between any two actors in a population (Figure 7.9).

- *Positive relationship* (+). In these kind of relations people tend to help each other, cooperate and trust each other—although the extent to which this is the case depends on tie-strength. Examples of positive ties are a friendship relation, marriage, cohabitation, but also the weaker ties between individuals; all sorts of relationships—strong and weak—which are generally evaluated as positive between two persons.

Image 7.2 How cohesive are personal networks?

Figure 7.9 Three possible relationships between any two actors.

- *Negative relationship* (–). These kind of relations indicate that two persons have a conflict, or they dislike each other, or don't trust the other person. Similar to positive ties, negative ties are also a matter of degree. These ties can be relatively mild but also very strongly negative. In weakly negative relations: (1) persons are not willing to help each other, (2) they put some effort into harming and obstructing the goals of the other person, (3) they tend to distrust each other. When the tie becomes more strongly negative, the distrust is higher and efforts to harm or obstruct the other also increase.
- *No/neutral relationships*. Relationships between two people need not be either positive or negative. Sometimes, people simply don't know each other. Or they might not be friends, but neither are they foes or enemies to each other.

With this in mind, you can see that if you take a representative sample of individuals in society and study the positive and negative relationships in personal networks, you would be able to aggregate your findings to the societal level and draw conclusions about the cohesiveness of its social structure. You could say whether, generally speaking, people are positively connected to each other, that relations have eroded or that negative ties prevail.

Sociologists study the cohesiveness of personal networks in various areas of research (Nieuwenhuis, Völker, & Flap, 2013). To give you an impression of this, consider the following three areas: family, youth and organizations.

Family sociology

There is a longstanding interest in sociology studying the cohesiveness of family ties (Amato, 2000; McLanahan & Sandefur, 1997; Straus, Gelles, & Steinmetz, 2017 [1980]). This includes the various relationships between the actors in the family, i.e., between parents and their children, between parents, sibling relations and so forth. Examples of questions that are central in this area of work are: are parent–child relationships positive or negative? What is the quality of the parent–child relationship? Do fathers and mothers spend time with their children and provide social support when needed? When and under what conditions do negative relationships emerge—such as the neglect or abuse of children? How many people are cohabiting or formally married? Do married couples have a positive relationship with each other or are there many conflicts? How often do marriages end up in a divorce? Are the number of marriages that end in divorce increasing over time? As you can see, answering these questions tells us something about the cohesiveness of networks within the family.

Sociology of adolescence and youth

Adolescents and youth develop ties outside their family setting, with peers for example, and many of those ties are formed at school. Sociologists study these kind of personal relationships. Do children develop close friendships with peers at school? Why do some children not develop ties with other children? How often and why do children bully each other in school (Faris & Felmlee, 2011; Veenstra et al., 2005) and how common is cyberbullying (Smith et al., 2008; Tokunaga, 2010)? This literature is informing us about social cohesion among adolescents and youth in schools.

Organizational sociology

People also develop ties in various settings outside the family and school context. An important context is the organization in which they work. What kind of informal connections are there at the work setting? Do people have positive relationships with their colleagues? Do they trust each other, cooperate well in teams and is there solidarity at the work place? Or is there distrust and lack of cooperation among colleagues? How often do people become victims of gossip, bullying and other negative encounters during work (Ellwardt, Labianca, & Wittek, 2012; Grosser, Lopez-Kidwell, & Labianca, 2010)? These and related questions are concerned with the cohesiveness of networks within organizations.

In conclusion, sociologists study the structure of positive and negative social ties in personal networks in various areas (family, youth, organizations, neighborhoods, etc.). The more prevalent positive relationships are in these domains, the more cohesive these social structures are. However, the concept of *social cohesion* encompasses more than the cohesion observed in personal networks—as we will see in Chapter 8 (Groups). Social cohesion is a complex concept (Chapter 3), which means that it consists of several dimensions.

Personal relationships capture one *dimension* of social cohesion. Let's call this dimension **personal network cohesion**. Personal networks are said to be more cohesive the more positive social connections individuals have in their social network. Say that we study the social network of John and we see that he has a good relationship with his parents, he is married, he has a number of friends and also many valuable connections in the neighborhood, at work and on Facebook. That is a much more cohesive network than someone who has very few connections and is socially isolated (McPherson et al., 2006), or whose social ties are mainly negative. Generally speaking, the more common positive ties are in personal networks, as opposed to negative ties, the higher the personal network cohesion. The cohesion of

personal network cohesion the degree to which someone's personal network consists of (strongly) positive relationships as opposed to no/neutral relationships or even (strongly) negative relationships.

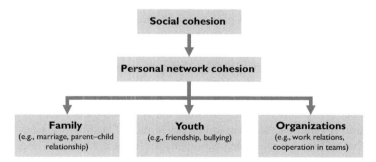

Figure 7.10 Personal network cohesion as one dimension of social cohesion; three examples of areas of research to study network cohesion.

personal networks is therefore one important dimension of the social cohesion in society at large (Figure 7.10). And network cohesion, so we have seen, is empirically examined in various areas of research, such as in the sociology of the family, youth and organizations.

7.8 Networks and social capital

The study of social networks has often been linked to the concept of "social capital." Inspired by the foundational work of Mark Granovetter (1973, 1974, 1985), Pierre Bourdieu (1980, 2010 [1979]; Bourdieu & Passeron, 1990 [1977]), James Coleman (1988, 1990), Robert Putnam (2000), Ronald Burt (1992, 2005, 2010) and Nan Lin (1999, 2001; Lin, Cook, & Burt, 2001; Lin & Erickson, 2008), hundreds of articles and books have been written about social capital (Castiglione, Van Deth, & Wolleb, 2008; Flap & Volker, 2004; Häuberer, 2011; Hsung, Lin, & Breiger, 2009; Portes, 1998).

In the words of Putnam, the "core idea of social capital theory is that social networks have value" (Putnam, 2000). However, it has been noted that "although the idea seems relatively straightforward, once explored, the concept raises a host of issues" (Kadushin, 2012). Indeed, the literature on social capital has been criticized for not coming up with a commonly accepted and clear definition of "social capital," for not articulating propositions and for poor measurement of the key concepts.

Claude Fischer, for example, argued that social capital "is not much different from saying that social capital is everything psychological and sociological about a person" (Kadushin, 2012). As a past editor of the journal *Contexts* he put "social capital" on his do-not-use style sheet (Fischer, 2005). Lin, Fu and Hsung noted that "without a clear conceptualization, social capital may soon become a catch-all term broadly used in reference to anything that is 'social'" (Lin, Fu, & Hsung, 2001). They argued that "without a clear measurement, it will be impossible to verify propositions or to accumulate knowledge" (Lin, Fu, & Hsung, 2001). Häuberer stated that "Almost everything ranging from social relationships via norms up to tolerance is termed social capital" (Häuberer, 2011).

To get some understanding of the sociological literature on social capital, two issues are important to realize. First, there does not exist a *single* social capital theory, in the sense of a single coherent set of propositions. Rather, there are multiple social capital theories, each using different conceptions of "social capital" and different propositions—albeit sometimes loosely formulated. These theories are based on a common *perspective* on social capital, a "research paradigm" (Lin & Erickson, 2008). The core idea of the **social capital paradigm** is that social networks have some sort of "value," that networks matter for certain desirable outcomes.

> **social capital paradigm** perspective according to which social networks have some sort of value.

Second, the social capital theories focus on different *outcomes*. It is not the case that these social capital theories explain the same thing, such as well-being. It is therefore critical to consider what the "value," the outcome, is of the social capital theory. For example, whereas one social capital theory is explaining "trust," another social capital theory aims at understanding "finding a job" and yet another social capital theory is about "health." Clearly, "trust," "finding a job" and "health" are not the same phenomena; different mechanisms underlie these outcomes and therefore it is useful to clarify what a certain social capital theory is actually about.

Viewed in this way, one can distill *multiple* social capital theories, which, despite carrying the same name, aim to explain *different* outcomes. Elsewhere, I will introduce you to four social capital theories that explain inequality in the labor market, namely the one proposed by Bourdieu (Chapter 9) and by Granovetter, Burt, and Lin (Chapter 10). Below, we will take a closer look at various social capital theories developed to explain three outcomes: (1) social norms, (2) trust and (3) health and well-being.

Social norms

Let's start with the social capital theory of social norms. We have seen that social norms can benefit the collective (Chapter 6). But a key difficulty with social norms is to make people conform to them, especially when the norm is rather new and there has been insufficient time for people to internalize the social norm such that it has become a moral norm. Social control theory argues that norm conformity is a function of expected social sanctions and approval. These subjective expectations, in turn, depend on people's perceptions of being monitored. This means that, if people do not sufficiently monitor each other's behavior, they can get away with free-rider behavior and the norm will not be enforced.

Social norms, therefore, critically depend on monitoring. But what determines monitoring? We have seen (Chapter 6) that Durkheim's theory on suicide stated that "in more cohesive groups, people more strongly conform to the norm which prohibits suicide" (Durkheim, 1961 [1897]). In cohesive groups, so it was argued, people are more strongly monitored and thus sanctioned in case of norm-deviance.

The social capital theory developed by Coleman (1988, 1990) elaborates on these classic sociological insights by introducing social network terminology. Specifically, the connection between the "cohesiveness" of social structures and monitoring can be captured with social network topologies. To see how, consider Figure 7.11. The figure presents two networks, (1) and (2), both consisting of four persons. A tie between two persons indicates that they know each other. The difference between the two networks is that network (1) is more "cohesive" than network (2). In network (1) there are 6 realized ties and the number of possible ties is also (4(4–1)/2 =) 6. This means that the density of network (1) is 1.0. Everyone is connected to everyone else. It is called a *clique*, such as often seen among adolescents' closest friends in school.

Coleman indicates such cohesive social webs with the concept of **network closure**, and he argues that in such a highly connected, dense and clustered network people strongly monitor each other's behavior. For example, if person A tends to free-ride and cheat, both B, C and D notice such behavior and sanction A. Now compare this with network (2), in which people are more loosely connected to each other. The density of this network is (3

network closure highly connected, dense, network.

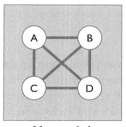 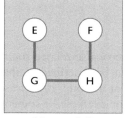

Network 1 **Network 2**

Figure 7.11 Network with (1) and without (2) closure.

realized ties/6 possible ties =) 0.5. In such a network without closure, people less strongly monitor each other's behavior. For example, if person E wanted to free-ride, only person G would be able to notice this. Consequently, social norms can be better enforced in networks with closure than networks without closure.

Networks (1) and (2) are stylized examples, of course. In reality, networks may vary along a continuum of closure, ranging from a completely connected network (density = 1) to networks that are completely disconnected (density = 0). But the idea remains the same: in more closed networks, that consist of more ties, people monitor each other's behavior more, which results in better enforcement of social norms. We can formulate Coleman's **network closure and norms** proposition as follows:

> P. The degree of closure in a certain network has a positive effect on the conformity to the social norms of that network. (*network closure and norms*)

Coleman illustrates the proposition with the norms parents impose on their children. Consider Figure 7.11 again. Suppose that now node A represents the parents of C and node B is the parents of D. Let's assume that parents A and B want their children to do well in school, that their children do their homework, do not drop-out of school and do not become involved in criminal activities. To enforce these social norms they monitor the behavior of their children. But because parents A and B also know each other, including the children of the other parent, they are better able to monitor the behavior of the children. For example, parents A and B may discuss who is keeping an eye on the children, sharing information on what they are doing outside school hours, with whom their children hang around and so forth. If child C hangs around with child D, then parents A know that parents B will keep an eye on not only their own child D but also on C. This is a case of what Coleman calls *intergenerational* closure.

In networks with lower levels of closure, such as in network (2), parents E and parents F are less able to monitor their children G and H. The parents do not know each other. This means that parents can take care of their own children, but cannot help others in monitoring their children. In such cases, enforcing social norms is more problematic and, according to Coleman, this can lead to undesirable collective outcomes, such as crime and school drop-out.

The concept of closure has become important in the social capital theory on the importance of networks for norms. The ideas can be traced back to the writings of Durkheim, but Coleman has articulated how a network approach helps to apply these ideas. The attractive feature of capturing Durkheim's ideas on the cohesiveness of groups with the network terminology on closure is that you can apply the network closure argument more broadly. You can establish the degree of closure in any type of network, i.e., personal networks, organizational networks, networks in the neighborhood, the family and so forth.

Trust

Social capital theories have also related social networks to trust. In the words of Freitag and Traunmüller, trust "can be described as the expectation that others will contribute to the well-being of a person or a group, or at least will refrain from harmful actions" (Freitag & Traunmüller, 2009). For example, if someone asks you to loan him some money and you agree to do so, you trust that person will return the money. That person can abuse your trust and never pay you back, so there is an element of risk involved. According to social capital theory, social networks play a role in generating trust.

To begin, consider trust between two individuals, ego and alter. At this dyadic level, trust is argued to be simply a function of (positive) tie strength (Blau, 2017 [1964]; Burt,

2005). Based on past experiences of positive (negative) encounters, ego and alter build trust (distrust) in each other. To illustrate, consider Figure 7.11 again and assume that each line represents a strong tie. Now compare two dyadic relations, namely between persons A and B, and between persons E and H. Who is more likely to trust each other? Persons A and B have a strong tie with each other, which means that—following Granovetter—they are emotionally close to each other, have a history of repeated interactions and tend to reciprocate favors. This is the type of dyadic relationship in which people trust each other. Person E and H do not have a strong tie with each other, which could mean that they have a weak positive tie or that they have a negative relationship. Clearly, E and H would distrust each other most when they have a strongly negative relationship. This leads us to the *tie strength and trust* proposition:

> P. The more positive the relationship between ego and alter, the more they trust each other. (*tie strength and trust*)

Does local network structure affect trust too? Let's compare relation AB with EG. Would A trust B as much as E would trust G? At the *dyadic* level the relations are the same: both are strong ties. However, the relationships are embedded in different *network structures*. Again, the concept of network closure helps to describe the difference. Whereas AB is part of a closed network, EG belongs to a more open network. Following the classic ideas of Simmel (1902), Granovetter argued that trust is more likely between people with mutual friends:

> My mortification at cheating a friend of long standing may be substantial even when undiscovered. It may increase when the friend becomes aware of it. But it may become even more unbearable when our mutual friends uncover the deceit and tell one another. (Granovetter, 1992)

Whereas AB have friends in common (namely C and D), EG do not. Simmel, Granovetter, Coleman and other scholars have argued that when the network in which ego and alter are embedded is more closed, such that they have more mutual friends or other strong positive third-party ties in common, ego and alter trust each other more (Coleman, 1990; Granovetter, 1992; Krackhardt, 1999, 2003; Simmel, 1902). This gives us the *network closure and trust* proposition:

> P. The higher the degree of closure in the network shared by ego and alter, the more ego and alter trust each other. (*network closure and trust*)

Dense webs of interconnected ties promote trustful relations between people in these networks. This type of trust is called *particularized trust*, or *thick trust*, and it is distinguished from *generalized trust*, or *thin trust* (Delhey, Newton, & Welzel, 2011; Fukuyama, 1995; Gambetta, 1988; Putnam, 2000; Uslaner, 2002; Yamagishi & Yamagishi, 1994). The difference is one of radius and scope. Particularized trust is trust in the smaller circle of closely related people, which typically include friends, family members and others with whom one frequently interacts, and who are embedded in the communities of interrelated ties to which one belongs. Generalized trust is trust one places in people in general, beyond one's friends and immediate social surroundings, such as strangers and political leaders.

How network structures impact generalized trust is a topic of discussion among scholars. Granovetter coined the idea that when people are strongly embedded in locally cohesive networks, when there is a high transitivity and many community-bonding ties, people may not trust political leaders because they may lack the (indirect) ties that connect them to these leaders (Granovetter, 1973). In his view, community-bridging ties (in this context often called *bridging social capital*), which create these links to other communities, thereby play an important role in overcoming the problem of trusting people outside one's own community.

More recently, scholars have argued that community-bonding ties can also promote generalized trust. Frequent interactions with friends, family members and other connections within one's community create generalized trust, because such trust is inferred from ongoing social experiences (Glanville & Paxton, 2007; Macy & Skvoretz, 1998; Paxton, 2007). Regular positive encounters with your friends—even though they are community-bonding ties—can foster the perception that people in general can be trusted. Let's formulate this idea as the **social ties and generalized trust** proposition:

> P. The more social interactions people have with friends, family members and other community members, the stronger their generalized trust. (*social ties and generalized trust*)

Research findings, based on both cross-sectional and longitudinal surveys, are generally in line with the *social ties and generalized trust* proposition (Delhey & Newton, 2003; Glanville, Andersson, & Paxton, 2013; Glanville & Paxton, 2007; Li, Pickles, & Savage, 2005; Welch, Sikkink, & Loveland, 2007). Also in line with this proposition and the mechanisms underlying it is the study of Freitag and Traunmüller, in which they find that people who place higher levels of *particularized* trust also tend to have more *generalized* trust (Freitag & Traunmüller, 2009).

Health and well-being

A third line of social capital theories focuses on health and well-being. There exists a large area of research which examines the consequences of social networks for these outcomes (Smith & Christakis, 2008). What are the key ideas in this field?

One line of theorizing is about the impact of people's personal network cohesion. Social connections, such as the ties people have with friends, spouse, peers and neighbors, are argued to be important for one's health and well-being. These ties, as we have seen, may be strong or weak and they may be positive, neutral or negative. The type of ties people have in their network is argued to affect people's health and well-being. It has been argued that if people have more strong ties rather than weak ties and positive ties rather than negative ties then they will have better health and higher well-being (Smith & Christakis, 2008). The mechanism underlying this proposition is that strong ties provide social and emotional support more so than do weaker ties. And positive ties, obviously, provide more support than negative ties, which can be stressful and undermine personal health and well-being. We can summarize the **network cohesion and health** proposition as follows:

> P. The higher someone's network cohesion, the better their health and well-being. (*network cohesion and health*)

To test this proposition, researchers have derived various testable hypotheses. To illustrate, let's consider three of them. These hypotheses rest on the assumption that network cohesion is: (1) higher among the married than the unmarried (divorced, single), (2) lower for widowers than non-widowers, (3) lower among those who are bullied. There is compelling evidence which supports this proposition:

H. Married people have better health and well-being than non-married people (*marriage and health effect*). In line with this hypothesis, research finds that married persons have lower mortality and lower depressive symptoms than the unmarried (Amato, 2000; Zick & Smith, 1991). On closer inspection, research findings suggest the negative consequences of divorce (exit) are far larger than the positive gains from marriage (entry) (Kalmijn, 2017).

H. Non-widows have better health and well-being than widows (*widowhood and health effect*). The loss of a spouse has been found to lead to a short-term rise in mortality and this effect is more pronounced in men (Elwert & Christakis, 2006).

H. Students who are not bullied in school have better health and well-being than students who are the victims of bullying in school (*bullying and health effect*). In line with this hypothesis, research findings suggest that being the victim of bullying in school substantially increases the risk of depression later in life (Ttofi, Farrington, Lösel, & Loeber, 2011).

The second proposition on the impact of social networks on health concerns not so much the connections people have, but rather the *attributes* of one's connections. Specifically, it is argued that the better the health and well-being of one's friends, spouse and other network ties, the better one's own health and well-being. Two mechanisms underlie this idea. First, people may copy the behavior of people in their environment. If one's friends have an unhealthy lifestyle, such as that they smoke, drink, use drugs and do little exercise, people may copy such unhealthy behavior. Second, being exposed to, or taking care of, friends and peers who are in bad health and well-being can be a source of stress. For these reasons the **network health and health** proposition states that:

P. The better the health and well-being of people's network ties, the better their own health and well-being (*network health and health*).

We have already (in Chapter 5, Opinions) reviewed evidence for this proposition in the peer influence literature. Specifically, research findings indicate that unhealthy behaviors, such as smoking and drinking, but also depressive moods, are transmitted from peer to peer. Other research findings also find consistent support for the proposition. Consider the following observations:

- Hospitalization of one spouse increases the risk of death of the other (Christakis & Allison, 2006).
- Caring for a sick spouse is associated with increased risk of illness and death (Schulz & Beach, 1999).
- Parental depression increases the risk of depression in offspring (Goodman et al., 2011; Jacob & Johnson, 1997).
- Parental physical health problems increase depression and poor physical health in offspring (Armistead, Klein, & Forehand, 1995).

In summary, research findings suggest that social networks impact people's health and well-being. Those who have more cohesive personal networks and those whose social network ties are healthier and happier tend to have better health outcomes.

7.9 Chapter resources

Key concepts

Graph	Strong tie	Community
Sociogram	Weak tie	Community-bonding tie
Nodes	Name generator	Community-bridging tie
Edges	Hub	Small-world network
Personal network	Network density	Social cohesion
Dyad	Triad	Personal network cohesion
Adjacency matrix	Transitivity	Social capital paradigm
Indegree	Triadic closure	Network closure
Outdegree	Forbidden triad	

Key theories and propositions

- Strength-of-weak-ties
- Loss-of-community
- Network closure and norms
- Tie strength and trust
- Network closure and trust
- Social ties and generalized trust
- Network cohesion and health
- Network health and health.

Key stylized facts

- Friendship paradox
- Personal network size in the US
- Hubs in personal networks
- Transitivity tendency
- Forbidden triad tendency
- Small-world phenomenon.

Summary

- Social networks are a set of actors (nodes) and the ties between them (edges).
- Personal networks present all the ties of a certain person (ego) with other persons (alters).
- One could present a network as a graph and adjacency matrix.
- In network studies a common distinction is made between strong ties and weak ties.
- Personal networks are characterized by hubs and transitivity. The ties that people have cluster together in communities.
- The small-world phenomenon is due to a combination of local clustering of social relations in communities and the existence of community-bridging ties.
- The strength-of-weak-ties proposition posits that weak ties more often create bridges to other communities than do strong ties.
- The loss-of-community proposition states that people are less strongly embedded nowadays in dense clusters of social ties.
- The study of social networks is often related to the complex concept of social cohesion. Personal network cohesion is one subdimension of social cohesion.

- Social networks are also linked to the concept of social capital. At the core of the social capital paradigm is the idea that networks have some sort of value, such as for creating trust and promoting health.

References

Amato, P. R. (2000). The consequences of divorce for adults and children. *Journal of Marriage and Family*, 62(4), 1269–1287.

Armistead, L., Klein, K., & Forehand, R. (1995). Parental physical illness and child functioning. *Clinical Psychology Review*, 15(5), 409–422.

Arnaboldi, V., Conti, M., Passarella, A., & Dunbar, R. I. (2017). Online social networks and information diffusion: The role of ego networks. *Online Social Networks and Media*, 1, 44–55.

Backstrom, L., Boldi, P., Rosa, M., Ugander, J., & Vigna, S. (2012). Four degrees of separation. Paper presented at the *Proceedings of the 4th Annual ACM Web Science Conference*, 33–42.

Barabasi, A. L. (2016). *Network science*. Cambridge, UK: Cambridge University Press.

Barabasi, A. L., & Albert, R. (1999). Emergence of scaling in random networks. *Science*, 286(5439), 509–512.

Bernard, H. R., Johnsen, E. C., Killworth, P. D., McCarty, C., Shelley, G. A., & Robinson, S. (1990). Comparing four different methods for measuring personal social networks. *Social Networks*, 12(3), 179–215.

Blau, P. (1977). *Inequality and heterogeneity: A primitive theory of social structure*. New York, NY: Free Press.

Blau, P. (2017 [1964]). *Exchange and power in social life*. Abingdon, UK: Routledge.

Boase, J., Horrigan, J., Wellman, B., & Rainie, L. (2006). *The strength of internet ties*. Washington, DC: Pew Internet and American Life Project. Retrieved from www.pewinternet.org/2006/01/25/the-strength-of-internet-ties/

Bonacich, P., & Lu, P. (2012). *Introduction to mathematical sociology*. Princeton, NJ: Princeton University Press.

Bourdieu, P. (1980). Le capital social: Notes provisoires. *Actes De La Recherche En Sciences Sociales*, 31, 2–3.

Bourdieu, P. (2010 [1979]). *Distinction: A social critique of the judgement of taste*. Abingdon, UK: Routledge.

Bourdieu, P., & Passeron, J. (1990 [1977]). *Reproduction in education, society and culture*. London: Sage.

Bruggeman, J. (2013). *Social networks: An introduction*. Abingdon, UK: Routledge.

Burt, R. S. (1984). Network items and the General Social Survey. *Social Networks*, 6(4), 293–339.

Burt, R. S. (1992). *Structural holes: The social structure of competition*. Cambridge, MA: Harvard University Press.

Burt, R. S. (2005). *Brokerage and closure*. Oxford: Oxford University Press.

Burt, R. S. (2010). *Neighbor networks: Competitive advantage local and personal*. Oxford: Oxford University Press.

Byrne, D. (1971). *The attraction paradigm*. New York, NY: Academic Press.

Cartwright, D., & Harary, F. (1956). Structural balance: A generalization of Heider's theory. *Psychological Review*, 63(5), 277–293.

Castiglione, D., Van Deth, J. W., & Wolleb, G. (Eds.). (2008). *The handbook of social capital*. Oxford: Oxford University Press.

Christakis, N. A., & Allison, P. D. (2006). Mortality after the hospitalization of a spouse. *New England Journal of Medicine*, *354*(7), 719–730.

Christakis, N. A., & Fowler, J. H. (2010). Social network sensors for early detection of contagious outbreaks. *PloS ONE*, *5*(9), e12948.

Coleman, J. S. (1988). Social capital in the creation of human capital. *American Journal of Sociology*, *94*, S95–S120.

Coleman, J. S. (1990). *Foundations of social theory*. Cambridge, MA: Harvard University Press.

Davis, J. A. (1970). Clustering and hierarchy in interpersonal relations: Testing two graph theoretical models on 742 sociomatrices. *American Sociological Review*, *35*(5), 843–851.

Davis, J. A., Holland, P., & Leinhardt, S. (1971). Comments on professor Mazur's hypothesis about interpersonal sentiments. *American Sociological Review*, *36*(2), 309–311.

de Sola Pool, I., & Kochen, M. (1978). Contacts and influence. *Social Networks*, *1*(1), 5–51.

Degenne, A., & Forsé, M. (1999). *Introducing social networks*. London, UK: Sage.

Delhey, J., & Newton, K. (2003). Who trusts? The origins of social trust in seven societies. *European Societies*, *5*(2), 93–137.

Delhey, J., Newton, K., & Welzel, C. (2011). How general is trust in "most people"? Solving the radius of trust problem. *American Sociological Review*, *76*(5), 786–807.

DiPrete, T. A., Gelman, A., McCormick, T., Teitler, J., & Zheng, T. (2011). Segregation in social networks based on acquaintanceship and trust. *American Journal of Sociology*, *116*(4), 1234–1283.

Dodds, P. S., Muhamad, R., & Watts, D. J. (2003). An experimental study of search in global social networks. *Science*, *301*(5634), 827–829.

Dunbar, R. I. M., Arnaboldi, V., Conti, M., & Passarella, A. (2015). The structure of online social networks mirrors those in the offline world. *Social Networks*, *43*, 39–47.

Durkheim, E. (1961 [1897]). *Suicide*. New York, NY: Free Press.

Easley, D., & Kleinberg, J. (2010). *Networks, crowds, and markets: Reasoning about a highly connected world*. New York, NY: Cambridge University Press.

Ellwardt, L., Labianca, G. J., & Wittek, R. (2012). Who are the objects of positive and negative gossip at work? A social network perspective on workplace gossip. *Social Networks*, *34*(2), 193–205.

Elwert, F., & Christakis, N. A. (2006). Widowhood and race. *American Sociological Review*, *71*(1), 16–41.

Faris, R., & Felmlee, D. (2011). Status struggles: Network centrality and gender segregation in same-and cross-gender aggression. *American Sociological Review*, *76*(1), 48–73.

Feld, S. L. (1981). The focused organization of social ties. *American Journal of Sociology*, *86*(5), 1015–1035.

Feld, S. L. (1991). Why your friends have more friends than you do. *American Journal of Sociology*, *96*(6), 1464–1477.

Fischer, C. S. (1982). *To dwell among friends: Personal networks in town and city*. Chicago, IL: University of Chicago Press.

Fischer, C. S. (2005). Bowling alone: What's the score? *Social Networks*, *27*(2), 155–167.

Flap, H., & Volker, B. (Eds.). (2004). *Creation and returns of social capital*. London, UK: Routledge.

Freitag, M., & Traunmüller, R. (2009). Spheres of trust: An empirical analysis of the foundations of particularised and generalised trust. *European Journal of Political Research*, *48*(6), 782–803.

Fukuyama, F. (1995). *Trust: The social virtues and the creation of prosperity*. New York, NY: Free Press.

Gambetta, D. (Ed.). (1988). *Trust: Making and breaking cooperative relations*. Oxford, UK: Basil Blackwell.

Girvan, M., & Newman, M. E. (2002). Community structure in social and biological networks. *Proceedings of the National Academy of Sciences of the United States of America*, 99(12), 7821–7826.

Glanville, J. L., Andersson, M. A., & Paxton, P. (2013). Do social connections create trust? An examination using new longitudinal data. *Social Forces*, 92(2), 545–562.

Glanville, J. L., & Paxton, P. (2007). How do we learn to trust? A confirmatory tetrad analysis of the sources of generalized trust. *Social Psychology Quarterly*, 70(3), 230–242.

Gonçalves, B., Perra, N., & Vespignani, A. (2011). Modeling users' activity on Twitter networks: Validation of Dunbar's number. *PloS ONE*, 6(8), e22656.

Goodman, S. H., Rouse, M. H., Connell, A. M., Broth, M. R., Hall, C. M., & Heyward, D. (2011). Maternal depression and child psychopathology: A meta-analytic review. *Clinical Child and Family Psychology Review*, 14(1), 1–27.

Granovetter, M. (1973). The strength of weak ties. *American Journal of Sociology*, 78(6), 1360–1380.

Granovetter, M. (1974). *Getting a job: A study of contacts and careers*. Cambridge, MA: Harvard University Press.

Granovetter, M. (1985). Economic action and social structure: The problem of embeddedness. *American Journal of Sociology*, 91(3), 481–510.

Granovetter, M. (1992). Problems of explanation in economic sociology. In N. Nohria & R. G. Eccles (Eds.), *Networks and Organizations* (pp. 25–56). Boston: Harvard Business School Press.

Grosser, T. J., Lopez-Kidwell, V., & Labianca, G. (2010). A social network analysis of positive and negative gossip in organizational life. *Group & Organization Management*, 35(2), 177–212.

Grund, T. (2014). Why your friends are more important and special than you think. *Sociological Science*, 1, 128–140.

Guiot, J. M. (1976). A modification of Milgram's small world method. *European Journal of Social Psychology*, 6(4), 503–507.

Häuberer, J. (2011). *Social capital theory: Towards a methodological foundation*. Wiesbaden, Germany: Springer.

Heider, F. (1946). Attitudes and cognitive organization. *The Journal of Psychology*, 21(1), 107–112.

Hill, R. A., & Dunbar, R. I. (2003). Social network size in humans. *Human Nature*, 14(1), 53–72.

Homans, G. C. (2017 [1951]). *The human group*. Abingdon, UK: Routledge.

Hsung, R., Lin, N., & Breiger, R. L. (Eds.). (2009). *Contexts of social capital: Social networks in markets, communities and families*. New York, NY: Routledge.

Jackson, M. O. (2008). *Social and economic networks*. Princeton, NJ: Princeton University Press.

Jacob, T., & Johnson, S. L. (1997). Parent–child interaction among depressed fathers and mothers: Impact on child functioning. *Journal of Family Psychology*, 11(4), 391.

Kadushin, C. (2012). *Understanding social networks: Theories, concepts, and findings*. New York, NY: Oxford University Press.

Kalmijn, M. (2017). The ambiguous link between marriage and health: A dynamic reanalysis of loss and gain effects. *Social Forces*, 95(4), 1607–1636.

Kleinfeld, J. S. (2002). The small world problem. *Society*, 39(2), 61–66.

Korte, C., & Milgram, S. (1970). Acquaintance networks between racial groups: Application of the small world method. *Journal of Personality and Social Psychology*, 15(2), 101–108.

Krackhardt, D. (1999). The ties that torture: Simmelian tie analysis in organizations. *Research in the Sociology of Organizations*, 16(1), 183–210.

Krackhardt, D. (2003). The strength of strong ties. In N. Nohria & B. Eccles (Eds.), *Networks and organizations* (pp. 216–239). Boston: Harvard Business School Press.

Laumann, E. O. (1973). *Bonds of pluralism: The form and substance of urban social networks.* New York, NY: J. Wiley.

Li, Y., Pickles, A., & Savage, M. (2005). Social capital and social trust in Britain. *European Sociological Review, 21*(2), 109–123.

Lin, N. (1999). Social networks and status attainment. *Annual Review of Sociology, 25,* 467–487.

Lin, N. (2001). *Social capital: A theory of social structure and action.* New York, NY: Cambridge University Press.

Lin, N., Cook, K., & Burt, R. S. (Eds.). (2001). *Social capital: Theory and research.* New Brunswick, NJ: Transaction Publishers.

Lin, N., & Erickson, B. H. (Eds.). (2008). *Social capital: An international research program.* Oxford, UK: Oxford University Press.

Lin, N., Fu, Y., & Hsung, R. (2001). The position generator: Measurement techniques for investigations of social capital. In N. Lin, K. Cook, & R. S. Burt (Eds.), *Social capital: Theory and research* (pp. 57–81). New Brunswick, NJ and London, UK: Aldine Transaction.

Louch, H. (2000). Personal network integration: Transitivity and homophily in strong-tie relations. *Social Networks, 22*(1), 45–64.

Lubbers, M. J., Molina, J. L., & Valenzuela-Garcia, H. (2019). When networks speak volumes: Variation in the size of broader acquaintanceship networks. *Social Networks, 56,* 55–69.

Lundberg, C. C. (1975). Patterns of acquaintanceship in society and complex organization: A comparative study of the small world problem. *Pacific Sociological Review, 18*(2), 206–222.

Mac Carron, P., Kaski, K., & Dunbar, R. (2016). Calling Dunbar's numbers. *Social Networks, 47,* 151–155.

Macy, M. W., & Skvoretz, J. (1998). The evolution of trust and cooperation between strangers: A computational model. *American Sociological Review, 63*(5), 638–660.

Marsden, P. V. (1987). Core discussion networks of Americans. *American Sociological Review, 52*(1), 122–131.

Marsden, P. V., & Campbell, K. E. (1984). Measuring tie strength. *Social Forces, 63*(2), 482–501.

McCormick, T. H., Salganik, M. J., & Zheng, T. (2010). How many people do you know? Efficiently estimating personal network size. *Journal of the American Statistical Association, 105*(489), 59–70.

McLanahan, S., & Sandefur, G. (1997). *Growing up with a single parent: What hurts, what helps.* Cambridge, MA: Harvard University Press.

McPherson, M., Smith-Lovin, L., & Brashears, M. E. (2006). Social isolation in America: Changes in core discussion networks over two decades. *American Sociological Review, 71*(3), 353–375.

Milgram, S. (1967). The small world problem. *Psychology Today, 1,* 61–67.

Mollenhorst, G., Völker, B., & Flap, H. (2011). Shared contexts and triadic closure in core discussion networks. *Social Networks, 33*(4), 292–302.

Newman, M. E. J. (2010). *Networks: An introduction.* New York, NY: Oxford University Press.

Nieuwenhuis, J., Völker, B., & Flap, H. (2013). "A bad neighbour is as great a plague as a good one is a great blessing": On negative relationships between neighbours. *Urban Studies, 50*(14), 2904–2921.

Paik, A., & Sanchagrin, K. (2013). Social isolation in America: An artifact. *American Sociological Review*, 78(3), 339–360.

Paxton, P. (2007). Association memberships and generalized trust: A multilevel model across 31 countries. *Social Forces*, 86(1), 47–76.

Portes, A. (1998). Social capital: Its origins and applications in modern sociology. *Annual Review of Sociology*, 24, 1–24.

Price, D. D. S. (1965). Networks of scientific papers. *Science*, 149(3683), 510–515.

Price, D. D. S. (1976). A general theory of bibliometric and other cumulative advantage processes. *Journal of the Association for Information Science and Technology*, 27(5), 292–306.

Putnam, R. (2000). *Bowling alone: The collapse and revival of the American community*. New York, NY: Simon & Schuster.

Robinson, D. T., & Balkwell, J. W. (1995). Density, transitivity, and diffuse status in task-oriented groups. *Social Psychology Quarterly*, 58(4), 241–254.

Schnettler, S. (2009a). A small world on feet of clay? A comparison of empirical small-world studies against best-practice criteria. *Social Networks*, 31(3), 179–189.

Schnettler, S. (2009b). A structured overview of 50 years of small-world research. *Social Networks*, 31(3), 165–178.

Schulz, R., & Beach, S. R. (1999). Caregiving as a risk factor for mortality: The caregiver health effects study. *JAMA*, 282(23), 2215–2219.

Scott, J. (2017 [1991]). *Social network analysis* (4th ed.). London, UK: Sage.

Simmel, G. (1902). The number of members as determining the sociological form of the group. *American Journal of Sociology*, 8(1), 1–46.

Smith, K. P., & Christakis, N. A. (2008). Social networks and health. *Annual Review of Sociology*, 34, 405–429.

Smith, P. K., Mahdavi, J., Carvalho, M., Fisher, S., Russell, S., & Tippett, N. (2008). Cyberbullying: Its nature and impact in secondary school pupils. *Journal of Child Psychology and Psychiatry*, 49(4), 376–385.

Straus, M. A., Gelles, R. J., & Steinmetz, S. K. (2017 [1980]). *Behind closed doors: Violence in the American family*. London and New York: Routledge.

Tokunaga, R. S. (2010). Following you home from school: A critical review and synthesis of research on cyberbullying victimization. *Computers in Human Behavior*, 26(3), 277–287.

Tönnies, F. (1957 [1887]). *Community and society*. East Lansing, MI: Michigan State University Press.

Travers, J., & Milgram, S. (1969). An experimental study of the small world problem. *Sociometry*, 32(4), 425–443.

Ttofi, M. M., Farrington, D. P., Lösel, F., & Loeber, R. (2011). Do the victims of school bullies tend to become depressed later in life? A systematic review and meta-analysis of longitudinal studies. *Journal of Aggression, Conflict and Peace Research*, 3(2), 63–73.

Uslaner, E. M. (2002). *The moral foundations of trust*. Cambridge, UK: Cambridge University Press.

Veenstra, R., Lindenberg, S., Oldehinkel, A. J., De Winter, A. F., Verhulst, F. C., & Ormel, J. (2005). Bullying and victimization in elementary schools: A comparison of bullies, victims, bully/ victims, and uninvolved preadolescents. *Developmental Psychology*, 41(4), 672–682.

Wang, H., & Wellman, B. (2010). Social connectivity in America: Changes in adult friendship network size from 2002 to 2007. *American Behavioral Scientist*, 53(8), 1148–1169.

Wasserman, S., & Faust, K. (1994). *Social network analysis: Methods and applications*. Cambridge, UK: Cambridge University Press.

Watts, D. J. (1999). *Small worlds: The dynamics of networks between order and randomness.* Princeton, NJ: Princeton University Press.

Watts, D. J. (2003). *Six degrees: The science of a connected age.* New York, NY: W. W. Norton & Company.

Watts, D. J., & Strogatz, S. H. (1998). Collective dynamics of 'small-world' networks. *Nature, 393,* 440–442.

Welch, M. R., Sikkink, D., & Loveland, M. T. (2007). The radius of trust: Religion, social embeddedness and trust in strangers. *Social Forces, 86*(1), 23–46.

Wellman, B. (1979). The community question: The intimate networks of East Yorkers. *American Journal of Sociology, 84*(5), 1201–1231.

Yamagishi, T., & Yamagishi, M. (1994). Trust and commitment in the United States and Japan. *Motivation and Emotion, 18*(2), 129–166.

Zheng, T., Salganik, M. J., & Gelman, A. (2006). How many people do you know in prison? Using overdispersion in count data to estimate social structure in networks. *Journal of the American Statistical Association, 101*(474), 409–423.

Zick, C. D., & Smith, K. R. (1991). Marital transitions, poverty, and gender differences in mortality. *Journal of Marriage and the Family, 53*(2), 327–336.

Chapter 8

Groups

Chapter overview

To which groups do you belong? How important are groups to you? Sociologists have long recognized that the theme of social relations entails more than the study of networks. The study of social relations also includes examination of group formation and intergroup relations. People belong to groups; they have group affiliations and identities. Groups may unite people and serve common interests, but they may also divide societies and create conflicts (8.1). I will review literature which suggests that the groups to which we belong affect who we befriend and marry, that social ties are segregated by group affiliations. Individuals who belong to the same groups (e.g., religion, race, ethnicity) tend to associate with each other more frequently, creating group segregation in societies (8.2). I then review several causes that give rise to this phenomenon of group segregation in friendship ties and marriages (8.3). Subsequently, I will show that group segregation is part of a broader pattern. Whether you study friendship ties, attitudes or cooperation, you'll see that people have more positive relations to in-group members than out-group members, a pattern called in-group favoritism (8.4). Beyond this baseline universal tendency of intergroup relations, however, there are also deviations. Sometimes, intergroup relations erode and conflicts emerge and yet other groups appear to be more cooperative towards each other. Research findings reveal that intergroup cohesion is contingent on social conditions (8.5). In order to understand why intergroup cooperation and conflict depends on contextual conditions, I will discuss group threat theory (8.6).

Learning goals

After reading this chapter, check if you are able to:

- Describe and use key sociological concepts on groups.
- Relate intergroup cohesion and organizational cohesion to social cohesion.
- Describe and explain the phenomenon of group segregation.
- Describe the phenomenon of in-group favoritism.
- Describe the minimal group paradigm and social identity theory.
- Describe and apply group threat theory.

8.1 Groups unite and divide

To which groups do you belong? Most people indicate that they belong to at least one group. Indeed, scholars argue that people have a fundamental need to belong to groups (Baumeister, 1991). You may enthusiastically support your favorite sports team, for example, feel gratification as an active member of a political party or identify with an ethnic group. Belonging to a group gives positive affect, a "we-feeling," a sense of being connected to other people—even unknown people—who belong to the same group. Participation in group meetings, such as attending a soccer game, a political party event or an ethnic-religious gathering, generates positive energy (Durkheim, 2001 [1912]).

Moreover, we-feeling can promote the production of collective goods and mitigate problems of human cooperation. Ever since humans have been organized in small-scale groups, as hunter-gatherers, people have shown a greater willingness to help in-group members. Research findings consistently reveal that a "we-feeling" increases cooperative behavior in social dilemma situations (Brewer & Kramer, 1986; Kollock, 1998; Simpson, 2006). People are less likely to free-ride in situations that create a tension between individual and collective benefits once they realize that they belong to the same group as the other people. Parochial cooperation occurs, for example, between supporters of the same soccer team, between party members and between co-ethnics. Groups can be sources of social and emotional support, financial assets, protection and well-being.

What actually is a "group?" A common definition of a **group** is that of a social category to which people could be affiliated. This means, for example, that we can consider "FC Barcelona" as a (soccer) group, the "Democratic Party" in the US as a (political) group and the Maori in New Zealand as an (ethnic) group. The social category "women" is a group and so is "university students." In sociology, groups are also called **affiliation networks** (Wasserman & Faust, 1994; White, 2008), i.e., a network of people affiliated to the same group. Individuals typically belong to multiple groups. In the words of Simmel, we "belong to a web of group

group (also **affiliation network**) social category with which people can affiliate.

affiliations" (Simmel, 1955). The intersection of all the affiliations to which you belong (e.g., sports club, political party, ethnicity, gender) is part of who you are.

When do we say that someone is "affiliated" to a group? Group affiliations are generally assigned in three different ways: as *membership*, *participation* and *identification*. Consider affiliation with a soccer club, say FC Barcelona. One way you could belong to this group is to become an official member. You pay fees and you get membership benefits, such as the club magazine. Seen in this way, researchers could get an "objective" indication of group affiliation by listing all the members of that soccer club, i.e., those who pay a contribution, for example, or who are officially registered. But group affiliation may also be interpreted in another way, namely by considering people who are actively engaged and attend meetings of the club. For example, if you attend the matches of FC Barcelona you are (actively) affiliated to that group and so, too, are you if you join activities organized by the club. However, you may even be affiliated to FC Barcelona while not being a member of the club nor ever having attended their matches or participated in their activities. This third way of looking at group affiliation is more subjective: you're affiliated with the club if you identify with it. If you feel connected to the club in a more personal, emotional way, if you are, say, a supporter at home when you watch their games then you subjectively identify as being affiliated to FC Barcelona. We can thus conceptualize group affiliation as having three subdimensions: "objective" affiliation (group membership), participation (group activity) and subjective identification (group identity).

THINKING LIKE A SOCIOLOGIST 8.1

With which groups do you identify? How important are these groups for you?

Some groups have an organizational structure, such that their members can actively participate, whereas others have not—or not on their own. For example, "university students" is such a social category, a group that may or may not have an organization connected to it. There may be a "student association" at your university and, if so, you may actively become engaged in it. These groups that have some sort of organization structure are called *voluntary associations* or common-interest group (Olson, 2009 [1965]). A political party is an example of a common-interest group, but so is a church, a sports club, a labor union, an environmental association, a social movement group, a yoga club and a student association—to name only a few. What defines voluntary common-interest groups is that these are groups with organizational structure and which serve the common interest of those who are affiliated. A sports club, for example, allows its members to play their favorite sports, say soccer or tennis—something people would be unable to do on their own, i.e., if there were no organization. Similarly, a political organization unites people who share the same political views and, as an organized group, they can collectively serve their interests much more, of course, than when they do so on their own.

The collective benefits generated by groups when they organize themselves has attracted scholarly attention. A classic study is Putnam's *Making Democracy Work* (Putnam, Leonardi, & Nanetti, 1993). Putnam studied the effectiveness of governmental institutions in Italy, drawing a sharp contrast between south and north Italy. Putnam argued that institutions work less efficiently in the southern parts of the country and that this region developed less well economically than the more affluent northern part of Italy. The reason for this north–south difference, Putnam posits, is that in the north there is more of a **civil society**, i.e., a society (region) consisting of a cohesive web of voluntary associations. In the north there are more sports clubs, music clubs and other voluntary associations than in the south and people in the north actively participate in these groups. According to Putnam, such a vibrant associational life promotes cooperation, solidarity, trust and norm enforcement, which are necessary elements for well-functioning, efficient democratic institutions.

> **civil society** society consisting of a cohesive web of voluntary associations.

Because voluntary associations are seen as a key ingredient of social cohesion in society, creating a "we-feeling" and enabling group cooperation, scholars have studied them in more detail. Putnam, in *Bowling Alone*, provided evidence to suggest that associational life in the US had been diminishing between 1950 and 2000 (Putnam, 2000). For example, during this period, there was a significant decline in membership rates of labor unions. Another classic study on associational life is that of the French sociologist Tocqueville in *Democracy in America*. Tocqueville, while travelling through the United States in the 19th century, noticed that there were far more religious organizations, social clubs and other kinds of voluntary organizations over there than in his home country of France (De Tocqueville, 2002 [1889]). Such over-time and cross-country differences in voluntary association involvement has become an important topic of research in sociology (Plagnol & Huppert, 2010; Ruiter & De Graaf, 2006; Schofer & Fourcade-Gourinchas, 2001). The most prominent type of groups in the world that have organizational structure are religious groups. In Chapter 13 I will take a closer look at religious groups and discuss in more depth why religious groups are more common in some societies than in others and how we can understand religious change.

The degree of *voluntary association involvement* in society can be seen as another dimension of social cohesion: the stronger the degree of associational involvement in society, the stronger its social cohesion. This particular type of social cohesion will be indicated as **organizational cohesion**. This dimension of social cohesion is analytically different from *personal network cohesion*, which was introduced in Chapter 7, and it differs from *intergroup cohesion*

> **organizational cohesion** degree of voluntary association involvement.

(Figure 8.1). When people organize themselves into sports clubs, political parties and other voluntary organizations, social relations in society become more than a collection of individuals and their personal networks. Indeed, when sociologists examine the overall cohesiveness of social relations in society—its social cohesion—they also consider the vibrancy of associational life. Without voluntary organizations, there would be no sports clubs, music clubs, religious organizations and so forth. In such a society there could still be strong personal network cohesion (Chapter 7)—people could be positively connected to each other in their personal networks—but at the group level the society is not cohesive at all and this means that it lacks voluntary organizations that serve common interests.

So far, we have seen that groups have the capacity to unite people: "Me" becomes part of something bigger, "Us." Merely belonging to the same social category can foster cooperation, a "we-feeling," and when groups get some organizational structure people are able to work together efficiently towards common goals. However, groups may also divide people into a world of Us versus Them, in-groups and out-groups, and undermine the well-being of out-group members. In the 19th century, racist White Americans began to self-organize into what was called the Ku Klux Klan (KKK) and they used their collective force to kill thousands of Blacks. Therefore, associational organizational cohesion may undermine social cohesion in society if such organizations cause out-group members harm (Paxton, 2007). But also merely

Figure 8.1 Three dimensions of social cohesion.

identifying with a certain group may result in Us versus Them thinking. Effectively, in these cases, intragroup cohesion undermines intergroup cohesion. Groups can become a basis for intergroup distinctions, cleavages and conflict in society.

Scholars therefore study **intergroup cohesion** as a third dimension of social cohesion, i.e., the degree to which (members of different) groups in society have positive relations with each other as opposed to negative relations. It is important to differentiate organizational cohesion from intergroup cohesion because these different dimensions of social cohesion do not necessarily overlap. A society can have strong organizational cohesion and yet weak intergroup cohesion.

intergroup cohesion degree to which (members of different) groups in society have positive relations with each other as opposed to negative relations.

How do we know whether intergroup cohesion is strong or weak? When do we say that (members of different) groups have positive relations with each other? When is there a strong Us–Them divide and when not? The study of intergroup relations is spread over four areas of research, each looking at different aspects and different indicators of Us versus Them intergroup relations in society (Figure 8.2):

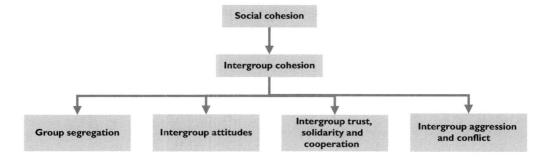

Figure 8.2 Intergroup cohesion as one dimension of social cohesion; four areas of research to study intergroup cohesion.

- *Group segregation.* Scholars study friendships, marriage and cohabitation and other types of positive social ties between people of different groups. Intergroup cohesion is stronger when members of different groups befriend each other and when intermarriages are common. When people instead create friendship bonds with in-group members, when group segregation emerges in social life, it is an indicator of weakened intergroup cohesion.

- *Intergroup attitudes.* Scholars study intergroup attitudes, a more subjective indicator of social distance between groups. The Us–Them divide is stronger when people have strong positive views about their own group and think very negatively about the out-group.
- *Intergroup trust, solidarity and cooperation.* Scholars examine how much people trust in- and out-group members, how much cooperation and solidarity there is between Us and Them.
- *Intergroup aggression and conflict.* Finally, scholars study acts of aggression and conflict, and when such acts are more common between groups they are a clear signal that intergroup cohesion is undermined.

In the following section I will review the literature on Us–Them divides and intergroup cohesion. I will discuss the main findings and theories on (1) *group segregation* and then relate this to research on (2) *intergroup attitudes* and (3) *intergroup trust, solidarity and cooperation.* I will show that, when bringing these literatures together, we are able to identify a common pattern of intergroup relations.

8.2 Group segregation

One way to examine intergroup cohesion in society is to look at personal ties. How strong are personal relations divided by group affiliations? Do your friends belong to the same group as you do? How many contacts do you have with out-group members? Scholars have long argued that group affiliation is a primary basis for social interaction, that Us–Them divides can be seen when we study friendships, marriages and other personal relations (Breiger, 1974; Watts, Dodds, & Newman, 2002). How can we empirically study such group divides? Consider Figure 8.3, which presents a social network of eight fictitious individuals and their friendship ties. As you can see, the networks separate into two communities: a clique of friends A–D and a clique of friends E–H.

But the network members also have group affiliations. In this example, all of them are affiliated to a religious group, either Muslim or Christian. Given these group affiliations, there are two possibilities for any social tie. A tie between two individuals who belong to the same group is called a **group-bonding tie**. An example

group-bonding tie tie between two individuals who belong to the same group.

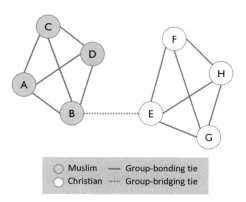

Figure 8.3 Friendship network and group affiliation: scenario 1.

is the friendship between A and B: as they are both Muslim, their friendship is a group-bonding tie. A tie between two members who are affiliated to different groups is called a **group-bridging tie**, also called a cross-cutting tie (Blau & Schwartz, 1984). In this friendship network there is only one such tie, namely the friendship between B and E.

group-bridging tie tie between two individuals who belong to a different group.

These social ties reveal something important to us about intergroup relations. In Figure 8.3, individuals have predominantly group-bonding ties and there are very few group-bridging ties. This means that personal networks are highly segregated between groups: friends are mainly from the religious in-group and few have friends from the religious out-group. Muslims are befriended with Muslims and Christians befriend other Christians—a sign that there is a divide between Us and Them. The two groups are segregated into two different communities.

It is helpful to have a measure of the degree of group segregation so that we can assess more precisely how strongly the social relations between members of any two groups are segregated. A simple and straightforward measure is the *group segregation index*:

$$Group\ segregation\ index = \frac{N\ group\text{-}bonding\ ties}{N\ group\text{-}bonding\ ties + N\ group\text{-}bridging\ ties} \qquad (8.1)$$

The group segregation index ranges from 0 (there are only group-bridging ties) to 1 (only group-bonding ties). If the group segregation index is in between these two extremes, the index is 0.50. In that case, there are as many group-bonding as group-bridging ties. In Figure 8.3 there are 12 group-bonding ties and there is only 1 group-bridging tie, which means that the group segregation index is (12/(12+1) =) 0.92. It is close to 1, which indicates strong segregation of social ties between the two groups, i.e., there are mostly group-bonding ties and few group-bridging ties.

Now consider this network again, but with the group affiliation distributed differently (Figure 8.4). Figure 8.4 presents again the social network of eight individuals and, as you can see, the network structure is identical to Figure 8.3. There are again two communities: clique A–D and clique E–H. However, the group segregation is completely different: rather than having two groups living in two different communities, there are many friendships between

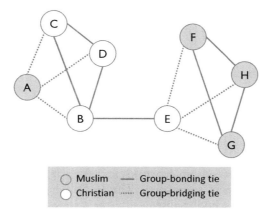

Figure 8.4 Friendship network and group affiliation: scenario 2.

members of the different groups. There are many more group-bridging ties than in Figure 8.3. The group segregation index is (7/(7+6)=) 0.53, which reveals that friendship ties are not segregated by group affiliations.

What do the empirics tell us about Us–Them group divides in social relations? Are individuals living in segregated groups in contemporary societies? One popular area of research on group segregation is the study of marriage patterns (Kalmijn, 1998). When marriages mainly occur among members of the same group, group segregation is said to be strong. When members of different groups often marry each other, it indicates stronger intergroup cohesion. In the literature on marriage, specific labels have been attached to the distinction between group-bonding and group-bridging ties. Researchers talk about **endogamy** when people marry someone from their own group. When people marry with a member of an out-group one speaks about **exogamy**, **intermarriage** or **mixed marriage**.

endogamy marriage between two individuals who belong to the same group.

exogamy (also **intermarriage**, or **mixed marriage**) marriage between two individuals who belong to different groups.

Group segregation is examined empirically by examining the endogamy rate, i.e., the number of within-group marriages as a percentage of all marriages (i.e., endogamous and exogamous). Often, scholars use the concept of a *marriage market* to study this. A marriage market is a cross-classification of married males and females, identified by a certain group, such as ethnicity or religion (Kalmijn, 1998). Consider Table 8.1, which illustrates this approach with two groups: Blacks (B) and Whites (W). To compute the endogamy rate in this population you have to divide the number of endogamous marriages among Blacks (C_{BB}) and Whites (C_{WW}) by the total number of marriages (T).

Table 8.1 Illustration of marriage market with two groups: Blacks and Whites.

	Females		Total
Males	*Black*	*White*	
Black	C_{BB}	C_{BW}	M_B
White	C_{WB}	C_{WW}	M_W
Total	F_B	F_W	T

There is overwhelming empirical evidence which shows that, as a general tendency, endogamy is more common in the population at large than exogamy (Kalmijn, 1998; Lucassen & Laarman, 2009; McPherson, Smith-Lovin, & Cook, 2001). This has been found with respect to multiple groups: racial groups (Kalmijn, 1993; Qian, 1997), ethnic groups (Jones & Luijkx, 1996), religious groups (Kennedy, 1944) and socio-economic-status groups (Kalmijn, 1994).

Sociologists also look at friendship networks, in particular among adolescents and youth in school classes, to study group segregation. The pupils who participate in the study are asked to name their friends at school. Subsequently, the researchers can study whether friendships are more common between adolescents who belong to the same group. What these studies find is that, generally speaking, the friendship networks of adolescents at school are rather homogenous (McPherson et al., 2001). In particular, it has been found that friendships are segregated by gender: boys name boys as friends and girls befriend girls. But also ethnicity and race appear to strongly segregate friendship networks at school, as has been found in the United States (Moody, 2001; Mouw & Entwisle, 2006), the Netherlands (Baerveldt, Van Duijn, Vermeij, & Van Hemert, 2004; Smith, Maas, & Van Tubergen, 2014; Stark & Flache, 2012) and Germany (Leszczensky & Pink, 2015; Windzio, 2012).

THINKING LIKE A SOCIOLOGIST 8.2

How homogenous is your core network? How similar are your friends to you with respect to age, gender, race/ethnicity, religion and social class?

Literature on the small-world phenomenon has also revealed that social ties are strongly segregated by groups. A recurrent finding of research on the small-world phenomenon is that when the starting person belongs to a *different group* than the target person, it proves more difficult to connect the two (i.e., longer chains, lower success rate) than when they are affiliated to the same group. For example, if the first person who is asked to forward the message is a Christian and the person to whom the message should be delivered is a Muslim, then in many cases the target person cannot be found. In the case where the starting person and the target person are from the same group (e.g., both Christian), such failures to reach the target are less common. This suggests the existence of group segregation as people simply don't know persons from other groups, not even via their connections. Evidence for group segregation in the small-world literature has been found with respect to race and gender in the US (Korte & Milgram, 1970; Lin, Dayton, & Greenwald, 1978; Milgram, 1967) and in a study of Ashkenazi and Oriental Jews in Israel (Weimann, 1983).

What is the take-away message from these studies on marriages, friendships and small-world research? They teach us the same lesson, namely that the Us–Them divide in social ties is a common pattern, a universal stylized fact. People tend to befriend and marry in-group members more often than out-group members. This empirical pattern has been found with respect to racial groups, ethnic groups, religious groups, status groups, but also with respect to gender, age and education (McPherson et al., 2001). The friends we have are often from the same groups as the ones we belong to ourselves and this is not only true for face-to-face relations but also online (Hofstra, Corten, Van Tubergen, & Ellison, 2017). Let's summarize this social phenomenon of ***group segregation*** in personal relations such as marriage, friendships and other contacts as a stylized fact.

STYLIZED FACT 8.1

Group segregation
People tend to have more frequent group-bonding ties than group-bridging ties.

This well-known empirical regularity is expressed in the popular sayings "*birds of a feather flock together*" and "*like associate with like*." In the scientific literature it has also been called *homogeneity bias*, *network homogeneity* and *network autocorrelation*. Sometimes it is called (baseline) *homophily* but, following other scholars (Wimmer & Lewis, 2010) and more in line with the original meaning (in Greek) of the term "homophily" (as we will see below), I will preserve the concept of homophily to designate a theoretical mechanism that helps to explain *why* group segregation exists rather than naming the stylized empirical pattern itself homophily.

8.3 The causes of group segregation

How can we explain the phenomenon of *group segregation* in social ties? Why do people have mainly friends who belong to their in-group? Why do we see that, as a general tendency, boys befriend boys, Muslims marry Muslims and higher educated people predominantly know other higher educated people? Why are friendship relations in society divided by group affiliations? Scholars have identified different mechanisms that underlie this phenomenon. I will review the two most important ones first: *opportunities* and *homophily*, loosely called "constraint-" and "choice-based" mechanisms. After that I will briefly discuss two more mechanisms: *transitivity* and *third party effects*.

Constraint: structural opportunity

It seems intuitive to explain group segregation with the idea that this is just what people want. If you see that Christians befriend Christians and Muslims befriend Muslims, why not say that this is because Christians *prefer* to befriend Christians and Muslims *prefer* Muslims above Christians? This seems a plausible explanation, but you cannot infer from the phenomenon of group segregation that this is due to in-group preferences.

The key element you would thereby overlook is that social ties are made in context and social contexts can constrain the choices we make. The theory that elaborates on this idea, which was largely developed by the sociologist Peter Blau, is **structural opportunity theory** (Blau, 1977, 1994; Blau, Blum, & Schwartz, 1982; Blau & Schwartz, 1984). In essence, the theory argues that group segregation arises as a result of (unequal) meeting opportunities between members of different groups. Figure 8.5 visualizes the main arguments of this theory in a multilevel framework.

At the individual level (arrow c), the theory simply argues that relationships between people are determined by the opportunity of people to meet each other. The higher the chances

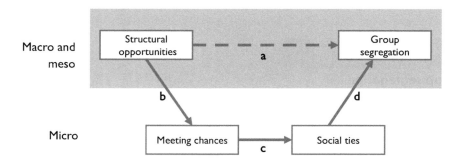

Figure 8.5 Structural opportunity theory.

of person A interacting with person B, the more likely it is that A and B will develop a social relationship. Think about your own friends. Presumably you met them at school, in your neighborhood or in another setting in which you both participated. If you had been raised in, say, another part of the country, you would have had no opportunity to meet them and you would have had other friends.

When you meet someone every day you're more likely to become friends than with someone you have hardly seen. This might sound like a trivial statement but the importance of such meeting chances is often overlooked and the consequences are far from trivial. All relationships we make are shaped by opportunity: out of the available pool of people we meet, we select our friends, partner and so forth. As the saying goes: "there is no mating without meeting." This is the micro-level foundation of opportunity theory.

The second argument of opportunity theory connects the social context (macro and meso) to the micro level. It states that the "pool of people" we meet is dependent on "structural opportunities" (arrow b), i.e., the meeting opportunities created by the social context in which people participate. Thus, the opportunity theory argues that the contexts in which people participate generally constrain their possibilities to meet people from other groups (arrow b), that such reduced intergroup meeting chances result in the development of group-bonding ties at the individual level (arrow c) and that from this process group segregation emerges (arrow d).

So, what determines the opportunities for meeting in- and out-group members? Blau introduces several structural constraints. One of these is *group size*, i.e., groups differ in how many members they have. The mere size of a group can be a key contextual condition that shapes meeting opportunities. Members of larger groups have ample opportunities to interact with in-group members, whereas people who belong to smaller groups have more restricted opportunities for meeting and interacting with in-group members. One consequence of this is that members of larger groups tend to marry more often with in-group members than do those of smaller groups (Kalmijn, 1998). Another structural constraint is **consolidation**, which refers to the degree of overlap ("correlation") between groups with respect to a certain dimension. To illustrate, consider race and income. If we simplify reality and differentiate between two racial groups only and two income categories, we get a cross-classification of race by income (Table 8.2).

consolidation degree of overlap, correlation between groups with respect to a certain dimension.

Suppose that there are 500 Whites and 500 Blacks and that Whites have a much higher income than Blacks. There are 400 Whites with a high income whereas this is true for only 100 Blacks. This means that race is strongly correlated with income, a high degree of "consolidation." High levels of consolidation restrict opportunities for intergroup ties (Blau & Schwartz, 1984; Centola, 2015). It means that members of different groups navigate in different **foci**, i.e., social

foci social settings in which people participate and that create the pool of people we meet.

Table 8.2 Illustration of consolidation between race and income.

	Low income	High income
Black	400	100
White	100	400

settings such as schools, workplaces and neighborhoods in which people participate and that create the pool of people we meet (Feld, 1981). Opportunity theory states that these local contexts often do not contain a random sample of the population but are more segregated instead. In other words, the structural opportunities to establish bonding ties are more prevalent than the opportunities to form bridging ties.

Specifically, if race and income correlate, then meso-level contexts such as schools, workplaces and neighborhoods tend to be segregated in terms of racial composition and socioeconomic class. This means that people more often meet someone from their own race or socioeconomic class in school, at work and in their neighborhood. Literature has found that, indeed, the segregated composition of foci tend to contribute to the emergence of group segregation in social ties (Kalmijn, 1998; Mollenhorst, Völker, & Flap, 2008; Mouw & Entwisle, 2006). In other words, structural opportunities constrain the formation of group-bridging ties and contribute to the fact that people's social connections tend to be mainly with in-group members.

Choice: homophily

Although structural opportunities indeed play a key role in generating group segregation, people also make choices within the constraints they face. According to **homophily theory**, we should consider the role of *similarity-based preferences*. The intellectual roots of this idea can be traced in the work of Lazarsfeld and Merton in the 1950s (Lazarsfeld & Merton, 1954) and in the work on the "attraction paradigm" by Byrne in the 1970s (Byrne, 1971). The name *homophily* is composed of the Greek words *"homo"* (meaning "same") and *"philos"* ("love"). As the meaning of this word already suggests, the homophily theory states that people *prefer* those who are the *same* as themselves. In other words, it argues that people selectively choose to interact with and befriend others who are socially similar to them at the expense of contacts and friendships with people who belong to out-groups. Contrary to the popular saying that *"opposites attract,"* the homophily proposition states that *"like prefers like."*

There are several assumptions that underlie this idea of homophily. One is that interaction with in-group members is sometimes easier in terms of *coordination* of actions. Say, for example, that you want to attend meetings of the political party you are affiliated with and you'd like to do so together with friends, then you can more easily coordinate this when you and your friends belong to the same political party. Similarly, attending meetings of a religious group, a student association and so forth is much easier to coordinate with your friends if they belong to the same group as you do. More generally, all the activities, rituals and practices that are unique and specific to each group imply that group-bonding contacts are easier to coordinate than group-bridging ties.

Another mechanism underlying the homophily hypothesis is the idea that, generally speaking, interactions with in-group members are more *psychologically rewarding* than contacts with out-group members. As we have seen, human populations have cultures and opinions and corresponding behavior cluster together in groups. This means that groups differ in, for example, what is seen as right and wrong, gender values, norms about appropriate behavior and so forth. Because of the human need for behavior approval, people will seek social ties with in-group members as these co-members will confirm that their cultural beliefs, values and behavior are right. In contacts with out-group members, by contrast, people expose themselves to different perspectives and practices. Their views may become subject to critique from out-group members, which is psychologically more challenging. Let's write down the general proposition from *homophily theory*.

P. People prefer to interact with members from their in-group as opposed to members of out-groups. (*homophily*)

According to this proposition, we should expect to see that people prefer the formation of in-group ties above out-group ties. For example, Muslims *prefer* to interact with Muslims, boys *want* to hang around with boys, higher educated people *prefer* to befriend higher educated people and so forth. The homophily theory can contribute to our understanding of group segregation: when people selectively form ties to in-group members, at the expense of out-group members, then personal ties are more segregated by groups compared with a situation in which people do not select ties based on group preferences. According to homophily theory the empirical phenomenon of group segregation ("like *associate* with like") is at least partly due to the tie-generating mechanism of *homophily* ("like *prefer* like").

What are the empirically testable hypotheses that can be derived from the homophily theory? What does empirical research tell us? Do people prefer social contacts with in-group members and selectively avoid out-group members? Is group segregation indeed a result of such choices? There are two sources of evidence for homophily, namely: *indirect* and *direct*. The indirect evidence comes from studies which rely on actual marriage and friendship data and from this they make inferences about revealed preferences. The direct evidence relies on data on people's stated preferences for social ties.

Indirect evidence: revealed preferences

Research that provides indirect evidence for homophily theory comes from data on actual marriages and friendships. A key challenge for researchers using such data is to disentangle opportunity from choice. For example, suppose we observe that in a certain country Muslims tend to marry Muslims and Christians marry Christians. Is this due to opportunities (constraints) or to homophily (choice)? Or both? To examine whether homophily plays a role, researchers compare the *actual* marriages with what would happen if people were "group blind" and *randomly* marry another person in the population. What would happen under random choice is determined by structural opportunities of marrying in- and out-group members (e.g., the constraints associated with group size and consolidation). If actual choices show a strong tendency of selecting people who are from the in-group, *as compared with what would be expected under random choice* (given the structural constraints), then this gives evidence for the proposition that people *prefer* to interact with similar others. Although preferences for marriage partners are not asked about, by studying the behavior of people as compared with random choices, one could infer their *revealed preferences*. More details about this research strategy are provided in the online Appendix for this chapter.

What do studies using observational data on marriages find? The literature has found consistent evidence for ethnic/racial homophily (Fu, 2001; Kalmijn & Van Tubergen, 2006; Qian & Lichter, 2007; Quillian & Campbell, 2003), religious homophily (Hendrickx, Lammers, & Ultee, 1991; Kalmijn, 1991), status homophily (Kalmijn, 1991) and other forms of in-group homophily in marriage markets (Kalmijn, 1998). There is, equally, evidence for homophily in studies on friendship choices in school (Kandel, 1978; McPherson et al., 2001). In particular, research has shown evidence for strong ethnic/racial homophily in the US (Goodreau, Kitts, & Morris, 2009; Moody, 2001; Mouw & Entwisle, 2006; Wimmer & Lewis, 2010), Germany (Leszczensky & Pink, 2015; Windzio, 2012) and the Netherlands (Baerveldt et al., 2004; Smith, Van Tubergen, Maas, & McFarland, 2016; Stark & Flache, 2012). In addition, gender homophily appears strong and homophily in other social categories has also been found (Leszczensky & Pink, 2017; Smith et al., 2014).

A related literature on revealed in-group preferences comes from the study of dissolution of social ties. If the homophily theory is true, so scholars argue, then couples and friendships that are from different groups should be more likely to end than relationships in which two persons are from the same group. This hypothesis is confirmed in empirical research. It has been shown that couples are more likely to divorce when they are of dissimilar ethnicity or race (Smith, Maas, & Van Tubergen, 2012; Zhang & Van Hook, 2009). Similarly, longitudinal research on adolescent friendships has shown that cross-race ties are more likely to be ended than same-race friendships (Hallinan, 1979; Hallinan & Williams, 1989).

Direct evidence: stated preferences

The empirical support for the homophily theory would be more convincing if the evidence was more direct. Such direct evidence exists and it comes from stated preferences in research on (online) dating. Several scholars have examined whether people tend to indicate preference to date in-group members as opposed to out-group members. To do so, they analyzed the stated preferences of singles in (on-line) dating. These data are perfectly suited to test the homophily theory because they give a direct measure of people's in-group preference for a dating candidate.

In line with the homophily theory, studies on internet dating show that people prefer to date others who are from their own ethnic and racial group (Feliciano, Lee, & Robnett, 2011; Hitsch, Hortaçsu, & Ariely, 2010a, 2010b; Lin & Lundquist, 2013; Potârcă & Mills, 2015; Robnett & Feliciano, 2011) and that people also prefer to date someone from their own status group, as indicated by their education (Skopek, Schulz, & Blossfeld, 2011). Other, related, research asked people to rank fictitious persons in terms of how much they are personally attracted to them. These studies have consistently found that people feel more attracted to persons who are more similar to them (Byrne, 1971; Montoya, Horton, & Kirchner, 2008; Singh & Ho, 2000; Singh & Teoh, 1999).

These insights from research on dating and personal attraction, marriage markets, friendships in schools and divorce point in the same direction: homophily is a key tie-formation mechanism (McPherson et al., 2001). In conclusion, the homophily theory is strongly confirmed empirically, as studies have consistently shown that people *prefer* in-group ties as opposed to out-group ties—at least with respect to marriages, friendships and other stronger social ties (Newman, 2003). This phenomenon is called *assortative mixing* (Newman, 2003), *inbreeding homophily* (McPherson et al., 2001) and *choice homophily* (Kossinets & Watts, 2009; McPherson & Smith-Lovin, 1987). The tie-formation process of homophily helps to understand why group segregation emerges in social relationships. The hypotheses derived from the homophily theory have been overwhelmingly supported, which means that we can summarize the **homophily phenomenon** as a stylized fact.

 STYLIZED FACT 8.2

Homophily phenomenon
People prefer to interact with members from their own group as opposed to members of other groups.

Other mechanisms: transitivity and third party effects

The choice-constraint framework is commonly used to explain group segregation. The friendships that people create are made in social contexts such as schools and neighborhoods that constrain intergroup friendships and, within these constraints, people tend to prefer in-group ties. The fact that opportunities for meeting out-group members are typically less common than opportunities for meeting in-group members and that people prefer in-group ties above out-group ties already create powerful tendencies towards group segregation. This is particularly so when the two forces become interdependent. This happens when people deliberately sort themselves into those settings (schools, neighborhoods) that maximize exposure to in-group members and minimize opportunities for meeting out-group members. Beyond these two forces, there are two other mechanisms that play a role in creating group segregation (Wimmer & Lewis, 2010).

One has to do with *transitivity*, i.e., the fact that your connections tend to know each other as well. This tendency can reinforce group segregation (Mouw & Entwisle, 2006). Suppose, for example, that you have made two new friends. Chances are high that they tend to be similar to you—say both are doing the same university program as you. Then chances are high that those two friends will subsequently also get to know each other because you introduce them to each other. The transitivity tendency will therefore amplify group segregation.

Another social force that further strengthens group segregation has to do with the role of third parties (Kalmijn, 1998). According to **third party theory**, relationships are not made in a social vacuum: there are other actors (hence the label "third" party) that interfere with the relationship between two persons. *Third parties* can be formal institutions, such as the state, but also informal parties such as peers, parents, other relatives and group members. The idea of third party theory is that these parties prescribe norms that approve, disapprove or even prohibit relationships between members of certain groups and that these third parties also monitor behavior and sanction in case of norm-violations. The third party theory can be seen as an application of *social control theory* (Chapter 6).

In many cases, so third party theory assumes, third parties tend to encourage within-group relations and discourage the formation of group-bridging ties. Ranging from parents and peers to religious and ethnic communities, group-bridging ties are more often disapproved of than bonding ties. Even the state sometimes prohibits relations between persons from different groups. Well-known are the laws that prohibited racial intermarriage in the United States, which were abolished in all states in 1967. Similar laws against Black–White relationships had been implemented under the Apartheid regime in South Africa (1948–1990), including the law against racial intermarriage and the law against having sexual intercourse with people of a different race. Although in contemporary western societies such laws against intermarriage or interethnic relations do not exist anymore, other laws have been implemented which are directed towards relationships that travel across countries. For example, as a response to the large flow of immigrants from the 1960s onwards, many western countries implemented laws that prohibited importing partners from abroad, thereby controlling the marital choices that people could make.

Third parties can play a role informally, promoting the segregation of group relations in subtle ways. During adolescence, dyadic relationships are affected by peers, who can approve or disapprove the choices that people make. If we think about a positive relationship between persons A and B, then there are three possibilities when a third party is involved (Figure 8.6).

Person C is the third party here, a peer that could approve or disapprove of the relationship between A and B. It could be that persons A and B are friends (+), but that person

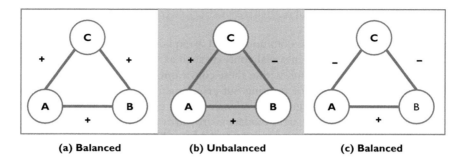

(a) Balanced   **(b) Unbalanced**   **(c) Balanced**

Figure 8.6 Structural balance: each labeled triangle must have one or three positive edges.

C interferes with their relationship. In condition (a), C is friends with both A and B, so C approves of their relationship. In condition (c), both A and B have a negative relationship (-) with C, and this common "enemy" will therefore not threaten the relationship between A and B. Conditions (a) and (c) are called *balanced*.

In condition (b), however, things are different and the triangle is *unbalanced*. A and B are friends, but they differ in their relationship with C. Whereas A and C are friends, B and C are enemies. This means that C, as a third party, has an incentive to change the relationship of A with B. Person C could disapprove of their relationship, perhaps threaten to withdraw from his or her relationship with A or perform other acts to strive for a balanced situation. Such structurally unbalanced relations are more likely to happen in a case where A and B belong to different groups, e.g., when they differ in race or religion. So, in subtle ways, group segregation is thus promoted by third parties such as peers.

Parents can also play a role in the homogeneity of friendship and dating relations. Parents can select suitable candidates for their children or disapprove of certain group-bridging relationships that their children have. In modern nations the role of parents has diminished, but there are still religious and ethnic groups in which parents are an important third party. In a similar way, relatives could interfere with dyadic relationships and so too could members of the religious or ethnic group to which people may belong.

8.4 In-group favoritism

Sociological studies provide strong evidence to suggest there is an Us–Them divide in social relations. People tend to hang around with friends from their in-group and they more often marry with in-group members. This group segregation phenomenon is not only due to structural forces that restrict opportunities to establish intergroup ties and facilitate in-group ties, but also results from the preference to interact with in-group members and additional processes such as transitivity and third party effects. How do these findings on personal, intimate social ties relate to other research findings on the Us–Them divide? What do research findings suggest when we look at other indicators of intergroup cohesion? Let's review key empirical findings on two related areas of intergroup research, namely (1) *intergroup attitudes* and (2) *intergroup trust, solidarity and cooperation*.

Intergroup attitudes

Intergroup attitudes capture the subjective distances between members of different groups, i.e., people's (positive or negative) feelings about their own group and about other groups (Allport, 1954). In studies on intergroup attitudes, scholars measure people's sentiment towards their in-group and out-groups in various ways. For example, respondents are asked to subjectively rate each group in terms of a thermometer, i.e., "how warm or cold they feel towards each group" (Wilcox, Sigelman, & Cook, 1989), or by asking if they would object to interacting with out-group members (Bogardus, 1933). These measures are seen as indicators of the subjective "social distance" from other groups.

One particular area of research on intergroup attitudes focuses on the attitudes people have towards their ethnic in-group and ethnic out-groups. Evidence from a myriad of sources suggests that people have more positive views about their ethnic in-group compared with out-groups (Bohman & Hjerm, 2016; Bubritzki, Van Tubergen, Weesie, & Smith, 2018; Ceobanu & Escandell, 2010; Scheepers, Gijsberts, & Coenders, 2002; Semyonov, Raijman, & Gorodzeisky, 2006). It is more generally found that people have a tendency to hold positive attitudes towards their own group than towards other groups. This tendency is sometimes called *ethnocentrism* (Sumner, 1906).

Intergroup trust, cooperation and solidarity

Another research area looks at the Us–Them group divide by considering trust, cooperation and solidarity with in- and out-group members. We have already seen that shared group membership increases cooperative behavior in social dilemma situations (Brewer & Kramer, 1986; Kollock, 1998; Simpson, 2006). Generally speaking, it is found that people trust in-group members more than they do out-group members. For example, research findings indicate that people trust co-ethnics more than they trust members of other ethnic groups, a pattern found in studies conducted in Russia (Bahry, Kosolapov, Kozyreva, & Wilson, 2005) and the US (Glaeser, Laibson, Scheinkman, & Soutter, 2000).

Relatedly, an overwhelming literature exists that consistently documents favored treatment of the in-group and discrimination of out-groups in access to valuable resources such as jobs and housing (Pager & Shepherd, 2008). The evidence for this conclusion comes from a myriad of sources, including field experimental studies. In a common experimental setup (Chapter 3), fictitious and identical resumes are created for a job vacancy and group membership (such as race or gender) is randomly assigned to a resume and typically signaled via names. It appears that the fictitious out-group members have systematically lower chances of being hired than in-group members (Riach & Rich, 2002; Zschirnt & Ruedin, 2016).

Taken together, this area of research suggests strong evidence for Us–Them divides with respect to trust, cooperation and solidarity. A key question addressed in this literature is whether such Us–Them divides occur only among groups that have some pattern of established social ties and a history of intergroup tensions, or that, alternatively, such prior intergroup relations are not a necessary condition to create Us–Them distrust and discrimination. To find out, the social psychologist Henry Tajfel and colleagues designed a series of pioneering studies on what is called the **minimal group paradigm** (Billig & Tajfel, 1973; Tajfel, 1970; Tajfel & Turner, 1979).

minimal group paradigm studies which reveal that arbitrarily created groups which have no interaction between members already reveal in-group favoritism.

275

The typical set up of these laboratory studies consists of two phases. In the first phase, participants in the experiment are divided into two groups, "group A" and "group B." The allocation of individuals to either group A or B was entirely random and ostensibly based on irrelevant criteria such as their preference for paintings from "Klee" or "Kandinsky," or flipping a coin. In the second phase, participants are asked to allocate some valuable resources (either real or symbolic) between the other participants. However, they have no idea who these other participants are, as the only information available to them is an anonymous ID number and group membership (e.g., "participant 12, group B"). There are no interactions between group members and each participant fills in the allocated resources individually and anonymously. Participants are informed that, after the task is completed, they will receive the resources allocated to them by the other participants. Because participants cannot allocate resources to themselves, individual interests are not affected by their choices.

Findings of these minimal group experiments reveal that participants allocate more resources to in-group members than to out-group members, even though these groups are artificially created, participants are assigned to a group by pure chance and group members do not know each other and are completely anonymous (Brewer, 1979; Tajfel, 1970). Thus, if you randomly sort people into two groups, either belonging to the "blue" or "yellow" group, then subsequently they will have more positive views on their own (blue or yellow) group and trust and cooperate more with in-group members than with out-group members. Furthermore, findings from these minimal group experiments suggest that participants give relatively more resources to in-group members than to out-group members, even when they could have obtained more resources in absolute terms by allocating more resources to the out-group.

Social identity theory

How can we understand these empirical findings from literature on (1) intergroup attitudes and (2) trust, cooperation and solidarity? Why do people, generally speaking, have more positive views of their own group and think more negatively about other groups? Why do people trust in-group members more and allocate more resources to in-group members, even when they have no personal ties to them?

One influential answer to these questions is provided by *social identity theory*, which was developed by Tajfel and Turner in the 1970s and 1980s (Tajfel, 1982; Tajfel & Turner, 1979). Social identity theory assumes that people strive to maintain or enhance their self-esteem, that, in other words, they strive for a positive self-concept. People's self-concept depends not only on their *personal identity* (i.e., someone's unique abilities) but also on their **social identity**.

Social identity that part of our self-concept corresponding to group identification.

What matters less, according to social identity theory, is that individuals belong to a group in an objective sense (e.g., group membership or participating in some group activity), which may be assigned by "others," and what matters more is that individuals subjectively identify with a certain group. People strive to maintain or enhance a positive social identity, which can be realized by making favorable comparisons between the in-group and the out-group. The aim of in- and out-group differentiation is to maintain or achieve superiority over an out-group on some dimensions. According to this theory, so Tajfel and Turner posit, "when social identity is unsatisfactory, individuals will strive either to leave their existing group and join some more positively distinct group and/or to make their existing group more positively distinct" (Tajfel & Turner, 1979).

In-group favoritism

Where are we now? We have reviewed findings and theories from three areas of research on intergroup relations. What can we conclude? It appears that the picture that emerges from these three areas of research is very similar. Based on research findings from literature on (1) group segregation in friendships and marriages, (2) intergroup attitudes and (3) intergroup cooperation, trust and solidarity, we can distill a common tendency that people tend to have more positive in-group relations than out-group relations. Generally speaking, people prefer to have intimate ties with in-group members rather than out-group members. This *homophily* tendency, in conjunction with constraints on meeting out-group members, gives rise to group segregation in social connections. Similar to homophily in the tie-formation process, research on intergroup attitudes finds that people tend to have positive attitudes towards their own group and think less well of other groups. And, finally, cooperation and trust is more common with in-group members than with out-groups and this even happens when people are randomly assigned to artificial groups.

In short, we may conclude that the common pattern, the *baseline* of intergroup relations, is that people have more positive in-group relationships than out-group relationships. This phenomenon is known under different names depending on the specific area of research and scientific discipline. Commonly used concepts, with very similar meanings, are: homophily, ethnocentrism, parochial cooperation, Us–Them divide, in-group bias and in-group favoritism. Some scholars call this phenomenon *tribalism* and argue that frequent in-group cooperation and trust and the problem of Us–Them divides comes from evolved tendencies and is part of our emotional and largely unconscious and "irrational" System I (Greene, 2014). Let's summarize this *baseline* empirical pattern of **in-group favoritism**.

 STYLIZED FACT 8.3

In-group favoritism
There is a general tendency that individuals have more positive in-group relationships than out-group relationships, as observed in research on intra- and intergroup (1) social ties, (2) attitudes and (3) trust, cooperation and solidarity.

8.5 Social context and in-group favoritism

In-group favoritism is the baseline condition in intergroup relations. We witness this phenomenon in many encounters between members of different groups. However, sometimes we see that groups deviate from this baseline condition, that members do not have "mild" in-group preferences but that in-group favoritism becomes particularly pronounced, that people refrain from having intergroup contact, that intergroup attitudes become extremely hostile and that acts of intergroup aggression and conflicts emerge. If this is the case, intergroup cohesion is strongly undermined and society may become fragmented in isolated, or even conflicting, groups.

Empirical research shows that intergroup relations are not fixed, universal patterns and that they sometimes deviate from the common pattern of baseline in-group favoritism. Intergroup cohesion is a matter of degree. Sometimes it is strong and, at other times, it tends to be rather weak. Furthermore, the cohesion between groups A and B in society can be strong but, in the same society, group A may be in conflict with group C. And intergroup cohesion can change over time; groups in conflict may find peace after some time and new intergroup conflicts may emerge. More generally, we may say that intergroup cohesion is *contingent upon social contexts*, i.e., it appears that the cohesion between any two groups can vary across social contexts. In other words, beyond the baseline of in-group favoritism, we see that the degree of intergroup cohesion differs from context to context.

Let's review some case studies that reveal the contingent nature of intergroup cohesion:

- Dutch society was highly divided into various groups in the 1950s, in particular between Catholics, Protestants and socialists. In this "pillarized" society, people lived in segregated worlds, in their own "pillar." For example, if you were from a Catholic family, you would attend a Catholic school, go to a Catholic scouting club and read Catholic newspapers. Intergroup sentiments were strongly negative at that time and if you were Catholic you would have only Catholic friends and marry a Catholic spouse. In a couple of decades, however, these pillars largely disappeared and intergroup relations became more cohesive (Hendrickx et al., 1991).

- In the US, a highly ethnically diverse society, some groups are more "socially distant" from each other than other groups. For example, scholars find that the intergroup cohesion between "Whites" and "Asians" is stronger than between Whites and Blacks. Research on marriage, for instance, reveals that intermarriages between Whites and Asians are more common than marriages between Whites and Blacks (Qian, 1997; Qian & Lichter, 2007). Intergroup cohesion between Whites and Blacks has increased over time, however. Although racial endogamy is still strong, the number of White–Black intermarriages has increased since the 1960s (Fryer, 2011; Rosenfeld, 2002).

- In Israel, it was found that there is systematic mistrust towards eastern-origin Jews—even among members of that group. The evidence for this conclusion comes from an experiment called the "trust game" (Fershtman & Gneezy, 2001). In this two-player game, Player A receives a certain amount of money and she is asked whether she wants to transfer any of it to Player B and, if so, how much. Any money given to Player B is tripled by the experimenter, who gives it to Player B. Then, Player B decides whether to give money back to Player A and, if so, how much. The key idea of this game is that both players can gain from collaborating, but they need to trust each other to make this happen. Players were then paired and the ethnic identities of the two groups (i.e., Ashkenazi and eastern-origin Jews) were signaled via names (which are a good indication of ethnic affiliation in that context). It was found that mistrust of players of eastern origin was common not only among Ashkenazic players but also among eastern players who themselves mistrusted players from their own group (Fershtman & Gneezy, 2001).

- In western European societies it has been observed that ethnic majority populations tend to have negative views of ethnic out-groups, i.e., "ethnic minorities" and "immigrant groups" (Semyonov et al., 2006). This is in line with baseline in-group favoritism. However, scholars have also noted that the intergroup views are not a constant. Instead, studies reveal that interethnic attitudes fluctuate *over time* within societies (Bohman & Hjerm, 2016; Meuleman, Davidov, & Billiet, 2009) and that they vary across *out-groups*:

some ethnic out-groups are disliked more than others (Bubritzki et al., 2018; Savelkoul, Scheepers, Tolsma, & Hagendoorn, 2010) and that attitudes towards the same ethnic out-group vary across *regions* within the same country (Schmidt-Catran & Spies, 2016; Semyonov & Glikman, 2009).

● Sometimes group boundaries escalate into a spiral of large-scale inter-group aggression and violence (Horowitz, 1985; Wimmer, 2013) such as, in certain episodes in time, between Protestants and Catholics in Northern Ireland; Hindus and Muslims in India; Christians and Muslims in Nigeria, the Philippines and Indonesia; Blacks and Whites in the United States and South Africa; Hutus and Tutsis in Rwanda; ethnic majority and Muslim minority group relations in Europe.

Out-groups can also be "created" and, as "scapegoats," they become the subject of collective aggression for certain moments in time. In early modern Europe, spanning the period between 1450 and 1750, "witches," often women, became such an out-group (Ben-Yehuda, 1980). The belief in the existence of a group of witches and their witchcraft practices gained widespread acceptance (Gaskill, 2010). Many people at that time thought that witches had demonic powers and used their magic to do harm to the in-group, such as killing children and

Image 8.1 Francesco Maria Guazzo, Compendium Maleficarum (1610 edition). This image expresses the common belief in early modern Europe that witches could change into animals.

making people ill. People thought that the group of witches had made a pact with the devil and that they could fly on a broomstick to attend a sabbath—a collective gathering where witches feed the devil with bodies of infants and have sexual intercourse with him. Also, it was believed that witches could transform themselves into animals, especially wolves.

People thought witches were everywhere in great numbers. For example, in 1587, in the French village of Brieulles, a judge claimed that he had "evidence of 7,760 witches in the single duchy of Rethelois" (Levack, 2006 [1986]). At that time, witchcraft was seen as a crime and thousands of people were accused of practising witchcraft, prosecuted and executed. In some regions the witch craze and the resulting witch hunt was massive. For example, in 1589, in the lands of the convent of Quedlinburg (Germany), 133 witches were executed in just one day. Overall, between 1450 and 1750, around 90,000 people were officially prosecuted for witchcraft in Europe, of which 45,000 were executed (Levack, 2006 [1986]). Other estimates of the number of executions of witches, stretching over a wider period of witch-hunting in Europe, are considerably higher—up to 500,000 (Ben-Yehuda, 1980). Importantly, these are the *official* records: it is unknown how many witches lost their lives as a result of lynching and other forms of *unofficial* sanctions.

In this European witch-hunt, interrogatory torture was common practice and used to obtain the confession of the witch during trial. This procedure is seen as brutal when judged by contemporary standards. Accused witches were tortured with the use of various horrifying instruments, such as thumb screws, strappado, leg screws and head clamps. Although innocent, many accused people confessed to witchcraft in order to stop further torture—even when the result was that they were sentenced to death. The official documents on witch trials which have survived give us insight into the accusations, trials and convictions of the witch craze. The historian Henry C. Lea has collected and annotated hundreds of these case studies (Lea, 1939). Here is a typical example:

> The still existing documents of a case in Vienna, 1583, show that a sixteen-year-old girl of Mank in the Viertl above the Wiener Wald suffered from cramps. She was pronounced to be possessed and was sent to Vienna, where she was exorcised in the Jesuit chapel of St. Barbara. After eight weeks of labor the Jesuits expelled 12,652 living demons. She chanced to mention that she often accompanied her grandmother, Elisabeth Pleinacher, to weddings and church consecrations, but only in Lutheran places; so she was brought to state that her grandmother had kept the demons in the shape of flies in glass bottles and had made them take possession of her. The Viennese Bishop, Kaspar Neubeek, had the grandmother, a women of seventy, imprisoned and tortured until she confessed to him that it was so and that the devil had intercourse with her in the shape of a goat, or of a little cat, and often as ball of thread; that for fifty years she had frequented the Sabbat; and that by her inducement the devil had entered an apple which she had given her granddaughter to eat. Whereupon she was tied to a horse's tail, dragged to the Richtplatz at Erdberg near Vienna, and there burnt alive.
>
> (Lea, 1939)

The take-away message of these case study findings is that, beyond the baseline tendency of in-group favoritism, *intergroup cohesion is contingent and varies across social contexts*. The theory question that follows up on these empirical findings is, of course: *why* is intergroup cohesion contingent on social contextual conditions? How can we explain that intergroup relations vary over time and across social contexts? Why do some group boundaries disappear over time? Why do "mere" group boundaries sometimes escalate into large-scale intergroup conflicts?

8.6 Group threat theory

One influential sociological theory that explains the contingent nature of intergroup cohesion is called **group threat theory**. A famous study, which is often seen as an important source of early development of group threat theory, was conducted by Sherif and his colleagues in the summer of 1954 (Sherif, Harvey, White, Hood, & Sherif, 1961). The subjects of the *Robbers Cave Experiment*, as the classic is known today, are 24 11-year-old boys. These boys did not know each other nor were they aware of the fact that they were subjects of an experiment. The boys were taken to a large isolated camp in a densely wooded area in the Sans Bois Mountains of southeastern Oklahoma in the US. The researchers had randomly divided the boys into two groups equal in size, so each group had 12 members. The groups arrived separately from each other in the camp, in different areas, so that they could not see or hear each other and would not become aware of each other's existence. The experiment ran for three weeks and was carefully planned by a large team of researchers.

In the first week, the research staff organized all kinds of activities, separately for both groups, so that the boys within each group started to know each other. Spontaneously, the boys emphasized the need to give their own group a name, one group calling themselves "Eagles" while the other group named themselves "Rattlers." In addition, the Eagles and Rattlers invented a flag that represented their group and several social norms in the group emerged. In the second week, the research staff revealed for the first time to the boys that there was another group in the camp and that they would compete with that group in a tournament. The winners of the two groups would receive knives and medals, the losing team would get nothing. For over four days the Eagles and Rattlers fiercely competed with each other in competitive games such as baseball, tug-of-war, football and tent pitching.

The research aim of introducing these competitive games in the second week was not to see which of the two groups would eventually win. Rather, the idea behind introducing these games was to experimentally see whether, under these competitive conditions, negative intergroup relations would emerge. The research staff, who continuously observed the behavior of the two groups and who took more than 12,000 pictures in three weeks, found evidence for this idea. For example, they observed that immediately after the first game the Eagles did not want to eat together with the Rattlers and that derogatory name calling started. After losing several games, the Eagles set the flag of the Rattlers on fire, after which the Rattlers burned the flag of the Eagles and organized a raid in commando style (e.g., darkening faces and arms) in which they turned the Eagles' beds over and ripped screens on the windows. The Eagles were furious and retaliated by messing up the Rattlers' cabin. On multiple occasions staff had to prevent physical fighting between the Eagles and Rattlers.

In the third week, the researchers ended the competition between the two groups to see how intergroup relations would evolve. At first they created intergroup contact opportunities for the Eagles and Rattlers. They organized attending a movie together and having joint meals. Intergroup contacts were promoted for several days, but without much change in intergroup relations. Hostile remarks and garbage fights were observed by the research staff. Then the researchers introduced a series of "superordinate goals," i.e., problems which confronted both Eagles and Rattlers and which could only be solved by cooperating together. For example, the researchers experimentally created a "drinking water problem" in the camp, which the Eagles and Rattlers solved by collaborating with each other. Research staff observed a notable improvement in intergroup cohesion and, on the last evening, the groups were entertaining *each other*.

The dramatic relations between Eagles and Rattlers under competitive conditions (week 2) and the remarkable shift towards improved intergroup relations after introducing superordinate goals (week 3) also became evident after studying friendships and intergroup attitudes. The researchers asked the boys at the end of the second week to indicate who their friends were from the entire camp (so they could nominate boys not only from their own group but also from the out-group). In the Eagles group, 93% of the friends were with in-group members; in the Rattlers group this was 94%. Hence, group segregation was strong: very few indicated that they saw anyone outside their own group as a friend (group-bridging ties); most of them had only group-bonding ties. But then the researchers asked the same question again at the end of the third week and they noticed a significant change in friendships. In the Eagles group, the percentage of in-group friends decreased from 93% to 77%; in the Rattlers group it diminished from 94% to 64%.

The researchers also asked both groups how they thought about their in-group and the out-group. They asked the boys to indicate their attitudes on a five-point scale, ranging from 1 (most unfavorable category) to 5 (most favorable category), using three favorable terms (brave, tough, friendly) and three unfavorable ones (sneaky, smart alecs, stinkers). At the end of week 2 both groups had extremely strong positive views of their own group (Table 8.3). Among the Eagles, 94% were very positive about their own group and among the Rattlers this was even more positive at 100%. Both groups were thinking negatively about the out-group. Only 15% of the Eagle ratings of Rattlers were favorable and only 35% of the ratings of Rattlers about Eagles were positive. This changed dramatically in week three, after the competitive games ended and when superordinate goals were introduced. Within a week, both groups tended to think much more positively about the out-group.

Table 8.3 Ratings of in-group and out-group, % favorable attitude (category 4 or 5, five-point scale).

| | Evaluated group | | | |
| | End of week 2 | | End of week 3 | |
Rating group	Eagles	Rattlers	Eagles	Rattlers
Eagles	94	15	87	68
Rattlers	35	100	86	96

Source: Sherif et al., 1961.

The *Robbers Cave Experiment* highlighted the key role of *group competition* for creating intergroup tensions. This finding is at the core of group threat theory. Other early contributions to group threat theory were made by Herbert Blumer (1958), Lewis Coser (1956) and Hubert Blalock (1967). More recently, the theory has been developed further by other scholars (Bobo, 1999; Ceobanu & Escandell, 2010; Olzak, 1994; Quillian, 1995; Scheepers et al., 2002; Schlueter & Scheepers, 2010). There are, to be sure, slightly different versions of "group threat theory" and scholars sometimes use different names too, such as "conflict theory," "group position theory," "ethnic competition theory," "realistic group conflict theory" and "symbolic threat theory." They present a family of closely related, often overlapping, ideas and mechanisms. Drawing on this literature, I will present several core propositions, assumptions and research findings.

In Figure 8.7 I represent group threat theory in a multilevel framework. As you can see, the key outcome to be explained is *the degree of intergroup cohesion*. Group threat theory posits that actual group competition in a certain social context decreases intergroup cohesion (arrow *a*), i.e., intergroup cohesion will erode under conditions of group competition. It means that, if the level of competition between groups rises, there will be (1) an increase in group-bonding ties and a decrease in group-bridging ties, (2) intergroup attitudes will become more negative, (3) members of different groups will distrust each other more and refuse cooperation with out-group members and (4) intergroup aggression and conflicts will become more likely. Note that this is an ecological relationship (Chapter 4), i.e., a relationship at the collective (group) level: the higher the actual competition between *groups*, the lower will be cohesion between *groups*.

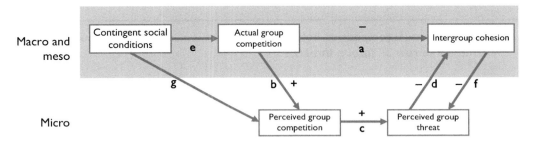

Figure 8.7 Representation of group threat theory in a multilevel framework.

Why would actual competition between two groups result in decreasing intergroup cohesion? How can we make this ecological relationship "understandable" (Chapter 4)? According to group threat theory this happens because, first of all, people identify with their in-group. This element comes from social identity theory and is integrated in group threat theory (Scheepers et al., 2002). People have social identities, which means that the rise of group competition affects people's perception of being in competition with other groups (arrow *b*). They see their own group in competition with other groups over certain scarce resources. That is to say, individuals not only perceive themselves, as individuals, in competition with other individuals, but they also categorize individuals as belonging to groups and perceive their in-group being in competition with out-groups.

These individual-level perceptions of (increased) group competition, in turn, result in (increased) personal feelings of group threat (arrow *c*); people are afraid of the danger created by out-groups. They fear that members of the competing group will take away their scarce resources, and the resources of other in-group members they care about. And they think that their own misfortune—and that of their own group—is caused by out-groups. Consequently, people will tend to think more negatively of the out-group; out-group antagonism and hate emerges; people more and more avoid out-group members; they distrust them more than ever before and so forth. These changing intergroup attitudes and behaviors result, at the collective level, in weakened intergroup cohesion (arrow *d*).

We can summarize the presumed impact of actual group competition on intergroup cohesion with three propositions: (1) a *social context effect*, which argues that actual competition affects perceived competition, (2) a *micro-level relationship* stating that such individual perceptions of group competition result in feelings of group threat and (3) *a simple aggregation effect*—the idea that perceived threat in turn weakens intergroup cohesion—which is an aggregation from the individual to the group level. We can represent this coherent set of propositions in a theory schema:

P.   The more actual competition between groups, the more strongly in-group members perceive group competition (arrow *b*).

P.   The more strongly in-group members perceive group competition, the more strongly they feel threatened by the out-group (arrow *c*).

P.   The more strongly in-group members feel threatened by out-groups, the weaker the intergroup cohesion will be (arrow *d*).

P.   The more actual competition between groups, the weaker the intergroup cohesion (arrow *a*). *(group threat)*

Theory schema 8.1 Group threat theory.

A key question is when do actual competitive conditions emerge? In the *Robbers Cave Experiment* the researchers created competitive conditions by introducing a tournament in which one group would win whereas the other group would get nothing. In that case the valuable scarce resources were knives and medals. How would we apply and test this theory in real-life situations? Scholars commonly make a distinction between *economic* and *cultural* competitive conditions.

Economic competitive conditions

To begin, groups compete for scarce economic resources. The theory assumes that people have, first and foremost, basic physiological needs, i.e., they want food, water, warmth, shelter. Then people strive for status and prestige. Jobs and high-status positions in the labor market are scarce goods. People want to have a job, in particular a high-status job, but there is competition among individuals to obtain jobs and in particular high-status jobs. Likewise, groups compete for housing. Everyone wants to live in a house, especially a nice one, but this is a scarce resource, which is therefore subject to competition as well.

When is there more actual competition between groups for these scarce economic resources? This depends on *contingent social conditions*—situations that are specific to a certain place, time, location or setting. The contingent social conditions determine the level of economic competitive conditions (arrow *e*) and, ultimately thereby, affect the contingent intergroup cohesion. Examples are changes in food production, poverty levels, the unemployment rate and housing shortages. A population that is affected by long periods of extreme weather (resulting in drought or floods) can suffer from limited food production (e.g., poor harvest), which increases the competition over scarce economic goods (food). Similarly, if more and more people are unemployed in society or if the poverty rate goes up or housing shortages increase, then the degree of economic competition between groups increases. This should weaken intergroup cohesion, according to the theory, because people perceive their in-group in competition with out-groups for the scarce jobs and houses. They feel threatened by out-groups, who they think will take away their jobs and houses.

We can derive this *economic competition* proposition in the following way:

P. The more actual competition between groups, the weaker their intergroup cohesion. (*group threat*)

P. The actual competition between groups is a function of economic scarcity in the population (e.g., food, water, warmth, shelter).

P. The more economic scarcity in the population, the weaker the intergroup cohesion. (*economic competition*)

> **Theory schema 8.2** Economic competition proposition derived from group threat theory.

Scholars have empirically tested this economic competition proposition in numerous ways, across many societies, using both historical and contemporary data sources. Several studies find that the *presence or inflow of large groups of immigrants*, which increase economic competition over jobs and housing, result in stronger anti-immigrant attitudes (Meuleman et al., 2009; Olzak, 1994; Schlueter & Scheepers, 2010; Schmidt-Catran & Spies, 2016). Other studies report that rising *unemployment levels, economic recessions and GDP contraction* are associated with increasingly negative sentiments towards immigrant out-groups (Meuleman et al., 2009; Meuleman, Davidov, & Billiet, 2018; Polavieja, 2016; Quillian, 1995). It has also been found that *deteriorating weather conditions* (e.g., extreme weather, temperature changes), which severely lower food production, result in increases in out-group violence. This link has been observed in research on large-scale aggression against Jews that took place in the period between 1100 and 1800 (Anderson, Johnson, & Koyama, 2017). Jewish minorities have suffered from social segregation, suppression, discrimination and collective violence and murder as a result of stereotypical beliefs about their group (Bauman, 2005 [1989]). But violence against Jewish minorities appears particularly common under conditions of economic scarcity, for which they are blamed.

Likewise, deteriorating weather conditions have been related to rising witchcraft trials in early modern Europe (Oster, 2004). The outburst of violence against witches can be understood in light of increasingly harsh economic conditions, which creates intergroup tensions and the need to find scapegoats that are blamed for these conditions. Witches became the target for blame. Early modern Europe was confronted with a Little Ice Age from the beginning of the 14th century, creating noticeably lower temperatures than in the 400 years before. Around that time, from 1450 onwards, witchcraft trials emerged. Analysis of data covering a number of regions in Europe between 1520 and 1770 shows that witchcraft trials increased as temperatures dropped (Oster, 2004). Using more contemporary data on Tanzania, studies come to similar conclusions. It has been found that in years when there is extreme weather (either too little or too much rain) the number of witch murders is significantly increased in Tanzania (Miguel, 2005). Harsh economic conditions foster intergroup violence (Hsiang, Burke, & Miguel, 2013).

Cultural competitive conditions

Groups can compete with each other for cultural (symbolic) reasons too. Culture, as we have seen, consists of a set of opinions, norms and corresponding practices. Importantly, groups can have distinctive cultures, such as having different languages, religions, values and norms. According to group threat theory, such cultural distinctiveness can become a source of "symbolic" threat. Group members may fear that the culture of the out-group will undermine their own culture; that the cultural values, norms and traditions of their own group will be challenged and restricted by the out-group or even disappear and be replaced by the culture of the out-group.

Such a cultural threat will not happen between any two groups, of course. According to group threat theory, intergroup conflicts will not be likely when the cultures of two groups largely overlap (say between an ethnic majority Christian population and a Christian ethnic minority group) or if cultural differences are trivial (e.g., between a tennis association and a soccer club). Instead, the theory stipulates that symbolic threats are more intense when the *cultural distance* between two groups is more pronounced. To illustrate, suppose that we can rank groups in how their members, on average, think about gender norms. We order them from 0 (highly progressive: "men and women have equal rights and roles") to 10 (highly conservative: "men and women have completely different rights and roles"). The cultures of groups can then be positioned on this continuum, e.g., group A may get a score of 2 (highly progressive), group B scores 5 (moderate) and group C scores 8 (highly conservative). Group threat theory predicts that, in this case, intergroup cohesion is weaker between groups A and C than it is between AB and BC.

We can derive the *cultural competition* proposition in the following way:

P.   The more actual competition between groups, the weaker the intergroup cohesion. (*group threat*)

P.   The actual competition between groups is a function of their cultural distance (i.e., opinions, norms and corresponding practices).

P.   The more cultural distance between two groups in the population, the weaker the intergroup cohesion. (*cultural competition*)

> **Theory schema 8.3** Cultural competition proposition derived from group threat theory.

Contingent social conditions determine the cultural distance between groups and, consequently, the perceived threat and boundaries between any two groups. One such contingent fact is that some ethnic minority groups in Western Europe are predominantly Christian whereas others are from Muslim countries (Van Tubergen & Sindradóttir, 2011). Given that Western European ethnic majorities are largely Christian and increasingly secular (Bruce, 2002), the large cultural difference between the ethnic majority group and predominantly Muslim ethnic minorities can result in perceptions of symbolic threat among the ethnic majority population. In line with the cultural competition proposition, it has been found that in Western Europe the intergroup cohesion between the ethnic majority group and Muslim groups is weaker than between the ethnic majority group and other ethnic minority groups. This pattern has been found, for example, in studies on negative interethnic attitudes (Savelkoul et al., 2010; Sniderman & Hagendoorn, 2007; Strabac & Listhaug, 2008; Valentino et al., 2019) and in research on intergroup marriages and friendships (Kalmijn & Van Tubergen, 2006; Leszczensky & Pink, 2017).

*

In conclusion, the group threat theory is able to understand the contingent nature of intergroup cohesion. It tells us that intergroup relations typically become particularly tense under conditions of economic competition and hardship and also when groups strongly differ in their cultural beliefs, values and norms. In addition to these core elements of group threat theory, two insights are often mentioned in the literature.

First, ever since the development of group threat theory, scholars have noted that *actual* competitive conditions and people's *perceptions* of competition (arrow *b*) may not always correspond. It is reasonable to assume that, as a general tendency, there is a link between objective competitive conditions and subjective perceptions of competition (Blalock, 1967). However, people's perceptions may also be wrong. As we learned from the Thomas and Thomas theorem (Chapter 5), people will act as if their perceptions correspond to reality. For this reason, scholars study not only actual competitive conditions but also *perceived* competitive conditions and *perceived* group threat (Blumer, 1958; Bobo & Hutchings, 1996).

To illustrate, let's consider people's perceptions of the numbers of Muslims in their country. Many western societies, traditionally being largely Christian and/or secular, have seen a rise in the Muslim population in their countries because of immigration and fertility. The actual numbers of Muslims may not be known to everyone. People may over-estimate how many Muslims there are in their own country, for example, and this may foster feelings of cultural threat. In 2016 a cross-national survey was conducted in which respondents were asked "Out of every 100 people in your country, about how many do you think are Muslim?" (Ipsos, 2019). Table 8.4 shows the average subjective estimates, as well as the actual numbers, for a number of predominantly Christian-secular societies. As becomes immediately clear

Table 8.4 Perceptions of the share of Muslims in own society, 2016.

Country	Average guess	Actual
France	31	7.5
Italy	20	3.7
Germany	21	5.0
Belgium	23	7.0
US	17	1.0
Russia	24	10.0
Canada	17	3.2
Sweden	17	4.6
Netherlands	19	6.0
Spain	14	2.1
Great Britain	15	4.8
Denmark	15	4.1
Australlia	12	2.4
Norway	12	3.7
Poland	7	<0.1
Hungary	6	<0.1

Source: Ipsos, 2019.

when you look at this table, in many societies people over-estimate how many Muslims live in their society—often by a large margin. At the top of public misperceptions is France, where people think that 31% of their country's population is Muslim whereas, in reality, it is 7.5%. Of course not all citizens in France have exactly the same perception, but generally speaking they are collectively wrong in their perception of how many French people are Muslim.

People may not always accurately perceive actual competition. They may over- or under-estimate the size of out-groups, the unemployment rate or the cultural distance with out-groups, for example. This means that intergroup cohesion may be undermined even in the absence of actual competition—as long as people perceive strong levels of intergroup competition. What matters in the end in creating intergroup threat is not objective conditions of competition but people's perceptions of competition (Kuntz, Davidov, & Semyonov, 2017; Pottie–Sherman & Wilkes, 2017). As a general tendency, one can assume that there is at least some correspondence between objective competitive conditions and subjective perceptions of competition, but scholars also note that there can be significant deviations from this pattern. Perceptions may be affected by other contingent conditions (arrow g) than actual group competition (arrow b). Research findings indicate that (mis)perceptions of group competition and out-group threat can be significantly affected by media messages (Boomgaarden & Vliegenthart, 2007, 2009; Legewie, 2013; Schlueter & Davidov, 2013; Van Klingeren, Boomgaarden, & De Vreese, 2017; Van Klingeren, Boomgaarden, Vliegenthart, & De Vreese, 2015).

There is a second way in which scholars have elaborated on the core propositions of group threat theory. It has been argued that weakened intergroup cohesion may subsequently lead to stronger perceptions of group threat (Figure 8.7: arrow f). This has been argued most prominently with respect to acts of violence and aggression by out-group members towards the in-group. These are a *sign* of weak intergroup cohesion, but such acts can also further increase perceptions of out-group threat (arrow f). In that case, the threat of the out-group is neither economic nor cultural, but rather one of *physical safety*: people become concerned that they, or their friends or relatives, will be the next victim of the violence of the out-group. These perceptions could result in a feedback effect (arrows d and f): in-group members will perceive the out-group as more threatening, leading to more negative out-group attitudes, which can lead to increased aggression, thereby further increasing out-group threat and so forth. In the *Robbers Cave Experiment*, staff members prevented such a downward spiral of weakening intergroup cohesion and increasing aggression between the Eagles and Rattlers. Such a feedback process (arrows d and f) could, in principle, result in a spiral of increasing inter-group violence—and it sometimes does, as in Hindu–Muslim violence in India and the Protestant–Catholic conflict in Northern Ireland, to name only a few cases that followed this pattern. Relatedly, research findings indicate that terrorist attacks in the name of Muslim extremists resulted in more negative views towards Muslims in several European countries (Legewie, 2013) and the 2004 Al Qaeda terrorist bombing in Madrid, which killed 191 people, resulted in a tendency of Spaniards to avoid living in close proximity to Arab immigrants (Edling, Rydgren, & Sandell, 2016).

8.7 Chapter resources

Key concepts

Group	Group-bonding tie	Foci
Affiliation network	Group-bridging tie	Minimal group paradigm
Civil society	Endogamy	Social identity
Organizational cohesion	Exogamy	
Intergroup cohesion	Consolidation	

Key theories and propositions

- Structural opportunity theory
- Homophily theory
- Third party theory
- Social identity theory
- Group threat theory.

Key stylized facts

- Group segregation
- Homophily phenomenon
- In-group favoritism.

Summary

- Individuals belong to groups, also called affiliation networks. Group affiliation can be assigned in different ways: as membership, participation and identification.
- Groups have the capacity to generate collective benefits, such as overcoming problems of cooperation. For this reason, scholars study organizational cohesion.
- However, strong organizational cohesion, which gives rise to a civil society, is analytically different from intergroup cohesion.
- To empirically study intergroup cohesion, scholars examine four aspects to it, namely: (1) group segregation in social ties, (2) intergroup attitudes, (3) intergroup trust, solidarity and cooperation and (4) intergroup aggression and conflict.
- The stylized fact of group segregation in friendship ties and marriages can be explained by structural opportunity theory and homophily theory in conjunction with transitivity and third party theory.
- The minimal group paradigm reveals that people have more positive views of, and act more cooperatively towards, in-group members as compared with out-group members, even when they have no personal ties to them and groups are created randomly.
- According to social identity theory, people strive for a positive self-concept and for positive evaluations of the in-group, which is part of their social identity and contributes to a positive view of self.
- Taken together, research reveals a general tendency in intergroup relations that is called in-group favoritism.
- At the same time, however, scholars also note that intergroup relations are not fixed universal patterns and sometimes deviate from the common pattern of baseline in-group favoritism.
- To understand the social contextual variation in intergroup cooperation and conflict, scholars have developed group threat theory.

References

Allport, G. W. (1954). *The nature of prejudice*. Cambridge, MA: Addison-Wesley Publishing Company.

Anderson, R. W., Johnson, N. D., & Koyama, M. (2017). Jewish persecutions and weather shocks: 1100–1800. *The Economic Journal*, 127(602), 924–958.

Baerveldt, C., Van Duijn, M. A. J., Vermeij, L., & Van Hemert, D. A. (2004). Ethnic boundaries and personal choice: Assessing the influence of individual inclinations to choose intra-ethnic relationships on pupils' networks. *Social Networks*, 26(1), 55–74.

Bahry, D., Kosolapov, M., Kozyreva, P., & Wilson, R. K. (2005). Ethnicity and trust: Evidence from Russia. *American Political Science Review*, 99(4), 521–532.

Bauman, Z. (2005 [1989]). *Modernity and the holocaust*. Cambridge, UK: Polity Press.

Baumeister, R. F. (1991). *Meanings of life*. New York, NY: The Guilford Press.

Ben-Yehuda, N. (1980). The European witch craze of the 14th to 17th centuries: A sociologist's perspective. *American Journal of Sociology*, 86(1), 1–31.

Billig, M., & Tajfel, H. (1973). Social categorization and similarity in intergroup behaviour. *European Journal of Social Psychology*, 3(1), 27–52.

Blalock, H. M. (1967). *Toward a theory of minority group relations*. New York, NY: Wiley.

Blau, P. (1977). *Inequality and heterogeneity: A primitive theory of social structure*. New York, NY: Free Press.

Blau, P. (1994). *Structural contexts of opportunities*. Chicago, IL: University of Chicago Press.

Blau, P., Blum, T., & Schwartz, J. (1982). Heterogeneity and intermarriage. *American Sociological Review*, 47(1), 45–62.

Blau, P., & Schwartz, J. (1984). *Crosscutting social circles*. Orlando, FL: Academic Press.

Blumer, H. (1958). Race prejudice as a sense of group position. *The Pacific Sociological Review*, 1(1), 3–7.

Bobo, L. (1999). Prejudice as group position: Microfoundations of a sociological approach to racism and race relations. *Journal of Social Issues*, 55(3), 445–472.

Bobo, L., & Hutchings, V. L. (1996). Perceptions of racial group competition: Extending Blumer's theory of group position to a multiracial social context. *American Sociological Review*, 61(6), 951–972.

Bogardus, E. S. (1933). A social distance scale. *Sociology & Social Research*, 17, 265–271.

Bohman, A., & Hjerm, M. (2016). In the wake of radical right electoral success: A cross-country comparative study of anti-immigration attitudes over time. *Journal of Ethnic and Migration Studies*, 42(11), 1729–1747.

Boomgaarden, H. G., & Vliegenthart, R. (2007). Explaining the rise of anti-immigrant parties: The role of news media content. *Electoral Studies*, 26(2), 404–417.

Boomgaarden, H. G., & Vliegenthart, R. (2009). How news content influences anti–immigration attitudes: Germany, 1993–2005. *European Journal of Political Research*, 48(4), 516–542.

Breiger, R. L. (1974). The duality of persons and groups. *Social Forces*, 53(2), 181–190.

Brewer, M. B. (1979). In-group bias in the minimal intergroup situation: A cognitive-motivational analysis. *Psychological Bulletin*, 86(2), 307–324.

Brewer, M. B., & Kramer, R. M. (1986). Choice behavior in social dilemmas: Effects of social identity, group size, and decision framing. *Journal of Personality and Social Psychology*, 50(3), 543.

Bruce, S. (2002). *God is dead: Secularization in the west*. Oxford, UK: Blackwell Publishing.

Bubritzki, S., Van Tubergen, F., Weesie, J., & Smith, S. (2018). Ethnic composition of the school class and interethnic attitudes: A multi-group perspective. *Journal of Ethnic and Migration Studies*, 44(3), 482–502.

Byrne, D. (1971). *The attraction paradigm*. New York, NY: Academic Press.

Centola, D. (2015). The social origins of networks and diffusion. *American Journal of Sociology*, 120(5), 1295–1338.

Ceobanu, A. M., & Escandell, X. (2010). Comparative analyses of public attitudes toward immigrants and immigration using multinational survey data: A review of theories and research. *Annual Review of Sociology*, 36, 309–328.

Coser, L. A. (1956). *The functions of social conflict*. Abingdon, UK: Routledge.

De Tocqueville, A. (2002 [1889]). *Democracy in America*. Washington, DC: Regnery Publishing.

Durkheim, E. (2001 [1912]). *The elementary forms of the religious life*. Oxford, UK: Oxford University Press.

Edling, C., Rydgren, J., & Sandell, R. (2016). Terrorism, belief formation, and residential integration: Population dynamics in the aftermath of the 2004 Madrid terror bombings. *American Behavioral Scientist*, 60(10), 1215–1231.

Feld, S. L. (1981). The focused organization of social ties. *American Journal of Sociology*, 86(5), 1015–1035.

Feliciano, C., Lee, R., & Robnett, B. (2011). Racial boundaries among Latinos: Evidence from Internet daters' racial preferences. *Social Problems*, 58(2), 189–212.

Fershtman, C., & Gneezy, U. (2001). Discrimination in a segmented society: An experimental approach. *The Quarterly Journal of Economics*, 116(1), 351–377.

Fryer, R. (2011). The importance of segregation, discrimination, peer dynamics, and identity in explaining trends in the racial achievement gap. *Handbook of Social Economics*, 1, 1165–1191.

Fu, V. K. (2001). Racial intermarriage pairings. *Demography*, 38(2), 147–159.

Gaskill, M. (2010). *Witchcraft: A very short introduction*. Oxford University Press.

Glaeser, E. L., Laibson, D. I., Scheinkman, J. A., & Soutter, C. L. (2000). Measuring trust. *The Quarterly Journal of Economics*, 115(3), 811–846.

Goodreau, S. M., Kitts, J. A., & Morris, M. (2009). Birds of a feather, or friend of a friend? Using exponential random graph models to investigate adolescent social networks. *Demography*, 46(1), 103–125.

Greene, J. (2014). *Moral tribes: Emotion, reason, and the gap between us and them*. London: Atlantic Books.

Hallinan, M. T. (1979). Structural effects on children's friendships and cliques. *Social Psychology Quarterly*, 42(1), 43–54.

Hallinan, M. T., & Williams, R. A. (1989). Interracial friendship choices in secondary schools. *American Sociological Review*, 54(1), 67–78.

Hendrickx, J., Lammers, J., & Ultee, W. (1991). Religious assortative marriage in the Netherlands, 1938-1983. *Review of Religious Research*, 33(2), 123–145.

Hitsch, G. J., Hortaçsu, A., & Ariely, D. (2010a). Matching and sorting in online dating. *The American Economic Review*, 100(1), 130–163.

Hitsch, G. J., Hortaçsu, A., & Ariely, D. (2010b). What makes you click? Mate preferences in online dating. *Quantitative Marketing and Economics*, 8(4), 393–427.

Hofstra, B., Corten, R., Van Tubergen, F., & Ellison, N. B. (2017). Segregation of social networks: A novel approach using Facebook. *American Sociological Review*, 82(3), 625–656.

Horowitz, D. L. (1985). *Ethnic groups in conflict*. Berkeley, CA: University of California Press.

Hsiang, S. M., Burke, M., & Miguel, E. (2013). Quantifying the influence of climate on human conflict. *Science*, 341(6151), 1235367.

Ipsos. (2019). Perils of perception. Retrieved from https://perils.ipsos.com/index.html

Jones, F. L., & Luijkx, R. (1996). Post-war patterns of intermarriage in Australia: The Mediterranean experience. *European Sociological Review*, 12(1), 67–86.

Kalmijn, M. (1991). Shifting boundaries: Trends in religious and educational homogamy. *American Sociological Review*, 56(6), 786–800.

Kalmijn, M. (1993). Trends in Black/White intermarriage. *Social Forces*, 72(1), 119–146.

Kalmijn, M. (1994). Assortative mating by cultural and economic occupational status. *American Journal of Sociology*, 100(2), 422–452.

Kalmijn, M. (1998). Intermarriage and homogamy: Causes, patterns, trends. *Annual Review of Sociology*, 24, 395–421.

Kalmijn, M., & Van Tubergen, F. (2006). Ethnic intermarriage in the Netherlands: Confirmations and refutations of accepted insights. *European Journal of Population*, 22(4), 371–397.

Kandel, D. B. (1978). Similarity in real-life adolescent friendship Pairs. *Journal of Personality and Social Psychology*, 36(3), 306–312.

Kennedy, R. J. R. (1944). Single or triple melting pot? Intermarriage trends in New Haven, 1870-1940. *American Journal of Sociology*, 49(4), 331–339.

Kollock, P. (1998). Social dilemmas: The anatomy of cooperation. *Annual Review of Sociology*, 24(1), 183–214.

Korte, C., & Milgram, S. (1970). Acquaintance networks between racial groups: Application of the small world method. *Journal of Personality and Social Psychology*, 15(2), 101–108.

Kossinets, G., & Watts, D. J. (2009). Origins of homophily in an evolving social network. *American Journal of Sociology*, 115(2), 405–450.

Kuntz, A., Davidov, E., & Semyonov, M. (2017). The dynamic relations between economic conditions and anti-immigrant sentiment: A natural experiment in times of the European economic crisis. *International Journal of Comparative Sociology*, 58(5), 392–415.

Lazarsfeld, P. F., & Merton, R. K. (1954). Friendship as a social process: A substantive and methodological analysis. *Freedom and Control in Modern Society*, 18(1), 18–66.

Lea, H. (1939). *Materials towards a history of witchcraft* (Vol. 3). Philadelpia: University of Pennsylvania Press.

Legewie, J. (2013). Terrorist events and attitudes toward immigrants: A natural experiment. *American Journal of Sociology*, 118(5), 1199–1245.

Leszczensky, L., & Pink, S. (2015). Ethnic segregation of friendship networks in school: Testing a rational-choice argument of differences in ethnic homophily between classroom- and grade-level networks. *Social Networks*, 42, 18–26.

Leszczensky, L., & Pink, S. (2017). Intra-and inter-group friendship choices of Christian, Muslim, and non-religious youth in Germany. *European Sociological Review*, 33(1), 72–83.

Levack, B. P. (2006 [1986]). *The witch-hunt in early modern Europe*. Abingdon, UK: Routledge.

Lin, K., & Lundquist, J. (2013). Mate selection in cyberspace: The intersection of race, gender, and education. *American Journal of Sociology*, 119(1), 183–215.

Lin, N., Dayton, P. W., & Greenwald, P. (1978). Analyzing the instrumental use of relations in the context of social structure. *Sociological Methods & Research*, 7(2), 149–166.

Lucassen, L., & Laarman, C. (2009). Immigration, intermarriage and the changing face of Europe in the post war period. *The History of the Family*, 14(1), 52–68.

McPherson, M., & Smith-Lovin, L. (1987). Homophily in voluntary organizations: Status distance and the composition of face-to-face groups. *American Sociological Review*, 52(3), 370–379.

McPherson, M., Smith-Lovin, L., & Cook, J. M. (2001). Birds of a feather: Homophily in social networks. *Annual Review of Sociology*, 27, 415–444.

Meuleman, B., Davidov, E., & Billiet, J. (2009). Changing attitudes toward immigration in Europe, 2002–2007: A dynamic group conflict theory approach. *Social Science Research*, 38(2), 352–365.

Meuleman, B., Davidov, E., & Billiet, J. (2018). Modeling multiple-country repeated cross-sections: A societal growth curve model for studying the effect of the economic crisis on perceived ethnic threat. *Methods, Data, Analyses*, 12(2), 185–209.

Miguel, E. (2005). Poverty and witch killing. *The Review of Economic Studies*, 72(4), 1153–1172.

Milgram, S. (1967). The small world problem. *Psychology Today*, 1, 61–67.

Mollenhorst, G., Völker, B., & Flap, H. (2008). Social contexts and core discussion networks: Using a choice-constraint approach to study similarity in intimate relationships. *Social Forces*, 86(3), 937–965.

Montoya, R. M., Horton, R. S., & Kirchner, J. (2008). Is actual similarity necessary for attraction? A meta-analysis of actual and perceived similarity. *Journal of Social and Personal Relationships*, 25(6), 889–922.

Moody, J. (2001). Race, school integration, and friendship segregation in America. *American Journal of Sociology*, 107(3), 679–716.

Mouw, T., & Entwisle, B. (2006). Residential segregation and interracial friendship in schools. *American Journal of Sociology*, 112(2), 394–441.

Newman, M. E. (2003). Mixing patterns in networks. *Physical Review E*, 67(2 Pt 2), 026126.

Olson, M. (2009 [1965]). *The logic of collective action*. Cambridge, MA: Harvard University Press.

Olzak, S. (1994). *The dynamics of ethnic competition and conflict*. Stanford, CA: Stanford University Press.

Oster, E. (2004). Witchcraft, weather and economic growth in renaissance Europe. *The Journal of Economic Perspectives*, 18(1), 215–228.

Pager, D., & Shepherd, H. (2008). The sociology of discrimination: Racial discrimination in employment, housing, credit, and consumer markets. *Annual Review of Sociology*, 34, 181–209.

Paxton, P. (2007). Association memberships and generalized trust: A multilevel model across 31 countries. *Social Forces*, 86(1), 47–76.

Plagnol, A. C., & Huppert, F. A. (2010). Happy to help? Exploring the factors associated with variations in rates of volunteering across Europe. *Social Indicators Research*, 97(2), 157–176.

Polavieja, J. G. (2016). Labour-market competition, recession and anti-immigrant sentiments in Europe: Occupational and environmental drivers of competitive threat. *Socio-Economic Review*, 14(3), 395–417.

Potârcă, G., & Mills, M. (2015). Racial preferences in online dating across European countries. *European Sociological Review*, 31(3), 326–341.

Pottie–Sherman, Y., & Wilkes, R. (2017). Does size really matter? On the relationship between immigrant group size and anti–immigrant prejudice. *International Migration Review*, 51(1), 218–250.

Putnam, R. (2000). *Bowling alone: The collapse and revival of the American community*. New York, NY: Simon & Schuster.

Putnam, R., Leonardi, R., & Nanetti, R. Y. (1993). *Making democracy work: Civic traditions in modern Italy*. Princeton, NJ: Princeton University Press.

Qian, Z. (1997). Breaking the racial barriers: Variations in interracial marriage between 1980 and 1990. *Demography*, 34(2), 263–276.

Qian, Z., & Lichter, D. T. (2007). Social boundaries and marital assimilation: Interpreting trends in racial and ethnic intermarriage. *American Sociological Review*, 72(1), 68–94.

Quillian, L. (1995). Prejudice as a response to perceived group threat: Population composition and anti-immigrant and racial prejudice in Europe. *American Sociological Review*, 60(4), 586–611.

Quillian, L., & Campbell, M. E. (2003). Beyond Black and White: The present and future of multiracial friendship segregation. *American Sociological Review*, 68(4), 540–566.

Riach, P. A., & Rich, J. (2002). Field experiments of discrimination in the market place. *The Economic Journal*, 112(483), F480–F518.

Robnett, B., & Feliciano, C. (2011). Patterns of racial-ethnic exclusion by Internet daters. *Social Forces*, 89(3), 807–828.

Rosenfeld, M. J. (2002). Measures of assimilation in the marriage market: Mexican Americans 1970-1990. *Journal of Marriage and the Family*, 64, 152–162.

Ruiter, S., & De Graaf, N. D. (2006). National context, religiosity, and volunteering: Results from 53 countries. *American Sociological Review*, 71(2), 191–210.

Savelkoul, M., Scheepers, P., Tolsma, J., & Hagendoorn, L. (2010). Anti-Muslim attitudes in the Netherlands: Tests of contradictory hypotheses derived from ethnic competition theory and intergroup contact theory. *European Sociological Review*, 27(6), 741–758.

Scheepers, P., Gijsberts, M., & Coenders, M. (2002). Ethnic exclusionism in European countries: Public opposition to civil rights for legal migrants as as response to perceived ethnic threat. *European Sociological Review*, 18(1), 17–34.

Schlueter, E., & Davidov, E. (2013). Contextual sources of perceived group threat: Negative immigration-related news reports, immigrant group size and their interaction, Spain 1996–2007. *European Sociological Review*, 29(2), 179–191.

Schlueter, E., & Scheepers, P. (2010). The relationship between outgroup size and anti-outgroup attitudes: A theoretical synthesis and empirical test of group threat and intergroup contact theory. *Social Science Research*, 39(2), 285–295.

Schmidt-Catran, A. W., & Spies, D. C. (2016). Immigration and welfare support in Germany. *American Sociological Review*, 81(2), 242–261.

Schofer, E., & Fourcade-Gourinchas, M. (2001). The structural contexts of civic engagement: Voluntary association membership in comparative perspective. *American Sociological Review*, 66(6), 806–828.

Semyonov, M., & Glikman, A. (2009). Ethnic residential segregation, social contacts, and anti-minority attitudes in European societies. *European Sociological Review*, 25(6), 693–708.

Semyonov, M., Raijman, R., & Gorodzeisky, A. (2006). The rise of anti-foreigner sentiment in European societies, 1988-2000. *American Sociological Review*, 71(3), 426–449.

Sherif, M., Harvey, O. J., White, B. J., Hood, W. R., & Sherif, C. W. (1961). *Intergroup conflict and cooperation: The Robbers Cave Experiment*. Norman, OK: University Book Exchange.

Simmel, G. (1955). *Conflict and the web of group affiliations*. New York, NY: Free Press.

Simpson, B. (2006). Social identity and cooperation in social dilemmas. *Rationality and Society*, 18(4), 443–470.

Singh, R., & Ho, S. Y. (2000). Attitudes and attraction: A new test of the attraction, repulsion and similarity–dissimilarity asymmetry hypotheses. *British Journal of Social Psychology*, 39(2), 197–211.

Singh, R., & Teoh, J. B. P. (1999). Attitudes and attraction: A test of two hypotheses for the similarity–dissimilarity asymmetry. *British Journal of Social Psychology*, 38(4), 427–443.

Skopek, J., Schulz, F., & Blossfeld, H. P. (2011). Who contacts whom? Educational homophily in online mate selection. *European Sociological Review*, 27(2), 180–195.

Smith, S., Maas, I., & Van Tubergen, F. (2012). Irreconcilable differences? Ethnic intermarriage and divorce in the Netherlands, 1995–2008. *Social Science Research*, 41(5), 1126–1137.

Smith, S., Maas, I., & Van Tubergen, F. (2014). Ethnic ingroup friendships in schools: Testing the by-product hypothesis in England, Germany, the Netherlands and Sweden. *Social Networks*, 39, 33–45.

Smith, S., Van Tubergen, F., Maas, I., & McFarland, D. A. (2016). Ethnic composition and friendship segregation: Differential effects for adolescent natives and immigrants. *American Journal of Sociology*, 121(4), 1223–1272.

Sniderman, P. M., & Hagendoorn, A. (2007). *When ways of life collide: Multiculturalism and its discontents in the Netherlands*. Princeton, NJ: Princeton University Press.

Stark, T. H., & Flache, A. (2012). The double edge of common interest: Ethnic segregation as an unintended byproduct of opinion homophily. *Sociology of Education*, 85(2), 179–199.

Strabac, Z., & Listhaug, O. (2008). Anti-Muslim prejudice in Europe: A multilevel analysis of survey data from 30 countries. *Social Science Research*, 37(1), 268–286.

Sumner, W. G. (1906). *Folkways: A study of the sociological importance of usages, manners, customs, mores and morals*. Boston: Ginn and Company.

Tajfel, H. (1970). Experiments in intergroup discrimination. *Scientific American*, *223*(5), 96–103.

Tajfel, H. (Ed.). (1982). *Social identity and intergroup relations*. Cambridge, UK: Cambridge University Press.

Tajfel, H., & Turner, J. C. (1979). An integrative theory of intergroup conflict. In W. G. Austin & S. Worchel (Eds.), *The social psychology of intergroup relations* (pp. 33–47). Monterey, CA: Brooks/Cole.

Valentino, N. A., Soroka, S. N., Iyengar, S., Aalberg, T., Duch, R., Fraile, M., Hahn, K. S., Hansen, K. M., Harell, A., Helbling, M., Jackman, S. D., & Kobayashi, T. (2019). Economic and cultural drivers of immigrant support worldwide. *British Journal of Political Science*, *49*(4), 1201–1226.

Van Klingeren, M., Boomgaarden, H. G., & De Vreese, C. H. (2017). Will conflict tear us apart? The effects of conflict and valenced media messages on polarizing attitudes toward EU immigration and border control. *Public Opinion Quarterly*, *81*(2), 543–563.

Van Klingeren, M., Boomgaarden, H. G., Vliegenthart, R., & De Vreese, C. H. (2015). Real world is not enough: The media as an additional source of negative attitudes toward immigration, comparing Denmark and the Netherlands. *European Sociological Review*, *31*(3), 268–283.

Van Tubergen, F., & Sindradóttir, J. Í. (2011). The religiosity of immigrants in Europe: A cross–national study. *Journal for the Scientific Study of Religion*, *50*(2), 272–288.

Wasserman, S., & Faust, K. (1994). *Social network analysis: Methods and applications*. Cambridge, UK: Cambridge University Press.

Watts, D. J., Dodds, P. S., & Newman, M. E. (2002). Identity and search in social networks. *Science*, *296*(5571), 1302–1305.

Weimann, G. (1983). The not-so-small world: Ethnicity and acquaintance networks in Israel. *Social Networks*, *5*(3), 289–302.

White, H. C. (2008). *Identity and control: How social formations emerge*. Princeton, NJ: Princeton University Press.

Wilcox, C., Sigelman, L., & Cook, E. (1989). Some like it hot: Individual differences in responses to group feeling thermometers. *Public Opinion Quarterly*, *53*(2), 246–257.

Wimmer, A., & Lewis, K. (2010). Beyond and below racial homophily: ERG models of a friendship network documented on Facebook. *American Journal of Sociology*, *116*(2), 583–642.

Wimmer, A. (2013). *Ethnic boundary making: Institutions, power, networks*. New York, NY: Oxford University Press.

Windzio, M. (2012). Integration of immigrant children into inter-ethnic friendship networks: The role of 'intergenerational openness'. *Sociology*, *46*(2), 258–271.

Zhang, Y., & Van Hook, J. (2009). Marital dissolution among interracial couples. *Journal of Marriage and Family*, *71*(1), 95–107.

Zschirnt, E., & Ruedin, D. (2016). Ethnic discrimination in hiring decisions: A meta-analysis of correspondence tests 1990–2015. *Journal of Ethnic and Migration Studies*, *42*(7), 1115–1134.

Part 4

Inequality

Chapter 9

Stratification and mobility

What are your chances of getting a good job after finishing your education? Do your parents play a role in your chances of success in education and the labor market? These are questions about inequality and in this chapter I will take a closer look at two subthemes of inequality, namely social stratification and social mobility. This chapter's objective is to introduce you to some important concepts, empirical patterns and theories. I will start with research showing how strongly happiness, life-expectancy and standards of living differ across societies (9.1). I will continue with a discussion of stratification within societies, introducing the concepts of social class and social status (9.2). Then I will address stylized findings of contemporary stratification in income and wealth (9.3) and identify key long-term developments in stratification (9.4). Subsequently, I will introduce the concept of social mobility, which refers to the changing positions people can take in the stratification system (9.5). I will discuss Blau and Duncan's well-known status attainment model, with which they examined the degree to which social mobility was due to "ascription" and "achievement" (9.6). Then I introduce the modernization process, which may have had significant impact on status attainment. I will review two ideas that make competing predictions about the role of modernization. These are: the modernization and mobility theory (9.7) and the cultural reproduction theory (9.8). At the end of this chapter I discuss the relationship between "social stratification" and "social mobility" (9.9).

> **Learning goals**
>
> After reading this chapter, check if you are able to:
>
> - Describe and use key sociological concepts on stratification and mobility.
> - Describe stylized facts on stratification and mobility.
> - Describe the difference between absolute and relative mobility.
> - Use the Blau-Duncan status attainment model to identify patterns of ascription and achievement.
> - Describe and apply the modernization and mobility theory.
> - Describe and apply the cultural reproduction theory.

9.1 What makes you happy?

What is important for becoming a happy person? Why are some people happier and more satisfied with their life than others? If you ask people this question, most would probably not come up with the idea that "the country in which someone was born" matters a great deal. Yet, from a sociological perspective, you may consider the place of birth as a factor determining someone's happiness. According to the *World Happiness Report*, which has a longstanding tradition in carefully measuring happiness and well-being across the world, some populations are indeed significantly happier than others. The happiest people in the world are living in Norway, Denmark, Iceland and Switzerland. Specifically, in the period between 2015–2017, citizens in those happy countries evaluated their happiness at around 7.5 to 7.6 on a scale running from 0 (worst possible life) to 10 (best possible life). In sharp contrast to this score are the much lower ratings of citizens from Burundi, Central African Republic and Liberia (Table 9.1). The populations of these countries rate their life happiness lower than 4 on average. In Burundi, where the least happy people of the world live, the average score is 2.9. Where you are born strongly impacts your chances of living a happy life.

Why are people in Norway, Denmark, Iceland and Switzerland so much happier than people born in Burundi, Central African Republic and Liberia? Happiness is strongly related to economic standards of living, i.e., to the economic development in a country. In Table 9.1, the countries are ranked in terms of GDP PPP (*Gross Domestic Product at Purchasing Power Parity*) per capita, which is an often-used indicator of economic standard of living. You can see the huge discrepancy in standards of living between the happy and unhappy nations in the world. In the affluent countries of Norway, Denmark, Iceland and Switzerland the GDP per capita amounts to over $53,000. This contrasts sharply with the GDP per capita of less than $1,500 per year in Burundi, Central African Republic and Liberia. Research findings reveal that in rich nations people are substantially happier than in poorer nations (Hagerty & Veenhoven, 2003; Sacks, Stevenson, & Wolfers, 2012).

Table 9.1 10 (very) rich and 10 (very) poor countries in the world.

Country	GDP per capita, PPP (2017) (US dollars)	Life expectancy at birth (2017)	Happiness score (average 2015–2017)
Ireland	76,744	81.4	7.0
Switzerland	66,307	83.5	7.5
Norway	62,182	82.0	7.6
United States	59,927	79.5	6.9
Iceland	55,322	83.1	7.5
Netherlands	54,422	82.0	7.4
Denmark	54,356	80.7	7.6
Austria	53,879	82.0	7.3
Germany	52,555	81.5	7.0
Sweden	51,404	82.7	7.3
...	...	...	...
Afghanistan	1,976	61.4	3.6
Ethiopia	1,903	65.6	4.4
Uganda	1,868	60.5	4.2
Madagascar	1,558	66.3	3.8
Liberia	1,285	61.9	3.5
Mozambique	1,250	56.1	4.4
Niger	1,018	62.7	4.2
Congo, Dem. Rep.	889	63.8	4.3
Burundi	735	57.9	2.9
Central African Republic	727	52.9	3.1

Source: Helliwell, Layard, & Sachs, 2018; World Bank, 2017a; World Population Review, 2017.

Why is there such a strong link between economic development and happiness? In poor countries, people suffer from poor health, diseases, poverty, crime and corruption, amongst other things, which can induce high levels of stress, insecurity and physical pain too. Basic medical facilities are often not available and housing conditions are problematic. Such daily living conditions matter a great deal for life satisfaction. In a project called *Dollar Street*, Rosling and colleagues (Rosling, Rosling, & Rosling Ronnlund, 2018) visited 264 families in 50 countries and collected 30,000 photos of their homes, beds, kitchen, toys, toilets, pets and much more. They then sorted the homes by four income levels (1 being poorest income levels in the world and 4 being the richest). To illustrate, consider the pictures that were taken of people's homes and toilets for four different income levels (Image 9.1).

Level 1   Level 2   Level 3   Level 4

Image 9.1 Homes and toilets of families from four different income levels.

In poor nations, people do not live as long as people in affluent nations. Diseases, poor nutrition and bad health conditions significantly reduce life expectancy at birth. To illustrate, life expectancy at birth in 2017 was 83.5 years in rich and happy Switzerland, as compared with only 57.9 years in poor and unhappy Burundi. The life expectancy in the top ten richest countries is around 80 years, as compared with around 60 years in the poorest nations in the world. This means that, on average, those born in poor countries live 20 years fewer than people born in rich nations. The strong positive association between economic development and life expectancy is known as the *Preston Curve*, named after the demographer Samuel Preston who described it in 1975 (Preston, 1975). Figure 9.1 illustrates this relationship with 2017 data. As you can see, people in richer countries live longer—on average, of course, because there are countries that deviate from the common pattern. The strongest gains in life expectancy are at the lower levels of per capita income. But it is also the case in richer countries that additional gains in income are associated with higher life expectancy. However, these further gains involve much larger absolute increases in income than in a poor country to get the same change in years of life expectancy (Deaton, 2013).

In summary, what these findings tell us is that the world in which you and I live today is highly "unequal." People born in Switzerland tend to be happy, rich and live a long time, whereas those born in Burundi are unhappy, poor and live 25 years fewer. Where you were born matters a great deal for *well-being*, *living standards* and *health*. These are key dimensions of what are called **valuable goods**, "something" that people value. People want to be happy and satisfied with their life (well-being), they want to have food, a house and a decent toilet (living standards), they want to visit a doctor who can help them when they are ill and to live without pain (health).

valuable goods something that people value.

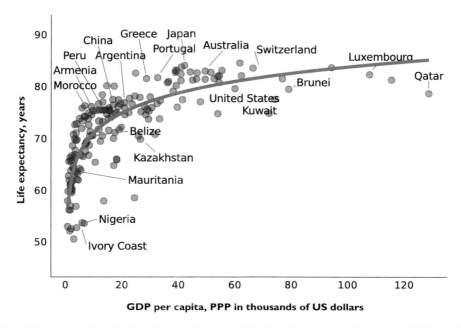

Figure 9.1 The Preston Curve: the association between life expectancy at birth and GDP per capita in 2017.

Source: World Bank, 2017a; World Population Review, 2017.

9.2 Social class and status

The sociological study of stratification is concerned with the study of the unequal distribution of valuable goods (Grusky, 2001). Stratification is thus about some sort of ranking, ordering and hierarchy. When we compare Switzerland with Burundi, how they differ in happiness, income and life expectancy, we are ranking these countries. People in Switzerland have more valuable goods than those in Burundi. These kinds of inequalities are called **between-country stratification**. But when we compare countries in this way, such as with respect to their economic prosperity, we are comparing country averages. For example, we compare the living standards of the *average* Swiss with the living standards of the *average* citizen in Burundi.

between-country stratification unequal distribution of valuable goods between countries.

When making such comparisons, although insightful, one does not pay attention to the stratification that may occur *within* countries. It was the work by sociologists Karl Marx and Friedrich Engels (Marx, 2008 [1867]; Marx & Engels, 2002 [1847]) in the 19th century that gave such questions on **within-country stratification** a prominent place on the agenda of sociologists and that, since then, has received continuous interest (Piketty, 2014). Societies consist of various vertical strata and societies can be more, or less, strongly stratified. A primary objective of sociological studies into inequality is charting the extent, as well as

within-country stratification unequal distribution of valuable goods within countries.

the developments, of stratification in a society. A major question then comes up: how do we rank individuals, or groups, in society? There are various ways to do so, but two commonly used bases of social stratification are *social class* and *social status* (Chan & Goldthorpe, 2007; Weber, 1978 [1922]).

Let's discuss **social class** first. Classical work on social class is that of Marx and Engels. As they grew up in a time of rapid industrialization in Europe, they became aware that industrialization went hand in hand with an unequal distribution between the rich businessmen who owned the machines and factories (the capital) and the laborers that worked for a low income. To them, what mattered most was therefore the distinction between two social classes: *capitalists* and *laborers*. Stratification within societies was such that capitalists were having the more favorable social class positions than laborers.

social class group of people who hold similar occupational positions.

The sociologists Erikson and Goldthorpe define social classes, in their study *The Constant Flux* (Erikson & Goldthorpe, 1992), as aggregates of social positions "that are identified in terms of relationships within labor markets and production units." Thus, social class considers someone's occupation—or clusters of occupations that are similar to each other along one or more dimensions—as the key base of social stratification, i.e., in getting access to money and power. From a social class perspective, people are stratified by occupation. Occupations create a ranking, a hierarchy of classes, such that the "higher" classes have more access to valuable resources than the "lower" classes. Social class tends to be associated with access to valuable goods such as *well-being*, *living standards* and *health*. This means that people who belong to the same social class have (more or less) similar access to these valuable goods.

In follow-up work to that of Marx and Engels, sociologists have developed more refined social class schemes, going beyond a simple dichotomy between capitalists and laborers. A prominent example is the so-called *Erikson-Goldthorpe-Portocarero* (EGP) class scheme, which differentiates (in an often-used collapsed version) seven social classes: *service class, routine non-manual, petty bourgeoisie, farmers, skilled workers, non-skilled workers* and *agricultural laborers* (Erikson & Goldthorpe, 1992). In the EGP class scheme, occupations are grouped into the same social class based on various criteria, such as (1) the *skills* required for the occupation, (2) the *sector* of employment and (3) the divide between *manual* and *non-manual* work. This means that people with different occupations can be grouped together in the same social class, depending on how they score on such criteria.

To illustrate, consider a study that was conducted in England and Wales in the late 1990s. In this study the researchers classified people in social classes and the researchers then examined their life expectancy. The social class that is at the top of the hierarchy, so-called *professionals* in this study, had a life expectancy of 78.5 (males) and 82.8 (females) years (Table 9.2). The lowest social class, *unskilled workers*, had a life expectancy of 71.1 (males) and 77.1 (females) years. Hence the study finds that, in England and Wales at that time, the higher class lived on average around 6–7 years longer than the lower class. This pattern—that higher social classes have a longer life expectancy than lower classes—is observed worldwide; what varies is the *degree* to which social class makes a difference (Antonovsky, 1967). A famous link between social class and life chances was noted when researchers analyzed the passengers of the *Titanic*, the luxury liner that rammed an iceberg and then sank. Statistics showed that, among the passengers, 62% of the first class survived, as opposed to 41% among the second class and only 25% among the third class.

Although social class schemes are often used, it has also been argued that there are some drawbacks to it (Ganzeboom, Treiman, & Ultee, 1991). One issue is that such social class categories can be quite heterogeneous. This means that people who fall into the same social class

Table 9.2 Life expectancy at birth by gender and social class in England and Wales, 1997–1999.

Social class	Examples of occupation	Males	Females
Professional	Doctors, engineers	78.5	82.8
Managerial and technical/ intermediate	Managers, school teachers	77.5	81.5
Skilled non-manual	Clerks, cashiers	76.2	81.2
Skilled manual	Plumbers, electricians	74.7	79.2
Partly skilled	Warehousemen, security guards	72.7	78.5
Unskilled	Cleaners, messengers	71.1	77.1

Source: Donkin, Goldblatt, & Lynch, 2002.

category (e.g., unskilled workers) can be quite different from each other, with notable variations in income, health and well-being. Thus, although unskilled workers earn less and have lower standards of living *on average* than, say, professionals, at the same time there are disparities in earnings and living standards *within* this group of unskilled workers. In an attempt to overcome these problems, sociologists have developed the so-called *socio-economic index of occupational status* (Ganzeboom, De Graaf, & Treiman, 1992). The socio-economic index of occupational status ranks *each* occupation along a continuum rather than grouping them together in broader *clusters* of occupations in heterogeneous social class schemes. Specifically, the index is constructed as a function of the average education and income of individuals within each occupation. Thus, those occupations that are characterized by highly educated workers who earn a lot are seen as occupations with a high *socio-economic* status.

Social class does not capture all bases of social stratification. A second base for stratification in society is **social status**, i.e., the subjective ranking of individuals or groups in terms of honor, esteem and respect (Correll & Ridgeway, 2003; Gould, 2002; Ridgeway, 2014; Weber, 1978 [1922]). Whenever individuals come together, status differentiation emerges. In the *Robbers Cave Experiment* (Chapter 8), for example, both the Eagles and the Rattlers had a leader, a few mid-level individuals and a set of followers (Sherif, Harvey, White, Hood, & Sherif, 1961). Within school classes, some students are highly popular and receive much respect from the other peers (Pál, Stadtfeld, Grow, & Takács, 2016). Status differentiation is also typical of organizations, in which some individuals have more authority and prestige than others. Also groups are stratified by status: ethnic groups, religion, race, gender, age, education and so forth are often ordered in terms of social status. For example, some people can believe that "men need to be more respected than women" and that "Whites have more prestige than Blacks."

social status subjective ranking of individuals or groups in terms of honor, esteem and respect.

In explaining the concept of social status as a base for social stratification, sociologist Cecilia Ridgeway mentions the following:

> When we think of inequality as merely a structural struggle for power and resources, we forget how much people care about their sense of being valued by others and the society to which they belong – how much they care about public acknowledgement of

their worth. This is status. People care about status quite as intensely as they do money and power. Indeed, people often want money as much for the status it brings as for its exchange value. An airport shoe-shine man once asked me what I did. When I told him, he said, "My daughter wants to go to Stanford and be a physician. What I do is just for her; I want her to be someone." Now, what was that about? Power? Not so much. Money? Yes, a bit. But above all it is about public recognition of his daughter's social worth. It is about social status.

(Ridgeway, 2014)

Social status differences can be related to someone's occupation, although, obviously, social status does not depend on someone's occupation alone. One can rank all occupations in some meaningful way, such that those occupations on the top are seen as more desirable than those at the bottom. A pioneering study that did precisely this was Treiman's *Occupational Prestige in Comparative Perspective*, which appeared in 1977 (Treiman, 1977). In this work, Treiman designed a new measure to rank occupations that was based on

> **occupational prestige** subjective ranking of occupations in terms of prestige and respect.

occupational prestige. Simply put, he asked respondents to rank occupations in terms of their prestige. Each occupation gets a "prestige score"—the higher the score, the more strongly it is seen as a prestigious occupation. Hence, one could rank individuals in society using their occupations and the corresponding prestige scores.

To illustrate this occupational ranking, consider Table 9.3, which gives the top five and lowest five prestigious occupations in the US in the year 1989. Among the most prestigious occupations are physicians, lawyers, computer system analysts and scientists. Ushers, maids, housemen and vehicle washers receive much lower scores.

The work by Treiman and others has revealed several striking patterns (Hodge, Siegel, & Rossi, 1964; Nakao & Treas, 1994; Treiman, 1977). First, it appears that the ranking of occupations is independent of the exact *wording* of the questionnaire that is used to acquire

Table 9.3 Occupational prestige in the US (1989): top five and lowest five.

Occupation	Prestige score
Physicians	86
Lawyer	75
Computer systems analyst or scientist	74
Teachers/college professors	74
Physicist or astronomer	73
...	...
Ushers	20
Maids and housemen	20
News vendors	19
Vehicle washers and equipment cleaners	19
Miscellaneous food preparation occupations	17

Source: Nakao & Treas, 1994.

prestige scores (Treiman, 1976). In other words, you get the same ranking of occupations no matter whether you ask respondents about the "prestige," "social standing" or "respect" of occupations. Second, you may think that the prestige ranking will turn out very differently for different groups of people in society. Maybe university professors give different ratings than car mechanics. This is not what the research shows. Different *groups* in society give the *same* prestige score. Whether one asks the educated or uneducated, young or older people, men or women, one gets the same ranking of occupations. Third, the ranking of occupation is highly similar across *space and time*. For example, lawyers are not only seen as highly prestigious in the US in 1989, they have always been seen that way—and in other countries this is the case as well. In short, occupational prestige rankings appear very robust. You get the same ranking no matter what words were used, no matter to whom one asks these questions and no matter in which country or time period you conduct the study. These findings were discovered and worked out most systematically in Donald Treiman's work, which is why scholars nowadays refer to this stylized pattern as the ***Treiman constant*** (Hout & DiPrete, 2006).

STYLIZED FACT 9.1

Treiman constant
Occupational prestige rankings are highly similar over time, across countries and have strong agreement between raters.

Analytically, social class and social status capture different dimensions of stratification (Chan & Goldthorpe, 2007). At the same time, it is also acknowledged that someone's social class position and social status can overlap. For example, research findings reveal that there is not a strong difference in the rankings of occupations by prestige (i.e., social status) and socio-economic status (i.e., social class). It appears that occupational prestige ratings strongly correlate with the socio-economic status of occupations (Ganzeboom et al., 1992). This means that the more prestigious jobs are also the occupations that require higher education and that result in higher income. In conclusion, class and status are analytically different, but people who have a high social class position tend to get more respect and prestige.

9.3 Income and wealth

Social class and status are typically seen as core bases of social stratification, i.e., the unequal distribution of valuable goods. But how strongly are valuable goods actually distributed within societies? A key area of research focuses on economic outcomes, in particular income and wealth. Individuals and households can be ranked in a hierarchy, a social ladder, depending on their income and wealth. We may then wonder about the *degree* of stratification of societies at large. For example, if we take the income of an entire country together, how much of it falls into the hands of the richest 10%? How much do the poorest 10% get? If society is fully equal, without any form of income stratification, the richest 10% hold as much income as the poorest 10% and there is no stratification. However, in a country where the top 10% hold, for instance, 40% of the total income, there is income stratification.

Image 9.2 Scholars research the degree of income stratification in societies: how great is, for instance, the inequality of income between the rich and the poor?

One measure that scholars often use to assess the degree of over-all income stratification in society is the **Gini coefficient**. The Gini is a summary measure of stratification, which runs from 0—in which case all citizens have the same income (or wealth, etc.)—to (almost) 100—in which case a country's entire income (or wealth, etc.) is in the hands of one single person. The Gini measure is commonly used for quantifying the degree of income (or wealth) stratification in society and has the advantage that it summarizes the *overall* stratification in society in a single number.

gini coefficient measure of stratification in society which runs from 0 (minimum) to 100 (maximum).

How much income stratification is there within countries? How great are the differences between the poor and the rich within countries? Table 9.4 presents Gini statistics on income stratification from the World Bank for a select number of countries. It is immediately noticeable that in each country the Gini exceeds 0, which means that there is at least some stratification. Another conclusion is also evident from the data: the degree of within-country income stratification is not a constant, but varies. Countries having strong income stratification include Brazil (Gini: 51) and, even more so, South Africa (63). In Sweden (29) and Denmark (28), there is much less income stratification.

The Gini index is a measure of *overall* stratification. Sometimes it is more informative to take a closer look at the income shares of certain strata. How much do the top 10% earn, for example? Or the lowest 20%? Table 9.5 presents data on the income of the top 10% taken from *The World Inequality Report 2018* (Alvaredo, Chancel, Piketty, Saez, & Zucman, 2018). The study differentiates between certain regions and countries in the world. The study reveals that in each region/country the top 10% have a larger share of the total income than

Table 9.4 Income stratification (Gini coefficient, 0–100).

	Gini coefficient (year)
North America	
United States	41.5 (2016)
Canada	34.0 (2013)
Mexico	43.4 (2016)
South America	
Argentina	42.4 (2016)
Brazil	51.3 (2015)
Asia	
China	42.2 (2012)
India	35.1 (2011)
Indonesia	39.5 (2013)
Japan	32.1 (2008)
Pakistan	33.5 (2015)
Africa	
Nigeria	43.0 (2009)
Egypt	31.8 (2015)
South Africa	63.0 (2014)
Europe	
Denmark	28.2 (2015)
France	32.7 (2015)
Germany	31.7 (2015)
United Kingdom	33.2 (2015)
Italy	35.4 (2015)
Russia	37.7 (2015)
Sweden	29.2 (2015)
Oceania	
Australia	34.7 (2010)

Source: World Bank, 2017b.

10%, but their excess in income differs strongly across regions. It is lowest in Europe, where the share of total national income accounted for by the top 10% of earners was 37% in 2016. It was higher in China (41%), Russia (46%) and US/Canada combined (47%). The highest income stratification was observed in the region of the Middle East, where the top 10% had 61% of the national income.

Evidence suggests that, even among the group of rich people making up the 10%, there is considerable stratification. Those who are *very* rich, the top 1%, have substantially more than the rest of the top 10% (Keister, 2014). Being very rich is more than having high income, however. The use of *income* as a measure for stratification ignores the fact that people may also have other forms of *wealth*, such as financial assets, real estate and savings.

Table 9.5 Top 10% national income share across the world, 2016.

Country/Region	Share of National Income (%)
Europe	37
China	41
Russia	46
US & Canada	47
Sub-Saharan Africa	54
Brazil	55
India	55
Middle East	61

Source: Alvaredo et al., 2018.

Media reports reveal that extreme wealth is in the hands of only a few persons. In 2013, business magazine *Forbes* informed us that the American Bill Gates had some $72 billion dollars at his disposal. This made the Microsoft entrepreneur the richest man in the world at that time. In 2018 his net worth had further increased to $97 billion dollars but, meanwhile, another American, Jeff Bezos, the owner of Amazon, had taken over the number one position with an estimated net worth of $153 billion dollars (Table 9.6). Their wealth contrasts sharply with the tens of millions of poor people in America who struggle with debts and with making ends meet. According to the US Census Bureau, 16% of all Americans lived their lives in poverty in 2012. Oxfam estimated that in the year 2016 the eight richest men in the world owned the same amount of wealth as the poorest half of the world (Hardoon, 2017).

Table 9.6 Top ten richest persons in the world in 2018.

Ranking	Name	Net worth (USD, billion as of August 7, 2018)	Nationality
1	Jeff Bezos	153 b	United States
2	Bill Gates	97 b	United States
3	Warren Buffett	86 b	United States
4	Bernard Arnault	77 b	France
5	Mark Zuckerberg	74 b	United States
6	Amancio Ortega	70 b	Spain
7	Carlos Slim	63 b	Mexico
8	Larry Page	60 b	United States
9	Sergey Brin	58 b	United States
10	Larry Ellison	55 b	United States

Source: (Bloomberg, 2019)

The distribution of income and wealth is extremely skewed: a handful of people are incredibly rich. Today, scholars describe the extreme concentration of income and wealth in the hands of the few as the phenomenon of the *one percent*.

STYLIZED FACT 9.2

The one percent

The within-country stratification in income and wealth in contemporary societies is highly skewed and much of the wealth is in the hands of the top 1 percent.

These are the stylized facts, i.e., the findings on stratification coming from reliable sources. They tell us something about the *objective* reality of stratification in contemporary societies. This objective reality need not necessarily overlap with people's *perceptions* of stratification in their society. People have their personal intuitions and beliefs and they may over- or underestimate the degree of stratification in their society (Arsenio & Willems, 2017; Eriksson & Simpson, 2012; Evans & Kelley, 2017; Norton & Ariely, 2011; Norton, Neal, Govan, Ariely, & Holland, 2014). Furthermore, their beliefs about stratification may or may not concur with their ideal stratification, which is part of their *values and preferences*. Research findings from literature on people's perceptions of and preferences for stratification suggest that people prefer a more egalitarian distribution of wealth than the one they believe exists in their country (Arsenio, 2018). Thus, many people perceive the degree of stratification in society as too high relative to what they think is fair and just.

BOX 9.1

Social inequality and social problems: is there a causal effect or not?

In 2009, the British social epidemiologists Richard Wilkinson and Kate Pickett published a remarkable book called *The Spirit Level: Why More Equal Societies Almost Always Do Better* (2009). In this study they came up with a controversial hypothesis that is the topic of a large debate among sociologists, epidemiologists and other scientists. The key proposition advanced in the book, as the title suggests, states that "the higher the income inequality in a social context, the more social problems there are in that social context." In their book, Pickett and Wilkinson present ample evidence that is in line with predictions based on this general proposition.

For example, they compiled an "index" that takes together different kinds of "social problems," such as lower life expectancy, lower literacy rates, higher infant mortality, homicide rates and other such problems. They then presented evidence suggesting that social problems are associated with income stratification within societies (Figure 9.2).

Figure 9.2 The relationship between income inequality and social problems.

Source: Wilkinson & Pickett, 2009.

Figure 9.2 shows that in countries with a low income inequality, such as Japan and Norway, there are not many social problems. In these countries there are fewer homicides, teenage births, obesity is lower and so forth. Countries with higher levels of inequality, however, such as the UK and Portugal, score high on this index of problems. The extreme case is the United States, which has the highest income stratification of all countries in their study and also ranks highest in terms of social problems.

Sociologists and other social scientists debate on the question of whether these and other observations indeed suggest that there is a *causal* effect of income stratification, X, on social problems, Y (Goldthorpe, 2010; Lynch et al., 2004; Pickett & Wilkinson, 2015; Pinker, 2018). In other words, how strong is the *internal validity* of the study (Chapter 3)? Most scholars agree that one criterion for causality is satisfied, i.e., there appears to be a correlation between income stratification (X) and social problems (Y). Correlation, however, does not prove causation. What about the issue that X should precede Y in time? And also that their relationship should be non-spurious? Some scholars argue that the observed relationship may go in the opposite direction: it may well be the case that social problems (Y) influence income stratification (X), rather than the other way around. Others suggest that it could also be the case that the relationship is spurious and that other variables ("Z") could explain why there is a correlation between income inequality and social problems.

9.4 Long-term changes in stratification

Has the degree of stratification we witness today been there forever? How much change is there in stratification over time? A key question in the sociology of stratification is the degree of change within societies.

Table 9.7 Top 10% income share across the world, 1980–2015.

Country/region	1980	1985	1990	1995	2000	2005	2010	2015
Middle East	–	–	65.86	65.98	62.55	61.09	58.78	60.91
Brazil	–	–	58.09	55.97	54.03	55.08	55.55	55.33
Africa	–	–	55.27	55.18	54.38	54.72	54.69	54.48
China	27.24	29.52	30.41	33.55	35.56	41.86	42.60	41.42
India	31.49	34.79	33.48	38.52	39.87	45.46	52.17	55.46
US-Canada	34.23	36.63	38.68	40.63	43.87	45.03	45.70	46.96
Russia	21.02	22.37	23.58	42.45	48.19	47.40	46.84	45.51
Europe	32.60	33.00	33.80	33.40	33.90	33.50	33.60	36.70

Source: Alvaredo et al., 2018.

What has happened in past decades? Taking the year 1980 as our starting point, we see that in many countries income stratification is increasing (Table 9.7). In India, for example, the share of the total income of the top 10% was 32% in 1980 and this increased to 40% in 2000 and to 55% in 2015. In Russia, the top 10% had 21% of the total income in 1980 and in 2015 this was 45%. In European countries, the increase in income stratification has not been as strong as in India and Russia but the trend is in the same direction nevertheless. The only exceptions to this pattern are the countries and regions that already had high levels of income stratification. In the Middle East, for example, the share of the total income taken by the top 10% was 65% in 1990 and this decreased to 61% in 2015. Taken together, these two trends suggest that countries that had low income stratification are moving towards the high income stratification frontier (Alvaredo et al., 2018).

Roughly the same picture emerges when you study wealth instead of income. Since the 1980s, the top 1% has seen their share of the total personal wealth increasing in many countries (Table 9.8). For example, in the US the top 1% owned 23% of the total wealth in 1980 and this increased to 38% in 2010. Although other nations do not have exactly the same figures, the direction in which they move is often the same: increasing within-country wealth stratification since the 1980s.

Table 9.8 Top 1% wealth shares across the world, 1920–2015.

Country	1920	1930	1940	1950	1960	1970	1980	1990	2000	2010	2015
China	–	–	–	–	–	–	–	–	19.6	30.5	29.6
France	50.5	49.6	34.8	33.4	31.4	20.3	17.2	17.2	28.1	23.5	–
Russia	–	–	–	–	–	–	–	–	39.2	34.3	42.6
UK	57.3	56.9	51.0	43.0	35.0	27.4	18.8	16.3	18.5	–	–
US	35.7	43.4	37.7	28.5	27.8	25.9	22.5	26.7	32.3	37.6	–

Source: Alvaredo et al., 2018.

Thus, the within-country stratification has increased in many countries since the 1980s, except for those countries that already had high levels of income stratification to begin with. At the same time, the within-country stratification in wealth is equally on the rise since the 1980s. However, when you look back further in history, you can see that inequality within countries has not been steadily increasing. For example, in 1980 the top 1% owned 17% of the total wealth in France, but in 1950 this was 33% and in 1920 it was even higher: 51%.

Looking even deeper into history, back to the 13th century, scholars have made two stylized observations with respect to stratification. First, evidence suggests that within-country stratification is cyclical (Álvarez-Nogal & De La Escosura, 2013; Milanovic, 2016). This means that stratification waxed and waned over time, increasing and decreasing in certain periods. There is, therefore, no evidence suggesting either a linear increase or decrease of stratification in human history—at least not since the 13th century (from which moment scholars have collected reliable data). Second, in an attempt to understand this cyclical nature of stratification, scholars have argued that epidemics and wars may have played a substantial role (Scheidel, 2017). Before countries had well-developed health care institutions, epidemics could kill large shares of the population. For example, scholars estimate that as many as 25–45% of the people in Europe died of the Black Death (Scheidel, 2017). The loss of so many people resulted in a labor shortage. As a consequence, the more affluent people, i.e., employers and businessmen, had to increase the wages, thereby reducing stratification. Wars had a similar "egalitarian" effect, although in a different way. Wars caused great losses to the rich people. Wars do much damage to the property, assets and wealth of the affluent, affecting them more than ordinary people.

9.5 Social mobility

The theme of "social inequality" is not solely concerned with the degree of stratification in a society. It may be that the country is strongly stratified, say the bottom 20% have only 1% of the national income, but the poorer people in that country can also easily build a career for themselves—which makes their society more "open" and less unequal. If, say, the people who belong to the poorest 20% of the country have a good chance of climbing the social ladder within a short span of time, there is less social inequality than if they have virtually no chance of escaping from poverty.

The second sub-theme of inequality examined by sociologists is, therefore, *social mobility* in a society (Grusky, 2001). Whereas the study of *stratification* is concerned with the unequal distribution of valued goods, the study of *mobility* focuses on *changes* between social positions. One can think of the social system as completely "closed" or "rigid," in which case it is impossible to climb or descend from one stratum to another. For instance, people who were born into a poor family will then remain poor for their entire life. In reality, societies are virtually never fully rigid and there is always at least some mobility, which means that people are able to step from one stratum to the next, i.e., they can climb the social ladder. Mobility is a matter of degree, a continuum which ranges from (almost completely) *rigid* to (almost completely) *open*. The extent to which mobility is possible, therefore, differs in both space and time. The more closed societies are, and so the less mobility there is, the greater the inequality present.

Sociologists map out the mobility in societies in two ways (Figure 9.3). They first look into **intergenerational mobility**: the change in the position between parents and their children. Such mobility emerges if the position of children in the stratification system differs from that of their parents, for instance when it comes to their

intergenerational mobility changing position between parents and their children in the stratification system.

Image 9.3 Apart from questions about stratification, sociologists also ask about social mobility in a society. Do children have the same jobs as their parents? Can newspaper boys become millionaires?

occupational status, income, wealth, life expectancy, the rights that they have or the prestige that they enjoy. According to the well-known belief in the "American Dream," this type of mobility is characteristic of the United States, where children born from poorer families can climb up the ladder to become a millionaire. Second, sociologists investigate **intragenerational mobility**, which boils down to the posi-

intragenerational mobility changing position in the stratification system over the life course.

tion changes that individuals go through in the course of their lives. Someone who was, for instance, a salesperson and who is then promoted and eventually works her way up to become the director of a major company has a great measure of (intragenerational) mobility.

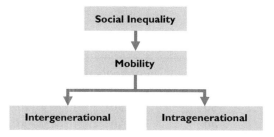

Figure 9.3 Mobility: inter- and intragenerational.

Of the two types of mobility, intergenerational mobility is studied most often by sociologists. Many studies have examined how much social mobility there is across generations in societies. But how do sociologists assess how much intergenerational mobility exists in society? One common way to do so is to make use of a **mobility table**, which cross-classifies *origins* and *destinations*. When examining intergenerational mobility, origins refer to the social position of the parent(s), such as their social class, whereas destinations indicate the social position of the child(ren). One can then use this table to study patterns of intergenerational mobility in occupational status, social class, income, wealth, education, health and so forth.

> **mobility table** table which cross-classifies origin and destination position in the stratification system.

To illustrate how a mobility table can shed light on intergenerational mobility, consider Table 9.9. This table shows a fictitious example in which the social class of the parents (origin) is cross-classified by the social class of the child (destination). In this case the society is stratified into three social class categories: high, intermediate, low. In reality, of course, you could make more refined distinctions. One way to understand this particular mobility table is to think about how it can tell you something about a certain group of children who come from three different backgrounds: higher class, intermediate class and lower class. The key question for sociologists interested in mobility is, then, where do these children end up?

In answering this question, sociologists commonly differentiate between absolute and relative (intergenerational) mobility. **Absolute mobility** indicates the total number of positional changes. You can find this kind of mobility by considering the numbers in the off-diagonal cells. This, in turn, partitions into those children who are *upwardly* mobile (i.e., their destination is "higher" than their origin)

> **absolute mobility** total number of positional changes.

and those children who are *downwardly* mobile (i.e., their destination is "lower" than their origin). In this example, upward mobility amounts to (40 + 60 + 90/1000) *100 = 19% of the children. Downward mobility pertains to (30 + 20 + 30/1000) * 100 = 8% of the children. Together, this makes 27% of the children having a social class position different from that of their parent(s). Consequently, the remaining group of 73% is "stable" (i.e., 150 + 230 + 350/1000).

It seems intuitive to use these numbers (27% mobile versus 73% stable) as indicating the degree of "openness" in society. To a certain degree, this is a valid conjecture: after all, when absolute mobility levels are high, the social positions of parents and their children differ. However, it is important to realize that this absolute mobility is partly due to

Table 9.9 Illustration of intergenerational mobility.

Social class parents (origin)	Social class child (destination)			
	High	Intermediate	Low	
High	150	30	20	200
Intermediate	40	230	30	300
Low	60	90	350	500
	250	350	400	1000

structural mobility. By this, sociologists mean that due to changes in the "volumes" ("margins") of social positions across generations, mobility is inevitable. To illustrate, consider again Table 9.9, in which you may have noticed the different volumes in social positions among origins and destinations. For example, among the parental generation (origins), there were 500 lower class positions. But among the next generation (destinations), there are only 400 such positions. This means that among the 500 children who come from a lower-class background, only 400 can occupy the same position as their parents: the remaining 100 are "pushed into" another class because of changing labor market structure.

structural mobility mobility that is due to changes in the volumes (margins) of available social positions.

To get a better understanding of the true openness in society across generations, its *social fluidity*, sociologists argue that we need to examine **relative mobility** (Box 9.2). This indicates the degree of inequality between children who come from various backgrounds (origins) in their opportunity to access social positions (destinations). This kind of inequality would emerge, for example, if children from lower-status backgrounds have limited opportunities to access higher-status positions.

relative mobility inequality between children from (different) social origins in their opportunity to access social positions.

BOX 9.2

Relative mobility and odds ratios

In what way can you determine if there are unequal chances for children to get access to higher status positions? To answer this question you can use the *odds ratio* (See Chapter 8, online Appendix). For example, let's answer this question: do children from a low-class origin have equal odds of getting a high-status position (relative to a low-status position) as compared with children who have a high-status origin? To answer this question (and using figures from Table 9.9), you can take these three steps:

1. Compute the odds for children from a high-social-class origin to obtain a high-class position relative to a low-class position. This is: 150/20 = 7.5.
2. Now, do the same for children from a lower-class background. This gives us: 60/350 = 0.17.
3. Finally, you need to compare the two figures, which gives you the odds ratio: 7.5/0.17 = 41.

An odds ratio of 1 indicates that the odds for the two origins are the same. In other words, if the odds ratio was 1 in this case, it would mean that lower- and higher-class children have equal odds of ending up in the high-class position. If that was the case then the society would be open in terms of relative intergenerational mobility. However, clearly this is not the case in the example here. An odds ratio beyond 1 indicates that children from a high-class origin are more likely to move into a high-class position than low-class children—and the higher the odds ratio, the stronger is this kind of inequality.

9.6 Ascription and achievement

In the classic study *The American Occupational Structure* (1967), sociologists Blau and Duncan argued that investigations that sociologists conduct into social mobility can be placed under the general question of the role of **ascription** ("ascribed characteristics") and **achievement** ("effort," "performance") (Blau & Duncan, 1967). Societies may have great inequality according to ascribed characteristics. If this is the case, the inequalities are largely set at birth and little can be achieved through people's efforts, hard work and performance. This happens when relative mobility is rare or, in other words, when the family into which you are born (*"origin"*) largely predicts the position

> **ascription**
> characteristics set at birth, such as family origin and ethnic origin.
>
> **achievement**
> personal effort, skills, talent and performance.

you will occupy in the labor market (*"destination"*). It is, however, also possible that it is not so much the ascribed characteristic of social origin that plays a role, but that it is actually people's personal talents, doing your best in school, hard work and creativity that are decisive and determinant for success. The study by Blau and Duncan gave great impetus to the sociological investigation of the importance of "ascription" versus "achievement" in social mobility.

The Blau-Duncan study has become famous not only because they explicitly placed the ascription–achievement question on the agenda but also, and perhaps more so, because of the simplicity and elegancy with which they theoretically and empirically answered this question. They introduced a new conceptual model to represent the *status attainment process*, i.e., the process by which people acquire a certain position, such as an occupation. Most importantly, they added education of the child (*E*) to the relationship between the socio-economic status of the parents—*origin* (*O*)—and the occupational status of the child—*destination* (*D*). Figure 9.4 presents a simplified version of their conceptual OED model, using a (more contemporary) multilevel framework. Note that in this figure, parental "socio-economic status" refers to an index that captures parent's educational level, socio-economic status of their occupations and income. The "occupational status" of the child refers to the socio-economic status of their occupation.

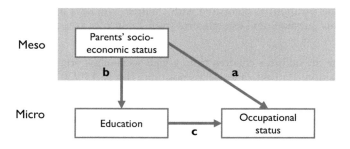

Figure 9.4 Status attainment process.

Using their conceptual model, Blau and Duncan were able to say more about how important the family into which someone is born is for being successful in education and getting access to prestigious jobs. And they were able to detect how much personal effort and merit played a role. Specifically, if family origin (ascription) matters, then the following propositions should be true:

> *P.* The higher the socio-economic status of the parents, the higher someone's occupational status (*arrow a*).

P. The higher the socio-economic status of the parents, the higher someone's educational level (*arrow b*).

If personal effort and talent are important for being successful in the labor market, then, so Blau and Duncan argued, we should expect:

P. The higher someone's education level, the higher someone's occupational status (*arrow c*).

In a fully rigid, ascribed society, one's family origin completely determines one's education (*arrow b*) and occupation (*arrow a*). It would mean that children born in affluent families would get access to prestigious education and get high-status, high-income jobs, whereas children born in poor families would remain poor for the rest of their life. In societies in which family origin plays no role at all and all that matters is personal merit (*arrow c*), the chances of getting highly prestigious jobs depend more on one's talents and personal efforts. These are extreme cases, of course, and Blau and Duncan were interested to see *how much* of a role ascriptive forces play (*arrow a and b*) and how much achievement (*arrow c*).

Blau and Duncan, using data on the US, found that the status attainment process was driven by a combination of both ascription and achievement. Children from higher-socio-economic-status families were more likely to obtain higher levels of education (*arrow b*) as well as higher-status jobs (*arrow a*) than those from lower-status backgrounds. This is evidence for the idea that people's labor market position is determined partly by ascription. But they also observed that education mattered for getting ahead (*arrow c*), hence people's own talents and skills mattered as well. Thus, at the time of their study (post WWII), the US appeared to be a society in which both family origin and educational achievements affected occupational careers.

9.7 Modernization and mobility theory

The Blau-Duncan study focused, by design, on a specific context, namely the US in the 1960s. A key question that has pre-occupied sociologists of mobility in the footsteps of the Blau-Duncan study is whether the importance of *ascription* (*arrow a + b*) vis-à-vis the impact of *achievement* (*arrow c*) is contingent on social context. For example, do children whose parents are lawyers or physicians have equally high chances of getting prestigious jobs today as they had in the 1960s? Are there any changes over time? And, if so, why would this be the case? There are two major theories proposed that attempt to answer these questions: the modernization and mobility theory and the cultural reproduction theory.

The ***modernization and mobility theory*** has its roots in the Blau-Duncan study (Blau & Duncan, 1967), it was elaborated on by Treiman in 1970 (Treiman, 1970) and has been the subject of numerous publications since then (Ganzeboom et al., 1991; Hout & DiPrete, 2006; Knigge, Maas, Van Leeuwen, & Mandemakers, 2014). It is also called the *industrialization theory*, *modernization theory* or the *increased merit selection hypothesis* (Whelan & Layte, 2002). The theory states that modernization in society will bring along changes in the labor market, such that people's personal skills and talents become the key determining factors whereas ascribed characteristics become less and less important. It is argued that modernization changes the status attainment process in the following two ways:

1 *Ascription becomes less important*. Modernization is argued to reduce the impact of someone's family origin. Whether your parents are rich or poor, high or low educated, lawyer or truck driver, matters less today than in the past for your chances of getting a good job. This means that parents' socio-economic status has less of an effect on (1) their children's education (*arrow a*) and (2) their children's occupational status (*arrow b*). In modern nations, social origin matters less for where you end up in your career.

2   *Achievement becomes more important.* Modernization also changes the role of education. Specifically, the theory posits that education is playing an increasing role in determining your chances in the labor market. This means that we should expect to see that the impact of someone's education on their occupational status (*arrow c*) has become more pronounced over the years.

We can integrate these ideas in the Blau-Duncan status attainment model (Figure 9.5). In this expanded multilevel framework, modernization represents changing macro-level conditions, the socio-economic status of parents (family) are contextual conditions at the meso level and the education and occupation of the children are micro-level characteristics. The modernization process acts as a moderator variable, as it changes (1) the impact parents have on their children and (2) the influence of education on labor market outcomes.

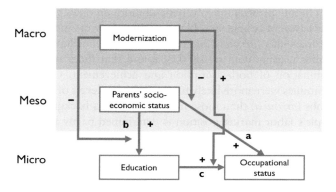

Figure 9.5 Modernization and mobility theory.

The reasons for expecting these changes with modernization are diverse. Modernization, as you will see in more detail in Chapter 12 (Modernization), refers to a set of interrelated changes in society. These processes reduce the importance of ascriptive forces and increase the importance attached to personal achievement. Consider the following modernization processes that alter the status attainment process (Knigge et al., 2014; Treiman, 1970):

1   *Increasing specialization.* Modernization encompasses accumulation of technological knowledge and innovations. Higher levels of technology—such as a shift from agriculture to industrial society—goes hand in hand with increasing specialization. New jobs emerge, which require new skills and talents, meaning that children can no longer simply inherit the same job as their parents (*arrow a* becomes less important), that they have to learn the required skills in school and that formal education is needed to get a job (*arrow c* becomes more important).

2   *Educational expansion.* Modernization also means educational expansion—more and more people attend primary and secondary education and increasingly people obtain university degrees. Education is no longer an exclusive privilege for the higher class but—due to lower school fees—increasingly open to those with lower-class origins (*arrow b* becomes less important). As larger segments of the population become educated, employers are in a stronger position to select employees in terms of their skills and educational qualifications rather than on ascribed characteristics—such as having a high-status origin *(arrow c* becomes more important).

3   *Increasing geographical mobility.* Another societal change associated with moderniza-
    tion is that transport becomes more readily available due to improved infrastructure.
    This results in increasing geographical mobility, opening up opportunities for people
    to find work outside the local community in which they were born and raised. People
    become less and less restricted to following in the footsteps of their parents, inheriting
    their jobs, and they need no longer search in the limited pool of occupations in their com-
    munity. As the market becomes broader in scope, employers are less and less recruiting
    people they know personally—instead they select on skills and talents (*arrow c* becomes
    more important).

For these and other reasons, modernization is expected to change the status attainment process. Let's write down the most general proposition from the modernization and mobility
theory.

> *P.* The more modernized a society, the stronger the impact of achieved characteristics
> and the weaker the impact of ascribed characteristics on labor market position in
> that society. (*modernization and mobility*)

The question, of course, is whether this proposition is true or not. How could you assess
this? Sociologists have come up with various ways to test it. One of these hinges on the
assumption that, *over time*, societies have become more modern—in particular, the Industrial
Revolution is often seen as a major moment in history reflecting accelerated technological
growth and economic development. Consequently, it is expected that, from the 19th century
onwards, we should observe a clear trend in the status attainment process: ascription is
becoming less important whereas achievement is getting more important. Thus, the following
prediction on trends in intergenerational mobility has been derived.

P.	The more modernized a society, the stronger the impact of achieved characteristics and the weaker the impact of ascribed characteristics on labor market position in that society. (*modernization and mobility*)
C.	Industrialization (from the 19th century onwards) has resulted in more modernized societies.

H.	From the 19th century onwards, societies have witnessed a weaker impact of ascribed characteristics and an increasing impact of achieved characteristics on labor market position. (*industrialization and mobility*)

> **Theory schema 9.1** Industrialization and mobility hypothesis derived from modernization and mobility theory.

This so-called ***industrialization and mobility hypothesis*** has been studied in various
countries and findings are mostly in line with it. It has generally been found that, over time,
ascription has become less important whereas achievement has increased in importance from
the 19th century onwards. This conclusion was reached in studies covering various countries,
each of which studied trends in mobility over time and the changing role of ascribed and

achieved characteristics. Examples include studies on Sweden (Breen & Jonsson, 2007), the Netherlands (Graaf & Luijkx, 1992; Knigge et al., 2014), Australia (Marks & Mooi-Reci, 2016) and the US (DiPrete & Grusky, 1990). In line with this, comparative studies covering multiple nations have found that, for the majority of countries, there was a declining impact of social origin on education (Breen, Luijkx, Müller, & Pollak, 2009; Marks, 2014), a smaller influence of origin on occupation (Marks, 2014) and an increasing influence of education on occupation (Marks, 2014). Clearly, the conclusion does not hold for *every country* or for *each specific period* within countries: there are exceptions (Hout & DiPrete, 2006). But as a *general pattern*, the conclusion we can draw is that ascription is becoming less and less important whereas achievement has become more important since the 19th century.

A second way in which sociologists have tested the modernization and mobility theory is to examine more directly the role of macro-level characteristics of modernization. Thus, rather than studying *trends* in ascription and achievement, these studies directly measure the degree of modernization in a country and investigate whether modernization is then associated with the decreasing importance of social origin. If the modernization and mobility theory is true, one should find that higher levels of economic development result in the lower importance of ascription and a growing impact of achievement. Cross-national and over-time comparative studies have indeed found that higher levels of economic development are associated with a lower impact of ascription and a more pronounced role of achievement (Ganzeboom & Treiman, 2007; Sieben & De Graaf, 2001; Yaish & Andersen, 2012).

9.8 Cultural reproduction theory

Although the evidence for the modernization and mobility theory seems convincing, researchers have also pointed out some findings that are not in line with predictions derived from it (Bernardi & Ballarino, 2016; Hout & DiPrete, 2006). Thus, in some countries and time periods, despite modernization (such as increasing levels of economic development and technology), there is no shift from ascription to achievement. These findings need not directly falsify the theory as it might well be the case that other social forces operate at the same time as modernization. If these social processes work in opposite directions then, even if the modernization and mobility theory is true, such counter processes can result in opposite trends and findings.

Are there indeed such counterforces and, if so, which ones? Some scholars have emphasized the role of political regimes and state interventions. Most prominently, it has been posited that countries under socialist or communist rule strongly increase social fluidity and the impact of achievement (Sieben & De Graaf, 2001). This means that if a society transitions from socialism or communism into a liberal democracy, one would expect to see a growing importance of ascription. And if this force is stronger than modernization processes—such as economic development—then over time one may not see a shift from ascription to achievement, despite modernization.

Another counterforce to the process of modernization was suggested by Bourdieu in the 1970s and 1980s in his classic works *Reproduction in Education, Society and Culture* (Bourdieu & Passeron, 1990 [1977]) and *Distinction* (Bourdieu, 2010 [1979]). In these studies, Bourdieu posits the idea that families strive for *status maintenance and distinction*, i.e., higher-class, higher-status families attempt to maintain their high social class and status position (cf. Chapter 6). Thus, when societal changes such as modernization pose a risk to higher-status families, making social origins less important, higher-status families will respond to this by increasing their investments in the education of their children. As education is becoming an increasingly important source of societal success (*arrow c* becomes more important), parents anticipate the potential decline of social origin by making the educational career of their children a success (*arrow b*). Thus, as modernization threatens to erode their high status, parents respond by investing more in the education of their children. Higher-status families can then maintain their high status: by increasing their impact on the education of their children (*arrow b*) they compensate for the loss of the direct impact they might have on the labor market outcomes of their children (*arrow a*).

In what way might higher-status parents be able to realize this? Bourdieu's **cultural repro-**
duction theory emphasizes the (increasing) transmission of *cultural capital* from parents to children. Although scholars have criticized Bourdieu for not providing a clear definition of this concept (Jæger & Breen, 2016), a common and useful way to think about cultural capital is that it refers to resources that come from (1) the affinity with higher status values, beliefs, norms and corresponding practices (e.g., high-status cultural activities like visiting museums) and (2) language competencies. Thus, cultural capital encompasses, first, "good taste": being familiar with the dominant values, ideas and behavior that are assumed to be typical of the school setting. For example, children who have visited museums with their parents, who have been taken to theaters and who have listened to classical music at home are more familiar with a school culture in which such high-status cultural values, norms and behaviors are dominant. But cultural capital also encompasses knowledge and, in particular linguistic competence. Being able to speak and write well in various languages is a key component of cultural capital.

> **compensatory mechanism** strategic behavior of high-status parents to maintain their high status in times of modernization.

According to cultural reproduction theory, cultural capital can act as a **compensatory mechanism**, i.e., the strategic behavior of high-status parents to maintain their high status in times of modernization. Let's review the various propositions contained in cultural reproduction theory in more detail. Figure 9.6 combines Bourdieu's theory with the Blau-Duncan status attainment model.

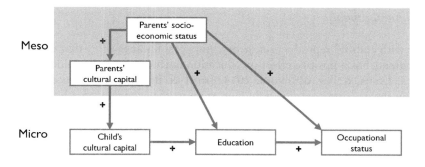

Figure 9.6 Cultural reproduction theory and status attainment.

According to cultural reproduction theory, the following propositions should hold. First, parents who have higher socio-economic status have more cultural capital. This means that parents—and people in general—with higher education, higher income and better-paid jobs tend to have more cultural resources, such that they have greater affinity with higher-status values, beliefs, norms and corresponding practices. They more often engage in high-status cultural activities, like visiting museums, listening to classical music and reading books, as compared with parents who have a lower socio-economic status. This has been confirmed in empirical work (De Graaf, 1986). Let's summarize this proposition.

P. The higher people's socio-economic status, the more cultural capital they will have.

Second, cultural reproduction theory states that parents transmit their cultural capital to their offspring. Parents invest in the cultural capital of their children, realizing that the possession of such resources may work to the advantage of their children in school. But such transmission may also occur less strategically. Parents may enjoy going to museums, for example, and their children may simply copy their behavior and internalize such activities in their preferences. Either way, the theory states that, as higher-status parents possess more cultural capital, their children will have more cultural capital as well. This happens by taking them to museums, theaters, by reading books and so forth. Empirical studies have shown that cultural capital is indeed transmitted from parents to children (Georg, 2004; Jæger & Breen, 2016; Kraaykamp & Van Eijck, 2010; Yaish & Katz-Gerro, 2010). The parent–child transmission of cultural capital can be regarded as a special case of parental transmission and conformity (Chapter 5). The second proposition specifies this social context effect.

P. The more cultural capital parents have, the more cultural capital their children will acquire.

In the third step, cultural reproduction theory proposes a micro-level proposition. It states that the more strongly children are equipped with cultural capital, the better they will perform in school. The idea is that children will transition more easily into the school environment, as they are more familiar with the dominant cultural codes of the school and because of better language skills. Empirical studies tend to support this conjecture, finding that the cultural capital of children has a positive effect on their academic achievement and educational attainment (DiMaggio, 1982; Gaddis, 2013; Jæger & Breen, 2016). This is the so-called ***cultural capital*** proposition.

P. The more cultural capital children possess, the better their educational outcomes. (*cultural capital*)

In line with cultural reproduction theory, empirical findings show that the cultural capital of the parents has a positive effect on education outcomes of their children (Andersen & Jæger, 2015; Evans, Kelley, & Sikora, 2014; Jæger & Breen, 2016). According to cultural reproduction theory, therefore, these findings support the argument that high-status parents are able to maintain their status by investing in the education of their children. Being confronted with a threat to their status, they invest in the cultural capital of their children. They will invest more than ever before in high-status cultural activities that promote their good taste—visiting museums and theaters—as well as their language skills. In doing so, their children will be equipped with much cultural capital, which will bring success in their educational career. In the end, high-status families are thereby able to maintain their high status, namely via (increasing) investments in their children's education.

9.9 The *Great Gatsby* Curve

Increasingly, scholars have become interested in the relationship between the two sub-themes of inequality that I have identified so far, namely: *stratification* and *mobility* (Torche, 2015). The *overall* inequality in a society, so you could say, would be more severe if it is characterized by both (1) high levels of stratification *and* (2) lack of mobility. More egalitarian societies are those with lower levels of stratification and higher levels of mobility. Thus, it is important to find out what the relationship between stratification and mobility might be, if any.

In this context, comtemporary research has discovered an empirical pattern which is called the "Great Gatsby Curve". What does this pattern show? Let's begin with the origins of the name of the curve.

In 1925, the American author F. Scott Fitzgerald published the famous novel *The Great Gatsby*. The title of the book refers to one of the main characters, Jay Gatsby, a millionaire who holds extravagant parties for the upper class. At that time, in the Roaring Twenties, the stratification in the US in terms of wealth was very strong and much of it was in the hands of a small elite. But there was a widespread perception that, if you did your best and worked hard, you could make it. Indeed, this belief was expressed in the novel too. Gatsby, born in a poor family, climbed up the social ladder and eventually became very rich. It represents the American Dream, the idea that *anyone* can get a good job, or even become a millionaire, as long as you do your best and work hard.

Does the American Dream correspond to reality? Are children born in families with lower socio-economic status, such as Gatsby, able to make it to the top? Is intergenerational mobility in the US—as a highly stratified society—different from mobility in Denmark—a country with considerably less stratification? In which country do children from lower-status backgrounds have the most chance to climb up the social ladder and get a high income?

THINKING LIKE A SOCIOLOGIST 9.1

What are your ideas about this? Do you think it is easier in the US to climb the social ladder than in Denmark? Do children from poor families in the US have more opportunities to get a high income than in Denmark? Why (why not)?

One way to answer these questions is to examine social class and occupational groups. Research findings reveal that relative intergenerational class mobility does not differ so much between countries (Erikson & Goldthorpe, 1992). Consequently, scholars have argued that the two sub-dimensions of inequality (stratification and mobility) are not related to each other and that, more generally, intergenerational mobility in social class and occupation is rather similar across societies. But social class and occupational groups are broad aggregate categories and so another way to look at this issue is to focus on income mobility.

Let us take a closer look at this kind of mobility. How strong is intergenerational mobility in income? In order to answer this question, scholars use a specific measure called *intergenerational elasticity* (IGE). Intergenerational elasticity measures the extent to which the relative position of parents in income distribution is a determinant for the relative position of their children in income distribution. The higher the IGE is, the lower the intergenerational mobility in income. If IGE is 0, the income of children is fully independent from that of their parents; if IGE is 1, the relative income position of the children is exactly equal to that of their parents. In other words, higher IGE means that the position of your family is more predictive of your income. If the American Dream is true, IGE should be low in the US and, if there is something distinct about this Dream being typically American, then the IGE should be lower in the US than in, say, Denmark.

What does empirical research find? Figure 9.7 presents IGE estimates for a number of countries. A first observation is that intergenerational income mobility strongly differs across societies (Corak, 2006, 2013). In other words, where you are born matters a great deal for your chances of climbing the social ladder. In some countries, children born in poor families remain so themselves, whereas in other countries, there is much more opportunity for social mobility. To illustrate, let's compare Brazil and Finland. The IGE is 0.52 in Brazil, which means that if the income of a child's parents was 40% higher than the average income of other persons of the same generation as these parents, then the child's income would be 20% (40% x 0.52) higher than that of its own generation. In other words, approximately 50% of the advantage (or disadvantage) of growing up with parents on a high (or low) income is passed on to the next generation in Brazil. In Finland, by contrast, there is much more inter-generational mobility in income. In Finland, children of parents with a 40% higher than aver-age income will have an 8% (40% x 0.20) higher income than that of their own generation.

That intergenerational mobility is higher in Finland than it is in Brazil is in line with a more general pattern discovered by scientists. When you rank the 12 countries in Figure 9.7 in terms of their intergenerational mobility and compare this with their income stratification, you see that in countries with great income stratification between the poor and the rich, social heritage was shown to be *more* determinant for economic success than in countries where such income inequalities are smaller. The correlation between the two variables is 0.90, which means that countries that have higher levels of income stratification tend to have higher levels of intergenerational elasticity (and thus lower levels of intergenerational mobil-ity). The United States is a country with relatively high levels of social stratification and low intergenerational income mobility. In the US, children born in poor families less often climb the social ladder and get a high income than in Denmark and other Scandinavian countries.

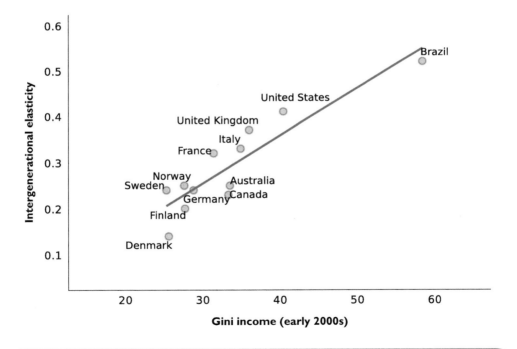

Figure 9.7 Intergenerational elasticity (IGE) and income stratification (Gini) in 12 nations.

Source: IGE (Blanden, 2013); Gini income (World Bank, 2017b).

In other words, if you want to live the American Dream you should move to Denmark or Finland (Wilkinson & Pickett, 2009), where intergenerational mobility is much stronger than in the United States.

In follow-up studies to these, scholars have also used parental education rather than parental income to predict the offspring's earnings. The findings from this work point in the same direction: (1) there is cross-national variation in the degree of intergenerational mobility and (2) countries that have stronger income stratification also have lower levels of intergenerational mobility (Jerrim & Macmillan, 2015). This means that parental education has a stronger impact on children's earnings in countries that have higher levels of income stratification. The exception to the linkage between income stratification and intergenerational mobility appears to be the transition economies (such as Russia, Poland, Czech Republic). When excluding these countries from the analysis, studies using parental background find a correlation coefficient between income stratification and intergenerational mobility of -0.86 (Jerrim & Macmillan, 2015). This empirical pattern—the strong association between income stratification and (lack of) intergenerational mobility—is today known as the *Great Gatsby Curve* (Corak, 2013; Jerrim & Macmillan, 2015), after Fitzgerald's novel.

STYLIZED FACT 9.3

Great Gatsby Curve
In contemporary societies, higher within-country income stratification is associated with lower intergenerational mobility in that country.

The empirical association between stratification and mobility seems paradoxical. Why is the income position of children more strongly associated with that of their parents in countries that have higher levels of income stratification? Why is it more difficult for children from poor families in the US and Brazil to climb the social ladder than for children from poor families in Denmark and Finland? These are important and difficult questions and are the subject of ongoing research. Although there is no definite answer to these questions yet (Gregg, Jonsson, Macmillan, & Mood, 2017), scholars have made the following relevant observations.

First, it has been noted by several scholars that in more stratified countries, a lower proportion of the national wealth goes into education (Jerrim & Macmillan, 2015). In highly stratified countries like the US and, in particular, Brazil, a larger share of children attend a private school and university tuition fees are higher than in more egalitarian countries like Denmark and Sweden.

Second, in more stratified societies, where private education plays a more prominent role and tuition fees are higher, parental financial resources become more important for getting access to education and (prestigious) universities (Jerrim & Macmillan, 2015). Indeed, research findings suggest that when income stratification increases, inequality in parental investments in their children increases as well (Schneider, Hastings, & LaBriola, 2018). In highly-stratified social contexts, the gap between the investments of high-income families and low-income families increases for such things as fees for recreational lessons, student rooms, school meals, books and equipment for school, tuition and childcare (such as costs for babysitting and nannies).

If, in more stratified societies, a larger share of the children attend private education and tuition fees are higher, and parental resources therefore become more important in getting a good education, as research seems to suggest, then it means that in these more stratified societies parental resources may strongly impact one's chances in the labor market. In strongly stratified societies, social origin can still have a major influence on children's position in the labor market, albeit indirectly—via the increasing inequality in financial investments of parents in their children's education.

Thus, as educational attainment becomes the key motor to success in modernizing countries (*achievement*) and thereby potentially reduces the overall impact of family origin (*ascription*), a counterforce emerges in countries that are characterized by high levels of (rising) income stratification. Higher-income families invest more than before in their children's education and, as low-income families do not have the same resources to do so, the result is that social positions are transmitted from generation to generation despite modernization. These insights thereby reveal a different potential counterforce to modernization to the one signaled by cultural reproduction theory. Higher-status families may not only maintain their status by transmitting cultural capital like good taste and language abilities (i.e., cultural resources), they may also invest more than before in the education of their children. In highly stratified societies such as the US and Brazil, higher-status families can use their *financial resources* to get a good education and thus a good job and income for their children.

9.10 Chapter resources

Key concepts

Valuable goods	Gini coefficient	Relative mobility
Between-country stratification	Intergenerational mobility	Ascription
Within-country stratification	Intragenerational mobility	Achievement
Social class	Mobility table	Compensatory mechanism
Social status	Absolute mobility	
Occupational prestige	Structural mobility	

Key theories and propositions

- Modernization and mobility theory
- Industrialization and mobility hypothesis
- Cultural reproduction theory
- Cultural capital.

Key stylized facts

- Treiman constant
- One percent
- Great Gatsby Curve.

Summary

- You can study stratification both between countries (between-country stratification) and within countries (within-country stratification).
- Two bases of social stratification are social class and social status.

- The phenomenon named the one percent reveals that within-country stratification in income and wealth in contemporary societies is highly skewed and much wealth is in the hands of the top 1%.
- Sociologists study two different dimensions of social mobility, namely between generations (intergenerational mobility) and over the life course (intragenerational mobility).
- With a mobility table you can identify patterns of absolute mobility (i.e., total number of positional changes), structural mobility (i.e., the mobility that is due to changes in the volumes of social positions) and relative mobility (i.e., the degree of inequality to move from one social position to another).
- The Blau-Duncan status attainment model of social mobility helps you to distinguish ascription from achievement.
- The modernization and mobility theory posits that modernization results in ascription becoming less important for status attainment and achievement becoming more important.
- The cultural reproduction theory, however, states that modernization leads to counterforces, such that high-status parents (increasingly) transmit their cultural capital to their children. This compensatory mechanism may result in the continuing significance of ascription.
- Growing income stratification since the 1980s may also provide a counterforce to modernization and increasing openness. The Great Gatsby Curve describes the phenomenon that in more stratified societies there is less intergenerational mobility.

References

Alvaredo, F., Chancel, L., Piketty, T., Saez, E., & Zucman, G. (2018). *World inequality report 2018*. Retrieved from https://wir2018.wid.world.

Álvarez-Nogal, C., & De La Escosura, L. P. (2013). The rise and fall of Spain (1270–1850). *The Economic History Review*, 66(1), 1–37.

Andersen, I. G., & Jæger, M. M. (2015). Cultural capital in context: Heterogeneous returns to cultural capital across schooling environments. *Social Science Research*, 50, 177–188.

Antonovsky, A. (1967). Social class, life expectancy and overall mortality. *The Milbank Memorial Fund Quarterly*, 45(2), 31–73.

Arsenio, W. F. (2018). The wealth of nations: International judgments regarding actual and ideal resource distributions. *Current Directions in Psychological Science*, 27(5), 357–362.

Arsenio, W. F., & Willems, C. (2017). Adolescents' conceptions of national wealth distribution: Connections with perceived societal fairness and academic plans. *Developmental Psychology*, 53(3), 463.

Bernardi, F., & Ballarino, G. (Eds.). (2016). *Education, occupation, and social origin*. Cheltenham, UK: Edward Elgar Publishing.

Blanden, J. (2013). Cross-country rankings in intergenerational mobility: A comparison of approaches from economics and sociology. *Journal of Economic Surveys*, 27(1), 38–73.

Blau, P., & Duncan, O. D. (1967). *The American occupational structure*. New York, NY: Free Press.

Bloomberg. (2019). Bloomberg billionaires index. Retrieved from www.bloomberg.com/billionaires.

Bourdieu, P. (2010 [1979]). *Distinction: A social critique of the judgement of taste*. Abingdon, UK: Routledge.

Bourdieu, P., & Passeron, J. (1990 [1977]). *Reproduction in education, society and culture*. London: Sage.

Breen, R., & Jonsson, J. O. (2007). Explaining change in social fluidity: Educational equalization and educational expansion in twentieth-century Sweden. *American Journal of Sociology, 112*(6), 1775–1810.

Breen, R., Luijkx, R., Müller, W., & Pollak, R. (2009). Nonpersistent inequality in educational attainment: Evidence from eight European countries. *American Journal of Sociology, 114*(5), 1475–1521.

Chan, T. W., & Goldthorpe, J. H. (2007). Class and status: The conceptual distinction and its empirical relevance. *American Sociological Review, 72*(4), 512–532.

Corak, M. (2006). Do poor children become poor adults? Lessons from a cross country comparison of generational earnings mobility. In J. Creedy & G. Kalb (Eds.), *Dynamics of Inequality and Poverty* (pp. 143–188). Bingley: Emerald Group Publishing Limited.

Corak, M. (2013). Income inequality, equality of opportunity, and intergenerational mobility. *The Journal of Economic Perspectives, 22*(3), 79–102.

Correll, S. J., & Ridgeway, C. L. (2003). Expectation states theory. In J. Delamater (Ed.), *Handbook of social psychology* (pp. 29–51). New York, NY: Kluwer Academic/Plenum Publishers.

De Graaf, P. M. (1986). The impact of financial and cultural resources on educational attainment in the Netherlands. *Sociology of Education, 59*(4), 237–246.

Deaton, A. (2013). *The great escape: Health, wealth, and the origins of inequality*. Princeton, NJ: Princeton University Press.

DiMaggio, P. (1982). Cultural capital and school success: The impact of status culture participation on the grades of US high school students. *American Sociological Review, 47*(2), 189–201.

DiPrete, T. A., & Grusky, D. B. (1990). Structure and trend in the process of stratification for American men and women. *American Journal of Sociology, 96*(1), 107–143.

Donkin, A., Goldblatt, P., & Lynch, K. (2002). Inequalities in life expectancy by social class, 1972–1999. *Health Statistics Quarterly, 15*(5), 15.

Erikson, R., & Goldthorpe, J. H. (1992). *The constant flux: A study of class mobility in industrial societies*. New York, NY: Oxford University Press.

Eriksson, K., & Simpson, B. (2012). What do Americans know about inequality? It depends on how you ask them. *Judgment and Decision Making, 7*(6), 741–745.

Evans, M. D. R., & Kelley, J. (2017). Communism, capitalism, and images of class: Effects of reference groups, reality, and regime in 43 nations and 110,000 Individuals, 1987–2009. *Cross-Cultural Research, 51*(4), 315–359.

Evans, M. D. R., Kelley, J., & Sikora, J. (2014). Scholarly culture and academic performance in 42 nations. *Social Forces, 92*(4), 1573–1605.

Gaddis, S. M. (2013). The influence of habitus in the relationship between cultural capital and academic achievement. *Social Science Research, 42*(1), 1–13.

Ganzeboom, H. B. G., De Graaf, P. M., & Treiman, D. J. (1992). A standard international socio-economic index of occupational status. *Social Science Research, 21*, 1–56.

Ganzeboom, H. B. G., & Treiman, D. J. (2007). Ascription and achievement in occupational attainment in comparative perspective. Paper presented at *The Sixth Meeting of the Russell Sage Foundation/Carnegie Corporation*, UCLA.

Ganzeboom, H. B. G., Treiman, D. J., & Ultee, W. C. (1991). Comparative intergenerational stratification research: Three generations and beyond. *Annual Review of Sociology, 17*, 277–302.

Georg, W. (2004). Cultural capital and social inequality in the life course. *European Sociological Review, 20*(4), 333–344.

Goldthorpe, J. H. (2010). Analysing social inequality: A critique of two recent contributions from economics and epidemiology. *European Sociological Review, 26*(6), 731–744.

Gould, R. V. (2002). The origins of status hierarchies: A formal theory and empirical test. *American Journal of Sociology, 107*(5), 1143–1178.

Graaf, P. M. D., & Luijkx, R. (1992). Van'ascription'naar'achievement'? Trends in statusverwerving in Nederland Tussen 1930 En 1980. *Mens En Maatschappij, 67*(4), 412–433.

Gregg, P., Jonsson, J. O., Macmillan, L., & Mood, C. (2017). The role of education for intergenerational income mobility: A comparison of the United States, Great Britain, and Sweden. *Social Forces, 96*(1), 121–152.

Grusky, D. B. (2001). The past, present, and future of social inequality. In D. B. Grusky (Ed.), *Social stratification in sociological perspective: Class, race & gender* (2nd ed., pp. 1–51). Boulder, CO: Westview Press.

Hagerty, M. R., & Veenhoven, R. (2003). Wealth and happiness revisited–Growing national income does go with greater happiness. *Social Indicators Research, 64*(1), 1–27.

Hardoon, D. (2017). An economy for the 99%: Oxfam briefing paper. Retrieved from https://oxf.am/2FOD0hK

Helliwell, J. F., Layard, R., & Sachs, J. D. (2018). World happiness report. Retrieved from https://s3.amazonaws.com/happiness-report/2018/WHR_web.pdf

Hodge, R. W., Siegel, P. M., & Rossi, P. H. (1964). Occupational prestige in the United States, 1925–63. *American Journal of Sociology, 70*(3), 286–302.

Hout, M., & DiPrete, T. A. (2006). What we have learned: RC28's contributions to knowledge about social stratification. *Research in Social Stratification and Mobility, 24*(1), 1–20.

Jæger, M. M., & Breen, R. (2016). A dynamic model of cultural reproduction. *American Journal of Sociology, 121*(4), 1079–1115.

Jerrim, J., & Macmillan, L. (2015). Income inequality, intergenerational mobility, and the Great Gatsby Curve: Is education the key? *Social Forces, 94*(2), 505–533.

Keister, L. A. (2014). The one percent. *Annual Review of Sociology, 40*, 347–367.

Knigge, A., Maas, I., Van Leeuwen, M. H., & Mandemakers, K. (2014). Status attainment of siblings during modernization. *American Sociological Review, 79*(3), 549–574.

Kraaykamp, G., & Van Eijck, K. (2010). The intergenerational reproduction of cultural capital: A threefold perspective. *Social Forces, 89*(1), 209–231.

Lynch, J., Smith, G. D., Harper, S. A., Hillemeier, M., Ross, N., Kaplan, G. A., & Wolfson, M. (2004). Is income inequality a determinant of population health? Part 1. A systematic review. *Milbank Quarterly, 82*(1), 5–99.

Marks, G. N. (2014). *Education, social background and cognitive ability: The decline of the social*. Abingdon: Routledge.

Marks, G. N., & Mooi-Reci, I. (2016). The declining influence of family background on educational attainment in Australia: The role of measured and unmeasured influences. *Social Science Research, 55*, 171–185.

Marx, K. (2008 [1867]). *Capital [Das Kapital]*. New York, NY: Oxford University Press.

Marx, K., & Engels, F. (2002 [1847]). *The communist manifesto*. London, UK: Penguin Books Ltd.

Milanovic, B. (2016). *Global inequality: A new approach for the age of globalization*. Cambridge, MA: Harvard University Press.

Nakao, K., & Treas, J. (1994). Updating occupational prestige and socioeconomic scores: How the new measures measure up. *Sociological Methodology, 24*, 1–72.

Norton, M. I., & Ariely, D. (2011). Building a better America-one wealth quintile at a time. *Perspectives on Psychological Science, 6*(1), 9–12.

Norton, M. I., Neal, D. T., Govan, C. L., Ariely, D., & Holland, E. (2014). The not-so-common-wealth of Australia: Evidence for a cross-cultural desire for a more equal distribution of wealth. *Analyses of Social Issues and Public Policy, 14*(1), 339–351.

Pál, J., Stadtfeld, C., Grow, A., & Takács, K. (2016). Status perceptions matter: Understanding disliking among adolescents. *Journal of Research on Adolescence*, 26(4), 805–818.

Pickett, K. E., & Wilkinson, R. G. (2015). Income inequality and health: A causal review. *Social Science & Medicine*, 128, 316–326.

Piketty, T. (2014). *Capital in the twenty-first century*. Cambridge, MA: Harvard University Press.

Pinker, S. (2018). *Enlightenment now: The case for reason, science, humanism, and progress*. New York, NY: Penguin Books.

Preston, S. H. (1975). The changing relation between mortality and level of economic development. *Population Studies*, 29(2), 231–248.

Ridgeway, C. L. (2014). Why status matters for inequality. *American Sociological Review*, 79(1), 1–16.

Rosling, H., Rosling, O., & Rosling Ronnlund, A. (2018). *Factfulness*. London, UK: Sceptre.

Sacks, D. W., Stevenson, B., & Wolfers, J. (2012). The new stylized facts about income and subjective well-being. *Emotion*, 12(6), 1181.

Scheidel, W. (2017). *The great leveler: Violence and the history of inequality from the stone age to the twenty-first century*. Princeton, NJ: Princeton University Press.

Schneider, D., Hastings, O. P., & LaBriola, J. (2018). Income inequality and class divides in parental investments. *American Sociological Review*, 83(3), 475–507.

Sherif, M., Harvey, O. J., White, B. J., Hood, W. R., & Sherif, C. W. (1961). *Intergroup conflict and cooperation: The Robbers Cave Experiment*. Norman, OK: University Book Exchange.

Sieben, I., & De Graaf, P. M. (2001). Testing the modernization hypothesis and the socialist ideology hypothesis: A comparative sibling analysis of educational attainment and occupational status. *The British Journal of Sociology*, 52(3), 441–467.

Torche, F. (2015). Analyses of intergenerational mobility: An interdisciplinary review. *The Annals of the American Academy of Political and Social Science*, 657(1), 37–62.

Treiman, D. J. (1970). Industrialization and social stratification. *Sociological Inquiry*, 40(2), 207–234.

Treiman, D. J. (1976). A standard occupational prestige scale for use with historical data. *The Journal of Interdisciplinary History*, 7(2), 283–304.

Treiman, D. J. (1977). *Occupational prestige in comparative perspective*. New York, NY: Academic Press.

Weber, M. (1978 [1922]). *Economy and society: An outline of interpretive sociology*. Oakland, CA: University of California Press.

Whelan, C. T., & Layte, R. (2002). Late industrialization and the increased merit selection hypothesis: Ireland as a test case. *European Sociological Review*, 18(1), 35–50.

Wilkinson, R., & Pickett, K. (2009). *The spirit level: Why more equal societies almost always do better*. London: Allen Lane.

World Bank. (2017a). GDP per capita, PPP. Retrieved from https://data.worldbank.org/indicator/NY.GDP.PCAP.CD?year_high_desc=true

World Bank. (2017b). GINI index. Retrieved from https://data.worldbank.org

World Population Review. (2017). Life expectancy by country. Retrieved from http://worldpopulationreview.com/countries/life-expectancy-by-country/

Yaish, M., & Andersen, R. (2012). Social mobility in 20 modern societies: The role of economic and political context. *Social Science Research*, 41(3), 527–538.

Yaish, M., & Katz-Gerro, T. (2010). Disentangling 'cultural capital': The consequences of cultural and economic resources for taste and participation. *European Sociological Review*, 28(2), 169–185.

Chapter 10

Resources

Chapter overview

How can we understand inequality in the labor market? Why do, for example, men have more prestigious jobs than women? In this chapter I will review the role of various types of "resources" or "capital" in the labor market. I will begin with human capital theory, which emphasizes the importance of "what you can do," i.e., your skills and knowledge (10.1). Then I will discuss social capital theories, which instead argue that what matters is "who you know" (10.2). Subsequently, I will address the idea that "who you belong to," your group affiliation, is key, because of discrimination in the labor market (10.3). After having discussed these three types of resources (human capital, social capital and group affiliation), I will show how they help us in understanding why someone's social background (e.g., gender, ethnic group, neighborhood) is related to inequalities in the labor market (10.4). I will illustrate this, in more detail, for gender inequality (10.5).

> ## Learning goals
>
> After reading this chapter, check if you are able to:
>
> - Describe how various resources can explain inequality in the labor market.
> - Describe and apply human capital theory.
> - Describe and apply various social capital theories.
> - Describe statistical and taste-based discrimination.
> - Relate inequality of outcomes to inequality of opportunity and inequality of returns.
> - Give various explanations for gender inequality.

10.1 Human capital

What plays a role in finding a new job? How do you get a good job? Why do some people get prestigious jobs and earn a lot, whereas others have low-paid jobs or remain unemployed? How can we understand inequality in the labor market? Blau and Duncan, as we have seen (Chapter 9), argued that someone's family origin plays a role (Blau & Duncan, 1967). If your parents have a higher socio-economic status, then it is more likely that you will find your way more easily into the labor market. One reason for this, so Blau and Duncan showed, is that children from higher socio-economic-status parents get more education. Having more education, in turn, helps you in finding a (good) job in the labor market.

In follow-up studies to the seminal work of Blau and Duncan, scholars have looked more in depth into the causes of inequalities in the labor market. What these studies have in common is that they point to the role of various "resources" or "capital" that help people to obtain their desired position in the labor market. In the Blau-Duncan model, "education" is such a resource: if you possess "more" of it, if you have obtained a university degree, for example, then you are more likely to get a high-status, high-paid job. Whoever possesses "more" of a certain resource has better chances in the labor market. There are various types of resources or capital and in this chapter we will review them one by one.

Let's begin with the resource called "human capital." When Blau and Duncan examined the impact of education on labor market outcomes, they were looking into the role of what is today called **human capital** or "human resources" (Becker, 1964). Human capital refers to people's knowledge and skills insofar as these are relevant to the labor market. In other words, whoever possesses a lot of relevant knowledge and skills will quickly find a job and earn a great deal of money. In contemporary industrialized societies, people acquire much of their knowledge and skills in (formal) education. It is in school that

> **human capital** people's knowledge and skills insofar as these are relevant to the labor market.

people acquire all types of knowledge and learn skills that are relevant for the labor market. Consequently, those who have spent more time in education and who have attained higher grades and credentials are typically seen as more attractive workers by potential employers.

Employers seek candidates for new positions within their company and they are primarily interested in candidates with the most human capital. With the right knowledge and skills employees are very well able to carry out their duties, to perform properly and to be productive, and that is good for the company. They are attractive to employers who, after all, are competing with other employers and their companies. Employers are looking for candidates who have the best knowledge and skills for the vacant position, for that would mean a very efficient employee and high labor productivity. How do employers know which employees have the most relevant knowledge and skills? An important source of information for employers is the candidate's resume. Whoever applies for a job is often asked to enclose their resume, which briefly describes the knowledge and skills the candidate possesses. The employer compares the resumes of the candidates that have applied and will use them to select the most suitable applicants for an interview. Someone's educational credentials provide clear signals for an employer on what kind of knowledge and skills a candidate has acquired.

The *human capital theory*, developed by economist Becker, argued that, precisely because education is a "resource" or "capital," and it is such an important determinant for getting a (good) job in the labor market, people deliberately make investments in their educational resources (Becker, 1964). In the Blau–Duncan status attainment model, as we have seen, someone's educational level was argued to depend on parents' socio-economic status. In the human capital theory, educational outcomes are regarded as a decision made by individuals who have "agency." The decision is based on weighing costs and benefits of educational investments. On the one hand, getting more education pays off in the labor market in terms of prestige and earnings. These are long-term gains. On the other hand, however, education is costly; there may be tuition fees and while you are in education you cannot work a lot (these are called "opportunity costs"). If people think that long-term benefits of educational investments outweigh the costs, so human capital theory argues, people are more likely to make such investments.

Education is thus an important human resource for getting ahead in the labor market because it increases someone's productivity. But the human capital theory posits that someone's productivity depends on more than education. Most prominently, *work experience* and *health* are also seen as important. Relevant knowledge and skills are often acquired in the workplace, during an internship or on a course taken in regular employment. This is referred to as on-the-job training: people learn in practice. Within an organization, people learn how to perform in a team and they acquire the specific skills needed within the company. Furthermore, personal health can affect someone's productivity as individuals suffering from mental or physical problems may not be able to work efficiently, or as efficiently as they could without such health problems. According to the theory, the human capital of potential candidates is a function of their *education, work experience* and *health* (Card, 1999; Mincer, 1974, 1958). These are the main human capital ingredients on which employers in industrialized societies base their selection of candidates and assess their productivity. The *human capital and job outcomes* proposition can be summarized as follows:

> P. The higher people's human capital, the better their labor market position. (*human capital and job outcomes*)

The human capital and job outcomes proposition is a proposition at the micro level. The importance of human capital is often acknowledged in sociological studies, and is used as a starting point for research looking into the role social contexts play in labor market inequalities. Human capital can be conceived as an individual resource but, as you will see, getting a (good) job also depends on resources that are more socially embedded.

10.2 Social capital

Whereas human capital theory focuses on the role of your personal skills and resources, on "what you can do," social capital theories instead consider the influence of social contexts, on "who you know." In Chapter 7 (Networks) we have reviewed various social capital theories that argue that social networks can have important consequences for various outcomes: social norms, trust, health and well-being. Scholars have also proposed social capital theories which relate social networks to labor market outcomes. Let's review three prominent social capital theories which did exactly that and which find their origins in the work of (1) Mark Granovetter (1973, 1974, 1985), (2) Ronald Burt (1992, 2005, 2010) and (3) Nan Lin (1999, 2001; Lin, Cook, & Burt, 2001; Lin & Erickson, 2008).

Granovetter's theory: strong and weak ties

A starting point of social capital theories on labor market outcomes is the seminal work of Mark Granovetter. In 1974 he published the highly acclaimed book *Getting a Job: A Study of Contacts and Careers* (Granovetter, 1974). A key question of this study, as the title indicates, is to find out how people get their jobs and whether social contacts play a role therein. If contacts such as friends and acquaintances somehow influence who gets a job, then this would question some of the hidden assumptions of human capital theory. Specifically, human capital theory regards the labor market as a "matching" process between employers and possible candidates, in which the employers post vacancies and candidates go through the vacancies and apply for those they consider attractive to them. This view implicitly assumes that employers and candidates have comprehensive information on candidates and vacancies, respectively, and that people use only *formal methods* such as advertisements to find jobs. Thus, according to theory, employers post vacancies and candidates respond to these advertisements.

But what about reality? Granovetter wanted to find out and so he interviewed 282 employees in Newton (Massachusetts, United States). Granovetter asked these workers how they had found their jobs. Did they use formal methods such as advertisements or did some of them also find their jobs using personal connections, i.e., *informal methods*? Table 10.1 presents the results of his study. His research showed that only 19% of the jobs had been found through *formal* channels, for instance by responding to advertisements or through employment agencies. More than 55% of the respondents in his study had acquired the job via *informal* channels, such as family members, friends and acquaintances. Another 19% had found their job via direct application, so without using personal connections or advertisements. All in all, the results of Granovetter's study suggested that personal networks are important for finding a job.

The study by Granovetter was reasonably small scale (only 282 employees participated) and only conducted among specific job groups ("professional," "technical" and "managerial workers"). A key question therefore concerns external validity (Chapter 3): should we take his study as being representative for the United States? The various replication studies that have been conducted since Granovetter's study, and which relied on larger and more representative samples, have revealed that informal methods are indeed important in finding a job. In a second edition of the original publication, which appeared in 1994, Granovetter reviewed 20 years of follow-up studies to his 1974 work, covering such nations as the US, UK, Japan and Germany. He concludes that around 30–50% of the jobs in these and other highly developed nations were found via informal channels (Granovetter, 2018). A great

Table 10.1 How did people find their job? Results from the Granovetter 1974 study.

Method	Definition	%
Formal means	Use of impersonal intermediary (advertisements, employment agencies, etc.)	18.8
Personal contacts	Some individual is known personally to the respondent, with whom that person originally became acquainted in some context unrelated to a search for job information, from whom that person has found out about the new job or who recommended that person to someone who then contacted that person.	55.7
Direct application	One who goes to or writes directly to a firm.	18.8
Other		6.7

Source: Granovetter, 1974.

number of languages even have a specific word for the role that family and other social ties play in finding jobs, such as *guanxi* in Chinese (Bian, 1997) and *wasta* in Arabic (Murphy, 2012). Apparently, the conclusion is that the labor market is not simply a matching process whereby candidates respond to formal vacancies. Instead, social networks (family, friends and so forth) play a key role in finding jobs. *Informal job finding* is thus a stylized fact.

 STYLIZED FACT 10.1

Informal job finding
In highly developed nations, a considerable share of the jobs (30–50%) are found informally, via friends, family, acquaintances and other social ties.

Granovetter looked more deeply into the finding that so many jobs are actually found via personal networks. Intuitively, you may be tempted to think that most jobs are found via friends or other close ties. But Granovetter empirically verified whether this is indeed the case. He asked his respondents who their social connections were, via whom they had acquired the job. A surprising outcome of Granovetter's (1974) study was that the respondents had found relatively few jobs through their *strong* connections and actually quite often through their *weak* connections. To be precise: of all the jobs that were found through informal channels, a mere 17% had found a job through contacts that they often met (i.e., at least twice a week), 56% through contacts that they met occasionally (at least once a year) and 28% through contacts that they rarely saw (less than once a year). Therefore, the *weaker ties*—acquaintances and other persons with whom people rarely have contact—were somehow more "useful" to jobseekers than their *strong ties*—best friends and family. Let's summarize this stylized fact, *jobs via weak ties*.

STYLIZED FACT 10.2

Jobs via weak ties

People more often find a job via one of their weaker ties than via one of their stronger ties.

Why is that? Why are you more likely to find a job via one of your *weaker* connections than via one of your *stronger* connections? Granovetter believed that this has to do with weak ties having more relevant job information than strong ties. Weak ties, as we have seen (Chapter 7), are more likely to create a bridge to other communities than strong ties (Granovetter, 1973, 1974). Thus, a weaker tie more often connects someone to a cluster of personal ties to whom the person (ego) has no direct ties. Weak ties could then potentially be very useful, as they can give ego novel and important information on relevant jobs. Figure 10.1 illustrates how this works.

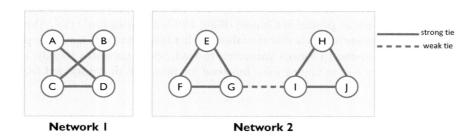

Network 1   Network 2

strong tie
weak tie

Figure 10.1 Illustration of the role of strong ties and weak ties.

The relationship of person G to person I can be valuable for persons G and I. This weak tie provides a bridge to another community and such community-bridging ties give access to job information that is *less likely to be obtained already* via the connections people have in their own community. Information acquired via weaker ties is, therefore, probably unique and highly valuable. Job information acquired via strong ties, however, is often not so useful according to Granovetter. The information your friends may give you about jobs circulates in the friendship network because of high local clustering (transitivity): your friends are often befriended as well. This means that the information they share with you will greatly overlap.

For example, look at Figure 10.1 again and suppose you are person G. Your friend E may have a suggestion for a job for you, but chances are high that your friend F comes up with more or less the same suggestion, because your friends E and F know each other and share information. Granovetter says that the information obtained through strong ties is often *redundant* and hence less useful. Thus, from the strength-of-weak-ties proposition, which states that weaker ties often create bridges to other communities, Granovetter infers that such weaker ties can be more useful as they generate information advantages. We can summarize this ***weak ties and job information*** proposition as follows:

> P. Weaker ties have more useful, less redundant job information than strong ties. (*weak ties and job information*)

The presumed link between tie strength and job information seems like a plausible explanation for the observation that people more often find a job via one of their weaker ties than via one of their stronger ties. However, we should realize that this is a possible explanation. We cannot infer from the fact that people often find jobs via weaker ties that this is *because* weaker ties have more useful information. A stylized fact needs to be considered here: people have only a few strong ties and many more weak ties (Chapter 7). People's strong tie network consists of roughly five alters if you look at the core network, or 15 alters if you take in the sympathy network. But people's *overall* network includes roughly 500 persons, which means that most of our connections are "weak ties." By pure chance you would therefore expect to see that people more often hear about new jobs via one of their numerous weaker ties than via their few stronger ties.

The key question, then, is: what are the odds of finding a job via a *single* weak tie as compared with a *single* strong tie? Say if you were to compare one of your friends with someone you have met only a few times, via whom are you more likely to find a job? Recent studies have used data from Facebook to answer this question, finding that a *single* strong tie is more important in getting a job than a *single* weak tie (Gee, Jones, & Burke, 2017; Gee, Jones, Fariss, Burke, & Fowler, 2017). These studies suggest that although people more often find a job via one of their weaker ties than via one of their stronger ties (in line with the stylized fact ***jobs via weak ties***), this empirical pattern does not arise because each weak tie is more valuable than each strong tie. They are just more numerous.

The finding that a single strong tie is more valuable for finding a job than a single weak tie does not necessarily refute Granovetter's claim that strong ties provide redundant job information more often than weaker ties. It is still very possible that Granovetter's *weak ties and job information* proposition is right—that strong ties more often provide redundant information than weaker ties. To explain this puzzle we need to consider that when we compare strong ties and weak ties what matters is not only the job information they possess. It may indeed be the case that a typical strong tie has less useful job information than a typical weak tie, but this "information disadvantage" can be compensated for in other ways. There may be one or more *counterforce(s)* at work in the opposite direction to offset the information disadvantage of strong ties.

One such counterforce was mentioned by Granovetter himself: strong ties are more "motivated to help" each other than weaker ties (Granovetter, 1974). Thus, your best friends are more willing to help you in finding a job than someone else you barely know. Friends and other close ties in your personal network may put more effort in to searching for appropriate jobs and share their information with you than weaker ties.

Furthermore, people have (by definition) more frequent contacts with strong ties, which create more opportunities to share information. Granovetter argued that the information advantage of weak ties would offset their lower willingness to help and the fewer opportunities to share information. It turns out that this is probably not the case: even if strong ties tend to have redundant information more often, a single strong tie is more important than a single weak tie and this is probably because they are more willing to help and see each other more often. This is what I call the ***strong ties and job outcomes*** proposition.

> P. A single strong tie is more important in getting a job than a single weak tie. (*strong ties and job outcomes*)

Burt's theory: structural holes

Ronald Burt (1992, 2005, 2010) elaborated on the theoretical and empirical work of Granovetter. Key concepts in his writing on social capital are "structural holes" and "brokerage." To understand the meaning of these concepts, consider again Figure 10.1. According to Burt, a structural hole exists between the community consisting of EFG and the community HIJ. There is a **structural hole** because there are few links between these two different communities. Compare this with the community consisting of ABCD. In this clique there are no structural holes, no missing connections that could have been there. Everyone is connected to everyone else and the network is closed.

> **structural hole** social network characteristic which refers to the lack of social ties between communities.

Why would structural holes matter for understanding inequalities in the labor market? Burt argues that in organizational contexts structural holes play a role in someone's earnings, promotion chances and so forth. Specifically, he states that people who are located in the social network of an organization as the *brokers*, the people who link separated communities and who are therefore able to "over-

> **brokerage** network position which connects (otherwise disconnected) communities.

come" the structural hole between these communities, are in a strategically advantageous position, which gives them favorable prospects. To illustrate, in Figure 10.1 person G is a broker, as G connects EF with HIJ. Such a **brokerage** position gives control and information advantages. Suppose E and F want to do business with HIJ, but they don't know them personally. The only way to do business is via the help of G, which gives G more control and power. Furthermore, elaborating on Granovetter's ideas, Burt argues that brokerage may also give information advantage. The connections G has to HIJ gives novel, interesting information which G did not receive yet via E and F. G is therefore exposed to a more diverse set of ideas and opinions than someone who is embedded in a closed network, such as E and F, and certainly everyone in the clique ABCD. We can summarize the ***brokerage and job outcomes*** proposition as follows.

> *P.* People who have a brokerage position in the social network of an organization have more favorable job outcomes. (*brokerage and job outcomes*)

In line with hypotheses derived from this proposition, Burt (1992, 2005, 2010) finds that brokerage is associated with favorable job outcomes, such as higher earnings and promotion.

In one of his studies, Burt takes a closer look at the information advantage, which is a mechanism underlying the link between brokerage and economic outcomes (Burt, 2004). If brokers do indeed have an information advantage, so Burt reasoned, it should mean that they have better ideas and more creative solutions than people who are embedded in a closed network. Being regularly exposed to diverse opinions gives brokers this information advantage. To test this idea, Burt asked a group of 673 managers who ran the supply chain in 2001 for one of America's largest electronics companies. Using social network techniques, Burt measured for each of these managers their network position in their organization, enabling him to identify who are the brokers. He then asked each manager "from your perspective, what is the one thing that you would change to improve [the company's] supply-chain management?" The survey elicited 455 ideas.

Burt handed over these ideas to two senior managers, who were asked to evaluate them independently. The judges did not know the source of the ideas as the ideas were made anonymous to them. Both judges had to rate, on a five-point scale, how much value could be generated if the idea was well executed. In line with Burt's theory, the study found that managers who are in a brokerage position came up with more valuable ideas. The ideas of managers who were more embedded in a closed network were more often dismissed by both judges (Burt, 2004).

Lin's theory: social resources

A third prominent social capital theory which links social networks to inequalities in the labor market was developed by Nan Lin (1999, 2001; Lin et al., 2001; Lin & Erickson, 2008). Lin considered the role of **social resources**, which in this context refers to valuable labor-market-related resources that are embedded in personal networks. These are all kinds of resources relevant for getting ahead in the labor market. Granovetter, as we have seen, argued that the job information of your connections is a very important resource (Granovetter, 1974). Lin and others have argued that social connections may also possess other resources relevant to the labor market. For example, friends may help with writing a good application letter and they may know how to present in a job interview (Aguilera & Massey, 2003). Furthermore, your connections may persuade employers or committee members to hire you or they may put in a good word for you. Thus, social ties may be useful for getting ahead in the labor market because of their knowledge of job vacancies, their information about the hiring process and the influence they can exert on the hiring procedure. We can write down Lin's *social resources and job outcomes* proposition as follows:

social resources valuable labor-market-related resources that are embedded in personal networks.

> *P*. The more people's social resources, the better their labor market position. (*social resources and job outcomes*)

According to Lin, individuals differ in their social resources (Lin, 2000). Some have an extensive network of friends, family members and acquaintances and are connected to people who have important job positions and labor market information, whereas others may have a smaller network and not know so many people who can help them in getting ahead in the labor market. To capture the concept of social resources, Lin developed a measure which is called the **position generator** (Lin & Dumin, 1986). This measure is constructed by presenting respondents with a list of occupations, ranging from high-status to low-status jobs. Respondents are then asked to indicate whether any of their relatives, friends or acquaintances have such an occupation. The idea behind this procedure is that if someone knows many people across the list of occupations shown to them, then that person has a large network of people who possess useful social resources.

position generator measure of social resources which captures the occupational positions of respondents' connections.

In his pioneering study on a sample of 399 males aged 20–64 in the New York area in 1975, Lin presented respondents with a list of 20 occupations (Lin & Dumin, 1986). Table 10.2 shows this list of occupations—ranked by occupational status—and how many respondents had access to them via their social network. For example, 45% of the respondents knew someone in their social network who was a lawyer. Lin and his colleagues discovered that, on average, the respondents had access to 8.5 out of the 20 occupations, but there was also considerable variation around this average; some people knew a considerable number of people having such occupations whereas others hardly did so. This,

Table 10.2 Access to occupations through social ties; New York, 1975.

Occupation	Socioeconomic status score	% access
Lawyer	92	45
Engineer	87	45
Manager	75	34
Department head	71	51
Insurance agent	66	44
Small business owner	62	54
Secretary	62	52
Union official	60	29
Foreman	50	48
Salesman	49	40
Office machine operator	45	26
Office clerk	44	50
Teacher	44	49
Skilled worker	44	58
Mechanic	27	48
Machinist	21	39
Guard	18	23
Waiter	17	37
Janitor	13	27
Laborer	8	55

Source: Lin & Dumin, 1986.

then, is seen as an indicator of social resources; those who personally know more people with (high-status) occupations have more social resources.

Having developed a measure of social resources using the position generator, the next step is to examine whether people who possess many social resources subsequently do better in the labor market. A large literature of empirical studies has emerged since the seminal work of Nan Lin in the 1970s, in which the impact of social resources on labor market positions, such as in getting a job and acquiring higher-status occupations, was examined. Studies have been conducted in a wide range of countries, such as China (Bian, 1997; Shen & Bian, 2018), Taiwan (Chen, 2009), United States (Mouw, 2003), Australia (Huang & Western, 2011), Belgium (Verhaeghe, Van der Bracht, & Van de Putte, 2015) and Chile (Contreras, Otero, Díaz, & Suárez, 2019), to name only a few. Although many studies do indeed find support for the social resource proposition (Lin, 1999), some findings do not show the presumed positive effect of social resources on labor market outcomes (Mouw, 2003). The merits and evidence for the social resource proposition are still a topic of discussion (Chen & Volker, 2016; Flap & Volker, 2004; Hsung, Lin, & Breiger, 2009; Lin, 1999; Lin & Erickson, 2008; Lin, Fu, & Chen, 2014).

The position generator is not the only measure used to capture social resources. Another way of measuring social resources is to consider the resources embedded in people's strong ties. People more often interact with their spouse and close friends than with people they know less well and such strong ties are also more willing to share information and to help you. Strong ties may therefore provide important social resources. However, individuals differ in how resourceful their strong ties are. As an indicator of their resources, scholars often consider two characteristics: (1) level of education and (2) employment position. Friends and a partner who have received more education and who are employed and occupy high-status positions have more valuable resources related to the labor market than friends and a partner who have received little education, who are unemployed and/or who have low-status jobs. For example, if someone has predominantly unemployed friends, that person will lack social resources that can help in receiving important information on jobs or contacts that can exert some influence on the hiring procedure. In line with social resource theory, a number of studies find that people who have a partner and close friends who are higher-educated and more economically resourceful have better chances in the labor market (Bernardi, 1999; Bernasco, De Graaf, & Ultee, 1998; Blossfeld & Drobnic, 2001; Rözer & Brashears, 2018; Verbakel & De Graaf, 2008, 2009).

10.3 Group affiliation and discrimination

We have seen so far that scholars explain inequalities in the labor market with two types of resources, namely *human capital* ("what you can do") and *social capital* ("who you know"). The third type of resource considers group affiliation ("who you belong to"). People belong to groups, i.e., social categories like ethnic groups, religion, gender and age. Group affiliation can be thought of as a resource—or barrier—for getting ahead. Group affiliation can become a source of inclusion and exclusion in the labor market when employers rely on group affiliation to make decisions about hiring, promotion and so forth. We speak of **labor market discrimination** to signal employers' unequal treatment of individuals with the same human capital, based on their group affiliation. If we mention the word discrimination we are always talking about behavior, in this case the behavior of employers who do, or do not, invite someone to an interview or hire someone. In other words, discrimination is not about what people think, experience, feel or want; it is always about behavior. Labor market discrimination is about decisions made by employers *not* based on human capital characteristics—which may be regarded as very legitimate reasons to select candidates.

> **labor market discrimination** employer's unequal treatment of individuals with the same human capital, based on their group affiliation.

Labor market discrimination may have various causes. One prominent cause is called *taste-based discrimination* (Becker, 2010), emphasizing that employers prefer in-group members above out-group members. This cause of discrimination is strongly related to the broader human tendency called *in-group favoritism*, reviewed in Chapter 8. People have more positive views about, and social ties with, their own group and more negative attitudes towards and ties to other groups, and this impacts the decisions that people—including employers—make. Employers prefer to hire in-group members because they have more positive in-group attitudes in general; they trust in-group members more and they have more ties to them. Variations in the *degree* of in-group favoritism, as we have seen, can be explained with group threat theory (Chapter 8). This means that if employers strongly perceive certain out-groups to be threatening to their own group's cultural and economic interests, they will discriminate against members of these out-groups more strongly.

The mechanism of taste-based discrimination may also work in other ways, however. Employers may act on the grounds of discrimination by their employees (*co-worker discrimination*). If, for instance, the employees dislike Black people and hiring Black people would lead to unrest in the workplace, employers may be taking this into account in their selection policy. But an employer may also consider in-group preferences among the company's customers (*customer discrimination*). If customers are, for instance, racist and would hesitate in buying a TV set from a Black salesman, the employer may decide not to hire Black people for that reason. Especially for jobs with frequent contact with clients, this could be an important mechanism for discrimination. In other words, taste-based discrimination can arise from employers' in-group favoritism, but also from that of their employees or customers.

Another perspective on discrimination comes from *statistical discrimination theory* (Phelps, 1972). This theory argues that discrimination arises from *poor information* that employers have when it comes to the candidates' knowledge and skills. If employers had access to all the information about the productivity of all the candidates, discrimination would not occur. The problem is that, in reality, employers have little information about the potential employees' abilities. In their search for candidates with the most human capital, employers have to make do with the information included in the resume or provided in the interview with the candidate. This information provides some insight into what candidates should be able to do, but a resume of a few pages only gives limited insight into what they can actually do in practice. A cover letter or a reference from someone else helps acquire more information, but still the information that employers have on their candidates remains incomplete. They can never be sure about the candidates' abilities.

To better estimate abilities, so statistical discrimination theory argues, employers use the (perceived) characteristics of the group to which a candidate belongs—such as age, sex, religion or ethnic and racial group. If a candidate is an older woman, and the employer believes that older people and women are generally less productive than youngsters and men, this information about the groups to which the candidate belongs may be used to gauge the candidate: "this older woman will not be very productive." According to the statistical discrimination theory, such group-based inferences about individual productivity explain the occurrence of discrimination. Employers, who cannot be sure about the candidates' true productivity, use information about the (perceived) average productivity of the relevant groups (meso level) in order to better gauge the productivity of the individual candidate (micro level). Perceptions of group-level productivity are based on the human capital composition of the group, such as average education, language proficiency and health.

Irrespective of its precise causes—taste-based or statistical—scholars have pointed out that discrimination may occur in various stages of someone's career (Blank, Dabady, & Citro, 2004). We use the term **cumulative discrimination** to indicate that members of a certain group are discriminated against at multiple transitions over their life course. Women, for instance, can be discriminated against at the "first transition," the job application stage, when they receive fewer invitations for a job interview than their male counterparts. Discrimination can also occur later, however. Say that some women do receive invitations for job interviews, but they are then rejected more often than men with an equal amount of human capital. This is also discrimination, but then at the job entry stage. Discrimination can also occur within organizations, for instance if men are awarded more permanent contracts than women, are offered higher salaries, receive more bonuses, get promoted sooner, have better secondary work conditions, etc. This is the job mobility stage.

cumulative discrimination discrimination that occurs in multiple transitions in the life course.

Discrimination can have negative consequences for labor market integration; it can hamper someone's occupational career. When someone is systematically less often invited for job interviews and rejected more often in interviews because of group affiliation, that person has to compensate for this by applying more often. Consequently, repeated discrimination means that someone has longer periods of job search and job inactivity. The prolonged period of inactivity and unemployment is itself an increasing risk for further unemployment (Heckman & Borjas, 1980), as employers may perceive this as a lack of productivity, effort and quality. And suffering from many rejections can also discourage people from making further efforts (Loury, 2009). They may decide not to send application letters any more, or send fewer, and they may invest less in their human capital. As a consequence, they will become less attractive to employers—a negative feedback spiral has emerged. Furthermore, there can be spillover effects across domains (Blank et al., 2004). For instance, if members from a certain group are discriminated against in the housing and credit market, it can reduce their opportunities to settle in desirable neighborhoods and cities, resulting in more limited labor market prospects. Let's formulate the ***discrimination and job outcomes*** proposition:

> P. The more strongly the groups to which people belong are discriminated against in the labor market, the worse their labor market position. (*discrimination and job outcomes*)

When you apply the *discrimination and job outcomes* proposition to understand inequalities in the labor market, it is important to consider the groups to which job seekers and employers belong. In contemporary western societies, for example, employers and managers are more often "men" and "ethnic majority." Consequently, belonging to these two particular groups (men, ethnic majority) can then be a "resource" in the labor market for men and ethnic majority members. At the same time, group affiliation can act as a constraint for women and ethnic minorities due to discrimination of out-groups by male ethnic majority employers and managers.

10.4 Inequality of outcomes, opportunities and returns

Resources play a key role in generating labor market inequalities. How easy it is for you to find a job and get access to prestigious occupations depends on your human capital, social resources and group affiliations. Scholars have argued that, in addition to these three types of resources, other resources play a role as well in the labor market. In Chapter 9 we have already reviewed the idea of cultural capital and financial resources and how they are related to education and employment outcomes. At the end of this chapter we will review one more type of resource that has to do with social norms and aspirations. Taken together, sociologists argue that *various* resources cause inequalities in the labor market. Individuals who possess *more* resources (of whatever type) will have more favorable labor market outcomes. If you have more human capital and social resources, for example, you will have more chances to get a job, higher earnings and so forth.

We can relate the role resources play in the labor market to patterns of social stratification and mobility (Chapter 9). Figure 10.2 presents a conceptual model that clarifies their relationship. First, the model includes *social background* characteristics. This includes characteristics set by birth or features of the situation in which someone is currently embedded. Key examples are: gender, ethnic group, race, social origin (i.e., socio-economic status of the parents), family size (e.g., number of siblings), family structure (e.g., broken families) and the neighborhood in which someone was born and raised.

inequality of outcomes the relationship between social background and labor market outcomes.

Sociological studies find that these social background characteristics are related to labor market outcomes. This is called **inequality of outcomes** (*arrow a* in Figure 10.2). For example, as we have seen

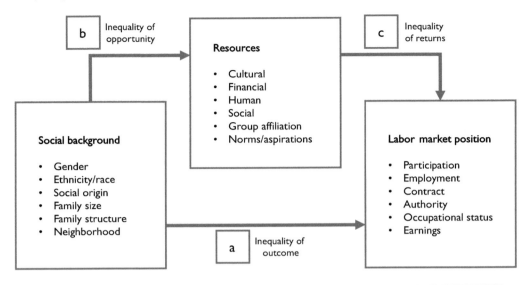

Inequality of opportunity

Figure 10.2 Conceptual model of the role of resources in explaining the relationship between social background and labor market position.

(Chapter 9), Blau and Duncan showed that children born in higher status families (social background) do better in the labor market (Blau & Duncan, 1967). Similarly, people born in deprived neighborhoods (social background) are less likely to find a good job (Wilson, 1987). Children from broken families (social background) do less well in the labor market (McLanahan & Sandefur, 1997). Your social background is therefore related to your position in the stratification system and chances of social mobility (Hout, 2015).

How can we understand inequality of outcomes? Here, the key role of resources comes in. First, there is **inequality of opportunity** (*arrow b*), i.e., social background characteristics impact the chances of accessing resources. Social background characteristics, like being a woman or an ethnic minority member, but also the neighborhood in which you grow up, influence access to human capital, social resources and so forth. For example, if you grow up in a poor neighborhood, it may not only be difficult to obtain good education (human capital) but also to build up a social network of friends who have useful information about the labor market (social resources).

inequality of opportunity the relationship between social background and access to resources.

The second process is called **inequality of returns** (*arrow c*), i.e., if you have more resources, you get more in return in the labor market. We have seen that having more human capital, more social resources,

inequality of returns the relationship between resources and labor market outcomes.

but also belonging to certain groups positively influences the chances of individuals in getting (good) jobs. The returns of these various types of resource may not be the same and they may vary across social contexts. For example, it could be that human capital is more important than social capital for getting ahead in the labor market, or that human capital is particularly important in one country whereas in another country social capital is more relevant.

To illustrate this conceptual model of the causes of labor market inequalities, let's consider family structure. A well-known finding is that children from broken families do less well in the labor market than children raised in intact families (McLanahan & Sandefur, 1997). How can we explain this inequality of outcomes? We may argue that children from broken families have less access to resources (inequality of opportunity). These children may not perform well in school and, because those who have more education have more chances in the labor market (inequality of returns), they may do less well in the labor market. In summary, *inequality of outcomes* (i.e., between social background characteristics such as family structure) can be understood as resulting from the combination of *inequality of opportunity* (i.e., access to resources) and *inequality of returns* (i.e., the influence of resources on labor market outcomes).

10.5 Gender inequality

Can we also use this conceptual model to understand gender inequality in the labor market? Gender stratification, or gender inequality of outcomes, is the topic of many sociological investigations (Charles & Grusky, 2004; Grusky, 2001). Let us first take a descriptive look to establish this pattern of gender inequality.

In 2017 the International Labour Office (ILO) published the *World Employment Social Outlook* and this report contains figures on gender inequality of outcomes (ILO, 2017a). To start, consider labor force participation and unemployment rates (Table 10.3). One pattern

Table 10.3 Labor force participation and unemployment among men and women, 2017.

	Labor force participation			Unemployment rate		
	Men	Women	Gender gap (absolute)	Men	Women	Gender gap (absolute)
World	76.1	49.4	−26.7	5.5	6.2	0.7
Northern Africa	74.1	22.9	−51.2	9.5	20.0	10.5
Sub-Saharan Africa	76.3	64.6	−11.7	6.2	8.3	2.1
Latin America and the Caribbean	78.3	52.7	−25.6	7.0	10.4	3.4
Northern America	68.3	56.2	−12.1	5.3	4.9	−0.4
Arab States	76.4	21.2	−55.2	8.3	21.2	12.9
Eastern Asia	76.8	61.3	−15.5	5.1	3.7	−1.4
South-Eastern Asia and the Pacific	81.2	58.8	−22.4	3.8	3.9	0.1
Southern Asia	79.4	28.6	−50.8	3.8	5.0	1.2
Northern, Southern and Western Europe	63.8	51.3	−12.5	8.8	9.3	0.5
Eastern Europe	68.1	53.0	−15.1	6.4	5.8	−0.6
Central and Western Asia	73.5	44.1	−29.4	8.9	9.6	0.7

Source: ILO, 2017a.

emerges from the findings: on average, women have lower labor force participation rates than men. The differences are smallest in sub-Saharan Africa (men: 76%, women: 65%) and highest in the Arab States (men: 76%, women: 21%). When we look at unemployment rates, however, the gender gap is much more modest in most regions in the world and sometimes even favors women. Two regions, however, stand out: in Northern Africa 20% of women were unemployed in 2017 as against 9.5% of men; in the Arab States 21% of women participating in the labor market had no job, as compared with 8% of men. But, generally speaking, the gender gap in labor force participation is much more pronounced than gender inequalities in employment rates.

Table 10.4 Female share in managerial positions, 2012–2017.

	(%)
North America	
United States	40.5
Canada	35.5
Mexico	36.7
South America	
Argentina	31.6
Brazil	39.9
Asia	
India	12.9
Indonesia	27.5
Japan	13.2
Pakistan	2.9
Africa	
Nigeria	30.3
Egypt	6.4
South Africa	32.1
Europe	
France	33.4
Germany	29.2
United Kingdom	36.2
Italy	27.5
Russia	41.3
Oceania	
Australia	38.7

Source: ILO, 2017b.
* The data is extracted from the period 2012–2017 (most recent for each country).

Participating in the labor market and getting a job are the first steps in a labor market career. What do we know about the positions men and women occupy in the labor market hierarchy? Again, the ILO provides valuable statistics on this question. One measure of having a more prestigious, high-paid job is having a managerial position, as such a position typically means having responsibilities over employees, higher earnings and prestige. If there was no gender inequality of outcomes, women would occupy 50% of these positions. Table 10.4 presents the findings for a number of countries. As you can see, women were underrepresented in managerial jobs in each country. However, there are also considerable differences across countries in the gender gap. For example, the share of women in managerial positions was much higher in Russia (41.3%) and the US (40.5%) than it was in Pakistan (2.9%) and Egypt (6.4%).

Another way to look at gender inequalities in the labor market is to compare earnings (Table 10.5). If there was no gender stratification in earnings, then women would earn as much as men do. In some countries this is (almost) the case. In Mexico, for example, women earn 34.36 Mexican pesos per hour (local currency) and men 34.99, which means that women earn ((34.36/34.99) *100) 98% of the earnings of men. In Italy gender differences in earnings are also relatively minor, as compared with countries in which gender pay gaps are more pronounced, such as in Germany and Russia. In each country, however, women earn less than men.

Table 10.5 Gender gaps in hourly earnings (2014–2017).

| | Hourly earnings (local currency) | | |
	Men	Women	Gender gap (relative)
Germany	19.87	15.44	77.7
UK	16.61	13.19	79.4
France	18.78	15.87	84.5
Russia	217	164	75.6
Italy	15.85	14.88	93.9
Pakistan	74	66	89.2
Brazil	14.4	12.1	84.0
Mexico	34.99	34.36	98.2

Source: ILO, 2017c.
* The data is extracted from the period 2014–2017 (most recent for each country).

Let's summarize the stylized finding of *gender inequality* in outcomes.

STYLIZED FACT 10.3

Gender inequality

In contemporary societies, women participate less often in the labor market than men and, when they do, they have occupations with lower prestige and lower wages.

Based on this finding, we can pose the following theoretical question:

> *Q(t)*. Why do men have better labor market positions than women in contemporary societies? (*gender inequality*)

According to the conceptual model (Figure 10.2), gender inequality of outcomes (*arrow a*) is due to two processes, namely: (1) inequality of opportunities between men and women in getting access to resources (*arrow b*) and (2) inequality of returns (*arrow c*). Let's focus on the three types of resources we have reviewed in this chapter, namely: human capital, social resources and group affiliation/discrimination (Figure 10.3). After we have discussed the role of these resources in understanding gender inequality, we will address a resource not introduced yet, namely gender norms and aspirations.

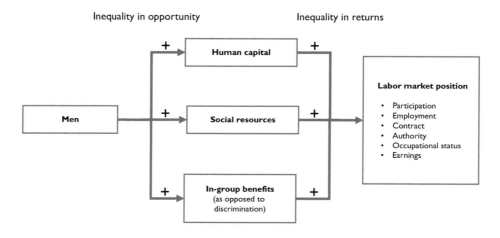

Figure 10.3 The role of human capital, social resources and group affiliation in explaining gender inequality.

Human capital

We have seen that there is inequality in returns of human capital, i.e., those possessing more human capital have more advantageous positions in the labor market. Is gender inequality partly due to women possessing less human capital than men? For a long time period women were typically less educated than men and this indeed contributed to the disadvantaged position of women in labor markets. Times have changed, however, and in past decades women have increasingly gained access to education in many countries, even surpassing men in some (Charles, 2011).

Table 10.6 presents tertiary education (completed) for women and men, for a number of countries, in the years 1950 and 2010. The general trend is that women have made significant gains in education, more so than men. For example, whereas only 0.8% of women in the year 1950 in Germany had completed tertiary education, in 2010 this had increased to 12.0% (Table 10.6). This amounts to an increase of ((12.0 − 0.8)/0.8) 1400%. Although in the same period men had also increasingly gained access to tertiary education, their progress has not been as strong as that of women. In many countries women have made huge progress

Table 10.6 Population with completed tertiary education (% of population aged 25 and over).

	Men		Women		% increase 1950 → 2010	
	1950	2010	1950	2010	Men	Women
North America						
United States	8.6	31.6	6.4	30.6	267	378
Canada	6.2	27.8	3.9	27.4	348	603
Mexico	2.2	14.0	0.4	12.1	536	2925
South America						
Argentina	1.7	2.5	0.2	4.4	47	2100
Brazil	1.4	6.7	0.1	9.3	379	9200
Asia						
China	0.2	2.8	0.0	2.0	1300	4900
India	0.8	8.5	0.1	3.7	963	3600
Japan	5.3	23.1	0.3	17.2	336	5633
Pakistan	0.9	6.8	0.2	3.8	656	1800
Africa						
Egypt	1.5	8.5	0.1	4.6	467	4500
South Africa	0.6	0.7	0.2	0.3	17	50
Europe						
France	2.4	13.6	0.3	10.3	467	3333
Germany	3.8	21.1	0.8	12.0	455	1400
United Kingdom	1.6	19.0	0.7	17.6	1088	2414
Italy	2.1	8.1	0.3	7.8	286	2500
Russia	3.4	28.8	0.8	23.2	747	2800
Oceania						
Australia	10.0	23.0	4.3	26.3	130	512

Source: Barro & Lee, 2013, 2018.

in getting access to secondary and tertiary education, resulting in a reduction of the gender gap in human capital.

The increasing educational level of women has had important consequences for their labor market position. Scholars have identified the considerably improved position of women in the labor market since WWII (England, 2005). Their increasing labor force participation is a case in point (Table 10.7). In Germany, for example, 45% of women aged 15 or older were active in the labor market in 1990. This increased to 55% in 2017, thereby resulting in a reduction of the (absolute) gender gap in labor force participation from 28% to 11%. This trend of decreasing gender inequalities in labor market participation is typical for many countries, although not all.

Table 10.7 Labor force participation rate (% of population aged 15+) (modeled ILO estimate).

	Men		Women		Gender gap	
	1990	2017	1990	2017	1990	2017
North America						
United States	75	68	56	56	19	12
Canada	76	70	58	61	18	9
Mexico	84	79	33	44	51	35
South America						
Argentina	76	73	43	49	33	24
Brazil	83	75	42	53	41	22
Asia						
China	85	76	73	61	12	15
India	85	79	35	27	50	52
Indonesia	82	82	44	51	38	31
Japan	77	71	50	50	27	21
Pakistan	84	83	14	25	70	58
Africa						
Egypt	72	74	21	22	51	52
Niger	90	91	68	67	22	24
Nigeria	65	60	48	50	17	10
South Africa	66	62	42	48	24	14
Europe						
France	66	60	46	51	20	9
Germany	73	66	45	55	28	11
United Kingdom	74	68	52	57	22	11
Italy	67	58	35	40	32	18
Russia	76	72	59	57	17	15
Oceania						
Australia	76	71	52	59	24	12

Source: World Bank, 2017.

Note: figures pertain to the population aged 15 and older. Among those aged 15–22, a considerable group of men and women are inactive in the labor market because they follow some sort of secondary or tertiary education. Among those aged 55 and higher, some have retired. This means that, if you use figures on those aged 25–55, you would find higher levels of labor force participation among men and women.

Social resources

Human capital theory can explain part of the gender inequality in labor market outcomes in contemporary societies and why gender inequality is decreasing over time. However, scholars have noted that human capital theory alone cannot fully explain gender inequality in the labor market. Possibly, social resources play a role as well. Whether women are at a disadvantage in getting access to social resources is a matter of scientific discussion. Studies find that, in some contexts, there is indeed evidence to suggest that women have less access to social resources, whereas this is not so in yet other contexts (Behtoui, 2007; Cross & Lin, 2008; Li, Savage, & Warde, 2008; Van Tubergen & Volker, 2015). Hence, it is not the case that studies reveal a clear cross-country pattern of female disadvantage in access to social resources.

Discrimination

Gender inequality in labor market outcomes can also be due to discrimination. Is there evidence for discrimination against women in the labor market? This is the topic of a great many discussions, both between scientists and in the public debate. Some believe that in Western countries and other "modern" societies, employers primarily base their selection on people's knowledge and skills and that actual discrimination does not occur or hardly ever occurs any more (Heckman, 1998). Others, on the other hand, believe that discrimination still is, in fact, an important factor (Pager & Quillian, 2005).

A key question is: how could you detect discrimination? Which method is appropriate? Clearly, asking people about their own experiences with discrimination is not a convincing approach because candidates have little to no insight into the experiences of their competitors. Maybe a candidate was rejected for the job interview and believes this is evidence for discrimination. But this need not be the case—maybe she was rejected not because she is a woman but because other candidates were more skilled. Asking employers whether they discriminate is not a good method either. They may discriminate in practice but decide not to reveal their true actions to the researcher. And they may also not be aware of their own discriminatory actions as this could happen unconsciously (Pager & Quillian, 2005).

The most convincing method to detect discrimination is the field experiment. These are, as we have seen (Chapter 3), experiments conducted in real-life settings. There are two main versions of this method when used for detecting discrimination, namely: *correspondence testing* and *audit testing* (Pager, 2007).

In the first one, **correspondence testing**, fictitious application letters with resumes are sent to companies with job vacancies. These letters and resumes have been created by the researchers themselves, in such a way that they strongly resemble each other in terms of qualifications. This means that the fictitious candidates are, objectively speaking, equally skilled for the job: they possess the same human capital, as can be seen from their education and work experience, for instance. Then the researchers match group affiliations *at random* to the letter and resume. For example, application I is matched to a male, whereas application II is a woman—this is a *random outcome*, i.e., it could have been the exact opposite. The researchers make sure that group affiliation (such as gender, age, ethnicity) is signaled clearly in the application letter and/or resume. In the case of gender and age this is straightforward, but ethnicity or national origin can also be signaled. For instance, the nationality of the applicant can be mentioned in the resume and the applicant's country of birth or even certain names could be used if sufficiently overlapping with ethnicity/national origin.

correspondence testing field experimental method which uses resumes to detect discrimination.

After sending the application letters to the organization(s), the correspondence-testing methodology allows researchers to discover discrimination at the application stage. After all, if members of one group (e.g., men) *consistently* receive more invitations for the job interview than members of another group (e.g., women), this is clear and convincing evidence for discrimination at the first stage. This can be illustrated as follows. Say we have two candidates who belong to two different groups: male and female. Both the man and the woman send ten application letters for the same positions. Both hope to be invited for an interview by at least one employer. The man and the woman possess the same human capital: they have the same education, work experience, language skills and health. The only difference between the two individuals is their gender. Imagine that the male applicant is invited for eight job interviews, whereas the woman receives no invitations. This is a case of gender discrimination: the two candidates have an equal amount of knowledge and skills (human capital) but they are unequally treated by employers because of their group affiliation.

Correspondence testing is subject to two limitations: it is only useful for discovering discrimination in *written* applications and it can only be used in the *first stage* (i.e., job application). To overcome these limitations, researchers also use **audit testing**, which supplements correspondence testing. With audit testing, researchers make use of actors who play the role of fictitious job seekers. The actors are carefully selected and trained to make sure that they resemble each other in every way except for their group membership. Thus, if the idea is to test discrimination based on gender, then it is important to make sure that the male and female actors are of the same age, use the same language and so forth. In this way, audit testing opens up new ways to test whether discrimination exists in the job application stage, for instance by letting the actors contact the organization by phone or by directly paying them a visit in person. Moreover, when using actors, researchers can also discover if discrimination exists in the job-entry stage. Specifically, when invited for a job interview, actors representing different groups can be treated unequally only because of their group affiliation.

audit testing field experimental method which uses actors to detect discrimination.

These kinds of field experiments emerged first in the 1960s, when British sociologists used them to detect ethnic and racial discrimination (Daniel, 1968; Jowell & Prescott-Clarke, 1970). Since then, they have been conducted in many countries around the world. Discrimination has been examined with respect to gender, but findings have been mixed at first sight (Riach & Rich, 2002). Sometimes it is found that women are discriminated against while at other times no gender discrimination is found, and some studies find that men are discriminated against more than women. On closer inspection, however, scholars have found discrimination against men in traditionally female-dominated jobs and discrimination against women in male-dominated jobs (Neumark, 2018). As these typically male jobs are better paid and more prestigious, gender discrimination may contribute to (persisting) gender inequality in the labor market.

Some studies have looked in detail at possible discrimination against mothers. It has been often observed that mothers have a less favorable position in the labor market than non-mothers—this has been called the **motherhood penalty** (England, Bearak, Budig, & Hodges, 2016; Oesch, Lipps, & McDonald, 2017). One possible explanation for this penalty is discrimination against mothers. In one field experimental study, conducted in a northeastern city in the United States, it was found that, compared with fathers and childless women, equally qualified mothers are less often invited for a job interview (Correll, Benard, & Paik, 2007). However, no such discrimination against mothers was found in field experimental studies that were done in Paris, France (Petit, 2007) and Sweden (Bygren, Erlandsson, & Gähler, 2017).

motherhood penalty finding that mothers have less favorable positions in the labor market than non-mothers.

Gender norms and aspirations

The three types of resources discussed so far—human capital, social resources and group affiliation/discrimination—help us in understanding gender inequality. However, scholars have also noted that there is more to it, that we need to consider yet other mechanisms to understand why men have a better position in the labor market than women. What is, in particular, puzzling is that, despite the significant gains of women in educational attainment, gender inequalities have not equally diminished (Charles, 2011; Charles & Grusky, 2004). There is an increase in the educational performance of women, but this trend is not reflected in women getting proportionally more higher-status jobs or better wages.

To understand this (persisting) gender inequality, scholars have argued that we need to consider the role of social norms and (internalized) aspirations, and how they (differentially) shape the careers of men and women. This explanation—which emphasizes the role of norms and aspirations—is called *preference theory* (Hakim, 2000) and *gender ideology theory* (West & Zimmerman, 1987). It can be seen as an application of *social control theory*. According to this theory, as we have seen earlier (Chapter 6), people's social environment influences their preferences and behavior via mechanisms of social sanctions in case of norm-deviance and approval in case of norm-compliance. Social environment is taken in its broad sense here, for instance parents, family members, friends and acquaintances, classmates, colleagues and neighbors.

Social control theory can be used to understand gender inequalities in the labor market. By doing so, it posits that the social environment can affect the *career ambitions* that men and women may harbor, the *value* they attach to income and status and their *preferences for certain jobs*. Social norms can prescribe different roles and ambitions for men and women. In many countries, although to a varying degree (Inglehart & Norris, 2003), norms prescribe that men should be the main breadwinner and hold a job with a high status, whereas women are more often supposed to take care of the children and the household. These norms can be broadly endorsed in society, involving not only parents but also other family members, peers, media, the spouse, employers, co-workers and so forth.

When such gender norms prevail, social control theory argues that two mechanisms can generate gender inequality in the labor market. When combined, the two mechanisms are powerful and provide a strong barrier to gender equality. First, deviations from the gender norms can result in *social sanctions*, whereas complying with such norms results in social approval. Such gender roles can be decisive in the career choices made by boys and girls and offer an explanation for the gender inequality in labor market positions. It could mean, for example, that even when women prefer to have a career, they refrain from doing so because of expected social sanctions.

Second, social norms can be *internalized*, which means that social norms become part of people's individual preferences, goals and values. Men and women comply with these norms even in the absence of social control because deviations from their moral norms results in feelings of guilt and shame, or such internalized norms have become part of people's personal values and preferences. Consequently, because of socialization processes, men and women will develop different ambitions and preferences for paid and unpaid work. In line with the idea that gender norms are internalized, studies find that males more than females value earnings and career promotions, leadership and power (Konrad, Ritchie Jr, Lieb, & Corrigall, 2000). Such deeply ingrained career ambitions and goals may thus drive gender inequality in labor force participation and occupational status. And they may explain why, despite the rising educational levels of women, gender inequalities remain so strong in the labor market.

Let's formulate this ***career ambitions and job outcomes*** proposition so that it reflects the mechanisms of social norms and internalized norms.

P. The higher people's career ambitions, and the more strongly these ambitions are approved in their environment, the better their labor market position (*career ambitions and job outcomes*).

We can use a conceptual model to clarify how gendered career ambitions and norms generate gender inequality in the labor market (Figure 10.4).

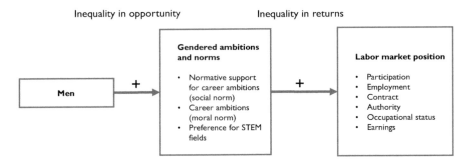

Figure 10.4 Gendered ambitions and norms as an explanation for gender inequality.

Sociologists Maria Charles and David Grusky state that there is actually a third way in which ambitions and norms generate gender inequality, which has to do with men more often preferring Science, Technology, Engineering and Mathematics (STEM). In what way does this affect gender inequality? Charles and Grusky point out that despite significant changes towards more gender equality in terms of educational attainment and labor force participation in the past decades, the occupational segregation of men and women in the labor market shows little change over time and remains very strong (Charles & Grusky, 2004). Men and women work in very different occupations. For example, a primary school teacher, secretary and nurse are typical female jobs, whereas construction worker, car mechanic and electrician are male-dominated occupations. Broadly speaking, women crowd into the non-manual/non-technical section and men crowd into the manual/technical sector (Charles & Grusky, 2004). According to Charles and Grusky, this kind of occupational segregation by gender is universal; it has been observed across all countries in the world (Hout & DiPrete, 2006).

The consequences of strong gender segregation in occupations are not trivial, as occupations are strongly affecting pay. Indeed, one study showed that 64% of the gender wage gap is due to occupational sex segregation (Petersen & Morgan, 1995). This means that, in order to understand gender stratification in wages, one needs to understand occupational sex segregation. But let us first identify the stylized fact of *gender hypersegregation*.

 STYLIZED FACT 10.4

Gender hypersegregation
Men and women work in very different occupations in contemporary societies.

Although gender hypersegregation is universal, the *degree* of this occupational sex segregation varies across countries. In some countries occupations are more segregated by gender than in other countries. Intuitively, one might think that in those countries in which gender conservative norms prevail, occupational sex segregation would be more prominent than in countries that have more gender egalitarian norms. However, consistent evidence emerges from multiple studies that the *opposite* is the case. Sweden, for example, is well-known for its progressive gender values and norms, exemplified by family-friendly policies and high levels of female educational attainment and labor force participation. But occupational sex segregation is very strong in Sweden, even more so than in more gender conservative countries (Blackburn, Jarman, & Brooks, 2000; Rosenfeld & Kalleberg, 1991).

These findings are counterintuitive, but they reflect a broader pattern: in more economically developed countries, like Sweden, occupational sex segregation is *more* pronounced than in poorer nations like Botswana. The route towards gender segregation in the labor market can already start with the choices that boys and girls make in education. Women are less represented in STEM jobs and this is because segregation emerges already in education. Gender segregation in the field of education is particularly strong in more economically advanced countries like Sweden. To illustrate, cross-national studies (Charles & Bradley, 2009) find that women are strongly underrepresented in graduate studies in math and natural sciences in countries that have a higher GDP per capita, such as Finland, Sweden and Denmark (Figure 10.5).

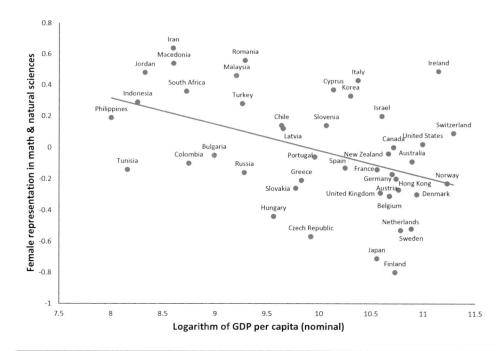

Figure 10.5 Relationship between economic development and gender representation in graduate studies in mathematics and natural sciences.

Source: Charles & Bradley, 2009.

Similar patterns were found in a study among more than 300,000 eighth-grade boys and girls in 53 countries (Charles, Harr, Cech, & Hendley, 2014). The study examined how boys and girls aspire to a math-related job, finding that boys generally aspire to such jobs more than girls in virtually all countries. But the size of this gender gap varies across countries and it does so in a consistent way: the gender gap in math-related occupational aspirations *increases* with economic development. This means that in highly developed countries such as the Netherlands and Belgium, many girls indicate that they do not want to have jobs that involve science, technology, engineering and mathematics (STEM)—as compared with how often boys in these countries dislike STEM. In poorer, more traditional countries like Indonesia and Ghana, this gender gap in STEM preferences is much less pronounced (Figure 10.6).

How can we explain these puzzling findings? Why do more economically developed countries have *higher* gender gaps in STEM fields and *higher* levels of occupational sex segregation? One explanation for this pattern emphasizes the role of cultural opinions (Charles & Grusky, 2004). Specifically, Charles and Grusky claim that, typically, many people uphold **gender essentialist beliefs**, i.e., the idea that there are *traits* that are distinctively male and female. For example, the idea that women excel in personal service, nurturance and interpersonal interaction, while men are presumed to excel in interaction with things and in physical labor. These gender

gender essentialist belief belief that there are traits that are distinctively male and female.

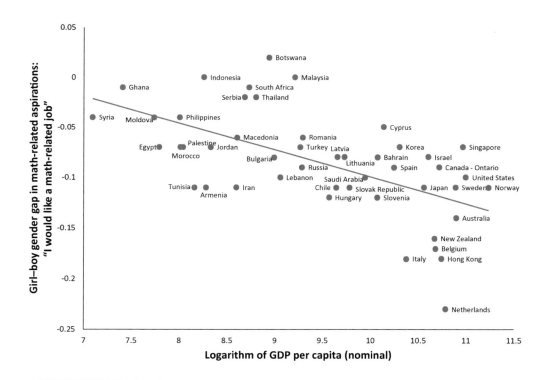

Figure 10.6 Relationship between economic development and boy–girl gap in attitudes toward mathematics.
Source: Charles et al., 2014.

stereotypes about men and women find their strong connection with *task requirements* of non-manual/service (female) occupations and manual/technical (male) occupations. Already in education boys and girls choose a field of study that is aligned to these occupational gender stereotypes, resulting in "horizontal" gender segregation in education and the labor market.

This gender gap becomes more pronounced in more economically developed countries because, in these countries, individual fulfilment and self-expression become increasingly important cultural values (Inglehart & Welzel, 2005). Higher levels of economic development reduce the prevalence of survival and collectivistic values and give rise to values emphasizing personal development, freedom and self-realization (Welzel, 2013). Given the universal pattern of gender essentialist beliefs, however, the boys and girls in these economically developed, culturally individualistic countries think that these (male and female) traits *belong to their core personality traits* and that, therefore, they will find fulfilment in acting according to these (gender) traits (Charles et al., 2014). In the poorer countries, which tend to have more collectivistic values, gender segregation in occupations is less strong because both men and women work to survive and make a decent income. But in more individualistic cultures, women (and men) want to acquire jobs in which they can personally develop themselves and this means they will emphasize typically female (and male) traits such as nurturance, personal service and interpersonal interaction (or working with things, physical labor and technical skills). In other words, "men and women are motivated by a desire to express their authentic (gendered) selves" (Charles et al., 2014). And in anticipation of their desired roles in the labor market, girls in more economically advanced societies like Sweden avoid STEM fields in education more so than girls in less economically advanced countries like Botswana.

10.6 Chapter resources

Key concepts

Human capital	Labor market discrimination	Correspondence testing
Structural hole	Cumulative discrimination	Audit testing
Brokerage proposition	Inequality of outcomes	Motherhood penalty
Social resources	Inequality of opportunity	Gender essentialist belief
Position generator	Inequality of returns	

Key theories and propositions

- Human capital theory
- Human capital and job outcomes
- Weak ties and job information
- Strong ties and job outcomes
- Brokerage and job outcomes
- Social resources and job outcomes
- Taste-based discrimination
- Statistical discrimination theory
- Discrimination and job outcomes
- Career ambitions and job outcomes

Key stylized facts

- Informal job finding
- Jobs via weak ties
- Gender inequality
- Gender hypersegregation

Summary

- Various types of "resources" or "capital" play a role in getting ahead in the labor market, such as human capital, social capital and group affiliation.
- Human capital refers to people's knowledge and skills insofar as these are relevant to the labor market.
- There are different theories on the role of social capital. Granovetter emphasizes the distinction between strong and weak ties, Burt focuses on structural holes and brokerage and Lin considers the impact of social resources.
- Group affiliation can also be regarded as a resource or a barrier. Discrimination can be due to statistical discrimination and taste-based discrimination.
- The impact of social background on labor market position (inequality of outcome) can be understood as resulting from the inequality of opportunity and inequality of returns. To illustrate, gender inequality (inequality of outcome) results from men and women having different access to resources, such as human capital and social resources, and the influence of these resources on labor market outcomes.
- In getting a deeper understanding of gender inequality, one should take account of the fact that men and women have very different occupations (gender hypersegregation).
- According to some scholars, gender hypersegregation may be the result of gender essentialist beliefs.

References

Aguilera, M. B., & Massey, D. S. (2003). Social capital and the wages of Mexican migrants: New hypotheses and tests. *Social Forces*, 82(2), 671–701.

Barro, R., & Lee, J. (2013). A new data set of educational attainment in the world, 1950–2010. *Journal of Development Economics*, 104(184), 198.

Barro, R., & Lee, J. (2018). Barro-Lee data. Retrieved from www.barrolee.com.

Becker, G. S. (1964). *Human capital*. New York, NY: National Bureau of Economic Research.

Becker, G. S. (2010). *The economics of discrimination*. Chicago, IL: University of Chicago Press.

Behtoui, A. (2007). The distribution and return of social capital: Evidence from Sweden. *European Societies*, 9(3), 383–407.

Bernardi, F. (1999). Does the husband matter? Married women and employment in Italy. *European Sociological Review*, 15(3), 285–300.

Bernasco, W., De Graaf, P. M., & Ultee, W. C. (1998). Effects of spouse's resources on occupational attainment in the Netherlands. *European Sociological Review*, 14(1), 15–31.

Bian, Y. (1997). Bringing strong ties back in: Indirect ties, network bridges, and job searches in China. *American Sociological Review*, 62(3), 366–385.

Blackburn, R. M., Jarman, J., & Brooks, B. (2000). The puzzle of gender segregation and inequality: A cross-national analysis. *European Sociological Review*, 16(2), 119–135.

Blank, R. M., Dabady, M., & Citro, C. F. (Eds.). (2004). *Measuring racial discrimination*. Washington, DC: National Academies Press.

Blau, P., & Duncan, O. D. (1967). *The American occupational structure*. New York, NY: Free Press.

Blossfeld, H., & Drobnic, S. (Eds.). (2001). *Careers of couples in contemporary society: From male breadwinner to dual-earner families*. Oxford, UK: Oxford University Press.

Burt, R. S. (1992). *Structural holes: The social structure of competition*. Cambridge, MA: Harvard University Press.

Burt, R. S. (2004). Structural holes and good ideas. *American Journal of Sociology*, 110(2), 349–399.

Burt, R. S. (2005). *Brokerage and closure*. Oxford: Oxford University Press.

Burt, R. S. (2010). *Neighbor networks: Competitive advantage local and personal*. Oxford: Oxford University Press.

Bygren, M., Erlandsson, A., & Gähler, M. (2017). Do employers prefer fathers? Evidence from a field experiment testing the gender by parenthood interaction effect on callbacks to job applications. *European Sociological Review*, 33(3), 337–348.

Card, D. (1999). The causal effect of education on earnings. *Handbook of Labor Economics*, 3, 1801–1863.

Charles, M. (2011). A world of difference: International trends in women's economic status. *Annual Review of Sociology*, 37, 355–371.

Charles, M., & Bradley, K. (2009). Indulging our gendered selves? Sex segregation by field of study in 44 countries. *American Journal of Sociology*, 114(4), 924–976.

Charles, M., & Grusky, D. (2004). *Occupational ghettos: The worldwide segregation of women and men*. Stanford, CA: Stanford University Press.

Charles, M., Harr, B., Cech, E., & Hendley, A. (2014). Who likes math where? Gender differences in eighth-graders' attitudes around the world. *International Studies in Sociology of Education*, 24(1), 85–112.

Chen, C. J. (2009). The distribution and return of social capital in Taiwan. In R. Hsung, N. Lin, & R. L. Breiger (Eds.), *Contexts of social capital: Social networks in markets, communities, and families* (pp. 193–215). New York and London: Routledge.

Chen, Y., & Volker, B. (2016). Social capital and homophily both matter for labor market outcomes–evidence from replication and extension. *Social Networks*, 45, 18–31.

Contreras, D., Otero, G., Díaz, J. D., & Suárez, N. (2019). Inequality in social capital in Chile: Assessing the importance of network size and contacts' occupational prestige on status attainment. *Social Networks*, 58, 59–77.

Correll, S. J., Benard, S., & Paik, I. (2007). Getting a job: Is there a motherhood penalty? *American Journal of Sociology*, 112(5), 1297–1338.

Cross, J. L. M., & Lin, N. (2008). Access to social capital and status attainment in the United States: Racial/ethnic and gender differences. In N. Lin & B. H. Erickson (Eds.), *Social capital: An international research program* (pp. 364–393). Oxford, UK: Oxford University Press.

Daniel, W. (1968). *Racial discrimination in England*. Middlesex, UK: Penguin Books.

England, P. (2005). Gender inequality in labor markets: The role of motherhood and segregation. *Social Politics: International Studies in Gender, State & Society*, 12(2), 264–288.

England, P., Bearak, J., Budig, M. J., & Hodges, M. J. (2016). Do highly paid, highly skilled women experience the largest motherhood penalty? *American Sociological Review*, 81(6), 1161–1189.

Flap, H., & Volker, B. (Eds.). (2004). *Creation and returns of social capital*. London, UK: Routledge.

Gee, L. K., Jones, J., & Burke, M. (2017). Social networks and labor markets: How strong ties relate to job finding on Facebook's social network. *Journal of Labor Economics*, *35*(2), 485–518.

Gee, L. K., Jones, J. J., Fariss, C. J., Burke, M., & Fowler, J. H. (2017). The paradox of weak ties in 55 countries. *Journal of Economic Behavior & Organization*, *133*, 362–372.

Granovetter, M. (1973). The strength of weak ties. *American Journal of Sociology*, *78*(6), 1360–1380.

Granovetter, M. (1974). *Getting a job: A study of contacts and careers.* Cambridge, MA: Harvard University Press.

Granovetter, M. (1985). Economic action and social structure: The problem of embeddedness. *American Journal of Sociology*, *91*(3), 481–510.

Granovetter, M. (2018). *Getting a job: A study of contacts and careers (2nd edition).* Chicago, IL: University of Chicago Press.

Grusky, D. B. (2001). The past, present, and future of social inequality. In D. B. Grusky (Ed.), *Social stratification in sociological perspective: Class, race & gender* (2nd ed.), (pp. 1–51). Boulder, CO: Westview Press.

Hakim, C. (2000). *Work-lifestyle choices in the 21st century: Preference theory.* Oxford: Oxford University Press.

Heckman, J. J. (1998). Detecting discrimination. *The Journal of Economic Perspectives*, *12*(2), 101–116.

Heckman, J. J., & Borjas, G. J. (1980). Does unemployment cause future unemployment? definitions, questions and answers from a continuous time model of heterogeneity and state dependence. *Economica*, *47*(187), 247–283.

Hout, M. (2015). A summary of what we know about social mobility. *The Annals of the American Academy of Political and Social Science*, *657*(1), 27–36.

Hout, M., & DiPrete, T. A. (2006). What we have learned: RC28's contributions to knowledge about social stratification. *Research in Social Stratification and Mobility*, *24*(1), 1–20.

Hsung, R., Lin, N., & Breiger, R. L. (Eds.). (2009). *Contexts of social capital: Social networks in markets, communities and families.* New York, NY: Routledge.

Huang, X., & Western, M. (2011). Social networks and occupational attainment in Australia. *Sociology*, *45*(2), 269.

ILO. (2017a). *World employment social outlook.* Geneva: ILO.

ILO. (2017b). *SDG labor market indicators.* Retrieved from www.ilo.org/ilostat.

ILO (2017c). *Earnings and labor income.* Retrieved from: www.ilo.org/ilostat.

Inglehart, R., & Norris, P. (2003). *Rising tide: Gender equality and cultural change around the world.* Cambridge, UK: Cambridge University Press.

Inglehart, R., & Welzel, C. (2005). *Modernization, cultural change, and democracy: The human development sequence.* Cambridge, UK: Cambridge University Press.

Jowell, R., & Prescott-Clarke, P. (1970). Racial discrimination and white-collar workers in Britain. *Race & Class*, *11*(4), 397–417.

Konrad, A. M., Ritchie, J. J., Lieb, E., & Corrigall, E. (2000). Sex differences and similarities in job attribute preferences: A meta-analysis. *Psychological Bulletin*, *126*(4), 593.

Li, Y., Savage, M., & Warde, A. (2008). Social mobility and social capital in contemporary Britain. *The British Journal of Sociology*, *59*(3), 391–411.

Lin, N. (1999). Social networks and status attainment. *Annual Review of Sociology*, *25*, 467–487.

Lin, N. (2000). Inequality in social capital. *Contemporary Sociology*, *29*(6), 785–795.

Lin, N. (2001). *Social capital: A theory of social structure and action.* New York, NY: Cambridge University Press.

Lin, N., Cook, K., & Burt, R. S. (Eds.). (2001). *Social capital: Theory and research.* New Brunswick, NJ: Transaction Publishers.

Lin, N., & Dumin, M. (1986). Access to occupations through social ties. *Social Networks*, *8*(4), 365–385.

Lin, N., & Erickson, B. H. (Eds.). (2008). *Social capital: An international research program*. Oxford, UK: Oxford University Press.

Lin, N., Fu, Y., & Chen, C. J. (2014). *Social capital and its institutional contingency: A study of the United States, China and Taiwan*. New York: Routledge.

Loury, G. C. (2009). *The anatomy of racial inequality*. Cambridge, MA: Harvard University Press.

McLanahan, S., & Sandefur, G. (1997). *Growing up with a single parent: What hurts, what helps*. Cambridge, MA: Harvard University Press.

Mincer, J. (1958). Investments in human capital and personal income distribution. *Journal of Political Economy*, *66*, 281–302.

Mincer, J. (1974). *Schooling, experience, and earnings*. Cambridge, MA: National Bureau of Economic Research.

Mouw, T. (2003). Social capital and finding a job: Do contacts matter? *American Sociological Review*, *68*(6), 868–898.

Murphy, C. (2012). *A Kingdom's future: Saudi Arabia through the eyes of its twentysomethings*. Washington, DC: Wilson Center.

Neumark, D. (2018). Experimental research on labor market discrimination. *Journal of Economic Literature*, *56*(3), 799–866.

Oesch, D., Lipps, O., & McDonald, P. (2017). The wage penalty for motherhood: Evidence on discrimination from panel data and a survey experiment for Switzerland. *Demographic Research*, *37*, 1793–1824.

Pager, D. (2007). The use of field experiments for studies of employment discrimination: Contributions, critiques, and directions for the future. *The Annals of the American Academy of Political and Social Science*, *609*(1), 104–133.

Pager, D., & Quillian, L. (2005). Walking the talk? What employers say versus what they do. *American Sociological Review*, *70*(3), 355–380.

Petersen, T., & Morgan, L. A. (1995). Separate and unequal: Occupation-establishment sex segregation and the gender wage gap. *American Journal of Sociology*, *101*(2), 329–365.

Petit, P. (2007). The effects of age and family constraints on gender hiring discrimination: A field experiment in the french financial sector. *Labor Economics*, *14*(3), 371–391.

Phelps, E. S. (1972). The statistical theory of racism and sexism. *The American Economic Review*, *62*(4), 659–661.

Riach, P. A., & Rich, J. (2002). Field experiments of discrimination in the market place. *The Economic Journal*, *112*(483), F480–F518.

Rosenfeld, R. A., & Kalleberg, A. L. (1991). Gender inequality in the labor market: A cross-national perspective. *Acta Sociologica*, *34*(3), 207–225.

Rözer, J. J., & Brashears, M. E. (2018). Partner selection and social capital in the status attainment process. *Social Science Research*, *73*, 63–79.

Shen, J., & Bian, Y. (2018). The causal effect of social capital on income: A new analytic strategy. *Social Networks*, *54*, 82–90.

Van Tubergen, F., & Volker, B. (2015). Inequality in access to social capital in the Netherlands. *Sociology*, *49*(3), 521–538.

Verbakel, E., & De Graaf, P. M. (2008). Resources of the partner: Support or restriction in the occupational career? Developments in the Netherlands between 1940 and 2003. *European Sociological Review*, *24*(1), 81–95.

Verbakel, E., & De Graaf, P. M. (2009). Partner effects on labour market participation and job level: Opposing mechanisms. *Work, Employment and Society*, *23*(4), 635–654.

Verhaeghe, P., Van der Bracht, K., & Van de Putte, B. (2015). Inequalities in social capital and their longitudinal effects on the labour market entry. *Social Networks*, *40*, 174–184.

Welzel, C. (2013). *Freedom rising: Human empowerment and the quest of emancipation.* Cambridge, UK: Cambridge University Press.

West, C., & Zimmerman, D. H. (1987). Doing gender. *Gender & Society, 1*(2), 125–151.

Wilson, W. J. (1987). *The truly disadvantaged: The inner city, the underclass, and public policy.* Chicago, IL: University of Chicago Press.

World Bank. (2017). Labor force participation rate. Retrieved from https://data.worldbank.org.

Part 5

Topics

Chapter 11

Immigration and integration

Chapter overview

Were you or your parents born in another country? Do you have personal connections to children of immigrants? How ethnically diverse is the society in which you live? The topic of immigration and integration is relevant more than ever before. International migration has resulted in increasingly ethnically diverse societies and questions arise about the integration of immigrants and their offspring. In this chapter, I will first discuss how issues of immigration and integration are addressed as social problems (11.1). Then I will review broad patterns of international migration, explaining key terminology (11.2). After that, I will discuss the topic of integration and distinguish three dimensions of this complex concept: cultural integration, social integration and economic integration (11.3). Subsequently, I will review the immigrant integration proposition, which posits that integration is a process that unfolds over time (11.4). I will then show that the integration process depends on social contextual conditions and that, in particular, there are notable differences between ethnic groups in their integration process (11.5). To illustrate the role of contextual conditions in shaping the integration process, I take a closer look at a case study on the so-called "culture of honor" (11.6). Subsequently, I examine the three dimensions of integration (cultural, social, economic) in relation to each other and highlight that these dimensions may work interdependently (11.7). Finally, I will discuss the segregation of ethnic minority and majority groups into different neighborhoods and cities (11.8).

> ## Learning goals
>
> After reading this chapter, check if you are able to:
>
> - Describe and use key sociological concepts on immigration and integration.
> - Describe dimensions and indicators of the concept of integration.
> - Describe and apply the immigrant integration proposition.
> - Explain why the integration process depends on social context effects.
> - Describe integration spillover effects.
> - Describe the Schelling segregation model.

11.1 Immigration and integration: a social problem?

International migration is regarded as a social problem in many contemporary societies. Immigration is affecting both developing and developed nations, creating challenges to societies in various ways. One aspect of the problem is that so many people move "involuntarily" because of conflict and violence in their region of living (Castles, De Haas, & Miller, 2013). The displacement of people can result in broken families, children growing up in insecure conditions and loss of personal belongings and employment. Moreover, the process of migrating can be life-threatening. The *Missing Migrants Project* of the International Organization for Migration estimated that, in the year 2016, more than 5,000 people died in the Mediterranean region when trying to reach European borders (International Organization for Migration, 2019).

International migration also creates social problems in terms of integration in host societies. Large groups of newcomers need to find their way in their new country of residence and this can be challenging. For example, immigrants may be confronted with lack of knowledge of the official language and they may not have the right qualifications to find their way into the labor market. The receiving "ethnic majority" population can be reluctant to accept newcomers, which may result in ethnic discrimination in the labor market and extreme right-wing sentiments. The ethnic majority population can also become increasingly divided and polarized about their opinions towards immigration. Some may be more accepting of allowing refugees and other immigrants to enter their country, while others may strongly oppose immigrant-friendly policies.

What is the role of sociologists in this debate? Sociologists provide valuable knowledge to policy makers and the public at large in three ways—in line with the three aims of sociology (Chapter 1). First, sociologists aim to come up with accurate *descriptions* of immigration and integration—which is very much needed to correct biased personal and public perceptions. For example, sociologists collect data to get a clear view of how many immigrants are actually unemployed. Second, sociologists construct theories and *explanations* that attempt to identify causes of immigration and integration. These theories are then rigorously tested. This means, for example, that sociologists study why immigrants may struggle finding jobs or which conditions fuel anti-immigrant sentiments. Third, sociological knowledge can be fruitfully *applied*. Useful predictions can be made regarding projected immigration flows or evidence-based interventions can be implemented to foster the integration of immigrants and their children.

Sociological research on immigration and integration is not always directly motivated by social policy concerns, of course. Studies are also conducted in view of scientific relevance. The motivation of the research is then to elaborate on current scientific knowledge in the field, to improve previous theories and methods, for example. Either way, the topic of *immigration and integration* is core to sociological research. Recent insights from this field can be found in books and specialized journals. Examples of key journals in this area of research include: *Journal of Ethnic and Migration Studies*, *International Migration Review*, *Demography*, *Ethnicities* and *Ethnic and Racial Studies*.

Broadly speaking, the sociological questions in the field can be divided into two broad clusters. First, sociologists ask questions about the topic of *international migration*: how many people migrate and for what reasons? What types of immigrants can be distinguished? What are the consequences of international migration for the populations in the countries of origin? How serious are problems of human trafficking? How does immigration change the ethnic diversity and demographics of host societies? Second, sociologists ask questions about the topic of *integration*: how well are immigrants and their offspring integrated in the host societies? How well do immigrants acquire the official language? Do they integrate in the labor market? How do ethnic majority populations treat newcomers? Does immigration become a topic of polarization?

In this chapter, I will introduce these two areas of research, identifying key concepts, theories and empirical patterns. We will use insights gained from "Thinking like a sociologist" (Part 1) and the CSI themes (Parts 2–4).

11.2 International migration

International migration has been on the agenda in the past decades. But international migration is not a new phenomenon, of course. Around 50,000 years ago, *Homo sapiens* migrated out of Africa, settled in different parts of the world and migration has continued ever since (Harari, 2014). It is common to distinguish the more recent history of international migration in four different periods (Massey et al., 1993).

In the *mercantile period* (1500–1800), colonization resulted in the settlement of Europeans in Africa and Asia, and subsequently in the Americas and Oceania. The European colonists set up a system of large-scale slavery, leading to the forced migration of an estimated 12.5 million African slaves to the Americas before 1850—most of them arriving in the Caribbean and South America (Eltis & Richardson, 2015). In the *industrial period* (1800–1914), the slave system came to an end. However, this created a demand for cheap labor because of shortages and the colonial authorities set up large-scale migration for indentured workers, particularly from Asia. It is estimated that around 12 to 37 million workers migrated, sometimes by force, in this slavery-like trade (Potts, 1990). Around the same time, around 48 million Europeans emigrated to the Americas (particularly to Argentina, Canada and the US) and Oceania (Australia and New Zealand), hoping to find better economic prospects there. At that time, then, the inflow of newcomers to the US was overwhelmingly from Europe: between 1820–1920, 88% of the immigrants in the US were from Europe (Castles et al., 2013). With the outbreak of WWI, emigration from Europe largely stopped. The *period of limited migration* (1914–1945) was characterized by economic crisis and hostility towards immigrants in many countries (Castles et al., 2013).

In the *post-industrial period* (1945–present), international migration again increased in volume and also became a more global phenomenon. Whereas in the industrial period migrants mainly originated from Europe and they typically settled in former European colonies, in the new era both the sending and receiving countries were more diversified (Massey et al., 1993). After World War II, more and more people from Africa, Asia and Latin America have migrated, thereby fundamentally changing the inflow of immigrants in western societies. For example, the US used to attract mainly European immigrants before WWII, but after WWII the major sources of origin were Asia, Mexico and South America. Furthermore, besides the traditional immigrant-receiving countries like Canada, the United States, Argentina, Australia and New Zealand, new immigrant-receiving countries began to emerge.

Between 1945 and 1973, several Western European countries, such as Germany, France, Belgium and the Netherlands, attracted many "guestworkers," typically low-skilled immigrants who were needed to fulfill labor shortages. Britain, France and the Netherlands furthermore witnessed an increase of immigrants from their former colonies, such as from Pakistan (Britain), Algeria (France) and Suriname (Netherlands). But new immigrant-receiving countries were emerging elsewhere, in Asia and Africa. After the oil-price rise of 1973, oil-producing countries of the Persian Gulf, such as Iraq, Kuwait and Saudi Arabia, attracted foreign workers from a variety of countries, in particular Egypt, Jordan/Palestine, India, Sri Lanka, Pakistan and Bangladesh (Castles et al., 2013).

In addition to these migration developments, another increasing source of international migration has to do with people who seek refuge elsewhere, because of conflict, violence and/or water/food shortages in their region of living. The United Nations Refugee Agency (UNHCR) keeps records of the mass displacements in the world that are due to such causes. Their estimates of "populations of concern to UNHCR" (i.e., refugees, asylum-seekers, internally displaced persons (IDPs), returnees (refugees and IDPs), stateless persons and others of concern to UNHCR), counted 32 million people in 2007. This number doubled to 64 million in 2015. Major origin countries of displaced persons in 2015 were the Syrian Arab Republic, Afghanistan and Iraq (UNHCR, 2016).

The United Nations regularly publishes statistics on the share of the **foreign-born population** per country, i.e., the number of immigrants in the country as a percentage of the entire population (i.e., both foreign-born and non-foreign born). Table 11.1 presents this data for the continents and a selected number of countries, giving the percentage of the population that are foreign-born, the so-called *migrant stock*, from 1990 to 2015. It shows that immigration has increased in the traditional immigrant-receiving countries like the US and Canada. It also appears that immigration is now a major social phenomenon in European societies, such as Germany. Not all countries show substantial increases in immigration and some nations even witness a decline in the migrant stock.

foreign-born population (also first generation) people born abroad.

The fact that some societies today have a low share of foreign-born population does not imply that these societies have no history of immigration. For this, we have to look back in time and also identify, as a start, among the non-foreign-born population those who are children of immigrants. It is conventional among social scientists to use the label **second generation** to indicate persons who were born in the host country but who have at least one foreign-born parent. By asking people about the parents' birthplace, scholars are able to identify this second generation. The foreign-born population is then called the **first generation**. Third and higher generation refers to those who were born in the host country and whose parents were

second generation people born in the host country, with at least one foreign-born parent.

Table 11.1 Migrant stock 1990–2015, percentage of total population.

	1990	2000	2010	2015
North America	**9.8**	**12.9**	**14.9**	**15.2**
United States	9.1	12.2	14.2	14.5
Canada	16.3	18.1	20.5	21.8
Mexico	0.8	0.5	0.8	0.9
South America	**1.6**	**1.2**	**1.4**	**1.5**
Argentina	5.0	4.2	4.4	4.8
Brazil	0.5	0.5	0.3	0.3
Asia	**1.5**	**1.3**	**1.6**	**1.7**
China	0.0	0.0	0.1	0.1
India	0.9	0.6	0.5	0.4
Indonesia	0.3	0.1	0.1	0.4
Japan	0.9	1.3	1.8	1.6
Pakistan	5.8	3.0	2.3	1.9
Africa	**2.5**	**1.8**	**1.6**	**1.7**
Nigeria	0.5	0.6	0.7	0.7
Egypt	0.3	0.3	0.4	0.5
South Africa	3.2	2.2	3.8	5.8
Europe	**6.8**	**7.7**	**9.8**	**10.3**
France	10.4	10.6	11.4	12.1
Germany	7.4	10.8	11.7	14.9
United Kingdom	6.4	8.0	11.3	13.2
Italy	2.5	3.7	9.7	9.7
Russia	7.8	8.1	7.8	8.1
Oceania	**17.5**	**17.3**	**19.6**	**20.6**
Australia	22.7	22.9	26.8	28.2

Source: United Nations, 2019.

also born in the host country. Table 11.2 presents the share of first and second generation for three traditional immigrant-receiving countries (Australia, Canada and US) and two more recent immigrant-receiving societies in Europe. As you can see, all countries have a significant second-generation population. In Australia, more than 20% of the population is the child of an immigrant parent.

Asking about the place of birth of the individual and that person's parents enables researchers to identify the first and second generation, and hence to get an understanding of the "migration history" of the country and the size of the group of immigrants and their children. Beyond the first and second generation, you could—in theory—also identify the immigrant offspring in the third generation (those who have at least one foreign-born grandparent)

Table 11.2 Percentage of first and second generation in the population, for the period 2005–2007.

	First generation	Second generation	Other (third generation +)
Canada	22	17	61
Australia	28	21	51
United States	12	13	75
Netherlands	12	11	77
France	16	11	74

Source: Australian Bureau of Statistics, 2019; Central Bureau of Statistics Netherlands, 2018; Kirszbaum, Brinbaum, Simon, & Gezer, 2009; Pew Research, 2013; Statistics Canada, 2019.

and also the fourth generation, fifth and so forth. However, such data are often time-consuming to gather and therefore rarely collected in surveys or censuses. For countries that have a truly long-term history of immigration, such as the United States, Canada and Australia, researchers are nevertheless interested in the diverse ethnic origins of the population in "the rest" category of "third generation and beyond." How do we measure these origins?

One way to measure these origins was invented by the 1980 Census of Population in the US, which asked, for the first time, about **ancestry**. Respondents were asked the open-ended question: "What is your ancestry?" They could fill in their ancestry in a blank line. Under this line the Census Bureau provided examples of appropriate responses:

> **ancestry** subjective identification with certain ethnic origin(s).

> For example: Afro-Amer., English, French, German, Honduran, Hungarian, Irish, Italian, Jamaican, Korean, Lebanese, Mexican, Nigerian, Polish, Ukrainian, Venezuelan, etc.

Furthermore, additional instructions were provided for the interviewer, to help the respondent understanding the question:

> Ancestry (or origin or descent) may be viewed as the nationality group, the lineage, or the country in which the person or the person's parents or ancestors were born before their arrival in the United States. Persons who are of more than one origin and who cannot identify with a single group should print their multiple ancestry (for example, German-Irish) … A religious group should not be reported as a person's ancestry.

Using the responses to the question about ancestry, sociologists could identify the ancestries of the American population in the population census of 1980 (Table 11.3).

Because respondents could indicate more than one ancestry, the figures add up to more than 100%. The largest ancestry groups at that time were the English (21.9%), German (21.5%) and Irish (17.8%). More than 9% indicated being "Afro-American," most of them the descendants of slaves. Another 2.9% identified themselves as "American Indian," the indigenous population of America. Close to 6% stated that they were "American" without further specifying a certain ancestry group. What this finding tells us, therefore, is that 94% of the American population in 1980 identified themselves with one or more different types of ancestry groups: some as the *indigenous population* (American Indian), some have their

Table 11.3 Ancestries of the American population in 1980.

Ancestry group	% of total population
English	21.9
German	21.5
Irish	17.8
Afro-American	9.3
American	5.9
French	5.7
Italian	5.5
Scottish	4.4
Polish	3.6
Mexican	3.4
American Indian	2.9
Dutch	2.8
Swedish	1.9
Norwegian	1.5
Russian	1.2
Spanish	1.0
Hungarian	0.8
Welsh	0.7
Danish	0.7
Puerto Rican	0.6
Czech	0.6
Portuguese	0.5

Source: Farley, 1991.

origin as European settlers or *voluntary migrants* (such as from England, Germany, Ireland), others as offspring of Black *slaves* or *involuntary migrants* (Afro-Americans).

The introduction of the ancestry question to the 1980 US Census created a new perspective on *ethnic origin*, i.e., origin (descent) beyond family roots (Fearon, 2003). First, the ancestry question is *supplemental* to questions about generations and national origins. Asking people to name their country of birth and the birthplace of their parents (and so forth) enables researchers to establish the *objective* ethnic origin of a respondent—typically up to two generations, but in principle beyond that as well. We have seen that when studying group affiliations (Chapter 8), you could use "objective" criteria (membership), but also more subjective affiliations (identification). The ancestry question is more "subjective" as it asks people to name the group with which they *identify*. The result is that the researchers collect data on *subjective* ethnic origins and thus ethnic group affiliation. This enables researchers to examine whether people who objectively belong to a certain ethnic group also identify themselves with that group. Furthermore, the ancestry question more easily captures the "third generation and beyond" ethnic group, capturing ethnic origins beyond the first and second generation. On the other hand, little is known about the ethnic origins of people who no longer identify themselves with a certain ethnic origin. For example, a child born in the United States with parents from Germany could identify as "American" rather than (a second generation) German. The result of this is that nothing is known about this person's ethnic roots. In principle, such not-identifying with the "true" ethnic roots could happen in every generation, even the first, although it is more frequent among later generations.

A second insight that came out of research on ethnic origins is that group identification is *multi-layered*. This became evident from the answers of the respondents to the ancestry question. As people were free to fill in any group they identified with as their ancestry (origin, descent) group, quite a few people filled in with groups other than national origin groups. Some people identified their ethnic roots as "Italian" but others identified as "Sicilian," "Tuscan," "Umbrian" or "Lombardian." The Census Bureau combined these within-national ancestries under the "Italian" rubric (Lieberson & Waters, 1988), but sometimes researchers use even broader ethnic origin categories such as "Europe." This creates a three-layered structure of ethnic origins: regional (Sicily), national (Italy), continental (Europe). In the US context, as in some other countries as well, it is also quite common to lump various specific ethnic groups together into broader "ethnic-racial" categories. Examples are: "Whites," "Asians," "Hispanics" and "Blacks." Both objectively and subjectively, ethnic origins can therefore be traced to different layers or levels.

Third, because ethnic origin is a social category, i.e., a group in the minimal sense of the word, an "ethnic group" need not necessarily be a *cohesive* ethnic group, a community with strong in-group favoritism and social norms. People living in the US whose ethnic origin is Italian, for example, do not necessarily make up a cohesive Italian group and/or have a shared Italian culture. This could be the case, but this is not a requisite for ethnic group affiliation. Whether people who are affiliated to the same Italian ethnic group often have face-to-face interactions with each other, whether they are organized in Italian ethnic organizations, speak the Italian language, whether they are (still) predominantly Catholic and so forth, is open to empirical investigations. In the words of Andreas Wimmer:

> When studying "Turks," "Swiss," or "Mexicans," however, one should be careful to avoid the ... fallacy of assuming communitarian closure, cultural difference, and shared identity. The study has to ask, rather than assume, whether there is indeed community organization, ethnic closure in networking practices, a shared identity, etc. (Wimmer, 2009)

When we speak about **ethnic groups**, therefore, we refer to people who are affiliated to the same origin (descent) beyond family roots. One could use objective or subjective criteria to determine to which ethnic group(s) people belong; one could differentiate different layers of ethnic groups (local, national, continental), but these ethnic groups do not necessarily imply groups in the *strong* sense, i.e., as communities whose members share beliefs, values and norms. We can speak of the social relations within ethnic groups (e.g., how cohesive is the group?) and about its culture (e.g., do members speak the Italian language?), but these are *characteristics* of the ethnic group—and do not define being an ethnic group in the first place.

ethnic group
people affiliated to the same origin beyond family roots.

Given the continuous stream of migration across the globe, researchers have become highly interested in studying the degree of **ethnic diversity** of societies. One way to capture the ethnic diversity of a society would be to simply count the number of ethnic groups

ethnic diversity
ethnic heterogeneity of a population.

present in society. However, this would ignore the size of the various groups. If there were, for example, ten ethnic groups in society and the biggest of these groups made up 20% of the total population, this would be something different than if this group were only 0.2% of the total. Therefore, a better way to capture ethnic diversity is to consider both the number and the size of ethnic groups. This is done in the so-called *ethnic diversity index* (ED) (Alesina, Devleeschauwer, Easterly, Kurlat, & Wacziarg, 2003):

$$ED_j = 1 - \sum_{i=1}^{N} p_{ij}^2$$

where P_{ij} is the proportion of ethnic group i ($i = 1 ... N$) in country j. The ED thereby measures the diversity of ethnic groups in society as one minus its degree of ethnic concentration, whereby the amount of concentration is captured by taking the sum of the squared proportions of each ethnic group in society. To illustrate how the diversity index (also called a *fractionalization* index) works, Table 11.4 gives several examples. In the case where there is only one ethnic group in society (country H), $ED_H = 1-1^2 = 0$. This would be a completely *ethnically homogenous* society. In country G there are two groups: 95% of the population are affiliated to one group, the other 5% to the other group. This means that $ED_G = 1 - 0.95^2 - 0.05^2 = 0.1$. Intuitively, this ethnic diversity index can then be interpreted as that the probability that two randomly selected individuals from country G belong to a different ethnic group is 0.1. In country E in Table 11.4 this probability is 0.5 and this can be easily seen as there are two groups equal in size. In theory, if there were as many groups as there were individuals in society (so every ethnic group has size 1), then ethnic diversity would be at its maximum and so ED would be 1.

Table 11.4 Illustrations of the ethnic diversity index.

Country	Structure	ED_J
A	*n* groups = *n* individuals	1.0
B	*n* groups (0.48, 0.01, 0.01, ...)	0.76
C	4 groups (0.25, 0.25, 0.25, 0.25)	0.75
D	3 groups (0.33, 0.33, 0.33)	0.67
E	2 groups (0.5, 0.5)	0.50
F	2 groups (0.8, 0.2)	0.32
G	2 groups (0.95, 0.05)	0.10
H	1 group	0

Source: Fearon, 2003.

Now that we have a measure of ethnic diversity, you may wonder how ethnically diverse contemporary societies are. This question has been addressed in several studies. One study, initiated by Alesina and colleagues, collected data on 650 ethnic groups in 190 countries, around the year 2000 (Alesina et al., 2003). Their findings should be taken with great caution, however, because of the uncertainties involved in collecting data on the size of ethnic groups in each of these 190 nations (Fearon, 2003). That said, the results are illustrative and even suggest some surprising broader empirical patterns that warrant further research.

Table 11.5 presents the results of the Alesina et al. study for a few selected cases, ranked by their ethnic diversity. It also shows the share of countries of the study with certain levels of ethnic diversity. As can be seen, 1% of the countries examined had very high levels of ethnic diversity: $ED > 0.9$. Uganda and Liberia are the two ethnically most diverse nations which together make up this upper category. The ethnic diversity index exceeding 0.9 means that when you compare two randomly selected individuals in Uganda, for example, the probability that they belong to a different ethnic group is more than 0.9. Somewhat lower in the ethnic diversity ranking we find Mexico, Brazil, Switzerland, the United States and India, examples of countries with moderately high levels of ethnic diversity ($0.4 < ED < 0.6$). Compared with these nations, ethnic diversity levels around the year 2000 were lower in Germany, China, the UK, Austria and France ($0.1 < ED < 0.2$). Examples of the least ethnically diverse societies were Japan, South Korea, Yemen, Portugal and Norway.

Table 11.5 Ethnic diversity around the year 2000.

Ethnic diversity	ED_J	%	Examples
Highest	0.9–1.0	1.05	Uganda, Liberia
Very high	0.8–0.9	6.84	Madagascar, Congo, Kenya, Nigeria, Ivory Coast
High	0.6–0.8	25.26	Libya, Angola, Afghanistan, South Africa, Indonesia
Moderate	0.4–0.6	22.63	Mexico, Brazil, Switzerland, United States, India
Low	0.2–0.4	18.95	Zimbabwe, Israel, Taiwan, Argentina, Russia
Very low	0.1–0.2	14.21	Germany, UK, Austria, France, China
Lowest	0–0.1	11.05	Japan, South Korea, Yemen, Portugal, Norway

Source: Alesina et al., 2003.

On a more general level, it is concluded in the study that, around the year 2000, the European continent was the most ethnically homogenous of all continents, whereas Africa was the most ethnically diverse (Alesina et al., 2003). The most ethnically diverse countries are to be found in Sub-Saharan Africa. Whether such a conclusion still holds today, given the changes in immigration that occurred after the year 2000 in Europe and elsewhere, is open to empirical scrutiny. What is evident, however, is that European countries have become more ethnically diverse since that time and that, in particular, there is a strong increase of the first and second generation population (Castles et al., 2013).

11.3 Integration: what does it mean?

The increasing ethnic diversity of many societies in past decades has made the topic of integration ever more pressing. How well are immigrants and their children integrated in the host society? To answer questions on *integration*, we first need to clarify this concept. In public discourse the term is used in different ways and in the social sciences (sociology, psychology, anthropology, economics) there are various interpretations of the concept of "integration" and related concepts like "incorporation," "acculturation" and "assimilation" as well (Alba & Nee, 1997; Berry, 1997). The disagreement over the definition of the concept of integration relates to three elements (Alba & Nee, 2003; Drouhot & Nee, 2019; Jonsson, Kalter, & Van Tubergen, 2018).

Normative or empirical?

Integration can be conceptualized as a normative issue (social problem) or as a social phenomenon (scientific problem). From a normative perspective, integration is something that is seen as desirable or undesirable, depending on one's political views. But integration can also be regarded as a social phenomenon, without making claims that integration should or should not be achieved, or in which way. Sociologists study integration as a social phenomenon whereas, in public discourse, integration is often interpreted from a normative perspective.

One-sided or multi-sided?

Another point of differentiation is whether one regards integration as something that concerns only ethnic minorities (*one-sided*), or if it is thought that integration is about ethnic minority and ethnic majority populations (*multi-sided*). For example, one can consider language learning of immigrants and argue that integration is about how well immigrants and their children speak and write the official language. In such a one-sided view, the only actors that can contribute to integration are ethnic minorities—the ethnic majority population is left out of the question about integration. Sociologists commonly take a multi-sided perspective (Alba & Foner, 2015b; Alba & Nee, 2003, 1997). In a multi-sided perspective integration refers to the degree of intergroup acceptance and similarity between ethnic minority and ethnic majority groups with respect to key dimensions. The opposite of integration can thus be thought of as the distance between (members of) both groups. This means, for example, that ethnic majority members can undermine integration by distancing themselves from ethnic minority members. Distances between ethnic minority and majority groups can increase if, for example, majority members do not befriend minorities, or if majority parents send their children to ethnic majority schools (Jonsson et al., 2018).

Unidimensional or multidimensional?

Integration can be regarded as a unidimensional and a multidimensional phenomenon. For example, one could equate integration with *economic* similarities between ethnic minority and majority groups and examine such indicators as labor force participation, employment and income. However, it is more common to think in sociology that integration is multidimensional (Gordon, 1964), a *complex concept* (Chapter 3). This means that integration can be *conceptualized* (Chapter 3) as consisting of various dimensions that are analytically distinct from each other (Alba & Nee, 1997; Drouhot & Nee, 2019). Hence, integration along one dimension does not imply integration along other dimensions. Three dimensions are typically distinguished and they relate to the CSI themes outlined in this book: culture, social relations and inequality (Drouhot & Nee, 2019).

Topics

- **Cultural integration** relates to the theme of culture. It indicates the degree of similarity between members of ethnic minority and majority groups with respect to cultural opinions, norms and corresponding practices. Obviously, neither members of ethnic minority groups nor members of ethnic majority populations tend to have the same cultural opinions, norms and practices. Therefore, when thinking of cultural integration, it makes sense to acknowledge that groups have tendencies towards certain cultural traits (Polavieja, 2015). To illustrate, suppose we have a measure of "gender values" ranging from 0 (very conservative) to 10 (very progressive). Then we compare ethnic groups A and B with an ethnic majority group C. Assume that members of ethnic minority group A score 3 on average on this scale and 95% of the members of this group score within the range between 2 and 4. Ethnic group B scores much higher on this scale, it has a mean of 7 (95% within range 6–8), and the ethnic majority group scores even higher, with 9 on average (95% within range 8–10). Clearly, if you then compare these groups based on this gender values scale, we would conclude that groups B and C are more culturally similar, more "culturally integrated," than groups A and C, which are more culturally distinct.

  > **cultural integration** degree of similarity between members of ethnic minority and majority groups with respect to cultural opinions, norms and corresponding practices.

- **Social integration** refers to the theme of social relations. It indicates the degree of intergroup cohesion between members of different ethnic groups. The cohesion between ethnic groups is stronger when (1) interethnic ties are more common, (2) interethnic attitudes are more positive, (3) intergroup cooperation, trust and solidarity is stronger and (4), intergroup aggression and violence is reduced. When, instead, ethnic groups have predominantly group-bonding ties (and few group-bridging ties), when interethnic sentiments are strongly negative, when ethnic groups distrust each other and when aggression and violence between ethnic groups emerges, social integration is clearly undermined. Similar to what we said about cultural integration, it is important to realize that, when we speak of social integration, we should acknowledge that there can be within-group differences. For example, when an ethnic group A is negatively perceived by the ethnic majority group C, it can be the case that there are also ethnic majority members who have positive attitudes towards group A. Nevertheless, when 95% of ethnic majority group C thinks negatively about ethnic group A and only 10% thinks negatively about group B, then we can say that, based on interethnic attitudes, members of group B and C are socially closer to each other, more "socially integrated," than members of groups A and C.

  > **social integration** degree of intergroup cohesion between members of different ethnic groups.

- **Economic integration** relates to the theme of inequality. It indicates the degree of similarity between ethnic minority and majority members in realizing valued goals. If we say that an ethnic group is not fully integrated economically, it means that there are unequal chances between ethnic groups in realizing their goals. If this is the case, societies are hierarchically ordered and stratified by ethnic groups. Such ethnic inequalities can arise with respect to, for example, education, employment, income, wealth, housing, health and well-being. And, similar to the concepts of cultural and social integration, the concept of economic integration also considers diversity within ethnic groups (Spörlein & Schlueter, 2018). If, say, a few members of ethnic minority group A have high-status jobs and outperform ethnic majority members in the labor market, it may still be that, on average, the chances to get such jobs are typically much smaller for members from ethnic minority group A than for ethnic majority members.

  > **economic integration** degree of similarity between ethnic minority and ethnic majority groups in realizing valued goals.

In summary, a common sociological approach to the topic of **integration** is to consider it as a multi-sided, multidimensional social phenomenon.

11.4 Integration: changes over time?

The theoretical and empirical literature on integration started at the beginning of the 20th century, after the great migration to the United States (1880–1920). It was shortly after that massive migration movement that various scholars started to formulate theories on the process of integration. One well-known idea is that the (social, cultural and economic) integration of immigrants and their offspring is a process that takes time (Gordon, 1964; Park & Burgess, 1969 [1921]). Initially, when immigrants arrive in their new country, most are hardly integrated. With increasing "length of stay," so the argument goes, immigrants and their offspring become more integrated.

> **integration** degree of cultural similarity (cultural integration), intergroup cohesion (social integration) and similarity in realizing valued goals (economic integration) between ethnic groups.

The concept of "length of stay" can be interpreted in two ways, namely: (1) as a *life-course* effect and (2) as a *generation* effect. First, the process of increasing integration can unfold over the life course, i.e., within someone's generation. This means that, within their life course, the opinions and norms of immigrants will converge with those of the mainstream culture, that immigrants will establish more social ties with ethnic majority members and that immigrants will work their way into the labor market. Second, increasing integration can also be expected to occur between generations. This would mean that the children of immigrants will be more socially, culturally and economically integrated than their parents, and this process of increasing integration continues with each successive generation. Either way, the ethnic majority population is expected to become more accepting of newcomers over time and to also overcome initial barriers to integration.

Let's write down this idea, which I will refer to as the ***immigrant integration*** proposition:

> P. With increasing length of stay of an ethnic minority group in a certain country, this ethnic minority group becomes more integrated. (*immigrant integration*)

In the literature, ideas very similar to this proposition are called the "assimilation model," "straight-line assimilation," "immigrant incorporation" and "adaptation" (Alba & Nee, 1997; Drouhot & Nee, 2019). However, some scholars have made a distinction between the concepts of "integration" and "assimilation" (Berry, 1997). I use the term ***immigrant assimilation*** to indicate a "stronger" version of the immigrant integration proposition, namely the proposition that, over time, the ethnic minority and majority groups become indistinguishable, fully "assimilated," and eventually ethnic group affiliation is no longer a meaningful social categorization. The difference between the two propositions is thus that the immigrant integration proposition argues that ethnic groups become more similar to each other over time, that groups tend to converge and accept each other, but that complete assimilation need not be the end state. The integration proposition leaves open the possibility of maintaining distinct cultural heritage and ethnic group identities.

The integration proposition (and its strong version: the assimilation proposition) has been a key starting point of theoretical and empirical studies of cultural, social and economic integration (Alba & Foner, 2015b; Alba & Nee, 1997; Bean & Stevens, 2003; Esser, 2004; Waters & Jiménez, 2005). As you can see, these propositions are not normative judgments, i.e., they do not say that ethnic minority groups should integrate. The propositions are theoretical statements that can be tested empirically. Both propositions can be related to each dimension of integration, i.e., cultural, social and economic integration.

In order to empirically test whether the propositions are true, researchers rely on indicators of each dimension (Figure 11.1). For example, scholars study language proficiency and usage as indicators of cultural integration. When immigrants and their children are more proficient in the official language of the host country, and when they use that language more often in daily conversations, it is a sign that they are more culturally integrated. Other indicators of cultural integration are religion, social norms and values. For each dimension of integration (cultural, social, economic) scholars examine multiple indicators.

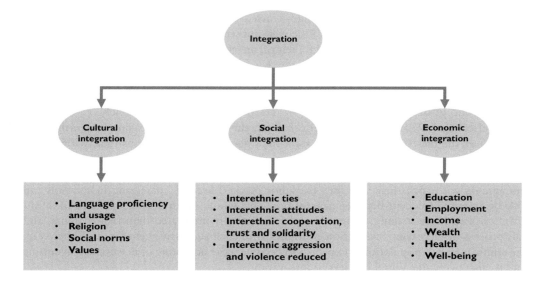

Figure 11.1 Indicators of the three dimensions of integration.

What do empirical studies tell us about the integration and assimilation propositions? Let's start with *cultural* integration. We have seen (Chapter 6) that cultural opinions, norms and corresponding practices that prevailed in the country of origin of ethnic minorities are passed on from generation to generation within the ethnic group in the country of destination, but with each generation they become less prevalent—until they largely disappear as successive generations adopt the mainstream culture (Giavazzi, Petkov, & Schiantarelli, 2019; Greeley & McCready, 1975; Rice & Feldman, 1997). Studies also suggest that immigrants and their offspring adjust their religious practices to mainstream religious practices among the ethnic majority population (Connor, 2008; Van Tubergen, 2006b). For example, ethnic minorities from strongly religious Muslim societies who migrated to more secular western European societies tend to become less religious over time with successive generations (Diehl & Koenig, 2009; Maliepaard & Lubbers, 2013; Maliepaard, Lubbers, & Gijsberts, 2010; Van de Pol & Van Tubergen, 2014).

Many immigrants are not very proficient in the official language of the destination country upon arrival. What happens over time? Scholars have consistently found both life course and generation changes. Immigrants gradually acquire the "second language" (L2) with length of stay, i.e., with years of residence in the host country immigrants become more proficient in speaking, writing, listening to and reading the official language (Bean & Stevens, 2003; Espinosa & Massey, 1997; Hwang & Xi, 2008; Mesch, 2003; Stevens, 1999; Van

Tubergen & Kalmijn, 2005). Many of them, however, never become fully proficient in L2 (Van Tubergen & Kalmijn, 2009a). The children of immigrants, however, make a significant step towards becoming fluent in L2 (Bean & Stevens, 2003).

Language proficiency does not imply that one also actively *uses* the language. But scholars find that being proficient in a certain language goes hand in hand with using the language—for example in daily conversations or when watching the news. A common pattern found among ethnic minority groups is the *three-generation language shift* (Alba, Logan, Lutz, & Stults, 2002; Veltman, 1983). The first generation (i.e., foreign-born) has limited knowledge of L2 and, although they then improve their L2 language skills with length of stay, most continue to use their first language (L1), i.e., the language of their origin country (*mother tongue*). The second generation acquire L1 from their parents and ethnic group, but they don't become as proficient in L1 as their parents and they learn L2 in school. They are *bilingual*, i.e., they use both L1 and L2. By the third generation, most ethnic minority members have entirely shifted to using L2 only (Esser, 2006; Portes & Hao, 1998; Portes & Rumbaut, 2006; Rumbaut, Massey, & Bean, 2006).

Similarly, scholars have observed that *social* integration unfolds over time. For example, when they arrive in a new country, ethnic minorities tend to identify strongly and exclusively with their ethnic group but, over time and in particular across generations, they identify more strongly with the host society, which is a sign of increasing intergroup cohesion (Diehl & Schnell, 2006). Likewise, interethnic contacts and friendships are rather uncommon upon arrival but, both within the life course (Martinovic, Van Tubergen, & Maas, 2009) and across generations, interethnic ties become more prevalent (Diehl & Schnell, 2006). Similar patterns are observed for ethnic intermarriage—another key indicator of social integration. Studies generally report that among the foreign-born population endogamy rates are high: many immigrants marry someone from their own ethnic group. But this changes across generations. The second generation has lower levels of endogamy and higher rates of exogamy than the first generation, a pattern found among ethnic groups in the US (Lichter, Qian, & Tumin, 2015; Qian & Lichter, 2007; Rosenfeld, 2002) and in Europe (Kalmijn & Van Tubergen, 2006; Kalter & Schroedter, 2010; Lucassen & Laarman, 2009). With successive generations, ethnic intermarriage becomes gradually more prevalent (Lieberson, 1980; Spörlein, Schlueter, & Van Tubergen, 2014).

Regarding *economic* integration, studies in western societies typically find that foreign-born immigrants tend to be less educated than the ethnic majority population. However, this educational gap becomes smaller over time and with successive generations (Drouhot & Nee, 2019). Children of immigrants are typically more educated and more often attend college than their parents. Studies in the US typically find that there is an increase in educational attainment across immigrant generations, such that they converge to the ethnic majority population or sometimes outperform them (Duncan, 2018; Farley & Alba, 2002; Kao & Thompson, 2003; Tran, 2018). Also in Europe, such gains in educational attainment by immigrant children have been observed (Heath & Brinbaum, 2014; Heath, Rothon, & Kilpi, 2008; Li, 2018). With respect to labor market position, studies of ethnic groups in the US similarly note initial disadvantages in employment, occupational status and income, and a steady progress in each immigrant generation in their position (Bean & Stevens, 2003; Luthra & Waldinger, 2010; Waters & Pineau, 2015). In Europe, such generational changes in labor market positions are more difficult to make because the second generation in European countries is still relatively young (Heath et al., 2008). However, recent studies generally report higher occupational status among the second generation than the first generation, and convergence to the native majority (Lessard-Phillips, Fibbi, & Wanner, 2012; Li & Heath, 2016; Pichler, 2011).

When we take together the literature on cultural, social and economic integration, the general picture that emerges from scientific studies is that, generally speaking, there is increasing integration with length of stay (Alba & Nee, 2003). With the passage of time, ethnic minorities acquire the host language, they use the official language more often, their opinions and norms are adjusted to what is common in the host society, interethnic friendships and marriages between ethnic minority and majority groups become more prevalent, ethnic minorities tend to think of themselves more as being members of the host country and, with successive generations, ethnic disadvantages with respect to education and employment diminish. We can summarize the findings from the literature as a stylized fact called the *integration process*.

STYLIZED FACT 11.1

Integration process
With increasing length of stay of an ethnic minority group in a certain country, this ethnic minority group becomes more integrated.

This stylized fact provides empirical support for the immigrant integration proposition. Empirical findings indicate that there is a general *tendency* towards increasing cultural, social and economic integration over time, which means that the process may take many generations or even stabilize at some point. The stronger version of this proposition, that immigrants become assimilated and indistinguishable, is more contested. Ethnic minority groups may, even after several generations, still identify themselves as such: as an ethnic group that is different from the host society. Cultural traits may be passed on from generation to generation and also become part of the cultural diversity in society.

11.5 Integration: social context effects?

When I say that empirical findings indicate that there is a general tendency towards increasing integration, I mean that this pattern is *typically* seen for *most* ethnic groups, in *most* host societies. It is the *baseline* pattern. However, scholars have noted that there are notable deviations from this common trend: some ethnic groups are more integrated than other groups and host countries differ in the degree of integration of ethnic groups too. In some countries ethnic groups are better integrated than in other countries. An important insight scholars have made is that the integration process depends on *social contexts*, such as the ethnic group, the receiving context and the interplay between the two (Crul, Schneider, & Lelie, 2012; Portes & Rumbaut, 2006; Van Tubergen, Maas, & Flap, 2004).

To illustrate, consider the notable differences between ethnic groups in their language proficiency and usage. In the multi-ethnic United States, studies consistently find that some ethnic groups speak better English (L2) and use L2 instead of their mother tongue (L1) more than other ethnic groups. For example, Mexican immigrants and their offspring typically show slower levels of L2 acquisition than other ethnic groups. One study using data from the 2000 US Census reports that, among Mexicans who were between 13–34 years of age when they arrived in the US, only 15% speak English "very well" (Portes & Rumbaut, 2006). In comparison, among those who came from the Philippines (and who also arrived when they were 13–34 years old), 70% speak English very well and among German immigrants this is even higher at 82%. Another study found that, by the third generation, 64% of the children with Mexican origins speak only English at home and no other language (Alba et al., 2002), thereby suggesting that one third still used some Spanish in the third generation. Language shift goes faster among other ethnic groups. For example, among the Chinese, by the third generation 91% speak only English at home, among the Japanese this is 97% and among Filipinos it is 96%. Such ethnic group differences in the speed of change from L1 to L2 have been found consistently across countries, such as in Canada (Lieberson, 1970), France (Tribalat, 1995) and Israel (Beenstock, 1996; Raijman, Semyonov, & Geffen, 2015).

Such ethnic group differences in the integration process are not limited to language. In fact, ethnic group differences have been found for each dimension of integration: cultural, social and economic (Drouhot & Nee, 2019). For example, scholars have noted significant differences in intermarriages across ethnic groups, with some groups having higher endogamy rates than others (Alba & Foner, 2015a; Lucassen & Laarman, 2009). Ethnic group differences have been found for interethnic friendships (Wimmer & Lewis, 2010), religion (Van Tubergen & Sindradóttir, 2011), education (Kroneberg, 2008; Levels, Dronkers, & Kraaykamp, 2008) and labor market outcomes (Fleischmann & Dronkers, 2010; Gorodzeisky & Semyonov, 2017; Heath, 2008; Kogan, 2006).

Why do ethnic group differences in the process of integration emerge? Why, for example, do Mexicans in the US have lower English language proficiency and use English less often than other ethnic groups? To answer this question we should look at the *characteristics* of ethnic groups. From the very moment when they arrive in their destination country, ethnic groups can differ in numerous important ways, such as in their *religion* (e.g., Christian, Muslim, other), *education* (e.g., low-skilled, high-skilled), *migration motives* (e.g., political, family, labor), *skin color* (e.g., black, white) and *official language* of their origin country (e.g., English or Chinese). Ethnic groups can also differ in the *historical relations* to the host country (e.g., former colonies, neighboring countries) and in the *number* of group members residing in the host country (e.g., smaller and larger ethnic groups). These ethnic group characteristics can impact the integration trajectory.

To see how, consider again the fact that Mexicans have lower L2 proficiency and use L2 less often than other groups. One key characteristic of ethnic groups that plays a role here is their size. Some ethnic groups have sizeable numbers of migrants in a certain country, such as Mexicans in the US, while other groups may be smaller. Some have only recently settled in the host society whereas other groups are more established—possibly over many generations. The size of an ethnic group is a contextual condition which impacts the speed with which ethnic group members acquire L2. We can represent this idea with a multilevel framework (Figure 11.2).

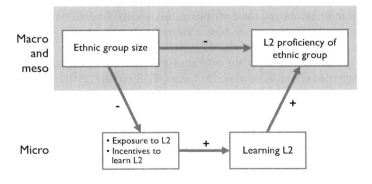

Figure 11.2 Influence of ethnic group size on L2 proficiency.

Ethnic group size is a contextual condition that influences *exposure* to L1 and L2 and the *incentives to invest* in L2 (Chiswick & Miller, 1996, 2001). Larger ethnic groups provide more opportunities for their members to communicate in their own ethnic language (L1), such as with neighbors, colleagues and friends (Stevens, 1992). Consequently, members of larger ethnic groups are relatively often exposed to L1 and less exposed to L2, and this limited exposure makes it more difficult to acquire L2. Members of smaller ethnic groups, by contrast, have many interethnic contacts, which implies greater exposure to L2 and they thereby acquire L2 more quickly. Moreover, ethnic group size affects the incentives to learn L2. Language is part of human capital (Espenshade & Fu, 1997). Learning a new language is difficult and costly, of course, and investments in human capital are subject to weighting costs and benefits. In larger ethnic groups members more often have jobs in ethnic enclaves and in co-ethnic businesses, for which they don't need to be proficient in L2. Hence, members of larger ethnic groups may have fewer incentives to invest in learning L2.

In line with these two arguments, studies consistently find that there is an inverse relationship between, on the one hand, ethnic group size in the country and, on the other hand, L2 proficiency and L2 usage, i.e., the larger the ethnic group, the less proficient their members are in L2 and the less often they use L2 (Hwang & Xi, 2008; Van Tubergen & Kalmijn, 2005, 2009a).

Group size is an important contextual condition that helps to explain why Mexicans in the US speak L2 less well than do other groups. In the US they are a very large group, in particular when taking into account the fact that their mother tongue (Spanish) is also common among many other ethnic minority groups. But, if you study Mexican immigrants in another country, in which there are only a few of them, such as in Australia or Canada, then very likely Mexicans in these destinations will acquire the host country language more rapidly.

In fact, group size matters not only for language learning. Group size also impacts intergroup cohesion, as we have seen before (Chapter 8) and thus social integration. Specifically, group size constrains the opportunity to meet members of outgroups (group-bridging ties) and instead promotes developing friendships and marriages with ingroup members (group-bonding ties). Group size also fosters perceptions of ethnic competition and threat, leading to more negative intergroup attitudes, aggression and violence.

In conclusion, integration trajectories differ across ethnic groups and we can understand such group differences by considering contextual conditions, such as group size. But contextual conditions may also be more generally related to the host country, to the context of reception (Portes & Rumbaut, 2006). Countries and regions can impact the process of immigrant integration as well. For example, integration policies in the host society may or may not be favorable to the integration of immigrants and their offspring. It is widely debated whether multicultural policies would improve integration in the host country or, rather, impede the process of integration (Koopmans, 2010, 2013; Kymlicka & Banting, 2006). Countries also differ in their anti-immigrant sentiments and support for anti-immigrant political parties, and such negative views can also change over time (Akkerman, De Lange, & Rooduijn, 2016; Bohman & Hjerm, 2016). When anti-immigrant sentiments are strong, it may undermine the development of intergroup friendships and widespread discrimination creates barriers of labor market integration.

Countries can also differ in certain institutional and labor market conditions (Kogan, 2006). For example, educational systems vary across countries in the timing of selection into different school types. In some countries this happens at an early age (e.g., age 10 in Germany) and in other countries this occurs much later. Some scholars have argued that early tracking hampers the educational attainment of the second generation because it gives them little time to escape from their disadvantaged starting position (Crul & Vermeulen, 2003). Indeed, one study found that in countries that use early education tracking, children of immigrants had lower educational attainment as compared with countries that apply such selection events at a later age (Van de Werfhorst, Van Elsas, Heath, & Brinbaum, 2014).

In summary, contemporary research on integration studies the role of contextual effects. The ethnic group, the receiving context and the interplay between these two provide social conditions that moderate the integration process. By considering characteristics of ethnic groups, such as their size, we can better understand why some ethnic groups more easily integrate into society than other groups. Similarly, we can explain differences across receiving contexts by examining the impact of integration policies and institutional and labor market conditions.

11.6 Case study: culture of honor

To illustrate the role contextual conditions can play in moderating the integration process, let's consider one specific case in more detail. In the 18th century, the US faced large-scale inflows of immigrants from two origins: Ulster (Scots-Irish) and the Scottish Highlands. At that time, inhabitants of these two regions of origin endorsed a **culture of honor**, a culture which strongly values reputation in the community and the right to self-defense in case one's honor is threatened (Oyserman, 2017). These honor values were adaptations to pastoral and lawless areas and were formed in the absence of formal law enforcement when people had to protect their own family and property, such as their own herds. This means that it was important to show strength, to keep up a good reputation and to punish others when they threatened your status and honor. Ulster and the Scottish Highlands were the most violent areas in Europe at that time.

> **culture of honor**
> culture which strongly endorses/ values reputation and the right to self-defense in case one's honor is threatened.

The immigrants from these regions of origin, therefore, had deeply ingrained culture of honor values when they arrived in the US in the 18th century. This ethnic-origin condition determined the situation of their members at the moment they entered the US. There is ample evidence that, after their arrival, immigrants from these two groups were using violence more so than other ethnic groups (Roth, 2012). Then, ethnic group conditions come into play: immigrants from Ulster and the Scottish Highlands were numerous and they tended to cluster together in certain areas and so did their children. Because of parental influence, their culture of honor was transmitted within the ethnic group, from those who were born in Ulster and the Scottish Highlands (first generation), to their children (second generation) and so forth—from generation to generation.

In the 19th century, however, third-party law enforcement became stronger in the North of the US than in the South. These changes in the receiving context impacted the integration process in the North: for all ethnic minority members—irrespective of their origin—it became less rewarding and more costly to protect oneself (violently, if needed). Consequently, the culture of honor and its associated use of violence became more sanctioned and less needed in the North than in the South (Wyatt-Brown, 2001)—as people became more strongly protected by the state. In other words: the honor values were no longer needed in the North and people in the North adjusted their values to these changing circumstances, an illustration of the adaptation bias (Chapter 5). In the South, however, formal control was less strongly developed and hence it was more valuable to use violence for self-protection. Hence, culture of honor values made more sense there.

It is illustrative to see that certain values, inherited from the country of origin culture, may pass on from generation to generation within an ethnic group—and only slightly adjusting to the culture of the host country. For how many generations did culture of honor—brought to the US in the 18th century—survive in the South? According to Nisbett and Cohen, it may have lasted for more than 200 years, albeit not as vividly as when the first immigrants from Ulster and the Scottish Highlands arrived in the US (Nisbett & Cohen, 1996).

In 1994, they discovered a surprising regional pattern in the readiness to use violence in the United States (Cohen & Nisbett, 1994). Using a nationwide survey conducted in 1972, these authors compared Whites living in the South ("Southerners") with Whites in the non-South ("Northerners") in their attitudes towards using violence for self-protection. Figure 11.3 presents their findings. A striking outcome of their study was that Southerners appeared more positive towards the right to kill someone for purposes of self-defense. For example, 80% of Southerners agreed "a great deal" that a man has the right to kill a person to defend his family. Among non-South, only 67% said so.

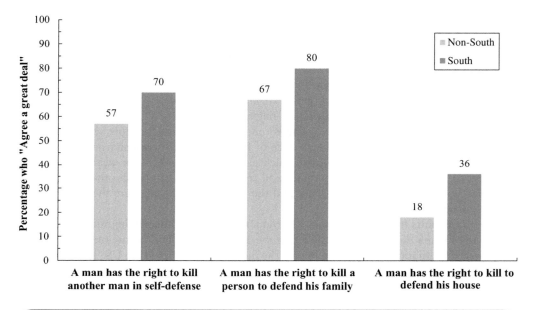

Figure 11.3 Attitudes towards use of violence in South and non-South in the US.
Source: Cohen & Nisbett, 1994

According to Nisbett and Cohen, this finding may reveal that the culture of honor in the South of the United States was still traceable in 1972, about two centuries after it was imported. Within a culture of honor, people are strongly concerned about their own reputation in the community. When their reputation is threatened, violence is seen as an acceptable behavioral response. In the South, people are generally more positive towards using violence as a means to protect themselves, their family and their belongings. It is seen as important to be tough and not to show evidence of weakness. Nisbett and Cohen argue that this culture of honor is still more widespread in the South than it is in the non-South.

Can we trust this conclusion? What about the issue of false positives and the role of replication (Chapter 3)? To validate their claim, Nisbett and Cohen carried out several follow-up studies, using different methods. In one study they used lab experiments. The participants were University of Michigan students who grew up either in the South or the North (Cohen,

Nisbett, Bowdle, & Schwarz, 1996). On their way to what the students assumed to be the experiment, they were insulted by a confederate who bumped into each participant and called the student an "asshole." The students were not aware of the fact that this confederate was an actor and that this incident was set up by the professors. For the researchers, this incident was the true experiment and the key question for them was: would Northerner and Southerner students respond differently to this insult? If the idea of a Southern culture of honor was true, then the students who were born in the South would react more aggressively to the confederate than their peers who were born in the North. Their study showed that Northerners were relatively unaffected by the insult, whereas Southerners felt more stressed and responded violently. Amongst other findings, the research showed that the cortisol levels (indicating stress) and testosterone levels (indicating aggression) of Southerners strongly increased after the insult, whereas this was not the case for Northerners. These findings suggest a deeply ingrained, emotional inclination and preference among Southerners to use violence for self-protection.

In yet another follow-up study on the culture of honor in the South, Nisbett and Cohen conducted a field experiment (Cohen & Nisbett, 1997). They created fictitious letters which they then sent to employers, inquiring about a job. All applicants had the appropriate qualifications. However, the fictitious applicants were also convicted for honor-related homicide. This is how the issue was phrased in the letter they sent to the employers:

> There is one thing I must explain, because I feel I must be honest and want no misunderstandings. I have been convicted of a felony, namely manslaughter. You will probably want an explanation for this before you send me an application, so I will provide it. I got into a fight with someone who was having an affair with my fiancée. I lived in a small town, and one night this person confronted me in front of my friends at the bar. He told everyone that he and my fiancée were sleeping together. He laughed at me to my face and asked me to step outside if I was man enough. I was young and didn't want to back down from a challenge in front of everyone. As we went into the alley, he started to attack me. He knocked me down, and he picked up a bottle. I could have run away and the judge said I should have, but my pride wouldn't let me. Instead I picked up a pipe that was laying in the alley and hit him with it. I didn't mean to kill him, but he died a few hours later at the hospital.

The letters were sent to 912 businesses across the country. In total, Nisbett and Cohen analyzed 112 responses. In line with expectations about the Southern culture of honor, they found that employers in the South (and West) responded more positively and with more sympathy to the honor-related homicide than employers in the North. Apparently, then, using violence for honor-related issues is more accepted in the South than in the North.

What can we conclude from these studies? The strength of the Nisbett and Cohen research is that they used different methods of inquiry to study the same phenomenon (Nisbett & Cohen, 1996). Their mixed-method approach consisted of: (1) a nationwide *survey* of attitudes among the general population, (2) a *lab experiment* among students and (3) a *field experiment* among employers. The three different sources of evidence point to the same social phenomenon: in the South, culture of honor values are *more common* among Whites than they are among Whites in the North. It is not that in the North there is no support for culture of honor at all, but rather that this culture is more widespread in the South. Because the evidence is coming from different sources, we can be more confident that there is indeed a stronger culture of honor in the South.

Because Southerners are generally more positively minded towards using violence when reputation is at stake, conflicts and disputes end up more often in (deadly) violence (Nisbett

& Cohen, 1996). It is well-known historically that the homicide rates in the South of the US have been higher than in the North and scholars have argued that this is a likely outcome of the culture of honor tradition in the South (Gastil, 1971). Even today, the chances of being murdered are three times as high in the "Deep South" (e.g., Florida, Arizona) as they are in the North of the US (Grosjean, 2014).

11.7 Integration: selective or spillover effects?

We have seen that there is a tendency towards increasing cultural, social and economic integration over time. The integration process is a baseline trend, however, something we typically see for most ethnic groups, in most countries. We have also seen that the integration process is moderated by contextual conditions, such as the ethnic group and the receiving context. Depending on the ethnic group to which someone belongs or host country conditions, this process may work out slower or faster. What we have not discussed so far, however, is what the relationship is between the different dimensions of integration. Implicitly, we have assumed that processes of cultural, social and economic integration are entirely independent from each other. Analytically, these dimensions are different, but is this also the case empirically?

Scholars have come up with various ideas (Berry, 1997; Gordon, 1964; Portes & Zhou, 1993; Van de Rijt, 2014; Zhou, 1997). According to the idea of *selective integration* ("selective acculturation"), the three dimensions of integration (cultural, social and economic) may work out rather independently, and this may even be true for indicators that belong to the same dimension (Portes & Zhou, 1993). For example, immigrants and their children may deliberately invest in learning the language of the host country as it can pay off economically, but also decide to maintain strong attachments to the religious practices inherited from their parents. It may also be the case that, at least sometimes, there are interdependencies between certain integration dimensions (Van de Rijt, 2014), in which case stronger integration in one dimension (or indicators thereof) goes hand in hand with other dimensions (or indicators). If this is the case, we speak of *integration spillover effects*.

Let's take a closer look at cases of integration spillover effects, as they deviate from the assumption that the three integration dimensions are independent from each other. We can focus on the dimension of economic integration and wonder: does economic integration depend on cultural and social integration? A consistent finding in research on economic integration is that, in western societies, non-western ethnic groups do less well than other ethnic groups and, in particular, they do less well in comparison with the ethnic majority population (Fleischmann & Dronkers, 2010; Gorodzeisky & Semyonov, 2017; Heath, 2008; Kogan, 2006; Spörlein & Van Tubergen, 2014; Van Tubergen, 2006a). Let's formulate this stylized finding of *ethnic inequality*.

> ### STYLIZED FACT 11.2
>
> **Ethnic inequality**
> Ethnic majority members have better labor market positions than non-western ethnic minority groups in contemporary western societies.

How can we understand ethnic inequality in the labor market? A useful approach to answer this question is to rely on the conceptual model introduced in Chapter 10, which highlights the key role of resources (Figure 10.2). Using this model, you can then proceed in three steps. First, ethnic inequality can be thought of as inequality of *outcomes*: ethnic majority members have better positions in the labor market than non-western ethnic minority members. Second, in order to explain this phenomenon, you can examine inequality of *opportunity*: do ethnic majority members have better access to resources than non-western minority members? Third, if this is the case, consider inequality of *returns*: how important are these resources for getting positions in the labor market? You can use the theories that were introduced before (Chapter 10), i.e., human capital theory, social resource theory and group affiliation/discrimination, to explain ethnic inequality. If spillover effects play a role here, then you should find that the (poor) economic integration of non-western ethnic groups depends on their more limited cultural and social integration—and that both cultural and social integration are related to the resources that matter in the labor market.

Human capital

Let's start with the first resource which was mentioned in Chapter 10: human capital. As we have seen, human capital plays a major role in finding your way in the labor market. It is without doubt a key resource, thus there is no question about inequality of *returns* to human capital: those who possess a lot of human capital get more in the labor market than those who have less. In order to apply the human capital theory to explain ethnic inequality, we need to assume that there is inequality of *opportunity* between these two groups: ethnic majority members have more human capital than non-western ethnic minority members. The human capital explanation for ethnic inequality can be formulated as follows.

P.   The higher people's human capital, the better their labor market position. (*human capital and job outcomes*)

C.   Ethnic majority members have more human capital than non-western ethnic minority members in contemporary western societies.

O.   Ethnic majority members have better labor market positions than non-western ethnic minority groups in contemporary western societies. (*ethnic inequality*)

> Theory schema 11.1 Explanation of ethnic inequality with human capital theory.

How much truth is there in the assumption we have made? What do studies tell us? Scholars have pointed out that non-western ethnic groups have a disadvantage in terms of human capital at entry into the host society: generally speaking, non-western ethnic minorities are lower-educated than ethnic majority members (Heath, 2008) and they tend to have lower language proficiency. Language skills are crucial for many occupations and language deficiencies hamper labor market integration of immigrants (Chiswick & Miller, 1995). On top of that, education acquired in the country of origin appears less relevant for employers in their new host societies and/or these acquired skills are of lower quality (Kanas & Van Tubergen,

2010; Lancee & Bol, 2017). Thus, non-western ethnic groups typically face deficiencies in their education and language skills upon *entry*: (1) they are *less* educated than the majority population and (2) they have limited proficiency in the host country language. In summary, inequalities in human capital between ethnic majority members and non-western minority members and the strong returns of human capital in the labor market partly explain ethnic inequality.

When attempting to overcome such barriers in human capital at entry, immigrants could invest in learning the language and getting additional education. If immigrants acquire more education, their chances in the labor market after graduation increase. Importantly, this implies that various aspects of economic integration do not operate independently, but are, rather, associated. Education—one aspect of economic integration—goes together with labor market position—another aspect of economic integration. Acquiring the official language of the host country (cultural integration) significantly improves one's prospects in the labor market (Dustmann & Fabbri, 2003), which means that the processes of cultural and economic integration do not always work independently from each other.

Social resources

Does economic integration also depend on social integration? According to the social resource and job outcomes proposition, this may well be the case. Lin's theory on social resources, as we have seen (Chapter 10), argues that the resources embedded in one's personal network play a role in finding (good) jobs. We can use this theory to formulate the following explanation of ethnic inequality.

P. The more people's social resources, the better their labor market position. (*social resources and job outcomes*)

C. Ethnic majority members have more social resources than non-western ethnic minority members in contemporary western societies.

O. Ethnic majority members have better labor market positions than non-western ethnic minority groups in contemporary western societies. (*ethnic inequality*)

> **Theory schema 11.2** Explanation of ethnic inequality with Lin's theory of social resources.

When immigrants arrive in the country, they often benefit from support from members of their own ethnic group, who can help them with finding jobs. Living in an ethnic enclave, in which many members of their own ethnic group reside, may therefore be helpful in the beginning (Damm, 2009). However, in the long run, such ethnic bonding ties may hamper integration in the host society as they do not connect well with accessing higher-status occupations (Kalter & Kogan, 2014). Ethnic group-bonding ties are prevalent and this means that members of non-western ethnic groups tend to have social ties within their own ethnic group. These in-group members, however, have fewer resources: they are less educated, are less proficient in the host language and they have less knowledge about how the labor market works than do ethnic majority members.

For these reasons, establishing group-bridging ties (Chapter 8), i.e., friendships and other contacts with ethnic majority members, can be critical for non-western ethnic groups in getting access to valuable resources, such as knowledge about the labor market. Indeed, a number of studies show that when members of (non-western) ethnic groups develop more interethnic ties with ethnic majority members, their chances in the labor market increase (De Vroome & Van Tubergen, 2010; Kanas, Chiswick, Van der Lippe, & Van Tubergen, 2012). This is another case of integration spillover effects, i.e., increasing social integration (as indicated by interethnic group ties and reduced group segregation) leads to better economic integration.

Several studies have examined social resources of ethnic groups using the position generator (Chapter 10). Support for the assumption that ethnic minority groups in general have less social resources than ethnic majority members was found in studies in the US (Cross & Lin, 2008), Netherlands (Van Tubergen, 2014; Van Tubergen & Volker, 2015) and the UK (Li, Savage, & Warde, 2008), though the evidence was more mixed in studies on ethnic minority groups in Sweden (Behtoui, 2007; Hällsten, Edling, & Rydgren, 2017) and Belgium (Verhaeghe, Van der Bracht, & Van de Putte, 2015). Overall, therefore, research findings indicate that in several social contexts fewer social resources available to ethnic minority groups contribute to understanding their worse position in the labor market (Lin, 2000).

Discrimination

Economic integration may depend on social integration in yet another way. Ethnic inequalities can also arise as a consequence of ethnic majority members upholding negative views of ethnic minority groups. In-group favoritism can result in ethnic discrimination in the labor market, which would create barriers for immigrants and their offspring to find (good) jobs. The discrimination and job outcomes proposition (Chapter 10) can explain ethnic inequality under the following conditions.

P . The more strongly the groups to which people belong are discriminated against in the labor market, the worse their labor market position. (*discrimination and job outcomes*)

C . The ethnic majority group is less discriminated against than non-western ethnic minority groups in contemporary western societies.

O . Ethnic majority members have better labor market positions than non-western ethnic minority members in contemporary western societies. (*ethnic inequality*)

> Theory schema 11.3 Explanation of ethnic inequality with discrimination processes.

What do the research findings tell us? The most convincing evidence about discrimination comes from field experiments. Using field experimental data, studies have consistently found evidence that non-western ethnic minority groups are discriminated against in contemporary western labor markets. This has been observed in Germany (Kaas & Manger, 2012), Belgium (Baert, Cockx, Gheyle, & Vandamme, 2015), the Netherlands (Blommaert, Coenders, & Van Tubergen, 2014), Sweden (Bursell, 2014, 2007), Finland (Ahmad, 2019),

Ireland (McGinnity, Nelson, Lunn, & Quinn, 2009), Australia (Booth, Leigh, & Varganova, 2012), and Canada (Oreopoulos, 2011). In the US, it has been observed that in particular Blacks are confronted with labor market discrimination (Bertrand & Mullainathan, 2004; Pager & Quillian, 2005; Quillian, Pager, Hexel, & Midtboen, 2017). Two consistent findings have been observed in this research area (Neumark, 2018; Riach & Rich, 2002; Zschirnt & Ruedin, 2016): (1) there is substantial discrimination against ethnic and racial minority groups in western labor markets, (2) discrimination is cumulative, as it occurs at multiple stages (i.e., application stage and job-hiring stage).

STYLIZED FACT 11.3

Ethnic and racial discrimination
There is substantial, cumulative discrimination against ethnic and racial minorities in contemporary western labor markets.

Using the same field experimental methods, scholars have found that discrimination of ethnic and racial minorities occurs not only in the *labor market* but in other *domains* as well (Pager & Shepherd, 2008). For example, studies show that ethnic and racial minorities face discrimination in *housing markets* (Ahmed & Hammarstedt, 2008; Andersson, Jakobsson, & Kotsadam, 2012), *credit markets* (Munnell, Tootell, Browne, & McEneaney, 1996) and *consumer markets* (Ayres & Siegelman, 1995). This means, for example, that Blacks in the US and ethnic minorities in Europe not only have lower chances of getting a job interview, they are also more likely to suffer from discrimination when searching for a new house (e.g., being steered into less wealthy neighborhoods), when trying to secure a mortgage (e.g., higher rejection rates) and when buying a new car (e.g., higher prices). Hence, ethnic and racial minorities experience discrimination across various social domains.

Research on discrimination provides yet another example of integration spillover effects. In-group favoritism and anti-ethnic minority sentiments contribute to ethnic inequalities, which means that better intergroup cohesion (social integration) has a positive impact on economic integration.

In conclusion, research findings indicate that the three dimensions of integration do not work independently. Although they are analytically distinct, in reality the process of economic integration depends on the process of social and cultural integration. When immigrants and their offspring acquire the official language, when group-bridging ties become more common, when intergroup sentiments becomes more positive and discrimination reduces, the chances of getting access to (better) jobs increases as well. Such spillover effects also emerge with respect to social and cultural dimensions of integration (Van de Rijt, 2014). For example, ethnic minority members' frequency of interethnic contacts is positively associated with L2 acquisition (Martinovic, Van Tubergen, & Maas, 2011; Van Tubergen & Kalmijn, 2009b). Presumably, this association is bi-directional: when immigrants develop more ties to ethnic majority members they are exposed to L2, thereby fostering L2 learning. But, increasing L2 proficiency also works the other way, namely when immigrants speak L2 better, they more easily establish contacts to ethnic majority members. The overall conclusion is therefore that although analytically distinct, in reality the three dimensions of integration are often associated with each other.

11.8 The dynamics of residential segregation

The integration process, as we have seen, depends on social contexts—such as the ethnic group to which someone belongs. The integration process, such as economic integration, also depends on integration in other domains, such as social integration—this is the spillover effect. But the integration process can also depend on the *dynamic interplay* between ethnic minority and majority groups. If this is the case, then ethnic group members respond to actions initiated by members of their own group as well as those of the other group, thereby creating intergroup dynamics.

An example of where this can happen is **residential segregation**, the *unequal* distribution of groups across geographical areas. When immigrants arrive in their new country they settle in a certain location within that country, such as a certain city, for example, and a certain neighborhood within that city. When their children grow up and leave the parental home they may stay nearby, in their

residential segregation unequal distribution of groups across geographical areas.

hometown, but they may also move to a location further away. And with each generation such locational choices are made. An important area of research is to study how the various ethnic groups are distributed spatially. If an ethnic group strongly clusters together in certain areas, whereas ethnic majority members live in other areas, this pattern may be seen as an indication of lack of integration. Ethnic residential segregation is linked to ethnic inequality (Massey & Denton, 1993), limited interethnic contacts (Blau, 1994) and development of intergroup prejudice (Allport, 1954).

How strong is ethnic residential segregation? And what causes it? To illustrate research on ethnic residential segregation, let's consider the case which has received most attention in the literature, namely Blacks in the US. And to get some intuition about their level of residential segregation in past decades, let's focus on the year 1980. We get the following descriptive question:

> Q(d). To what degree were Blacks residentially segregated in the United States, around the year 1980?

To answer this question, we have to decide, first, on how to define Blacks. Let's rely on the subjective identifications as captured by the ancestry question in the 1980 Census of Population. Second, we have to make a decision on at which geographical scale we capture residential segregation. As a start, we take the largest scale, namely the nine major geographical areas in the US. Table 11.6 presents the geographical distribution of Blacks, together with other ethnic groups, in the US in 1980. As you can see, of all Blacks in the US, 1.8% lived in New England, which is clearly below the average of the total US population who resided in that area (5.5%). Blacks were overrepresented in South Atlantic: 29% lived there, as opposed to 16.3% of the US population. Among the other four ethnic groups, it appears that, in particular, the Irish were fairly evenly distributed across the nine regions. Of all Italians, 43.8% lived in Mid Atlantic (as compared with 16.2% of the total population).

One could discuss the share of each group in each area, but it would be more helpful to capture the degree of residential segregation in a single overall measure. Scholars have developed various such segregation measures (Massey & Denton, 1988). The most common measure is the *Dissimilarity Index* (D) (Duncan & Duncan, 1955). This measure captures how evenly members of a certain group are distributed across certain geographical areas. D ranges between 0 (perfect integration) to 1 (perfect segregation). Conceptually speaking, it represents the proportion of group members that would have to move to another geographical area to achieve an even distribution (Massey & Denton, 1988). Using this measure, it

Table 11. 6 Geographical distribution of five ethnic groups in the United States in 1980 (%).

	Black	English	German	Irish	Italian	US total
New England	1.8	5.9	2.2	7.2	13.1	5.5
Mid Atlantic	16.5	10.6	16.8	17.1	43.8	16.2
East North Central	17.2	16.5	27.2	18.0	14.0	18.4
West North Central	3.0	6.8	13.9	8.3	2.3	7.6
South Atlantic	28.9	19.9	11.5	14.9	8.3	16.3
East South Central	10.8	9.1	3.2	6.4	1.1	6.5
West South Central	13.3	10.6	7.1	10.4	3.3	10.5
Mountain	1.0	6.6	5.4	4.7	3.0	5.0
Pacific	7.5	14.1	12.6	13.0	11.0	14.0
D	0.23	0.11	0.21	0.04	0.37	

Source: Lieberson & Waters, 1988. Note: column totals may not add up to 100% because of rounding. D = Index of dissimilarity (range 0–1).

appears that, of the five ethnic groups considered, the Italians were the most segregated group at the broadest geographical level. The value of 0.37 means that 37% of the Italians had to move to another major geographical area in 1980 to achieve an even distribution. The English and Irish were very evenly distributed. Blacks and Germans were moderately segregated.

When analyzed at this broad level, however, nothing can be said about the degree of ethnic segregation at lower levels. Sociologists agree that, in fact, at the more local level, Blacks were the most segregated group around 1980. To illustrate, consider Table 11.7, which presents the average dissimilarity index, D, of the 60 largest standard metropolitan statistical areas (SMSAs) in the US in 1980. For Blacks, D was 0.69, which means that 69% of Blacks had to move to another neighborhood to achieve an even distribution with Whites. The dissimilarity scores for Hispanics (0.44) and Asians (0.34) are still substantial, but much lower compared with Blacks. In some cities, such as Chicago, the residential segregation of Blacks was extremely high.

Table 11.7 Residential dissimilarity from "Whites" in 60 US Metropolitan Areas, 1980.

	Blacks	Hispanics	Asians
Average	.69	.44	.34
Chicago	.88	.64	.44
Los Angeles	.81	.57	.43
Miami	.78	.52	.30
New York	.82	.66	.48
San Francisco	.72	.40	.44

Source: Massey & Denton, 1987, 1989.

Extreme levels of residential segregation ($D > 0.6$) are called hypersegregation (Massey & Denton, 1989). Such was the reality for Blacks not only in 1980, as we have seen, but also before and after that time. Research has shown that, at least during the period between 1970 and 2000, Blacks were hypersegregated from Whites at the neighborhood level (Farley & Frey, 1994; Lichter, Parisi, & Taquino, 2015). Let's formulate this as a stylized fact, which I call **Black hypersegregation in the US**.

STYLIZED FACT 11.4

Black hypersegregation in the US

In the period between 1970 and 2000, Blacks in the US lived in extremely segregated neighborhoods (D > 0.6).

Now that we have established an important social phenomenon—Black hypersegregation in the US—we can address the following theoretical question:

Q(t). Why were Blacks in the US living in extremely segregated neighborhoods ($D > 0.6$) in the period between 1970 and 2000?

Various sociological theories have been proposed to explain ethnic residential segregation, and that of Black (hyper)segregation in particular (Charles, 2003). One of these theories is the famous Schelling model, named after economist Thomas Schelling. His ideas about this model were first published in the second issue of the *Journal of Mathematical Sociology* in 1971 (Schelling, 1971) and subsequently in his seminal book *Micromotives and Macrobehavior*, which appeared in 1978 (Schelling, 2006 [1978]). The Schelling segregation model has become a classic, not only because it gives an explanation of Black residential segregation, but also, and perhaps even more so, because his model showed the usefulness of social simulation, often called *Agent Based Modelling* (see the Online Appendix for Chapter 11). You can use this tool to understand certain social phenomena—not just residential segregation (Macy & Willer, 2002; Squazzoni, 2012).

An early application is the work of Granovetter, who used social simulation to understand collective outcomes such as riots (Granovetter, 1978; Granovetter & Soong, 1983). With the use of Agent Based Modelling (ABM) scholars aim to explain collective outcomes by explicitly considering the complex interplay between individuals and their social context (Bonabeau, 2002; Epstein & Axtell, 1996; Gilbert & Troitzsch, 2005; Macy & Flache, 2009; Mäs & Flache, 2013; Miller & Page, 2007; Squazzoni, 2012). It is a formal theory tool which is used by scholars to explain social phenomena whereby *social interdependency* plays a key role, i.e., situations in which people respond to what others do (Chapter 4). In such cases of interdependency, *simple aggregation* fails and we should instead think of *complex aggregation*.

Before we discuss the **Schelling segregation model**, it should be acknowledged that his ideas were actually not entirely new and that another scholar deserves credit too. Although commonly known as the "Schelling model," and it was he who received the Nobel Prize for this work, it was actually the much less-known James Sakoda who first came up with the ideas incorporated in this model (Hegselmann, 2017). Sakoda published, in the very first issue of the *Journal of Mathematical Sociology*, an article entitled "The checkerboard model of social interaction"

(Sakoda, 1971). This publication contains the essential elements of what has become famous as the Schelling segregation model. For these reasons, one may also call it the *Sakoda–Schelling segregation model*, named after its original founder and the scholar who popularized the model.

The idea of social simulation is quite simple. The aim of social simulation is to understand the emergence of collective outcomes (in this case: Black hypersegregation) by simulating the interplay between individuals and their social context. The question we ask is then: under which conditions does the collective outcome of Black hypersegregation emerge? Say we call Black hypersegregation "Z." With the help of social simulation, you could ask yourself: if I assume A and B will happen, would social phenomenon Z then emerge? Or, would Z appear, if instead I assume C and D? If A and B do not result in Z, but C and D do, then we can say that, under conditions of C and D, the social phenomenon Z may emerge. Thus, we may wonder: when will Black hypersegregation occur? Under which social conditions does this phenomenon emerge?

Schelling explained Black hypersegregation with a social simulation model that takes into account the dynamic interplay between Blacks, Whites and their environment. He argued that even when both groups have only mild in-group favoritism to live in areas with at least some people from their own group, the consequence could be hypersegregation. How can that (counterintuitive) result happen? How can strong residential segregation emerge when people have only modest preferences to live with co-ethnics?

Schelling argued that this collective outcome can happen because of the interplay between individuals and their context. He illustrated his social simulation model with a chess board that has 64 squares. Table 11.8 gives an example of this, with random initial conditions, so that Blacks (B) and Whites (W) are scattered all over the board, without any clear evidence for residential segregation. Each individual has certain neighbors. Now, let's start with moving the actors and begin with one actor on the board: the White person at E2, i.e., column E and row 2. Assuming mild in-group preferences, Schelling stated that individuals will remain if more than one third of their neighbors are from the same race. The White person at E2 has five neighbors. One of them is White and four are Black, which makes it that only one fifth of his neighborhood is White. As this person is White, this person is clearly unhappy. Given the threshold of more than one third, there should be more White neighbors, and the consequence is that this person will move away to a White neighborhood, for example to square F3.

Table 11.8 Initial condition of spatial segregation between Whites (W) and Blacks (B) on a 64-square chess board.

	A	B	C	D	E	F	G	H
8		B		B	W	B		W
7	B	B	B	W		W	B	W
6		B	W			B	W	B
5		W	B	W	B	W	B	W
4	W	W	W	B	W	W	W	
3	B		B	B	B			W
2		B	W	B	W	B	W	
1		W		W			B	

Source: Schelling, 2006 [1978].

The migration of the White person to another neighborhood leaves an empty cell at E2 and this alters the racial composition of the neighborhood this person left behind and it also changes the composition of the neighborhood to which this person has moved. You can play this social simulation game using a chess board yourself. You will see that, over time, there will eventually be a situation in which all actors are happy, in the sense that they live in a neighborhood with more than 33% of their own race, and nobody wants to move anymore. Schelling showed that the end state will be strong residential segregation between Blacks and Whites. One such possible outcome is presented in Table 11.9.

Table 11.9 Stable segregated pattern obtained in several iterations of spatial segregation between Whites (W) and Blacks (B) on a 64-square chess board.

	A	B	C	D	E	F	G	H
8		B	B	B	W			W
7	B	B	B	W		W		W
6	B	B	W				W	
5		W		W		W		W
4	W	W	W	B	W	W	W	
3			B	B	B	W	W	W
2	W	B	B	B	B	B	B	B
1	W	W				B	B	B

Source: Schelling, 2006 [1978].

The table shows that the surprising result of these movements is that the two groups live as *highly segregated* in the end. Indeed, the collective outcome of the Schelling model is exactly the phenomenon we wanted to explain: *Black hypersegregation*. This means that Black hypersegregation emerges under the conditions that were specified in the Schelling model. These were, to repeat: there are two groups (Blacks, Whites) who can decide to stay in their neighborhood or move to another neighborhood and who have only *mild* in-group preferences (threshold > 33% same-race). The counterintuitive result of this simple Schelling model is therefore that extreme levels of segregation can emerge under conditions of mild in-group preferences. This collective outcome, moreover, is a *stable* situation, because everyone lives in a neighborhood that is satisfactory to themselves and there is no reason to move. Once a hypersegregated society is created, in other words, it is hard to change.

11.9 Chapter resources

Key concepts

Foreign-born population	Second generation	Ethnic group
First generation	Ancestry	Ethnic diversity

Topics

Culture of honor	Cultural integration	Economic integration
Integration	Social integration	Residential segregation

Key theories and propositions

- Immigrant integration
- Immigrant assimilation
- Selective integration
- Integration spillover effect
- Schelling segregation model

Key stylized facts

- Integration process
- Ethnic inequality
- Ethnic and racial discrimination
- Black hypersegregation in the US

Summary

- One can assess ethnic group affiliation in an "objective" way by considering national origin and generations. A common distinction is that between first and second generation.
- Ethnic group affiliation can also be identified more subjectively by considering self-identification and ancestry.
- Integration can be studied as a multi-sided, multi-dimensional social phenomenon.
- It is common to distinguish three dimensions of integration: cultural integration, social integration and economic integration.
- The immigrant integration proposition posits that with increasing length of stay, ethnic minority groups become more integrated. A stronger version of this idea is the immigrant assimilation proposition.
- Empirical findings are in line with the immigrant integration proposition, finding evidence for the presumed integration process.
- The integration process is an overall tendency, which is found for most ethnic groups, in most countries. However, the integration process also depends on social contexts, such as the ethnic group and host country.
- According to the idea of selective integration, the various integration dimensions operate independently.
- By contrast, integration spillover effects occur when dimensions of integration are not independent from each other, but reinforce each other.
- The integration process may also depend on the dynamic interplay between ethnic minority and majority groups. The Schelling segregation model reveals that the strong residential segregation between Blacks and Whites in the US may be due to such a dynamic interplay.

References

Ahmad, A. (2019). When the name matters: An experimental investigation of ethnic discrimination in the Finnish labor market. *Sociological Inquiry, in press.* doi:https://doi.org/10.1111/soin.12276

Ahmed, A. M., & Hammarstedt, M. (2008). Discrimination in the rental housing market: A field experiment on the internet. *Journal of Urban Economics*, 64(2), 362–372.

Akkerman, T., De Lange, S. L., & Rooduijn, M. (Eds.). (2016). *Radical right-wing populist parties in Western Europe: Into the Mainstream?* Abingdon, UK: Routledge.

Alba, R., & Foner, N. (2015a). Mixed unions and immigrant-group integration in North America and Western Europe. *The Annals of the American Academy of Political and Social Science*, 662(1), 38–56.

Alba, R., & Foner, N. (2015b). *Strangers no more: Immigration and the challenges of integration in North America and Western Europe*. Princeton, NJ: Princeton University Press.

Alba, R., Logan, J. R., Lutz, A., & Stults, B. J. (2002). Only English by the third generation? Loss and preservation of the mother tongue among the grandchildren of contemporary immigrants. *Demography*, 39, 467–484.

Alba, R., & Nee, V. (1997). Rethinking assimilation theory for a new era of immigration. *International Migration Review*, 31(4), 826–874.

Alba, R., & Nee, V. (2003). *Remaking the American mainstream: Assimilation and contemporary immigration*. Cambridge, MA: Harvard University Press.

Alesina, A., Devleeschauwer, A., Easterly, W., Kurlat, S., & Wacziarg, R. (2003). Fractionalization. *Journal of Economic Growth*, 8(2), 155–194.

Allport, G. W. (1954). *The nature of prejudice*. Cambridge, MA: Addison-Wesley Publishing Company.

Andersson, L., Jakobsson, N., & Kotsadam, A. (2012). A field experiment of discrimination in the Norwegian housing market: Gender, class, and ethnicity. *Land Economics*, 88(2), 233–240.

Australian Bureau of Statistics. (2019). Census of population and housing: Australia revealed, 2016. Retrieved from www.abs.gov.au.

Ayres, I., & Siegelman, P. (1995). Race and gender discrimination in bargaining for a new car. *American Economic Review*, 85(3), 304–321.

Baert, S., Cockx, B., Gheyle, N., & Vandamme, C. (2015). Is there less discrimination in occupations where recruitment is difficult? *Industrial Relations & Labor*, 68(3), 467–500.

Bean, F. D., & Stevens, G. (2003). *America's newcomers: Dynamics of diversity*. New York, NY: Russell Sage Foundation.

Beenstock, M. (1996). The acquisition of language skills by immigrants: The case of Hebrew in Israel. *International Migration*, 34, 3–30.

Behtoui, A. (2007). The distribution and return of social capital: Evidence from Sweden. *European Societies*, 9(3), 383–407.

Berry, J. W. (1997). Immigration, acculturation, and adaptation. *Applied Psychology*, 46(1), 5–34.

Bertrand, M., & Mullainathan, S. (2004). Are Emily and Greg more employable than Lakisha and Jamal? A field experiment on labor market discrimination. *American Economic Review*, 94(4), 991–1013.

Blau, P. (1994). *Structural contexts of opportunities*. Chicago, IL: University of Chicago Press.

Blommaert, L., Coenders, M., & Van Tubergen, F. (2014). Discrimination of Arabic-named applicants in the Netherlands: An internet-based field experiment examining different phases in online recruitment procedures. *Social Forces*, 92(3), 957–982.

Bohman, A., & Hjerm, M. (2016). In the wake of radical right electoral success: A cross-country comparative study of anti-immigration attitudes over time. *Journal of Ethnic and Migration Studies*, 42(11), 1729–1747.

Bonabeau, E. (2002). Agent-based modeling: Methods and techniques for simulating human systems. *Proceedings of the National Academy of Sciences of the United States of America*, 99(Suppl 3), 7280–7287.

Booth, A. L., Leigh, A., & Varganova, E. (2012). Does ethnic discrimination vary across minority groups? Evidence from a field experiment. *Oxford Bulletin of Economics and Statistics*, 74(4), 547–573.

Bursell, M. (2007). What's in a name? A field experiment test for the existence of ethnic discrimination in the hiring process. *SULCIS Working Paper 2007*, 7, 1–28.

Bursell, M. (2014). The multiple burdens of foreign-named men: Evidence from a field experiment on gendered ethnic hiring discrimination in Sweden. *European Sociological Review*, 30(3), 399–409.

Castles, S., De Haas, H., & Miller, M. J. (2013). *The age of migration: International population movements in the modern world*. New York, NY: Palgrave.

Central Bureau of Statistics Netherlands. (2018). Statline. Retrieved from www.cbs.nl.

Charles, C. Z. (2003). The dynamics of racial residential segregation. *Annual Review of Sociology*, 29, 167–207.

Chiswick, B. R., & Miller, P. W. (1995). The endogeneity between language and earnings: International analyses. *Journal of Labor Economics*, 13(2), 246–288.

Chiswick, B. R., & Miller, P. W. (1996). Ethnic networks and language proficiency among immigrants. *Journal of Population Economics*, 9(1), 19–35.

Chiswick, B. R., & Miller, P. W. (2001). A model of destination-language acquisition: Application to male immigrants in Canada. *Demography*, 38(3), 391–409.

Cohen, D., & Nisbett, R. E. (1994). Self-protection and the culture of honor: Explaining southern violence. *Personality and Social Psychology Bulletin*, 20(5), 551–567.

Cohen, D., & Nisbett, R. E. (1997). Field experiments examining the culture of honor: The role of institutions in perpetuating norms about violence. *Personality and Social Psychology Bulletin*, 23(11), 1188–1199.

Cohen, D., Nisbett, R. E., Bowdle, B. F., & Schwarz, N. (1996). Insult, aggression, and the southern culture of honor: An "experimental ethnography". *Journal of Personality and Social Psychology*, 70(5), 945–959.

Connor, P. (2008). Increase or decrease? The impact of the international migratory event on immigrant religious participation. *Journal for the Scientific Study of Religion*, 47(2), 243–257.

Cross, J. L. M., & Lin, N. (2008). Access to social capital and status attainment in the United States: Racial/ethnic and gender differences. In N. Lin & B. H. Erickson (Eds.), *Social capital: An international research program* (pp. 364–393). Oxford, UK: Oxford University Press.

Crul, M., Schneider, J., & Lelie, F. (Eds.). (2012). *The European second generation compared: Does the integration context matter?* Amsterdam, Netherlands: Amsterdam University Press.

Crul, M., & Vermeulen, H. (2003). The second generation in Europe. *International Migration Review*, 37, 965–986.

Damm, A. P. (2009). Ethnic enclaves and immigrant labor market outcomes: Quasi-experimental evidence. *Journal of Labor Economics*, 27(2), 281–314.

De Vroome, T., & Van Tubergen, F. (2010). The employment experience of refugees in the Netherlands. *International Migration Review*, 44(2), 376–403.

Diehl, C., & Koenig, M. (2009). Religiosität Türkischer migranten im generationenverlauf: Ein befund und einige erklärungsversuche. *Zeitschrift Für Soziologie*, 38(4), 300–319.

Diehl, C., & Schnell, R. (2006). 'Reactive ethnicity' or 'assimilation'? Statements, arguments, and first empirical evidence for labor migrants in Germany. *International Migration Review*, 40(4), 786–816.

Drouhot, L. G., & Nee, V. (2019). Assimilation and the second generation in Europe and America: Blending and segregating social dynamics between immigrants and natives. *Annual Review of Sociology*, 45(1), 177–199.

Duncan, B. (2018). *Socioeconomic integration of U.S. immigrant groups over the long term: The second generation and beyond*. Cambridge, MA: National Bureau of Economic Research.

Duncan, O. D., & Duncan, B. (1955). A methodological analysis of segregation indexes. *American Sociological Review, 20*(2), 210–217.

Dustmann, C., & Fabbri, F. (2003). Language proficiency and labour market performance of immigrants in the UK. *The Economic Journal, 113*(489), 695–717.

Eltis, D., & Richardson, D. (2015). *Atlas of the transatlantic slave trade*. New Haven, CT: Yale University Press.

Epstein, J. M., & Axtell, R. (1996). *Growing artificial societies: Social science from the bottom up*. Washington, DC: Brookings Institution Press.

Espenshade, T. J., & Fu, H. (1997). An analysis of English-language proficiency among US immigrants. *American Sociological Review, 62*, 288–305.

Espinosa, K. E., & Massey, D. S. (1997). Determinants of English proficiency among Mexican migrants to the United States. *International Migration Review, 31*(1), 28–50.

Esser, H. (2004). Does the "new" immigration require a "new" theory of intergenerational integration? *International Migration Review, 38*(3), 1126–1159.

Esser, H. (2006). *Migration, Sprache und Integration*. Berlin, Germany: WZB.

Farley, R. (1991). The new census question about ancestry: What did it tell us? *Demography, 28*(3), 411–429.

Farley, R., & Alba, R. (2002). The new second generation in the United States. *International Migration Review, 36*(3), 669–701.

Farley, R., & Frey, W. H. (1994). Changes in the segregation of Whites from Blacks during the 1980s: Small steps toward a more integrated society. *American Sociological Review, 59*(1), 23–45.

Fearon, J. D. (2003). Ethnic and cultural diversity by country. *Journal of Economic Growth, 8*(2), 195–222.

Fleischmann, F., & Dronkers, J. (2010). Unemployment among immigrants in European labour markets: An analysis of origin and destination effects. *Work, Employment and Society, 24*(2), 337–354.

Gastil, R. D. (1971). Homicide and a regional culture of violence. *American Sociological Review, 36*(3), 412–427.

Giavazzi, F., Petkov, I., & Schiantarelli, F. (2019). Culture: Persistence and evolution. *Journal of Economic Growth, 24*(2), 117–154.

Gilbert, N., & Troitzsch, K. G. (2nd ed.). (2005). *Simulation for the social scientist*. Maidenhead, UK: McGraw-Hill Education.

Gordon, M. M. (1964). *Assimilation in American life*. New York, NY: Oxford University Press.

Gorodzeisky, A., & Semyonov, M. (2017). Labor force participation, unemployment and occupational attainment among immigrants in West European Countries. *PloS ONE, 12*(5), e0176856.

Granovetter, M. (1978). Threshold models for collective behavior. *American Journal of Sociology, 83*(6), 1420–1443.

Granovetter, M., & Soong, R. (1983). Threshold models of diffusion and collective behavior. *Journal of Mathematical Sociology, 9*(3), 165–179.

Greeley, A. M., & McCready, W. C. (1975). The transmission of cultural heritages: The case of the Irish and the Italians. In N. Glazer & D. P. Moynihan (Eds.), *Ethnicity: Theory and practice* (pp. 209–235). Cambridge, MA: Harvard University Press.

Grosjean, P. (2014). A history of violence: The culture of honor and homicide in the US South. *Journal of the European Economic Association, 12*(5), 1285–1316.

Hällsten, M., Edling, C., & Rydgren, J. (2017). Social capital, friendship networks, and youth unemployment. *Social Science Research, 61*, 234–250.

Harari, Y. N. (2014). *Sapiens: A brief history of humankind*. New York, NY: Random House.

Heath, A. (Ed.). (2008). *Ethnic minority disadvantage: Comparative perspectives*. Oxford, UK: Oxford University Press.

Heath, A., & Brinbaum, Y. (Eds.). (2014). *Unequal attainments: Ethnic educational inequalities in ten European countries*. Oxford, UK: Oxford University Press.

Heath, A., Rothon, C., & Kilpi, E. (2008). The second generation in Western Europe: Education, unemployment, and occupational attainment. *Annual Review of Sociology*, *34*, 211–235.

Hegselmann, R. (2017). Thomas C. Schelling and James M. Sakoda: The intellectual, technical, and social history of a model. *Journal of Artificial Societies and Social Simulation*, *20*, 3. doi:10.18564/jasss.3511

Hwang, S., & Xi, J. (2008). Structural and individual covariates of English language proficiency. *Social Forces*, *86*(3), 1079–1104.

International Organization for Migration. (2019). Missing migrants project. Retrieved from https://missingmigrants.iom.int/

Jonsson, J. O., Kalter, F., & Van Tubergen, F. (2018). Studying integration: Ethnic minority and majority youth in comparative perspective. In F. Kalter, J. O. Jonsson, F. van Tubergen, & A. Heath (Eds.), *Growing up in diverse societies: The integration of immigrants in England, Germany, the Netherlands, and Sweden* (pp. 1–39). Oxford, UK: Oxford University Press.

Kaas, L., & Manger, C. (2012). Ethnic discrimination in Germany's labour market: A field experiment. *German Economic Review*, *13*(1), 1–20.

Kalmijn, M., & Van Tubergen, F. (2006). Ethnic intermarriage in the Netherlands: Confirmations and refutations of accepted insights. *European Journal of Population*, *22*(4), 371–397.

Kalter, F., & Kogan, I. (2014). Migrant networks and labor market integration of immigrants from the former Soviet Union in Germany. *Social Forces*, *92*(4), 1435–1456.

Kalter, F., & Schroedter, J. H. (2010). Transnational marriage among former labour migrants in Germany. *Zeitschrift Für Familienforschung - Journal of Family Research*, *22*(1), 11–36.

Kanas, A., Chiswick, B. R., Lippe, T., & Tubergen, F. (2012). Social contacts and the economic performance of immigrants: A panel study of immigrants in Germany. *International Migration Review*, *46*(3), 680–709.

Kanas, A., & Van Tubergen, F. (2010). The impact of origin and host country schooling on the economic performance of immigrants. *Social Forces*, *88*(2), 893–915.

Kao, G., & Thompson, J. S. (2003). Racial and ethnic stratification in educational achievement. *Annual Review of Sociology*, *29*, 417–442.

Kirszbaum, T., Brinbaum, Y., Simon, P., & Gezer, E. (2009). *The children of immigrants in France: The emergence of a second generation*. (Innocenti Working Papers No. inwopa574).IDEAS.

Kogan, I. (2006). Labor markets and economic incorporation among recent immigrants in Europe. *Social Forces*, *85*(2), 697–721.

Koopmans, R. (2010). Trade-offs between equality and difference: Immigrant integration, multiculturalism and the welfare state in cross-national perspective. *Journal of Ethnic and Migration Studies*, *36*(1), 1–26.

Koopmans, R. (2013). Multiculturalism and immigration: A contested field in cross-national comparison. *Annual Review of Sociology*, *39*, 147–169.

Kroneberg, C. (2008). Ethnic communities and school performance among the new second generation in the United States: Testing the theory of segmented assimilation. *The Annals of the American Academy of Political and Social Science*, *620*(1), 138–160.

Kymlicka, W., & Banting, K. G. (Eds.). (2006). *Multiculturalism and the welfare state: Recognition and redistribution in contemporary democracies*. New York, NY: Oxford University Press.

Lancee, B., & Bol, T. (2017). The transferability of skills and degrees: Why the place of education affects immigrant earnings. *Social Forces*, 96(2), 691–716.

Lessard-Phillips, L., Fibbi, R., & Wanner, P. (2012). Assessing the labour market position and its determinants for the second generation. In M. Crul, J. Schneider, & D. Lelie (Eds.), *The European second generation compared: Does the integration context matter?* (pp. 165–224). Amsterdam, Netherlands: Amsterdam University Press.

Levels, M., Dronkers, J., & Kraaykamp, G. (2008). Immigrant children's educational achievement in Western countries: Origin, destination, and community effects on mathematical performance. *American Sociological Review*, 73(5), 835–853.

Li, Y. (2018). Against the odds? A study of educational attainment and labour market position of the second-generation ethnic minority members in the UK. *Ethnicities*, 18(4), 471–495.

Li, Y., & Heath, A. (2016). Class matters: A study of minority and majority social mobility in Britain, 1982–2011. *American Journal of Sociology*, 122(1), 162–200.

Li, Y., Savage, M., & Warde, A. (2008). Social mobility and social capital in contemporary Britain. *The British Journal of Sociology*, 59(3), 391–411.

Lichter, D. T., Parisi, D., & Taquino, M. C. (2015). Toward a new macro-segregation? Decomposing segregation within and between metropolitan cities and suburbs. *American Sociological Review*, 80(4), 843–873.

Lichter, D. T., Qian, Z., & Tumin, D. (2015). Whom do immigrants marry? Emerging patterns of intermarriage and integration in the United States. *The Annals of the American Academy of Political and Social Science*, 662(1), 57–78.

Lieberson, S. (1970). *Language and ethnic relations in Canada*. New York, NY: John Wiley.

Lieberson, S. (1980). *A piece of the pie: Blacks and White immigrants since 1880*. Berkeley, CA: University of California Press.

Lieberson, S., & Waters, M. (1988). *From many strands: Ethnic and racial groups in contemporary America*. New York, NY: Russell Sage Foundation.

Lin, N. (2000). Inequality in social capital. *Contemporary Sociology*, 29(6), 785–795.

Lucassen, L., & Laarman, C. (2009). Immigration, intermarriage and the changing face of Europe in the post war period. *The History of the Family*, 14(1), 52–68.

Luthra, R. R., & Waldinger, R. (2010). Into the mainstream? Labor market outcomes of Mexican-origin workers. *International Migration Review*, 44(4), 830–868.

Macy, M. W., & Flache, A. (2009). Social dynamics from the bottom up: Agent-based models of social interaction. In P. Hedström & P. Bearman (Eds.), *The Oxford Handbook of Analytical Sociology* (pp. 245–268). Oxford, UK: Oxford University Press.

Macy, M. W., & Willer, R. (2002). From factors to actors: Computational sociology and agent-based modeling. *Annual Review of Sociology*, 28(1), 143–166.

Maliepaard, M., & Lubbers, M. (2013). Parental religious transmission after migration: The case of Dutch Muslims. *Journal of Ethnic and Migration Studies*, 39(3), 425–442.

Maliepaard, M., Lubbers, M., & Gijsberts, M. (2010). Generational differences in ethnic and religious attachment and their interrelation. A study among Muslim minorities in the Netherlands. *Ethnic and Racial Studies*, 33(3), 451–472.

Martinovic, B., Van Tubergen, F., & Maas, I. (2011). Acquisition of cross-ethnic friends by recent immigrants in Canada: A longitudinal approach. *International Migration Review*, 45(2), 460–488.

Martinovic, B., Van Tubergen, F., & Maas, I. (2009). Dynamics of interethnic contact: A panel study of immigrants in the Netherlands. *European Sociological Review*, 25(3), 303–318.

Mäs, M., & Flache, A. (2013). Differentiation without distancing: Explaining bi-polarization of opinions without negative influence. *PloS ONE*, 8(11), e74516.

Massey, D. S., Arango, J., Hugo, G., Kouaouci, A., Pellegrino, A., & Taylor, J. E. (1993). Theories of international migration: A review and appraisal. *Population and Development Review*, 19(3), 431–498.

Massey, D. S., & Denton, N. A. (1987). Trends in the residential segregation of Blacks, Hispanics, and Asians: 1970–1980. *American Sociological Review, 52*(6), 802–825.

Massey, D. S., & Denton, N. A. (1988). The dimensions of residential segregation. *Social Forces, 67*(2), 281–315.

Massey, D. S., & Denton, N. A. (1989). Hypersegregation in US metropolitan areas: Black and Hispanic segregation along five dimensions. *Demography, 26*(3), 373–391.

Massey, D. S., & Denton, N. A. (1993). *American apartheid: Segregation and the making of the underclass*. Cambridge, MA: Harvard University Press.

McGinnity, F., Nelson, J., Lunn, P., & Quinn, E. (2009). *Discrimination in recruitment: Evidence from a field experiment*. Dublin, Ireland: The Equality Authority and The Economic and Social Research Institute.

Mesch, G. S. (2003). Language proficiency among new immigrants: The role of human capital and societal conditions: The case of immigrants from the FSU in Israel. *Sociological Perspectives, 46*(1), 41–58.

Miller, J. H., & Page, S. E. (2007). *Complex adaptive systems: An introduction to computational models of social life*. Princeton, NJ: Princeton University Press.

Munnell, A. H., Tootell, G. M., Browne, L. E., & McEneaney, J. (1996). Mortgage lending in Boston: Interpreting HMDA data. *American Economic Review, 86*(1), 25–53.

Neumark, D. (2018). Experimental research on labor market discrimination. *Journal of Economic Literature, 56*(3), 799–866.

Nisbett, R. E., & Cohen, D. (1996). *Culture of honor: The psychology of violence in the south*. Boulder, CO: Westview Press.

Oreopoulos, P. (2011). Why do skilled immigrants struggle in the labor market? A field experiment with thirteen thousand resumes. *American Economic Journal, 3*(4), 148–171.

Oyserman, D. (2017). Culture three ways: Culture and subcultures within countries. *Annual Review of Psychology, 68*, 435–463.

Pager, D., & Quillian, L. (2005). Walking the talk? What employers say versus what they do. *American Sociological Review, 70*(3), 355–380.

Pager, D., & Shepherd, H. (2008). The sociology of discrimination: Racial discrimination in employment, housing, credit, and consumer markets. *Annual Review of Sociology, 34*, 181–209.

Park, R., & Burgess, E. (1969 [1921]). *Introduction to the Science of Sociology* (3rd ded. ed.). Chicago, IL: University of Chicago Press.

Pew Research. (2013). *Second-generation Americans: A portrait of the adult children of immigrants*. Washington, DC: Author.

Pichler, F. (2011). Success on European labor markets: A cross-national comparison of attainment between immigrant and majority populations. *International Migration Review, 45*(4), 938–978.

Polavieja, J. G. (2015). Capturing culture: A new method to estimate exogenous cultural effects using migrant populations. *American Sociological Review, 80*(1), 166–191.

Portes, A., & Hao, L. (1998). E pluribus unum: Bilingualism and loss of language in the second generation. *Sociology of Education, 71*, 269–294.

Portes, A., & Rumbaut, R. G. (2006). *Immigrant America: A portrait* (3rd ed.). Berkeley and Los Angeles, CA: University of California Press.

Portes, A., & Zhou, M. (1993). The new second generation: Segmented assimilation and its variants. *The Annals of the American Academy of Political and Social Science, 530*(1), 74–96.

Potts, L. (1990). *The world labour market: A history of migration*. London, UK: Zed Books.

Qian, Z., & Lichter, D. T. (2007). Social boundaries and marital assimilation: Interpreting trends in racial and ethnic intermarriage. *American Sociological Review, 72*(1), 68–94.

Quillian, L., Pager, D., Hexel, O., & Midtboen, A. H. (2017). Meta-analysis of field experiments shows no change in racial discrimination in hiring over time. *PNAS*, *114*(41), 10870–10875.

Raijman, R., Semyonov, M., & Geffen, R. (2015). Language Proficiency among post-1990 immigrants in Israel. *Journal of Ethnic and Migration Studies*, *41*(8), 1347–1371.

Riach, P. A., & Rich, J. (2002). Field experiments of discrimination in the market place. *The Economic Journal*, *112*(483), F480–F518.

Rice, T. W., & Feldman, J. L. (1997). Civic culture and democracy from Europe to America. *The Journal of Politics*, *59*(4), 1143–1172.

Rosenfeld, M. J. (2002). Measures of assimilation in the marriage market: Mexican Americans 1970-1990. *Journal of Marriage and the Family*, *64*, 152–162.

Roth, R. (2012). *American homicide*. Cambridge, MA: Harvard University Press.

Rumbaut, R. G., Massey, D. S., & Bean, F. D. (2006). Linguistic life expectancies: Immigrant language retention in Southern California. *Population and Development Review*, *32*(3), 447–460.

Sakoda, J. M. (1971). The checkerboard model of social interaction. *Journal of Mathematical Sociology*, *1*(1), 119–132.

Schelling, T. C. (1971). Dynamic models of segregation. *Journal of Mathematical Sociology*, *1*(2), 143–186.

Schelling, T. C. (2006 [1978]). *Micromotives and Macrobehavior*. New York, NY: WW Norton & Company.

Spörlein, C., & Schlueter, E. (2018). How education systems shape cross-national ethnic inequality in math competence scores: Moving beyond mean differences. *PloS ONE*, *13*(3), e0193738.

Spörlein, C., Schlueter, E., & Van Tubergen, F. (2014). Ethnic intermarriage in longitudinal perspective: Testing structural and cultural explanations in the United States, 1880–2011. *Social Science Research*, *43*, 1–15.

Spörlein, C., & Van Tubergen, F. (2014). The occupational status of immigrants in Western and Non-Western Societies. *International Journal of Comparative Sociology*, *55*(2), 119–143.

Squazzoni, F. (2012). *Agent-Based Computational Sociology*. Chichester, UK: John Wiley & Sons.

Statistics Canada. (2019). Generation status: Canadian-born children of immigrants. Retrieved from www12.statcan.gc.ca/nhs-enm/2011/as-sa/99-010-x/99-010-x2011003_2-eng.cfm

Stevens, G. (1992). The social and demographic context of language use in the United States. *American Sociological Review*, *57*, 171–185.

Stevens, G. (1999). Age at immigration and second language proficiency among foreign-born adults. *Language in Society*, *28*(4), 555–578.

Tran, V. C. (2018). Social mobility across immigrant generations: Recent evidence and future data requirements. *The Annals of the American Academy of Political and Social Science*, *677*(1), 105–118.

Tribalat, M. (1995). *Faire France: Une Enquete Sur Les Immigrès Et Leurs Enfants*. Paris, France: La Dècouverte.

UNHCR. (2016). Refugees. Retrieved from www.unhcr.org/refugees.html

United Nations. (2019). Trends in international migrant stock. Retrieved from www.un.org/en/development/desa/population/migration/data/estimates2/estimates15.asp

Van de Pol, J., & Van Tubergen, F. (2014). Inheritance of religiosity among Muslim immigrants in a secular society. *Review of Religious Research*, *56*(1), 87–106.

Van de Rijt, A. (2014). Selection and influence in the assimilation process of immigrants. In S. R. Thye & E. Lawler (Eds.), *Advances in group processes* (pp. 157–193). Bingley, UK: Emerald Group Publishing Limited.

Van de Werfhorst, H., Van Elsas, E., Heath, A., & Brinbaum, Y. (2014). Origin and destination effects on the educational careers of second-generation minorities. In A. Heath & Y. Brinbaum (Eds.), *Unequal attainments: Ethnic educational inequalities in ten Western countries* (pp. 245–272). Oxford, UK: Oxford University Press.

Van Tubergen, F. (2006a). Occupational status of immigrants in cross-national perspective: A multilevel analysis of 17 Western countries. In T. Smeeding & G. Parsons (Eds.), *Immigration and the transformation of Europe* (pp. 147–171). Cambridge, UK: Cambridge University Press.

Van Tubergen, F. (2006b). Religious affiliation and participation among immigrants in eight Western countries: A cross-national study of individual and contextual effects. *Journal for the Scientific Study of Religion*, 45, 1–22.

Van Tubergen, F. (2014). Size and socio-economic resources of core discussion networks in the Netherlands: Differences by national-origin group and immigrant generation. *Ethnic and Racial Studies*, 37(6), 1020–1042.

Van Tubergen, F., & Kalmijn, M. (2005). Destination-language proficiency in cross-national perspective: A study of immigrant groups in nine Western countries. *American Journal of Sociology*, 110(5), 1412–1457.

Van Tubergen, F., & Kalmijn, M. (2009a). A dynamic approach to the determinants of immigrants' language proficiency: The United States, 1980–2000. *International Migration Review*, 43(3), 519–543.

Van Tubergen, F., & Kalmijn, M. (2009b). Language proficiency and usage among immigrants in the Netherlands: Incentives or opportunities? *European Sociological Review*, 25(2), 169–182.

Van Tubergen, F., Maas, I., & Flap, H. (2004). The economic incorporation of immigrants in 18 Western societies: Origin, destination, and community effects. *American Sociological Review*, 69, 704–727.

Van Tubergen, F., & Sindradóttir, J. Í. (2011). The religiosity of immigrants in Europe: A cross-national study. *Journal for the Scientific Study of Religion*, 50(2), 272–288.

Van Tubergen, F., & Volker, B. (2015). Inequality in access to social capital in the Netherlands. *Sociology*, 49(3), 521–538.

Veltman, C. (1983). *Language shift in the United States*. New York, NY: Mouton.

Verhaeghe, P., Van der Bracht, K., & Van de Putte, B. (2015). Inequalities in social capital and their longitudinal effects on the labour market entry. *Social Networks*, 40, 174–184.

Waters, M. C., & Jiménez, T. R. (2005). Assessing immigrant assimilation: New empirical and theoretical challenges. *Annual Review of Sociology*, 31, 105–125.

Waters, M. C., & Pineau, M. G. (Eds.). (2015). *The integration of immigrants into American society*. Washington, DC: The National Academies Press.

Wimmer, A. (2009). Herder's heritage and the boundary-making approach: Studying ethnicity in immigrant societies. *Sociological Theory*, 27(3), 244–270.

Wimmer, A., & Lewis, K. (2010). Beyond and below racial homophily: ERG models of a friendship network documented on Facebook. *American Journal of Sociology*, 116(2), 583–642.

Wyatt-Brown, B. (2001). *The shaping of Southern culture: Honor, grace, and war, 1760s-1890s*. Chapel Hill, NC: The University of North Carolina Press.

Zhou, M. (1997). Segmented assimilation: Issues, controversies, and recent research on the new second generation. *International Migration Review*, 31(4), 975–1008.

Zschirnt, E., & Ruedin, D. (2016). Ethnic discrimination in hiring decisions: A meta-analysis of correspondence tests 1990–2015. *Journal of Ethnic and Migration Studies*, 42(7), 1115–1134.

Chapter 12

Modernization

Chapter overview

Do you think the world is getting worse? Is crime on the rise and is the world becoming less safe? In this chapter I will address long-term changes in human societies. We will discover that the majority of the world population is rather pessimistic about social change, believing that the world is indeed getting worse (12.1). In light of these public perceptions, I will review two "objective" societal developments. One is the growing wealth and improving health of human populations (12.2), another is that societies have become more peaceful and safer places to live (12.3). How can we understand these patterns of socio-economic progress? I will review the idea that, over time, cultures have become more rational, i.e., more efficient collective enterprises, thereby creating more wealth, health, peace and safety (12.4). I will review the empirics of this rationalization trend, focusing on three key indicators, namely: technological progress (12.5), the growth of science and education (12.6) and increasing rationality across domains in society (12.7). I will then take these two broader trends (i.e., socio-economic progress and rationalization) together, identifying them as interrelated dimensions of the overarching modernization trend. Subsequently, I will examine the consequences of modernization for value change (12.8) and population structures (12.9). At the end of the chapter I will reflect on the puzzle that people's perceptions of societal trends are more pessimistic than their view of their personal lives, and I will address the underlying dynamics of the rationalization process (12.10).

Learning goals

After reading this chapter, check if you are able to:

- Describe key concepts on the topic of modernization.
- Disentangle dimensions of modernization.
- Describe long-term trends in modernization.
- Describe and apply the rationalization proposition.
- Describe and apply the modernization and individualism proposition.
- Describe the impact of modernization on population structures.
- Reflect on the mechanisms that underlie the process of rationalization.

12.1 Is the world getting worse?

When you ask people what they think of changes going on in their society, most people say that things are getting worse. Their concern may be related to issues such as increasing crime rates, terrorism, conflicts and wars, the refugee crisis, teenage pregnancy, drugs, depression and mental health problems, social isolation and loneliness, suicide, societal polarization, oppression and the reduction of freedom, civil rights and liberties, increasing pollution and global warming, religious fundamentalism, unemployment, economic crises, poverty and inequality. These concerns about rising social problems are not limited to populations of certain countries, such as the poorer nations in the world. The idea that the world is getting worse is a widespread opinion.

In 2017, researchers conducted a cross-national survey that asked people about what they think is happening in the world. The 30 countries that participated in the study were not the poorest nations in the world, to be sure. The researchers asked representative samples from these countries the following question: "overall, do you think the world is getting better or worse, or neither getting better nor worse?" The findings of the study indicated that in each of those 30 countries, the majority of the population believed that things are getting worse (Figure 12.1).

One may argue that asking questions about changes in the world in such a general way may not give the same results as asking people about specific trends, such as changing crime rates. However, scholars find that people have the same pessimistic views about societal changes when asking more specific questions. For example, it appears that people believe that crime tends to get worse and that the world is becoming less safe. In 2017 a cross-national population survey was conducted in 38 countries, asking people "do you think the murder rate in your country is higher, lower, or about the same as it was in 2000?" On average, 46% of the populations across 38 countries thought that the murder rate in their country was higher in 2017 than it was in 2000, as compared with only 7% who believed the murder rate

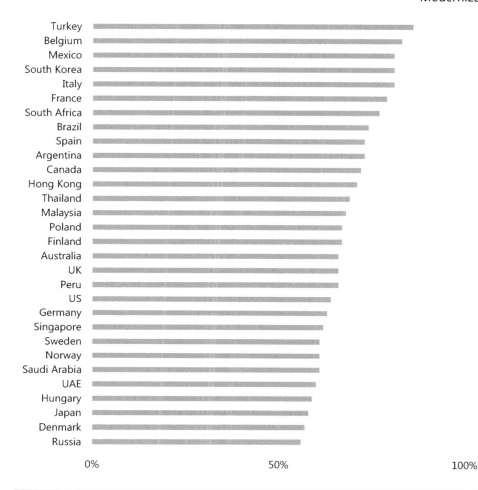

Figure 12.1 Percentage of the population that believes things are getting worse in the world.

Source: Gapminder, 2019; Rosling, Rosling, & Rosling Ronnlund, 2018.

had decreased (Figure 12.2). There is quite some country variation in these perceptions, but overall the pattern is clear: many more people tend to be pessimistic than optimistic about trends in murder rates.

A key question for sociologists is to find out how much truth there is in the public concerns about societal issues. Is the world indeed getting worse? To a certain extent, this is a *normative question* (Chapter 1)—it depends on one's values as to what one considers better and worse. The debate between pessimists and optimists may thus depend on one's value priorities. On the other hand, however, underlying one's opinions about the world getting better or worse are perceptions about changes. These perceptions may or may not be accurate. If people believe that the murder rate has increased, they may reason that the world is getting worse. But whether the number of murders has indeed increased in the past decades is something sociologists can study. By doing so, sociology can inform the public at large and policy making.

Topics

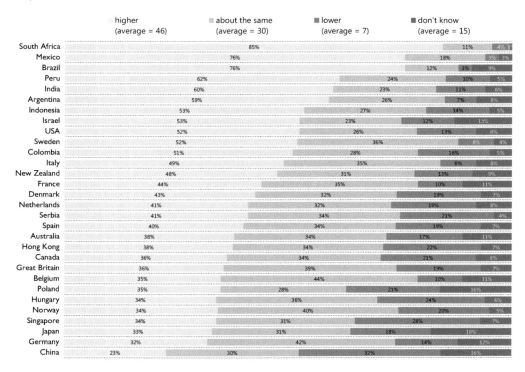

	higher (average = 46)	about the same (average = 30)	lower (average = 7)	don't know (average = 15)
South Africa	85%		11%	4% 1
Mexico	76%		18%	3% 3%
Brazil	76%		12%	3% 9%
Peru	62%	24%	10%	5%
India	60%	23%	11%	6%
Argentina	59%	26%	7%	8%
Indonesia	53%	27%	14%	5%
Israel	53%	23%	12%	13%
USA	52%	26%	13%	8%
Sweden	52%	36%	8%	4%
Colombia	51%	28%	16%	5%
Italy	49%	35%	8%	8%
New Zealand	48%	31%	13%	9%
France	44%	35%	10%	11%
Denmark	43%	32%	19%	7%
Netherlands	41%	32%	19%	8%
Serbia	41%	34%	21%	4%
Spain	40%	34%	19%	7%
Australia	38%	34%	17%	11%
Hong Kong	38%	34%	22%	7%
Canada	36%	34%	21%	8%
Great Britain	36%	39%	19%	7%
Belgium	35%	44%	10%	11%
Poland	35%	28%	21%	16%
Hungary	34%	36%	24%	6%
Norway	34%	40%	20%	5%
Singapore	34%	31%	28%	7%
Japan	33%	31%	18%	18%
Germany	32%	42%	14%	12%
China	23%	30%	32%	16%

> **Figure 12.2** Percentage of the population that believed in the year 2017 that the murder rate in their country is higher/lower/about the same as it was in 2000.
> *Source:* Ipsos, 2019.

In this chapter I will review key societal trends—some of these cover the past decades, others go more deeply into human history, spanning not decades but centuries or more. I start our empirical investigation at the birth of our species *Homo sapiens*, i.e., the species *sapiens* (meaning "wise") and the genus *Homo* (man). We are siblings to other humans, such as *Homo rudolfensis*, *Homo erectus* and *Homo neanderthalensis* (Harari, 2014). Humans evolved approximately 2.5 million years ago in East Africa, from the genus of apes called *Australopithecus*. Around 150,000 BC to 100,000 BC, *Homo sapiens* was born in the same region (Harari, 2014; Lenski & Nolan, 2006) and the other humans eventually became extinct. What has happened to *Homo sapiens* in the past 150,000 years? What are the major patterns of social change that we can distil?

12.2 Wealth and health

Nobody wants to live in poverty and be exposed to hunger, illnesses and existential threats. What are the changes in human history with respect to poverty and standards of living? How many people lived in poverty in the past and live in poverty today? Scholars have been able to look back over 200 years in history and found that, in 1820, almost 95% of the world lived in so-called "extreme poverty." What counts as "extreme poverty" is of course a matter

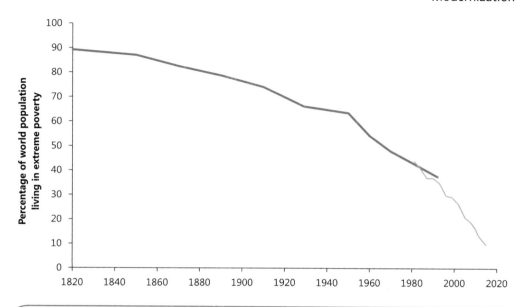

Figure 12.3 Extreme poverty, 1820–2015.
Source: Bourguignon & Morrisson, 2002; Roser & Ortiz-Ospina, 2017.

of definition, but in this case it means, in today's equivalent income, less than $1.90 a day. In the past 200 years, however, a historical change occurred: extreme poverty fell from 95% in 1820 to 10% today (Figure 12.3).

Poverty is an indicator of standards of living in a country. Another aspect of standards of living is economic development, conventionally measured with GDP per capita. Using this indicator, scholars have been able to track historical developments that go back more than 200 years (Table 12.1). Research suggests that, for a long time in human history, citizens tended to have more or less the same poor standards of living. Only in more recent times have significant changes in economic prosperity occurred (Milanovic, 2016). The economic progress occurred unevenly in the world, with what are today called *western societies* (Western European nations, Australia, Canada, US, New Zealand) taking the lead.

This divergence occurred from the year 1800 onwards and possibly even earlier, around 1500–1700—this is still a matter of scholarly debate (Clark, 2007; Pomeranz, 2009). To illustrate, in the year 1700 the GDP per capita in India was $1,200 and, 200 years later, in the year 1900, it was more or less the same: $1,131. By contrast, the GDP per capita in the UK in the year 1700 was $1,591, but this grew to $5,608 in 1900. Consequently, a major divergence emerged between the populations in India and the UK: whereas for generations the population in India remained at the same standard of living, citizens in the UK became more and more wealthy, thereby increasing the gap between these two nations. This historical phenomenon is called the *Rise of the West* (McNeill, 2009) and the *Great Divergence* (Pomeranz, 2009).

This trend towards a growing gap between the west and the non-west has not continued until the present day, however. Many non-western countries, including what were traditionally called "developing countries," have shown immense economic progress in the past decades—stronger than those in the more advanced western countries. An example of such an

Table 12.1 Long-term development of real GDP per capita (in 2011, US dollars).

Year	1500	1600	1700	1800	1900	1950	2000	2016
Germany	1,113	784	912	958	4,596	5,536	33,975	46,841
Spain	1,797	1,896	1,730	1,947	3,853	4,201	26,424	31,556
France	1,350	1,283	1,350	–	4,214	6,869	31,771	38,758
Italy	1,494	1,329	1,439	1,329	2,144	3,698	33,185	34,989
UK	–	–	1,591	2,205	5,608	9,441	34,390	39,162
USA	–	–	–	1,980	6,252	15,241	45,887	53,015
India		1,305	1,200	–	1,131	1,417	2,003	5,961
Japan	–	766	840	856	1,575	2,519	33,294	36,452
China	–	–	–	–	840	757	4,071	12,320
Brazil	–	–	–	600	606	1,549	8,316	13,479

Source: Bolt, Inklaar, de Jong, & van Zanden, 2018. Note: "-" indicates that no (reliable) data are available.

economically booming country is China, which showed a massive increase in GDP per capita from a "mere" $757 in 1950 to $4,071 in 2000, growing further to $12,320 in 2016. Although still behind the average GDP per capita in such western countries as Spain and Germany, the difference between these countries has strongly reduced. When seen from a global perspective, the empirical pattern is clear: the gap between western and non-western societies declined in the past decades (Milanovic, 2016). And, more generally, everywhere in the world, standards of living—as indicated by economic development—have improved (Deaton, 2013).

What about changes in health? What was the life expectancy of humans 150,000 years ago? How did it change over time? For most of human history, life expectancy was extremely low. Child mortality rates were high, there were poor health facilities and people suffered from extreme poverty. Scholars estimate that human life expectancy at birth was around 25–35 years throughout history. Even in the year 1800, findings suggest, the average life expectancy was around 27 years. This continued until around 1850, when life expectancy started to change dramatically (Clark, 2007; Lee, 2003). Only very recently in the history of *Homo sapiens* has life expectancy become substantially higher. It increased from 30 in 1880 to 45 in 1950 and to 65 in 2000 (Figure 12.4). In the year 2019, the average life expectancy in the world hit an unprecedented record, climbing further to 70.

We can summarize these empirical patterns as ***wealth and health progress***.

 STYLIZED FACT 12.1

The wealth and health progress

The history of *Homo sapiens* has witnessed changes in wealth and health, i.e., a decline of poverty, rising standards of living and increasing life expectancy.

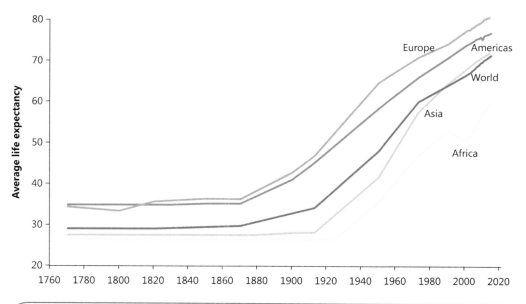

Figure 12.4 Life expectancy, 1771–2020.
Source: Pinker, 2018; Riley, 2005; Roser, 2019.

12.3 Peace and safety

Do you think your society has become less safe in past decades? The question of whether murders, crime and conflicts have increased or decreased over time has always been a matter of controversy. The 18th-century philosopher Rousseau claimed that the past was more peaceful than the present (Rousseau, 1999 [1755]). He believed that aboriginal humans lived harmoniously and that wars, murders and conflicts were uncommon. Only in more recent times, with the rise of property and inequality, have these human evils emerged. Hobbes, in contrast, believed that the "state of nature" was one of wars, conflicts and murders, a state in which every man was against every man, which made life "poor, nasty, brutish and short" (Hobbes, 1994 [1651]). He argued that in more recent times, with the formation of states, violence has declined.

Which of the two claims is correct? Criminologist Manuel Eisner collected data on homicide for several regions in Europe, going back as far as 800 years in human history (Eisner, 2014). Figure 12.5 presents his findings for Italy, Germany, England and Wales, as well as the average of 11 European regions for which he managed to find data. The homicide rate indicates the annual number of homicides per 100,000 people. His findings reveal two major trend periods. The first period covers the years from around 1200 to 1450. During this period homicide rates were around 25–30 per 100,000 inhabitants, with little change therein during these 250 years. But then, from the 15th century onwards, there is a steady decline in the homicide rates in the European regions, falling to 20 (1500–1549), 12 (1600–1649), 6 (1700–1749), 4 (1800–1825), 2 (1900–1925) and 1 (2000–2012). In 500 years, European homicide rates fell from 25–30 to 1.

Steven Pinker, in his book *The Better Angels of Our Nature*, presents evidence to suggest that violence has declined in human history (Pinker, 2011). He presents data from various

413

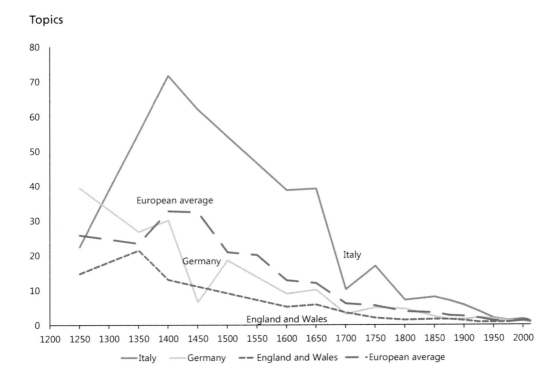

sources on violent deaths spanning even longer periods of time, including periods when most humans did not live in state societies, but in the "state of nature." This includes data from skeletons dug out of archaeological sites, which go back as far as 14,000 BC. He finds that in such non-state societies the death rate was on average 15%, which means that 15% of all deaths were caused by violence. In state societies, by comparison, the death rate due to violence is less than 1%. He draws similar conclusions when looking at homicide rates instead of the death rate. He finds an average homicide rate in non-state societies of 524 per 100,000 inhabitants. This is far larger than the homicide rate in European states in the period 1200–1450, which, as we have seen, was around 25–30.

These findings suggest Hobbes was right and that violence has substantially declined in human history (Eisner, 2003, 2014; Pinker, 2011). However, data on death causes that go back thousands of years are surrounded with much uncertainty. They are less reliable than statistics about more contemporary causes of death and may therefore strongly under- or overestimate the true violence rate. That said, we can be confident in the reliability of data from the 13th century onwards. The picture that emerges from trends is that, since the 15th century onwards, fewer people die because of murder or are the victims of non-lethal violence. The number of societies engaged on the battlefield has been declining for centuries and civil conflicts are less common. Of course, there were certain periods and settings in the past centuries in which there was no change or even an increase in violence. But these were temporary, or local, events. Globally, and taking a long-term perspective, the world has become more peaceful and safe in the past centuries.

The route towards increasing safety is not restricted to the decline in human violence. Pinker, in his more recent book *Enlightenment Now* (Pinker, 2018), shows that the trend is more general. To illustrate, Pinker shows statistics on the trend in the number of motor vehicle accident deaths in the US. In 1920 around 24 people died per 100 million motor vehicle miles. In 1950 this number had dropped to 7 and in 2015 it was close to 1. If you are a motor driver today, the chances of getting killed are 24 times lower than in 1920. Other trends for the US reveal the same pattern towards increasing safety. For example, after WWI the number of pedestrian deaths declined, there is a decline in occupational accident deaths and the number of deaths from drowning and fire go down as well. These patterns are not restricted to the US, but rather signal a global trend towards increasing safety. Thus, if you examine plane crashes in the world, for example, what you find is that the risk of getting killed in a plane crash has significantly diminished (Rosling et al., 2018). Or, to give another example, the chances that human beings die because of natural disasters have decreased as well (Rosling et al., 2018). The world is becoming an increasingly safe place.

Let's call these patterns *peace and safety progress*.

STYLIZED FACT 12.2

Peace and safety progress
From the 15th century onwards, human societies have become more peaceful and more safe.

12.4 Rationalization

The trends in wealth and health and in peace and safety go in the same direction. Let's take these two long-term developments together, which I will refer to as **socio-economic progress**. How can we explain this long-term trend? Why is there socio-economic progress? Why do we see improvement in wealth and health? Why has violence declined in history and has the world become a safer place?

socio-economic progress progress in wealth, health, peace and safety.

One reason behind socio-economic progress, so scholars have argued (Lenski & Nolan, 2006; Welzel, 2013), is that human beings strive for precisely this outcome. Individuals have agency, they act with purpose and basic human motives are to achieve wealth, to be healthy and to live in peace and safety—for oneself and for others. These universal human motives have always been there—even our ancestors who lived 150,000 years ago had these goals. Obtaining more wealth, having better health and living in peace and safety results in fewer constraints, more "human empowerment" and freedom in realizing one's goals.

The follow-up question, however, is why early *Homo sapiens* was not able to succeed in realizing these goals as much as contemporary human beings do. One prominent idea set forth by various scholars is that, over long periods of time, human cultures have been able to solve the problems of poverty, poor health, violence and unsafety (Lenski & Nolan, 2006; Weber, 1919). Cultures are the "secret of our success" (Henrich, 2015). Whereas individuals have always been striving for more wealth, health and safety, cultures can be seen as *collective* solutions to problems with which their members are confronted. We have seen that norms can generate collective benefits and help to overcome problems of coordination and cooperation (Chapter 6). Norms vary in how much they benefit the collective, of course. Some norms, as we have seen, may not be useful at all and instead harm people. Generally speaking, however, norms tend to adapt to changing social conditions and, over time, norms evolved that promoted conditions for socio-economic progress. In particular, the emergence of legal norms and the enforcement of these norms by formal authorities (Hobbes' *Leviathan*) in well-functioning institutions may be an important driver for socio-economic progress (Acemoglu & Robinson, 2012).

But there is another aspect of culture besides norms that sociologists have emphasized and which is important for understanding socio-economic progress. This is the idea that socio-economic progress depends on knowledge, on human reason, on "rationality" of *opinions* (Henrich, 2015; Lenski & Nolan, 2006; Pinker, 2018; Weber, 1919). If you want to produce an airplane or a smartphone you need to know how to do it. You may need tools, so then you need to know how to make these useful tools too. If you want to cure a disease, you can hope for the best, but you can also rely on theories, empirical data and—eventually—evidence-based medicine. If you want people to drive safely on the road, you need to know how to make cars that are safe and to know how you can create an infrastructure that minimizes risks.

People's opinions—perceptions, beliefs, cognition—can be more or less *rational* and the more rational opinions are, the better people are able to realize their goals, such as to increase wealth and improve their health and to reduce undesirable outcomes such as violence. Rationality is about human reason, about "opinions based on knowledge" (Pinker, 2018). But rationality is a matter of degree. Rationality is stronger the more you rely on *rational thinking*: you rely on scientific theories, you think logically and you use empirical evidence to evaluate hypotheses, rather than relying on authority, intuition, emotions or mysticism. When opinions are based on solid knowledge, they also become more *efficient*. This means that the goals that are set are better realized. Rationality also includes the idea that people are better able to *predict and control* their environment. Higher rationality means better understanding of what happens and why, knowing what the future will look like and being able to anticipate and control events such that ends are met.

There can be rationality at the individual and collective level. An individual can be very smart and skilled or not so and so, too, can we think of the rationality of collective cultures—the aggregate of people and their knowledge. Cultures are "collective brains" (Henrich, 2015), which can be more or less "rational." Highly rational cultures have deep understanding of how the world works; a high level of knowledge; a highly diverse, specialized and complimentary set of tools and skills. Highly rational collective brains are better able to realize fundamental human goals—wealth, health, peace, safety—more successfully than in cultures that are based on limited understanding of the world, in which perceptions and beliefs are based on authority and superstition instead of logic and empirics.

Collective rationality does not come out of the blue, as something one generation invents. Instead, collective rationality is the result of *cumulative processes*, in which one generation passes on knowledge to the next generation. Sometimes, knowledge gets lost but, according to Max Weber, one could distil a long-term process in which cultures become increasingly rational (Weber, 1919). That is to say, the collective opinions are becoming more and more accurate; they are increasingly based on empirical evidence and on logical thinking. Knowledge is becoming more scientifically grounded and rational. Increasingly, people adopt a scientific worldview, i.e., their perceptions and ideas are more and more shaped by scientifically informed empirical knowledge and logical thinking, on ideas that are more accurate and which can better explain how things work. Less and less so, Weber argued, cultural opinions are based on false perceptions, on ideas that are not true, on premises that do not match reality. But also, opinions that are not empirically testable (largely or entirely so) have lost their popularity. Hence, mythical thinking, superstition, religion and magic and other non-scientific beliefs have become more marginal over time. According to Weber "The fate of our times is characterized by rationalization and intellectualization" (Weber, 1919). Let's formulate Weber's hypothesis on the supposed long-term process called *rationalization*.

> H. Over time, cultures have become more and more rational, i.e., an increase in the rationality of opinions and corresponding products and practices. (*rationalization*)

This supposed rationalization process is a topic of investigation not only in sociology (Chase-Dunn & Lerro, 2016; Lenski & Nolan, 2006) but also in other scientific disciplines, most notably in evolutionary anthropology, biology and psychology (Boyd & Richerson, 1988, 2005; Henrich & McElreath, 2003; Mesoudi, 2011), economics (Clark, 2007), history (Harari, 2014; Landes, 1969; Morris, 2010) and geography (Diamond, 1997). Much empirical work has been done to describe this rationalization trend; how it varies across societies, when it accelerated, how it penetrates various domains in society (e.g., education, technology, politics, economy, sports), as well as on the theoretical understanding of the causes underlying this process.

Concepts related to rationalization are *industrialization* (Treiman, 1970) and *McDonaldization* (Ritzer, 2011). It has also been referred to as *cumulative culture*, to indicate the process in which knowledge from one generation is inherited by the next generation, which then adds new knowledge to the prior set of knowledge (Enquist, Ghirlanda, Jarrick, & Wachtmeister, 2008). The exact meaning of these concepts sometimes differs from the meaning of rationalization, but by and large they have much in common.

How could you empirically verify if Weber was right and that human cultures have become more rational? What are the empirical indicators we should look for? Rationalization is a complex concept and scholars commonly differentiate between three dimensions. If there is indeed a process of rationalization, then we should observe the following trends:

1 Accumulation of technological knowledge and innovations ("*technological progress*").
2 Growth of science and increasingly skilled and educated populations ("*scientization*").
3 Increasing rationality across social domains in society: economy, organizations, politics, sports, art and so forth ("*McDonaldization*").

These three presumed processes of rationalization are said to be an important driver of socio-economic progress. We may therefore wonder what empirics tells us about the supposed trends. Have human cultures become more rational? Let's review each supposed trend one by one.

12.5 Technological progress

I begin with the idea of technological progress. What does this mean? Cultural opinions are the things that "are in our heads"—the knowledge that we possess. Now, we can't look back in time and study the rationality of human beings 10,000 years ago or more. However, knowledge translates itself into the choices that we make, the things that we do and the products and tools that we make. Cultural knowledge can be applied, for instance, to build bridges and cars, to make telephones, print books, etc. We refer to technological knowledge, i.e., the knowledge needed for practical applications, and technology—the products that are based on this knowledge. Thus, although we cannot study how people were thinking thousands of years ago, we are able to investigate the technological tools and products they made.

Archaeological observations suggest that before *Homo sapiens* entered the field, some technological innovations were made and cumulative culture had already started. One of the oldest innovations was the usage of stones as tools. There is evidence that around 3.4 million years ago these tools were used in Ethiopia, presumably by *Australopiths* (Henrich, 2015). At the moment *Homo sapiens* was born, other innovations had also been passed on from generation to generation, in particular the hand ax, wooden spears, constructed shelters and colored pigments. Of critical importance was also the knowledge of how to control fire, which goes back to at least 800,000 BC, thus long before we, *Homo sapiens*, were born. Controlling fire was a particularly important innovation because it allowed humans to cook their food (Goudsblom, 1993; Wrangham, 2009). Although many of us do not realize it today, making and sustaining fire is actually a highly complex process, particularly under conditions of rainstorms and high winds (Henrich, 2015).

This knowledge acquired by other humans was passed on to *Homo sapiens* some 150,000 years ago. But then new technological innovations were made by *Homo sapiens*. The sociologists Gerhard Lenski and Patrick Nolan created an overview of the innovations that were made between 100,000–8,000 BC (Table 12.2). In the period between 100,000–40,000 BC,

Table 12.2 Examples of technological innovations between 100,000 BC and 8,000 BC.

Time period	Technological innovations		Innovations per thousand years
100,000 to 40,000 BC	Use of bone for tools Built-in handles on tools	Skin clothing Harpoon heads	0.07
40,000 to 10,000 BC **(Upper Paleolithic)**	Spear-thrower Lamps Fish gorges Needles with eyes Shovels or scoops Stone saws Spoons Jewelry Separate handles Boats Domestication of dog	Bow and arrow Pins or awls Cord Antler hammers Mattocks Graving tools Stone ax with hafted handle Pestles and grinding slabs Musical instruments Figurative art	0.70
10,000 to 8,000 BC **(Mesolithic)**	Beer Fish traps Adzes Plant cultivation Basketry Grinding equipment Paving Ice picks	Fishhooks Fishnets Sickles Domestication of sheep Cloth Leather-working tools Sledge Combs	8.0

Source: Lenski & Nolan, 2006.

they counted five innovations made by *Homo sapiens*, one of them being the use of bones for tools (Lenski & Nolan, 2006). As this period stretched over 60,000 years, it comes down to 0.07 innovations per thousand years. In other words, for thousands of years, there was very little if any change in the cultural knowledge of *Homo sapiens*. Cultures remained very similar from generation to generation, as humans used the same tools and they had the same practices and technological beliefs.

In the Upper Paleolithic period, which runs from 40,000 to 10,000 BC, we witness more changes, although there is still not a spectacular growth of knowledge. The innovation of the bow and arrow during this period greatly increases the efficiency of hunting. At the same time, existing tools were gradually refined and made more useful and efficient. In total, 21 innovations were made in this 30,000-year period according to Lenski, which means 0.7 innovations per thousand years.

In the Mesolithic period (10,000 BC–8,000 BC) we see that cultural knowledge was changing more rapidly. During this period, 16 further innovations were made. This included the domestication of sheep and plant cultivation. On average, this resulted in eight innovations per 1,000 years. Although this rate of innovation is more than in earlier eras, technological change is still very limited. For most humans at that time, they would not experience any change in technology during their whole life. They would pass on the tools and techniques they had inherited from their parents to their own children, without adopting any new innovation.

What does the long-term trend in innovations tell us? The increase in technological knowledge concurs with Weber's proposition on the rationalization of human cultures—even in the first thousands of years of *Homo sapiens* we find such a trend.

The accumulation of knowledge, according to the Lenski-Nolan counting, does not occur in a linear way. They posit that a striking pattern seems to emerge from Table 12.2, namely that the *rate* of innovations occurs at an *accelerating* pace. While in the period 100,000–40,000 BC there were only 0.07 innovations made per thousand years, this increased to 8 in the Mesolithic period. Obviously, these figures need to be taken with some caution. For one thing, it is not always clear what we should call an innovation. Often, minor improvements are made to existing tools instead of inventing something completely new. Furthermore, the further back we go in history, the more selective and uncertain our observations are: we are left with the facts that survived the passage of time and it might well be that innovations are made earlier than current evidence suggests and that our records of very old innovations are lost. On the other hand, however, scholars have used other data sources and reached the same conclusion: there is evidence to suggest a non-linear, accelerating increase in technological innovations over time (Basalla, 1988; Enquist et al., 2008).

Thus, the evolution of human cultures can be characterized by increasing levels of technological knowledge. Based on this trend, Lenski and Nolan classified different types of societies in terms of their primary mode of subsistence technology (Table 12.3). The hunting and gathering societies are the technologically most primitive cultures. The primary mode of subsistence in these cultures is the hunting of wild animals and foraging for uncultivated plant foods. With increasing knowledge and technology, people were able to cultivate plants (simple horticultural societies) and eventually they made use of metal tools (advanced horticultural societies). In simple agrarian societies people also know how to cultivate plants and how to make and use metal tools (bronze and copper), but in addition to that they also use plows. In advanced agrarian societies people use iron tools, which are stronger than bronze and copper. Finally, in industrial societies, people know how to use inanimate energy, like coal, petroleum, natural gas and nuclear power. These power sources are used for machine technology and lead to highly efficient modes of production.

Table 12.3 The technological evolution of human societies.

Type of society	Plant cultivation	Metallurgy	Plow	Iron	Inanimate energy
Hunting and gathering	–	–	–	–	–
Simple horticultural	+	–	–	–	–
Advanced horticultural	+	+	–	–	–
Simple agrarian	+	+	+	–	–
Advanced agrarian	+	+	+	+	–
Industrial	+	+	+	+	+

Source: Lenski & Nolan, 2006.

This classification of human societies is a simplification of all societies that have existed in human history. It is important to note that, in addition to the abovementioned societies, which are the major types, there are three other kinds of societies that are more marginal in human history, namely fishing, herding and maritime societies. Lenski and Nolan compared these three societies with the six major types of societies in terms of their technological development, i.e., the level of "information" or knowledge about technology (Figure 12.6). Fishing societies, for example, are slightly more technologically advanced than hunting and gathering societies, but less complex than horticultural societies. As you can see, the level of technological development is lowest in hunting and gathering societies and highest in industrial societies, which have the most productive and efficient subsistence technologies and which have the most "know-how."

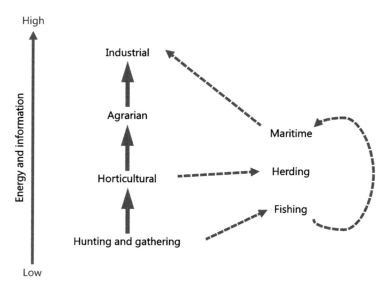

Figure 12.6 Level of technological development and patterns of evolution.
Source: Lenski & Nolan, 2006.

For seven million years the ancestors of *Homo sapiens* hunted for animals and gathered food and, for the most part of the history of *Homo sapiens*, we have lived in this type of technologically most primitive kind of society as well. Small-scale, technologically primitive societies predominated in the world of *Homo sapiens* from 150,000 BC until they were gradually replaced by horticultural and agricultural societies. In the 21st century, the hunting and gathering type of society has become very marginal, while other types of societies have become dominant and have effectively replaced technologically more primitive societies. Figure 12.7 visualizes in which type of society the world population has lived in the period between 15,000 BC and AD 2000.

It shows that, somewhere around 12,000 BC, fishing societies were first to develop after hunting and gathering societies. At that time and long thereafter, hunting and gathering remained the predominant type of society, however. This gradually changed with the rise of simple horticultural cultures between 10,000 BC and 8,000 BC (McNeill & McNeill, 2003). With the invention of metal tools, these societies developed into advanced horticultural societies in around 4,000 BC. Then, with the invention of the plow, simple agrarian societies came into existence in about 3,000 BC and these developed further into more advanced agrarian societies in 1,000 BC. The technological tools needed for the industrialization of societies were developed in the 18th century, but only at the beginning of the 19th century could some societies be classified as truly industrial societies.

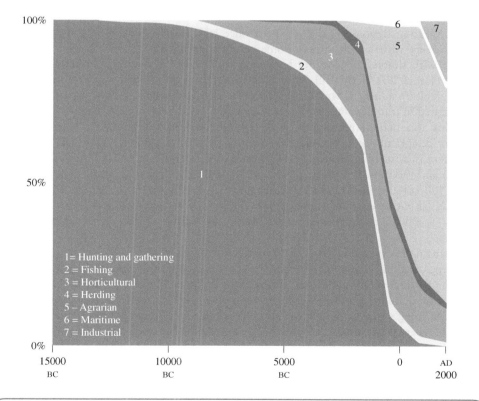

Figure 12.7 Percent of world population by type of society, 15,000 BC–AD 2000.

Source: Lenski & Nolan, 2006.

Topics

Although the Lenski-Nolan fine-grained overview of different types of societies in terms of primary subsistence technology is useful, other scholars tend to lump various societies together and adopt a more-simplified classification (Harari, 2014). This typology is based on a combination of the type of primary subsistence technology and other characteristics such as permanent settlement. This typology consists of three types of societies:

1 Hunting and gathering societies: from the birth of *Homo sapiens* (150,000 BC) until around 8,000 BC.
2 Agrarian societies: 10,000 BC–AD 1800. Starting with simple horticultural techniques, which subsequently developed into advanced agrarian cultures.
3 Industrial societies: from about AD 1800 to the present.

The hunting and gathering societies are the starting point for the other two types of societies that evolved afterwards. First came the more technologically advanced societies that are characterized by food production: the domestication of wild animals and plants and permanent settlement. This includes both the horticultural and agrarian cultures and in this classification no distinction is made between these two. The emergence of these food-producing societies is called the Agrarian Revolution, which happened in different areas in the world after 10,000 BC. This gradual shift from a nomadic lifestyle and hunting wild animals and gathering food to sedentary food production is considered one of the major changes in the history of human cultures, a change that, as we will see, affected the political, economic and social organization of human societies.

The Agrarian Revolution did not start once and in one place only. Instead, archaeological evidence reveals that at least some cultural innovations leading to agriculture (i.e., beginning with simple horticulture) happened *multiple* times and *independently* in several societies (Harari, 2014; McNeill & McNeill, 2003). It is presumed that the oldest area in which agriculture appeared was Southwest Asia, in the so-called "Fertile Crescent," a large region located in Iraq (around the Tigris River), Syria and Palestine. Archaeologists estimate that in this area plants and animals were domesticated around 8,500 BC. Later, elsewhere in the world, agriculture emerged independently as well. According to scholars (Diamond, 1997), there is compelling evidence to suggest that this happened in Eastern China (around 7,500 BC) and thousands of years later in Mesoamerica (3,500 BC), in the Andes and Amazonia (3,500 BC) and the eastern United States (2,500 BC). For other regions there is more uncertainty about whether the development of farming occurred independently. These are: the Sahel (5,000 BC), tropical West Africa (3,000 BC), Ethiopia (unknown) and New Guinea (7,000 BC).

In many more cases, however, the domestication of plants and animals was adopted from neighboring cultures (Diamond, 1997). That is to say, the techniques and practices were not independently discovered but learned from nearby cultures. In addition, what also happened was that simple hunting and gathering communities were surrendered by larger and more powerful farming societies. Either way, the knowledge and practices of agriculture diffused from areas where it was discovered independently to other locations. In this way, societies in Western Europe became agrarian around 6,000–3,500 BC and so did the Indus Valley in India in 7,000 BC and Egypt in 6,000 BC (Diamond, 1997).

In the past centuries, agrarian societies have developed into industrialized societies. The Industrial Revolution, which began around 1800 in England and then spread to other societies, consisted of various phases (Landes, 1969). It is common to differentiate between four of them (Lenski & Nolan, 2006). Table 12.4 gives an overview of these various stages, as well as some major innovations that belong to each of them.

Table 12.4 Four phases of industrialization.

Phase	Main innovations	Where and when started?
I	Steam engine, "spinning jenny"	England, 1760
II	Railroads, steamships	England, 1850
III	Internal combustion engine, telephone, radio, movies	Germany and US, 1890
IV	Television, computer, Internet, plastic	US, 1940

Source: Lenski & Nolan, 2006.

The Industrial Revolution started in England with innovations made in around 1760—most notably the steam engine and the "spinning jenny" (which replaced the traditional, less-efficient, spinning wheel). Hundreds of years later, the industrialization entered its second stage, with the coming of railroads, steamships, farm machines, steel and rubber. Still, England was the center of technological innovations in the world. This changed, however, in the decades thereafter, when Germany and the US took over as the regions of technological growth. It was in these societies that the car industry emerged (as a result of the invention of the internal combustion engine), the capacity of electricity rapidly increased and new communication technology was boosted (telephone, radio, moving pictures). The current phase of the Industrial Revolution—in which the gravity of technological innovations is located in the US—is often called the "information age" because of the numerous innovations that help to increase access to and dissemination of information (television, computer, Internet, mobile devices). At the same time, however, many other innovations have been made regarding materials such as plastic, nylon and polyester. Let's summarize the stylized fact of *technological progress*.

STYLIZED FACT 12.3

Technological progress
There is a rise in technological knowledge in human cultures from 150,000 BC to the present and the speed of growth in technological knowledge is increasing.

12.6 Scientization

When scholars study the rationalization process, they not only examine trends in technological knowledge. Another area of research is *science*: knowledge and skills based on more systematic theory formation, logical reasoning and empirical observations. Rationalization entails scientific progress, i.e., an increasing understanding of the world, predictions that are more and more in line with reality, increasing predictability and control of our environment. Inherent to scientific progress is the improvement of the scientific method itself, i.e., increasing *quantification* of phenomena, *standardization* of measures, more extensive *classifications*, improved *observations* and *tests*, *transparency*, *replication* and *evaluation* (Ritzer, 2011).

It is hard to say exactly when *Homo sapiens* started to do science. Possibly, we have always been observing the things around us, trying to understand them and predicting future events. And, presumably, people have relied on the knowledge acquired by previous generations and then gradually, step by step, they have tried to improve on it. However, systematic *scientific observations* were rather uncommon in most of human history and so were *scientific explanations*. According to historical records, and simplifying a bit, something special happened around the year AD 1450, just before Copernicus was born. It was the beginning of what is called the Scientific Revolution: a sudden and immense growth of scientific knowledge (Harari, 2014), which was particularly strong in Western Europe.

To be sure, in premodern times, in the tradition of Christianity, Islam and other religions and cultures, important scientific discoveries were made before this (Lindberg, 2010; Weinberg, 2015). However, for most of human history, theories were formulated in terms of stories rather than being worked out more systematically. The science that evolved after 1450 relied more heavily on mathematics, using abstract symbols and equations, and it featured a more quantitative approach to understanding reality. Moreover, the empirical testing of theories and hypotheses increased in accuracy through the invention of experimental methods. At the same time, the traditional dominance of religious, magical and aesthetic beliefs in explaining the world eroded and scientific research became more and more independent from such "irrational" belief systems (Weinberg, 2015).

The detailed historical records of the emergence of science suggest that around 1450 the Scientific Revolution started. To test whether this observation is confirmed by other evidence, scholars have quantified the number of major scientific discoveries that were made in the period 1000–1900 (Darmstaedter & DuBois-Reymond, 1904). Figure 12.8 shows that, indeed, few discoveries were made in the period between AD 1000–1500. In line with the idea of the Scientific Revolution, the number of discoveries strongly increases in the 16th century and then this rate accelerates further until 1900, suggesting an exponential increase in scientific discoveries (Darmstaedter & DuBois-Reymond, 1904; Lehman, 1947). More recent work shows that this accelerating trend in scientific discoveries continues until today, as exemplified by the enormous growth of scientific publications after 1950 (Drori, Meyer, Ramirez, & Schofer, 2003).

Weber's rationalization thesis states that, over time, human populations have become more skilled and "rational," a process we automatically associate with an increase in informal and formal education, with growing knowledge, abilities and skills. Science and education are often studied together, as there is a linkage between the two. On the one hand, there are scientific discoveries and insights made by individual scholars, or by teams of researchers at universities, as well as improvements in the scientific method (e.g., quantification, standardization). On the other hand, this growth of scientific knowledge finds its way into the population at large and may modify the perceptions, skills and abilities of many people. For instance, the changing common-sense beliefs about the relationship between the sun and earth emerged from the discoveries by scientists like Copernicus, Kepler and Galileo, who questioned the established views using scientific theories and exact measurements. These scientific insights gradually took root in the common-sense beliefs of the rest of the population. Such change in cultural opinions and skills primarily takes place in education, either informally (e.g., parent–child) or formally (i.e., in schools, colleges and universities). If Weber's rationalization hypothesis is true, we can expect to see a trend called scientization (Drori et al., 2003): the rise and increasing dominance of scientific knowledge and the scientific

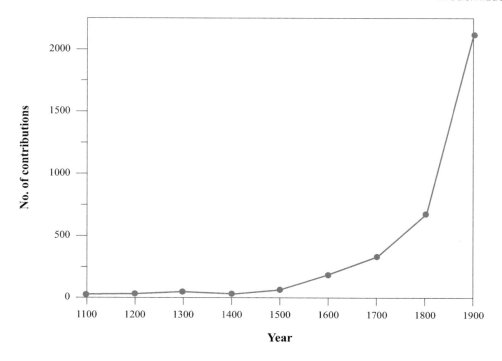

Figure 12.8 The number of scientific discoveries by century, 1000–1900.
Source: Darmstaedter & DuBois-Reymond, 1904.

method among the population at large. This implies a shift from informal to more formal education and the growing knowledge, skills and abilities of the population.

Is there evidence for the supposed trend called "scientization?" As a proxy for abilities and skills of human populations, we can use *literacy* levels, i.e., being able to read and write is often used as a measure of skills. Such literacy levels are attractive to study because observations go back several centuries and hence allow the study of longer time periods.

Table 12.5 presents statistics on literacy for the period between 1500 and 1885. It illustrates the increasing literacy skills of the citizens in England and Scotland, as indicated by their ability to sign the marriage certificate. The figures show that at the beginning of the 16th century only a small elite was able to write in England. The vast majority of the population could not provide their signature on the marriage record. Literacy rates steadily increased in England, from up to 45% of male adults in 1714 to 89% in 1885. Women lagged behind men for centuries until the end of the 19th century, when they reached equal literacy levels to men. Such a long-term increase in literacy levels has been found in Western Europe more generally (Buringh & Van Zanden, 2009; Clark, 2007).

In more recent times, there has been a shift from informal to formal education and from educating a small elite to the population at large. Scientific knowledge is disseminated to the public, starting at a young age and stretching over many years. The scientific method and worldview, based on logic, quantification, standardization and empirical evidence, is more and more becoming the standard cultural belief system across the world, at the expense of non-scientific sources of knowledge and approaches, traditional beliefs and magical-religious

IL VERO RITRATTO DI NICOLO COPERNICO

INCISO CIRCA IL 1650 DAL CELEBRE ARTISTA POLACCO GEREMIA FALCK DI DANZICA

Image 12.1 Copernicus (1473–1543) made a considerable contribution to scientific knowledge. His heliocentric theory went against the prevailing views and argued that the sun was the center of the solar system and earth and the other planets revolved around it.

Table 12.5 Percentage of adults able to sign their name at the marriage ceremony, England and Scotland 1500–1885.

Year	England		Scotland	
	Men	Women	Men	Women
1500	10	5		
1600	20	10		
1650	30		10–25	0–5
1714	45	25		
1754	60	40	40–65	23
1840	67	50		
1850	69	54	87	87
1870	80	73		
1885	89	87		

Source: Stephens, 1990.

thinking. Across the globe, the number of schools, colleges and universities has been increasing in past centuries and there is a parallel growth of people who follow formal educational training. More and more, people are exposed to science and rational cultural beliefs via formal education.

This trend is illustrated in Table 12.6. It shows that the average years of schooling in the population aged 25 and older has significantly increased for each country presented. For example, in 1950, the citizens in Egypt had attended on average 0.49 years in education. By the year 2010 this had increased to 6.55 years. In South Africa, it changed from 3.75 years in 1950 to 9.43 years in 2010. In other countries the increase in schooling is evident too, albeit that the magnitude of the change differs. Increasingly, people stay longer at school—the number of years people spend in school has grown enormously in just a few decades and this is a global phenomenon.

Conventionally, scholars make a distinction between *primary education* (approximately ages 6–11), *secondary education* (12–17) and *tertiary education* (18–21). Increasingly, people attend not only primary education but also secondary and tertiary education (Schofer & Meyer, 2005). Nowadays, many young people attend some sort of post-secondary education, such as higher vocational training or university. In Egypt, for example, only 1.1% of the population aged 25 and over had attended tertiary education in 1950 (Table 12.6). In 2010, this had increased to 10.1%. Globally, more and more people enrol in tertiary education.

In 1984, the scholar James Flynn published a study which provided evidence for the scientization trend using a surprising data source: IQ tests (Flynn, 1984). Flynn had collected the results of nationwide samples on how Americans performed on standardized IQ tests for the period between 1932 and 1978. The average of an IQ test is always standardized to 100 after all subjects have conducted the test. Flynn discovered that, over time, subjects were performing better and better. This means that if the same people are given two IQ tests, one normed in 1932 and the other in, say, 1935, they score higher on the earlier test. Because of the improved performance over time, the average score (100) in later years is capturing higher

Table 12.6 Educational enrolment of the population aged 25 and over, 1950–2010.

	Average years of schooling		Tertiary education, enrollment (%)	
	1950	2010	1950	2010
North America				
United States	8.13	13.42	13.6	57.3
Canada	7.39	12.56	8.8	47.7
Mexico	2.17	8.33	1.4	17.7
South America				
Argentina	4.60	9.48	1.2	11.7
Brazil	1.96	7.66	0.9	11.3
Asia				
China	0.65	7.53	0.2	3.6
India	0.92	5.39	0.7	9.1
Indonesia	0.74	7.26	0.1	7.5
Japan	5.91	11.52	4.5	30.1
Pakistan	0.85	4.45	0.7	6.7
Africa				
Egypt	0.49	6.55	1.1	10.1
South Africa	3.75	9.43	2.7	6.1
Europe				
France	4.31	10.64	1.7	24.4
Germany	6.71	12.69	2.8	24.3
United Kingdom	6.11	12.32	1.6	28.3
Italy	4.04	9.54	1.5	12.1
Russia	3.16	11.73	3.3	62.0
Oceania				
Australia	7.87	11.77	10.5	38

Source: Barro & Lee, 2013. The full data set can be found at: www.barrolee.com.

skills and abilities than in the years before. If people had taken the earlier test, they would have scored higher. Flynn discovered that in the period 1932–1978 the mean IQ score increased by 13.8 points. After he published this finding, Flynn examined whether the same pattern can be observed in other developed countries (Flynn, 1987). And this is, indeed, what he found: his 14-nation study showed that IQ scores had been increasing there as well. The empirical pattern is known as the **Flynn effect**, i.e., the gradual increase in skills and

flynn effect
gradual increase in skills and abilities of populations in developed countries between 1930 and 1995.

abilities of populations in developed countries between 1930 and 1995—as evident from increasing IQ scores in that period (Flynn, 2007). Note that after this period there is no clear evidence for further IQ improvement (Flynn & Shayer, 2018).

Let's summarize the trends we have observed: the growth of scientific knowledge, not only in terms of scientific discoveries but also in terms of formal education, literacy and skills of the population at large. The process called *scientization* is a stylized fact.

 STYLIZED FACT 12.4

Scientization

Over time, human cultures have become more science-oriented. There is a growth of scientific knowledge; more formal education; increasing literacy, knowledge and skills.

12.7 McDonaldization

We have seen that human cultures have witnessed a process of rationalization in terms of technology, science and education. In line with Weber's rationalization hypothesis, we have found that cultures have become more technologically advanced, more science oriented, that literacy has increased and that more and more people receive formal education. According to Weber, however, the rationalization process is not restricted to the domains of technology, science and education. To him, rationalization is a process that affects all segments of society. What we see, according to Weber, is that the economy, politics, sports, arts and other domains in society are becoming increasingly rationally organized as well. That is to say: the rationalization process—increasing scientific thinking, efficiency, prediction and control—is not limited to technological and scientific knowledge and their corresponding products and practices, but spreads out to many different *domains*.

This happens in (at least) two ways. First, technological products diffuse to various areas. For example, the invention of clocks and calendars, the increasing quantification and standardization of time (Crosby, 1997), subsequently diffused to organizations, which resulted in a more efficient and regulated organization of work and social relations (Zerubavel, 1985). Second, the scientific method itself—this rationalized worldview—becomes more the mainstream perspective outside academia. This method of scientific thinking and reason, which people have learned in education, sets the standard in the things we do: scientific and evidence-based, efficient and transparent (Drori et al., 2003; Schofer & Meyer, 2005). Inherent features of the scientific method are increasingly applied to areas outside academia, i.e., the growth of quantification, standardization, transparency and evaluation, testing and evidence-based products and practices. Taken together, this techno-scientific rationalized culture will be diffused to other sectors of society: to economic production, politics, organizations, sports, arts, health care and so forth.

In his work, Weber described how organizations have become more rational over time and how the elements of a rational culture gradually pervade modern, bureaucratic, organizations. Bureaucratization means, first of all, that processes become more efficiently organized, which results from division of labor and formalization of rules and procedures. Specialization is a core element of increasingly rationalized societies, i.e., more and more workers are experts in highly specific fields, well-defined tasks or certain skills. In bureaucratic organizations, quantification and standardization are key as they help employers to track the output and productivity of their personnel, to measure the efficiency of the organization and to increase sales and profit. As a result of formal rules and procedures, bureaucracies operate in a highly predictable manner. Employees know what they are expected to do and their customers know what to expect. Moreover, in a bureaucratic organization, employers exert control over their employees, as the rules, regulations and structures dictate to them what they should do. If an employee fails to perform a task, that employee can be replaced by another employee (or even by a machine) who can take over the specialized task. Although it might sound strange to say this nowadays, according to Weber, the bureaucratic organization is a highly rational organization. In practice, most of these "modern ideas" on how employers and managers could produce such highly rational and efficient work settings were known as "scientific management principles" and they were originally formulated by Frederick Taylor in the early 20th century (Taylor, 1914). Taylor was hired by several large-scale organizations to work out those ideas in practice (Ritzer, 2011) and scholars argue that even today such scientific management principles are still gaining in popularity (Drori, Meyer, & Hwang, 2006).

Elaborating on Weber's ideas, the sociologist Ritzer coined the term *McDonaldization* (Ritzer, 2011). The process of *McDonaldization* refers to the broader rationalization tendencies of societies, as found in organizations, sports, arts and so forth. McDonalds is a paradigmatic case of an organization that is characterized by high efficiency, predictability and control, which adopted the scientific method and hence the scientific management principles by standardizing, quantifying and evaluating almost everything. In his book *The McDonaldization of Society*, Ritzer gives many examples of how the rationalization process has unfolded in the consumer market, health care, sports and other sectors of society. He describes how, in 1958, the McDonalds' manual gave detailed instructions for operating a fast-food restaurant in a highly efficient and rational way:

> It told operators exactly how to draw milk shakes, grill hamburgers, and fry potatoes. It specified *precise* cooking times for all products and temperature settings for all equipment. It fixed *standard* portions on every food item, down to the *quarter ounce* of onions placed on each hamburger patty and the *thirty-two slices per pound* of cheese. It specified that French fries be cut at *nine thirty-seconds of an inch* thick … Grill men *were instructed* to put hamburgers down on the grill moving from left to right, creating *six rows of six* patties each.
>
> (Ritzer, 2011)

It is not only organizations and work settings that are increasingly subject to scientific principles and the rationalization process. According to Weber and Ritzer (Ritzer, 2011), these developments also affect other domains in society, such as sports. Today, more than ever, we count, compare, measure and quantify everything in sports. How this rationalization process unfolded in sports was noted by Guttmann in 1978:

> Modern sports are characterized by the almost inevitable tendency to transform every athletic feat into one that can be quantified and measured. The accumulation of statistics on every conceivable aspect of the game is a hallmark of football, baseball, hockey, and of track and field too, where the accuracy of quantification has, thanks to an increasingly precise technology, reached a degree that makes the stopwatch seem positively primitive.
>
> (Guttmann, 1978)

In summary, human cultures have become increasingly rational and thereby more effective and efficient in realizing the universal human goals of wealth, health, peace and safety. Knowledge is passed on from generation to generation in a cumulative way, with each generation adding new knowledge. Compared with thousands of years ago, contemporary human cultures are incredibly sophisticated and intelligent collective enterprises—producing such technological tools as smartphones and fMRIs, being able to understand complex biochemical reactions and particle physics, eradicating smallpox (a disease which killed 300 million people in the 20th century alone) and so forth. It is for this reason that scholars argue that culture is the secret of our success, the collective brains that enable human populations to understand, control and change the world in ways that satisfy their needs.

12.8 Value change

The process of rationalization which I have described is often taken together with the trend in socio-economic progress. Rationalization and socio-economic progress are actually seen as two dimensions of the concept of **modernization** (Inglehart, 1997). When scholars speak of modernization, they typically have in mind these two trends: rationalization and socio-economic progress (Figure 12.9). These trends, although analytically distinct, are not independent from each other in reality: the growth of technology, science and education enables populations to produce more wealth, better health, more peace and safety. It has been argued that rationalization enables socio-economic progress, but the reverse is likely also true: more prosperous, peaceful societies created opportunities for human cultures to become more rational, to invest more in science and education. Modernization refers to these co-occurring and interrelated trends, i.e., growth in technology, science, education and more wealth, health, peace and safety.

modernization
co-occurring and interrelated process of rationalization and socio-economic progress.

What are the consequences of modernization? What does the process of modernization mean for cultures (opinions, norms), social relations (networks and groups) and inequality (stratification, mobility and resources)? Putnam, as we have seen (Chapter 7), speculated that technological changes will bring about changes in personal networks, that modernization leads to a loss of community (Putnam, 2000). Blau and Duncan (Chapter 9) argued that modernization will change social mobility, such that achievement becomes more important

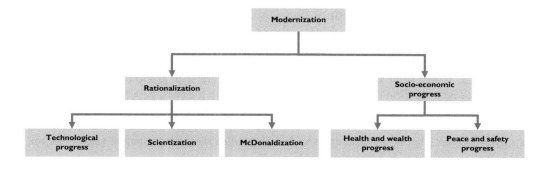

Figure 12.9 Rationalization and socio-economic progress as subdimensions of modernization.

and ascription less so (Blau & Duncan, 1967). Let's take a look at whether modernization has also influenced two other social phenomena, namely (1) value change and (2) population structures.

To begin with values. Does modernization result in a change of human values? Does progress in wealth, health, safety and peace, in combination with the rationalization process, result in a change of what people consider "valuable?" There exists a long tradition in sociology in which scholars have claimed that modernization results in a shift from "collectivistic" to "individualistic" values (Bell, 1976; Durkheim, 2014 [1893]; Tonnies, 1957 [1887]). What do these values mean? This question has been a topic of investigation since the 1970s (Rokeach, 1973). Since then, a tremendous amount of work on values has been done by three scholars in particular, each of them using completely different methods of observation:

- Ronald Inglehart investigated cultural values using the massive EVS/WVS survey data, starting in the early 1980s and continuing until the present day (Inglehart, 1990, 1997, 2015 [1977]; Inglehart & Baker, 2000).
- Geert Hofstede collected survey data among workers of one multinational business organization (IBM) in 1968 and 1972. In total, more than 116,000 questionnaires were distributed, spanning 72 countries (Hofstede, 2001 [1980]).
- Shalom Schwartz gathered survey data among (mostly) student and teacher samples in around 20 nations (Schwartz, 1992, 2006; Schwartz & Bilsky, 1987; Schwartz et al., 2012).

Importantly, these scholars worked rather independently from each other, using different samples and methods, and also invented their own measures to capture general values. The outcomes of their studies are, however, remarkably consistent. All three authors make the distinction between *individualistic values* (in short: **individualism**) and *collectivistic values* (**collectivism**) (Hofstede, 2001 [1980]; Oyserman, Coon, & Kemmelmeier, 2002; Triandis, 1995). Some scholars use different concepts that have (more or less) the same meaning: "autonomy" versus "embeddedness" (Schwartz, 2006), "loose" versus "tight" cultures (Gelfand et al., 2011), "post-materialism" versus "materialism" (Inglehart, 2015 [1977]) and "self-expression" versus "survival" values (Inglehart & Welzel, 2005). Studies have shown that these different concepts are strongly associated empirically (Datler, Jagodzinski, & Schmidt, 2013; Inglehart & Welzel, 2005; Welzel, 2013).

individualism (also emancipative values) individualistic values, such as emphasis on autonomy and personal choice.

collectivism collectivistic values, such as emphasis on group loyalty and authority.

When people have collectivistic values, loyalty to the group is regarded as of utmost importance and individuals are supposed to consider group interest first and foremost. In such collectivistic cultures, people are more extrinsically motivated as they seek to gratify the expectations of the group. People value respect for authority and they prefer in-group membership, fitting in, obedience and conformity. By contrast, in individualistic societies, people value autonomy, personal choice, freedom, independence and uniqueness. In these societies, people value autonomous human choices, i.e., self-orientation and creating equal opportunities for individuals are positively valued. That is why Christian Welzel also called these **emancipative values** (Welzel, 2013; Welzel, Inglehart, & Kligemann, 2003).

Individualistic and collectivistic values manifest themselves in specific values regarding family, school, politics and gender (Hofstede, 2001 [1980]; Triandis, 1995). It thereby creates *coherence* in values across domains, categories and issues. Table 12.7 presents some stylized differences between collectivistic and individualistic cultures.

<table>
<thead>
<tr><th>Table 12.7 Individualistic and collectivistic values.</th></tr>
</thead>
</table>

Specific domain	Collectivistic culture	Individualistic culture
Family	Divorce is bad	Divorce is OK
	Children should care for parents	Parents should care for themselves
	Marriage should be arranged by parents	Marriage should be based on love and free choice
School	Group work encouraged	Individual work encouraged
	Preferential in-group treatment is OK	Preferential in-group treatment is wrong
Organization	Employees should act in accordance with in-group interest	Employees should act to fulfil personal goals
	Loyalty to organization and employer highly valued	Personal development of employees is what matters
Politics	Important that political elite rules the country	Important that the mass public has political power
	Collective interests are more valuable than individual interests	Individual interests are more valuable than collective interests

The so-called ***modernization and individualism*** proposition states that with increasing levels of modernization in society, collectivistic values become less widespread as they are replaced by individualistic values:

> P. The higher the level of modernity in a society, the more widespread are individualistic values in that society. (*modernization and individualism*)

Is there evidence for this proposition? Scholars have tested this proposition in various ways, namely (1) *longitudinally*, by studying value change within societies and (2) *cross-nationally*, by comparing values in highly modern, western societies versus those in less modern, non-western societies. Let's first see how the proposition has been tested longitudinally.

P.   The higher the level of modernity in a society, the more widespread are individualistic values in that society. (*modernization and individualism*)

C.   In the period 1800–2015, societies have become more modern.

H.   In the period 1800–2015, individualistic values have increased. (*individualization*)

> **Theory schema 12.1** Hypothesis on individualization derived from the modernization and individualism proposition.

Is there evidence for a trend towards individualization? To answer this, consider values concerning gender. How strongly do gender values change over time? Values have a certain *direction*, i.e., values can be ranked along a continuum and people's values are located somewhere on that continuum. Sociologists often distinguish between "progressive" and "traditional" gender values. If a person has (more) progressive gender values, it means that that person feels it is important to have equal roles and rights for men and women, in the household, in education, in the labor market and in society at large. If, instead, a person has (more) traditional gender values, then that person prefers to have unequal roles for men and women, such that women take care of the children and household tasks, whereas men are more entitled to do paid work and to play a dominant role in society. Traditional gender values are an expression of more collectivistic values, as group loyalty and fitting in are seen as more important than individual freedom and autonomy for both genders—values that are more common in individualistic cultures.

The EVS/WVS data, which has been at the center of the work of Inglehart and Welzel (Inglehart, 1990, 1997, 2015 [1977]; Inglehart & Baker, 2000; Welzel, 2013), allow us to study gender values at the level of societies. We can do so because we can aggregate the individual-level responses to survey questions about gender values. In the EVS/WVS surveys, multiple questions and statements are addressed that are related to gender values. The following are three such statements:

● "When jobs are scarce, men should have more right to a job than women."
● "On the whole, men make better political leaders than women do."
● "A university education is more important for a boy than for a girl."

Respondents were asked to indicate how much they agree or disagree with each of these statements. The idea behind this is that (strong) agreement with these statements indicates traditional gender values, whereas (strong) disagreement indicates more progressive gender values. Combining the responses of respondents to these three items, Welzel (2013) created a scale for gender equality values ranging from 0 (strong traditional gender values) to 100 (strong progressive gender values).

Using this scale, Figure 12.10 presents a comparison over two periods in time, using the EVS/WVS data from two rounds. As you can see, for most countries, the collective gender equality values became slightly more progressive between the two time periods. For example, in Norway the gender equality score shifted from around 83 in the period 1995–2000 to 89 in 2007–2014. There are some countries, such as India, which have become more traditional between these two periods, but the overall pattern is that of increasingly progressive gender values. The rate of change, however, appears very modest. Cultural values tend to be rather stable within societies and only slowly change in a certain direction. But the path it follows, overall, is that of increasing emphasis on gender equality (Inglehart & Norris, 2003; Welzel, 2013).

This finding can be seen in a broader shift from collectivistic to individualistic cultural values. Studies have repeatedly documented this change over time, which occurs slowly but steadily in this direction. Besides the EVS/WVS surveys showing this change (Inglehart & Welzel, 2005; Welzel, 2013), other sources of data equally find this trend. For example, some scholars have studied the frequency of individualistic words (such as "I," "me," "unique") and collectivistic words ("obedience," "authority") in US presidential speeches, covering periods as large as from the year 1790 to the year 2012 (Chopik, Joshi, & Konrath, 2014). Others have examined the usage of individualistic and collectivistic words in American English books, using the Google Ngram viewer (Michel et al., 2011), over the period 1800–2000

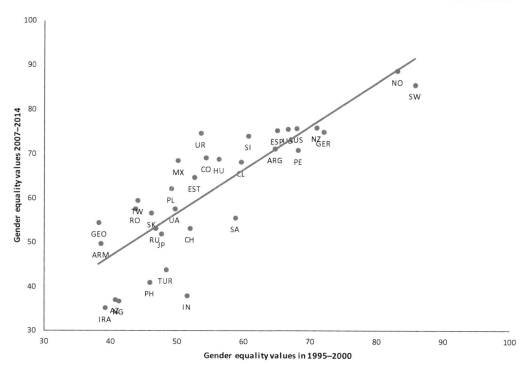

Figure 12.10 Gender equality values over time.

(Greenfield, 2013) and similarly for Chinese books between 1970 and 2008 (Zeng & Greenfield, 2015). All these studies point in the same direction, namely a gradual shift from collectivistic to individualistic cultural values. Based on this large body of research, the stylized fact called ***individualization*** can be distilled.

STYLIZED FACT 12.5

Individualization

In the period between 1800 and 2015 there was an increase in individualistic values at the expense of collectivistic values in societies.

The individualization trend is in line with the modernization and individualization proposition. However, it may also be that the trend towards individualism is not related to modernization, but actually to something else that has changed over time. Therefore, scholars also used another test of the modernization and individualism proposition. In this test, they compared the values in western countries with the values in non-western nations, on the assumption that western societies are more modern than non-western societies.

P . The higher the level of modernity in a society, the more widespread are individualistic values in that society. (*modernization and individualism*)

C . Western societies were more modern than non-Western societies in the period 1800–2015.

H . Western societies were more individualistic during the period 1800–2015 than non-Western societies. (*Western individualism*)

> **Theory schema 12.2** Hypothesis on Western individualism derived from the modernization and individualism proposition.

Are individualistic values more prevalent in western countries? What do the results show? Figure 12.11 presents the findings from the EVS/WVS data for the period between 2007 and 2014. The figure again uses the Welzel scale on gender values (0–100). As you can see, gender values strongly differ across nations. In some countries, like Norway and the Netherlands, many people have values that emphasize gender equality. In other nations, like Jordan, Iran and Egypt, this is much less so.

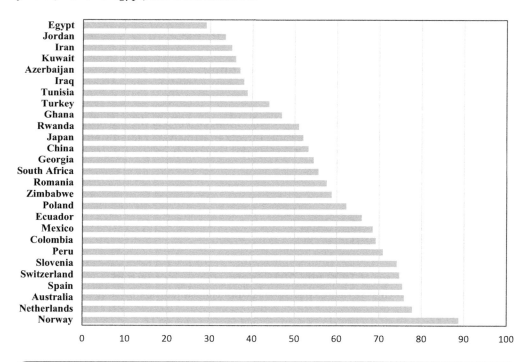

> **Figure 12.11** Gender equality values per country, 2007–2014.

It is not the case that only *gender* values are more individualistic in western societies. In western societies values regarding *family*, *religion*, *politics*, *organizations* and so forth are also more individualistic than they are in non-western societies. The individualistic, emancipative values that are so characteristic of western societies manifest themselves in all areas of life and they make up a rather coherent set of more specific values. This conclusion is corroborated in studies using the aforementioned cross-national surveys from the EVS/WVS project (Inglehart & Welzel, 2005; Welzel, 2013), studies using the comparative surveys among workers of IBM (Hofstede, 2001 [1980]) and research using survey data among students and teachers (Schwartz, 2006). We can call this empirical pattern *western individualism*.

STYLIZED FACT 12.6

Western individualism

Individualistic values are more widespread in Western societies than in non-Western societies.

Using cross-national comparative data, scholars have tested the modernization and individualization proposition even more directly. Rather than comparing western and non-western countries with each other, they studied the direct link between human development in a country and the prevalence of individualistic values. Figure 12.12 illustrates this link, using data on EVS/WVS and the Human Development Index (HDI) which gives a good measure of modernization in society. The HDI ranges from 0 to 1; the higher the index, the more modernized a society.

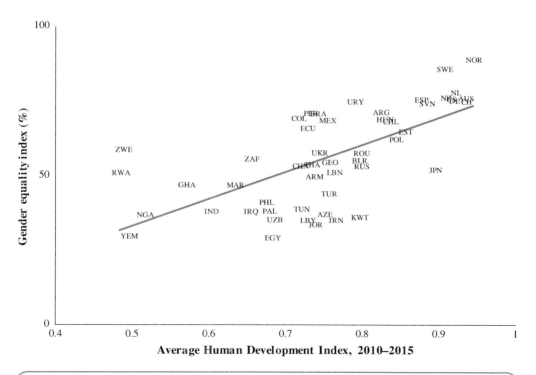

Figure 12.12 The relationship between HDI and gender equality values.

Empirical research has found strong evidence for the modernization and individualization proposition. When societies become more technologically advanced, more science oriented, higher educated and more prosperous and safe, then cultural values shift from collectivistic to individualistic. This conclusion is drawn in studies using EVS/WVS data (Inglehart & Welzel, 2005), the IBM study (Hofstede, 2001 [1980]) and the Schwartz data on students and teachers (Schwartz, 2006).

Does individualism mean more egoism and selfishness? Welzel, in his book *Freedom Rising* (Welzel, 2013), has argued and indeed found that individualistic, emancipative values are actually associated with "pro-civic" orientations. Following Tocqueville (De Tocqueville, 2002 [1889]), Welzel defines civicness as "a benign mentality characterized by a concern for the well-being of the outer world beyond one's ego and in-group". Civicness in this sense includes:

- an *unselfish* orientation toward others and the environment,
- a *trustful* orientation that bridges group boundaries,
- a *humanistic* orientation that welcomes people's diversity.

Welzel finds evidence to suggest that emancipative values promote pro-civic orientations. In turn, so Welzel argues, the rise of these emancipative values and pro-civic orientations has subsequently contributed to the emergence of legal norms (laws) that protect people's citizen rights (Welzel, 2013). Thus, an increasing demand to guarantee human rights has stimulated the emergence of formal norms that protect these civil rights. Such rights have not been protected in autocracies, in which people were treated unequally and in which violence towards and torture of citizens was not uncommon. Welzel argues that the rise of emancipative, pro-social values explains why autocratic governments have become less common over time and gradually replaced by democracies.

Indeed, empirical findings reveal a gradual increase in democracy. Figure 12.13 presents data from 1800 to today, averaging the autocracy–democracy score for sovereign states with a population greater than 500,000. The scale runs from complete autocracy (score –10) to a perfect democracy (10). The democratization process started around 1800 and, despite some fluctuations and periods of rising autocracy, the long-term development is that of rising democracies.

Democracies empower people; they secure their public freedom (political participation rights) and private freedom (personal autonomy rights) (Welzel, 2013). Within established democracies this process of empowering people has developed ever since. Most notably, since the second half of the 20th century, the rights of common people have strongly intensified. This **rights revolution** includes, amongst others, growing civil rights, women's rights, children's rights, gay rights and animal rights (Pinker, 2011).

rights revolution increase of human rights in the second half of the 20th century.

Why does, generally speaking, modernization go hand in hand with a reduction of collectivistic values? Why do individualistic, emancipative values emerge more strongly in societies that become more technologically advanced, prosperous and safe? Better theories, so we have seen (Chapter 2), are those that are more general and wider in *scope*, i.e., they are more *informative*. So, if we can come up with a theory that explains why modernization results in a reduction of collectivistic values, we can also understand the conditions under which this general pattern does not occur.

How can we explain the ecological relationship between *modernization* and *individualism*? How can we make this macro-level relationship "understandable" (Chapter 4)? One answer to this question is provided by the so-called ***existential insecurity theory***, which has its origin in the works of several authors (Inglehart & Welzel, 2005; Triandis, 1995). I will

discuss this theory in more detail in Chapter 13 (Religion). The existential insecurity theory, when applied to value change, can be presented in a multilevel framework (Figure 12.14).

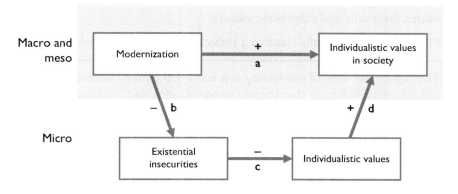

Figure 12.14 Explanation of existential insecurity theory for the modernization and individualistic values link.

To understand the link between modernization and value change, we need to look at each relationship, one by one:

a   *Ecological relationship.* At the macro level, it is shown that modernization generally results in the rise of individualistic values in society (arrow a). This is the *modernization and individualism* relationship.

b   *Social context effect.* Now, in order to understand this social change at the macro level (a), the theory postulates a social context effect: modernization generally results in a reduction of existential insecurities (arrow b). Technological progress results in more control over nature and in more material and economic resources. Poverty levels are reduced, people are healthier, all sorts of existential insecurities and threats diminish. In modern societies people do not have to struggle for survival as much as they did in the past.

c   *Shifting value priorities.* These reduced existential insecurities result, in turn, in changing priorities of values (arrow c). This is a micro-level relationship. When people face continuous existential threats, much depends on loyalty to their group. That's why Inglehart also called these "survival" values, very much borrowing his ideas from Maslow's hierarchy of needs, which emphasized that people first want to secure their physiological and safety needs and group belonging before they come to emphasize esteem and self-actualization. With growing control over nature, more personal resources and increasing securities, such collectivistic "survival" values become less useful. Instead, the utility of individualistic "emancipative" values increases, at the expense of the utility of collectivistic values (Welzel, 2013). People become less dependent on their group for survival and that opens up opportunities to prioritize new values, such as self-expression, making autonomous choices, equality of opportunities and other individualistic values. People adapt their values to the changing conditions.

d   *Aggregation.* Finally, as individuals are changing their value priorities in society so, together, as a population, the *collective, aggregated values in society* are changing.

The existential insecurity theory, when applied to values, can be formulated in a theory schema.

P.   The more strongly people are confronted with existential uncertainties, the more strongly they prioritize collectivistic values instead of individualistic values. (*insecurity and collectivistic values*)

C.   Modernization generally leads to a reduction in existential uncertainties.

P.   The higher the level of modernity in a society, the more widespread are individualistic values in that society. (*modernization and individualism*)

Theory schema 12.3 Explanation of the link between modernization and individualism with the existential insecurity theory.

12.9 Population change

The modernization process also has consequences for population structures. Increasing health care has dramatically changed life expectancy, as we have seen. But modernization has also changed fertility levels and, together, these patterns have changed population structures.

To begin, the average number of children women give birth to has decreased over time. This happened more recently than the drop in mortality. In 1700 a woman gave birth to around 6 children and this declined only slightly to 5 in 1950 (Table 12.8). From then on, a rapid decline started: in 2000 the fertility rate dropped to 2.7 and it is projected to further decrease to 2 in 2050 (Lee, 2003).

Two long-term patterns in human population structure can be distilled, namely: (1) a decrease in mortality and (2) a decrease in fertility. Demographers often take these two

Table 12.8 World life expectancy, fertility rate and age composition: trends and prediction, 1700–2050.

Year	Life expectancy (years at birth)	Total fertility rate (births per woman)	Population aged < 15 (% of total pop.)	Population aged > 65 (% of total pop.)
1700	27	6.0	36	4
1800	27	6.0	36	4
1900	30	5.2	35	4
1950	47	5.0	34	5
2000	65	2.7	30	7
2050	74	2.0	20	16

Source: Lee, 2003; United Nations, 1999, 2003.

population-level changes together and call them the **demographic transition**, i.e., the transition within a population from high fertility and high mortality to low fertility and low mortality (Caldwell, 1976; Kirk, 1996). Such worldwide patterns, however, hide the considerable heterogeneity across societies in the timing of the demographic transition. In some societies, the demographic transition has just begun, whereas in other societies this happened already a long time ago. It has been well-documented in the literature that the demographic transition—declining fertility *and* declining mortality—started in Western Europe around the year 1800 and other societies followed thereafter (Lee, 2003). Let's formulate these demographic changes as a stylized fact of *demographic transition in Western Europe*.

demographic transition transition within a population from high fertility and high mortality to low fertility and low mortality.

 STYLIZED FACT 12.7

Demographic transition in Western Europe
The demographic transition started first in Western Europe around the year 1800 and then other countries followed.

Sociologists and demographers have observed that, after the 1960s, fertility levels in some Western European countries have become so low that they fall below the replacement level of around 2.1 children per woman (Morgan & Taylor, 2006). This means that, in the long run, and in the absence of counter-forcing mechanisms, the population size of these countries will shrink. Such a societal trend is called the **second demographic transition** (Lesthaeghe, 2010; Van de Kaa, 1987), i.e., the change within a population towards extremely low fertility levels. Many Western European countries have undergone this change. There is much research on whether, outside Europe, other countries are also undergoing such a second demographic transition. Let's sum up what empirics show us, namely the phenomenon of the *second demographic transition in Western Europe*.

second demographic transition change within a population towards extremely low fertility levels.

STYLIZED FACT 12.8

Second demographic transition in Western Europe
In the period between 1960 and 2015, fertility levels in Western European countries strongly decreased.

Why did the first and second demographic transition start off in Western Europe and not elsewhere? Why did fertility levels decrease so dramatically since the 1960s in this part of the world? This is a matter of discussion among scholars, but one idea, coined by Van de Kaa (1987) and Lesthaeghe (1995), states that this has to do with modernization and changing values. In an early formulation of this idea, Lesthaeghe argued as follows:

> The steep decline in marital fertility after the early 1960s in the West is ... also a recent indicator of the autonomous progression of an individualistically oriented Western value system: it coincides with the legitimation of cohabitation outside marriage, voluntary childlessness, nonconformist sexual behavior, abortion, and euthanasia.
>
> (Lesthaeghe, 1983)

The fertility decline is, according to Van de Kaa and Lesthaeghe, related to modernization and changing values and, in fact, is part of a more general change in family preferences and behavior. European countries have become more affluent over time, particularly after WWII, which decreased the support for collectivistic values—emphasizing conformity to family and survival strategies—and gave rise to individualistic values—focusing on the needs of the individual. Hence, collectivistic family values that emphasize the importance of marriage and having large families have become less popular, whereas individualistic family values—cohabitation instead of marriage, having children for pleasure instead of necessity—have become more common. These ideas can be seen as a specific application of the modernization and individualism proposition. Van de Kaa and Lesthaeghe extend this proposition with the idea that these individualistic values, in turn, result in a drop in *fertility*. Let's summarize this idea using a theory schema.

P .   The higher the level of modernity in a society, the more widespread are individualistic values in that society. (*modernization and individualism*)

P .   The more individualistic values people have, the lower their fertility rate.

P .   The higher the level of modernity in a society, the lower the fertility rate.

C .   In the period between 1960 and 2015, there was a strong increase in economic development and technology in Western Europe.

O .   In the period between 1960 and 2015, fertility levels in Western European countries strongly decreased. (*second demographic transition in Western Europe*)

Theory schema 12.4 Explanation of the second demographic transition in Western Europe with the modernization and individualism proposition.

As you can see, the modernization and individualism proposition, in conjunction with the idea of Van de Kaa and Lesthaeghe, offers an explanation for the dramatic decrease in Western European fertility levels. Whether this explanation is indeed true is still a matter of discussion among scholars—there is no consensus on this issue yet. It is debated, as the explanation goes, whether higher economic development lowers fertility levels or not (Bongaarts & Sobotka, 2012; Bryant, 2007; Myrskylä, Kohler, & Billari, 2009). In addition, whether such a relation between modernization and fertility, when found, can be attributed to the decline of collectivistic family values is also a matter of controversy (Zaidi & Morgan, 2017).

What is not controversial among scholars is that the sharply decreasing fertility levels in Western European societies, and also in quite a few other societies (e.g., Japan, Taiwan), are a *game changer*. As a consequence of reduced fertility and increased longevity, there are fewer young people and more elderly. An aging society significantly changes the conditions in the labor force (e.g., more inactive people), family relations (e.g., multiple generations, taking care of grandparents), health care (e.g., rising demand), to name only a few. The changing age composition in society is a key example of how demography impacts our lives.

From a long-term perspective, increasing life expectancy has dramatically changed population size. In the very far past of *Homo sapiens*, around 150,000 BC, there were, according to one estimate, around 800,000 people. Such "guestimates" should be taken with great caution, of course, but even the upper-limit estimates of world population size at that time do not exceed a few million. Other scholars estimate that, at that time, there were in fact no more than 100,000 people on earth (Clark, 2007). The earth, at that time, was a quiet place. And that remained so for a considerable period of time: even around 10,000 BC there were no more than 2 million people living on the entire planet. With the invention of horticulture and, subsequently, agriculture, however, populations started to grow more rapidly. In 1800, there were almost 1 billion people and this increased even more rapidly to 1.6 billion in 1900, 6 billion in 2000 and 7.5 billion in 2017 (Table 12.9).

Table 12.9 World population size: 150,000 BC–2017.

Year	Population size (millions)
150,000 BC	0.8
40,000 BC	1.2
10,000 BC	2
5,000 BC	18
0	188
500	210
1000	295
1500	461
1600	554
1700	603
1800	989
1900	1,654
1950	2,545
2000	6,145
2017	7,555

Source: Hassan, 1981; Klein Goldewijk, Beusen, & Janssen, 2010; Lenski & Nolan, 2006; United Nations, 2017.

Thus, population growth remained modest until around 1900 because of low life expectancy. The huge increase in life expectancy was the major driver of the population expansion in past decades. Child mortality had significantly decreased, more women were able to give birth to children and people lived longer. Worldwide human population growth did not really commence until industrialization. Before the Industrial Revolution "life was short, births were many, growth was slow and the population was young" (Lee, 2003). If life expectancy had changed and high birth rates had continued until today, then worldwide population figures would have increased even more. This did not happen, however. Consequently, these lower fertility rates diminish the growth of human populations.

Population growth has changed human societies. Hunting-gathering societies typically consisted of around 40 people (Table 12.10), with larger societies not exceeding a few hundred people. Within such small-scale societies, everyone was connected to everyone else. In horticultural societies population size increased to a few thousand people and then further increased to more than 100,000 people in agrarian societies. Still, however, these are very small numbers when compared with contemporary industrialized societies, which typically have more than 10 million people. China and India, the two countries with the largest populations today, have more than 1.3 billion citizens; more than one-third of the current world population lives in one of these two nations.

Table 12.10 Median population size of societies, by type of society.

	Median population size
Hunting and gathering	40
Simple horticultural	1,500
Advanced horticultural	5,250
Agrarian	100,000
Industrial	10,500,000

Source: Lenski & Nolan, 2006.

12.10 The dynamics of modernization

What can we conclude from this chapter? The history of human societies reveals a pattern called modernization. There is increasing technological knowledge, growth of science and education—*rationalization*—and improved health, wealth, more peace and safety—*socio-economic progress*. Modernization results in changing values—from collectivistic "survival" values to individualistic "emancipative" values and to changing population structures. These broad historical trends raise certain questions: (1) why are human beings actually so pessimistic about societal changes? (2) how can we explain the rationalization trend? and (3) why do we see exponential increase?

1 Why are human beings so pessimistic about societal changes?

At the beginning of this chapter we have seen that most people in the world are pessimistic about societal developments. Most of us think things have got worse and that the future will bring no good. In the perception of many, crime rates have increased and the world has become less safe. Why do people think so when social science shows that these opinions are not in line with reality? The crime rate, as we have seen, is significantly *declining* not increasing: the world used to be more murderous and unsafe than it is today. Interestingly, when asked about their *personal* lives, people are more optimistic. Studies show that many people rate their personal lives as comfortable and pleasant, safe and peaceful. When asked, they think their own economic situation will improve in the coming years but, when asked about the country's economic situation, they think things will get worse. People are more satisfied and optimistic with their personal lives than they are about their society.

This phenomenon is called the **optimism gap** (McNaughton-Cassill & Smith, 2002; Whitman, 1998). How can we explain this puzzle? Several scholars have suggested that people have personal knowledge about the things in their immediate environment, but derive their views about society from the media, which tends to present *negative* news (Whitman, 1998). Thus, there are rarely news reports on rising life expectancy in the world or about declining poverty levels. Instead, news focuses on current negative events and incidents, such as terrorist attacks or a plane crash. When people are then asked to give their opinion about societal changes, they think about the information they gather from the news.

optimism gap situation in which people are more positive about their personal lives than they are about society.

The cognitive bias called **availability heuristic** (Kahneman, 2011), which in the dual-process model of cognition belongs to System I (Chapter 5), comes into play: the judgment of the probability of events, or the frequency of a kind of thing, depends on the ease with which people can think of certain information. This means that, because people are strongly exposed to negative news about society, when asked to give their opinion about societal developments they will tend to strongly rely on the information they received from the media to give their judgment. Thus, the optimism gap can be explained by news selectively reporting on negative events rather than on progress and positive news, thereby giving a distorted view on societal change.

availability heuristic cognitive bias that people's judgment of the probability of events, or the frequency of a kind of thing, depends on the ease with which people can think of certain information.

Some studies suggest that news has become more negative over time. One study used a technique called sentiment analysis to quantify the tone of articles and broadcasts (Leetaru, 2011). Some words, such as *good* and *nice*, have positive connotations, whereas others, such as *bad* and *hate*, express negative connotations. By counting the number of positive and negative words over time, one could examine changes in negativity of news over time. The study applied this method to articles published in *The New York Times* between 1945 and 2005 and to broadcasts from 130 countries between 1979 and 2010. The findings reveal that news has become more negative over time (Leetaru, 2011). If this trend continues and news reports more and more selectively on negative events and ignores positive developments, it could imply that the optimism gap will become even more pressing.

2 How can we explain the rationalization process?

You may wonder how we can explain the rationalization process. How can we understand the fact that our collective brains have become smarter? The long-term development of increasing knowledge and rationality of opinions can be understood with social learning theory (Chapter 5) in combination with individual learning (Henrich, 2001; Henrich & McElreath, 2003). A multilevel framework helps us to clarify the argument (Figure

12.15). At time *t*, individuals have certain beliefs and perceptions, a certain understanding of how things work. They experiment on their own to increase their knowledge. There is, in other words, *individual* learning in the population, i.e., individuals learn on their own, trial-and-error-wise, leading to new ideas and to products and practices based on these new insights. Such new insights or innovations are then *aggregated* to the collective, which then become part of the collective knowledge: a mixture of old and new ideas, skills and knowledge.

Then a social context effect emerges, such that, via the process of *social learning* (via imitation or teaching), those who do not possess the new knowledge copy this from others at *t+1*. However, as stated by propositions on social learning biases, people do not copy randomly any kind of knowledge. Some opinions are more likely to be adopted than others. The likelihood of adoption, as we have seen (Chapter 5), is affected by the attractiveness of the opinion (and the attractiveness of its corresponding practice and product). The *adaptation bias* mechanism states that the more certain opinions are adapted to the social environment, the more likely it is that people will conform to those opinions. When certain ideas and beliefs are based on good grounds—i.e., they are more rational—they can be seen as more adaptive. Even though people are prone to *confirmation bias*—which will slow the process of change—in the end people are open to innovations if it makes their life better.

Rational beliefs and innovations are more strongly based on logic and empirical evidence (as opposed to magical thinking, superstition, false beliefs, etc.) and these ideas result in more efficient and convenient products and practices. They are more attractive and hence more likely to be adopted at *t+1* than ideas which make less sense. So, there is an evolutionary mechanism, a social learning bias, towards the successful transmission of more accurate and more rational beliefs and more efficient and convenient products and practices. Via the well-known S-shaped diffusion process, eventually the entire population (or most of them) adopts these more accurate beliefs, products and practices.

When taking a long-term historical perspective, the process of selectively adopting rational beliefs is repeated over and over and passed on from generation to generation. The body of cultural knowledge (and its applications) at a certain moment *t* is stored (with the

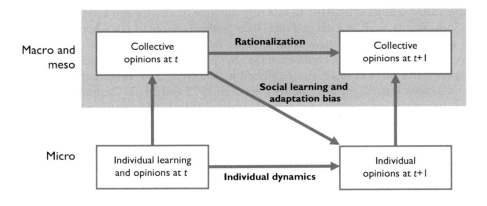

Figure 12.15 Social learning theory explains the rationalization process.

help of human memory, books, articles, computers, etc.) and then used as a starting point for the next generation. Just as scientific growth is the gradual accumulation of empirical and theoretical insights, so too do cultural opinions, products and practices more generally become more rational and adaptive. Innovations that are made are added to the existing knowledge and passed on to future generations (Lenski & Nolan, 2006). New innovations lead to an increase in the efficiency with which tasks are performed or goals are obtained, and to an increase in the amount of knowledge that a society possesses. New generations replace less efficient tools or techniques with more efficient ones and new possibilities are added to old ones. This results in a growth of knowledge, from one generation to the next, in what is called the rationalization process in the words of Weber.

3 Why exponential growth?

Weber was right about the rationalization process. However, he did not foresee that the rationalization was—at least sometimes—*non-linear*; that in some periods in time there were very few innovations and little change in science and technology and that, over time, there is an *increasing rate* of scientific discoveries and technological innovations. Why is the growth of knowledge accelerating over time, such as is seen in technological progress (Stylized fact 12.3) and scientific progress (Stylized fact 12.4)?

There is much discussion in the literature about the right answer to this question and scholars have not reached consensus yet. One idea is that the exponential growth of knowledge and technology is due to a *self-reinforcing process*. Another idea is that this phenomenon is caused by *improved cultural transmission*. None of these ideas are contradictory to social learning theory, but rather elaborate on its major premises.

Self-reinforcing process

According to Lenski and Nolan, growth of knowledge is exponential because it is a self-reinforcing process (Lenski & Nolan, 2006). They argue that a major part of innovations are what they call *inventions*, i.e., combinations based on already existing elements of knowledge. The potential for such inventions is therefore a function of the number of *elements* (pieces of information, cultural items) that already exist. Table 12.11 illustrates how the number of possible combinations depends on the number of elements. Thus, if a certain culture possesses knowledge of the elements A and B (i.e., two elements), it can only combine them in one way. When knowledge expands to cultural element C, this opens up many new possibilities. Now, A and B can be combined, or A and C, or B and C, or even all three together: A, B and C. Thus, with three elements there are suddenly four combinations possible instead of one. If the number of elements increases to four (A, B, C and D), then 11 combinations are possible and so forth. With 10 elements there are 1,000 combinations and with 20 elements there are already over a million. The growth of possibilities is therefore exponential. Hence, this idea of collective knowledge being a self-reinforcing force via the mechanism of combining elements of knowledge in new ways has the potential to explain the increasing rate of technological and scientific knowledge.

Improved cultural transmission

The Lenski-Nolan model seems particularly relevant for understanding the explosive growth of technological innovations. But what about the rise of science? Can this phenomenon also be explained with the idea that increasing numbers of cultural elements are combined? Possibly it can. However, and perhaps more importantly, how can the idea that knowledge is

> **Table 12.11** Number of combinations possible for various numbers of elements.

Number of elements	Total number of combinations					Total
	2 at a time	3 at a time	4 at a time	5 at a time	6 at a time	
2	1	0	0	0	0	1
3	3	1	0	0	0	4
4	6	4	1	0	0	11
5	10	10	5	1	0	26
6	15	20	16	6	1	57

Source: Lenski & Nolan, 2006.

self-reinforcing account for the fact that science strongly progressed after the 15th century? What was so peculiar about that period? Some scholars have claimed that exponential cumulative culture can happen because of changes in the way information is transmitted between individuals.

In the standard social learning theory, as well as in the Lenski-Nolan model, the assumption is made that all individuals in the population are aware of the knowledge possessed by all other individuals in the same population. Using the terminology of the Lenski-Nolan model, one could say that if the collective knowledge of a population consists of cultural elements (information) A, B, C and D, then *each* individual in the population knows about A, B, C and D. However, this assumption might not be realistic. Particularly, early in history, in the hunting-gathering societies, people lived in small communities that were isolated from each other. Under these conditions, it could very well be the case that one group knows A and B and another group—living 30 kilometers away—knows C and D. Because the groups do not share their information, knowledge and technological innovations, the cultural elements remain in their own group. The next generation in the first group still knows only A and B and the next generation in the other group only C and D.

In this case, the cultural transmission between individuals in the same population is highly inefficient. It might be that *improved transmission* of knowledge could explain the increasing rate of knowledge growth. What happened in the course of history is a change from **one-to-one transmission**, via **one-to-many transmission**, to **many-to-many transmission** (Mesoudi, 2011). In the case of *one-to-one transmission*, the person who possesses certain knowledge, both old and new, transmits this knowledge to one person—or to just a few. This is the typical **vertical diffusion** of knowledge from parents to their children, from one generation to the next generation. In small-scale hunting-gathering communities most of the information was transmitted in this

one-to-one transmission knowledge transmitted from one person to another.

one-to-many transmission knowledge transmitted from one person to many persons.

many-to-many transmission knowledge transmitted from many persons to many persons.

vertical diffusion knowledge transmitted from parents to children, from one generation to the next generation.

vertical way, from the parental generation to the children. Over time, however, groups have become increasingly interconnected with one another because of increasing mobility integration in larger societies. This has opened up the way to learn not only from parents but also from others: friends, peers, acquaintances, teachers and so forth. It is this **horizontal diffusion** of knowledge that allows for *one-to-many transmission*. Using mass media (books, newspapers, TV, radio), for example, information can be transmitted to many people at once.

horizontal diffusion knowledge transmitted within generations.

Research shows that under conditions of one-to-one transmission, the growth of knowledge and technology is very low as new innovative ideas only spread to a small group (Mesoudi, 2011). When there is one-to-many transmission instead, great ideas can reach a much bigger group and cultures rapidly become more rational (Cavalli-Sforza & Feldman, 1981). Via many-to-many transmission almost everyone in the world is able to share their opinions with almost anyone else in the world. The increasing interconnectedness of humans has thereby created the possibility to share information on a large scale.

At certain points in history the scope of cultural transmission was greatly enhanced and possibly provides part of the explanation of the great leap forwards in science from the 15th century. It was at that time that the printing press was invented in Europe. Although early discoveries and techniques to make printed books go back to the old Han Dynasty in China (206 BC–AD 220), they had the problem that they only allowed small-scale production of books. With the invention of the printing press in 1450 by the German printer Johannes Gutenberg, the production of books in large numbers became possible. This technological innovation resulted in a sharp increase in the number of printed books in Europe from the 15th century onwards (Buringh & Van Zanden, 2009). The printing press, in itself a cultural innovation, thereby contributed to the improved social transmission of knowledge and cultural innovations across people, regions and cultures in Europe.

Clearly, with the invention of the printing press, the one-to-many diffusion of knowledge was greatly improved and possibly contributes to the explanation of the exponential growth in science since the 15th century. In more recent periods in history, other innovations have further improved the one-to-many transmission. One important innovation was the *newspaper*. The technology to produce newspapers existed in the 17th century, but it was only from the 19th century onwards that newspapers became available to a larger audience. *Radio* and *TV* (i.e., broadcast media) found their way into the homes of people after the 1950s; first in a small group of predominantly rich families in developed nations, to be followed by a larger audience in the 1960s and 1970s, and nowadays billions of people have access to broadcast media.

In short, the *cultural transmission* of knowledge has greatly increased in scope and efficiency over time. In the small hunting-gathering societies, innovations would remain in their own community, where they would be passed on from parents to children. Over time, however, due to increased mobility and interconnectedness of people, innovations could find their way into larger populations, reaching out to many more people. In particular, with the inventions of the printing press, newspapers, scientific journals and broadcast media and the Internet, knowledge could spread rapidly and reach out to many people. Today, when a scientist invents something new, this could reach an audience of millions of people within only a day, as the information could spread via modern communication technologies. Under these conditions, the Lenski-Nolan idea of exponential growth is indeed possible, as now everyone can spread their ideas to the entire (scientific) population, instead of to only a few people.

12.11 Chapter resources

Key concepts

Socio-economic progress	Rights revolution	One-to-one transmission
Flynn effect	Demographic transition	One-to-many transmission
Modernization	Second demographic	Vertical diffusion
Individualism	transition	Horizontal diffusion
Collectivism	Optimism gap	Many-to-many transmission
Emancipative values	Availability heuristic	

Key theories and propositions

- Rationalization
- Modernization and individualism
- Existential insecurity theory.

Key stylized facts

- Wealth and health progress
- Peace and safety progress
- Technological progress
- Scientization
- Individualization
- Western individualism
- Demographic transition in Western Europe
- Second demographic transition in Western Europe.

Summary

- The long-term development called modernization consists of two dimensions, namely: socio-economic progress and rationalization.
- Socio-economic progress is evident from wealth and health progress and peace and safety progress.
- Technological progress, scientization and McDonaldization are indicators of the rationalization process.
- The modernization and individualism proposition states that modernization has contributed to changing values, i.e., from collectivism to individualism.
- Modernization may also affect population structures by lowering fertility levels and giving rise to the second demographic transition.
- The optimism gap relates to the fact that, despite modernization, many people feel pessimistic about societal changes whereas they are more positive about their own lives.
- Social learning theory provides an explanation for the rationalization process.

References

Acemoglu, D., & Robinson, J. A. (2012). *Why nations fail: The origins of power, prosperity, and poverty*. New York, NY: Crown Publishers.

Barro, R., & Lee, J. (2013). A new data set of educational attainment in the world, 1950-2010. *Journal of Development Economics*, 104(184), 198.

Basalla, G. (1988). *The evolution of technology*. Cambridge, UK: Cambridge University Press.

Bell, D. (1976). *The coming of the post-industrial society*. New York, NY: Basic Books.

Blau, P., & Duncan, O. D. (1967). *The American occupational structure*. New York, NY: Free Press.

Bolt, J., Inklaar, R., de Jong, H., & van Zanden, J. L. (2018). Rebasing "Maddison": New income comparisons and the shape of long-run economic development. *Maddison Project Database, Maddison Project Working paper 10*.

Bongaarts, J., & Sobotka, T. (2012). A demographic explanation for the recent rise in European fertility. *Population and Development Review, 38*(1), 83–120.

Bourguignon, F., & Morrisson, C. (2002). Inequality among world citizens: 1820-1992. *American Economic Review, 92*(4), 727–744.

Boyd, R., & Richerson, P. J. (1988). *Culture and the evolutionary process*. Chicago, IL: University of Chicago Press.

Boyd, R., & Richerson, P. J. (2005). *The origin and evolution of cultures*. Oxford, UK: Oxford University Press.

Bryant, J. (2007). Theories of fertility decline and the evidence from development indicators. *Population and Development Review, 33*(1), 101–127.

Buringh, E., & Van Zanden, J. L. (2009). Charting the "Rise of the West": Manuscripts and printed books in Europe, a long-term perspective from the sixth through eighteenth centuries. *The Journal of Economic History, 69*(2), 409–445.

Caldwell, J. C. (1976). Toward a restatement of demographic transition theory. *Population and Development Review, 2*(3/4), 321–366.

Cavalli-Sforza, L. L., & Feldman, M. W. (1981). *Cultural transmission and evolution: A quantitative approach*. Princeton, NJ: Princeton University Press.

Chase-Dunn, C., & Lerro, B. (2016). *Social change: Globalization from the stone age to the present*. Abingdon, UK: Routledge.

Chopik, W. J., Joshi, D. H., & Konrath, S. H. (2014). Historical changes in American self-interest: State of the union addresses 1790 to 2012. *Personality and Individual Differences, 66*, 128–133.

Clark, G. (2007). *A farewell to alms: A brief economic history of the world*. Princeton, NJ: Princeton University Press.

Crosby, A. W. (1997). *The measure of reality: quantification in Western Europe, 1250–1600*. Cambridge, UK: Cambridge University Press.

Darmstaedter, L., & DuBois-Reymond, R. (1904). *4000 Jahre Pionier-Arbeit in De Exacten Wissenschaften*. Berlin, Germany: Stargardt.

Datler, G., Jagodzinski, W., & Schmidt, P. (2013). Two theories on the test bench: Internal and external validity of the theories of Ronald Inglehart and Shalom Schwartz. *Social Science Research, 42*(3), 906–925.

De Tocqueville, A. (2002 [1889]). *Democracy in America*. Washington, DC: Regnery Publishing.

Deaton, A. (2013). *The great escape: Health, wealth, and the origins of inequality*. Princeton, NJ: Princeton University Press.

Diamond, J. (1997). *Guns, germs, and steel: The fates of human societies*. New York, NY: WW Norton & Company.

Drori, G., Meyer, J. W., Ramirez, F. O., & Schofer, E. (2003). *Science in the modern world polity: Institutionalization and globalization*. Stanford, CA: Stanford University Press.

Drori, G. S., Meyer, J. W., & Hwang, H. (2006). *Globalization and organization: World society and organizational change*. Oxford, UK: Oxford University Press.

Durkheim, E. (2014 [1893]). *The division of labor in society*. New York, NY: Simon and Schuster.

Eisner, M. (2003). Long-term historical trends in violent crime. *Crime and Justice, 30*, 83–142.

Eisner, M. (2014). From swords to words: Does macro-level change in self-control predict long-term variation in levels of homicide? *Crime and Justice, 43*(1), 65–134.

Enquist, M., Ghirlanda, S., Jarrick, A., & Wachtmeister, C. (2008). Why does human culture increase exponentially?. *Theoretical Population Biology, 74*(1), 46–55.

Flynn, J. R. (1984). The mean IQ of Americans: Massive gains 1932 to 1978. *Psychological Bulletin, 95*(1), 29.

Flynn, J. R. (1987). Massive IQ gains in 14 nations: What IQ tests really measure. *Psychological Bulletin, 101*(2), 171.

Flynn, J. R. (2007). *What is intelligence? Beyond the Flynn effect*. New York, NY: Cambridge University Press.

Flynn, J. R., & Shayer, M. (2018). IQ decline and Piaget: Does the rot start at the top? *Intelligence, 66*, 112–121.

Gapminder. (2019). Retrieved from www.gapminder.org/data.

Gelfand, M. J., Raver, J. L., Nishii, L., Leslie, L. M., Lun, J., Lim, B. C., ... Yamaguchi, S. (2011). Differences between tight and loose cultures: A 33-nation study. *Science, 332*(6033), 1100–1104.

Goudsblom, J. (1993). *Fire and civilization*. London, UK: Penguin Books.

Greenfield, P. M. (2013). The changing psychology of culture from 1800 through 2000. *Psychological Science, 24*(9), 1722–1731.

Guttmann, A. (1978). *From ritual to record*. New York, NY: Columbia University Press.

Harari, Y. N. (2014). *Sapiens: A brief history of humankind*. New York, NY: Random House.

Hassan, F. A. (1981). *Demographic archaeology*. New York, NY: Academic Press.

Henrich, J. (2001). Cultural transmission and the diffusion of innovations: Adoption dynamics indicate that biased cultural transmission is the predominate force in behavioral change. *American Anthropologist, 103*(4), 992–1013.

Henrich, J. (2015). *The secret of our success: How culture is driving human evolution, domesticating our species, and making us smarter*. Princeton, NJ: Princeton University Press.

Henrich, J., & McElreath, R. (2003). The evolution of cultural evolution. *Evolutionary Anthropology: Issues, News, and Reviews, 12*(3), 123–135.

Hobbes, T. (1994 [1651]). *Leviathan*. Indianapolis, IN: Hackett Publishing.

Hofstede, G. (2001 [1980]). *Culture's consequences: Comparing values, behaviors, institutions and organizations across nations* (2nd ed.). Thousand Oaks, CA: Sage Publications.

HumanProgress. (2019). Democracy versus autocracy over time. Retrieved from https://humanprogress.org/

Inglehart, R. (1990). *Culture shift in advanced industrial society*. Princeton, NJ: Princeton University Press.

Inglehart, R. (1997). *Modernization and postmodernization: Cultural, economic, and political change in 43 societies*. Princeton, NJ: Princeton University Press.

Inglehart, R. (2015 [1977]). *The silent revolution: Changing values and political styles among Western publics*. Princeton, NJ: Princeton University Press.

Inglehart, R., & Baker, W. E. (2000). Modernization, cultural change, and the persistence of traditional values. *American Sociological Review, 65*(1), 19–51.

Inglehart, R., & Norris, P. (2003). *Rising tide: Gender equality and cultural change around the world*. Cambridge, UK: Cambridge University Press.

Inglehart, R., & Welzel, C. (2005). *Modernization, cultural change, and democracy: The human development sequence*. Cambridge, UK: Cambridge University Press.

Ipsos. (2019). Perils of perception. Retrieved from https://perils.ipsos.com/index.html

Kahneman, D. (2011). *Thinking, fast and slow*. New York, NY: Farrar, Straus and Groux.

Kirk, D. (1996). Demographic transition theory. *Population Studies, 50*(3), 361–387.

Klein Goldewijk, K., Beusen, A., & Janssen, P. (2010). Long-term dynamic modeling of global population and built-up area in a spatially explicit way: HYDE 3.1. *The Holocene*, *20*(4), 565–573.

Landes, D. S. (1969). *The unbound Prometheus: Technological change and industrial development in Western Europe from 1750 to the Present*. Cambridge, UK: Cambridge University Press.

Lee, R. (2003). The demographic transition: Three centuries of fundamental change. *Journal of Economic Perspectives*, *17*(4), 167–190.

Leetaru, K. (2011). Culturomics 2.0: Forecasting large-scale human behavior using global news media tone in time and space. *First Monday*, *16*, 9. doi:https://doi.org/10.5210/fm.v16i9.3663

Lenski, G. & Nolan, P. (2006). *Human societies: An introduction to macrosociology* (10th ed.). Boulder, CO: Paradigm Publishers.

Lehman, H. C. (1947). The exponential increase of man's cultural output. *Social Forces*, *25*(3), 281–290.

Lesthaeghe, R. (1983). A century of demographic and cultural change in Western Europe: An exploration of underlying dimensions. *Population and Development Review*, *9*(3), 411–435.

Lesthaeghe, R. (1995). The second demographic transition in Western countries: An interpretation. In K. O. Mason & A. M. Jensen (Eds.), *Gender and family change in industrialized countries* (pp. 17–62). Oxford, UK: Clarendon Press.

Lesthaeghe, R. (2010). The unfolding story of the second demographic transition. *Population and Development Review*, *36*(2), 211–251.

Lindberg, D. C. (Ed.). (2010). *The beginnings of Western science: The European scientific tradition in philosophical, religious, and institutional context, prehistory to AD 1450* (2nd ed.). Chicago, IL: University of Chicago Press.

Marshall, M. G., Gurr, T. R., & Jaggers, K. (2016). Polity IV project: Political regime characteristics and transitions 1800-2015. Retrieved from www.systemicpeace.org/inscrdata

McNaughton-Cassill, M. E., & Smith, T. (2002). My world is ok, but yours is not: Television news, the optimism gap, and stress. *Stress and Health*, *18*(1), 27–33.

McNeill, J. R., & McNeill, W. H. (2003). *The human web: A bird's-eye view of world history*. New York, NY: W.W. Norton & Company.

McNeill, W. H. (2009). *The rise of the West: A history of the human community*. Chicago, IL: University of Chicago Press.

Mesoudi, A. (2011). *Cultural evolution: How Darwinian theory can explain human culture and synthesize the social sciences*. Chicago, IL: University of Chicago Press.

Michel, J. B., Shen, Y. K., Aiden, A. P., Veres, A., Gray, M. K., Google Books Team, Pickett, J. P., Hoiberg, D., Clancy, D., Orwant, J., Pinker, S., Nowak, M. A., Aiden, E. L. (2011). Quantitative analysis of culture using millions of digitized books. *Science*, *331*(6014), 176–182.

Milanovic, B. (2016). *Global inequality: A new approach for the age of globalization*. Cambridge, MA: Harvard University Press.

Morgan, S. P., & Taylor, M. G. (2006). Low fertility at the turn of the twenty-first century. *Annual Review of Sociology*, *32*, 375–399.

Morris, I. (2010). *Why the West rules-for now: The patterns of history and what they reveal about the future*. London, UK: Profile Books.

Myrskylä, M., Kohler, H., & Billari, F. C. (2009). Advances in development reverse fertility declines. *Nature*, *460*, 741–743.

Oyserman, D., Coon, H. M., & Kemmelmeier, M. (2002). Rethinking individualism and collectivism: Evaluation of theoretical assumptions and meta-analyses. *Psychological Bulletin*, *128*(1), 3–72.

Pinker, S. (2011). *The better angels of our nature: A history of violence and humanity.* London: Penguin.

Pinker, S. (2018). *Enlightenment now: The case for reason, science, humanism, and progress.* New York, NY: Penguin Books.

Pomeranz, K. (2009). *The great divergence: China, Europe, and the making of the modern world economy.* Princeton, NJ: Princeton University Press.

Putnam, R. (2000). *Bowling alone: The collapse and revival of the American community.* New York, NY: Simon & Schuster.

Riley, J. C. (2005). Estimates of regional and global life expectancy, 1800–2001. *Population and Development Review, 31*(3), 537–543.

Ritzer, G. (2011). *The McDonaldization of society* (6th ed.). Los Angeles, CA: Pine Forge Press.

Rokeach, M. (1973). *The nature of human values.* New York, NY: Free Press.

Roser, M. (2019). Life expectancy. Retrieved from https://ourworldindata.org/life-expectancy

Roser, M., & Ortiz-Ospina, E. (2017). Global extreme poverty. Retrieved from https://ourworldindata.org/extreme-poverty

Rosling, H., Rosling, O., & Rosling Ronnlund, A. (2018). *Factfulness.* London, UK: Sceptre.

Rousseau, J. (1999 [1755]). *Discourse on the origin of inequality.* Oxford: Oxford University Press.

Schofer, E., & Meyer, J. W. (2005). The worldwide expansion of higher education in the twentieth century. *American Sociological Review, 70*(6), 898–920.

Schwartz, S. H. (1992). Universals in the content and structure of values: Theoretical advances and empirical tests in 20 countries. *Advances in Experimental Social Psychology, 25,* 1–65.

Schwartz, S. H. (2006). A theory of cultural value orientations: Explication and applications. *Comparative Sociology, 5*(2), 137–182.

Schwartz, S. H., & Bilsky, W. (1987). Toward a theory of the universal content and structure of values: Extensions and cross-cultural replications. *Journal of Personality and Social Psychology, 58*(5), 878–891.

Schwartz, S. H., Cieciuch, J., Vecchione, M., Davidov, E., Fischer, R., Beierlein, C., Ramos, A., Verkasalo, M., Lönnqvist, J.-E., Demirutku, K., Dirilen-Gumus, O., & Konty, M., (2012). Refining the theory of basic individual values. *Journal of Personality and Social Psychology, 103*(4), 663–688.

Stephens, W. (1990). Literacy in England, Scotland, and Wales, 1500-1900. *History of Education Quarterly, 30*(4), 545–571.

Taylor, F. W. (1914). *The principles of scientific management.* New York, NY: Harper & Brothers.

Tonnies, F. (1957 [1887]). *Community and society.* East Lansing, MI: Michigan State University Press.

Treiman, D. J. (1970). Industrialization and social stratification. *Sociological Inquiry, 40*(2), 207–234.

Triandis, H. C. (1995). *New directions in social psychology: individualism & collectivism.* Boulder, CO: Westview Press.

United Nations. (1999). *The world at six billion.* New York: Author.

United Nations. (2003). *World population prospects: The 2002 revision.* New York: Author.

United Nations. (2017). World population prospect: The 2017 revision. Retrieved from https://population.un.org/wpp/

Van De Kaa, D. J. (1987). Europe's second demographic transition. *Population Bulletin, 42*(1), 1–59.

Weber, M. (1919). *Wissenschaft Als Beruf.* Munich: Duncker & Humblodt.

Weinberg, S. (2015). *To explain the world: The discovery of modern science*. London, UK: Penguin Books.

Welzel, C. (2013). *Freedom rising: Human empowerment and the quest of emancipation*. Cambridge, UK: Cambridge University Press.

Welzel, C., Inglehart, R., & Kligemann, H. (2003). The theory of human development: A cross-cultural analysis. *European Journal of Political Research*, 42(3), 341–379.

Whitman, D. (1998). *The optimism gap: The I'm Ok–they're not syndrome and the Myth of American decline*. New York, NY: Walker and Company.

Wrangham, R. W. (2009). *Catching fire: How cooking made us human*. New York, NY: Basic Books.

Zaidi, B., & Morgan, P. S. (2017). The second demographic transition: A review and appraisal. *Annual Review of Sociology*, 43, 473–492.

Zeng, R., & Greenfield, P. M. (2015). Cultural evolution over the last 40 years in China: Using the Google Ngram Viewer to study implications of social and political change for cultural values. *International Journal of Psychology*, 50(1), 47–55.

Zerubavel, E. (1985). *Hidden rhythms: Schedules and calendars in social life*. Berkeley, CA: University of California Press.

Chapter 13

Religion

Chapter overview

How important is religion in your life? Why are people in some societies highly religious, whereas religion plays little role in other societies? The topic of religion has been one of the key topics studied by the founding fathers of sociology, such as Durkheim, Weber, Marx and Comte. In this chapter, you will see that the classical sociologists had rather similar ideas about religion. They supposed a deep and intrinsic connection between modernization and religion, such that, with increasing modernity, religious involvement declines. Today, more than 100 years after the classical sociologists developed their arguments, this idea is still at the core of the discussion in the sociology of religion. In this chapter, I guide you through this discussion, presenting the main questions, theoretical arguments and empirical findings in the sociology of religion. This begins with a brief discussion of what we mean by "religion" and relating religion to the themes on culture and social relations (13.1). Then I address the potential role religions have played in establishing human cooperation a long time ago—when large-scale societies emerged (13.2). Subsequently, we come to learn more about the stickiness factor of religion—the phenomenon that religions remain rather stable over time and geography (13.3). After that, we will see that, despite this stickiness, religions can sometimes change and we look in more detail at secularization in Western Europe (13.4). Then I discuss how modernization forces explain this pattern of secularization in Western Europe (13.5). Finally, I review the existential insecurity theory, which attempts to explain more generally patterns of religious stability and change in the world (13.6).

> **Learning goals**
>
> After reading this chapter, check if you are able to:
>
> - Describe key concepts on the topic of religion.
> - Relate the topic of religion to sociological themes on culture and social relations.
> - Describe why religious groups can solve cooperation problems.
> - Describe and explain the phenomenon of religious stickiness.
> - Describe the secularization process in Western Europe.
> - Relate religious change to cohort effects.
> - Describe and apply the modernization and secularization proposition.
> - Describe and apply the existential insecurity theory.

13.1 What is religion?

I guess that everyone has an intuition about what religion is. Perhaps you belong to a religious group yourself or you know of a friend who goes to religious meetings. Being affiliated to a religion is very likely in religious nations, of course, but, even in more secular countries, religion is present somewhere. Although each of us has an intuition about what religion is and probably knows someone who belongs to a religion, it is important to precisely define the concept of religion. In contemporary literature on religion it is common to think of religion as a complex concept, which consists of multiple dimensions (Hall, Meador, & Koenig, 2008; Stark & Glock, 1970). This idea is reflected in the definition given by Johnstone in his renowned textbook on the sociology of religion:

> Religion can be defined as a system of beliefs and practices by which a group of people interprets and responds to what they feel is sacred, and usually, supernatural as well.
> (Johnstone, 2016 [1975])

This definition emphasizes the idea that religion consists of two dimensions: it can be studied as a "group" phenomenon, hence as an aspect of *social relations*, but it can also be seen as "a system of beliefs and practices," that is, as *culture*. Let's elaborate on both dimensions.

Belonging: religion as a group phenomenon

A religion is, first of all, a group to which people can be affiliated. When we speak of "Christians," for example, we refer to the group, the social category, of Christians, which we can distinguish from other groups, such as Muslims. But religious groups also have, often, an organizational structure in which members can participate. They are more than merely a social category. Religious groups are an example of voluntary associations which serve the common interest of their members. As with any type of voluntary organization, people can not only be *affiliated* with the organization, they can *participate* in it. People can actively participate in meetings of the religious group and attend religious rituals.

Taken together, you could study, at the individual level, a person's degree of **religious belonging**, i.e., the degree of social integration of an individual in the religious group. When a person is affiliated to a religious group and also participates actively in this group, it indicates strong religious belonging—much more so than when a person is not affiliated to a religious group and/or when a person does not attend meetings regularly. A high degree of religious

religious belonging
degree of social integration of an individual in the religious group.

belonging of many individuals in the population aggregates into a high degree of *religious organizational cohesion* at the collective level. This means that you could study the degree of religious organizational cohesion by examining how many individuals in the population are affiliated to religious groups and how frequently individuals attend religious meetings.

To get an impression of religious organizational cohesion in the entire world, let's consider religious affiliation (Table 13.1). Empirics show that many people in contemporary societies belong to a religious group. Specifically, in 2015, the Pew research organization estimated that around 84% of the world population belonged to a certain religious group (self-identified) and only 16% did not identify with any religious group (i.e., atheists, agnostics). The largest group is Christians, which make up around 31% of the world population. The second largest group is Muslims (24%), followed by Hindus (15%), Buddhists (7%) and Folk religionists (6%). The "other religious" category contains a variety of smaller religions, such as Baha'i faith, Taoism, Jainism, Shintoism, Sikhism, Tenrikyo, Wicca, Zoroastrianism and many others.

Importantly, people may not identify themselves in terms of these broader social categories. For example, they may not see themselves as belonging to the group of "Christians," but rather to the religious group of "Protestants" (37% of Christians fall into this sub-group) and

Table 13.1 Religious affiliation in the World in 2015.

Religious group	Number of adherents (affiliated)	Percentage of world population
Christians	2,276,250,000	31.2
Muslims	1,752,620,000	24.1
Hindus	1,099,110,000	15.1
Buddhists	499,380,000	6.9
Folk religionists	418,280,000	5.7
Jews	14,270,000	0.2
Other religion	59,710,000	0.8
No religion	1,165,020,000	16.0

Source: Pew Research Center, 2019.

thereby distinguish themselves from other Christian sub-groups, such as Catholics (50%), Orthodox Christians (12%) and other Christian groups (1%). And even within these sub-groups further distinctions are not uncommon. For example, within Protestantism there are many sub-groups, such as "Calvinism," "Lutheranism," "Methodism," to name only a few.

As with other types of voluntary associations, sociologists study the origins, development and eventual popularity or decline of religious groups (Kaufmann, 2010; Norris & Inglehart, 2004). Religious groups start with a few initiators, they are then followed by a handful of supporters and, when successful, they attract more and more followers. Some religious groups remain local, whereas others—such as Hinduism, Buddhism, Christianity and Islam—become groups with followers all over the world. Sociologists examine this rise and spread of religious groups and thereby study patterns of religious organizational cohesion.

Next to the study of within-group cohesion of religions, one could also examine inter-group cohesion. Religious groups are a source of intergroup boundaries too. As with any type of group, people distrust more those who do not belong to their own religious group, they are less willing to cooperate with such out-group members, they develop fewer friendships and social ties with them and, in extreme cases, there are intergroup tensions and conflict. Examples are the Protestant–Catholic conflict in Northern Ireland, the negative attitudes of secular Christian majority populations in Western Europe towards Muslim immigrants in particular and Christian–Muslim conflicts in India and Indonesia. Relatedly, it has been found that in the United States—a quite religious society—the group of non-religious people ("atheists") are distrusted most (Edgell, Gerteis, & Hartmann, 2006).

In summary, you could study religion as a group phenomenon, hence relating the topic of religion to the sociological theme of social relations (Figure 13.1).

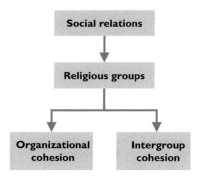

Figure 13.1 Religion as a group phenomenon.

Believing: religion as a cultural phenomenon

Religions can also be studied as a cultural phenomenon (Figure 13.2). Religions are a system of cultural opinions, norms and corresponding practices. Many religions, scholars argue, contain a set of religious *beliefs* or statements to which their members could adhere. Religion is, very often, a worldview that contains descriptions and explanations of life, death, nature and human interaction. These are beliefs in the sense that they are claims about reality, about what is possible and impossible, about what happens in life and after life, and they provide explanations for why things happen. For example, the Old Testament contains ideas about the origins of life and the earth in the telling of the story of Adam and Eve. Many religions have statements which say that "there is a God" or that "supernatural powers exist" or that "there is an afterlife" in some form (a heaven or hell in the Christian tradition). Buddhism has the idea of reincarnation. Islam and other religions contain yet other religious statements, which their followers may or may not believe in.

Religions also consist of a set of values and social norms—although not all religious groups have these cultural elements. Religious values and norms are often related to what is considered *sacred*, i.e., that which is regarded as something special, holy, and which is contrasted with the *profane*, ordinary, mundane (Durkheim, 2001 [1912]; Johnstone, 2016 [1975]). Religions can prescribe social norms that specify how people should live in order to honor the divine power (or powers). Religious groups can define a set of values, i.e., what the group considers good and bad, beautiful and ugly, desirable and undesirable. For example, religions may approve or disapprove of homosexuality and divorce; they can urge their members to take care of the poor; they may prohibit murder and crime and so forth.

In summary, religions can be seen as cultural phenomena, as a more or less coherent set of cognitive beliefs, values, norms and corresponding practices (Figure 13.2). Sociologists study the origins and development of these cultural traits. They examine patterns of **religious believing**, i.e., the degree to which individuals in a population adhere to religious beliefs and values. A person is a (strong) religious believer if that person (strongly) agrees with the ideas and values of a religious group. At the collective level, you could study how many individuals in the population are religious believers.

> **religious believing** degree to which an individual adheres to religious beliefs and values.

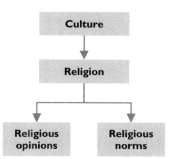

Figure 13.2 Religion as a cultural phenomenon.

Religiosity: belonging and believing

Now that we have distinguished two dimensions of religion, we need to ask the question: what is the relationship between the two? Can there be "religious believing without religious belonging?" Are there societies that show high levels of religious involvement but low levels of religious believing?

When studying religion, the social dimension (religious belonging) and the cultural dimension (religious believing) need not always go hand in hand. For example, a person could adhere to religious beliefs but not participate in religious activities (Davie, 1990). Or someone could actively attend religious meetings but not be a religious believer. Analytically, therefore, the two dimensions are different and they need not necessarily go together. That said, however, empirically, sociologists have shown that the social and cultural dimensions of religion often *do* go together in the same person: those who are more strongly involved in a religious group are also those who more strongly subscribe to the beliefs, values and norms of that group (Voas & Crockett, 2005). Although the two dimensions of religion are theoretically distinctive, empirically they often go hand in hand. When a person is strongly involved in a religious group, that person will also more strongly adhere to the beliefs and values of that religious group than another person who is less strongly involved in the group.

Sociologists speak of **religiosity** to indicate the degree to which an individual is involved in a religious group (i.e., religious affiliation and participation) and the degree to which that person adheres to the beliefs and values of that religious group (Stolz, 2009). When scholars study "religiosity" they refer to both the *belonging* and *believing* dimensions of religion. As you can see from the definition, religiosity is not a matter of yes or no, but rather a matter of degree. On one side of the continuum we find those who are "irreligious" or "atheists," i.e., for whom religion has no meaning in their life, who do not believe in religious statements, who have no religiously inspired values and who do not attend religious meetings at all. On the other side of the continuum we find the highly religious, extremely devout persons, for whom religion means everything, who believe everything that is written in the holy books and who bring religious values into practice. In between these two extremes we find the rest of the population, who are more or less religious. Thus, if a person strongly adheres to the statements in the Bible, that person is said to be *more* religious than someone who expresses doubt about the validity of these statements. Similarly, if someone attends church every week, that person is *more* religious than someone else who attends church once a year or less frequently. In ordinary life we often capture the idea of highly individual religiosity by saying that a person is deeply attached to a religion, that a person feels close to a religious group or that a person is strongly involved in a religion.

> **religiosity** degree of religious belonging and believing.

13.2 Did religions solve the problem of human cooperation?

We have seen that people who belong to the same group tend to cooperate more easily with each other and trust each other more (Chapter 8). According to some scholars, religious groups may have been critically important for establishing large-scale cooperation when human populations transitioned from small groups into large-scale anonymous societies (Norenzayan, 2015). This transition—from small-scale hunter–gathering populations to agrarian societies— is puzzling, because at that time there were no efficient governments established that could sanction people if they harmed other people or in any other way acted as a "free-rider." When societies are small—as in hunter–gatherer societies, where most belong to the same family and kin and people repeatedly interact with each other over long periods of time—people cannot easily operate as free-riders because, if they do so, then this would become common knowledge in the group: the free-rider gets a bad reputation and will be excluded from the group or otherwise punished. The problem of cooperation is solved in such small groups, as everyone monitors everyone else and free-rider behavior will be easily detected and sanctioned.

But in large-scale non-state societies, people have to interact with many more people—not just the small in-group of family and kin. They also interact with anonymous strangers, with whom they have to trade or do business, for example, and whom they possibly meet only once. In such situations, people are tempted to free-ride. In the absence of an efficient government, it is attractive for individuals under these conditions to free-ride because they can get the benefits from their free-riding behavior without getting sanctions from others. And as this kind of behavior is attractive for each individual in the population, the collective result is that of a society in which people do not cooperate with each other and in which distrust is common.

However, somehow humans managed to establish cooperation even in large-scale anonymous societies without governments. How could that happen? Insights into this puzzle can be found in a classic study published by Durkheim in 1912: *The Elementary Forms of Religious Life* (2001 [1912]). In it, Durkheim argued that religious groups—and groups in general—have the capacity to unite people. He argued that when people belong to the same religious group, they trust each other more and are more willing to cooperate with each other. Importantly, religious identities can be broader than family/kin/clan identities. Hence, sharing religious identities makes possible solidarity, trust and cooperation with in-group members beyond the small hunting-gathering community. People would do business with strangers if they belonged to the same religious group; they would trust them in business transactions.

Elaborating on Durkheim's idea, scholars have argued that people converted to the most attractive religious group—the one that attracts most members and/or the group that is closest—to benefit from the shared trust among in-group members, which would then facilitate opportunities for business, social interaction, support and so forth (Norenzayan, 2015). In this way, some religious groups started to grow more and more, making cooperation possible on a large scale.

This may seem to be a plausible explanation for the emergence of large-scale human cooperation, but it also raises the question of whether religious identities could not just be faked. How do you know whether another person belongs to your group? The potential power of religious in-group trust could be undermined when members are not "true followers," but rather fake their religious identity and get away with the benefits of belonging to the religious group. For example, an individual could be said to be a "Christian" in an opportunistic, instrumental way, in order to be seen by other Christians as an in-group member and thereby use their false belief for personal advantage.

Durkheim had already identified this issue and he argued that religions typically overcome this problem by initiating all kinds of religious meetings in which the members come together as a group. Durkheim named these shared religious activities **collective effervescence** and examples include collective religious rituals, jointly making music and dancing together. Such collective religious activities create strong emotional energy among the members; it promotes in-group solidarity and reduces temptations to fake religious identities. Durkheim and other scholars, such as Randall Collins (1992 [1982]), argued that these joint activities which promote in-group solidarity are not unique to religion but can also be observed among other groups. Thus, this idea argues that in-group cooperation and trust become especially strong when members actively participate in religious gatherings.

> **collective effervescence** shared religious activities.

More recently, scholars have argued that such religious activities are just *one example* of *signaling* religious identities (Henrich, 2009). When members participate in religious meetings, they send out a signal to other members that they belong to the religious group. However, such religious activities are restricted in time and space, which means that people cannot always infer from each other that they belong to the same religious group when they do not jointly participate in such activities. Some scholars claim that this is the reason for **credibility-enhancing displays** (CREDs), i.e., behaviors that signal that people are genuine believers (Henrich, 2009).

> **credibility-enhancing displays** behaviors which signal that people are genuine believers.

For example, people might wear symbols that express their religious identity, such as a cross necklace (Christians), a headscarf (Muslims) or keppel (Jews).

The more "costly" such CREDs are to the individual, however, the more strongly they send out a signal to their group members that they are true believers, that they are committed to their religion and that they can be trusted (Iannaccone, 1994). According to this logic, self-restricting behavior such as fasting during Ramadan, not drinking any alcohol, not eating pork and praying five times per day, as in Muslim traditions, clearly signals that one is a true Muslim. Extravagant behavior, such as ritualized public self-castrations of male priests of the goddess Cybele and public crucifixion among Roman Catholics in the Philippines, can be seen as more extreme and more costly expressions of the very same idea of signaling religious commitment (Iannaccone, 1994; Norenzayan, 2015). Although these are extreme cases of very costly CREDs, many religions contain self-restricting behaviors that help to signal that one is a genuine believer and that in-group members can be trusted. For these reasons, authors believe that religions may have played a key role in establishing human cooperation in large-scale societies without strong governments (Norenzayan, 2015).

13.3 The stickiness factor of religion

When you look at a map of contemporary religions in the world, you cannot escape from the conclusion that religions are strongly *geographically clustered* (Norris & Inglehart, 2004). Take a country in Northern Africa or the Middle East and you'll find that the population is predominantly Muslim. Randomly select an individual from Indonesia and chances are high that that person belongs to the Muslim group as well. India is the homeland of Hindus; in China you'll find many people affiliated with Buddhism and indigenous religions; in North and South America, Europe and Oceania those who are religious are most often Christian; in Israel, the majority is Jewish. There are, of course, exceptions to these patterns, partly as a result of international migration but, generally speaking, religious groups tend to be highly clustered geographically.

This pattern is not something that is characteristic of the present moment and that changes every year or so. On the contrary, if you consider an older map of religions in the world, the distribution of religions across countries would be more or less the same. For example, if you look at countries in Northern Africa and the Middle East in the year 2000, or even further back in history, say 1950, then you'll see that they were predominantly Muslim societies at that time as well. Religions are thus not only highly clustered in the world, they also tend to be rather stable over time. Christian societies tend to remain Christian; Muslim societies remain Muslim.

Also, when you consider religiosity more generally, beyond group affiliation, you'll see that persistence and stability is a common pattern. If you look at religious involvement then you discover that, over time, populations tend to remain rather stable (Hout & Fischer,

2014). To put it differently: if you want to predict how often individuals in a certain population attend religious meetings in year *t*, then you can very well do so by taking the figures for *t-1*. Year by year the figures tend to be rather similar and, even stretched over longer time periods, say five to ten years, you'll see quite stable patterns. Societies in which 80% of the people attend religious activities weekly in year *t* did not suddenly emerge as highly religious societies. On the contrary, they were already highly religious societies before that time and just remained so.

These patterns of stability at the collective level are mirrored in the life-courses of individuals. For example, individuals who were socialized as a Christian tend to stay Christian for the rest of their life, rather than suddenly switching to another religion every now and then, such as becoming Muslim. Similarly, highly devout persons tend to remain so, instead of becoming non-religious. And, vice versa, young people who were not raised religious are unlikely to become highly religious persons later in life. Thus, scholars have observed that intra-generational *stability* of religion is the common pattern, rather than strong changes within people's life-course (Hout & Fischer, 2014).

Of course, these are general patterns. At a certain point in time religions were non-existent and then they emerged a long time ago and spread globally (Finke & Stark, 2008; Kaufmann, 2010). And, similarly, individuals can change in their religiosity over the life-course. But, setting this aside for the moment, the broad pattern is that of persistent religious identities of human populations. Taken together, in these empirics we have identified what we may call *religious stickiness*.

STYLIZED FACT 13.1

Religious stickiness
Religiosity tends to be rather stable over time and geographical areas.

How can we explain the stickiness factor of religion? Why do Catholic societies tend to remain Catholic? What explains the stability of highly religious societies over time? One answer to these questions can be given with the stylized fact of *conformity* (Chapter 5), i.e., the general human tendency to copy the opinions and corresponding practices from one's social environment. The stickiness factor of religion is part of this broader pattern. People tend to copy what others are doing and so, too, do people copy the *religious* traits of the actors with whom they interact. And if they do so *very strongly* then it will result in religious stability over time and clustering of certain religions within geographical areas.

Research shows that *parental transmission* of religion plays a major and enduring role in people's own religious group identity, practices, beliefs and values. Thus, it is found that children strongly copy the religious identity of their parents and that, when parents are highly religious, their children will be very religious as well. In fact, scholars agree that parents are *the* most important source of one's religiosity. And this means that the religiosity of one generation is passed over to the next generation, creating religious stability of societies—at least in the short run. Studies on the self-reported importance of religious socializing consistently show that people rank parents as having the most important influence (Hunsberger &

Brown, 1984). And also studies in which the religiosity of parents and their children were compared find that religious identity and religiosity are strongly transmitted from parents to their children (Brañas-Garza, Garcia-Munoz, & Neuman, 2011; Güngör, Fleischmann, & Phalet, 2011; Hayes & Pittelkow, 1993; Myers, 1996; Need & De Graaf, 1996; Regnerus, Smith, & Smith, 2004; Ruiter & Van Tubergen, 2009; Sherkat, 1998; Te Grotenhuis & Scheepers, 2001; Wilson & Sandomirsky, 1991). Thus, children of Christian parents are very likely to become Christians themselves rather than, say, Muslims or non-religious. Similarly, highly devout parents tend to produce strongly religious children whereas secular parents breed secular children.

This pattern of strong parental transmission of religion creates stability of religiosity in societies over time. But it is not the only factor causing this. Researchers have found that the stickiness of religion is also reinforced by *peer transmission*. Peers—who themselves inherited the same religiosity of their parents—again influence the religious behavior and beliefs of individuals as well, although less strongly than parents do. It has been found that adolescents are affected by their peers in school; when their friends are (highly) religious, they are more likely to be religious than when their peers are more secular (Regnerus & Smith, 2005; Regnerus et al., 2004). Similarly, studies have found that people are affected by the religiosity of their spouse, such that people adjust their own religiosity to that of their partner (Te Grotenhuis & Scheepers, 2001). Thus, individuals born in *highly* religious societies tend to become *highly* religious persons themselves, because the previous (parental) generation transmits their high religiosity both directly (parent–child, "vertical" transmission) and indirectly (peer–peer, "horizontal" transmission).

Image 13.1 Parental transmission plays a key role in understanding religious stickiness.

THINKING LIKE A SOCIOLOGIST 13.1

Why do you think parental transmission of religion is so strong? How can we explain the strong inheritance of religion? Which sociological theory can explain this empirical fact?

You may wonder, then, how can we explain the religious transmission from parents to children and from peer to peer? Why is this kind of social influence so pronounced? Why are, for example, the religious values, beliefs and (corresponding) religious behavior so strongly transmitted from parents to their children? Why is this happening? Why do children copy the religious identities (e.g., "Christian"), involvement (e.g., weekly attendance), beliefs (e.g., "God exists") and values (e.g., "marriage is important in life") from their parents?

According to social control theory (Chapter 6), the answer to these questions is that people copy the religiosity of their parents and peers because of normative pressure. Thus, children who are raised by religious parents, or who interact with religious peers, may be faced with social norms like these:

- *Affiliation*: "you <u>should</u> be a Christian."
- *Involvement*: "you <u>should</u> go to church every week."
- *Beliefs*: "you <u>should</u> believe in the existence of God."
- *Values*: "you <u>should</u> value the importance of marriage."

According to social control theory, members are socialized, controlled and possibly sanctioned by their religious group in case of norm-deviance (Sherkat, 1997; Sherkat & Wilson, 1995). This means that, if children do not copy the religious affiliation of their parents, they might be sanctioned by them. Conversely, obeying the social norms of the religious group results in approval of the parents. When children live with their parents, monitoring and control mechanisms are strong. Later in life, when children leave the parental home and are less and less monitored by their parents, they still adhere to the religious norms inherited by their parents because the social norms have been internalized as moral norms and internalized preferences.

In summary, people strongly inherit their religiosity from their parents and from the previous generation more generally. In this way, religion is passed on from generation to generation, resulting, over time, in stability of religiosity at the individual and collective level. Parents and religious groups prescribe a set of social norms that require that the next generation (i.e., the children of group members) should become group members as well, that they should follow the standards of religious participation common to the group, that they should agree with the system of beliefs and values of the group. Additionally, earlier on we observed the phenomenon of cultural inertia (Chapter 6), i.e., the time lag that can exist between changing social conditions and adapting to new norms and opinions that are better suited to the new conditions. Cultural norms and values slowly change over time and, thus, religious norms and values also tend to change only incrementally. At the collective level, these forces of social control and cultural inertia tend to result into religious stability over periods of time and across generations. And they explain why, if a certain religious group (say Catholicism) is established in a certain geographical area, it will tend to remain there. These processes of conformity and social control can explain the stickiness factor of religion.

13.4 Secularization in Western Europe

The *baseline* pattern of religiosity in the world is that of stability and continuity within societies, as we have seen. There are strong social forces which lead to such patterns of stability. However, this common pattern does not exclude the possibility that in some societies and in some specific periods in time there is religious change. New religions emerge, some religious groups become more popular than other groups and entire populations may become less religious or more religious. Let's see one well-known example of religious change, namely that which occurred in Western Europe in the past decades. We address the following descriptive question:

> Q(d). To what extent has religious belonging (i.e., religious affiliation and attendance) as well as religious believing (i.e., religious beliefs, values) changed in Western Europe between 1950 and 2015?

To answer this question, sociologists have used, first of all, survey data on religious attendance. Norris and Inglehart analyzed religious trends for the period between 1970 and 1996 (Table 13.2). Consider the trend for Belgium. Yearly changes in religious attendance are subject to fluctuations in survey estimates, but the long-term trend can be interpreted with more confidence. The direction of the trend is clear, namely that of declining participation. In the 1970s around 40–50% attended religious meetings once a week or more. This diminished to 30–40% in the 1980s, and to 20–30% in the 1990s. Thus, in a period of roughly 25 years, weekly religious attendance dropped from around 45% to 25%. This general trend of declining religious attendance is not unique to Belgium. It is a pattern more commonly observed in Western-European societies. When considering all countries presented in Table 13.2, it appears that, overall, there is a statistically significant trend towards declining religious participation.

Sociologists have observed that not only has religious group involvement decreased over time in Western Europe, but so has the adherence to the corresponding religious beliefs and values, i.e., religious believing. Fewer people in Western Europe today, for example, believe in God or in life after death (Norris & Inglehart, 2004). When the religious group structure erodes so does its corresponding culture—they go "down" hand in hand. The overall picture, then, is that after WWII the population in Western Europe has become less involved in religious groups and also subscribes less to religious beliefs and values (Brañas-Garza, 2004; Bruce, 2001, 2002; Crockett & Voas, 2006; Lechner, 1996; Te Grotenhuis & Scheepers, 2001; Voas, 2003; Voas & Crockett, 2005).

How should we interpret this religious change? There are three potential factors. First, such change can be due to *period effects*, which means that periodic changing events bring about religious change. An example of a period effect would be that when the unemployment rate increases in a certain year, people become more religious. Second, there can be *age* effects, which means that religious changes are associated with aging. An example of an age effect would be that, as people become older, they become more religious. Third, there can be **cohort effects**, which refer to generational changes. For example, it could be that more recent cohorts—people born more recently—are less religious than people born a longer time ago.

cohort effect societal changes that are due to generational replacement.

In studies on the interpretation of religious change, scholars have therefore disentangled these three effects (Hout & Fischer, 2014). An example is the study of Voas and Chaves for Great Britain (Voas & Chaves, 2016). Figure 13.3 presents some findings of their study. It

Table 13.2 Religious attendance in Western-Europe, 1970–1996.

	France	Belgium	Netherlands	Germany	Italy	Luxembourg	Denmark	Ireland	Great Britain	Northern Ireland
1970	23	52	41	29	56	.				
1971	27	58	49	39	58	.				
1973	19	38	33	22	48	48	.		.	.
1975	22	45	44	26	39	44	5	91	16	.
1976	23	45	45	30	37	40	6	93	8	59
1977	22	50	48	26	37	42	6	93	17	60
1978	18	45	45	23	36	39	5	91	17	56
1980	14	38	31	21	37	41	5	90	10	64
1981	13	36	29	20	35	36	5	91	9	69
1985	12	27	24	19	37	32	7	91	7	59
1988	13	31	36	19	42	30	6	88	8	58
1989	14	29	34	18	44	28	6	85	7	61
1990	13	30	36	21	46	32	4	83	10	60
1991	10	24	35	19	46	28	4	85	13	62
1992	9	22	22	17	43	29	4	82	13	61
1993	12	27	33	15	45	27	3	79	6	54
1994	11	27	28	16	41	22	4	81	7	.
1996	5	10	14	15	39	17	3	77	12	.
							4	65	4	46

Source: Norris & Inglehart, 2004.
Note: Percentage attending religious services "several times a week" or "once a week," as measured from the question "Do you attend religious services several times a week, once a week, a few times during the year, once a year or less, or never?"

gives the percentage of the population that is affiliated to a religion compared across birth decades and over time. If period effects play a role, then you would expect to see strong (yearly) fluctuations within the same cohort. But within cohorts there is actually not so much change. This also takes away the idea of age effects. If there are such effects, you would expect to see that, within a cohort, there is an increase (or decrease) of religious affiliation.

What matters most are cohort effects. There are noticeable differences between people born in different cohorts. Those born in the oldest decade (1905–1914) have the highest rate of affiliation, i.e., around 83%. This birth cohort remained rather stable over time, i.e., there are very few fluctuations over time. If you then take the next generation that comes after this one (i.e., those born in 1915–1925), it appears that they are slightly less often affiliated to a religion (around 80%). Again, we see that, within this cohort, there are few over-time changes. With each successive (younger) generation, you see that the percentage that are affiliated to a religion goes down. Even if you compare people of the same age, but who are from different birth cohorts, you see that the younger cohorts are less religious. In the youngest generation, less than 30% is still affiliated. Thus, *across* generations, there is a decline in religious affiliation from 83% to 30%.

The conclusion scholars draw from analyses like these for Great Britain and other societies in Western Europe is that the over-time decline in religiosity in Western-European societies is largely due to cohort effects. Specifically, each younger generation in Western Europe is becoming somewhat less religious than the previous one (Crockett & Voas, 2006; Voas, 2008; Voas & Crockett, 2005). It is not so much the case that the decline in religiosity is due

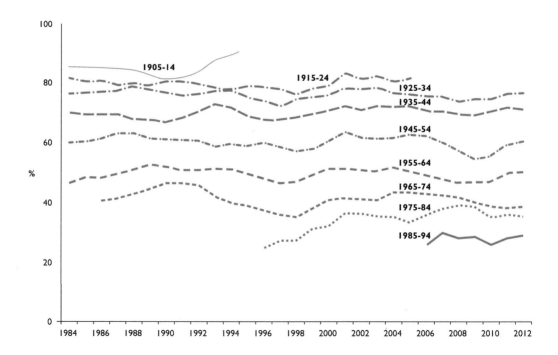

Figure 13.3 Percentage affiliated to a religion by decade of birth in Great Britain, 1983–2013.

Source: Voas & Chaves, 2016.

to changes *within* people's life course, or to *periodic events* that suddenly alter the religiosity of each generation. Instead, each new generation is slightly less religious than the previous one and, as each previous generation is only slowly replaced by new generations, the over-time changes in Western-European societies tend to occur *slowly* over long periods of time rather than quickly and in short periods of time.

This pattern of change is called **secularization**, i.e., declining religious belonging (i.e., fewer religious affiliations and less religious attendance) and diminishing religious believing (i.e., less support of religious beliefs and values) within societies over time. Secularization is thus a trend and this societal change is well-documented for Western Europe, at least for the period between 1950 and 2015 (Bruce, 2001, 2002; Crockett & Voas, 2006; Lechner, 1996; Molteni & Biol-

> **secularization**
> diminishing
> religiosity, i.e.,
> decline in religious
> belonging and
> believing.

cati, 2018; Norris & Inglehart, 2004; Voas, 2008; Voas & Crockett, 2005). It remains a matter of scientific debate whether the secularization trend in Western Europe started before that period (De Graaf, 2013; Stark, 1999) and whether it can also be observed in other nations and regions in the world (Brauer, 2018; Brenner, 2016; Greeley & Hout, 1999; Hout & Fischer, 2002; Hout & Greeley, 1987; Schnabel & Bock, 2017; Voas & Chaves, 2016, 2018). That discussion set aside, we can be confident in formulating the following stylized fact of *secularization in Western Europe*.

STYLIZED FACT 13.2

Secularization in Western Europe

Western European populations have become more secular between 1950 and 2015. This is seen with respect to *religious belonging* (fewer people are affiliated to a religious group and religious participation levels have declined) and *religious believing* (fewer people subscribe to "religious" beliefs and values).

Related to this secularization trend, sociologists have observed the increasing *functional differentiation* of religious groups in Western Europe (Dobbelaere, 1999). This means that more and more religious groups are treated as autonomous subsystems, rather than imposing their own system of religious beliefs and practices on other institutions, such as politics, economy, science, medicine and education (Dobbelaere, 1999). In contemporary Western Europe, more so than in the past, religious groups have little to say about these non-religious institutions. For example, universities are seen as autonomous institutions, which define their own goals, rules and methods without interference from religious authorities. The separation of church and state, and the lack of religious authority in other areas outside of a religious community, signify functional differentiation (Chaves, 1993).

13.5 Modernization and secularization

Now that we have established the stylized fact of secularization in Western Europe, you may wonder what is driving this trend. Explaining the secularization trend in Western Europe is a first step towards understanding why religiosity can change within populations despite strong

counterforces towards religious stability and continuity. It will give us insights into the underlying forces of religious change, not only in Western Europe but in societies more generally.

> *Q(t)*. Why have Western-European populations become more secular between 1950
> and 2015?

Several theories have been proposed in the literature which explain religious change (De
Graaf, 2013). A well-known theory links the process of secularization to the process of *modernization* (Chapter 12). The origins of this **modernization and secularization theory** can be
traced in the works of Durkheim, Weber, Marx, Engels and Comte, amongst others. For one
thing, each of them studied religion in a different context and with different purposes, and
they certainly did not witness the secularization trend after WWII in Western Europe. That
said, they had in common the intuition that, in the long run, religion would become less and
less important. Hence, they predicted the pattern of secularization which we have seen taking
place in Western Europe.

Moreover, the classical sociologists had in mind that this secularization trend was
affected by the "modernization" process. The modernization and secularization theory
argues that when societies become more modern, religiosity declines. In Chapter 12 we saw
that modernization consists of two interrelated changes: (1) rationalization (i.e., growth of
technology, science, education) and (2) socio-economic progress (i.e., improved health and
wealth, safety and peace). We can summarize these intuitions more formally with a theory
schema to explain the stylized fact.

P. The more modernized a society, the more secular people are in that society.
    (modernization and secularization)

C. Between 1950 and 2015, Western Europe has become more modernized.

O. Between 1950 and 2015, Western European populations have become more
    secular. *(secularization in Western Europe)*

> **Theory schema 13.1** Explanation of secularization in Western Europe with
> modernization and secularization theory.

Western-European countries have generally become more technologically advanced and
prosperous (i.e., increasing modernity), so the explanation makes sense. That said, it is only a
possible explanation. We do not know whether modernization forces are indeed the cause of
secularization—maybe something else caused the secularization in Western Europe?

A next step, then, is to test this modernization and secularization proposition. Scholars
have done so by comparing the relationship between the level of religiosity in a country and
its degree of modernization. Now if Western-European countries have become so secular
because they have become so modern, it is important to not only focus on Western-European
countries. Instead, one should also consider countries that have lower levels of technological
and economic development.

Scholars have examined the modernization-secularization link with the EVS/WVS data,
which encompasses many more countries, as we have seen (Norris & Inglehart, 2004). They
have tested this proposition in two ways: (1) by considering the degree of *technology* in a
country and (2) by examining *economic development*.

Technology and religiosity

To examine the association between technological development in society and religiosity, Norris and Inglehart classified countries into three groups according to their level of technology: "agrarian," "industrial" and "postindustrial." If the proposition is true, one should see the lowest levels of religiosity in postindustrial societies and the highest levels in agrarian countries.

The results of their analysis of the EVS/WVS data, which covers more than 60 nations, is presented in Figure 13.4. The percentage of the population that attends religious meetings at least weekly drops from 44% in agrarian societies, to 25% in industrial countries, to 20% in postindustrial countries. Likewise, we see that, with increasing technological development, fewer people pray daily and fewer people say that religion is very important in their life. This confirms the theory.

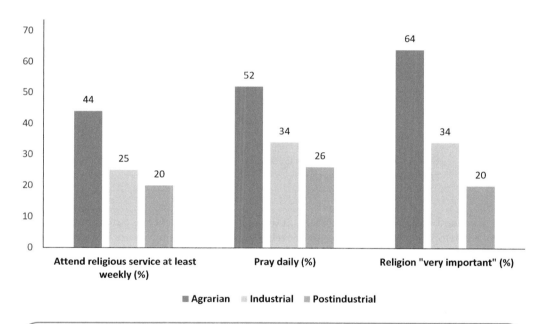

Figure 13.4 Religiosity by type of society.
Source: Norris & Inglehart, 2004.

Economic development and religiosity

Norris and Inglehart have also used the EVS/WVS data to test whether there is a link between economic development and religiosity (Norris & Inglehart, 2004). They classified each of the more than 60 nations according to their (logged) GDP per capita (as a measure of economic development) and related this to the religiosity of the population in the country. Results of analyses on the EVS/WVS data are presented in Figure 13.5.

There is a general tendency that those countries that are more prosperous appear to be less religious. The results show a bivariate correlation coefficient between, on the one hand, (logged) GDP per capita and, on the other hand, religious participation and frequency of

Topics

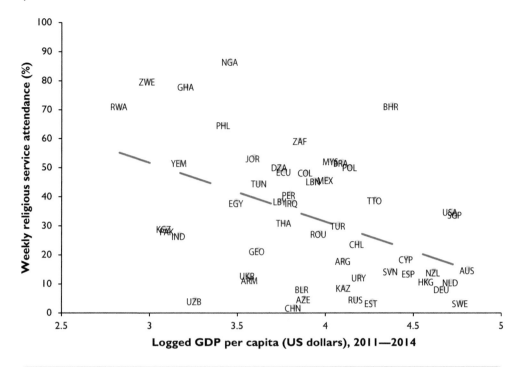

Figure 13.5 Relationship between economic development and % weekly religious attendance.

prayer of around -.50 (Norris & Inglehart, 2004). There is ample evidence that the degree of economic development in a country and the religiosity of its inhabitants are negatively associated (Herzer & Strulik, 2017; Paldam & Gundlach, 2013; Ruiter & Van Tubergen, 2009; Storm, 2017; Te Grotenhuis, Scholte, de Graaf, & Pelzer, 2015).

The modernization-secularization theory is empirically supported in studies that compare the religiosity across countries: more modern, technologically advanced, wealthy countries are generally less religious. Given that the association between modernization and secularization is well-established, we can identify the ***modernization and secularization*** regularity as a stylized fact.

 STYLIZED FACT 13.3

Modernization and secularization
The more modernized a society, the more secular the people in that society.

At the same time, we have also seen that the modernization-secularization link is not an iron law (Norris & Inglehart, 2004). It is a tendency: *generally speaking*, those countries that are more modern are less religious. There are deviations from this pattern, from the "slope," as we can see in Figure 13.5. This means that the relationship between GDP per capita and religiosity is not perfect; there are countries that deviate from the general pattern.

A case in point is the United States. Figure 13.5 shows that inhabitants of the US attend religious meetings more frequently than is common for other countries with similar levels of economic development. Some scholars have asked themselves: "How could such a highly modern, wealthy and technologically-advanced country as the US have such a highly religious population?" The empirical puzzle that the citizens in the US are strongly religious has been labeled *US exceptionalism*, as it deviates from the pattern predicted by the modernization and secularization theory.

This single deviation, however, does not refute the modernization and secularization theory. Although the religiosity in the US may indeed be higher than expected by the modernization proposition, there is firm evidence that, *in general*, when examined over a large number of countries, modernization is negatively correlated to religiosity in a country by around -0.5. Even with some exceptions, such as the US, the theory is supported. The connection between modernization and secularization is a general tendency, a probabilistic relation, not an iron law.

Nevertheless, the exceptional case of the US remains puzzling. It is a technologically highly advanced and wealthy society and yet, at the same time, a highly religious country—at least more so than countries similar to the US. It therefore provides an interesting challenge to the modernization and secularization theory. And, like the US, there are other countries that deviate from the general pattern. And this raises the question as to how we can explain these deviations. Why are some countries relatively modern and yet highly religious? And why are there other nations that are not so modern but unexpectedly secular? When we are able to answer these questions we can understand under what conditions modernization forces result in secularization and when they don't. In other words, such a theory would have a broader scope; it would be more informative than the modernization and secularization theory. It would tell you under which conditions the modernization and secularization links occurs and when it does not. In short, it gives a *deeper explanation* (Chapter 2).

THINKING LIKE A SOCIOLOGIST 13.2

Why do we call an explanation for the modernization-secularization theory a 'deeper explanation'? If you don't know, check Chapter 2.

In summary, we address the following theoretical question:

> *Q(t)*. Why is it the case that, generally speaking, modernization results in secularization, and under which conditions does modernization not have this effect?

13.6 Existential insecurity theory

One way scholars explain the modernization-secularization relationship is with the *existential insecurity theory* (Burger & Lynn, 2005; Keinan, 1994, 2002), which was introduced in Chapter 12. Here, I describe how this theory has also been applied to explain patterns of religiosity.

The existential insecurity theory has become influential in the sociology of religion, in particular after the publication of the book *Sacred and Secular* in 2004, written by Pippa Norris and Ronald Inglehart, in which the theory was forcefully proposed and systematically tested. The origins of this idea can be traced previously in the writings of the anthropologist Malinowski, who argued that "both magic and religion arise and function in situations of emotional stress" (Malinowski, 2004). In anthropology (Sosis & Handwerker, 2011), but also in psychology (Baumeister, 1991; Hogg, Adelman, & Blagg, 2010), similar thoughts on the importance of "uncertainty," "existential threats" and "stress" for understanding religiosity have been developed as in sociology, but insights from these disciplines have remained largely separated from each other. In the following section, I integrate these fragmented research lines into a single theory of insecurity.

The starting point of the theory is that people are confronted with *existential insecurities* in their environment, both personally as well as for their friends and relatives. Humans are confronted with illnesses, death, poverty, violence and loss of beloved ones. According to existential insecurity theory, people turn to religion as a way to cope with these difficulties. This happens in two ways.

1 *Group support.* First of all, religions can provide support as a group. As we have seen, belonging to a group generates membership benefits. It fulfills the human need to belong to a group (Baumeister, 1991) and the emotional pleasure from collective effervescence—participating in group activities—as we have learned from Durkheim. Engaging in rituals (such as religious meetings) and other types of repetitive and predictive behavior (such as praying) gives a sense of control. Moreover, people can count on social support from in-group members, including cooperation, trust and protection from in-group members. This can be emotional support, but also financial assets, physical protection and other kinds of social security. In short, religious groups provide group support, as they protect members from poverty, violence and suffering.

2 *Supernatural support.* But religions also provide a set of cultural beliefs and values. Key to many religions is that they posit the existence of supernatural powers, which control the world and the afterworld. This gives meaning: even when things seem extremely difficult to accept—such as the loss of a relative—people can find comfort and meaning in the idea of an order created by supernatural beings and the existence of an afterlife or reincarnation. Religious meanings can make sense out of the pain and suffering of the individual or those who are close to them. In many religions, group members also have the ability to "negotiate" actively with these supernatural beings: they can "invest" in them and turn to them for a favor, for example by praying to them, giving them sacrifices and performing other kinds of rituals that serve them (Stark & Bainbridge, 1987; Stark & Finke, 2000). In return for that, people believe they will attain certain goals (with the help of God)—such as that their sick child will be cured or that they will have something to eat tomorrow.

Taken together, insecurity theory argues that religious groups share the common interests of their group members: they provide *group support*, as in-group members protect each other from risks to safety and property; and *supernatural support*, in the sense of a belief system which gives meaning and which opens up opportunities to control things that group members cannot and which are in the hands of supernatural beings. In short, religion gives people control over outcomes they find desirable and which are otherwise uncontrollable (Burger & Lynn, 2005).

So, how can the existential insecurity theory explain that, in general, modernization results in a decline in religiosity? To see how, consider Figure 13.6, which presents the explanation using a multilevel framework. The modernization and secularization proposition relates the modernity in a country to the religiosity of its population. This is depicted as arrow "a" which stipulates that modernization (independent variable) impacts the religiosity of the country (dependent variable). Both are variables at the *macro level*, i.e., "modernization" is a property of a country and so is "the religiosity of a country." You have seen that there is empirical support for this ecological relationship. Both technological development and economic development (as two key indicators of modernity) negatively relate to religiosity in the population. This macro–macro (ecological) relationship is not perfect, however, it is a *tendency*.

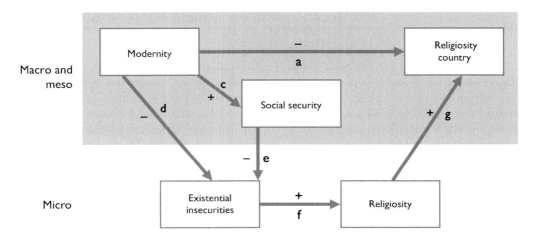

Figure 13.6 The relationship between modernity and religiosity according to insecurity theory.

Why is there such a link between modernization and religiosity? How does modernization exactly change the religiosity of a population? Existential insecurity theory argues that *in general* modernity lowers *existential insecurities* (arrow d). People in primitive, poor nations face strong existential threats, such as high poverty rates and life-threatening violence. They are deprived of adequate medical facilities and, consequently, mortality rates are high and deceases cannot be controlled very well. The *insecurity and religiosity* proposition then posits a micro-level relation between people's experience of existential insecurity and their religiosity. Uncertain and competitive conditions create high amounts of stress and religions provide valuable group—and supernatural—support to cope with this. People will seek comfort in religions, they need to belong to a religious group to gain the benefits from cooperation with group members. Hence, under conditions of survival, people strongly attach to a religion and firmly support their belief and value system (f), which leads to high levels of religiosity in society (g).

As a consequence of technological advances and economic development, existential insecurities are more and more reduced and people are less and less confronted with highly stressful situations and the need to cooperate with in-group members to realize their goals. This lowers the personal need for religion. Therefore, in the end, modern societies become less religious, although the aggregation process happens slowly and is delayed because changes happen through cohort replacement and not so much because of instantaneous events. Thus, existential insecurity theory argues that modernization impacts religiosity of societies in the *long run*. Let's summarize this thinking with a theory schema.

P . The stronger the existential insecurities with which people are confronted, the more strongly their religiosity. (*insecurity and religiosity*)

C . Modernization generally results in a reduction of existential insecurities.

P . The more modernized a society, the more secular the people in that society. (*modernization and secularization*)

> **Theory schema 13.2** Explanation of the link between modernization and secularization with the existential insecurity theory.

In providing a more secure place to live, highly modernized societies reduce the need for religion as a control and copying mechanism. This is partly so because the technologically more advanced and more prosperous societies develop social security systems (arrow c) that protect their citizens from all kinds of risks and reduce existential uncertainties (arrow e). In generous welfare states, such as in Scandinavian countries like Sweden and Denmark, people are strongly protected by the government to ensure financial stability. Thus, citizens are protected from poverty, from loss of income when they are unemployed and there is extensive health insurance and so forth. By contrast, in countries with less extensive welfare spending, such as Nigeria and Sudan, people are more vulnerable to all kinds of economic risks. This means that people born and raised in welfare states will find it less attractive to belong to and believe in a religion compared with those who were raised in countries without a strong safety net (Norris & Inglehart, 2004). Strong governments have taken over the task of religious groups to protect people and to establish cooperation in large-scale societies (Norenzayan, 2015). The following hypothesis can be derived.

P . The stronger the existential insecurities with which people are confronted, the more strongly their religiosity. (*insecurity and religiosity*)

C . Social security generally results in a reduction of existential insecurities.

H . The more social security in a society, the more secular the people in that society. (*social security and secularization*)

> **Theory schema 13.3** Hypothesis on the link between social security and secularization, derived from existential insecurity theory.

Are empirical findings in line with this hypothesis? One study found that changes in social welfare spending in nine highly developed European countries over a short period of time (1980–1998) did not result in immediate changes in the religiosity of the populations in these nations during that short period (Te Grotenhuis et al., 2015). Other studies have found similar results (Van Ingen & Moor, 2015) and when studies do find short-term effects of changes in social welfare spending (Storm, 2017), or proxies of (the lack of) welfare spending—such as high income inequality (Solt, Habel, & Grant, 2011)—the impact is relatively modest. These findings may be interpreted as evidence against the idea that short-term changes in welfare spending lead to short-term changes in religiosity (Te Grotenhuis et al., 2015). But, following existential insecurity theory, one could actually argue that no short-term changes in welfare spending will have an impact on religiosity, but that only in the long run will religion erode in well-developed welfare states.

Specifically, one may argue that short-term changes in social welfare spending are unlikely to strongly impact the existential insecurity and stress experienced by the population. Given the stickiness factor of religion, changes in welfare spending may have no or little short-term impact on religiosity, as such short-term changes do not significantly alter levels of stress and existential insecurity in the population. Because people strongly inherit the religiosity of their parents and religiosity remains rather stable within their life course, changes in welfare spending during their life course will not abruptly impact their religiosity at all. For these reasons, changes in social welfare spending may have no significant short-term impact.

The development of social welfare societies creates conditions that reduce the demand for religion in the population in the *long run*. That is, people born and raised in welfare states experience that the government will provide a safety net for them in case of economic hardships; that the state will secure their pensions, protect them from violence and so forth. That, in essence, the need to belong to a religious group that will protect them is now taken over by the government. Consequently, this experience is then transmitted to the next generation, to their children, such that in each generation their children will be raised less religiously. Consequently, although religiosity is rather stable over the life course, the population in (more generous) welfare states will become less religious over time—slowly, though, as it happens only through generational succession and within-generation stability remains a counterforce. Thus, only in the *long run*, through slow cohort changes (i.e., children being slightly less religious than their parents), populations in countries that have (strong) social welfare spending will become more and more secular. A number of cross-national comparative studies have been conducted and these studies do show that people born and raised in countries with more social welfare spending turn out to be more religious than those who grew up in societies with fewer security benefits—and this relationship remains even when taking into account other societal conditions such as economic development (Barber, 2011; Gill & Lundsgaarde, 2004; Immerzeel & Van Tubergen, 2011; Norris & Inglehart, 2004; Rees, 2009; Ruiter & Van Tubergen, 2009).

If there is indeed a connection between social welfare spending and religiosity, as some studies suggest, then it is not so exceptional that the US is more religious than other equally economically developed nations such as Sweden and Denmark. Based on existential insecurity theory, one may argue that Americans are more religious because the US has not developed a social welfare system to the same degree as in Western European societies and, correspondingly, income inequality is much higher over there (Norris & Inglehart, 2004; Ruiter & Van Tubergen, 2009). According to this idea, US citizens are more religious than in other modern countries because insecurity is more widespread in the US. To be sure, also in the US it has been observed that each new generation is less religious than the previous generation (Brauer, 2018; Voas & Chaves, 2016), thus secularization is also taking place there because of modernization and cohort replacement. But because modernity has not equally resulted in developing a strong social welfare state in the US (arrow c, Figure 13.6) as in Western Europe, the modernization forces are not reducing religiosity as strongly over there.

As you can see, the insecurity theory offers an explanation for the link between modernization and secularization. The theory is able to explain why, generally speaking, more modern nations tend to be less religious. And it can also explain why some modern nations—e.g., Denmark, Norway, Netherlands—are more secular than other equally modern countries like the US. That said, you should realize that this is *one* explanation—there may be other theories to explain the modernization-secularization link. And, moreover, the insecurity theory provides only a *possible* account for this link, but is it also true? To see whether there is any merit in the insecurity theory, scholars have derived new hypotheses from this theory. If these hypotheses are confirmed by empirical observations, then we can have more confidence that the theory is true.

In the literature you'll find various ways in which scholars have tested the existential insecurity theory. If the insecurity theory is true, then you would expect to see that people who are exposed to strong existentially threatening conditions are more religious. This impact can be long term, affecting subsequent generations, but also *immediate*, *short-term* consequences are expected, as long as the existential threats are *sudden* and of *high intensity*. I now discuss three such testable hypotheses.

P . The stronger the existential insecurities with which people are confronted, the stronger is their religiosity. (*insecurity and religiosity*)

C . The existential insecurities with which people are confronted are higher when:

C1 People are exposed more strongly to death in their direct environment.

C2 People are exposed more strongly to violence in their direct environment.

C3 People are exposed more strongly to natural disasters in their direct environment.

H . The more strongly people are exposed to death in their direct environment, the more religious they are. (*death and religiosity*)

H . The more strongly people are exposed to violence in their direct environment, the more religious they are. (*violence and religiosity*)

H . The more strongly people are exposed to natural disasters in their direct environment, the more religious they are. (*disasters and religiosity*)

Theory schema 13.4 Hypotheses derived from existential insecurity theory.

Hypothesis I: death and religiosity

The first prediction is that people who are more strongly exposed to death in their direct environment will be more religious. Is this hypothesis confirmed or refuted?

One answer to this question comes from an experiment that was conducted among American students (Norenzayan & Hansen, 2006). They were randomly divided into two groups and each group was confronted with a different situation. One group was exposed to an undesired existential outcome ("death"), over which people have little control of when it will happen to them. In this uncertain "mortality salient" ("experimental") condition, students had to respond to the open-ended question:

In the space below, write a paragraph about what will happen to you when you die. Write in some detail about the feelings that the thought of your own dying arouse in you.

In the "control" condition, students responded to the open-ended question:

> In the space below, write a paragraph about your favourite foods that you have enjoyed eating. Write in some detail about the feelings that these foods arouse in you.

After the students had completed their task, they received a short questionnaire in which they had to fill in demographic information and also indicate their religiosity, as measured by two questions: (1) "How strongly do you believe in God?" and (2) "How religious are you?" In line with the existential insecurity theory, the researchers found that the students in the mortality salient condition believed in God significantly more strongly and were also significantly more religious than the students who had to write something about food (the neutral condition). In subsequent experimental studies it was again found that students who were made aware of their own death or of that of someone else—such as the death of a child in a story they had to read— made them more religious (Norenzayan & Hansen, 2006). The main conclusion of the study was that, when people are confronted with undesirable existential outcomes over which they have no control, they turn to religion—in line with insecurity theory.

These studies rely on student samples and suffer from the WEIRD people problem and external validity (Chapter 3). Hence, it is important to see whether the analysis of other samples point to the same conclusion. One study used longitudinal data on widowed individuals and matched controls in the United States (Brown, Nesse, House, & Utz, 2004). A total of 103 widowed individuals were followed at 6 months, 24 months and 48 months after the loss. When the scientists compared post-loss religion with pre-loss data on religion, they found that widowed individuals were more likely than controls to increase their religious beliefs and church attendance. This is in line with existential insecurity theory, because one expects to see that people become more religious if they lose an intimate contact, which reminds people of death.

Hypothesis II: violence and religiosity

The second prediction states that the more strongly people are exposed to violence in their direct environment, the more religious they are. Several studies have looked into the consequences of terrorist attacks, which are obviously situations of increased exposure to violence. On September 11, 2001, suicide terrorists of Al-Qaida killed thousands of US citizens by using hijacked airplanes to destroy major buildings. This violent attack took many Americans by surprise, causing widespread feelings of insecurity among the population. A nationally-representative study, conducted three to five days after the attacks, found that 44% of US adults reported substantial symptoms of stress and 90% had one or more symptoms to at least some degree (Schuster et al., 2001). Did these widespread feelings of stress lead to an increase in religiosity in the US, as one would predict with insecurity theory? The answer is yes. From the same study, it was found that 90% of the US citizens had turned to prayer, religion or spiritual feelings after the attacks, and this was particularly the case among those with substantial stress (Schuster et al., 2001). This increase in religiosity in the US population has been confirmed in other studies as well (Ai, Tice, Peterson, & Huang, 2005).

Israel is another setting in which researchers have studied the consequences of the threat of terrorism. Scholars have shown that when people expected that their house would be hit in the 2006 Lebanon War, they had a higher probability of reciting psalms (Sosis & Handwerker, 2011). In another study among women in a northern Israeli town, it was found that knowing someone who was killed in the Second Palestinian Intifada or believing that their town would be attacked by terrorists were strong predictors of psalm recitation (Sosis, 2007).

In addition to the impact of present existential insecurities and people's expectations of the future, such uncertainties experienced during childhood can have an enduring impact on people's religion (Norris & Inglehart, 2004). Scholars have examined how growing up in times of war could have a lifetime impact on people's religion. In several studies it was found that people who grew up during a war in their youth later in life attended religious meetings more often and also prayed more frequently (Immerzeel & Van Tubergen, 2011), even when taking the religiosity of the parents and the religious environment during socialization into account (Ruiter & Van Tubergen, 2009). In line with these findings, another research study found that Muslim war refugees from Kosovo and Bosnia who were highly traumatized often used religion to cope with their emotional stress and trauma (Ai, Tice, Huang, & Ishisaka, 2005).

Hypothesis III: natural disasters and religiosity

The third prediction derived from the insecurity theory is that the more strongly people are exposed to natural disasters in their direct environment, the more religious they are. What do empirical observations show with respect to this hypothesis?

An early study that looked into this was carried out by Penick, who focused on one of the most powerful earthquakes in US history that occurred in the period between December 1811 and February 1812 (Penick, 1981). The epicenter of these earthquakes was in the state of Missouri, which means that US citizens living there, or nearby, were directly exposed to the natural disaster, whereas those who lived elsewhere were not. Penick observed that in the year after the earthquake the region that was affected showed a 50% increase in church membership, compared with an increase of 1% in the rest of the US.

Another study looked into what happened in New Zealand after the city of Christchurch experienced a massive earthquake on February 22, 2011. The earthquake caused extensive damage in the city and killed 198 people. The researchers Sibley and Bulbulia examined whether this may have impacted the religiosity of the people in Christchurch (Sibley & Bulbulia, 2012). They compared data from a longitudinal panel study, in which the same people were interviewed before the earthquake (in 2009) and again shortly after the earthquake (after February 2011). The researchers observed that the religiosity of the interviewed people in Christchurch was higher after the earthquake than it was before, whereas among those living elsewhere—and not being directly exposed to the earthquake—it decreased in the same period.

These two studies focus on particular settings—Missouri in the US and Christchurch in New Zealand—and you may ask yourself if the conclusions from these cases can be generalized to other societies and religions. More recent work has attempted to answer that question. Bentzen used EVS/WVS data on religiosity in 914 districts in 85 countries, covering most of the inhabited parts of the World (Bentzen, 2015). She then matched these data on religiosity in these districts to earthquakes, creating one measure of how strongly people in a certain district in a country are living near to a high-risk earthquake area, and another measure of actual earthquakes that occurred in their district shortly before the EVS/WVS interview. Her study finds that those living in or near to high-risk regions and those who recently experienced an earthquake were more religious compared with those who were not exposed to such natural disasters. This pattern is found worldwide, within different religions (Christianity, Islam, Hinduism) and within all countries. These studies, in conjunction with findings from yet other work (Ager & Ciccone, 2017), thereby support the *disasters and religiosity* hypothesis.

In conclusion, what can we say about existential insecurity and religion? We have reviewed the evidence and it appears that predictions derived from the theory are largely supported in the literature. The theory offers an explanation for the *modernization-secularization*

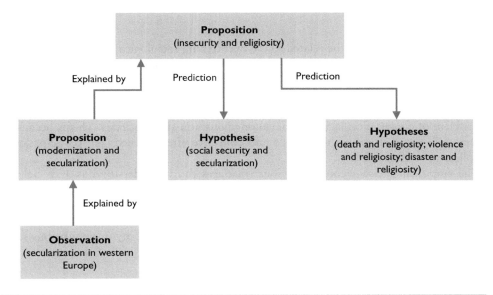

Figure 13.7 **Figure 13.7 Structure of existential insecurity theory of religion.**

link, for the *long-term* secularization consequences of growing up in social welfare systems and hypotheses derived on *short-term* effects of extreme existential threats are largely confirmed as well (Figure 13.7). To be sure, evidence for the existential theory largely comes from observational studies, which means that further testing is needed to examine internal validity. However, overall, the theory provides a coherent explanation of why and when religious change occurs in societies and research findings largely support the predictions derived from the theory.

13.7 Chapter resources

Key concepts

Religious belonging	Collective effervescence	Cohort effect
Religious believing	Credibility-enhancing	Secularization
Religiosity	displays	

Key theories and propositions

- Modernization and secularization theory
- Existential insecurity theory

Key stylized facts

- Religious stickiness
- Secularization in Western Europe
- Modernization and secularization

Summary

- The topic of religion can be related to the overarching sociological themes of social relations and culture.
- Sociologists study religiosity as the degree of religious belonging and the degree of religious believing.
- Scholars argue that the evolution of religion and religious groups may have solved the problem of cooperation in large-scale anonymous non-state societies. This is because of trust and cooperation within groups and collective effervescence, i.e., participation in collective religious rituals.
- The empirical phenomenon of religious stickiness can be understood as a special case of conformity and social control theory: religion is passed on from parents to children, from generation to generation, and subject to normative pressures, social sanctions and approval.
- Despite the baseline tendency of religious stickiness, the religiosity of populations sometimes changes over time. In Western Europe, secularization is a well-documented phenomenon, a process of gradual religious decline after WWII.
- According to the modernization and secularization theory, this process of secularization is due to modernization forces. Empirically, research findings indeed indicate that modernization is associated with lower levels of religiosity.
- To understand this relationship between modernization and secularization, we can turn to existential insecurity theory. According to this theory, modernization generally results in a reduction of existential securities thereby decreasing people's demand for religious believing and belonging.

References

Ager, P., & Ciccone, A. (2017). Agricultural risk and the spread of religious communities. *Journal of the European Economic Association*, 16(4), 1021–1068.

Ai, A. L., Tice, T. N., Huang, B., & Ishisaka, A. (2005). Wartime faith-based reactions among traumatized Kosovar and Bosnian refugees in the United States. *Mental Health, Religion & Culture*, 8(4), 291–308.

Ai, A. L., Tice, T. N., Peterson, C., & Huang, B. (2005). Prayers, spiritual support, and positive attitudes in coping with the September 11 national crisis. *Journal of Personality*, 73(3), 763–792.

Barber, N. (2011). A cross-national test of the uncertainty hypothesis of religious belief. *Cross-Cultural Research*, 45(3), 318–333.

Baumeister, R. F. (1991). *Meanings of life*. New York, NY: The Guilford Press.

Bentzen, J. S. (2015). Acts of god? Religiosity and natural disasters across subnational world districts. *University of Copenhagen Department of Economics, Discussion Paper No. 15-06*.

Brañas-Garza, P. (2004). Church attendance in Spain: Secularization and gender differences. *Economics Bulletin*, 26(1), 1–9.

Brañas-Garza, P., Garcia-Munoz, T., & Neuman, S. (2011). Intergenerational transmission of 'religious capital': Evidence from Spain. *Revista Internacional De Sociologia*, 69(3), 649–677.

Brauer, S. (2018). The surprising predictable decline of religion in the United States. *Journal for the Scientific Study of Religion*, 57(4), 654–675.

Brenner, P. S. (2016). Cross-national trends in religious service attendance. *Public Opinion Quarterly*, 80(2), 563–583.

Brown, S. L., Nesse, R. M., House, J. S., & Utz, R. L. (2004). Religion and emotional compensation: Results from a prospective study of widowhood. *Personality and Social Psychology Bulletin, 30*(9), 1165–1174.

Bruce, S. (2001). Christianity in Britain, R.I.P. *Sociology of Religion, 62*(2), 191–203.

Bruce, S. (2002). *God is dead: Secularization in the West.* Oxford, UK: Blackwell Publishing.

Burger, J. M., & Lynn, A. L. (2005). Superstitious behavior among American and Japanese professional baseball players. *Basic and Applied Social Psychology, 27*(1), 71–76.

Chaves, M. (1993). Secularization as declining religious authority. *Social Forces, 72*(3), 749–774.

Collins, R. (1992 [1982]). *Sociological insight: An introduction to non-obvious sociology* (2nd ed.). New York, NY: Oxford University Press.

Crockett, A., & Voas, D. (2006). Generations of decline: Religious change in 20th-century Britain. *Journal for the Scientific Study of Religion, 45*(4), 567–584.

Davie, G. (1990). Believing without belonging: Is this the future of religion in Britain? *Social Compass, 37*(4), 455–469.

De Graaf, N. D. (2013). Secularization: Theoretical controversies generating empirical research. In R. Wittek, T. Snijders, & V. Nee (Eds.), *The handbook of rational choice social research* (pp. 321–354). Stanford, CA: Stanford University Press.

Dobbelaere, K. (1999). Towards an integrated perspective of the processes related to the descriptive concept of secularization. *Sociology of Religion, 60*(3), 229–247.

Durkheim, E. (2001 [1912]). *The elementary forms of the religious life.* Oxford, UK: Oxford University Press.

Edgell, P., Gerteis, J., & Hartmann, D. (2006). Atheists as "other": Moral boundaries and cultural membership in American society. *American Sociological Review, 71*(2), 211–234.

Finke, R., & Stark, R. (2008). *The churching of America, 1776–2005: Winners and losers in our religious economy.* New Brunswick, NJ: Rutgers University Press.

Gill, A., & Lundsgaarde, E. (2004). State welfare spending and religiosity. *Rationality and Society, 16*(4), 399–436.

Greeley, A. M., & Hout, M. (1999). Americans' increasing belief in life after death: Religious competition and acculturation. *American Sociological Review, 64*(6), 813–835.

Güngör, D., Fleischmann, F., & Phalet, K. (2011). Religious identification, beliefs, and practices among Turkish Belgian and Moroccan Belgian Muslims: Intergenerational continuity and acculturative change. *Journal of Cross-Cultural Psychology, 42*(8), 1356–1374.

Hall, D. E., Meador, K. G., & Koenig, H. G. (2008). Measuring religiousness in health research: Review and critique. *Journal of Religion and Health, 47*(2), 134–163.

Hayes, B. C., & Pittelkow, Y. (1993). Religious belief, transmission, and the family: An Australian study. *Journal of Marriage and the Family, 55*(3), 755–766.

Henrich, J. (2009). The evolution of costly displays, cooperation and religion. *Evolution and Human Behavior, 30*(4), 244–260.

Herzer, D., & Strulik, H. (2017). Religiosity and income: A panel cointegration and causality analysis. *Applied Economics, 49*(30), 2922–2938.

Hogg, M. A., Adelman, J. R., & Blagg, R. D. (2010). Religion in the face of uncertainty: An uncertainty-identity theory account of religiousness. *Personality and Social Psychology Review, 14*(1), 72–83.

Hout, M., & Fischer, C. S. (2002). Why more Americans have no religious preference: Politics and generations. *American Sociological Review, 67*(2), 165–190.

Hout, M., & Fischer, C. (2014). Explaining why more Americans have no religious preference: Political backlash and generational succession, 1987–2012. *Sociological Science, 1:* 423–447.

Hout, M., & Greeley, A. M. (1987). The center doesn't hold: Church attendance in the United States, 1940-1984. *American Sociological Review, 52*(3), 325–345.

Hunsberger, B., & Brown, L. B. (1984). Religious socialization, apostasy, and the impact of family background. *Journal for the Scientific Study of Religion*, 23(3), 239–251.

Iannaccone, L. R. (1994). Why strict churches are strong. *American Journal of Sociology*, 99(5), 1180–1211.

Immerzeel, T., & Van Tubergen, F. (2011). Religion as reassurance? Testing the insecurity theory in 26 European Countries. *European Sociological Review*, 29(2), 359–372.

Johnstone, R. L. (8th ed.). (2016 [1975]). *Religion in society: A sociology of religion*. Abingdon, UK: Routledge.

Kaufmann, E. (2010). *Shall the religious inherit the earth? Demography and politics in the twenty-first century*. London, UK: Profile Books.

Keinan, G. (1994). Effects of stress and tolerance of ambiguity on magical thinking. *Journal of Personality and Social Psychology*, 67(1), 48–55.

Keinan, G. (2002). The effects of stress and desire for control on superstitious behavior. *Personality and Social Psychology Bulletin*, 28(1), 102–108.

Lechner, F. J. (1996). Secularization in the Netherlands? *Journal for the Scientific Study of Religion*, 35(3), 252–264.

Malinowski, B. (2004 [1948]). *Magic, science and religion and other essays*. Whitefish, MT: Kessinger Publishing.

Molteni, F., & Biolcati, F. (2018). Shifts in religiosity across cohorts in Europe: A multilevel and multidimensional analysis based on the European Values Study. *Social Compass*, 65(3), 413–432.

Myers, S. M. (1996). An interactive model of religiosity inheritance: The importance of family context. *American Sociological Review*, 61(5), 858–866.

Need, A., & De Graaf, N. D. (1996). 'Losing my religion': A dynamic analysis of leaving the church in the Netherlands. *European Sociological Review*, 12(1), 87–99.

Norenzayan, A. (2015). *Big gods: How religion transformed cooperation and conflict*. Princeton, NJ: Princeton University Press.

Norenzayan, A., & Hansen, I. G. (2006). Belief in supernatural agents in the face of death. *Personality and Social Psychology Bulletin*, 32(2), 174–187.

Norris, P., & Inglehart, R. (2004). *Sacred and secular: Religion and politics worldwide*. Cambridge, UK: Cambridge University Press.

Paldam, M., & Gundlach, E. (2013). The religious transition: A long-run perspective. *Public Choice*, 156(1-2), 105–123.

Penick, J. L. (1981). *The new Madrid earthquakes*. Columbia, MO: University of Missouri Press.

Pew Research Center. (2019). The changing global religious landscape. Retrieved from www.pewforum.org/2017/04/05/the-changing-global-religious-landscape.

Rees, T. J. (2009). Is personal insecurity a cause of cross-national differences in the intensity of religious belief? *Journal of Religion and Society*, 11, 1–24.

Regnerus, M. D., & Smith, C. (2005). Selection effects in studies of religious influence. *Review of Religious Research*, 47(1), 23–50.

Regnerus, M. D., Smith, C., & Smith, B. (2004). Social context in the development of adolescent religiosity. *Applied Developmental Science*, 8(1), 27–38.

Ruiter, S., & Van Tubergen, F. (2009). Religious attendance in cross-national perspective: A multilevel analysis of 60 countries. *American Journal of Sociology*, 115(3), 863–895.

Schnabel, L., & Bock, S. (2017). The persistent and exceptional intensity of American religion: A response to recent research. *Sociological Science*, 4, 686–700.

Schuster, M. A., Stein, B. D., Jaycox, L. H., Collins, R. L., Marshall, G. N., Elliott, M. N., Zhou A. J., Kanouse D. E., Morrison J. L., & Berry, S. H. (2001). A national survey of stress reactions after the September 11, 2001, Terrorist attacks. *New England Journal of Medicine*, 345(20), 1507–1512.

Sherkat, D. E. (1997). Embedding religious choice: Preferences and social constraints into rational choice theories of religious behavior. In L. A. Young (Ed.), *Rational choice theory and religion: Summary and assessment* (pp. 65–82). New York, NY: Routledge.

Sherkat, D. E. (1998). Counterculture or continuity-competing influences on baby boomers' religious orientations and participation. *Social Forces, 76*(3), 1087–1114.

Sherkat, D. E., & Wilson, J. (1995). Preferences, constraints, and choices in religious markets: An examination of religious switching and apostasy. *Social Forces, 73*(3), 993–1026.

Sibley, C. G., & Bulbulia, J. (2012). Faith after an earthquake: A longitudinal study of religion and perceived health before and after the 2011 Christchurch New Zealand earthquake. *PloS ONE, 7*(12), e49648.

Solt, F., Habel, P., & Grant, J. T. (2011). Economic inequality, relative power, and religiosity. *Social Science Quarterly, 92*(2), 447–465.

Sosis, R. (2007). Psalms for safety. *Current Anthropology, 48*(6), 903–911.

Sosis, R., & Handwerker, W. P. (2011). Psalms and coping with uncertainty: Religious Israeli women's responses to the 2006 Lebanon War. *American Anthropologist, 113*(1), 40–55.

Stark, R. (1999). Secularization, RIP. *Sociology of Religion, 60*(3), 249–273.

Stark, R., & Bainbridge, W. S. (1987). *A theory of religion.* New York, NY: Peter Lang Publishers.

Stark, R., & Finke, R. (2000). *Acts of faith: Explaining the human side of religion.* Berkeley, CA: University of California Press.

Stark, R., & Glock, C. Y. (1970). *American piety: The nature of religious commitment.* Berkeley, CA: University of California Press.

Stolz, J. (2009). Explaining religiosity: Towards a unified theoretical model. *The British Journal of Sociology, 60*(2), 345–376.

Storm, I. (2017). Does economic insecurity predict religiosity? Evidence from the European Social Survey 2002–2014. *Sociology of Religion, 78*(2), 146–172.

Te Grotenhuis, M., & Scheepers, P. (2001). Churches in Dutch: Causes of religious disaffiliation in the Netherlands, 1937–1995. *Journal for the Scientific Study of Religion, 40*(4), 591–606.

Te Grotenhuis, M., Scholte, M., de Graaf, N. D., & Pelzer, B. (2015). The between and within effects of social security on church attendance in Europe 1980–1998: The danger of testing hypotheses cross-nationally. *European Sociological Review, 31*(5), 643–654.

Van Ingen, E., & Moor, N. (2015). Explanations of changes in church attendance between 1970 and 2009. *Social Science Research, 52*, 558–569.

Voas, D. (2003). Intermarriage and the demography of secularization. *The British Journal of Sociology, 54*(1), 83–108.

Voas, D. (2008). The rise and fall of fuzzy fidelity in Europe. *European Sociological Review, 25*(2), 155–168.

Voas, D., & Chaves, M. (2016). Is the United States a counterexample to the secularization thesis? *American Journal of Sociology, 121*(5), 1517–1556.

Voas, D., & Chaves, M. (2018). Even intense religiosity is declining in the United States: Comment. *Sociological Science, 5*, 694–710.

Voas, D., & Crockett, A. (2005). Religion in Britain: Neither believing nor belonging. *Sociology, 39*(1), 11–28.

Wilson, J., & Sandomirsky, S. (1991). Religious affiliation and the family. *Sociological Forum, 6*(2), 289–309.

Glossary

Absolute mobility   Total number of positional changes.

Academic sociology   The way academic institutions describe and explain the social world. Characteristic are the systematic way of gathering knowledge, making explanations public and subject to criticism, the development of coherent theories and rigorous testing.

Achievement   Personal effort, skills, talent and performance.

Adjacency matrix   A matrix representing who has a relation to whom in a network.

Administrative research   Research in which the researcher uses data on human populations that are provided by official institutions such as governments, schools or hospitals.

Affiliation network   See: Group.

Aggregation mechanism   Proposition which relates the individual level to collective outcomes.

Ancestry   Subjective identification with certain ethnic origin(s).

Application question   Type of scientific question targeted towards applying scientific knowledge.

Ascription   Characteristics set at birth, such as family origin and ethnic origin.

Audit testing   Field experimental method which uses actors to detect discrimination.

Availability heuristic   Cognitive bias that people's judgment of the probability of events, or the frequency of a kind of thing, depends on the ease with which people can think of certain information.

Background knowledge   The theories and observations that are known before the study commences.

Between-country stratification   Unequal distribution of valuable goods between countries.

Biased sample   Sample for which observations in the study cannot be generalized to the population.

Bidirectional relation   Relation between two variables X and Y, such that changes in X result in changes in Y, and changes in Y result in changes in X. Synonym: Feedback relation.

Big data research   Research in which the researcher uses (unstructured) data from the Internet, digital communication and digital traces.

Black Box explanations   Type of explanation in which Y is explained by X, but the theoretical mechanism linking X to Y is missing.

Brokerage   Network position which connects (otherwise disconnected) communities.

Bystander effect   Phenomenon in which people are less likely to help other people in a critical situation when passive bystanders are present.

Glossary

Case study research   Research that is an in-depth examination of an extensive amount of information about very few units or cases.

Causality   Idea that an independent variable (X) has an effect on a dependent variable (Y).

Civil society   Society consisting of a cohesive web of voluntary associations.

Cohort effect   Societal changes that are due to generational replacement.

Collective effervescence   Shared religious activities.

Collectivism   Collectivistic values, such as emphasis on group loyalty and authority.

Common sense   Everyday thinking, intuitions, beliefs and perceptions.

Community   A cluster of nodes that are more connected internally than externally, either directly and/or indirectly.

Community-bonding ties   Ties between people within the same community.

Community-bridging ties   Ties between people of different communities.

Comparative-case question   Question which includes some comparison of cases, such as multiple social contexts, multiple moments in time and/or multiple populations.

Compensatory mechanism   Strategic behavior of high-status parents to maintain their high status in times of modernization.

Complete mediation   The impact of X on Y is completely accounted for by a third variable, Z, such that there is no other way that X affects Y than via Z.

Complex aggregation   Idea that collective outcomes result from complex interplay between individuals and their social context.

Complex concept   Theoretical concept that consists of different dimensions.

Complex contagion   Diffusion of opinions that need more sources.

Concept   Hypothetical abstraction that contains certain categories. Synonym: Theoretical variable.

Conceptualization   The differentiation of various dimensions of theoretical variables. Relevant for complex concepts.

Conceptual model   Type of theory tool in which the causal relationships between concepts are visualized.

Condition   Assumption about the specific setting which relates propositions to observations and hypotheses.

Consolidation   Degree of overlap, correlation between groups with respect to a certain dimension.

Cooperation problem   Certain condition in which rational self-interest behavior results in collective problems. Synonym: Social dilemma.

Coordination problem   Certain condition in which people want to do the same thing, but are uncertain about the behavior of each other.

Correspondence testing   Field experimental method which uses resumes to detect discrimination.

Credibility-enhancing displays   Behaviors which signal that people are genuine believers.

Cultural inertia   Time-lag between changing social conditions and adapting new norms and opinions.

Cultural integration   Degree of similarity between members of ethnic minority and majority groups with respect to cultural opinions, norms and corresponding practices.

Cultural maladaptation   Norms and opinions which do not fit their social environment well.

Culture   Sociological theme on opinions, norms and corresponding behavior.

Culture of honor   Culture which strongly endorses/values reputation and the right to self-defense in case one's honor is threatened.

Cumulative advantage   Positive feedback process in which prior success increases likelihood of successive success. Synonym: Matthew effect.

Cumulative discrimination   Discrimination that occurs in multiple transitions in the life course.

Cumulative science   The practice that theories and observations of earlier studies are incorporated in the work of successive studies.

Decree   Top-down change in descriptive norm.

Deductive-nomological explanation   Form of explanation of phenomena using proposition(s) and conditions.

Deeper explanation   Type of explanation in which one proposition is explained by another, more general, proposition.

Demographic transition   Transition within a population from high fertility and high mortality to low fertility and low mortality.

Dependent variable   Variable which is affected by another variable (independent variable).

Descriptive norm   Statement specifying what a person is expected to do.

Descriptive question   Type of scientific question targeted towards describing phenomena.

Descriptive research   Research whose purpose is to come up with accurate descriptions of social phenomena.

Diffusion   The transmission and spread of something.

Dimensions   Aspects of theory variables.

Direct causal relationship   A relationship between two variables X and Y, such that changes in X have a direct effect on changes in Y.

Dominant strategy   Strategy that is favorable to choose irrespective of what other people do.

Dyads   Each (possible) relationship between ego and alter.

Ecological explanation   Type of explanation in which both the dependent and independent variable(s) are at the collective level (meso or macro).

Economic integration   Degree of similarity between ethnic minority and ethnic majority groups in realizing valued goals.

Edges   The ties in the network.

Emancipative values   See: Individualism.

Empirical success   The degree of empirical confirmation of a theory.

Empirical variable   See: Measure.

Endogamy   Marriage between two individuals who belong to the same group.

Ethnic diversity   Ethnic heterogeneity of a population.

Ethnic group   People affiliated to the same origin beyond family roots.

Exogamy   Marriage between two individuals who belong to different groups. Synonym: Intermarriage, Mixed marriage.

Experimental research   Research in which the researcher manipulates conditions for some research participants but not others and then compares group responses to see whether doing so made a difference.

Explanatory research   Research whose purpose is to rigorously test hypotheses.

Exploratory research   Research whose purpose is to discover new phenomena and to construct new theories.

External sanction   Sanctions imposed by third parties, i.e., other people of the group in which the social norm applies.

External validity   The validity of inferences about whether the results of the study are generalizable beyond a specific study.

False negative   A research finding which suggests the hypothesis is false, whereas in reality the hypothesis is true.

False positive   A research finding which suggests the hypothesis is true, whereas in reality the hypothesis is false.

False theoretical question   Theoretical question which aims to explain something that does not exist.

Feedback relation   See: Bidirectional relation.

First generation   See: Foreign-born population.

Flynn effect   Gradual increase in skills and abilities of populations in developed countries between 1930 and 1995.

Foci   Social settings in which people participate and that create the pool of people we meet.

Forbidden triad   A triad in which ego A has strong ties to alters B and C, but in which no tie exists between B and C.

Foreign-born population   People born abroad. Synonym: First generation.

Formal model   Type of theory tool in which theories are expressed with formalized language.

Formal sanction   Punishment for behavior diverging from legal norms.

Framework   See: Perspective.

Free-ride   Type of behavior in which one prefers personal gains above the interest of the group.

Gender essentialist belief   Belief that there are traits that are distinctively male and female.

Gini coefficient   Measure of stratification in society which runs from 0 (minimum) to 100 (maximum).

Graph   A visual representation of relations between actors in a network.

Group   Social category with which people can affiliate. Synonym: Affiliation network.

Group-bonding tie   Tie between two individuals who belong to the same group.

Group-bridging tie   Tie between two individuals who belong to a different group.

Habitus   Behavioral dispositions based on cognitions, moral norms, values and cultural scripts.

Horizontal diffusion   Knowledge transmitted within generations.

Hub   Highly connected central nodes in a network.

Human capital   People's knowledge and skills insofar as these are relevant to the labor market.

Hypothesis   Testable prediction, derived from theory.

Ill-defined question   Question which is vague and ambiguous. Such questions are contrasted with precise questions, which have clear interpretations.

Indegree   The number of nominations a person receives from others.

Independent variable   Variable which has an effect on another variable (dependent variable).

Indicator   See: Measure.

Individual learning   Things people try out themselves, without being influenced by others.

Individual-level effect   Type of propositions which refer to processes at the micro level.

Individual perspective   Type of explanation of human behavior which focuses on individual causes.

Individualism   Individualistic values, such as emphasis on autonomy and personal choice. Synonym: Emancipative values.

Induction   Inferences that are made from observations of only a limited number of cases to a more general, universal pattern.

Inequality   Sociological theme on social stratification, social mobility and resources.

Inequality of opportunity   The relationship between social background and access to resources.

Inequality of outcomes   The relationship between social background and labor market outcomes.

Inequality of returns   The relationship between resources and labor market outcomes.

Information content   The degree of theoretical precision and theoretical scope of a theory.

Informational social influence   Influence to accept information obtained from another as evidence about reality.

Injunctive norm   Normative statement specifying what a person should do or not do. Synonym: Prescriptive norm, Oughtness norm.

Innovation   A completely new belief, or some new practice or object that is based on new beliefs (knowledge), which is aimed to solve a certain problem.

Integration   Degree of cultural similarity (cultural integration), intergroup cohesion (social integration) and similarity in realizing valued goals (economic integration) between ethnic groups.

Interaction effect   See: Moderation effect.

Intergenerational mobility   Changing position between parents and their children in the stratification system.

Intergroup cohesion   Degree to which (members of different) groups in society have positive relations with each other as opposed to negative relations.

Intermarriage   See: Exogamy.

Internal sanction   Feeling of shame, guilt and bad conscience resulting from deviation from internalized norms.

Internal validity   The validity of inferences about whether an observed association between X (independent variable) and Y (dependent variable) reflects a causal relationship from X to Y.

Internalized norm   Norm that has become part of people's intrinsic set of things one should do or prefer to do. Synonym: Moral norm.

Intragenerational mobility   Changing position in the stratification system over the life course.

Labor market discrimination   Employer's unequal treatment of individuals with the same human capital, based on their group affiliation.

Law   See: Legal norm.

Legal norm   Formal, normative statement specifying what a person should do or not do. Synonym: law.

Glossary

Literature review Systematic overview of the theories and observations that are known (background knowledge), typically in a certain specialized field of research.

Macro level Social contexts that are broader than meso-level units. Examples: nations, groups of nations, continents.

Many-to-many transmission Knowledge transmitted from many persons to many persons.

Matthew effect See: Cumulative advantage.

Measure Variable used in empirical research. Synonym: Indicator, Empirical variable, Proxy.

Measurement quality Quality of the measures. This depends on the validity and reliability of the measures.

Measurement reliability The degree to which the measurement instrument gives the same result when repeating the observation of the same phenomenon.

Measurement validity The degree to which measures reflect the theoretical concept that they are intended to measure.

Mediator A variable Z that mediates the relationship between variables X and Y, such that changes in X impact changes in Z, which then results in changes in Y.

Meso level Social contexts at the intermediate level. Examples: families, neighborhoods, schools, organizations.

Micro level The level at which individuals operate. Commonly distinguished from meso level and macro level.

Minimal group paradigm Studies which reveal that arbitrarily created groups which have no interaction between members already reveal in-group favoritism.

Mixed marriage See: Exogamy.

Mobility table Table which cross-classifies origin and destination position in the stratification system.

Moderation effect The relationship between X and Y is dependent on variable Z. Synonym: Interaction effect.

Modernization Co-occurring and interrelated process of rationalization and socio-economic progress.

Modus tollens Logic rule which states that if it is hypothesized that A leads to B, and it is observed that B is not true, then A cannot be true either.

Monitoring The behavior of an individual within a group is visible to third parties.

Moral norm See: Internalized norm.

Motherhood penalty Finding that mothers have less favorable positions in the labor market than non-mothers.

Multilevel framework A framework which considers the interplay between individuals and their social environment.

Name generator A survey question which asks respondents to mention the names or initials of alters in their personal network.

Negative social influence Process by which people's opinions and behavior develop in the opposite direction to the opinions and behavior of other actors in their environment.

Network closure Highly connected, dense, network.

Network density The ratio of all realized ties in a network to the number of all possible ties in the same network.

Nodes Actors within the network. In social networks, these are often individuals.

Norm   Rules of the game in society.

Normative question   Question that entails value judgments.

Normative social influence   Influence to conform to the positive expectations of another.

Observational research   Research in which the researcher relies on non-experimental observations.

Occupational prestige   Subjective ranking of occupations in terms of prestige and respect.

One-to-many transmission   Knowledge transmitted from one person to many persons.

One-to-one transmission   Knowledge transmitted from one person to another.

Operationalization   Translation of theoretical variables (concepts) into empirical variables (indicators).

Opinion   Cognitive beliefs, preferences, attitudes and values.

Optimism gap   Situation in which people are more positive about their personal lives than they are about society.

Organizational cohesion   Degree of voluntary association involvement.

Oughtness norm   See: Injunctive norm.

Outdegree   The number of nominations a person makes.

Paradigm   See: Perspective.

Partial mediation   The impact of X on Y is partially accounted for by a third variable, Z, such that X affects Y via Z, but also via other variables.

Personal network   A network presenting all the ties that a certain person (ego) has to others (alters).

Personal network cohesion   The degree to which someone's personal network consists of (strongly) positive relationships as opposed to no/neutral relationships or even (strongly) negative relationships.

Personal trouble   Problem related to the personal life of an individual. Contrasted with social problem (public issue).

Perspective   Certain way of looking at things. Synonym: Framework, Paradigm.

Pluralistic ignorance   Situation in which the majority of people privately reject a certain norm, but incorrectly believe that others privately support the norm.

Population   The entire set of cases about which the researcher wants to draw conclusions.

Position generator   Measure of social resources which captures the occupational positions of respondents' connections.

Positive social influence   Process by which people's opinions and behavior develop in the same direction as the opinions and behavior of other actors in their environment.

Precise question   Question which has clear interpretation. Such questions are contrasted with ill-defined questions, which are vague and ambiguous.

Prescriptive norm   See: Injunctive norm.

Private sociologists   The way human beings, in daily life, make sense of the social world. As such they are prone to, among other things, intuitive thinking, implicit reasoning, development of incoherent and vague ideas, keeping knowledge private and searching for confirmations. Contrasted with academic sociology.

Probability sample   Sample drawn by giving individuals in the population equal chance to participate in the study.

Proposition   Universal statement, i.e., statement about the causal relations between two or more concepts.

Glossary

Proximate causes   Factors that are close to the phenomena to be explained. Proximate causes can be explained by ultimate causes.

Proxy   See: Measure.

Public good   Good that serves collective benefits, such as national safety and environmental protection.

Public issue   See: Social problem.

Question ingredients   Elements of a question which can be specified. These are: (1) behavior of interest, (2) social contexts, (3) period and (4) populations.

Relative mobility   Inequality between children from (different) social origins in their opportunity to access social positions.

Religiosity   Degree of religious belonging and believing.

Religious believing   Degree to which an individual adheres to religious beliefs and values.

Religious belonging   Degree of social integration of an individual in the religious group.

Replication   Redoing studies on the same topic, theory or hypothesis using different data, methods or measures.

Representative sample   Sample for which observations in the study can be generalized to the population.

Residential segregation   Unequal distribution of groups across geographical areas.

Resources   Capital, opportunities and power one can use to realize one's goals.

Rights revolution   Increase of human rights in the second half of the 20th century.

Sample   A small set of cases a researcher selects from the population.

Scientific question   Question that does not entail value judgments. There are three types of scientific questions, namely: descriptive, theoretical and application.

Scientific relevance   Relevance of sociological work for the accumulation of sociological knowledge.

Scope condition   Set of conditions to which a certain theory is applicable.

Second demographic transition   Change within a population towards extremely low fertility levels.

Second generation   People born in the host country, with at least one foreign-born parent.

Secularization   Diminishing religiosity, i.e., decline in religious belonging and believing.

Self-fulfilling prophecy   When behavior based on false beliefs about a situation cause that situation in the end.

Simple aggregation   Idea that collective outcomes are no more than the sum of their parts.

Simple concept   Theoretical concept that can be easily measured with empirical variables.

Simple contagion   Diffusion of opinions that need few sources.

Small-world network   A network that is characterized by a high level of local clustering and low average path length.

Social approval   Rewards and appreciation by other group members for following social norms.

Social capital paradigm   Perspective according to which social networks have some sort of value.

Social class   Group of people who hold similar occupational positions.

Social cohesion   The degree to which individuals and groups have (strongly) positive relationships with each other, as opposed to no/neutral relationships or (strongly) negative relationships.

Social context   Social environment in which people are embedded.

Social context effect   Influence of social conditions on individual outcomes.

Social dilemma   See: Cooperation problem.

Social dynamics   Ecological relationships and collective changes.

Social identity   That part of our self-concept corresponding to group identification.

Social influence   Process by which people's opinions and behavior are affected by others.

Social integration   Degree of intergroup cohesion between members of different ethnic groups.

Social interdependency   Situations in which actions of individuals affect those of yet other individuals.

Social intervention   Social policy measure.

Social learning biases   Conditions that modify the degree of conformity.

Social mobility   Movement of people from one position to another in the stratification system.

Social network   A set of actors and the ties between them.

Social norm   Informal, normative statement specifying what a person should do or not do.

Social phenomenon   Collective human behavior.

Social problem   Problem that: 1 goes beyond the personal troubles of the individual (it affects many people); 2 is an issue about which many people are concerned. Synonym: Public issue.

Social proof   The "evidence" individuals perceive which arises when a group of people in the environment does something in the same way.

Social relations   Sociological theme on social networks and groups.

Social resources   Valuable labor-market-related resources that are embedded in personal networks.

Social sanction   Punishment for behavior diverging from social norms.

Social status   Subjective ranking of individuals or groups in terms of honor, esteem and respect.

Social stratification   Unequal distribution of valued goods.

Societal relevance   Relevance of sociological work for the understanding of social problems.

Socio-economic progress   Progress in wealth, health, peace and safety.

Sociogram   See: Graph.

Sociological imagination   Type of explanation of human behavior which focuses on social causes. Synonym: Sociological perspective.

Sociological perspective   See: Sociological imagination.

Sociological subtheme   Subdimension of a sociological theme.

Sociological theme   Complex concept which helps to relate diverse, specific topics to each other in a more abstract way. Three main sociological themes are: culture, social relations and inequality.

Sociological topic   A specific subject matter in sociology. Examples: crime, ethnicity, globalization, gender.

Spiral of silence   People's tendency to remain silent and not express their private preferences when they believe that their private preferences deviate from the majority's preferences.

Standardization   Process of making identical procedures, questions, answer categories and other aspects of the measurement instrument.

Stratified sample   Sample based on dividing the population into subpopulations (strata).

Strong ties   Positive relationships in which people feel emotionally close to one another, trust each other and help each other out when needed.

Structural hole   Social network characteristic which refers to the lack of social ties between communities.

Structural mobility   Mobility that is due to changes in the volumes (margins) of available social positions.

Survey research   Research in which the researcher uses questionnaires to collect data from respondents.

Theoretical precision   The degree to which the theory excludes possibilities of what could happen with respect to a particular case.

Theoretical question   Type of scientific question targeted towards understanding phenomena.

Theoretical scope   The degree to which the theory is applicable to a wider range of cases: phenomena, populations and settings.

Theoretical variable   See: Concept.

Theory   Coherent set of propositions and assumptions about conditions which can explain certain phenomena and which generate hypotheses (predictions) on other (yet unobserved and hypothetical) phenomena.

Theory schema   Type of theory tool in which propositions, conditions, hypotheses and observations are written out as a coherent set of verbal statements.

Theory tool   Tool which helps to systematically present a theory. Three often-used theory tools are: theory schema, conceptual model and formal model.

Thick description   Detailed description of persons, their behaviors, motivations, social processes and personal relationships within a well-defined case.

Third party   Other members of the same group to which certain norms apply.

Thomas and Thomas Theorem   If men define situations as real, they are real in their consequences.

Transitivity   See: Triadic closure.

Triad   A network of three actors and the (possible) ties between them.

Triadic closure   The situation in which the two alters of one ego are also connected to each other. Synonym: Transitivity.

Typology   A way of classifying reality, often done by combining concepts.

Ultimate causes   Factors that underlie proximate causes.

Unpopular norm   Norm which is not serving collective benefits.

Valuable goods   Something that people value.

Value   Things that people want and appreciate.

Variable sociology   Type of sociology which focuses on causal relationships between variables.

Verstehen   Type of explanation in which subjective understanding plays a key role.

Vertical diffusion   Knowledge transmitted from parents to children, from one generation to the next generation.

Weak ties   A more superficial or instrumental relationship between two people who see each other not that often and are emotionally less close to one another.

WEIRD people   Typical participants in laboratory experiments in the social sciences are: Western, Educated, Industrialized, Rich and Democratic. Due to their specific characteristics, they are not representative of the larger population.

Within-country stratification   Unequal distribution of valuable goods within countries.

Index

absolute mobility 316; *see also* social mobility

academic sociology 30–1; *see also* private sociologists

acculturation 377; *see also* integration

achievement 318–19

adaptation bias 161–2; and culture of honor 385; and diffusion of innovations 167; and emergence of norms 193; and rationalization process 446; *see also* social learning biases

adjacency matrix 223

administrative research 94–6

affiliation network *see* group

age effect 468

agent based modelling 395–7

aggregation mechanism 131; *see also* multilevel framework

aims of sociology 16–19

analytical sociology 127

ancestry 372–4

anomie theory 61–2

Ansell, Christopher K. 94–5

application question 21; *see also* questions

arcs 223

Asch, Solomon 146–9, 153–5

ascription 318–19

assimilation 377; *see also* integration

assumption *see* condition

attitudes: and discrimination 343; intergroup 259–88; *see also* opinions

audit testing 354; *see also* discrimination

availability heuristic 445

background knowledge 32

bandwagon effect *see* popularity bias

Becker, Gary 334

beliefs *see* opinions

between-country stratification 303; *see also* social stratification

biased sample 83; *see also* sample

bidirectional relation 66

big data research 98–100

Black Box explanation 125

Black hypersegregation in the US 395

Blalock, Hubert 282

Blau, Peter 184, 268–9, 318–23, 334–5, 346, 431

Blumer, Herbert 282

Boudon, Raymond 126, 129

Bourdieu, Pierre 191, 206, 246, 322–4

brokerage 340; and job outcomes 340

Burt, Ronald 246, 336, 340–1

Byrne, Donn 270

bystander effect 204

capital *see* resource

career ambitions and job outcomes: proposition 355–6

case study research 91–4

causal explaining *see* Erklären

causal figure *see* conceptual model

causality 62–4; and causal explaining 123–5; and internal validity 87–8

Charles, Maria 356–9

Christakis, Nicholas 221

civil society 262

class *see* social class

climate change *see* global warming

climate crisis *see* global warming

cognitive biases: availability heuristic 445; *see also* social learning biases

Cohen, Dov 386–8
cohesion *see* social cohesion
cohort effect 468
Coleman, James 127–8, 170, 246–9
Coleman's boat *see* multilevel framework
collective effervescence 463
collectivism 432–40; *see also* value
Collins, Randal 463
common sense 26–31
community: bonding tie 238; bridging tie 239; definition of 238; and group segregation 264–5; and job finding 338; loss-of-community 240–2; and social cohesion 242–6; and structural hole 340; and trust 249–50
community-bonding tie 238–40; and loss-of-community 240–2; and trust 249–50; *see also* community
community-bridging tie 238–40; and job finding 338; and trust 249–50; *see also* community
comparative-case question 25; *see also* questions
compensatory mechanism 323
complete mediation 65
complex aggregation 132; *see also* multilevel framework
complex concept 79; *see also* simple concept
complex contagion 160; and diffusion of innovations 166–8; *see also* contagion
computational social science *see* big data research
Comte, Auguste 34, 110–12, 472
concept 58–62; complex 79; and definition 60; simple 78; and typology 60
conceptual model 64–8; and multilevel framework 129; *see also* theory tool
conceptualization 79
condition 42
confirmation bias 161; and diffusion of innovations 167–9; and private sociologists 31; and rationalization process 446; *see also* social learning biases
conflict theory *see* group threat theory
conformity 146–53; and collectivism 432; and cultural capital 324; in judgments 146–8; and religious stickiness 465–7; and social control theory 187–9; and

social influence 153–5; and social learning theory 156–62
consolidation 269–70
contagion 153; complex 160; simple 160; *see also* conformity
convention *see* descriptive norm
cooperation: and intergroup cohesion 274–7; as problem 193–7; and religion 462–4, 477–8; and we-feeling 260–2
coordination problem 197–9, 200–2; and group distinction 206–9
core network 225–35; and group segregation 267
correspondence testing 353; *see also* discrimination
Coser, Lewis 282
credibility-enhancing displays 464
crime: and administrative research 94; age-crime curve 18; and case study research 91–4; and Merton's typology of anomie and deviance 61–6; and network closure 248; perceptions of 408–10, 445; and poverty 301; and social control theory 183–4, 187; and social norms 182–3; as sociological topic 114–15; trends in homicide and violence 413–15; witchcraft as 280
cultural capital 323–4, 328, 345–6
cultural inertia 200–3; and religion 467
cultural integration: changes over time 379–82; definition of 378; and social context effects 382–5; and spillover effects 388–92; *see also* integration
cultural maladaptation 199–206
cultural reproduction theory 322–4
cultural transmission 153; *see also* conformity
culture: as sociological theme 115–18; definition of 117; *see also* norm; opinion
culture of honor 385–8
cumulative advantage 164–5
cumulative culture 417; *see also* rationalization
cumulative discrimination 344
cumulative science 32–34
customs *see* descriptive norm

De Tocqueville, Alexis 111–12, 262, 438
decree 198

deductive-nomological explanation 42
deeper explanation 56; and modernization and secularization theory 475; and multilevel framework 128–9; and Pygmalion effect 143; *see also* information content
demographic transition 441; in Western Europe 441
demography *see* population and demography
density *see* network density
dependent variable 62
descriptive norm 198–201; and group distinction 206–9; *see also* norm
descriptive question 20; *see also* questions
descriptive research 75; *see also* explanatory research; exploratory research
differential association theory 184
diffusion: definition of 166; horizontal 448–9; of innovations 165–70; vertical 448–9; *see also* conformity; social influence; transmission
digital data *see* big data research
digraph 223
dimension 79
direct causal relationship 65
directed ties 222–3
discrimination: and audit testing 354; and correspondence testing 353; cumulative 344–5; and ethnic inequality 391–2; and gender inequality 353–4; and in-group favoritism 275, 343; of Jewish minorities 285; and job outcomes 345; labour market 343; statistical 344; taste-based 343–4
distal cause *see* ultimate cause
Dohmen, Thomas 148–9
dominant strategy 194
dual-process model 156; and availability heuristic 445; and habitus 191; and internalized norms 190
Dunbar, Robin 228
Durkheim, Emile 6, 12–13, 32, 53–9, 94, 111–15, 124, 126–7, 150, 152, 184, 186–7, 206, 247–8, 463, 472, 476
Durkheim's integration and suicide theory 53–8; and network closure 247–8; and social control theory 187
dyads 222

echo chamber 161, 169
ecological explanation 124
economic integration: changes over time 379–82; definition of 378; and social context effects 382–5; and spillover effects 388–92; *see also* integration
edges 222
education: and cultural reproduction theory 322–4; and Flynn effect 427–9; and gender inequality 190, 350–1; and homophily 272; as human capital 334–5; of immigrants 381–3, 389–90; and intergenerational closure 248; and peer influence 150, 159; and scientization 423–9; and self-fulfilling prophecy 142–5; and social networks in school 223, 225, 233, 244–5, 247, 266–7, 269–73, 305; as sociological topic 114–15; and status attainment 318–22, 327–8, 345–7; and STEM fields 357–9; and timing of selection 384–5
Eisner, Manuel 413
Elias, Norbert 113, 206–9
emancipative values *see* individualism
empirical success 47
empirical variable *see* measure
endogamy 266
Engels, Friedrich 6, 111–13, 115, 303–4, 472
Erikson, Robert 304
Erklären 123–7; and multilevel framework 127–32
ethnic competition theory *see* group threat theory
ethnic diversity 374–5
ethnic group 374
ethnic inequality 388–92
ethnicity and race: and ancestry 372–4; and discrimination 343–5, 391–2; and group segregation 264–74, 278–9, 281–8; as groups 119, 261–2, 374; and international migration 369–376; as sociological topic 114–15; *see also* integration
ethnocentrism 275, 277
existential insecurity theory: and individualistic values 438–40; and religion 475–83
exogamy 266

experimental research 100–3

explanation *see* theory

explanatory research 75; *see also* descriptive research; exploratory research

exploratory research 75, 88–90; *see also* descriptive research; explanatory research

exposure bias 158–9; and confirmation bias 161; and diffusion of innovations 167; *see also* social learning biases

external sanction 184

external validity 82–6

Facebook 98–100, 161, 220–1, 228, 237, 339

false enforcement 205

false negative 105–6; *see also* false positive

false positive 105–6; *see also* false negative

false theoretical question 25; *see also* questions

family: and core networks 232; and cultural capital 322–4; and demography 440–4; and health 251; and individualistic-collectivistic values 432–3; and inequality 345–7; and intergenerational mobility 314–28; and loss-of-community 240–2; marriage and suicide 56–7; as meso level 11; and multilevel framework 129–30; and network closure 248; and parental transmission 148–9, 152, 188, 202, 448–9, 465–7; and personal networks 222–6; and small-world phenomenon 237; and social capital 336–9, 341–3; and social cohesion 244–6; and social control theory 184, 187; and social norms 182, 195; as sociological topic 114–15; and theme on culture 115–16, 122–3; and theme on inequality 120–3; and theme on social relations 118–19, 122–3; and trust 249–50; and welfare states 60; *see also* gender

feedback relation *see* bidirectional relation

Feld, Scott 221

fertility 440–4

Firebaugh, Glenn 91

Fischer, Claude 246

first generation *see* foreign born population

Flynn effect 427–9

foci 269–70

forbidden triad 233–5, 239

forbidden triad tendency 232–5

foreign-born population 370

formal model 68; *see also* theory tool

formal sanction 191

Fowler, James 221

framework *see* perspective

free-ride 194

Freitag, Markus 248, 250

friendship paradox 220–2

Galatea effect 143–4; *see also* Pygmalion effect

Gambetta, Diego 69

game theory 194

Gemeinschaft 240

gender: essentialist belief 358; and footbinding 201–2; as group 260–1, 343–5; and group segregation 266–7; and homophily 270–1; hypersegregation 356; inequality 347–59; and scapegoats 279–80; as sociological topic 114–15; and status 305; values 190, 432–7

gender essentialist belief 358

gender hypersegregation 356

gender ideology theory 355

gender inequality 347–59; and discrimination 353–4; and gender norms and ambitions 355–9; and human capital 350–2; and motherhood penalty 354; and social resources 352–3

Gesellschaft 240

Gini coefficient 308

global warming 16, 19, 161, 169, 194, 408

Goffman, Erving 125

Golder, Scott 100

Goldthorpe, John 82, 304

Granovetter, Mark 233–5, 239–40, 246, 249, 336–41, 395

graph 222

Great Gatsby Curve 324–8

Gross, Neal 167–9

group: affiliation and discrimination 343–5, 353–5; ancestry 372–3; and collectivism 432–3; definition of 119, 260; distinction 206–9; ethnic 373–4; and group threat theory 281–8, 343, 384; and homophily 270–2, 277; and in-group favoritism 274–7; and intergroup cohesion

263–4; and organizational cohesion 262–3; religious 458–60; and residential segregation 393–97; segregation 264–74, 281–8; and social class 304; and social control theory 183–9; and social identity 276, 283; and social norms 183; and social proof 158; and social status 305; and status bias 159–60; and structural opportunity theory 268–70; as subtheme of social relations 119
group position theory *see* group threat theory
group segregation: causes of 268–74, 281–8; empirics of 264–8; index 265
group threat theory 281–8, 384; and discrimination 343
group-bonding tie 264
group-bridging tie 265
Grusky, David 356–9

habitus 191
Hardin, Garrett 194
Harris, Marvin 201
Häuberer, Julia 246
health: and binge drinking 180–1, 205; child mortality 14–15, 311–12, 412, 444; and economic development 301–2; as human capital 335; networks and 250–1; obesity 4–10, 312; and self-fulfilling prophecy 142–3; and social class 304–5; as sociological topic 114–15
Hedström, Peter 127
Hobbes, Thomas 34, 110–12, 413–14
Hofstede, Geert 432
Homans, George 184
homo economicus 186
homo sociologicus 182, 186
homogeneity bias *see* group segregation
homophily: empirics 271–2; and group segregation 267–8; and in-group favoritism 277; phenomenon 272; theory 270–1; and transitivity tendency 233–5
horizontal diffusion 448–9; *see also* transmission
hub 229–30
hubs in personal networks: stylized fact 230
human capital 334–5, 343–6; and ethnic inequality 389–90; and gender inequality 350–1; and job outcomes 335; and language proficiency 384
hypothesis 45

ill-defined question 22; *see also* questions
imitation 153; *see also* conformity
immigrant assimilation: proposition 379
immigrant integration: proposition 379
immigration: and ethnic diversity 369–76; international migration 369–76; as sociological topic 114–15; *see also* ethnicity and race; integration
increased merit selection hypothesis *see* modernization and mobility theory
indegree 224
independent variable 62
indicator *see* measure
individual learning 156
individual perspective 4–13; *see also* perspective
individualism 432–40; *see also* value
individualization 435
individual-level effect 130; *see also* multilevel framework
induction 89
industrialization and mobility hypothesis 321
industrialization theory *see* modernization and mobility theory
inequality: definition of 120; as sociological theme 120–1; *see also* resources; social mobility; social stratification
inequality of opportunity 345–7; and ethnic inequality 389–92; and gender inequality 347–59
inequality of outcomes 345–7; and ethnic inequality 389–92; and gender inequality 347–59
inequality of returns 345–7; and ethnic inequality 389–92; and gender inequality 347–59
informal job finding: stylized fact 337
information content 48; *see also* theoretical precision; theoretical scope
informational social influence 153–5; *see also* social influence
Inglehart, Ronald 190, 203, 432, 434, 440, 468, 473, 476
in-group favoritism 274–7; contingent upon social context 277–80

injunctive norm 182–3; *see also* norm
innovation 165; diffusion of 165–70
institution 192; *see also* norm
integration: changes in 379–82; cultural
    378; and culture of honor 385–8;
    definition of 376–9; economic 378;
    and group segregation 264–74, 281–8;
    immigrant assimilation proposition 379;
    immigrant integration proposition 379;
    process 382; and residential segregation
    393–7; selective 388–92; social 378;
    and social context effects 382–5; and
    spillover effects 388–92
integration spillover effect 388–92
interaction effect *see* moderation effect
intergenerational mobility 314, 316–17; *see
    also* social mobility
intergroup cohesion: contingent upon
    social context 278–80; definition of
    263; dimensions of 263–4; and group
    segregation 264–74; and group threat
    theory 281–8; and in-group favoritism
    274–7; *see also* social cohesion
intermarriage *see* exogamy
internal sanction 190; *see also* internalized
    norm
internal validity 87–8
internalized norm 189–91; and career
    ambitions 355–6; and religion 467; *see
    also* norm
international migration 369–76
internet 96, 98, 159, 169, 241, 272, 449
interpretative sociology 125
intragenerational mobility 315; *see also*
    social mobility

jobs via weak ties: stylized fact 337–8

Kahneman, Daniel 156
Khaldun, Ibn 110, 112

labor market discrimination 343; *see also*
    discrimination
Laumann, Edward 231–2
law *see* legal norm
Lazarsfeld, Paul 28, 270
legal norm 191–2; and rights revolution
    438; *see also* norm

Lenski, Gerhard 418–22, 447–9
Lesthaeghe, Ron 442–3
Lin, Nan 246, 341–3
Lindenberg, Siegwart 129
literature review 24
Locke, John 111–12
loose cultures 432; *see also individualism*
loss-of-community 240–2

Mackie, Gerry 201–2
macro level 11–12
Macy, Michael 100
Malinowski, Bronislaw 476
many-to-many transmission 169–70, 448–9;
    see also transmission
marriage market 266
Marx, Karl 6, 19, 32, 111–15, 303–4, 472
Matthew effect *see* cumulative advantage
McClelland, David C. 127–9
McDonaldization 429–31
Mead, George Herbert 125
measure 78
measurement quality 76–82; *see also*
    measurement
measurement reliability 80–2; *see also*
    measurement
measurement validity 77–9; *see also*
    measurement
measurement: quality 76–82; reliability
    80–2; validity 77–9
media transmission 150–2; and conformity
    152
mediator 65
Merton, Robert 61–2, 142–6, 156, 165, 270
meso level 11–12
methods *see* research
micro level 11–12
Milgram, Stanley 236–7
Mills, C.W. 6
minimal group paradigm 275–6
mixed marriage *see* exogamy
mobility *see* social mobility
mobility table 316–17
moderation effect 67
modernization: and cultural reproduction
    theory 322–4; definition of 431; health
    progress 410–12; and loss-of-community
    240–2; McDonaldization 429–31; and

mobility theory 319–22; and optimism gap 444–5; peace and safety progress 413–15; and population change 440–4; rationalization 415–417, 445–9; and religion 471–5; scientization 423–9; as sociological topic 114–15; technological progress 417–23; wealth and value change 431–40

modernization and individualism: proposition 433

modernization and mobility theory 319–22

modernization and secularization: stylized fact 474; theory 471–5

modus tollens 46

monitoring 185; and network closure 247

moral norm see internalized norm

motherhood penalty 354

multilevel framework 127–32; and conformity 154; and cultural markets 164; and cultural reproduction theory 323; and existential insecurity and religiosity 477; and group threat theory 283; and individualistic values 439; and language proficiency 383; and modernization and mobility theory 320; and rationalization process 446; and self-fulfilling prophecies 145; and social learning biases 157; and status attainment process 318; and structural opportunity theory 268

name generator 227; see also position generator

negative social influence 153; see also social influence

network closure 247; and norms 248; and trust 249

network cohesion and health: proposition 250

network density 230–5; and network closure 247–8

network health and health: proposition 251

network homogeneity see group segregation

network see social network

Nisbett, Richard 386–8

nodes 222

Nolan, Patrick 418–22, 447–9

norm: and cultural integration 378, 380; and cultural maladaptation 199–206; and cultural reproduction theory 322–4; definition of 117; descriptive 198; emergence of 192–9; and gender inequality 355–9; and group distinction 206–9; social 182–3; injunctive 183; and institutions 192; internalized 189–91; legal 191–2, 438; and network closure 247–8; and religion 461, 467; and social control theory 183–9; as subtheme of culture 117–18; unpopular 199

normative question 20; see also questions

normative social influence 153–5; see also social influence

Norris, Pippa 468, 473, 476

North, Douglas 192

obesity 4–10, 312

observational research 100

occupational prestige 306

odds ratio 317

one percent: stylized fact 311

one-to-many transmission 448–9; see also transmission

one-to-one transmission 169, 448–9; see also transmission

operationalization 78

opinions: and adaptation bias 161–2, 167, 193, 385, 446; and availability heuristic 445; beliefs as 117; and collectivism and individualism 431–3; and complex contagion 160, 166–8; and confirmation bias 31, 161, 167–9, 446; and conformity 146–53, 324, 432, 465–7; and cultural integration 378; definition of 117; and diffusion of innovations 165–70; and dual-process model 156, 190, 191, 445; and exposure bias 158–9, 161, 167; and Galatea effect 143–4; and group distinction 206–9; media transmission of 150–2; parental transmission of 148–9, 152, 188, 202, 324, 465–7; peer transmission of 150, 152, 251, 466; and popularity bias 157–8, 162–5; and popularity of cultural products 140–1, 162–5; preferences as 117; and Pygmalion effect 143–4;

and rationalization 415–17, 445–9; and religion 460–1; and self-fulfilling prophecy 142–6; and simple contagion 160, 168; and social influence 153–5; and social learning theory 156–62; and social proof 158, 162, 169, 204; and status bias 159–60, 167; as subtheme of culture 117; and susceptibility bias 160–1; and Thomas and Thomas Theorem 144, 287; values as 117; and Werther effect 150–2

optimism gap 445

order *see* social cohesion

organizational cohesion 262–3; *see also* social cohesion

organizations: and administrative research 94; and authority and status 305; brokerage and 340–1; and case-study research 91–4; and discrimination 344; and individualistic and collectivistic values 432–3; and McDonaldization 429–31; as meso level 11, 26; and multilevel framework 129–30; and network density 231; and organizational cohesion 262–3; and on-the-job training 335; and personal network cohesion 245; religious groups as 459; and self-fulfilling prophecies 143; and social control theory 184, 187; and social norms 182–3; as sociological topic 114–15; and survey research 97; voluntary associations as 261–2; and weak ties 225

oughtness norm *see* injunctive norm

outdegree 224

Padgett, John F. 94–5

paradigm *see* perspective

parental socialization *see* parental transmission

parental transmission 148–9; and conformity 152; of cultural capital 324; of religion 465–7; and social control theory 188; and unpopular norms 202; and vertical diffusion 448–9

parochial cooperation 260, 277

partial mediation 65–6

path model *see* conceptual model

Patterson, Orlando 192

peace and safety progress 413–15

peer influence *see* peer transmission

peer transmission 150, 159; and conformity 152; of health 251; and horizontal diffusion 448–9; of religion 466

period effect 468

personal network 222–6; and group segregation 264–8; and hubs 229–30; size of 226–9; and tie-formation 233, 268–74

personal network cohesion 242–6; *see also* social cohesion

personal network size in the US: stylized fact 229

personal trouble 13

perspective: definition of 113; individual 4–13; and multilevel framework 127–32; origins of sociological 110–13; social capital paradigm 246; sociological imagination 4–13; and sociological themes 114–23

Phillips, David 150

Pickett, Kate 311–12

Pinker, Steven 413–15

pluralistic ignorance 203–6

Popper, Karl 30, 42, 45, 126–7

popularity bias 157–8; and popularity of cultural products 162–5; *see also* social learning biases

popularity of cultural products 140–1, 162–5

population 83; *see also* sample

population and demography: and international migration 369–76; population change 440–4; and residential segregation 393–7; *see also* health

position generator 341; *see also* name generator

positive social influence 153; *see also* social influence

poverty 14–15, 29, 111–12, 120, 122, 284, 301, 310, 314, 410–2, 440, 476–7

power *see* resource

precise question 22; *see also* questions

preferences *see* opinions

prescriptive norm *see* injunctive norm

Preston curve 302–3

private sociologists 30–1; *see also* academic sociology

probability sample 84; *see also* sample
proposition 42
proximate cause 10–11
proxy *see* measure
public good 195
public issue *see* social problem
Putnam, Robert 203, 241–3, 246, 261–2, 431
Pygmalion effect 143–4; *see also* Galatea effect

qualitative methods 91
quantitative methods 91
question ingredients 22–4; *see also* questions
questions: application 21; asking good 21–6; comparative-case 25; descriptive 20; false theoretical 25; ill-defined 22; ingredients of 22–4; normative 20; precise 22; relevant 26; scientific 20; theoretical 21

race *see* ethnicity and race
racism *see* discrimination
rational choice 127; and adaptation bias 162, 200; and conformity to norms 185–6; and cooperation problems 194; and dual-process model 156; and rationality of beliefs 416; and rationalization process 415–29, 445–9
rationalization 415–17; causes of 445–9; hypothesis 417; and McDonaldization 429–31; and scientization 423–9; as subdimension of modernization 431; and technological progress 417–23
realistic conflict theory *see* group threat theory
relative age effect 44–5, 47–8, 50; and Pygmalion and Galatea effect 143–4
relative mobility 317; *see also* social mobility
religion: believing 461; belonging 459; and cohort effects 468; and cooperation 462–4; and credibility-enhancing displays 464; and existential insecurity theory 475–83; and modernization 471–5; parental transmission of 465–6; peer transmission of 466; and secularization in Western Europe 468–71; and social

control theory 467; as sociological topic 114–15; stickiness 464–7
religiosity 462
religious believing 461
religious belonging 459
religious stickiness 464–7
replication 103–6
representative sample 84; *see also* sample
research: administrative 94–6; big data 98–100; case study 91–4; descriptive 75; experimental 100–3; explanatory 75; exploratory 75, 88–90; observational 100–3; qualitative and quantitative 91; survey 96–8
residential segregation 393–7; and Black hypersegregation in the US 395; and Schelling segregation model 395–7
resource: cultural 322–4; definition of 121; financial 327–8, 345–6; group affiliation as 343–5, 353–4, 391–2; human 334–5, 350–1, 384, 389–90; and norms and aspirations 355–9; social 336–43, 352–3, 390–1; as subtheme of inequality 121
revealed preferences 271
Ridgeway, Cecilia 305
rights revolution 438
Ritzer, George 430
Robbers Cave Experiment 281–2, 284, 288, 305
Rogers, Everett 169
Rosling, Hans 29, 301
Ryan, Bryce 167–9

Sakoda, James 395–6
Salganik, Matthew 162–5
sample: biased 83; definition of 83; and population 83; probability 84; representative 84; stratified 85
scapegoats 279, 285
Schelling segregation model 395–7
Schelling, Thomas 395–7
Schwartz, Shalom 432
scientific question 20; *see also* questions
scientific relevance 24; *see also* societal relevance
scientization 423–9
scope condition 56; *see also* information content

second demographic transition 441; in
Western Europe 441–2
second generation 370
secularization 468–71; and modernization
471–5
selective acculturation *see* selective
integration
selective integration 388–92
self-fulfilling prophecy 142–6
Sherif, Muzafer 281
signaling 157, 202, 205–7, 463–4
Simmel, Georg 6, 113, 206, 249, 260–1
simple aggregation 131; *see also* multilevel
framework
simple concept 78; *see also* complex concept
simple contagion 160; and diffusion of
innovations 168; *see also* contagion
six degrees of separation *see* small-world
phenomenon
small-world network 239
small-world phenomenon 235–40; and
group segregation 267
social approval 184
social capital: Bourdieu's theory of 322–4;
Burt's theory of 340–1; and ethnic
inequality 390–1; and gender inequality
352–3; Granovetter's theory of 336–9;
and health 250–1; and job outcomes
336–343, 352–3, 390–1; Lin's theory of
341–3; paradigm 246; and social norms
246–7; and position generator 341; and
trust 248–50
social capital paradigm 246
social class 303–7
social cohesion: definition of 242;
intergroup 263–88; personal network
242–6; organizational 262–3
social contagion *see* contagion
social context 6
social context effect 129; *see also* multilevel
framework
social control theory 183–9; and conformity
153–4, 185–9; and cooperation problem
195; and gender norms 355; and
internalized norms 189–90; and network
closure 247; and religious transmission
467; and third party theory 273
social dilemma 194
social dynamics 132

social fluidity 317
social identity: definition of 276; and group
threat theory 283; theory 276
social inequality *see* inequality
social influence: definition of 153; and
cultural reproduction theory 322–4; and
culture of honor 385–8; and diffusion of
innovations 165–70; and gender norms
355–9; and group distinction 206–9;
and health 251; informational 153–5;
negative 153; normative 153–5; and
popularity of cultural products 162–5;
positive 153; and rationalization 415–7,
445–9; and religious stickiness 465; and
social control theory 183–9; and social
learning theory 156–62; and unpopular
norms 202
social integration: changes over time
379–82; definition of 378; and social
context effects 382–5; and spillover
effects 388–92; *see also* integration
social interdependency 131
social intervention 18
social learning biases: adaptation bias
161–2, 167, 193, 385, 446; definition of
156; confirmation bias 31, 161, 167–9,
446; exposure bias 158–9, 161, 167;
popularity bias 157–8, 162–5; status bias
159–60, 167; susceptibility bias 160–1
social learning theory 155–62; and diffusion
of innovations 165–70; and dual-process
model 156; and popularity of cultural
products 162–5; and rationalization
process 445–9
social media 98–100, 161, 169, 228, 237,
241, 339
social mobility: absolute 316; and
ascription and achievement 318–19;
and cultural reproduction theory 322–4;
definition of 121; and Great Gatsby
Curve 324–8; intergenerational 314,
316–17; intragenerational 315; and
modernization and mobility theory
319–22; relative 317; structural 317;
as subtheme of inequality 120–1; table
316–17; *see also* resource
social network: and community 238–46;
definition of 119; density of 230–5;
and group segregation 264–8; and

hubs 228–30; and loss-of-community 240–2; personal network 222–6; size of 226–9; and small-world phenomenon 235–40; and social cohesion 242–6; as subtheme of social relations 119; and tie-formation 233, 268–74; and transitivity tendency 232–4; *see also* social capital

social norm 182–3; and cooperation problem 194–7; and cultural integration 380; and gender 355; and network closure 247–8; and religion 461, 467; and social control theory 183–9; *see also* norm

social phenomenon 7

social policy *see* social intervention

social problem 13–16; and aims of sociology 17

social proof 158; and diffusion of innovations 169; and pluralistic ignorance 204; and popularity of cultural products 162

social relations: definition of 119; as sociological theme 118–20; *see also* group; social network

social resources 341; and job outcomes 341–3; and position generator 341

social sanction 184

social simulation 395–7

social status 303–7

social stratification: between-country 303; definition of 120; long-term trends in 312–14; and one percent 311; perceptions of 311; and Preston curve 302–3; and social class 303–7; and social problems 311–12; and social status 303–7; as subtheme of inequality 120–1; and Treiman constant 306–7; within-country 303, 307–11; *see also* resource

social ties and generalized trust: proposition 250

societal relevance 19; *see also* scientific relevance

socio-economic progress 415

sociogram *see* graph

sociological imagination 4–13; *see also* perspective

sociological perspective *see* sociological imagination

sociological subtheme 115

sociological theme 114–23

sociological topic 114–23

solidarity *see* social cohesion

Spencer, Herbert 110, 112

spiral of silence 205

standardization 81

statistical discrimination theory 344

status attainment process 318

status bias 159–60; and diffusion of innovations 167; *see also* social learning biases

status *see* social status

strain theory 61–2

stratification *see* social stratification

stratified sample 85; *see also* sample

strength-of-weak ties 239–40; and job information 339

strong ties 224–6; and informal job finding 337–9; and job outcomes 339; *see also* weak ties

structural balance 273–4

structural hole 340

structural mobility 317; *see also* social mobility

structural opportunity theory 268–70

subjective understanding *see* Verstehen

survey research 96–8

susceptibility bias 160–1; *see also* social learning biases

Swedberg, Richard 89–90

symbolic interactionism 125

symbolic threat theory *see* group threat theory

Tarde, Gabriel 150, 166–9

Tarde's diffusion theory 167–70

taste based discrimination 343–4

technological progress 417–23

theme *see* sociological theme

theoretical precision 49; *see also* information content

theoretical question 21; *see also* questions

theoretical scope 50; and existential insecurity theory 438; and modernization and secularization theory 475; and multilevel framework 128–9; and social control theory 187; *see also* information content

theoretical variable *see* concept
theory: and causality 62–4; and
    concepts 58–62; definition of 46; and
    explanation 41–6; useful 46–52; *see
    also* theory tool
theory schema 42; *see also* theory tool
theory tool 64, 69; and conceptual model
    64; and formal model 68; and theory
    schema 42
thick descriptions 93
third party 184; *see also* third party theory
third party theory 273–4
Thomas and Thomas Theorem 144; and
    group threat theory 287
three-generation language shift 381
tie strength and trust: proposition 249
tight cultures 432; *see also* collectivism
Tönnies, Ferdinand 240–2
topic *see* sociological topic
Tragedy of the Commons 194
transitivity *see* triadic closure
transitivity tendency 232–4; and small-
    world phenomenon 238–9
transmission: and diffusion 165–70;
    horizontal 448–9; many-to-many 169–
    70, 448–9; media 150–2; one-to-many
    169, 448–9; one-to-one 448–9; parental
    148–9, 152, 188, 202, 324, 465–7; peer
    150, 152, 251, 466; vertical 448–9; *see
    also* conformity; social influence
Traunmüller, Richard 248, 250
Travers, Jeffrey 236–7
Treiman constant 306–7
Treiman, Donald 306–7, 319
triad 232
triadic closure 232–5
tribalism 277
trickle-down theory 206–9
trust 118, 143, 149, 159–60, 165, 167, 203,
    224, 226, 228–9, 240, 242–5, 248–50,
    262, 275–8, 283, 312, 343, 378, 438,
    460, 462–4, 476
trust game 278
Twitter 98–100, 161
typology 60

ultimate cause 10–11
undirected ties 222–3
unpopular norm 199; *see also* norm

validity: external 82–6; internal 87–8
valuable goods 302
value: change 431–40; collectivism 432–40;
    and cultural integration 378; and cultural
    reproduction theory 323–4; and cultural
    threat 285–6; and culture of honor 385;
    definition of 189; and gender ambitions
    355; and homophily theory 270;
    individualism 432–40; and internalized
    norms 189–91; as opinions 117; and
    social problems 13; and stratification
    311; and *The Protestant Ethic* 127–32
Van de Kaa, Dirk 442–3
variable sociology 124
Verstehen 123–7; and multilevel framework
    127–32
vertical diffusion 448–9; *see also*
    transmission

Watts, Duncan 28–9, 98, 162–5
weak ties 225–6; and informal job finding
    337; and job information 339; jobs via
    337–8; strength of 240; *see also* strong
    ties
wealth and health progress 410–2
Weber, Max 6, 32, 112–15, 125–8, 132,
    416–7, 419, 424, 429–30, 447, 472
WEIRD people 102; *see also* external
    validity
Welzel, Christian 190, 432, 434, 436, 438
Werther effect 150–2
western individualism 437
Whyte, Willem Foote 92–4
Wilkinson, Richard 311–12
Wimmer, Andreas 374
witchcraft 279–80, 285
within-country stratification: definition
    of 303; by income and wealth 307–11;
    long-term trends in 312–14; perceptions
    of 311; and social problems 311–12; *see
    also* social stratification